SECOND EDITION

The Economics of the Canadian Financial System

Theory, Policy & Institutions

SECOND EDITION

The Economics of the Canadian Financial System

Theory, Policy & Institutions

Ronald A. Shearer
Professor of Economics
The University of British Columbia

John F. Chant
Professor of Economics
Simon Fraser University

David E. Bond
Public Service of Canada

Prentice-Hall Canada Inc.,
Scarborough, Ontario

CANADIAN CATALOGUING IN PUBLICATION DATA

Shearer, Ronald A., 1932 —
  The economics of the Canadian financial system

Includes index.
ISBN 0-13-229799-X

1. Finance — Canada. 2. Money — Canada. 3. Finance,
Public — Canada. 5. Financial institutions — Canada.
I. Chant, John F., 1937 —   II. Bond, David E.
III. Title.

HG185.C2S52   332'.0971   C83-098579-4

© 1984 by Prentice-Hall Canada Inc.
Scarborough, Ontario

Prentice-Hall Inc., Englewood Cliffs, New Jersey
Prentice-Hall International Inc., London
Prentice-Hall of Australia, Pty., Ltd., Sydney
Prentice-Hall of India, Pvt., Ltd., New Delhi
Prentice-Hall of Japan, Inc., Tokyo
Prentice-Hall of Southeast Asia (PTE.) Ltd., Singapore
Editora Prentice-Hall do Brasil Ltda., Rio de Janeiro

Production Editor: Scott Olson
Copy Editor: Ernest Hillen
Illustrations: Helmut Weyerstrahs
Production: Monika Heike

ISBN 0-13-229799-X

    2   3   4   5   6   JD   89   88   87   86   85

Typeset by ART-U Graphics Ltd.
Printed and bound in Canada by John Deyell Company

To

JOSEPH A. CRUMB,
whose passionate interest in monetary economics attracted many students to the field

ROBERT E. HUKE,
whose inspired teaching and thirst for knowledge are an example to all

H.W. FOWLER,
who was confident we could understand

BEV, MARCIE AND CARMELLE,
with love

CONTENTS

PREFACE TO THE SECOND EDITION

The first edition was motivated by our dissatisfaction with the standard model of the money and banking textbook. We offered a book with a different approach, and were gratified by its reception by both instructors and students. In preparing this edition, we have not felt compelled to make major changes in our approach, but rather to respond to criticisms of parts of the analysis and to clarify certain ambiguities. Above all, we have updated the analysis in light of important advances in the professional literature of monetary economics and major changes in the legal and institutional environment of the Canadian financial system. Instructors who used the first edition will find that this is the same book.

Among the major changes from the first edition are the following: The microeconomic theory of financial markets has been revised to deal more effectively with the impact of inflation and taxation on equilibrium in financial markets, and to clarify the multidimensional concept of risk as it affects portfolio balance decisions; the material on Canadian financial institutions has been updated, and the analysis of microeconomic policy has been extensively revised in light of recent developments in Canada and the United States. Public policy in the two countries is considered in the context of the histories and structures of the two financial systems, and a new chapter explores the different paths followed by the two governments in seeking more competitive financial systems in an environment of rapid technological change. As in the first edition, the chapters on monetary theory and policy develop both Keynesian and monetarist models for closed and open economics. More attention is given to the analytical foundations of monetarism, and more emphasis to the determination of the price level. The material on the international aspects of the macro models has been reorganized and rewritten, to better integrate the analysis of fixed and flexible exchange rates and the implications of the monetarist model. A new concluding chapter considers the monetarist proposition about the desirability of a "monetary constitution," and explores the history of the quest for such a constitution internationally, from the gold standard through Bretton Woods and beyond.

David Bond found that his responsibilities with the Government of Canada prevented him from taking a major role in the revision. Fortunately, John Chant agreed to join as a co-author. As in the first edition, the co-authors take joint responsibility for all of the material in the book.

J.F.C.
R.A.S.
D.E.B.

PREFACE TO THE FIRST EDITION

This book is intended as a textbook for undergraduate courses in money and banking at Canadian Universities. The level of the analysis presumes the mastery of at least a standard course in the principles of economics.

Over the years, a rather standard format has developed for textbooks in money and banking. With some exceptions, most of the widely used books are variations on a basic theme. The structure and content of this book reflect our dissatisfaction with the standard model. We are critical of the model in general, but feel particularly strongly that it is inappropriate for courses concerned with Canadian financial institutions and Canadian monetary policies. We have consciously departed from it in several important respects.

First, we take the view that we must be concerned with microeconomics as well as macroeconomics. Indeed, to the limited extent that it is possible, the macroeconomic analysis should build on microeconomic foundations. The standard textbook does have a microeconomic section, but we believe that the relevant microeconomics is more than just a description of banking institutions and their operations.

Institutions must be described, and we have devoted considerable space to that task, but we do so on the presumption that the proper scope of the discussion is the whole financial system, including both the chartered banks and non-bank financial intermediaries of all types, and the money and capital markets in both their domestic and their international dimensions. At the same time, we have attempted to avoid presenting a mail-order catalogue of financial institutions. It is important that the institutions be viewed as an integrated system which performs certain basic economic functions (in the spirit of Gurley and Shaw). To this end, their operations must be interpreted in terms of a systematic body of economic theory. We have attempted to do so, using as our foundation an elementary and slightly modified version of what has come to be called portfolio balance theory.

We also take the view that the purpose of economic analysis is the exposition of public policy and policy alternatives. Therefore we have devoted considerable space to the discussion of the development of public policy with respect to the structure of the financial system, both in Canada and the United States, and to the discussion of some of the major issues which have been troubling economists concerned with microeconomic policy in this area. Inevitably we have paid considerable attention to the *Report* of the Royal Commission on Banking and Finance and the subsequent revisions of the *Bank Act*.

Our second major departure from the standard model is in our treatment of historical topics. The typical textbook has major sections on the history of money and of banking institutions, and perhaps an extended discussion of the history of monetary theory. Although we recognize the value of a historical perspective on theory and institutions, these are specialized topics with an already abundant and readily accessible literature. In this book, we could only add another superficial survey. While there are many historical references scattered throughout the texts, we have confined our historical chapters to the analysis of the evolution of the structure of the financial industry and the development of government policy toward the financial structure in Canada and the United States. Given the orientation of our microeconomic analysis, these are important topics and, unlike other historical topics, are less adequately developed in the literature which is readily available to undergraduate students.

Our third major point of departure from the standard textbook is in the treatment of international finance. Canada's is an open economy, and, what is more important from our present point of view, the Canadian financial system is likewise open. Canadian monetary economics, like Canadian monetary policy, must have an international orientation. In the standard textbook, international finance is discussed separately in a section at the end of the book, almost as an afterthought. It is our impression that many instructors never get to this section, or, if they do, deal with it very superficially.

We take the position that the discussion of international finance must be *fully integrated* with the discussion of monetary theory and monetary policy. There is no excuse for leaving the Canadian student with a model of monetary policy appropriate only for a closed economy. While our discussion of the macroeconomic aspects of international finance does come towards the end of the book, we have developed the analysis as an extension of the models of monetary policy developed in the previous chapters. We have attempted to adapt the familiar IS-LM model to demonstrate the balance of payments constraint on monetary policy in a regime of fixed exchange rates, and to explore the implications of a regime of flexible exchange rates. We have also explored such topics as speculation in foreign exchange markets and the international liquidity problem from the perspective of their implications for Canadian monetary policy.

Finally, as a fourth major departure, we take the view that wherever possible the conclusions of economic theory must be considered relative to the findings of empirical research. It is difficult and frustrating to attempt to interpret for undergraduate students the often conflicting findings of empirical researchers (the subtleties of methodological controversies defy explanation); however, wherever it seemed relevant, we have attempted to do so. We refer frequently to the results of empirical research, and the second to last chapter is entirely devoted to a survey of research on the effectiveness of monetary policy.*

Helpful comments from a number of people helped us to catch many errors before they reached print, though undoubtedly some will remain. Those that do are our fault alone. We must acknowledge particularly useful observations from Carol Clark, Basil Moore, Philip Neher, Douglas Purvis, John Chant, Tom Maxwell, A.A. Shapiro, and John Borcich.

---

*This has been changed in the second edition.

We have been extremely fortunate in having hard-working and imaginative research assistants and we owe a special debt of gratitude to George Temple, Richard Lewin, Tom Gussman, and John Dickenson. In addition, our typists Patricia Miller, Karen Wildie, Trish Purvin-Good, Julia Popp, Mary Shearer and Maria Rasonivic dealt effectively with often illegible manuscripts and strange spelling. They rendered loyal service indeed. Finally we owe much to our students in Economics 308, particularly in the year 1968-69. They suffered through the use of part of the manuscript in its earlier rough state and we profited from their finding our mistakes.

D.E.B.
R.A.S.

THE FUNCTIONS OF THE FINANCIAL SYSTEM 1

To the average citizen, finance, financial activities, and the financial system have an aura of mystery. Successful practitioners of the financial arts are widely held in awe — although it is also fair to say that many people regard these financial experts with somewhat the same skepticism as they do astrologers and fortune-tellers. On the one hand, reports of fortunes created overnight, almost magically, stir imaginations and gambling instincts. Likewise, reports of bankruptcies under mysterious circumstances and losses of life savings by "innocent" investors stir rumors, allegations, and public outcries for investigations of fraud and deceptive financial "manipulations." Some of these investigations, in fact, reveal practices which are either illegal or ethically suspect. Partly as a result, the financial industry is surrounded by more government rules and regulations than perhaps any other industry, and new laws are being added to the books almost every year. On the other hand, public forums on the somber issues of government economic policy are seldom considered complete unless they include the considered advice of bankers or investment analysts. Yet back-room discussion of the economic problems of our time commonly centers on the theme of the conspiracy of the bankers, domestic or international.

THE FINANCIAL INDUSTRY

Myths about finance are embedded in our culture and an anthropologist or sociologist could undoubtedly write a fascinating analysis of the social functions performed by invocations of the financial spirits. To an economist, however, the financial system is but another industry in the economy. True, it is a particularly important industry that frequently has a far-reaching impact on society and the economy, but stripped of its occult trappings, it is, like any industry, a group of firms which combine factors of production (land, labor, and capital) under the general direction of a management team, and produce a product or cluster of products for sale in financial markets. These markets have varying degrees of competition, and are regulated by the forces of supply and demand within a general context set by government laws and regulations. It is not quite the same thing as the widget industry, but the general principles applied to the analysis of the widget industry in introductory principles of economics courses can also be applied to the financial industry.

The Output of the Financial Industry

The product of the financial industry is not tangible, as are automobiles, food, or clothing. Rather, it is a service such as those produced in the barbering or laundry industry. Indeed, it is incorrect to refer to *the* product of the industry. We are not talking about a single service, but a collection of services. It is true that some financial firms specialize in the provision of a single service (or a cluster of very closely related services), but many, including some of the very largest, are complex multi-product firms. The industry as a whole, including specialized and diversified firms, produces a wide range of services, but all of these services are related directly or indirectly to assets and liabilities, i.e., *claims* on people, corporations, institutions, and governments. These are the forms in which people accumulate much of their wealth.

It is not important that we have a complete catalogue of the services offered by the industry, but it is useful to identify the most important ones. Basic to almost all the activities of financial firms is the systematic collection and interpretation of *information* on almost all aspects of economic activity. Some of this information is passed on to clients in the form of *professional advice* on investments and other personal economic problems. On the basis of such information certain financial firms will also undertake to manage the economic affairs of clients (or their estates) on a *trusteeship* basis. Comprehensive, detailed, and accurate information is an essential input into almost all the activities of a financial firm, including what we call brokerage and financial intermediation. Many financial firms serve as *brokers* in the same sense that they bring borrowers and lenders together, thus arranging a transaction (for a fee) without being a party to the transaction themselves. Perhaps more familiar are the activities of financial firms as *financial intermediaries.* In this capacity they act simultaneously as borrowers and lenders. Like a broker, a financial intermediary brings borrowers and lenders together, but unlike a broker it is a party to the transaction. The financial intermediary actually borrows from one group in society (who are often happy to trust the financial intermediary whereas they would not trust those to whom the intermediary lends) and lends to another, thus putting itself at risk should some of the loans be defaulted. The activities of a financial firm as an intermediary are sometimes confused in the popular mind with another service, the provision of *safekeeping* of valuable property. Thus, depositors in a bank frequently fail to recognize that they are creditors of the bank: they have, in fact, lent the bank money. Safekeeping is provided by the safety-deposit-box department of the bank, not by the deposit wickets. Furthermore, safekeeping is a minor service to customers, incidental to the main business at hand. Finally, we must note that the financial system provides facilities for the *transfer of purchasing power* from individual to individual, or from firm to firm, both within the country and internationally. It thus arranges the financial side of almost all exchanges consummated in markets in the economy and, in the process, provides a detailed set of *records* of transactions, both for the use of the individuals concerned and, in different forms, for government agencies and the public at large. The financial system is a primary source of statistics used in analyzing national and international economic activity.

Value Added in the Financial Industry

So much for the nature of the products of the financial industry. How important is this industry relative to the total economy?

The accepted measure of the aggregate output of the economy is the gross national product. Correspondingly, the appropriate measure of the output of any single industry is "value added" in that industry. "Value added" is defined as the difference between the market value of the product produced and sold by the industry, and the cost of all materials purchased from other industries (e.g., raw materials, component parts, fuel, advertising services, etc.). It is thus equal to the payments for the services of all factors of production directly employed in that industry (rents, wages, interest) plus any residual profit earned by the owners of the firms. In other words, it is the value of "income originating" in the industry. Since such a calculation avoids the error of double counting — of counting as output in one industry what is in fact the output of another industry, as when you simply add up the value of sales by industry — "value added" is the best measure of the relative contribution of any industry to aggregate national output.

In attempting to measure value added in the financial industry, certain complications arise which are discussed in books on national income accounting. The problem arises in the treatment of interest. In accounting for value added in a normal industry, interest received is deducted from the income of the firms on the grounds that this does not represent payment for services of capital employed in production in that industry. If this procedure is carried out for financial intermediaries the value added by the industry is almost invariably negative. According to national income accountants this answer is "unacceptable" so they resort to imputations; that is, they assign an arbitrary value to the services provided by the financial intermediaries to their customers. The resulting estimates are severely criticised by some economists, and must be regarded as approximations only. Further complications arise in attempting to use the published estimates since value added by the financial industry is not shown separately, but is included in the category "Finance, Insurance, and Real Estate." In recent years this category accounted for 11%-12% of gross national product. The financial industry proper (excluding real estate, but including insurance) probably accounted for 3%-5% of gross national product.

Put differently, the financial industry directly accounts for perhaps 1/30 of the gross output of goods and services produced in this nation. This clearly establishes it as a major industry. But can we take this as sufficient indication of the importance of the financial industry?

ECONOMIC FUNCTIONS OF THE
FINANCIAL SYSTEM _____

The economic significance of the financial system and its operations cannot be assessed in the same way as that of the widget industry. It is not simply a matter of adding up value added and expressing that as a proportion of national output. If the widget industry were removed from the economy, perhaps by an act of Parliament, repercussions might be felt in many segments of the economy. Suppliers of materials would find that part of their market had disappeared, and hence they would have to adjust the scale of their production. Employees in the widget industry, and probably in supplying industries, would have to seek new employment. Purchasers of widgets would have to make do with substitutes, and if the widget were an essential input into some other industry perhaps that industry would be faced with impossible difficulties. Depending on the size of the industry and the nature of its relations with other industries, the repercussions could be felt over a wide circle of economic activity. In some cases, the adjustments could be painful and protracted. However, given time, the economy would adjust. Without the widget industry, economic activity would be different, but it would carry on.

If the financial industry were removed in the same way, we could not be so optimistic about the outcome. Unlike the widget industry, the financial industry provides services which are essential to every industry in the economy. In this sense, financial activities are complementary to all other economic activities. While the financial industry may not be unique in this respect, it nonetheless means that the importance of the industry transcends that indicated by the relative size of value added in the industry. It performs certain essential functions for the economy, including the maintenance of the payments system, the collection and allocation of the savings of society, and the creation of a variety of stores of wealth to suit the preferences of individual savers.

The Payments System

The payments system is the set of institutional arrangements through which purchasing power is transferred from one participant in an exchange to another, i.e., from the buyer to the seller.

Why do we consider this to be an essential economic function? Ever since the discipline of economics was established as a systematic analysis of economic activity, economists have been asserting that specialization in productive activities is a necessary (but not sufficient) condition for the achievement of a high general standard of living. Without an elaborate division of labor into specialized tasks the application of modern technology would be inconceivable. But the counterpart of specialization is exchange. The man who specializes in the activity of dog-catching must somehow obtain the variety of goods and services which he and his family wish to consume. He must exchange his services for the products of other specialized producers. Efficient exchange also implies an intermediary which we call money. Money, in a sense, is generalized purchasing power: something which all of the participants in the economy are willing to accept in payment for goods and services, not because they want to consume it, but because they know that they can exchange it with some other person, now or later, for the things which they desire. The use of money in the exchange process is quite apart from any utility which the monetary medium itself might yield as a commodity. Indeed, it is not necessary that the monetary medium be something which is desired as a commodity: it can be marks on the books of a banker as well as some finite object such as pieces of gold or paper. We will return to the concept and properties of money later in the book. Suffice it to note at this point that any number of things have been used as money under varying circumstances. But whatever the instrument, and whatever the concrete historical circumstances of its evolution as the monetary medium, confidence that others would accept it in the normal course of business has always been a necessary condition for anything to serve as money.

It is difficult, but not impossible, to conceive of an exchange economy without money. All exchange would have to involve a direct bartering of goods for goods. But barter can only be an efficient method of exchange when there occurs a *double coincidence of wants,* that is, when each party to the exchange has precisely what the other party desires, at the time required, and in quantities appropriate to the exchange. In a large, complex society this implies a remarkable coincidence of events in time and space. Under other circumstances — that is, under normal circumstances — barter must involve a series of indirect exchanges. Each individual must take payment in kind, consume what he wishes, and store or perhaps transport the excess until the time and place are right for him to exchange it for the items which he requires. Clearly, such a system would be highly wasteful of time and resources.

What we have referred to as the payments system is simply a set of institutional arrangements for the transfer of money from person to person, frequently among persons widely separated geographically, often in different countries using different monies. Our interest in the payments system is that of an economist and not that of a financial expert, an accountant, or a geographer. We are not concerned with the techniques of effecting payments or with techniques of recording payments, or even with what the patterns of payments tell us about the geographical patterns of production and trade. Granted that a payments system is essential to an exchange economy, what further questions might an economist ask about it?

The answer is twofold: he must be concerned with the *efficiency* of the payments mechanism and with its *neutrality* with respect to the essential economic decisions of society.

As we have described it, effecting payments is essentially a mechanical activity, one increasingly performed by electronic equipment. Still, it is not a costless activity: it absorbs scarce resources (labor and capital) which have alternative uses. The less the labor and capital absorbed in effecting a given value of payments, the greater the efficiency of the payments system, the greater the supply of these scarce resources available for other productive employments, and hence the greater the potential output of the economy. This, then, must be a primary interest of economists in the payments mechanism.

Although efficiency is a primary interest of the economist, it must be only part of his concern with the payments mechanism. The economic system is, at root, a social mechanism for making certain decisions; for effecting social choices relating to what is to be produced, how and where it is to be produced, and to whom it is to be distributed.

As a mechanical counterpart of the exchange process the payments system is involved in this decision-making. But apart from the fact that the participants in the process must bear the cost of effecting transactions emanating from their decisions, the payments system itself should be essentially neutral as among possible outcomes. The operations of the payments mechanism should not discriminate among transactors or among types of transactions except on the basis of different marginal costs of effecting transactions. Given the pervasive involvement of the payments mechanism in the exchange processes of the economy, the economist must ask if this neutrality is in fact achieved.

Our discussion of the payments system in Chapter 2 is largely descriptive. In part this reflects the fact that description is a necessary preliminary to analysis. However, it also reflects the fact that little economic research has been done on the Canadian payments system. While we attempt to cast some light on the two important economic issues, we are doing so in the spirit of suggesting relevant fields for research rather than reporting on established research findings.

The Accumulation and Allocation of Savings

In principles of economics courses it is demonstrated that an exchange economy can be characterized as two reciprocal flows: a flow of real goods and services and a reverse flow of payments. The real flows are our ultimate concern. These are what determine our standard of economic well-being. However, the *financial flows* are not irrelevant for they *elicit and guide the real flows.*

Thus, consumer expenditures (or expectations of such expenditures) elicit production of appropriate items. Likewise, income payments from business firms elicit flows of productive services. On the real side of this scheme, households appear as consuming units with distinct preferences, and as providers of productive services with distinct characteristics. Business firms appear as producing units motivated by profits, and as units which absorb productive services to produce the goods and services demanded by households (and by other firms and government agencies). The government has an ambiguous role. In some respects it is a unit for collective consumption; in other respects it is a producer of goods and services; in still other respects it is a vehicle for the establishment and administration of public policies. Like other producing units it participates in the circular flow as an absorber of productive services. Unlike the consumer and business units, it does not normally respond to market indicators in its decisions on what to produce.

In real terms each of these groups of units has distinct functions and characteristics. However, they are all alike in that they are all *spending units;* all receive funds from various sources and spend funds for the purchase of goods and services. Each spending unit has sources of revenue: primarily the sale of productive services in the case of households; the sale of products in the case of business firms; and tax collections in the case of governments. In a general way, the expenditure of any spending unit is linked to its revenue. However, revenues do not have to control expenditures on goods and services during any period of time. A spending unit's revenues may well exceed its expenditures on goods and services, and in this sense it may have a *surplus* budget. But alternatively its expenditures on goods and services may exceed its revenues, and for that period it may have a *deficit* budget.

These financial surpluses and deficits have their counterparts in real terms. A financial surplus implies that during that period the spending unit has chosen not to acquire all of the goods and services which its revenues would permit. A financial deficit implies that during that period the spending unit has been able to acquire more goods and services than its revenues would permit. Taking the two together, there is a transfer of command over resources from the surplus spending units to the deficit spending units. The transfer is arranged through the financial system; and this then is the second major function of the financial system. *It collects the surpluses of the surplus spending units and makes them available to the deficit spending units.*

Stated this way, it sounds like a mechanical process similar in effect to the payments mechanism. There is much more involved than the mechanical acts of collection and transfer. The financial surpluses (and their real equivalents) are, after all, scarce resources capable of many alternative possible uses. It is necessary to adjust the total available supply and the total demand (either by adjusting the demand or the supply, or both), and to allocate the actual supply forthcoming among all of the competing demands. That is, the financial system must act like a market — a market in which prices are formed and adjusted to variations in supply and demand so as to clear the market. This is far from the mechanical type of process described in the discussion of the payments system.

The prices which are formed in financial markets are interest rates. While they perform the same general role, they have a significance somewhat different from other prices in the economy. Interest rates indicate the market rate of exchange between dollars for present use and dollars for use at some time in the future. In this sense they reflect the opportunity cost of funds devoted to current consumption by households, and thus should affect household decisions regarding the division of income between consumption and saving. Likewise, they represent the opportunity cost to corporations of funds devoted to particular capital projects. They provide a standard against which the probable profitability of any project can be assessed to determine whether the project should be undertaken. Thus, even if the agency of the financial system is not directly involved, the information provided by the financial system should be highly relevant to a broad range of economic decisions, i.e., those relating to the balancing of future gains and present costs.

Throughout this discussion (with one exception) we have studiously avoided the terms *saving* and *investment* in describing this function of the financial system. As a result, in place of the straightforward statement that the financial system transfers command over resources from savers to investors we have had to use the cumbersome phrase "from surplus spending units to deficit spending units." While it sounds pedantic, we have chosen this expression quite deliberately. Saving and investment are technical terms in economic analysis with important and widely recognized meanings. They are not necessarily the same as the financial surpluses and financial deficits to which we refer. Investment implies expenditures to acquire physical capital goods, to expand the productive capacity of the firm and hence of the economy. But a spending unit may be in deficit for reasons unrelated to capital formation. A household, for example, may require funds simply to support a level of consumption in excess of its current income. Likewise, a spending unit may save and yet not have a financial surplus in the sense of that term used here. This would be true, for example, of a firm which finances its capital formation (investment) out of its undistributed profits (savings).

It is true, however, that the bulk of the transfers to which we are referring are related to the process of capital formation. They involve the collection of the financial counterpart of the saving of the society and its allocation to competing demands for capital formation. This means that the operations of the financial system are vital to the pace and structure of the growth of the economy. However, we must not forget that some portion of the transfers are to households to acquire consumer goods and services and to governments for assorted purposes, including collective consumption.

What are the questions that an economist would ask about the functioning of the financial system as an allocative mechanism? The answer is quite simple: he would be concerned with its effectiveness in directing funds to uses with the highest social value at the margin, and doing so at least cost, and the mechanism's flexibility in adapting to changing patterns of demand and supply. Inevitably, as in any market, the quest for such information leads the economist to an analysis of competitive conditions in financial markets.

Again, much of our discussion must be descriptive. The financial system is incredibly complicated even in its purely domestic aspects. The fact that any student of the Canadian financial system must also immerse himself in international financial arrangements only adds to the complications. There is no escaping the fact that an analysis of the economic efficiency of the financial system must be predicated upon a reasonably full understanding of the complex interrelationships within the system. And again, as in the discussion of the payments system, our conclusions on the efficiency of the financial system as an allocative device may seem weak by contrast to our ambitions as set out here. The reason again is the paucity of professional research on the economics of the Canadian financial system.

Financial Intermediation

Assets, liabilities, and wealth are central concepts in our analysis of the financial system. These are familiar concepts to accountants; indeed, they are the stuff of which accounts are made. The terms refer to market values (even though the market value is frequently estimated rather than determined by actual transactions) measured in terms of the unit of value, or unit of account, the dollar. Thus, one's asset are the things of value owned. Assets derive their value either from the fact that they are capable of yielding income in the future (as a factory might yield income to its owners) or from the fact that they have qualities which are prized by others who are therefore willing to pay to obtain them (as a work of art might be prized and hence valuable). One's liabilities are the value of one's obligations, what one owes. Wealth is simply the difference between the value of assets and liabilities.

An individual, a family, or a nation becomes wealthy by the process of accumulating assets in excess of liabilities. This is normally done through the acts of saving and investing. If we leave aside the possibility of accumulating claims on residents of other countries, a nation can accumulate wealth in basically two forms: physical capital goods and the intangible skills, knowledge, organizational patterns, and work habits of its population (what is sometimes called human capital). These are the assets which are capable of producing output and hence income for the inhabitants of the nation in the future. However, through the financial system, any individual within the nation has a much wider range of choices open to him as to the forms in which he can accumulate wealth. He is not restricted to the accumulation of physical and human capital. He can hold financial instruments or securities which represent claims on other individuals or organizations. Hence, he can participate, directly or indirectly, in the income stream generated by the human and physical capital held by others. This indirect participation is made possible through the financial system.

You may well ask how significant is this fact? Is not our ultimate concern real income and wealth? Is it not true that, for society as a whole, income and wealth can only be produced by the underlying physical and human assets to which we referred earlier? Indeed, if we set out to measure the wealth of society, all of the complex layers of financial claims would cancel themselves out, leaving only the underlying human and physical capital assets. This follows because every claim which appears as some person's assets is simultaneously someone else's liability. When you measure the wealth of the two combined, the asset of one cancels out the liability of the other. Thus, if Jones owns a $1 million claim on Smith, and Smith owns a factory worth $2 million, the wealth of the two combined is $2 million, not $3 million, i.e., it is the value of the underlying capital asset. If we say Jones' wealth is $1 million, then Smith's is only $1 million, the value of his asset less the value of Jones' claim. We can push it a step farther by noting that if Smith and Jones could exchange promissory notes (promises to pay), each would acquire an asset, his claim on the other, and each would acquire a liability, the other's claim on him. In the extreme, they could create a truly staggering total of paper assets for each of them. Note, however, that in spite of all this financial activity no real wealth would be created. Can we not conclude, therefore, that as economists interested in the real income and wealth of society we can well afford to ignore the complex of claims and counter-claims generated through the financial system? Do they appear as a veil, obscuring the real processes of saving and investing which create the real wealth of society, but having no vital significance of their own? Perhaps we would do better to allocate our scarce analytical resources to the study of the real processes themselves.

Reverting to the Jones-Smith example, everyone would presumably agree that it is possible that without Jones' indirect participation Smith might not have had the resources to build the factory. In this sense the creation of financial claims may have some significance. But this is just another aspect of the process which we have already discussed. The financial system serves as a vehicle for collecting the surpluses of surplus spending units and transferring them to deficit spending units. The surplus unit (Jones) is given a financial instrument as evidence of its continuing command over the scarce resources of the economy. This is nothing new. This transaction simply amounts to Jones and Smith pooling their resources to achieve an objective which neither could achieve alone. It perhaps illustrates the point that financial instruments are *divisible* in a fashion in which real capital assets may not be, but that is about all.

The fact of *divisibility* is important, however. At a maximum it permits the pooling together of the small financial surpluses of many isolated individuals to finance a venture of considerable magnitude. Thus, divisibility is important for the efficient collection and use of the savings of society, especially where these savings occur in small, isolated quantities.

Beyond this, divisibility also permits a *diversification* of asset holdings which would not otherwise be possible. Let us refer to any individual's collection of assets as his *portfolio*. We have said nothing about the form of Jones' claim on Smith. Perhaps it takes the form of a claim to half of the profits earned by the factory. In agreeing to share in Smith's venture in this way Jones must recognize that the returns from the factory are conjectural. If they occur at all, they will occur in the future. The magnitude of the possible profits cannot be known now with any degree of certainty. Market conditions could emerge in which not profits, but rather heavy *losses*, are sustained by the venture. On the other hand, the returns could be much in excess of any expectations that the two men might have at the outset. There is some element of *risk* involved; returns may be large or small, and in the extreme the asset could become worthless. By holding only this asset in his portfolio, Jones bears the full burden of this risk. If the factory fails, his wealth is correspondingly reduced (of course, if the factory should prosper beyond all expectations, his wealth would increase correspondingly).

However, Jones does not have to commit all of his resources to Smith's venture. Even if he split his resources between two ventures which are in some sense equally risky, the total risk on his portfolio would be reduced, at least if the success of one of the ventures was not in some fashion related to the success of the other (i.e., if the risks were *independent* of each other). This follows because it is less likely that two independent ventures will fail at the same time than that either of them will fail individually. The risk on his portfolio could be reduced even farther by spreading the funds over a variety of ventures, each with risks independent of each other. The financial system makes such diversification feasible for even relatively small portfolios.

But the financial system goes even farther than that. It creates financial instruments which have properties completely unlike those of physical or human assets. It creates a variety of assets which are virtually — indeed, in the extreme, completely — free of the risks inevitably attached to the real capital assets upon which the value of the financial instruments ultimately rest.

As a step in that direction, we might again consider the claim which Jones has upon Smith, and particularly the *form* of that claim. So far, we have implicitly assumed that it took the form of a claim to a share of the potentially variable earnings of the venture. That is, we assumed that it was a *variable income security*. This is not the only form possible. The agreement between Smith and Jones might call for a specified dollar payment to Jones periodically (and perhaps a final payment on some date, after which the claim would no longer exist). Then the claim would take the form of a *fixed income security*. In the case of the variable income security, Jones bore part of the risk of fluctuation in the venture's earnings. In the case of a fixed income security, Smith bears all of this risk. Jones is entitled to a *certain* fixed payment, whether the earnings of the venture are large or small. Of course, there is a still larger risk which Jones cannot escape in this way. There is the risk that the venture will fail completely; that is, the risk that Smith will be unable to meet his commitment. This risk can only be hedged against by diversification. The certainty of payment on a fixed income security is only certainty in the small, i.e., in the absence of major catastrophes to the venture.

The financial system facilitates diversification in another way. Not only does it permit the division of real assets and income streams into smaller parcels, it also provides markets in which the financial instruments can be traded among individuals. Securities vary in *marketability* as the characteristics of the underlying concerns are or are not known to a wide circle of potential investors. However, through efficient, organized markets, millions of dollars worth of transactions in securities occur every day in Canada.

Our man Jones has wealth of $1 million at his disposal. He can obtain a considerable range of diversification among his assets, and yet have a significant sum invested in each venture. This is not true of the typical individual, who may have only a few thousand dollars at his disposal (over and above his own earning power, which is normally his major asset). However, what is possible for an individual through diversification of his portfolio is also possible for specialized financial institutions. We call such institutions *financial intermediaries,* and the function which they perform in the economy we call *financial intermediation.* These institutions hold a diversified portfolio of claims, each of which may have a substantial degree of risk, and issue their own liabilities which are largely (but not necessarily completely) devoid of such risk. Standing as an intermediary between the ultimate lender and the ultimate user of the funds, they absorb risk, and thus completely alter the range of investment opportunities open to individuals, and particularly the small investor. Financial intermediaries provide financial instruments which incorporate the advantages of portfolio diversification by being claims upon diversified portfolios.

Indeed, through the vehicle of the financial intermediary, the financial system carries the process a step farther. The system provides a variety of financial instruments — each of which is a claim on a diversified portfolio of claims — with widely varying characteristics designed to appeal to the specific preferences of very differently situated assetholders. We will have occasion to examine some of these later on, but one type of instrument requires special mention at this point. Financial intermediaries create assets which have the property of *liquidity,* or convertibility into a fixed amount of money on demand. Indeed, what we widely use as *money,* the demand deposit or chequing account, is precisely such a financial instrument. Many economists argue that this provision of liquidity is the most significant aspect of financial intermediation. While holding essentially illiquid assets themselves, intermediaries are able to create liquid assets to be held by the ultimate savers in the economy.

What then is the significance of the fact that the financial system creates a wide variety of financial instruments and markets on which they can be traded efficiently? What is the economic importance of financial intermediation? Have we really answered our earlier objection that all of this financial activity is so much window dressing, a curtain obscuring our view of the true processes of saving and investing in the economy? What is the economist's interest in it all?

Underlying our analysis is the assumption that individuals have preferences as to the *form* in which they accumulate their assets. By creating a diverse range of assets the financial system permits a more complete satisfaction of these preferences, and in this sense permits an increase in economic welfare. This includes making available relatively risk-free and highly liquid assets as well as assets in which the degree of risk is accentuated and which are therefore calculated to appeal to those with gambling instincts.

Beyond this are the implications for public policy designed to influence the level of income, employment, and prices in the economy. If individuals have preferences among assets, they presumably alter their portfolio choices as the characteristics of assets change, and particularly as the relative yields on assets change. Thus, a decline in the yield on a particular asset may induce many individuals to select something else. On one hand, a general decline in the rates of return on financial assets may well induce the selection of non-financial (real) assets in their place. On the other hand, the decline in rates may encourage some to borrow so as to acquire a real asset. Such *substitution effects* can have important implications for the level of economic activity.

We have discovered over time that the government, primarily through the agency of the central bank, is able to alter the supply of certain types of financial instruments, particularly money and claims upon the central government. This affects the rate of return on these assets, and hence produces substitution effects of the type noted above. The end product should be change in the demand for real capital assets, and hence an effect on aggregate demand, the level of income, employment, and prices in the economy. This suggests the possibility of a monetary policy, by which we mean a policy designed to use these financial linkages for constructive social purposes, particularly the stabilization of the economy. Proper policy proposals then, are a matter of major interest to the economist. How can such a policy be affected? What rules ought to guide it? How powerful will its effects be? How successful have we been in using this tool? These matters, of profound significance to every citizen, are the subject matter of Part III of this book.

THE SOCIAL INTEREST IN THE FINANCIAL SYSTEM

Following this rather academic discussion of the functions of the financial system, it may be worthwhile to extract the essence of what we have said about the social interest in the financial system. Why should students of economics be concerned with money, banking, and finance?

Our first proposition is that the payments mechanism is part of the financial system, and its efficiency affects the overall efficiency of the economy. Secondly, the financial system is a vehicle by which a scarce resource, savings, is allocated among alternative competing uses. The use of the flow of savings affects both the rate of growth of the economy and the structure of economic activity. It is a matter of basic importance. Thirdly, the financial system is the repository of the claims to wealth of most families in this country, who have selected financial assets partly because of their belief that these assets are safe. It is important that this not be an illusion, for the consequences of financial collapse are grave. Finally, we have suggested, the interrelationships within the financial system give rise to the possibility of monetary policy designed to influence the level of income and employment in the economy. This alone should be sufficient to create an interest in the economics of money and finance.

PART I

Microeconomics of the Canadian Financial System

The first part of this book (Chapters 2 — 12) is concerned with the micro-economics of the Canadian financial system. Microeconomics is that branch of economics which analyzes the processes involved in the allocation of resources and the distribution of income. These are vast and complex topics, and in our analysis we touch only a small but important corner. We are very narrowly concerned with the role of financial institutions and financial markets in the resource allocation process. In the Canadian economy, resource allocation occurs primarily through markets, which may be domestic or international in scope. Not surprisingly, our microeconomic analysis must also focus on markets, both financial markets *per se* and the interaction between financial institutions and other markets in the economy.

Among the fundamental microeconomic issues are the nature of money, and the role of money and of the payments system in the functioning of broader national and international markets in goods and services. These are considered in Chapter 2. However, financial markets also have importance in themselves, as vehicles for both the allocation of credit in the economy and the organization and reorganization of forms in which individuals hold their wealth. In Chapter 3 we explore the organization of major Canadian financial markets, and in Chapters 4 — 8 develop a theoretical analysis (with appropriate empirical support) of the functioning of these markets.

In one sense, financial markets are just like other markets in the economy. Although their stock in trade is somewhat unusual — pieces of paper which provide a link between the future and the present — they operate on the familiar principles of supply and demand, and prices are set and quantities change hands. Perhaps the most distinctive feature of financial markets is the presence of a group of institutions called financial intermediaries — institutions like banks, credit unions, and trust companies. These institutions are simultaneously principals on both sides of the market. They both borrow and lend. In any microeconomic analysis of the financial system, they require special attention. In Chapter 9 we develop a theory of financial intermediation, and in Chapters 10 — 12 explore the characteristics of the major Canadian intermediaries.

In our opinion, a major purpose for studying the microeconomics of the financial system is to provide a basis for the evaluation of governmental policy with respect to financial institutions and markets. This is a difficult subject. Clearly, a good understanding of the nature and theories of financial institutions and financial markets is basic to the criticism of policy. However, it is also important to see both the system and the policies in historical context — and it is useful to consider some alternative policies in other institutional and historical contexts. Building on the background of the chapters in Part I, these are the subjects considered in Part II of the book.

MONEY AND THE PAYMENTS SYSTEM 2

Money is a commonplace phenomenon. It is involved in all of our personal economic activities and is so much a part of our everyday life that we tend to take it for granted. Occasionally, perhaps following a casual visit to a numismatic shop or a discussion with a coin-collecting friend, we may be bemused by the diversity of things which have been used as money in different times and places. Or we may struggle with strange coins and unfamiliar denominations in another country, and wonder how such different "monies" can coexist in the world. But seldom do we stop and carefully consider how the "money system" works. Why can I obtain what I want at a store by handing over pieces of paper? Why will only certain pieces of paper do? How can I be sure that if I write and mail a cheque to pay a bill in a distant city (or perhaps another country) my creditor will in fact be paid? And if he is paid, what are the mechanics of the transfer? If we take pause, these and many similar questions may occur to us.

THE MONEY SUPPLY

Money Defined

What is money? A suitable definition might be *anything that is normally accepted when a transfer of purchasing power takes place.*

Long philosophical treatises have been written about the essence of "moneyness," attempting to explain why money is money — why certain objects are "normally accepted when a transfer of purchasing power takes place." Our definition, however, is pragmatic, not probing the essence of moneyness, but rather acknowledging as money anything that is in fact used as a customary and normal medium of exchange.

The words *customary* and *normal* are important. Our definition rules out things which may emerge on an occasional *ad hoc* basis as an intermediary in isolated and irregular exchange, but at the same time admits the possibility of a wide variety of objects performing this function in different times and different places: cigarettes in prisoner of war camps; cowrie shells in the primitive native trading economies of the precolonial Pacific Islands and the coasts of Africa; tobacco or warehouse receipts for tobacco in the colony of Virginia; playing cards in New France; gold and silver in the form of bullion, dust, or coins; and paper promissory notes of governments throughout the world.

What money is, then, is a matter of customary practice. The nature of the money supply in any particular area will evolve over time as customary practices adapt to changing circumstances. A list of items to be considered money at one time may be inappropriate at another. Moreover, at any given point, such a list may seem somewhat arbitrary. Whether a particular item qualifies as money or not involves a matter of judgment: is it a "normal and customary medium of exchange?"

Commodity vs. Fiat Monies

The story of the evolution of money in different historical, geographical, and cultural contexts is fascinating. Many people have sought general principles underlying this evolution, and it may be that such principles do exist. However, it is not part of our purpose to attempt to identify them, such a quest being more suited to the sociologist or anthropologist than the economist. As one scholar has noted, "Money does not exist in a vacuum. It is not a mere lifeless object, but a social institution."[1] However, we must take some interest in the form of the basic monetary medium because it affects the possibility for deliberate manipulation of the money supply as an aspect of government economic policy. The significant fact from this point of view is that while the process has been neither steady, one-directional, nor complete, the development of modern monetary systems has involved the displacement of *commodity monies* by intangible claims or *fiat monies.*

In early history, the object used as money tended to be one with intrinsic value as a commodity (as well as certain other desirable properties), or to be representative of such a commodity and freely convertible into it on demand. This commodity is normally referred to as the *standard money.* The most widely recognized monetary commodities are, of course, gold and, to a lesser extent, silver, and as a result the historical literature on monetary systems abounds with references to types of gold standards, silver standards, and bimetallic standards (with both metals as standard monies). Indeed, in spite of the passing of a formal gold standard, many people still regard gold as money *par excellence.*[2]

One effect of having a commodity base for the money supply was to place the size of the money supply largely (but seldom completely) beyond the control of the government. It was strongly influenced by forces governing the availability of the standard commodity. Thus, with a gold standard, the money supply would be affected by forces affecting the output of newly mined gold (including erratic discoveries of new rich deposits); the flow of gold in international trade; and the absorption of gold by industry for non-monetary purposes.

In modern times this link to a commodity has largely been broken. The coins issued by a modern state tend to be simply tokens, the value of the metal which they contain being far less than the value of the coin as a coin. Similarly, the notes which are issued as currency are generally not convertible on demand into any standard commodity (except in the sense that any holder of money can presumably purchase whatever commodities he prefers in the open market). Modern currencies are *fiat monies*. They are issued by governments, are not representative of any commodity, and are not redeemable in terms of such a commodity. By government fiat or decree, they are *legal tender*. That is, creditors are legally obligated to accept such currencies in settlement of debts. Since there is no legal link to a commodity, modern monetary systems are generally referred to as inconvertible paper standards. The possibilities for deliberate manipulation of the money supply — for good or evil — should be apparent.

There is another aspect of an inconvertible paper standard which also should be of interest to a student of economics. When the money supply is based on a commodity such as gold, an expansion of the money supply can only be accomplished by employing scarce productive resources to produce more of the commodity (or by attracting more of the commodity from alternative possible uses). A substantial economic cost is involved, equal, at the margin, to the value of the money created. With inconvertible paper money, the creation of more money is virtually (but not completely) costless. It does not absorb anywhere near the same value of scarce productive resources. As a result, by economizing on the scarce resources of the world, while performing exactly the same economic function, inconvertible paper money permits the attainment of a (slightly) higher overall standard of living.

In fact, in any modern economy, both token coins and fiat paper currencies constitute but a fraction of the money supply and account for an even smaller fraction of the total value of payments in the economy. By far the most important medium of exchange is the bank deposit which is convertible into currency on demand and is transferable among individuals by cheque. By our definition, these deposits are money, although they are not legal tender. They are "normally accepted when a transfer of purchasing power takes place." Yet they are completely intangible. They are claims on a private institution, a bank, taking the form simply of entries in a ledger book. Such money is commonly referred to as *bank money* or *credit money,* or, since it is based on trust in the soundness of the institution, *fiduciary money.*

The Canadian Money Supply

Armed with our pragmatic definition of money, what would we have to count if we set out to measure the Canadian money supply? The most obvious items, upon which we would all immediately agree, are the coins and notes used for hand-to-hand circulation. While the term *currency* is frequently used only with reference to the paper notes, we can properly use it to refer to both the coins and notes. In Canada, all currency is now issued by agencies of the Government of Canada.

Coins.   Coins are manufactured and issued by the Royal Canadian Mint, a branch of the Department of Finance. With rare exceptions (gold coins designed and sold as collectors' items rather than for actual circulation, although they are legal currency), these coins are intended to be *tokens*. That is, the face value of each coin is intended to be substantially greater than the market value of the metal contained in the coin. Since the coins are in effect sold to the public at their face value, the manufacture and issuance of coins is normally a profitable business. The difference between the face value of the coins and the value of the coins as metal is known as *seignorage,* and, after allowing for the other expenses related to the operation of the mint, it provides a (relatively minor) source of revenue for the government. In 1980, for example, the Royal Canadian Mint reported net gains on minting coins of approximately $17 million.

While coins are *intended* to be tokens, they do contain metal which has market value as a commodity. Since that market value can change under the combined pressures of supply and demand, it can happen that the value of the metal as a commodity comes to exceed the face value of the coin. This was dramatically illustrated in 1966 when the price of silver rose sharply in the open market, making the commodity value of Canada's silver coins exceed their value as coins. This not only made it unprofitable for the Mint to manufacture the traditional silver coins, but also made it profitable for private individuals to melt down the silver coins for their metal content (this is illegal, of course). As a result, the government reduced the silver content of new Canadian coins and in 1968 began to replace the silver coinage with pure nickel coins. Once again in the late 1970s the high world price for copper had raised the cost of producing a one-cent piece to between two and three cents each. To date, however the Mint has not taken steps to introduce a cheaper substitute for the traditional copper penny.

Paper currency.   The issuance of paper money in Canada is a government monopoly. It is the exclusive right and responsibility of the Bank of Canada, a crown corporation under the jurisdiction of the Minister of Finance.

The issuance of notes for circulation was not always a government monopoly in Canada. Prior to 1935, privately owned chartered banks had the right to issue paper currency. On December 31, 1934, of the total currency outstanding of $252 million, $119 million or 47%, were chartered bank notes. The balance was in coin and Dominion Notes issued by the Government of Canada. In 1935, the Bank of Canada began operations and assumed responsibility for the issuance of paper currency. (Initially privately owned, it was nationalized shortly after it was founded.) The chartered banks were required to gradually reduce the amount of their notes in circulation, and in 1950 the liability for such bank notes as were still outstanding (approximately $14 million) was assumed by the Bank of Canada in exchange for a corresponding payment to the Bank of Canada by the banks.

Bank of Canada notes are liabilities of the Bank of Canada, and until June 1970 they all bore the inscription, "The Bank of Canada will pay to the bearer on demand one dollar" (or "two dollars," or "five dollars," etc., as the case might be). This, however, was an essentially meaningless phrase, an anachronism that might have had some meaning if Canada had been on a gold standard under which the Bank was obliged to redeem all notes for an equivalent value of gold. Such is not the case today, nor has it been the case since the Bank of Canada was established.[3] If someone presents the Bank of Canada with some of its notes for payment "on demand," all that person can expect to receive is a different combination of Bank of Canada notes. In June 1970, as it began issuing a new series of notes, the Bank took the obvious step of removing this meaningless inscription. The new notes simply state: "This note is legal tender."

Paper currency in Canada is thus a form of government debt, but it is non-interest-bearing debt which need never be retired. Since the face value of Bank of Canada notes exceeds the value of the paper as a commodity, the government also earns seignorage on the issuance of paper money (Bank of Canada profits automatically revert to the government). We do not know the magnitude of this seignorage, but it is not as large as might be expected from the obvious nominal cost of a paper note. Paper currency wears out rapidly and must be continually replaced, significantly raising the costs of maintaining the outstanding volume of paper currency.

Bank Money.   As in other modern economies, the bulk of the money supply in Canada is bank money, the deposit liabilities of private banks. Just as paper currency is in effect government debt, so bank money is private debt. Bank depositors have made a loan to the bank. They are creditors, the banks, debtors. What happens in the payments process, therefore, is a transfer of ownership of the debts of banks.

There are many types of deposits (and we shall see later, many types of "banks"), not all which qualify as money in our definition. That is, not all deposits are designed to be used as a medium of exchange and hence not all deposits are customarily used as such. *The essential technical requirement for a deposit to be money in the narrow sense in which we have defined money is that the ownership of the deposit can be readily transferred from individual to individual, i.e., that it be chequable.*

A cheque is a written order from a depositor instructing his banker to pay a specified sum to a third party. It is the instrument through which the transfer of purchasing power is effected. Not all deposits can be transferred by cheque, and indeed, by focusing attention on this property we can readily identify three categories of deposits. In one category we have deposits which can only be withdrawn on a specified date or after a minimum period of notice. We would not want to classify these *term* or *notice* deposits as money. At the opposite extreme, and unequivocally money, are those deposits which can be withdrawn on demand and which are transferable among individuals by cheque, including *current account demand deposits, personal chequing accounts* and some (but not all) *personal savings accounts.* Although banks can legally require notice prior to the withdrawal of all personal savings deposits, in fact they do not.

A third type of deposit which can be withdrawn on demand, but only "over the counter," is the *non-chequable personal savings deposit.* However, it is debatable whether such deposits should be considered money or not. On our narrow formal definition they appear to be excluded. If they cannot be transferred by cheque, they are not designed and cannot be effectively used in their existing form as a medium of exchange. At the same time, it only takes a trip to the bank (indeed a phone call) to transfer the funds from such an account to a chequable account. If our concern was with the impact of the money supply on the behavior of firms and households, we would want to think twice about excluding such deposits. If they can be so readily transformed into "money," should not the holder of such an account behave as though he had money in his hands? Certainly if such deposits are not money, they are the nearest of *near monies.* The concept of near money will play a prominent role in our analysis in later chapters, when we will define it more precisely.

In referring to these deposits we have used the expression *bank money.* We might well ask if it is necessary for the deposits to be with a bank for them to be considered money. If we mean by a bank an institution which has a charter to engage in "the business of banking," issued by the federal government under the terms of the *Bank Act* (i.e. a "chartered bank"), then the answer is clearly no. There are, in Canada, a large number of institutions which accept deposits on essentially the same terms as chequable savings deposits with the chartered banks. These institutions are frequently called *near banks* and consist of certain trust companies, mortgage loan companies, credit unions, caisses populaires, Quebec savings banks, and certain provincially-owned financial institutions. We will examine their activities in greater detail in later chapters. What is relevant at the moment is that they hold deposits which are very close substitutes for personal savings deposits (chequable and non-chequable) with chartered banks. If we are to measure the money supply of Canada on the definition of money which we have proposed, then at least chequable deposits with such institutions must be included. They are normally and customarily accepted when a transfer of purchasing power occurs. Although they are not as important as bank deposits, they are a medium of exchange.

The Canadian Money Supply.   We are now in a position to answer the question which introduced this section: What should we count if we want to measure the Canadian money supply?

Our pragmatic definition of money says that we should include all of those items normally used when a transfer of purchasing power takes place. However, even this is a matter of degree. The items used most actively as media of exchange are currency (coins

**TABLE 2-1   The Canadian money supply, June 30, 1982
(\$ Millions)**

Payments money		
Currency (coin and notes)	\$ 10 673	
Demand deposits with chartered banks	15 185	
Payments money (narrow definition)		\$ 25 858
Chequable savings and time deposits with:		
Chartered banks	8 085	
Trust and loan companies	2 132	
Caisses populaires and credit unions	3 886*	
Payments money (broad definition)		39 961
Near money deposits		
Non-chequable deposits with:		
Chartered banks	138 871	
Trust and loan companies	54 354	
Caisses populaires and credit unions†	26 343*	
Payments money and near money		\$259 529

* March 31, 1982
† Term deposits and share capital.
SOURCE: *Bank of Canada Review;* Statistics Canada, *Financial Institutions*

and Bank of Canada notes in circulation outside banks) and demand deposits with chartered banks. We can refer to these items as payments money in the narrowest sense (and in measuring the money supply we will include only currency and deposits held by the public). Chequable savings deposits with chartered banks and near banks are also payments money, although they are used much less intensively in the payments stream. In Table 2-1, we have set out data on the Canadian money supply at mid-1982 on both definitions. As we will see later in the book, it is sometimes argued that a broader definition of money is appropriate for certain analytical purposes, including certain types of near money. Accordingly, Table 2-1 also includes data on near-money deposits with near banks.

The Composition of the Money Supply.   There are, then, several items which can be used as money in Canada. What determines the composition of the money supply? Is the composition constant over time?

In considering these questions, the important principle to keep in mind is that while the various types of money in use in Canada are not officially convertible into any commodity like gold or silver, they are *freely convertible into each other*. Thus, the holder of a demand deposit in a bank can, at any time (at least while the bank is open) convert his deposit into currency. Likewise, a holder of Bank of Canada notes can readily convert them into coins, or into a demand deposit, or into a personal savings deposit at any of the banks or near banks which hold such deposits. This means that the *composition* of the money supply depends simply on the relative demands of the public for each type of money. (We italicize the word "composition" because this is not true of the *size* of the total money supply.)

Why might the public have different demands for each type of money? A major explanation (apart from habit) must be that each type of money is efficient for different purposes.

As is evident from Table 2-1, deposits, transferable by cheque, constitute the largest part of the money supply: about 75% on the broader definition. This refers to the stock of money held at any point in time. What is not shown on the table is the fact that the actual transfer of such deposits accounts for an even larger portion of the total value of payments made in Canada. There are no data to which we can refer, but some authorities estimate that between 85% and 90% of the value of transactions are effected by cheques.

The users of money in Canada clearly find bank money the most convenient form for most purposes. As an asset, bank money is safer than currency. It can only be withdrawn by the owner of the deposit; whereas currency can be lost through theft, fire, natural disaster, etc. Therefore, there is a much smaller risk of loss as long as the bank itself is sound. (Note: in Canada, additional safety is provided by the fact that bank deposits are insured by government agencies up to a maximum $60 000 per deposit.) The cheque is a convenient and (at least for large transactions) relatively cheap method of making payment. It can be drawn for exactly the correct sum, and can be readily transported over long distances through the mail at very low cost. The shipment of currency, by contrast, can be very expensive, and in addition involves risk of loss. There are alternative transfer arrangements with currency, e.g., postal money orders or telegraphic transfers, but again these are relatively expensive as compared to cheques. It

Measuring the Money Supply: A Continuing Debate

Our concept of payments money would be unlikely to gain the endorsement of most economists as their preferred measure of the money supply. In fact, one of the most fiercely contested debates in economics in recent years has been over the appropriate definition of the money supply. The issues in the debate can be quite easily understood once it is recognized that the starting point for any measurement must be the purpose for which it is undertaken. When we are buying shoes we need to know the length and width of our feet but are less interested in their weight. In contrast, in buying meat, the length and width of a piece of steak is of less interest than its weight. When we measured the money supply earlier in this chapter, we were interested in determining the value of those items which are currently used in transferring goods and services among individuals. But as we will see, many measurements of the money supply are made for other purposes.

In following Milton Friedman, the most effective advocate of the modern approach to the quantity theory and Nobel prize winner for his work, we can view *money as a predictor* of money income. The quantity theory of money, as we show in more detail in Chapter 21, states that the money supply is one of the most important determinants of the level of overall money income in an economy. In the 1960s, when Friedman began to publish statistical studies of the relationship between the money supply and income in the United States, he distinguished between *M1*, a money supply measure consisting of currency in public circulation and demand deposits, and *M2*, which included, in addition to *M1*, time deposits at commercial banks. Even though his *M1* corresponds more closely with our payments money, Friedman chose to emphasize the relationship between *M2* and

income because *M2* appeared to explain movements in money income to a greater degree than did *M1*. Since the time of Friedman's initial work, economists of many persuasions have studied the relationship between various concepts of the money supply and aggregate income. One result of these studies has been a proliferation of different concepts of money which the various investigators have argued are superior in "explaining," in a statistical sense, movements in national income.

Another purpose for measuring the money supply is as a guide to central banks in conducting their monetary policy. As a consequence, we can view *money as a target* for central bank policy. In the 1970s, a number of central banks, in face of the mounting evidence of a close relationship between changes in the money supply and changes in national income, modified the emphasis of their operating procedures away from credit market conditions and, in particular, the level of interest rates, toward target levels of the money supply. The Bank of Canada's Governor, Gerald Bouey, announced the adoption of such a policy of *monetarism* in his so-called "Saskatoon Manifesto" speech of September 1975. The adoption of money supply targets by the Bank of Canada and other central banks raises a further dimension of the measurement of money. Which measure of the money supply should the central bank attempt to control?

This has proven to be a contentious issue. The central bank controls the money supply not as an end in itself but as a means to achieving superior macroeconomic performance as generally gauged by the stability and growth of national income and the stability of prices. Choice of a monetary target involves a trade-off between the closeness of the relationship between the money measure and national income and the degree of control by the central bank over the chosen monetary measure. Obviously, the central bank should choose a measure which appears closely related to national income, otherwise the attempt to stabilize national income by controlling a monetary aggregate would be jeopardized. In addition, the central bank must be concerned with its ability to control the chosen monetary aggregate. A monetary target which is closely related to national income would not be very useful if it could not be controlled. On the basis of these considerations, the Bank of Canada has designated its monetary target in terms of *M1*, the sum of currency and demand deposits at the chartered banks.

The Bank of Canada collects and publishes statistics on a variety of measures of the money supply in addition to *M1*, as shown in the table. *M1* includes only currency held by the public and demand deposits held at chartered banks. The next concept, *M1B*, includes, in addition to *M1*, all other chequable deposits at chartered banks. The most inclusive monetary measure published by the Bank is *M3* which consists of currency plus total privately held chartered bank deposits. This last measure does not differentiate be-

tween Canadian dollar and foreign currency deposits of Canadian residents, and includes both. We note that none of the Bank of Canada's measures correspond to our broader concept of payments money. All of the Bank's measures exclude the liabilities of near banks which are chequable and hence can be used for making payments but which are included in our measure.

We should not be too surprised that economists do not agree on a single measure of the money supply. After all, economists have different reasons for measuring it. Payments money need not be identical to "money as a target" or "money as a predictor." Even these latter two concepts need not be identical for controllability, which is obviously important for money as a target, but is not necessary for money as a predictor. Much confusion and needless controversy might have been avoided had economists made their purposes clear from the beginning. Still, we must be careful to avoid exaggerating the differences in views about the measurement of money. All three approaches — payments money, money as a predictor, and money as a target — are based on the view that those items that are generally accepted in exchange for goods and services have a special role in the functioning of our economy.

TABLE 2-2 **Alternative measures of the money supply, June 30, 1982 ($ Millions)**

Bank of Canada concepts		
Currency and demand deposits	M1	$ 25 858
Currency and all chequable deposits with chartered banks	M1B	33 943
Currency and all chequable, notice and personal term deposits with chartered banks	M2	128 722
Currency and all privately held chartered bank deposits	M3	176 612
Payments money (broad definition)		$39 961

SOURCE: *Bank of Canada Review;* Table 2-1.

is also worth noting that cheques leave a very convenient record for the firm or individual.

Bank money, then, is relatively convenient for most commercial purposes, but there is always some demand for currency from individuals who do not trust or do not understand banks. There is probably also some demand from individuals who find that the property of cheques of leaving a record of transactions is a disadvantage, e.g., persons trying to avoid income tax or persons engaged in illegal transactions.[4] Beyond that, currency is relatively convenient for small, local transactions. Given a standard bank charge per cheque (regardless of the magnitude of the cheque), cheques are relatively costly for small transactions. Moreover, the person drawing a cheque may have to go through the inconvenient and time-consuming routine of identifying himself and providing evidence that he indeed has an account with the bank in question. Also, coins have a particular use in automatic vending machines, which are of increasing importance in the retail trade. The active use of currency, therefore, is closely related to the retail trade, and particularly "small ticket" retail sales.

Little historical research has been done on the changing composition of the money supply in Canada. Research in the United States shows a relatively strong downward long-run trend in the ratio of currency to the total money supply, at least until 1930. There were major increases in the ratio in the depression of the 1930s (when there was a widespread loss of confidence in the banking system as a result of a wave of bank failures) and during World War II (perhaps because of increased foreign hoardings of U.S. dollars, and increased use of currency for illegal transactions and tax evasion). Although the long-run trend seemed to re-emerge after World War II, by the mid-1960s the ratio of currency to money was much higher than in the pre-war period (the 1920s, for example).

Within each year (and each month, and each week), there are also striking patterns in the use of currency relative to deposits, following mainly the retail trade (and for shorter time periods, payroll arrangements). Thus, the ratio of currency to money systematically rises to a peak in December with the burst of retail activity related to the Christmas season, and has several minor peaks during the year also related to retail activity.

THE PAYMENTS SYSTEM

Payment by currency is a straightforward affair about which little more need be said. However, as we have already pointed out, currency is a relatively inconvenient medium of exchange, except for small local transactions. In fact, transfers of currency probably account for a rather small share of the total value of transactions. The arrangements for transferring purchasing power by cheque are necessarily more complicated, although the principles involved are actually very simple.

Payment by Cheque

To illustrate the principle underlying payment by cheque we can trace what happens when you have purchased some major item, received the bill, and have written a cheque in payment. The cheque, you will recall, is nothing other than a written order to your banker to pay the appropriate amount to the merchant. If, as is the case for about 15% of cheque transactions, both you and the merchant have accounts with the same branch of the same bank all that happens is that the bank makes the appropriate entries on its books. The merchant's account is credited (increased) with the appropriate amount; your account is debited (decreased). Purchasing power is transferred with a few strokes of the bookkeeper's pen (or, more likely, an entry in the bank's computer).

If you have accounts with different branches of the same bank the transfer is only slightly more complicated. The merchant's branch credits the appropriate sum to his account and sends the cheque to your branch. After verification of the authenticity of the cheque, the appropriate sum is deducted from your account. Again, all that is involved is a series of bookkeeping entries, even though you and the merchant live in different cities.

But what if you do *not* have accounts with the same bank or indeed if you have accounts in another financial institution such as a credit union or trust company? The principle is just the same. If you mail a cheque from Vancouver on a Royal Bank account to a merchant in Montreal with an account at the Bank of Montreal, he will deposit it in his branch of the Bank of Montreal, which will forward it to your branch of the Royal Bank in Vancouver for verification and deduction from your account. The only important difference is that the Bank of Montreal ends up with a claim on the Royal Bank in the amount of your cheque, requiring an interbank settlement of this debt.

The Clearinghouse.   Banks and other financial institutions will not make separate interbank payments for each individual cheque. Rather, the branch receiving the cheque forwards it to its institution's clearing branch at the nearest of the regional clearing centers. Here, depending on the size of the center, cheques are exchanged among the institutions at least daily, and in larger centers virtually continually. Once a day, the representatives of each bank and other financial institutions that are members of the Canadian Payments Association will meet in a central location, called the *clearinghouse,* to simultaneously exchange an accounting of the cheques drawn on each other and received for deposit since the previous day's clearing. The claims of each bank or each institution on each of the others are totalled by the manager of the clearinghouse, and the institutions then settle the *net balance* due. In principle, the interbank settlements could be effected by payment of currency. In fact, this will not be done: all interinstitution transfers are ultimately effected through bookkeeping entries at the Bank of Canada.[5]

Each member of the Canadian Payments Association directly or indirectly maintains a deposit with the Bank of Canada (in this sense the Bank of Canada is a "bankers' bank") which is notified of the results of the daily clearings at each major clearinghouse. It then simply transfers the appropriate sums from the deposits of those institutions that have lost funds in the clearings to the deposits of those institutions that have gained funds.

The network of local and regional clearinghouses is obviously a vital element in the domestic payments system. In Canada these clearinghouses were established and operated for many years by the Canadian Bankers Association, an organization of all the chartered banks. It will be remembered that there are many other financial institutions which hold chequable deposits: institutions such as trust companies, caisses populaires, and credit unions, which we referred to collectively as near banks. Under the 1980 Bank Act, the Canadian Payments Association was created to administer the clearing system and, unlike the previous arrangements, included near banks in its membership. Near banks can continue to use other members of the clearing system as their agent for clearing on a fee basis. These near banks maintain accounts with the financial institution which serves as its agent. Cheques drawn on the near bank and deposited in another financial institution are presented to the near bank's clearing agent, through the clearinghouse as though they were cheques drawn on the clearing agent itself. The agent makes payments as on the near bank's cheques, and then arranges the appropriate settlement with the near bank. Other near banks may choose to become members of the Canadian Payments Association on exactly the same basis as the chartered banks.

Service Charges.   Payment by cheque is more efficient than payment by currency for many types of transactions. The use of currency is frequently inconvenient, risky, and costly. But we should not assume that the service provided by the bank is costless. Indeed, the costs associated with the servicing of demand deposits are among the major costs incurred by banks. In the United States it has been estimated that between 40% and 50% of all bank employees are assigned to the cheque-processing function. While we do not have comparable data, it is presumably approximately the same in this country. This should not be surprising since on an average business day millions of cheques will be written, and while the volume of activity depends on the size and location of the office, major bank offices will handle many thousands of cheques drawn on out-of-town branches and other banks. Thus, in the early 1980s, Canadian banks handled roughly 2 billion cheques per year, with an aggregate value in excess of $2000 billion.

The costs in question arise in connection with the handling of all the documents and bookkeeping entries involved in transferring funds by cheque. This has provided fertile grounds for automation, and while there are large numbers of items, the costs involved depend more directly on the *number* of cheques handled than on the total value of payments transferred. Thus, it costs no more to handle a cheque for $1 million than it does to handle a cheque for $1 (providing it is cleared through the same channels).

The banks attempt to recover the costs of handling these payments in two ways. They do not pay interest on current accounts. Thus, in effect the depositor makes an interest-free loan to the bank, foregoing interest income for the privilege of writing cheques. The bank can use the money to make loans or purchase securities, using the interest income to help cover the costs of providing chequing facilities. In the case of chequable personal savings deposits, the banks do pay interest, but at a lower rate than on non-chequable accounts, and they discourage the writing of a large number of cheques. In addition to the interest foregone, the depositor is normally assessed a *service charge* which is related to the number of cheques he writes.[6] The exact amount of the charge depends on the type of deposit, the size of the minimum balance maintained in the deposit (which affects the interest income the bank can earn on funds deposited), and the number of cheques written each month. The service charges bear relatively more heavily on cheques drawn for small sums of money than on cheques for large sums. This is one factor making the cheque a relatively more efficient instrument for large payments than for small ones.

An Alternate Clearing System: The United States

The principle of local clearinghouses is common to all banking systems. However, the arrangements for the clearing and collection of out-of-town cheques in the United States are sometimes significantly different from those which prevail in Canada. Partly because the institutions of the U.S. banking system have a direct and obvious importance to Canadians, and partly because the U.S. system contains features advocated by some economists for adoption in Canada, it is useful to make a brief comparison of the two methods of handling out-of-town cheques.

Branch Banking versus "Fragmented" Banking.   The most striking feature of the Canadian banking system is the relatively small number of banks, five of which account for over 90% of all deposits. Each of these five major banks has a network of branches in every major city in every province in the nation. Out-of-town cheques deposited in any branch are collected through the facilities provided by the nationwide network of branches. The local clearinghouses provide links between the nationwide branch banking organizations, but the collection of out-of-town cheques is essentially internal to each branch banking organization. While the central bank is involved in settling clearing balances, no external agency is involved in the cheque collection process.

In the United States such large-scale nationwide branch banking firms do not exist. In place of Canada's small number of nationwide banks, together with a few regional and specialized ones, the United States has some 15 000 banks. Many of these have extensive branch organizations in limited areas, but branching across state boundaries is not permitted.[7] While the term is not fully accurate (since there are many branch banking firms) the U.S. banking system is generally referred to as a *unit banking system.* Perhaps the term "fragmented" would be more descriptive.

A second distinctive feature of the U.S. banking system is that not all banks are required (or allowed) to maintain deposits with the central bank, i.e., the Federal Reserve System. The term "system" is quite appropriate. The central bank is in fact a network of 12 regional Federal Reserve Banks, coordinated by the Board of Governors of the Federal Reserve System in Washington, D.C. The fact that not all commercial banks belong to the Federal Reserve System is a product of the dual character of arrangements for chartering banks. Both the federal and state governments can issue bank charters. National banks are required to be members of the Federal Reserve System and to hold deposits with the regional Federal Reserve Bank. State banks, if they meet certain minimum requirements, are permitted to join the system, but they are not required to do so.

It should be obvious that the process of clearing and collecting cheques in the United States *must* be considerably more complicated than in Canada. It is not possible to rely on the facilities of nationwide branch-banking organizations — they do not exist. All clearings cannot be handled through the central bank — not all banks hold deposits with the central bank. Indeed, in one sense there is not one central bank, but 12, so arrangements must be made for each Federal Reserve Bank to settle clearing balances with each of the other Federal Reserve Banks.

In fact, there are two parallel systems for the collection of out-of-town cheques in the United States: the Federal Reserve System, and the correspondent banking system.

The Central Bank as a Cheque Collection Agency.   Unlike the Bank of Canada, the Federal Reserve System is actively involved in the collection of out-of-town cheques. Each Federal Reserve Bank will accept cheques from member banks (and under some circumstances from non-member banks also) which it will then forward to the appropriate cities for collection. The bank depositing the cheques for collection will receive appropriate credit in its deposit with the Federal Reserve Bank, and the corresponding adjustment will be made in the paying bank's deposit at the other end.

The Correspondent Banking System.   Although this cheque collection service is free, most out-of-town cheques are not collected through the agency of the Federal Reserve System. Evidence suggests that the larger banks rely on the Federal Reserve to collect a major portion of their out-of-town cheques; smaller banks are less reliant on the Federal Reserve facilities. The rest of the out-of-town cheques are collected through an alternative system, a network of correspondent banks.

Correspondent banking relations involve banks' maintaining deposits with each other and performing certain services for each other. Generally speaking, smaller banks in outlying areas maintain deposits with correspondent banks in larger cities in the region; these banks in turn hold deposits with correspondent banks in still larger cities. However, the structure of the system is not a simple pyramid. Many banks, and particularly larger ones in larger cities, hold deposits for other banks and also maintain deposits with these same correspondents. Moreover, the larger banks will have correspondent relations with many banks, including foreign banks.

City correspondent banks provide a variety of services for their country correspondents. This includes participation in loans too large for the small bank to handle, advice on investments, assistance in trading in government securities, and sometimes assistance in the recruitment and training of personnel. But the main service, and the only one of interest to us, is the clearing and collection of out-of-town cheques. Correspondent banks act as agents for other banks in the collection of cheques. Thus, instead of using the facilities of the Federal Reserve System, a bank receiving a cheque drawn on an out-of-town bank has the option of sending it to a correspondent bank in that city for collection, and having the proceeds deposited in its account with the correspondent. Similarly, a bank having to make payment in another city can do so by drawing drafts on its correspondent balances. In the Canadian banking system this same service would be provided by distant branches of the same bank. A branch-banking firm has its own built-in correspondent system. Thus, from the point of view of cheque clearing and collection and of a whole range of banking services and operations, branch banking and correspondent banking are substitutes.

Two clearing systems coexist in the United States partly because many banks do not belong to the Federal Reserve System. But even member banks make heavy use of the correspondent system. Because of the increased deposits which it provides to them, many city banks have found it profitable to compete actively for correspondent business. The result of their competition is fast, efficient service in collecting cheques (plus all of the other services that go along with correspondent relations), which many banks find preferable in some respect to the service provided by the central bank. In general, the Federal Reserve System is used most heavily to collect cheques drawn on very distant banks, and the correspondent system is used to collect cheques drawn on banks which are not so remote.

Some indication of the scope of correspondent relationships can be gained from examining the volumes of corresponding balances. As of June 30, 1981, some 362 banks each held at least $5 million correspondent balances on behalf of other banks. The total correspondent balances held by these banks were greater than $52 billion, with the largest correspondent balances at any bank exceeding $6 billion. At one time, a large New York City bank was reported to hold correspondent balances for over 4000 banks.

The correspondent banking principle is universal in banking. While the dominance of nationwide branch banking in Canada makes an elaborate network of correspondent relations unnecessary in domestic banking operations, the institution (although not called correspondent banking) can be seen in our description of the Canadian clearing system. It is the principle which underlies access for some near banks to the Canadian Payments Association clearinghouses. In addition, the smaller, regionally oriented Canadian banks maintain correspondent relations with their larger, nationwide counterparts. All Canadian banks have extensive correspondent relations with banks throughout the world.

Par Clearing.   The involvement of the Federal Reserve System in the cheque collection process has had another important effect in the U.S. payments system. The Federal Reserve System has insisted on what is called *par clearing*.

Until June 1970, Canadian banks levied a special charge, called an *exchange charge,* on all cheques cashed or deposited that were drawn on branches or banks outside the region serviced by the local clearinghouse. The charge was usually 1/8 of 1% of the face value of the cheque, with a minimum charge of 15 cents. The banks justified exchange charges on out-of-town cheques on the grounds that it is more costly to handle such cheques than it is to handle local cheques. They justified a fee based on the value of the cheque (rather than on the number of cheques) on the grounds that since the customer depositing the out-of-town cheque is given immediate credit for it, even though it may take the banks several days to collect the cheque from the person who wrote it, the bank in effect makes an interest-free loan to the person who deposits the cheque (and, incidentally, the bank runs some risk that the cheque may "bounce," giving rise to additional collection costs). Thus, until the later 1960s, the Canadian system involved *non-par clearing.* Out-of-town cheques were not necessarily accepted at their face value.

Exchange charges of this type were also common in the early banking system of the United States. However, throughout its history (since 1913) the Federal Reserve System has attempted to eliminate exchange charges and hence to impose the principle of par clearing. It has done this in two ways. Initially it made par clearing compulsory for member banks of the Federal Reserve System, and when this did not achieve the desired results (because many banks chose not to join the system), it gave non-member banks access to the federal cheque collection service on condition that they accept the par clearing principle. The Federal Reserve efforts have been largely successful.

Since, as we have already noted, the process of clearing and collecting cheques is far from costless, it can be argued that a charge for the service is both fair and economically efficient. It would be economically efficient on the grounds that those who use the scarce resources of the economy ought to pay a price equal to the value of those resources in their alternative uses, i.e., ought to pay a price equal to the marginal cost of the service. Why, then, has the Federal Reserve been so insistent on par clearing?

The Federal Reserve case rested largely on the social interest in an efficient, low-cost cheque payments system. The non-par clearing system led to circuitous routings of cheques to avoid exchange charges, with consequent delays in payments. Equally important, the exchange charges had discriminatory effects. Not all bank depositors were treated alike, and the differences were not necessarily related to costs. Banks were accused of exploiting whatever monopolistic power they had, making the charging of exchange charges a profitable activity. (It is still true that non-par banks are typically the only bank in any given town.) The principle that the recipient of a payment, rather than the remitter, is required to pay the cost of the payment can also be questioned. Perhaps the appropriate place to levy charges is on the deposit, with the charges related to the activity of the account.

Foreign Payments

So far we have examined how transfers of purchasing power are made possible within the confines of one nation. For a trading nation such as Canada, an important number of the total transactions involve payments to or from places outside the nation's boundaries. Such payments introduce two complications: The Canadian bank may not have branches in the relevant foreign center (although Canadian banks do have agencies in many important foreign financial centers), and the payment involves another currency besides the Canadian dollar.

The first of the complications is readily solved using the correspondent banking principle already examined in the context of the U.S. clearing system. To illustrate, assume that you live in Winnipeg and that a bill you owe in Minneapolis is payable in U.S. dollars. (The bill could just as well be made payable in London, Cairo, Tokyo, or Moscow.) You could use different methods to pay the bill. You could go to your local bank branch and buy U.S. currency in exchange for Canadian currency. The U.S. currency could then be mailed to Minneapolis, completing the transfer. This method involves a risk of theft or loss and would be suitable for small transactions only. More safely, you could purchase a bank draft payable in U.S. funds and send it to Minneapolis. This draft is in effect a check written by the Canadian bank upon an account it holds in a U.S. correspondent bank. The recipient of the check in Minneapolis deposits or cashes the draft and it is then put through the clearing system just as if it were any other check written on a U.S. bank. The Canadian bank reduced its holdings of U.S. dollars (i.e., its deposits with its Minneapolis correspondent) and increased its holdings of Canadian currency or reduced its deposits liabilities by an equivalent amount. For providing this service the bank charges a fee for the draft and a fee for exchanging Canadian dollars for U.S. dollars.

A second question that arises: How does the Canadian bank obtain the U.S. dollar deposits to sell to its customers? There are two possibilities. First, corresponding to the payment by Canadians to foreigners are reverse payments by foreigners to Canadians. To the extent that the Canadian recipients of these payments are customers of the bank, it has a flow of U.S. dollars out of which it can meet its customers' demands. Second, if the demands for U.S. dollars exceed the funds which the bank has available, it can enter the foreign exchange market and purchase the required U.S. funds from other banks which have a surplus. This market is an essential part of the international payments process. We will examine it in more detail in a later chapter.

In summary, the crucial institutions involved in international payments are an international network of correspondent banks and a foreign exchange market in which foreign monies can be bought and sold just as if they were commodities like wheat or rice.

THE EVOLUTION OF THE PAYMENTS SYSTEM[8]

We have seen the continuing evolution of the payments system, starting from a system of crude barter and developments, through the use of pure commodity money and paper money issued by government, to the present stage of primarily bank money in the form of deposits. As we will see shortly, each of these changes contributed to the increased efficiency of the payments system. As might be expected, the payments system continues to evolve. The most interesting current developments are the emergence of the general purpose payments card and the use of the computer in the electronic payments system.

The Payments Card

The payments card has been around in one form or another for some time. The earliest type of payments card was the merchant charge card, or credit card, issued by retail merchants such as department stores and oil companies, which entitled selected customers to make purchases on credit from the merchant who issued the card. The card's role, when present in these credit arrangements, was to identify those customers who were eligible to use the credit facilities to make their purchases. The advantage to customers of using the card was twofold. They were able through using the credit facility to spread payment for any purchases over an extended period of time. In addition, even if they did not use the credit facility they could make purchases without using cash and with the need to make only one payment per month.

The next stage in the evolution of the payments card was the appearance in the 1950s of the general payments cards issued by organizations such as American Express, Diners' Club, and Carte Blanche. These cards differed from the merchant credit cards in that they could be used to make purchases from a variety of merchants cooperating with the card issuer. As with the merchant card, the purchaser is extended credit by the card issuer in order to make the purchase; in contrast, however, the merchant does not extend the credit but rather is paid immediately by the card issuer who makes the loan to the purchaser. While in principle the general payments card could be viewed as quite close to our concept of payments money for making transactions, in practice it has been limited to use in a rather narrow range of transactions such as luxury goods and payments to hotels and restaurants.

The third stage in the evolution of the payments card has been the development of payments cards issued by banks. The use of the bank payments card for making payments involves the same process as with the general payments card in that the merchant receives payment from the issuing bank almost immediately and, as a result, the bank issuing the card supplies the credit which finances the transaction. Traditionally with bank payments cards, the purchaser has the option of paying the accumulated balance in total each billing period or paying only a portion of the balance and incurring interest charges on the remainder, usually at a rate comparable to that on other consumer loans. The banks issuing the payments cards also earn revenue through a discount charged to the merchant which ranges anywhere from 2 to 5.75% of the value of the sale according to the total volume and average size of the merchant's transactions.

Bank payments cards are generally issued by groups of associated banks. The two major bank cards are Visa, started in the 1960s by Bank of America as Bank Americard, and Mastercard. Four Canadian banks — Royal Bank of Canada, Canadian Bank of Commerce, Toronto Dominion Bank and the then Bank Canadian National (now National Bank of Canada) — introduced Visa's predecessor, Chargex, to Canada in 1967. Subsequently, in 1972, one other bank, the Bank of Nova Scotia, joined the Visa system and, in 1973, two other banks, the Bank of Montreal and the Provincial Bank (now merged with Bank Canadian National as part of National Bank of Canada), brought Mastercard to Canada. Now the caisses populaires in Quebec plus a number of trust companies also offer the use of the payments card to their customers.

By October 1981, about 9 million Visa cards and about 3.5 million Mastercharge cards were outstanding in Canada, while Visa was accepted by 215 000 merchants and Mastercharge by 140 000 merchants. It is estimated that during 1981 retail sales using bank payments cards totalled roughly $15 billion, with an average sale of approximately $40. Even though the value of sales through these payments cards is only a minor fraction of the value of total retail sales, the importance of the cards lies in their possible role in the payments system of the future.

Our examination of the payments card raises several important questions. What contribution does the payments card make to the efficiency of our payments system? What developments can we anticipate in terms of the payments cards and the future system of exchange? How should we treat the payments card in terms of our measure of the money supply?

The Efficiency of the Card.   We have already outlined the evolution of the payments system through a variety of stages: barter, commodity money, paper money, and bank money. Each of these changes can be understood in terms of the increased efficiency of the payments system that could be gained from its adoption. The movement to a commodity money permitted transactors to avoid the problem of double coincidence of wants involved in barter transaction whereby each transactor had to find someone else who was willing to accept exactly what the first transactor was willing to give up, and who was willing to give up exactly what the first transactor was willing to receive. Commodity money, in contrast, existed as a medium of exchange which was acceptable to both parties in the transaction. Sellers would accept commodity money in the confidence that people selling to them would in turn accept commodity money. Still, commodity money was not without its own difficulties. Transactors were required to determine the value of the commodity, such as the gold incorporated in the money, so as to ensure that they were gaining their desired price for the objects they were selling. Thus, the move to paper money permitted sellers to avoid the necessity of determining the commodity value of the money offered by the buyers. The use of paper money did not obviate the need for buyers and sellers to physically exchange the goods for money at the time of purchase. The actual physical possession of money imposed costs of safekeeping and security on people using money for making payments. Finally, the use of bank deposits allowed buyers and sellers to make exchanges without the physical presence of the medium of payment and the attendant problems of security.

Even with the advantages that bank money had over its predecessors, some problems still remained with respect to its general acceptability. Certainly, most transactors in a modern economy would willingly accept bank money in exchange for goods and services; the remaining problem was ascertaining that the cheque presented in payment was a valid claim on a bank deposit. This limitation meant that for most transactions bank money could only be used where the purchaser was known or could readily establish that the cheque would be paid. The bank card can be thought of as a form of payment guarantee: any merchant that follows the procedures established by the bank issuing the bank card is assured payment in full. For small payments, within the appropriate limit determined by the type of transaction, the merchant must determine that the card is valid by checking against a list of "hot" or invalid cards. For larger transactions, the merchant must gain authorization from the organization that issued the bank card. The use of bank cards has also allowed many businesses to avoid the security problems created by the use of currency. Many service stations, for example, during late night hours only accept either exact payment in currency, which then is put directly into a safe, or payment by a payments card. To some extent, the perceived advantages to merchants of payments cards is revealed by their willingness to accept the cards on the same terms as currency despite the discount given up in accepting this form of payment.

The Future of the Payments Card.   As we have seen, the bank payments card is a recent phenomenon in our system of making payments. In fact, we have strong reason to believe that the bank payments card has not yet achieved its full potential as an element in the payments system. To date, the development of the payments card has been closely tied to computer technology. The universal acceptability of the card, at least for large transactions, has required the merchant to verify that the cardholders remaining credit balance is sufficient to cover the transaction. For locally issued cards, the merchant phones a center operated by the card issuing bank where the cardholder's account can be readily consulted. For other cards, the merchant's bank contacts an authorization center which has access to the records of all card issuers participating in that payments card system. Clearly such a general payments system would be extremely costly in the absence of computer technology. We should expect to see the workings of the payments card system change in parallel with continuing advances in computer technology, a topic to be considered in more detail later in this chapter.

What future developments are on the horizon for the payments card? While it is always hazardous to attempt to forecast technical change, at least two developments have begun to emerge. First, a number of banks in the United States have offered a debit card as an alternative to the present credit card for making payments. Whereas the credit card requires the buyer to make payments by incurring a liability in the form of a debt to the card issuer, with a debit card the buyer is able to use an existing asset in the form of a deposit to make a payment. It appears that the debit card has come about because some card issuers want to avoid the cost of automatically granting free credit over the initial grace period that occurs under the existing payments card arrangements. In addition, the debit card may permit some households which do not qualify for a line of credit to gain access to the card payment system. With a debit card, they only have to establish a deposit balance which can be drawn down by card payment transactions. The second development is the prospect of a payments card which by itself would maintain a record of the customer's remaining line of credit or deposit account. Such a card would have a magnetic strip with such information in the form of coded electric charges. Each time a purchase was made with the card, the information on the magnetic strip would be revised to reflect the current payment. Periodically, card holders could take their cards to the financial institution which issued the card to have the remaining balance replenished by making the equivalent of a deposit into a conventional account. The advantage of such a card is that it would reduce the need for verification of payments cards for all transactions. Instead, the information encoded in such a card provides a basis for determining that the card use is within its acceptable limit.

The Payments Card and the Money Supply.   Our interest in the payments card arises from its possible role in the future evolution of the payments system. In particular, should we include the payments card and its accompanying institutional arrangements as part of the monetary system? The first issue to consider is the role of the card in the payments system. Here, we must distinguish between the instruments by which ownership of money is transferred, and the object, which is money itself. For some types of money, this distinction is not required. The coin is both the instrument used to transfer commodity money and the commodity itself. In contrast, a cheque is not money; rather, it is the means by which ownership of bank deposits, which are money, is transferred from buyer to seller. The payments card performs the same function as the cheque: it is the instrument used in the transfer of purchasing power from buyer to seller. In the case of the payments card, however, buyers increase their liabilities, in particular indebtedness to the card issuer, in making the payments, whereas with a cheque, buyers reduce their assets in the form of bank deposits. The recent emergence of so-called "debit" payment cards decreases this distinction. With the debit card, the buyer draws down deposit balances in making payments.

Recognition that payments cards are only instruments for the transfer of purchasing power raises the question of what measure of purchasing power should be included as part of the money supply. Under the existing institutional arrangements, transactions made by payments cards are paid from lines of credit granted to card holders by the card issuer. Inclusion of these credit lines would lead to a change in principle in measuring the money supply. Our present measures include only deposits which are assets of money holders; the equivalent measure for the payments card is a liability, a line of credit. Moreover, the liability is a potential liability in that it represents a line of credit on which the individual is permitted to draw in making transactions. This question of principle should not, however, stand in the way of attempting to reflect the use of payments cards in our measure of the money supply. The past has shown that what has been an appropriate measure of the money supply must at times be altered to reflect the change in payments practices.

A second issue in considering the role of the payments card in the payments system is the frequency with which it is used in making transactions. Recall that earlier in this chapter we defined money as anything that is normally accepted when a transfer of purchasing power takes place. The word "normally" helps us in deciding what to count as part of money. It permits us to exclude bus tickets and other tokens which can be used only for a very limited range of transactions. Clearly, payments cards are not acceptable for a wide range of payments. They cannot be used, for example, in vending machines or for most other small transactions, nor can they be used for large transactions such as buying a house or purchasing corporate stock. This less-than-complete acceptability of payments cards does not in itself rule out counting payments cards as a medium of exchange. When we examine other components of payments money, we find that none of them are acceptable for all transactions. In the evolution of the payments system, the older forms of money have generally remained acceptable over a range of specialized transactions. Commodity money, in the form of coins, is more useful than paper money and bank deposits for making purchases from vending machines, whereas currency and coin are impractical for large transactions. Whether payments cards are a medium of exchange, therefore, does not depend on any question of principle but rather on their degree of acceptability in transactions at any given time.

Our test for including payment card balances is purely a question of judgment. Are bank payment cards a generally acceptable means of payments? At present, some 250 000 merchants in Canada belong to either one or the other of the card systems.[9] Nevertheless, in a number of areas of merchandising payments cards are not acceptable. Most notably, these cards cannot be used for payments in food stores in some provinces as a result of government decree. However, the use of payments cards is sufficiently general, in particular as compared to the use of coin, to warrant modification of our definition of payments money to include balances that can be used for payments by means of the card. At present, we have chosen not to include these balances in our payments money for the practical reason of the lack of availability of adequate data on the size of these balances. This lack of data should not prevent us from realizing that bank payments cards do perform an important role in our payments and that this role can be expected to expand in the future.

Computer Technology and the Payments System

There are few areas of economic activity which computer technology has the potential to change as much as banking and the payments system. In particular, the accounting for millions of daily transactions and the storing of business and personal deposit records are tasks that are especially adaptable to computer use. Nevertheless, the so-called "chequeless revolution" has been slower in occurring than many early prophets had predicted. In this section we review the present uses of computer technology in banking and show some of the changes which have arisen from their use. We will also speculate about some future applications of computers in banking and try to anticipate policy issues which may arise from this extension in the use of computers.

Internal Applications of the Computer.   Most of the early applications of the computer in banking consisted of what might be called "backroom" applications in which the procedures for performing traditional banking functions are altered without changing the relationships between banks and their customers. The first applications of computer technology started in the 1950s and 1960s and were directed toward reducing the paperwork and processing time which accompanied the growth of the cheque payments system. One of the earliest changes that was visible to bank customers was the adoption by the Canadian Bankers Association in 1962 of magnetic ink character recognition (MICR) coding by which the information required for sorting the cheques of different banks and branches was printed on the bottom of the cheques in magnetic ink. While the MICR coding did not alter traditional banking practices, it did reduce the time required for processing cheques.

The most important internal computer application in banking to date has been the movement toward on-line banking in which the accounts of individual branches are held in a central computer. Terminals in the branches allow the branch staff to record each transaction in the appropriate accounts as it occurs. While the development of on-line banking in itself can be viewed as an internal innovation which must have as its justification the savings of costs in relation to traditional techniques, it has altered a number of traditional banking relationships. On the corporate banking side, on-line banking permits corporations to manage their cash balances much more closely than before so as to avoid the foregone interest returns from excessive cash balances or, alternatively, the interest expense of unnecessary borrowing. Many large corporations are able to consolidate their cash holdings into a central account each day and then adjust their short-term investments or bank loans so as to maintain a zero or near-zero balance. In some cases, the investment of any positive balance or the financing of any negative balance in the concentration accounts is automatic, with the interest rate tied to the bank's prime lending rate or 30-day wholesale deposit rate. Some indication of the implications of corporate cash management can be gained from examining the changing composition of corporate bank deposits. In 1970, business demand deposits accounted for 58% of total business deposits whereas by 1981 demand deposits had dropped to about 25% with a corresponding increase in the share of corporate savings deposits.

The movement to on-line banking has also changed the opportunities available to household customers of the banks. Perhaps the most significant change was the introduction of savings accounts which paid interest on the customer's daily minimum balance. Traditionally, the chartered banks had paid interest only on the minimum monthly balances, a practice which tended to limit the extent to which households could benefit from careful cash management. In order to gain any return from savings account balances, households were required to hold balances over an entire calendar month. On several occasions in the early 1970s, the federal government had attempted to legislate a move to payment of interest on daily balances but had been met with the protest from the banks that such a practice would be too expensive given their numerous widespread branches. Payment of interest on a minimum daily balance was initiated by near banks, in particular by some credit unions and trust companies which had been among the first financial institutions to have their branches on line with a central computer. Finally, in mid-1979, the five largest chartered banks offered savings accounts which paid interest on a daily minimum balance. Clearly, this move was made possible because most branches by then had their accounts maintained on a central computer. As might be expected, the banks paid a lower interest rate on the daily balance accounts by a margin of around 0.5%. The household whose savings account balance fluctuates over the month still stands to gain from the payment of the lower rate on the average of daily minimum balances as compared to the higher rate applied to the lowest balance held over the month.

Computers and Bank Customers. Computer technology has also brought about changes which alter fundamentally the traditional relationship between the bank and its customers. In the past, many banking services could only be performed through the physical presence of the customer at a bank branch during opening hours. Moreover, the business hours of bank branches were generally shorter than those of other businesses, limiting customers' access to banking services. The application of computer technology has reduced the dependence on personal presence in order to obtain banking services. In 1969, one of the chartered banks introduced cash dispensers which permitted customers to make withdrawals when banking offices were closed. Since that time other banks have installed cash dispensers and also automated teller machines which permit customers to perform a variety of transactions including deposits, withdrawals, and transfers among accounts in off banking hours. Moreover, computer technology has permitted the banks to eliminate the former identification of customers with a single bank; now many banks offer multi-branch banking through which their customers are permitted to conduct their business at any branch. So far, the automated teller machines operated by the banks have been located as part of existing bank branches. In the future, we may see the installation of these machines in locations such as airline terminals and shopping centers which are independent of branch locations. Eventually, banks may decide to consolidate branches by replacing some branches, where the majority of transactions are relatively routine, by sets of automated tellers. More complicated transactions would be offered to bank customers at central "parent" branches.

Future developments in computer technology may change our payments mechanism even more fundamentally than the developments to date. In particular, we can expect to see the emergence of an electronic payment system as an alternative to our two traditional patterns of payments. While use of cash allows the seller to gain purchasing power immediately and with certainty from the buyer, it requires the buyer to anticipate transactions by previously withdrawing cash from his bank. On the other hand, while payment by cheque allows the payer to transact without cash, it delays the transfer of purchasing power to the seller until the cheque clears. A third alternative, based on modern communication and computer technology, uses computer terminals sited in retail outlets. These point-of-sale terminals will be able to transfer funds immediately from the purchaser's account at one financial institution to the seller's account at another, with the purchaser having the choice of paying through the equivalent of a cheque — a reduction in a deposit account — or through a credit transaction much like current credit card payments. The electronic funds payment system based on point-of-sale terminals requires telecommunication links between retailers and financial institutions and similar links among financial institutions. A central component of such a system must be some form of computerized clearing facility for participating financial institutions to permit them to transfer electronically the debits and credits accumulated through their customers' transactions.

Some experiments with electronics payments using point-of-sale terminals are already in operation in the United States, involving a direct link between a bank's computer and a retailer's on-line terminals. Thus, the Chase Manhattan Bank of New York is linked to the Fortunoff Department stores, providing Visa authorizations on the basis of information from in-store terminals. Similarly, Macy's is linking 1800 terminals in New York to the American Express computer, and Montgomery Ward is developing a nationwide network which will have 25 000 on-line terminals.[10] While these developments fall short of a general means of payment based on electronic technology, they do show that the electronic payments system is an imminent development and not just a creation of science fiction.

Policy Implications of the Electronic Payments System

The emergence of an electronic payments system raises a number of policy issues different from those encountered in the existing system. While lawyers, economists, regulators, and consumer advocates have identified a wide range of issues, it is very difficult at the present time to judge their eventual importance. We will concentrate on those issues which are likely to be most important.

Documentation.   The present payments system based on cheques provides documentation of transactions in a retrievable form. Disputes between retailers and their customers or between financial institutions and their customers can frequently be resolved by the paper documentation inherent in the use of cheques. One source of savings inherent in a movement to an electronic payments system will be the elimination, or at least reduction, of the expensive processing of paper instruments. Consumers, however, may be uneasy about relying on a payments system which does not provide the degree of protection that exists in the present system. Some have argued that government involvement in the development of the electronic funds payment system is required to ensure that the consumer is given a degree of documentation equal to that inherent in the existing system. Other observers maintain that consumers will be unlikely to switch to a new payments system unless it offers advantages over the existing alternative; they also attribute the slower-than-expected emergence of the "chequeless" payments system precisely to consumer resistance to dispensing with paper-based documentation.

Consumer Access.   We also need to consider the question of access to any future electronic payment system. Will all consumers be able to use and benefit from a payment system based on point-of-sale terminals? Will the existing competitive advantage among financial institutions be altered by the development of an electronic payment system? So far, our discussion has been in terms of economic efficiency. There is little doubt that the development of computer technology will eventually produce a system more efficient than our present payment system based on paper. Even though economic efficiency is important, we must ensure that its attainment is not too costly in terms of jeopardizing other important objectives. For example, we may not be willing to adopt a policy which increases economic efficiency at the expense of extreme hardship for a few.

The question of consumer access to the electronic payment system arises because many people expect the point-of-sale payment system to be based on the present payments card. The card will provide the means for identifying qualified users and will activate the transfer of funds. Under present arrangements the status of the payments card as a credit card means that only consumers who have an acceptable credit rating are able to acquire a card. On the whole, the ineligibility of some consumers for the use of the payments card imposes little hardship under current conditions because the use of currency is an alternative means of payment for most goods and services. Still, even today payment for car rentals is much more convenient through payments cards.

While the problem of consumer access may be a source of some concern, it is unlikely to be an immediate problem in the development of the electronic payment system. As we have already seen, the development of new monies does not always displace the existing money in all uses nor does it always displace the existing money entirely in any given use. Today, for example, we could pay for a suit or a dress with currency, with bank money through a cheque, or with a payments card. We expect that, initially, the emergence of an electronic payment system based on point-of-sale terminals will be as a supplement to methods of payment which prove to be more efficient for many consumers for many uses. Its general acceptance will be sufficiently gradual that existing forms of money will continue to be acceptable for the majority of transactions for a long time to come. Moreover, a further development which will lessen the problem of consumer access is the use of debit cards. This form of payments card, as we have seen, permits consumers to use deposit balances rather than drawing on lines of credit to settle payments card transactions. Therefore, even consumers who are unable to qualify for a line of credit needed for a credit card may still be able to acquire one form of payments card and, as a result, be able to use point-of-sale terminals in making payments through an electronic payment system.

Institutional Access.   A more important policy problem arises from the issue of access to the electronic payments system to various types of financial institutions. In order to see the nature of the problem, we need to distinguish between the credit-granting function and the payment function of financial institutions. At present, individuals can be granted credit either by a financial institution, such as a bank, which offers deposits that serve as a medium of payment, or by lending institutions, such as finance companies or consumer loan companies, which do not offer deposits. The procedures, which in each case involve an interview and a credit check, are very similar. Some additional convenience, at the most, may be offered by the bank. Under an electronic payments system, the relative advantages of the institutions as credit grantors may be altered substantially. The customer will be able to activate through a point-of-sale terminal a previously approved line of credit from a financial institution participating in the system. In contrast, the use of credit from a non-participating financial institution will be more unwieldy. The customer may have to deposit the proceeds of any loan with a bank and then make payments from that account. Moreover, in the former case the consumer may only pay interest on the amount of credit actually used, whereas in the latter he would pay on the total amount borrowed even though part may remain unused in his bank account. This disadvantage of credit from non-participating institutions would be absent, of course, if the near banks were direct participants in the electronic payments system. Then their lines of credit would also be used to make payments through point-of-sale terminals.

Some representatives of near banks and other lending institutions fear that the development of the electronic payment system will occur in such a way so as to strengthen the competitive position of the banks at the expense of the near banks. Clearly, a large number of questions remain about the future of the electronic payments system. Who will develop it — the banks, a consortium of all interested financial institutions, the telecommunications industry, or the government?

The question of accessibility remains under any of these forms. A recent government study concludes:

> The exclusion of finance companies from POS networks will distort the payments system in favor of deposit-taking institutions. Consumer credit from EFT (electronic funds transfer) terminals would be restricted to banks, credit unions etc., and retailers. Possible competitors would be excluded by law, not by market decisions. Therefore *it is recommended that all financially sound credit institutions be given access to the POS terminals on an equal basis.* The ultimate EFT participants should be determined by competition between firms. Consumer preference will determine if finance companies are providing a valuable service. This is a case where regulation is unnecessary and the market can select the participants.[11]

We have already seen how direct access to the clearing system was once limited to only the chartered banks; this impediment to competition among banks and near banks was removed in the 1980 revisions to banking legislation. Adoption of the principle of free access to point-of-sale terminals in an electronic payments system would be in keeping with the same spirit.

MONEY AND THE FLOW OF PAYMENTS

In our later analysis, the concept of the demand for money will play a central role. Monetary policy — one of the central concerns of this book — involves manipulation of the supply of money.

What is the nature of the demand for money? What factors govern the quantity of money demanded at any point in time? We are not yet ready to examine these questions in detail. However, our discussion of money as a medium of payment does suggest one factor of consequence. Surely, if money is a medium of payment, then the quantity of money demanded must be related in some way to the value of payments to be made. This is correct, but the exact nature of the relationship is neither simple nor obvious.

The complication which arises in specifying the relationship between the value of transactions and the demand for money is that these are variables in different dimensions. The value of payments is a *flow variable*. It is something which occurs *over a period of time:* a day, a week, a month, or a year. By contrast, money is a *stock variable*. It is something which can be measured at a *point in time:* at a particular minute on a particular day. Thus, we cannot talk about the stock of money in the year 1983 in the same sense that we talk about the gross national expenditure in 1983. The stock of money must be measured at some particular point in time, such as the end of the business day, June 14, 1983. For purposes of analysis, of course, we might want to measure the *average* stock of money in existence during the year 1983. In principle, we should be measuring the average stock in existence at each successive instant during that year. In fact, we would probably only measure the stock once a week or once a month, and average these observations to obtain the annual average.

It is true that the flow of payments involves money. Payments are effected by money changing hands. However, over any given period of time — such as a year — the same piece of money can change hands many times. Thus, the total flow of payments during the year can be many times the average stock of money in existence during the year. If money changes hands rapidly — if it has a high *turnover rate* or *velocity of circulation* — a very small average stock of money can support a very large flow of payments. If velocity is high, each piece of money is held for a short time between payments. A small stock of money is required to support a given flow of payments. Clearly, we cannot derive the demand for money from a knowledge of the flow of payments without knowing something about the determinants of the velocity of circulation. That is a very complex topic which we are not yet ready to explore.

An analogy is sometimes helpful in thinking about these concepts. For example, a fountain continuously recirculates the same water supply by means of a mechanical pump. We might insert a meter into the pipe of the fountain and measure the total flow of water past that point in an hour. That would be analogous to the flow of payments in the economy in any period of time. The total flow of water past our meter is effected by the continuous recirculation of the same water supply, and the magnitude of that flow depends directly on the speed at which we run the pump — i.e., the velocity or rate of turnover of the water supply. We cannot say how much water we require in the reservoir for any given flow of water per hour unless we know how fast the pump runs.

ENDNOTES

1. P. Einzig, *Primitive Money* (London: Eyre & Spottiswoode, 1948), p. 25.
2. Why has gold been so widely selected as the commodity to be used as money? While there are clearly many cultural factors to be taken into account, early monetary economists argued that gold was technically superior to most commodities for this purpose. Gold is widely prized for decorative and other industrial purposes. Since it is also limited in supply, it has "intrinsic" value, i.e., it would have value as a commodity even if it were not used as money. The supply is physically limited, apart from occasional major gold discoveries, and it tends to maintain its value over time. It has a relatively high value in relation to its weight, and in this sense is relatively portable. It is virtually indestructible. It is homogeneous and readily divisible. Finally, it is quite easily recognizable. A classic exposition of the "technical" requirements for a monetary commodity is provided by W.S. Jevons, *Money and the*

Mechanism of Exchange (New York, 1902), pp. 29-39. How does paper money compare with gold in terms of these technical desiderata? (Remember that, while paper money is far from "indestructible," a worn-out note is easily and relatively cheaply replaced).

3. When the Bank of Canada was established in 1934 (it opened for business in 1935) Canada was nominally on the gold standard. However, the provision that Dominion Notes (the currency which Bank of Canada notes replaced) be convertible into gold on demand had been suspended in fact in 1929 and in law in 1931. Indeed, the gold standard was in suspension from 1914 except for the years 1926-1929. The Bank of Canada Act continued the nominal requirement for convertibility of legal tender into gold, and added the obligation that the Bank of Canada should hold reserves of gold, silver, or foreign exchange in the amount of 25% of its deposit and note liabilities. That requirement was also suspended in 1940. The revised Bank of Canada Act, passed in 1967, removed these provisions.

4. It is interesting to note that on January 1, 1981, some $326 million, or just over 3% of the value of Bank Canada notes outstanding, were in denominations of $1000. What is the explanation for this? Surely notes of this size are not widely used in normal retail transactions.

5. There are 10 major clearing centers in Canada, normally called cash clearing centers. These are Ottawa, the eight cities in which the Bank of Canada has an agency, and Quebec City. It is the clearings at these centers which are reported daily to the Bank of Canada and which are then settled on the books of the Bank of Canada.

6. In 1973, a number of banks offered plans under which a bundle of services was offered to depositors at a fixed monthly fee. Subsequently, some trust companies, credit unions, and banks have offered accounts on which bank charges are waived if the customer maintains an adequate minimum balance.

7. In the early 1980s some loose associations of banks incorporated in different states were formed which could offer their customers the same advantages as inter-state branching.

8. John W. Lambie, *Electronic Funds Transfer System in Canada: Emerging Issues and Recommendations* (Ottawa: Minister of Supply and Services, 1979), is a useful reference for the changing technology in the payments system. Much of the following section draws on Lambie's study.

9. This estimate takes into account merchants that belong to both systems.

10. *Ibid.*, p. 49.

11. *Ibid.*, p. 30.

FINANCIAL INSTRUMENTS AND FINANCIAL MARKETS 3

Nearly everyone is aware of financial markets from the masses of information on interest rates and stock market prices printed on the financial pages of our newspapers. However, few fully realize the role that these financial markets play in our economy through (1) gathering funds from lenders who are *surplus spending units* in that they wish to spend less than their current income and (2) allocating these funds among competing borrowers who are *deficit spending units* in that they wish to spend more than their current incomes. Individuals exchange their savings for *financial instruments* that are claims on borrowers which entitle the lenders to receive returns in the future. Depending on the lender and the instrument issued, these returns may be either certain or uncertain. The interaction of supply (from borrowers) and demand (on the part of lenders) in the market for financial instruments determines their market prices and in the process regulates the size, composition, and direction of financial flows in the economy. In this chapter we will discuss the characteristics of the most important types of financial instruments and some of the basic institutions of financial markets. In subsequent chapters we will develop a theoretical analysis of how these markets work.

THE CHARACTERISTICS OF FINANCIAL INSTRUMENTS

Definition

A financial instrument originates in an act of borrowing and lending — a transfer of purchasing power from a surplus spending unit to a deficit spending unit. It is what the borrower gives to the lender as evidence of the debt. In a more general way, we can define a financial instrument as *a claim to a future stream of payments*. It is a *contract* between a creditor (who will receive the payments) and the debtor (who will make the payments), and one which in general can be bought and sold in the market at a market-established price. Thus, the initial creditor need not remain a creditor. He can sell the claim to someone else. A major part of our problem is to explain the price at which such transactions will occur.

Our definition of a financial instrument is a general one. Individual instruments will differ in a number of ways. First, we have not specified the *number* of payments to be received. It can range between a single payment and an infinite number of payments. Second, we have not specified the *timing* of the payments, only that they be made in the future, or at some unspecified time in the future. Third, we have not specified the *magnitude* of the payments. They may be large or small, of equal or of different size, and indeed they may vary in size from time to time. Finally, we have not specified that the payments will necessarily be made. A financial instrument is a *claim* to such payments: that claim may in fact be honored in whole, in part, or not at all. At the moment we cannot know what will happen since the claim is for *future* payments.

Bonds as Financial Instruments

The most common of all financial instruments is what we shall call a *bond*. It has the amount of each payment and the number of payments (the length of the payments stream) specified in the contract. It is a *fixed income security*. We are using the term "bond" in a very broad, generic sense to include all fixed income securities, regardless of the term to maturity, the number and type of payments, or the various provisions for the security of the bondholder (which will be set in a "Deed of Trust" accompanying the bond). In fact, there are many types of bonds and, without attempting to provide a complete catalogue, it may be useful to note the characteristics of some of the major varieties.

Term to Maturity.   A major consideration in classifying bonds is the term to maturity, i.e., the time which must elapse before the final payment is due. At one extreme is a peculiar class of bonds issued by some governments, variously called *consols* or *perpetuities*. The contract calls for annual payments to the owner in perpetuity. By contrast, most bonds have a definite term to maturity. Those with a maturity date of 10 years or over are normally classed as *long-term* bonds, those with maturities in the range of three to 10 years might be called *intermediate-term* bonds, and those with a maturity less than three years, *short-term* bonds. The shortest-term bonds are those payable on demand, i.e., at any time specified by the holder.

Why is this classification by maturity important for our analysis? One of the characteristics of financial instruments is the responsiveness of market price to changing interest rates and, in general, movements of market price depend on the term to maturity. Those bonds with a short term to maturity tend to have a more stable price than those with a long term to maturity. This is a result of some importance which we will establish in Chapter 5.

Security of the Bondholder.   Another major consideration in classifying bonds is the provision for the security of the bondholder. Some bonds are secured by a formal pledge of certain physical assets of the debtor. These are *mortgage* bonds, and in modified form are well known in real estate transactions as mortgages. By contrast, some bonds are simply a charge against the general assets and earning power of the debtor, and are not secured by a pledge of any specific assets. These bonds are commonly called *debentures*, although if they are for a very short term they are more likely to be referred to as *promissory notes*, or *notes* for short. Some bonds also have a provision for a sinking fund, and hence are called *sinking fund bonds*. This form of bond requires that the debtor set aside a certain sum of money each year (frequently through the purchase of part of the outstanding issue of bonds) to provide for eventual retirement of the issue. This is supposed to provide additional security to the bondholder. Municipal governments generally issue *serial bonds* instead of sinking fund bonds to achieve the same purpose. A serial bond is, in fact, a package of bonds, each with a different maturity such that a portion of the total issue comes due for retirement each year during the term of the issue.

This brief survey hardly does justice to the variety of possible types of provisions for the security of bondholders, and hence to the possible types of bonds. However, they are only relevant in the present context because they have some bearing on the *risk* attached to the bond, and that is a factor of some interest for our analysis.

Credit Risk.   Our definition of a bond stresses that it is a claim to a series of payments of fixed magnitude to be made in the *future*. However, the future can never be known in advance. There will always be some *uncertainty* about whether the payments will ever be made. Circumstances may change so that even the most carefully formulated plans and expectations do not materialize; the debtor may be unwilling or unable to meet his obligation. In some cases this may only create costs of collection which cannot be fully recovered. In other cases, it may involve partial or total default on the obligation, with partial or complete loss to the creditor. In this event, the provisions for the security of the bondholder referred to in the previous section may take on more than academic significance.

We refer to the risk that the contractual payments may not be forthcoming as planned as the *credit risk*. In a sense, it is a one-sided risk. The actual payments may be less than those called for in the contract, but they will never be more.

For reasons which we will explore more fully in Chapter 5, credit risk enters into the determination of the market price of bonds. In brief, other things being equal, investors will normally prefer less risky securities to more risky securities. As a result, if the promised stream of payments is the same for two securities, investors will offer a higher price for the less risky one. But if risk is to enter the investment decision, investors must be able to assess differences in credit risk. This calls for specialized skills in financial analysis. As a result, an industry has developed as an adjunct of financial markets providing information and professional advice to investors.

Nature of the Payment Stream.   Another characteristic with respect to which bonds may differ is the nature of the stream of payments involved. In general, a bond will call for equal semiannual payments (the interest or coupon payments) and a larger lump-sum payment on the maturity date (variously called the *face* value, the *par* value or the *redemption* value of the bond). Bonds are normally issued in denominations of $1000 (although there are many exceptions to this). That is to say, the *redemption value* is

$1000. This should not be confused with the *market price* of the bond. A bond which has a redemption value of $1000 may trade in the market at a price either higher or lower than $1000. If its price is less than its face value the bond is said to be trading at a *discount,* and if its price is greater than its par value the bond is said to be trading at a *premium.* Bonds are frequently issued at a discount or a premium. Thus, the original issuer of a bond with a face value of $1000 does not necessarily receive $1000. He may receive less or more.

The annual interest payments (normally two coupons) can be expressed as a percent of the face value of the bond. Thus a $1000 bond, bearing semiannual coupons for $75 each, would normally be referred to as a 15% bond. That is, the annual interest payment of $150 is 15% of the face value of the bond. This is only a coupon rate of interest and does not reflect the effective rate of return to the investor. Just as the market price of the bond may depart significantly from its par value, so the true rate of interest to the investor (what we shall call the yield) may depart significantly from this coupon rate. Indeed, as we just noted, at the time the bond is first issued, the issuer may receive less than the face value of the bond (he may sell it at a discount). As a result, he pays a higher rate of interest on the money which he has actually obtained than that indicated by the coupon rate. The only significance of the coupon rate is to fix the size of the semi-annual coupon payments.

Not all the bonds will be in this coupon form, however. A particularly important variant is what we shall call a *bill.* This is a security calling for a single payment on a fixed date in the future. There are no periodic interest payments, only the final payment, the redemption value of the bill. Such bonds are normally very short-term, and perhaps the most important is the 91-day treasury bill issued by the federal government. It plays a particularly important role in the financial system and we will have occasion to refer to it frequently.

Bills always trade at a discount. The effective interest rate on a bill (the yield) depends on the relationship between its market price and its redemption value. For example, on January 6, 1981 newly issued Treasury bills which sold for $96.49 per $100 par value had an annual yield of 14.56% over their 90-day term to maturity. Approximately five months later, on August 5, 1981, newly issued Treasury bills had an annual yield of 21.07% and sold for $95.00.

Marketability.   Finally, it is necessary to mention another salient characteristic which may or may not be possessed by bonds and other financial instruments — *marketability.* This refers to the ability of the holder to sell the security to someone else on short notice at a reasonably predictable price. Some instruments are not marketable because they are not transferable. That is, the sale of the security to a third party is prohibited. For example, Canada Savings Bonds contain the condition: "This bond is not assignable nor transferable." Still, the owner of a Canada Savings Bond is able to have his bond redeemed by the government on demand. Other instruments are not marketable simply by virtue of the fact that an active market does not exist.

Such a statement must seem puzzling to a student of economics. A market exists whenever transactions occur. Thus, the very fact that the present purchaser of the security has purchased it must indicate that a market exists. Moreover, it is in general possible to find a buyer for most securities at some price. In effect, then, marketability is a question of degree. A bond is regarded as not marketable when the costs of finding a buyer preclude transactions for all practical purposes.

It is also useful to make a distinction between the primary and secondary markets for securities. By the *primary market* we mean transactions involving the issuance of new securities. By the *secondary market* we mean transactions in outstanding securities. Thus, the supply of securities in the primary market comes from individuals, firms, and government agencies raising money for diverse purposes. The supply of securities in the secondary market comes from assetholders selling securities out of their portfolios.

The range of securities continuously traded in significant volume in the secondary market is relatively limited. These tend to be securities of well-known creditors whose credit worthiness can be relatively easily assessed and of which a relatively large volume is outstanding. Only these securities can be said to be highly marketable. True, most other transferable securities can be sold at some price, but possibly only after considerable searching for a buyer, some delay, perhaps substantial cost, and possibly then only at a low price. The secondary market for such instruments is irregular and unorganized.

A marketable security is a security for which there is a developed secondary market in which there is a relatively large volume of continuous trading of the security.

Common Stock as a Financial Instrument

While the type of financial instrument which will occupy most of our attention in this book is the bond, there are other financial instruments in which the amount of each payment is not specified in the contract between creditor and debtor. The prototype of such securities is the *common stock* of corporations. Whereas a bond entitles its owner to a series of fixed payments, a share of common stock entitles its owner to a *pro rata* share of such dividends as may be declared from time to time by the directors of the corporation. Dividends are normally thought of as a share of profits, although they are not rigidly tied to profits. The directors of a corporation might decide to retain some or all of the profits to finance the growth of the corporation, and on occasion they may decide to pay dividends even though the corporation is not making profits or perhaps is suffering losses. In general, however, dividend payments will tend to reflect the profits of the corporation.

Also, unlike most bonds, common stock does not have a definite maturity date. There is no fixed lump-sum redemption value, although the stockholders own residual rights to the assets of the corporation (i.e., after all other claims are allowed for).

The important point for our analysis is that just as the profits of a corporation may vary from time to time, so the dividend payments to the stockholder may vary over a wide range. Accordingly, we refer to such a financial instrument as a *variable income security*.

Stockholders as Creditors.   Since our definition of financial instruments involves the concepts of debtor and creditor, it may seem as if we are stretching a point to include common stock. The owners of the common stock of a corporation are in law the owners of the corporation, not its creditors. Moreover, since they have a claim to a *pro rata* share of the profits (or better, the declared dividends) of the corporation, their "instrument" has many of the characteristics of titles to physical capital rather than what we might normally think of as a financial instrument.

These points are valid and important. However, we should distinguish between the corporation and its stockholders or owners; and it is *convenient* to treat the stockholders simply as creditors of the corporation with a particular type of claim on that corporation, a variable income claim. We should remember that the corporation is in itself a "legal person" with certain rights and obligations. The stockholders are not responsible for the actions and debts of the corporation, except to the extent that they may lose their investments in the corporation should it be unable to meet its obligations. Indeed, it is this fact of the "limited liability" of the stockholders — the fact of their divorcement from the obligations of the corporation — which makes the corporation such an effective form of business organization for ventures involving risk.

As a subsidiary point, it might be noted that while all stockholders have the right to vote at stockholders' meetings (which generally must be held at least once a year), in a typical corporation most do not participate actively in the management of that corporation. They treat their stock as an investment in someone else's venture; and they hold it in anticipation of a series of dividend payments whose magnitude is beyond their direct control. Even if a stockholder is in the management of the corporation, we should nonetheless regard his stock simply as a claim on a separate entity, the corporation. It is true that the fact of his ability to influence or control corporate policy may add an important dimension, a valuable characteristic, to that particular financial instrument; nonetheless, it is a financial instrument which provides a claim to a (probably variable) future stream of payments.

Other Variable Income Instruments. The common stock is the best known type of variable income security. However, there are several other types of instruments which have variable payments streams. Basically, they combine some of the features of common stock with some of the features of bonds. There are many subtle variations on the central principles, and we can only briefly mention some of the main types.

Perhaps the best known of such instruments is *preferred stock*. Unlike a bond, preferred stock does not have a fixed maturity, although it may be redeemable in the sense that the corporation has the option of retiring it on specified terms. The owner of preferred stock has a *prior claim* to dividends, up to a specified maximum rate, before any dividends can be paid on common stock. Moreover, some preferred stocks are participating; that is, they have the prior claim to dividends, but once dividends are paid on common stock at a certain specified rate the owners of the preferred stock share in any additional dividends declared. Thus, the specified rate is in this case a minimum rate, not a maximum.

There are also two classes of bonds which have variable payments streams, *income bonds* and *participating bonds*. These are bonds in the sense that they have a fixed redemption date and a fixed redemption value. However, in each case the annual interest payment is contingent on the earnings of the corporation, with participating bonds having the additional feature of a guaranteed minimum annual payment.

The endless varieties of financial instruments, with subtle differences in their characteristics, are evidence of the ingenuity of the participants in the financial system in designing instruments to suit the specific preferences of both debtors and creditors (including taking advantage of many complex provisions of tax laws).

Money as a Financial Instrument

In the previous chapter we offered a general definition of money as "anything which is normally accepted when a transfer of purchasing power takes place." Our concern was with the payments system, and our interest in money was as a *medium of exchange.* However, the very fact that money will normally be accepted in exchange for goods and services means that it is an asset. It is something which can be held as a *store of wealth.* In Canada today, money is simply one type of financial instrument which has the peculiar property of being acceptable at face value in exchange for goods, services, and other financial instruments.

To some students this may seem a paradox. Financial instruments are claims for future payment. Future payments will be made in money. How then can money be both the means of payment and a claim for payment? Are we simply talking in riddles?

Perhaps no problem arises in connection with *bank money.* Chequable bank deposits can be regarded as claims for payment in legal-tender money — claims which may be effected at the option of the depositor in whole or in part at any time in the future. We can take this as a limiting case in our definition of a financial instrument. It can be a claim for a *single payment* (the shortest possible stream of payments), payable *on demand* of the creditor (the shortest possible term to maturity).

This still leaves the problem of legal-tender money, however. As we noted in the previous chapter, legal tender in Canada in practice means notes issued by the Bank of Canada for use as currency, and these have the formal status as liabilities of the Bank of Canada. They are payable "on demand," although, as we have seen, this inscription on Bank of Canada notes is quite meaningless. In what sense, then, can we say that legal-tender money is a claim for payment?

Unit of Account.   In order to answer this question we require another concept, that of the *unit of account.* This is the abstract unit by which we measure, record, and compare market values, the unit in which we keep our personal and business accounts. In Canada, the unit of account is the dollar (which is subdivided into 100 cents).

It is sometimes said that one of the functions of money is to serve as a unit of account. However, such a statement confuses two concepts. *Money* is an object, a financial instrument or (at some times and in some places) a commodity. It is something which changes hands in the process of exchange. The *unit of account* is an arbitrary unit in which we measure market value, *including the value of money.* It should be thought of in the same vein as one thinks of the ounce as an arbitrary unit in which we measure weight and the degree as the arbitrary unit in which we measure temperature. It is true that money is normally issued in denominations corresponding to the unit of account. That is not necessary, however. For example, in England values are frequently measured in guineas, a unit of account for which there is no monetary counterpart.

Generalized Fixed-Price Claim.   In what sense, then is money (particularly legal-tender money) a claim for future payment? We should not regard it as a claim against any specific debtor (even though the government issues it). Rather, it is a claim for payment in that it is universally acceptable in exchange for goods, services or financial instruments of a given value, with the value measured in terms of the unit of account. A $10 Bank of

Canada note can always be exchanged for goods, services, or financial instruments whose market value equals $10. The Bank of Canada note — legal-tender money — is a general claim against society which can be effected at any time at the option of the holder.

It is important to remember that to say that the price of money is fixed in terms of the unit of account is not to say that the purchasing power of money is always constant. As the evidence of the 1970s showed, a given quantity of money may not always command a fixed quantity of goods and services, only a fixed market value of goods and services. The prices of goods and services measured in terms of the unit of account may rise over time, and money, which always commands a *fixed value* of goods and services, will buy a *smaller quantity* of those goods and services. The purchasing power of money will have fallen. This process is called inflation, and one of the major tasks of monetary theory is to explain its causes, consequences, and cures.

In summary, we can say that money is a peculiar type of financial instrument. Regardless of the form in which it appears, money should be regarded as a claim against society as a whole rather than against any single debtor. It is a financial instrument whose price, measured in terms of the unit of account, is fixed. This vital property is not possessed by most other financial instruments (or commodities). The holder of shares of corporate stock or of government bonds faces the risk that their market values will fall. By contrast, the holder of money faces no such risk. We describe this property of money by the term *liquidity* and will have more to say about it in Chapter 5.

THE INSTITUTIONS OF FINANCIAL MARKETS

To an economist, the concept of a market does not necessarily imply a fixed location, any particular set of institutional arrangements or pattern of organization of exchange. A market exists whenever buyers and sellers agree to exchange, regardless of whether they are located in the same physical place and regardless of how their mutual interests are brought together. The tangible evidence of a market is not a structure of buildings or a particular set of institutional arrangements; it is simply a series of exchanges. In this sense, then, an economist would consider the financial market to be conterminous with the entire financial system. The financial system is basically a set of markets for particular types of financial instruments.

Usually, when we use the term financial market we have a narrower concept in mind. We can divide all financial transactions into two types, loan transactions and investment transactions. In the former category we place all transactions involving face to face negotiations between borrowers and lenders. The promissory notes involved are not normally designed to be re-sold, and hence they tend to remain lodged in the lender's portfolio (although this is not necessary, of course). In the second category we place all transactions in "public issues," financial instruments designed to be sold on an impersonal basis to any and all buyers. Inevitably, the distinction between the two categories is fuzzy at the margin. It is not clear whether certain transactions (e.g., negotiated private placements of long-term marketable bonds with a single institutional lender) should be considered a loan or investment type transaction. There is, however, a difference of substance. When we speak of financial markets in the narrow sense, we make reference to the second type of transaction — impersonal transactions in marketable financial instruments.

For most purposes of economic analysis, complete details on the institutional arrangements of markets are not necessary. Indeed, such details frequently get in the way of clear analysis. While it is important to know that certain types of markets exist, and to understand the institutions of those markets in broad outline, it is seldom important that all of the details of those arrangements be understood. All that is required here is a brief overview of the major institutions involved in exchanging financial instruments.

Brokers, Dealers, and Underwriters

The central institutions of financial markets are a group of business firms called investment houses. They function as middlemen in the marketing process, as brokers, as dealers, or as underwriters.

A *broker* is a pure go-between in market transactions. He is not a party to any transaction himself. Rather, he acts as an *agent* for his clients, be they buyers or sellers. He uses his information on the market — the basic ingredient in his activities — and his contacts to bring buyers and sellers together, at mutually acceptable prices, and provides the technical facilities necessary for the execution of the transactions. For his services, the broker charges his clients a fee or *commission* which is normally related to the value of the transaction.

A *dealer* is also an intermediary in the exchange process. In contrast to the broker, the dealer actually becomes a party to market transactions. In the jargon of the trade, he "makes markets." He holds an inventory of securities, buys in the market to add to that inventory, and sells out of his inventory to other buyers, perhaps at a different time or place. He hopes to make a profit on a spread between buying and selling prices.

While techniques of underwriting vary depending on the circumstances, an *underwriter* is basically a dealer who handles new issues of securities. He buys them, and then sells them into the market hoping to make a profit on the spread between the selling and the buying price. Again, information and market contacts are the essential ingredients in the underwriter's activities.

Earlier in this chapter we distinguished between primary and secondary markets for securities. We can identify underwriting with the primary market, and the main operations of brokers and dealers with secondary markets. This is an oversimplification, in part, because not all new issues of securities go through a formal process of underwriting. Thus, one vitally important group of bonds, those of the Government of Canada, are sold in the first instance to a large list of "primary distributors" including the chartered banks as well as over 100 selected investment houses. If there is an underwriter, it is the Bank of Canada, but that hardly seems the appropriate designation of the Bank's activities. Similarly, a significant portion of corporate, provincial, and municipal bonds arc "direct placements" with large institutional lenders. The issuers negotiate directly with the lenders, generally with the assistance and advice of an investment house, but without benefit of an underwriting arrangement. This is an extension of the brokerage function to the new issue market.

The identification of underwriters with primary markets, and brokers and dealers with secondary markets is also an oversimplification, because it is difficult to separate the three activities. Investment houses in Canada, with some exceptions, do not narrowly specialize in one or the other line of activity. Thus, in the words of the Royal Commission on Banking and Finance:

> One of the distinguishing features of the Canadian industry is its relative lack of specialization. The largest and most profitable firms are fully integrated; they underwrite and distribute new issues, position and trade debt and other securities, sell wholesale and retail, operate in the money market, have membership in one or more stock exchanges, manage portfolios and in general perform the whole range of functions common to the industry.[1]

Moreover, the Commission noted, the "largest and most profitable" fully integrated firms dominate all aspects of the financial industry. This observation appears to be just as valid today as in the 1960s described by the Royal Commission. A more recent study observed:

> Four securities firms, operating nationally and internationally, dominate the primary market for Canadian issues and are active in all phases of the securities market as dealers and brokers.[2]

Patterns of Organization in Financial Markets

A study for the Royal Commission on Banking and Finance done in the early 1960s revealed that there were as many as 400 firms acting as brokers, dealers, and underwriters in Canada. More recent data suggest that this number is nearer 250 firms. Not all of these firms are independent. Many are specialized affiliates of other firms. Moreover, there is a marked degree of concentration in the business. A handful of integrated firms, with nationwide branch organizations, account for the vast majority of business done in all aspects of the industry. Nonetheless, taking the industry as a whole, we are talking about a comparatively large number of firms who trade among themselves (wholesale transactions) and with the general public (retail transactions). How are their activities organized so as to produce an effective national market in securities?

Over-the-counter Markets vs. Organized Exchanges.   Dealings with the general public are through a series of offices and branch offices throughout the country. Through salesmen or "customer's men" in these offices, an investment house takes orders for purchases or sales, whether as a dealer selling or buying for its own account or as a broker taking orders for transactions to be effected in the market. In this respect, the securities industry is organized much like any other retail sales industry.

Perhaps the best known — and certainly the most spectacular — institutional arrangement for dealings among investment houses is the organized stock exchange. In Canada, there are five such exchanges in operation, in Toronto, Montreal, Winnipeg, Calgary, and Vancouver. In 1981, both the Toronto Stock Exchange and the Vancouver Stock Exchange traded over 1.5 billion shares. The Toronto Stock Exchange was the leader in terms of the value of shares traded, accounting for $29.5 billion or 70% of the total value traded, compared to only $4.4 billion for the Vancouver Stock Exchange,

$3.4 for the Montreal Stock Exchange and less than $500 million for the Alberta Exchange.

A stock exchange is a corporation incorporated under provincial legislation. It provides a place where representatives of investment houses, admitted to membership in the exchange, can meet to buy and sell securities, on their own behalf or as agents for clients, and under rules established and enforced by the exchange. For the market to work effectively, of course, the traders on the floor must have almost instantaneous contact with their brokerage offices, and through these offices (and their branches throughout the country) indirectly with the firm's customers. Not all investment houses are members of organized exchanges (although many non-member brokers have access to the facilities of the stock exchanges through members, with whom they split the commissions). Thus, of an estimated 250 firms in the security business, perhaps 120 belong to one or more organized exchanges in Canada. Each exchange establishes its own rules governing membership, and in general each has established a fixed upper limit to the number of "seats" available. These seats can be bought and sold, but only with the approval of the exchange (and some members may own more than one seat). Over the 1970s, seats on the Toronto Stock Exchange have sold for more than $130 000 and for as little as $12 000.

Just as not all investment houses are members of organized exchanges, so not all securities are traded on these exchanges. There is a second type of marketing arrangement connecting investment houses, the so-called over-the-counter market. In Canada, all bonds and many stocks are traded on the over-the-counter market. In some cases stocks are not "listed" on one of the stock exchanges because the corporation cannot meet the requirements of the exchange for listing; in other cases it is a matter of deliberate choice on the part of the management of the corporation not to seek listing. However, in the case of bonds, the stock exchanges until recently have deliberately excluded bonds from trading on the floor of the exchange. The over-the-counter market is a telephone market. Deals are sought and consummated by telephone and telegraph, with the formal exchange of papers occurring subsequently. Much of the trading on the over-the-counter market involves dealers trading for their own account rather than as brokers.

A National and an International Market.   The investment houses, many of them with nationwide networks of branch offices, linked together through the stock markets and the over-the-counter markets in stocks and bonds, provide the institutional arrangements for a truly nationwide market in all types of securities. Changes in demand or supply in any one section of the country will be felt almost immediately in all others. In part, this transmission of market changes will result from formal arbitrage operations. *Arbitrage* involves the simultaneous purchase and sale of a security in two different markets. Thus, if a particular stock listed on both the Toronto and Vancouver markets should fall in price in Vancouver at a certain moment, an alert investment house (probably with seats on both exchanges) could buy shares in Vancouver and sell them in Toronto virtually simultaneously, making a profit in the transaction and tending to eliminate the price differential between the two markets.

Arbitrage of this sort appears to account for a small but significant portion of the activity in the organized stock exchanges. However, equally important in transmitting the changes in supply or demand among market areas are the activities of brokers and dealers on the over-the-counter market. In virtually constant communication with each other, traders at the leading investment houses seek out the best prices for their customers who wish to buy or sell, and are constantly alert for profitable buying and selling opportunities for the firm's own portfolio. The result is a fluid and continuous coast-to-coast market.

But the market connections established through the network of investment houses and formal stock exchanges are not confined to the boundaries of the nation. There are equally important international connections as well, and particularly strong connections with the financial markets of the United States. Thus, some Canadian stocks are traded on stock exchanges in the United States, and U.S. stocks in Canada. Leading Canadian investment houses have branch offices in the United States (and several other countries), and some investment houses operating in Canada are branch offices of U.S. firms. Canadian security dealers and brokers are in virtually continuous telephone and telegraphic contact with their counterparts in New York and elsewhere. These connections permit international arbitrage in both Canadian and foreign securities, and facilitate Canadian transactions in foreign securities and foreign transactions in Canadian securities. *The institutions of the financial markets are international as well as national in scope, and as a result market transactions flow easily across the country and across national boundaries.* This, as will become evident, is a fact of profound significance for Canadian monetary policy.

The Secondary Bond Market

As we will discover in a later section of this book, a major portion of the day-by-day operations of the Bank of Canada, including the implementation of monetary policy, involves purchases and sales of bonds in the open market. These are operations in the *secondary* bond market, and the nature and scope of that market can affect the magnitude, timing, and nature of the operations which the central bank can effectively carry out. Hence, since it has particular significance for our later analysis, before we leave our brief description of financial markets, we should examine the dimensions of the secondary bond market.

TABLE 3-1 **The secondary bond market in Canada, 1962 and 1977 ($ Billions)**

	1962		1977	
Security	*Amount outstanding*	*Secondary sales*	*Amount outstanding*	*Secondary sales*
Government of Canada Bonds				
Treasury Bills	$2.2	$6.5	$10.3	$29.7
Short-term bonds	4.2	5.5	7.7	3.3
Long-term bonds	8.1	2.0	13.8	11.8
Provincial government bonds	7.2	1.2	36.3	6.9
Municipal government bonds	3.1	0.4	8.9	0.9
Corporate bonds	6.0	1.2	23.0	7.2

SOURCE: Toronto Stock Exchange, *Bond Trading Study*, Part I.

The development of the secondary bond market is shown in Table 3-1. In 1962, the Canadian secondary bond market was not highly developed. The bulk of secondary trading was in Government of Canada bonds, particularly treasury bills and short-term bonds. Between 1962 and 1977 the volume of secondary trading expanded over threefold from $16.8 billion to $59.8 billion. Even though trading in government securities still accounts for almost three-quarters of total secondary trading, substantial expansion occurred in the trading of provincial government and corporate bonds.

The market in short-term government securities is part of what has come to be called the *money market,* an open market in the short-term securities of selected "blue chip" borrowers. The money market has taken on an institutional identity of its own and has developed a peculiar significance within the financial system.

THE MONEY MARKET

The money market is effectively organized by a small number of money market dealers (or "jobbers" as they are sometimes called). These are investment houses which "make markets" in money market instruments. That is, they hold inventories of short-term securities, and stand ready to buy and sell short-term securities to be taken into and out of their inventories hoping to make a profit on the spread between buying and selling prices. The money market dealers tend to be the larger, better-known bond dealers, with nationwide networks of branches and international connections. They have lines of credit with the major chartered banks, and with the Bank of Canada.

Money Market Instruments

The money market is an active open market in *selected* short-term financial instruments.

Treasury Bills. Perhaps most important are the short-term obligations of the Government of Canada, including treasury bills. In one sense there has been a money market in Canada for a long time. That is, there is a long history of some trading in short-term securities. However, as we will see later, a primary function of the modern money market is to serve as a place in which financial intermediaries (and increasingly non-financial corporations) can make adjustments to their liquidity positions. This calls not for occasional *ad hoc* trades but continuous trading in a broad active market, and such a market requires a continuous supply of suitable money market instruments. The origins of the money market in this sense are generally identified with the first offering of treasury bills by competitive tender in 1934, although it is probably more accurate to date the market from 1953 or 1954.

The introduction of regular competitive tenders for treasury bills provided part of the requirements for an active money market. It guaranteed the market a regular supply of suitable instruments. From 1937 through 1952, an auction of treasury bills was held fortnightly, and in early 1953 the frequency of the auctions was increased to weekly.

The introduction of the treasury bill itself could not guarantee an active money market, however. Until the mid-1950s the money market remained primarily a market in short-term government securities, particularly treasury bills, and it was essentially a triangular market. Treasury bills were traded among the Government of Canada (as issuer), the Bank of Canada, and the chartered banks. Throughout the years 1946-1952 the chartered banks and the Bank of Canada between them tended to hold in excess of 85% of the total amount of treasury bills outstanding, and as late as December 1951 they held almost 95% of the $450 million in outstanding treasury bills.

In 1953 and 1954, a number of institutional changes in money market arrangements were promoted by the Bank of Canada which facilitated the development of a more active and broader money market. Some of these changes related to the availability of short-term government securities. Thus, beginning in January 1952, treasury bills were auctioned weekly instead of fortnightly, and the total amount outstanding was sharply increased. In 1952 there was a fortnightly auction of $75 million of three-month treasury bills, with a total of $450 million outstanding at any one time. In 1953, the amount outstanding was increased to $650 million, and by late 1956 this had risen to $1600 million. In early 1982 the Government of Canada was holding a weekly auction of $700 million of three-month and $200 million of six-month treasury bills and a monthly auction of $250-million of one-year treasury bills.

The increase in the amount of treasury bills outstanding was accompanied in late 1955 by an arrangement between the chartered banks and the Bank of Canada under which the banks agreed to invest a portion of their funds in treasury bills. The banks agreed to invest, at a minimum, 7% of their Canadian dollar deposits in cash, day-by-day loans to security dealers, or treasury bills over and above the deposits which they had to maintain as cash reserves. This substantially increased the demand for treasury bills. The 1967 revision of *The Bank Act* formalized this arrangement and included a compulsory secondary reserve requirement.

Day-to-Day Loans.   Some of the changes in money market arrangements in 1954 related to the position of government security dealers in the market, and were designed to encourage these dealers to cultivate the market by holding inventories and actively trading money market instruments. Thus, certain bank charges arising out of inter-dealer transactions in securities were reduced and eventually eliminated in order to encourage active trading. The chartered banks were also encouraged to make low cost "day-to-day" loans to the dealers to permit them to carry inventories of government securities, and the Bank of Canada offered lines of credit to a selected list of such dealers. Day-to-day loans (or *day loans* for short) are demand loans to money market dealers, secured by short-term government securities. Such loans can be called by either party before noon for payment the same day. The rate of interest is determined by competitive forces in the market, but is normally substantially below the rate of interest on other money market instruments.

Bank of Canada Advances.   Day loans from the chartered banks quickly became a primary source of finance for the money market dealers. As the market developed, other private sources of funds emerged as well. We will turn to these shortly. However, the lines of credit with the Bank of Canada were little used. This was largely by design. The Bank of Canada sees its role as a supplier of funds to money market dealers as that of a "lender of last resort" — a residual source of the finance should other sources dry up unexpectedly. The purpose is to relieve temporary pressures on the market and hence prevent short-term instability in the market resulting from the forced liquidation of money market dealer inventories. In accordance with this role, the interest rate on advances had generally been set as a penalty rate above the current yield on treasury bills. Effective March 1980, the rate on advances was made identical to the Bank Rate which was set 1/4 of 1% above the average yield on three-month treasury bills. Other sources of finance are generally cheaper.

Advances from the Bank of Canada are in the form of "purchase and resale agreements," or "buy-backs." The securities are formally sold to the Bank of Canada, but the sale is accompanied by an agreement to repurchase the security on a specified date at a specified price. The difference between the price at which the dealer initially sells the security and that at which he agrees to repurchase it is calculated to yield the Bank of Canada the appropriate interest rate. This type of arrangement has broader applications in the money market as well.

Finance Paper, Commercial Paper, and Bankers' Acceptances.

The institutional changes of 1953 and 1954 did not produce the money market. They could only facilitate its development. The really active force was a general rise in the demand for funds, accompanied by a general rise in interest rates. This development brought many new participants into the market, both to invest temporarily idle funds for short periods of time, and to borrow funds on short-term instruments. The former development produced what has come to be called "country banking" in short-term instruments. The range of instruments actively traded on the market expanded rapidly.

Among the earliest participants in the market were a group of sales finance companies who issued short-term notes, commonly called "finance paper." In the later 1950s, an increasing number of non-financial corporations began raising funds through money market issues, so-called "commercial paper." These firms include several retail stores, grain merchants, oil companies, and other industrial firms. In general, these firms found they could raise funds somewhat cheaper in the money market than through bank loans, although they generally have a line of credit with chartered banks as insurance.

The issuing of commercial paper is generally confined to companies that have established a sound credit rating in the money market. In 1962, an instrument called a *bankers' acceptance* was introduced into the money market. The bankers' acceptance is an agreement by the borrower to make a payment on a specified date which has been "accepted" by a chartered bank. In effect, the acceptance of the chartered bank is a guarantee of payment, which means the financial instrument is secured by the credit of both the borrower and the accepting bank. The use of bankers' acceptances permits lesser known borrowers to participate in the money market. The costs to the borrower of using the bankers' acceptances are of two kinds. As with any other money market instrument, the borrower must pay interest to the lender supplying the funds. In addition, the borrower must pay an acceptance fee to the chartered bank which guarantees the acceptance. Clearly, the borrower would only use the bankers' acceptance if the total costs of borrowing through this means were cheaper than both a direct bank loan and the issuance of commercial paper without a bank's guarantee.

After its start in the early 1960s, the bankers' acceptance market developed very slowly. By 1970, total outstanding bankers' acceptances still remained below $400 million. Finally, in the late 1970s, the market for these instruments grew very rapidly, more than tripling in the three-year period from 1978 on to reach a level of $6.3 billion at the end of 1981.

In addition to finance paper, commercial paper, acceptances and short-term Government of Canada securities, there are a number of other instruments traded in the money market. Some of the major municipal and provincial governments raise money through issues of treasury bills. Some banks and trust companies also use the facilities of the money market to attract funds into term deposits. There is also trading in foreign securities from time to time, and foreign participation in the Canadian money market.

"Country Banks."   Finally, a development in the money market which has attracted some attention from time to time is the emergence of the *country bank*.

The role of the money market dealer in making markets in money market instruments is crucial to the efficient functioning of the money market. By standing ready to buy or sell securities, the dealers provide continuity and hence a margin of stability to the market, reducing the risks of illiquidity for all participants in the market. However, to perform this role, the dealer must be able to finance the acquisition and holding of inventories of securities. The dealer's own capital is one source of such finance but, in general, it only accounts for a small portion of the total funds used by money market dealers. As we have already seen, the chartered banks provide an important source of funds for money market operations through day loans. The banks also provide funds on conventional call-loans to investment dealers, some of whom will also be money market dealers. The Bank of Canada stands ready as a lender of last resort, but not as a continuing normal source of funds. The rest of the funds with which the dealers operate come from country banks: non-bank private lenders, mainly private corporations.

The typical country bank will be a corporation which has a large sum of money available for a short period of time, and which wishes to invest those funds in safe interest-bearing instruments. The investment dealer may bid for those funds on a competitive basis with banks and other possible short-term borrowers. These loans would be in the form of purchase and resale agreements, with the terms of the resale agreement tailored to the specific needs of the lender of the funds.

The Role of the Money Market

From its beginnings in the 1950s, the Canadian money market has developed into a substantial component of the Canadian financial system with, as shown in Table 3-2, $35 billion of outstanding securities and a variety of instruments to meet the needs of different lenders and borrowers. Nevertheless, it is still a wholesale market which caters to specialized borrowers. As can be seen in Table 3-2, the federal government accounts for more than 40% of the total outstanding issues, whereas the private borrowers are generally demanders of a large amount of funds who have developed the knowledge and skills required to operate in the market. Nevertheless, as the volume of outstanding issues shows, the market does provide an important alternative to finance through bank loans for this group of borrowers.

The basic function of all financial markets is to mobilize the financial surpluses of the nation and to allocate these among competing deficit spending units. The money market, however, has another important role to play in the financial system. It provides a place where spending units and financial intermediaries can adjust their liquidity

TABLE 3-2   The Canadian money market: short-term securities outstanding, June 30, 1982 ($ Millions Canadian)

	Denominated in:		
	Canadian dollars	Other currencies	Total
Government of Canada treasury bills (excluding Bank of Canada holdings)	$15 421	—	$15 421
Provincial and municipal treasury bills	821	—	821
Sales finance and consumer loan company paper	2 250	$281	2 531
Other commercial paper	6 991	672	7 663
Bankers' acceptances	12 284	—	12 284
TOTAL	$37 767	$953	$28 720

SOURCE: *Bank of Canada Review.*

positions, and where the central bank can adjust the liquidity position of the entire economy. The vital quality of the money market is its breadth, activity, and stability which can absorb substantial short-term shocks without excessive gyrations in market prices. Thus, corporations, banks, or other financial intermediaries with temporarily surplus cash can put it to work, at a competitive rate of interest, in the money market, and be reasonably secure in the knowledge that the funds can be recalled on very short notice if needed. Likewise, the corporations, banks, or other financial intermediaries which are short of cash can obtain it on short notice and for short periods of time, if that is desirable, by borrowing in the money market, or selling in the market any money market instruments that they may have been holding. The money market thus makes it possible for all types of firms and financial intermediaries to manage their financial affairs more efficiently, and particularly to economize on their holdings of money. It also provides a convenient point for the central bank to intrude into the operations of the financial system. The central bank can sell Treasury Bills and other short-term government securities in the money market in order to absorb what it might consider to be excess cash in the financial system. Likewise, it can purchase such money market instruments in exchange for cash if it feels that there is not sufficient cash in the system. We will have many occasions, as we progress through this book, to refer to the money market and its importance for financial intermediaries and the operation of monetary policy.

ENDNOTES

1. Royal Commission on Banking and Finance, *Report* (Ottawa: Queen's Printer, 1964) p. 302.
2. D. Shaw and R. Archibald, *The Canadian Securities Market: A Framework and a Plan.* Study Eight: The Management of Change in the Canadian Securities Industry (Toronto: Toronto Stock Exchange, 1977).

Elementary Theory of Financial Markets
PART 1: THE DEMAND
FOR WEALTH

4

In Chapter 3 we described the major instruments exchanged in financial markets, and discussed the more important institutions of these markets in Canada. It is now time to turn to the more difficult task of exploring the process by which prices are formed in such markets. That is the purpose of this and the following three chapters.

When asked, "What determines prices in a financial market?" the average economics student will instinctively respond, "Supply and demand." This is true in a general sense, since all prices are determined by supply and demand, but unless we can put some content into the concepts of supply and demand, such an answer will not take us very far down the road to understanding the behavior of financial markets.

THE DEMAND FOR FINANCIAL INSTRUMENTS

The Basic Decisions

The demand side of the market for financial instruments includes, at various times, virtually every spending unit in the economy — households, financial intermediaries, business firms, non-profit institutions, and government agencies. Any spending unit with a need or desire to accumulate wealth will probably enter this market from time to time.

The role of financial intermediaries in financial markets raises special issues which are best considered separately. We will discuss them in Chapter 9. At the outset we also prefer to leave aside discussion of the demands of business firms, non-profit institutions, and government agencies. With a few exceptions, particularly relating to the demand for money, they are peripheral to the main demand forces in financial markets. Thus, in this and the next chapter we will be focusing attention almost exclusively on household demands for financial instruments.

We will cast our analysis of household demands for financial instruments in terms of two basic decisions which every household must make:

(1) a decision on the *size* of total wealth holdings; and

(2) a decision on the *composition* of wealth holdings.

Wealth is the central concept in the analysis, Indeed, we will argue that financial instruments take on significance to households simply as forms in which wealth may be accumulated.

The first decision is the subject of this chapter, the second decision that of the next.

WEALTH AND SAVING

If wealth is to be the central concept in the analysis of demands for financial assets, then the first task must be to define the concept of wealth and to explore the process by which wealth is accumulated. Our objective is the development of a theory of wealth accumulation.

The Concept of Wealth

As a start, we might define the household's wealth as *the value of the household's net equity in the things which the household owns.* While complex, this definition is designed to emphasize three essential elements. First, the concept of wealth relates to things which have value in the economic sense, i.e., *market value.* Second, it implies *ownership* — the right of the household to exclude others from the enjoyment of these valuable things. Finally, the definition recognizes that the household may formally "own" valuable things of greater aggregate value than the total wealth of the household. The difference is the aggregate value of the debts or obligations of the household. Thus, to cite the most familiar example, a family may "own" its house, and at the same time have an outstanding debt or mortgage against it, equal to a substantial portion of the market value of the house. The contribution of the house to the family's wealth is the difference between the value of the house and the value of the mortgage — the family's *equity* in the house.

The Accounting Framework

Three basic accounting relationships provide a simple framework for our analysis of the demand for wealth. Each of these can be expressed in the form of an equation, but an equation which is an *identity.* The two sides of the equation are equal by definition. One can take the left-hand side of each equation as a formal definition of the variable on the right-hand side. Unlike equations which embody *functional relationships,* identities do not tell us anything substantive about the demand for wealth. They do not purport to describe the behavior of participants in the financial system. Rather, they specify *constraints* on behavior. They tell us that certain combinations of events or activities are logically impossible. For example, the first identity tells us that it is impossible for a household's assets to increase while both its liabilities and its net worth are falling.

The Balance Sheet Identity.   *Assets* are values which the household owns. *Liabilities* are the values which it owes. The difference between assets and liabilities is the equity in the value of things owed — the household's net worth or *wealth*. This fundamental relationship can be expressed in the balance sheet identity:

$$\text{ASSETS} - \text{LIABILITIES} = \text{WEALTH} \qquad (4.1)$$

Wealth need not always be positive. The assets of the household could exceed or fall short of liabilities, and accordingly wealth could be positive or negative. If wealth is positive, we can refer to the household as a *net creditor,* and if wealth is negative we can refer to it as a *net debtor.*[1]

The Saving Identity.   The second basic identity is a definition of net saving. For every household, and indeed for the nation as a whole, it is true by definition that:

$$\text{INCOME} - \text{CONSUMPTION} = \text{SAVING} \qquad (4.2)$$

This identity is simply a statement of the fact that consumption and saving are alternative uses of the same scarce resources, the household's (or the nation's) income. In order to save, the household must choose to forego current consumption, and in this very basic sense current consumption foregone is the cost of saving. The decisions on consumption and on saving are two sides of the same coin. If you explain one, you explain the other.

There is nothing in the saving identity which says that saving must be positive. Saving can be negative as long as current consumption exceeds current income (negative saving is sometimes called dissaving). Thus, saving is an economic variable which must be assigned an algebraic sign as well as a magnitude.

The Accumulation Identity.   Assets, liabilities and wealth are *stock variables.* They are values measured at a point in time. Income, consumption, and saving are *flow variables.* They are values measured over a period of time. The third identity — the accumulation identity — establishes a logical link between the stocks and the flows. It simply states that during any given period of time:[2]

$$\text{SAVING} = \Delta \text{ WEALTH} \qquad (4.3)$$

where Δ wealth means the *net change* in wealth.

The logic of this equation should be self-evident. If it is not, consider briefly what is involved in the act of saving. If the saving of a given household is positive during some month, the household receives more income than it spends on consumption during that month. What can the household do with the balance of its income? There are three possibilities. It might use this portion to acquire real or financial assets. This is a non-consumption use of the household's income, which results in an increase in its net asset holdings and hence its wealth. Alternatively, the household might use this portion of its income to pay off debts. Again, this is a non-consumption use of its income which, by reducing liabilities, increases the household's wealth. If it neither purchases assets nor pays off liabilities then the household must simply accumulate money in the amount of the excess of its income over its consumption. But money is also an asset. Its accumulation implies an equal increase of the household's wealth. *Positive saving implies a corresponding increase in wealth.*

The same points can be made regarding negative saving. If consumption is to exceed income, the household must somehow finance its deficit budget. It must either borrow, and thereby increase its liabilities and hence reduce its wealth, or it must draw down its assets, whether money or other assets, with the same effect on its wealth. *Negative saving implies a corresponding reduction in wealth.*

THE ECONOMIC THEORY OF THE SAVING DECISION

On any particular date which we can choose arbitrarily as the starting point for our analysis, each household in the population will have a measurable stock of wealth (positive or negative), and will expect a certain flow of income during the following time period, say one year. The household may plan to increase, decrease, or make no change in its wealth holdings over that year. For our analysis, this is the fundamental decision to be made by each household — a decision about the size of its wealth holdings.

Equation 4.3 tells us that saving is the method by which any household adjusts the size of its wealth. This suggests that we should call this fundamental decision the *saving decision.* (It is important to remember that saving may be either positive or negative; wealth may be increased or decreased).

Specific Motives for Saving

If we asked people why they save part of their income we would probably be given a great variety of specific motives. It is quite likely that we would discover many instances in which saving was alleged to be quite *fortuitous* — an unplanned, inadvertent, and perhaps random event. Aside from such short-term aberrations, however, we would probably discover that most households had in mind a fairly deliberate plan for saving. In some cases it might involve a general *income objective,* like the provision of a pension during years of retirement from active participation in the labor force or otherwise to increase the household's income in later years. In other instances we might be told about some specific *target* which the household has in mind, such as the purchase of a new house, a new automobile, or some other major durable good, or even an intangible item such as a prolonged vacation, perhaps involving a trip to "the old country," or a university education, or a legacy for the household's children. In other instances we might discover that saving was simply an attempt to provide for general or specific *contingencies* which might occur in the future. Thus, a household might buy life or disability insurance on the main income earner, or it might build up a bank account "against a rainy day," or take advantage or unexpected future opportunities.

The variety of possible motives for saving is virtually endless, and no single theory can encompass all of them in detail. The problem is to distill from the endless complexities of reality a few generalizations which capture the "essence" of the behavior of saving. In recent years, this has been the subject of much theoretical and empirical research. Without attempting a detailed review of the resulting literature, it is pertinent to note some of the highlights.

Income and the Saving Decision

The Keynesian Hypothesis.   The theory of saving developed in most principles of economics textbooks is that embodied in the Keynesian consumption function. Its originator, J. M. Keynes, asserted that "the amount of aggregate consumption mainly depends on the amount of aggregate income," and this relationship exists because there is a:

> fundamental psychological law, upon which we are entitled to depend with great confidence, both *a priori* from our knowledge of human nature and from the detailed facts of experience . . . that men are disposed, as a rule and on the average, to increase their consumption as their income increases, but not by as much as the increase in their income.[3]

As equation 4.2 demonstrates, consumption and saving are complements. They are alternative possible uses of income, and if you explain one you necessarily explain the other. Thus, Keynes' consumption function can be readily translated into a saving function which says that "the amount of aggregate saving mainly depends on the amount of aggregate income," and "men are disposed, as a rule and on the average, to increase their saving as their income increases, but not by as much as the increase in their income." In most elementary economic theory it is assumed that the relationship between aggregate income and saving can be described by a straight line, such as that depicted in Figure 4.1. At low levels of income, saving is negative. At higher levels of income it is positive, and is an increasing function of income. The portion of income saved (the average propensity to consume) thus depends on the level of income, but the increase in saving is always a constant proportion (the marginal propensity to consume) of any increase in income.

This assumed relationship between income and saving seems plausible enough. Since the accumulation of wealth is but one among the many competing demands on the limited income of each household, it would be surprising if the level of saving in the household was not affected by the household's income. Households with relatively high incomes are able to buy more of everything, including wealth, than are households with relatively small incomes. Moreover, at a low level of income, present consumption needs are likely in general to seem relatively more urgent than future requirements. We would therefore expect low-income households to save a smaller portion of their income than high-income families.

As it has been used in economic theory, the Keynesian hypothesis is primarily a relationship between *aggregate* income and *aggregate* saving. It is clear, however, for his "fundamental psychological law" that Keynes thought of his relationship applying at the *microeconomic* level as well — as in explaining differences in individual household's saving. The validity of the hypothesis has been tested at both levels in a large number of studies. The aggregative studies have examined the relationship

FIGURE 4-1   Aggregate saving function: Keynesian hypothesis

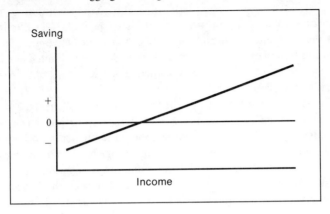

between income and saving for the nation as a whole over varying time periods extending well over half a century in length. The microeconomic studies, by contrast, examine the saving behavior of a cross-section of households during a given period of time, normally one year.

At first glance, both the micro and macro studies appear to confirm the Keynesian hypothesis, at least in a general way. While the relationship may not be strictly linear, there is a clear, unmistakable positive relationship between saving and income, both in the aggregate and on the average for a cross section of the population. The latter is illustrated in Table 4-1. However, in spite of this evidence, many economists have lingering doubts about the adequacy of the hypothesis.

These doubts are based, in part, on theoretical reasoning involving the relationship between saving and wealth accumulation which we have already established. A low-

TABLE 4-1   Income and saving of families in Canadian urban areas, 1978

Family income (before taxes)	All classes	Under $6000	$6000 -7999	$8000 -11 999	$12 000 -15 999	$16 000 -19 999
1. Average net income after taxes	$17 462	$ 4 117	$ 6 736	$ 9 049	$12 128	$15 186
2. Consumption	15 231	4 999	7 294	9 089	11 893	14 331
3. Saving	2 231	−882	−554	−40	+235	+856
Saving ratio	+12.7	−21.4	−8.2	−0.4	+1.9	+5.6

	$20 000 -24 999	$25 000 -29 999	$30 000 -34 999	$35 000 and over
	$18 654	$22 346	$25 672	$36 332
	16 487	19 421	20 651	27 301
	+2 167	+2 925	+5 021	+9 031
	+11.6	+13.1	+19.6	+24.9

SOURCE: Statistics Canada, *Familiy Expenditure in Canada* (1981), pp. 2-3.

income household which is dissaving must be simultaneously reducing its wealth, either by disposing of assets or increasing liabilities. The assumption that saving depends solely on income (if it is to conform to the facts of Table 4-1) implies a further assumption that households with chronically low incomes have unlimited means to finance consumption in excess of income. They must have unlimited assets which can be sold, or they must be able to increase their debts without limit. In general, this assumption is implausible.

Households with incomes above the zero saving level must be accumulating wealth. This includes the bulk of the households in the population. The hypothesis that saving depends only on the level of income implies the further hypothesis that households whose income remains continuously in this range have an insatiable demand for wealth. While it does not do as much violence to our pre-conceptions about the world as does the first assumption (unlimited credit or assets for sale), this is also implausible. Households presumably demand wealth for any of the variety of purposes which we have noted earlier. None of these suggests an insatiable demand for wealth at moderate to high-income levels regardless of all other considerations.

Empirical research appears to confirm these theoretical doubts. A careful sifting of the evidence shows that the Keynesian hypothesis does not adequately explain all of the significant variations in saving behavior among households, or all of the significant fluctuations in national saving behavior. The Keynesian hypothesis appears to identify one important consideration in household saving, but as a total theory of saving it is at best only a first approximation.

The Permanent Income Hypothesis.   One of the interesting regularities discovered in cross-sectional studies is that the saving behavior of households which have recently experienced a significant *change* in income is different from the behavior of households with the same present income level but which have not experienced a change in income. Households which have experienced a decline in income tend to save less than comparable households with a steady income, and households which have experienced a rise in income tend to save more than comparable households with a stable income. One possible explanation for this phenomenon is to be found in the so-called *permanent income hypothesis.*

An important element to this theory, as might be expected, is the concept of "permanent income." This concept is somewhat complex, and a formal definition is beyond our present exposition. However, we can roughly interpret it as that level of income which the household has come to expect as its normal income. The actual income may fall short of or exceed permanent income as a result of random "transitory" factors.

Illness or unexpected unemployment might reduce income below permanent income. Similarly, an unexpected gift or a sudden rise in the market price of a product produced and sold by members of the household would raise current income above permanent income. Thus, income has a permanent component (planned or expected) and a transitory component (a product of unexpected chance variations).

According to this hypothesis, a household's consumption does not depend directly upon the household's current income. Rather, if we ignore a random or "transitory" component in consumption expenditures, it depends upon the household's permanent income.[4] In effect, consumption expenditures are expected to remain relatively stable at the level determined by permanent income while current income fluctuates as a result of transitory factors. Thus, the high rate of consumption to income at low incomes in Table 4-1 would be interpreted to mean that the current income of these households was below their permanent income because of some unforeseen circumstances. Similarly, the low proportion of consumption to income at high income means that these families received incomes above their permanent income.

The permanent income hypothesis is normally presented as a theory explaining the behavior of consumption expenditures. However, equation 4.2 permits us to interpret it as a theory of saving. In the long run, permanent saving, just like permanent consumption, depends on permanent income. In the short run, the relationship is more complex. Consumption, as we will recall, is assumed to remain stable at a level determined by permanent income while current income varies because of transitory factors. Equation 4.2 tells us that if consumption remains stable while income varies, the level of savings must respond to the movements of income. The permanent income hypothesis puts saving in the role of a shock absorber in the short run. Thus, we see in Table 4-1 that saving is very low and even negative at low levels of income where negative transitory components can be expected to be substantial. Conversely, at high levels of income where positive transitory income is more likely, saving is a substantial proportion of income.

The permanent income hypothesis, if correct, provides a fundamentally different interpretation of the relationship between income and saving than does the Keynesian hypothesis. Moreover, the difference is a matter of considerable consequence for economic policy, as we will see in later sections of the book. Tests of the hypothesis have thus has a relatively high priority in empirical economics in recent years. Unfortunately, none of the variables involved — permanent income, permanent consumption, or permanent saving (or, for that matter, the corresponding transitory components) — can be observed directly. They are theoretical constructs. As a result, all of the tests have had to be indirect. Perhaps for this reason we must regard the formal statistical tests as inconclusive. Much of the evidence is favorable to the hypothesis, but the evidence is far from decisive.

The Life Cycle Hypothesis.   In the simple form in which we have presented it, the permanent income hypothesis does not provide us with many insights into the saving decision. It only tells us that in part the saving decision is deliberate and in part a product of chance variations in income. It does not tell us what considerations govern the level of planned saving. (By definition, we cannot have a theory to explain the "random" component.) This is not a fault of the theory, but of our exposition, since we have not explored the theoretical foundations of the hypothesis.

The theory of household behavior underlying the permanent income hypothesis is in all essentials the same as that underlying another contemporary theory of saving behavior, the so-called *life cycle hypothesis,* which starts with the familiar assumptions that households seek to maximize utility, and that they derive utility only from the consumption of goods and services (and perhaps from leaving bequests to the next generation). However, households have a normal life span well beyond one year. Hence, the household will presumably seek to maximize the utility which it derives from

FIGURE 4-2   The life cycle: income, consumption, saving, and wealth

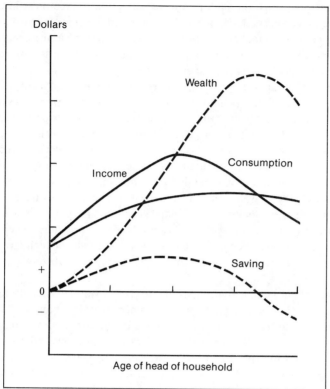

consumption over its entire life span. This calls for a lifetime plan for consumption expenditures in the light of expected lifetime income.

A basic fact of life which the household must recognize is that the lifetime pattern of income which the household expects to receive will probably not correspond exactly to the most desirable pattern of consumption. A typical life cycle is illustrated in Figure 4-2. In the early working years, household income is relatively low. As the household grows older, its income typically rises because of increased work experience and seniority. Income usually reaches a maximum sometime during middle age depending on occupation. Finally, income from employment drops in later years and ceases at retirement. Consumption also exhibits a characteristic pattern over a lifetime. In early years, as the household is formed, acquires the necessary durable goods and raises and educates children, it is quite probable that income will not exceed planned consumption by a substantial margin, and in many cases may fall considerably short of planned consumption.[5] In the middle years of the life span, by contrast, planned consumption will normally fall substantially short of earned income, as the children grow up and leave home. In later years, income from employment will probably drop significantly,

FIGURE 4-3   The life cycle: income and wealth of families and
unattached individuals, 1977

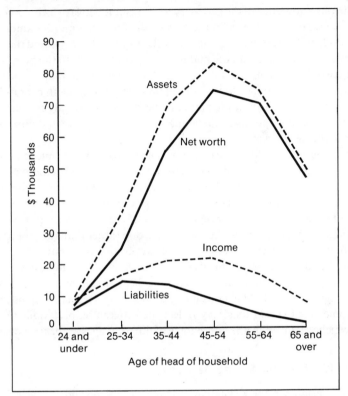

Source: Statistics Canada, *The Distribution of Income and Wealth, 1977*, Ottawa, 1979, p. 34.

particularly following retirement. Planned consumption will then greatly exceed income from employment. A typical life cycle of income and consumption is illustrated in Figure 4-2.[6]

Under these circumstances, the maximization of utility from consumption requires a redistribution of purchasing power between years of "surplus" income and years of "deficient" income. In addition, the household may wish to accumulate a reserve for contingencies, such as illness or unemployment, which might have a short-term impact on either income or consumption expenditures. The method of achieving both of these objectives is through saving. From equation 4.2 we know that current saving equals the difference between current income and current consumption. The rate of saving which corresponds to the income and consumption for the household at each age is also shown in Figure 4-2.

Finally, our equation 4.3 showed that the level of saving determines, and is identical to, the change in household wealth. In years of surplus income the household can accumulate wealth (positive saving); in years of deficient income wealth is reduced, either through a reduction in asset holdings or an increase in liabilities (negative saving).

The pattern of wealth over the life time implied by our patterns of income and consumption is shown in the lower panel of Figure 4-2.

From our knowledge of the necessary relationships between income, consumption, savings, and wealth, we should find certain predictable relationships among the panels of Figure 4-2, and indeed we do. Only two will be noted. First, we find that the point at which saving becomes zero in the middle panel corresponds to the point in the upper panel where income equals consumption and, moreover, and more important for our purposes, it also corresponds to the household's maximum wealth over its life span. In addition, we should note that the point at which income exceeds consumption by the greatest amount corresponds to the points where saving is greatest and where wealth increases at the fastest rate.

Some aspects of the life cycle in income and wealth for a sample of households are illustrated in Figure 4-3. These data tend to conform fairly well to the expectations that would be derived from the life cycle hypothesis. We see that income rises through the early age groups and reaches its peak at the age group of 45-54 years. Net worth, the measure of wealth also grows throughout most of the life-cycle, but in contrast to our expectations reaches a peak for the 45-54 age group rather than the group which is just prior to retirement. We should remember, however, that these data do not correspond exactly to the concepts used in the life cycle hypothesis. The sample covers households of different ages at a point in time, whereas the theory explains patterns of savings and wealth of a given household over its life cycle. The imperfect correspondence between the data and our expectations may reflect the different expectations about lifetime income which were held by the households of different ages at the time of the survey.

Expected Yield and the Saving Decision

The central variable in the Keynesian, permanent income and life cycle hypotheses is income. While the relationship between income and saving will depend in part on transitory factors and in part on the household's stage in the life cycle, it is conceded in general that the higher the level of income the higher will be the level of saving. There is also a second variable affecting the saving decision which has received much attention in the literature; this is the *expected yield on assets.*

Expected yield is the interest rate implicit in the relationship between the stream of future payments and the market price of the asset which provides those payments. A more precise formulation of the concept is developed in the Appendix to Chapter 5. However, in a very crude sense it is the ratio of the expected future payments to the current cost of the asset.

That expected yield should be a primary determinant of the demand for wealth should not be surprising. As we have already noted, the accumulation of wealth implies the sacrifice of current consumption in order to accumulate the means for larger future consumption. Depending on preferences between future and present consumption, saving — and hence, the net demand for wealth — should be more or less sensitive to changes in the yield on assets.

While saving should be sensitive to yields on assets, the direction of the effect is not always clear. From one perspective, the effect of higher yields is to provide a larger stream of future benefits from any given present sacrifice (e.g., a larger pension, or a larger estate for one's heirs). Since larger benefits are to be preferred to smaller, higher yields should stimulate saving. From a different perspective, however, the higher the yield the smaller the current sacrifice which is necessary to achieve any given future objective (e.g., a new house, or a round-the-world tour). A higher yield could conceivably reduce the incentive to save on the part of "target savers."

There is also another aspect to any increase in expected yields on assets. Higher yields also imply higher costs of borrowing funds (an interest cost to the borrower is an expected yield to the lender). The higher cost of credit should deter households from borrowing, and hence increase saving.

In summary, higher expected yields mean more favorable "terms of trade" between future and present. This should induce saving and hence increase the demand for additions to wealth. However, households with fixed targets for wealth accumulation can now achieve those targets with less saving. While the effect of higher yields could thus be perverse, most economists assume that higher yields lead to marginally higher saving rates (empirical evidence is somewhat equivocal).

Socio-Economic Factors in the Saving Decision

Current income, permanent income, stage in the life cycle, and expected yield are all "objective" factors affecting the saving decision. They are factors in the outside world to which the household reacts. We should not ignore the "subjective" or personal elements in the decision as well. The tastes or preferences of households as between future and present consumption and with respect to the provision of an estate for future generations may differ markedly. In technical terms, they may have very different "time preferences." Some differences in time preference may be related to other social or economic characteristics. Thus, survey researchers have discovered many interesting differences in saving behavior as between urban and rural families, home-owners and tenants, and persons with different occupations, levels of education, or racial backgrounds.

The Economic Theory of the Saving Decision: A Summary

The theory of demand developed in elementary economic theory has its foundations in the concept of utility. People demand goods and services because the consumption of these goods and services yields utility directly to the consumer. In general, however, financial instruments are not in this category. They do not yield utility directly in the same sense that the consumption of a cup of coffee or a candy bar yields utility. The demand for financial instruments is a demand for something to be held — an asset —not a demand for something to be consumed. If households seek to maximize the utility derived from the use of their limited incomes, why then should they allocate part of their limited incomes to the accumulation of non-utility-yielding financial instruments? Is their behavior inconsistent with the general assumption of utility maximization? Are asset-accumulating households acting irrationally?

In general, the answer to this last question is no. It may be quite rational for a household which is seeking to maximize utility to devote part of its limited income to the accumulation of financial instruments, even though these instruments are not objects of consumption and hence do not yield utility directly in the same sense as do consumer goods. The rational head of the household must take a lifetime perspective on utility maximization, and plan the household's expenditures with an eye to the future as well as the present. It may seem rational to deliberately reduce the consumption of the household below its potential levels at present in order to permit higher levels of consumption in the future. Such a redistribution of income and consumption from the present to the future requires an accumulation of wealth, and one of the basic forms in which wealth may be accumulated is in the form of financial instruments. *The demand for financial instruments has at its roots a desire to accumulate wealth, and the desire to accumulate wealth is in turn based on the desire to redistribute income and consumption over time.*

ENDNOTES

1. This accounting definition of wealth is deceptively simple. We are in fact glossing over many of the complexities in the measurement of wealth, particularly in the measurement of the value of assets. In particular, we have ignored intangible assets, like the earning power of the members of the household — what some economists call human wealth. The measurement of the value of human assets is complicated by the fact that markets for such assets do not exist and as a result it is impossible to quote market values. Markets exist for the services of human beings, of course, but since the abolition of slavery there are no markets in which the *asset* which yields the services can be traded. This does not mean that the measurement of the value of the human asset is impossible. In the appendix to the next chapter we develop the concept of present value. The measurement of the value of a human resource — like the measurement of the value of any resource — is a problem in the calculation of present value.

    If the value of human assets is included in the household's balance sheet, it is less likely that wealth could ever be negative.

2. The validity of this identity depends on the appropriate definitions of income and consumption in equation 4.2, and hence the definition of saving. Problems arise because of three elements in the household's financial accounts: gifts, taxes, and changes in the market values of assets (capital gains or losses). We must make adjustments for each of these items. Capital gains and losses and gifts received must be counted as income (capital losses reduce income, of course). Gifts made by the household might be considered as a consumption use of income, but it is probably better to group gifts together with taxes paid as a deduction from income to obtain the household's disposable income.

3. J. M. Keynes, *The General Theory of Employment, Interest and Money,* (New York: Harcourt, Brace & Co., 1936), p. 96.

4. This is not a fully accurate statement of the position of the permanent income theorists. They argue that the ratio of permanent consumption to permanent income is independent of the level of permanent income. It does depend on a variety of other factors, however, including the level of interest rates and the household's "tastes and preferences for consumption versus additions to wealth." In the latter category, such objective factors as the size and age composition of the family and the variability of the household's income are suggested as important considerations. However, with all of these factors given, then the ratio of permanent saving to permanent income will be the same at all levels of permanent income. Cf., M. Friedman, *A Theory of the Consumption Function,* (Princeton: Princeton University Press, 1957), p. 26.

5. It should be noted that the statistical relationship between age and savings depends on the definition of saving. This is particularly true in the early stages of the life cycle when the household is typically making heavy expenditures on durable consumer goods, including the purchase of a house. If all consumer durables are considered to be assets and hence included in the measurement of net worth, then only the "consumption" (i.e., depreciation) of these assets will be included in consumption expenditures. Saving is less likely to be negative under these circumstances than if these goods are not included in the measurement of net worth. Most statistical studies omit most of these consumer durables, largely because of the lack of reliable data. About the only durable good commonly included is the owner's equity in his house. This is the definition of assets used in measuring net worth as plotted in Figure 4-3, i.e., the household's equity in its house plus the value of its financial assets.

6. We should note that we are trying to explain real consumption and real saving. Thus the life cycle patterns shown in Figure 4-2 do not reflect the increases in money income and consumption that can be expected to occur in periods of inflation. Rather, they reflect money income deflated by some measure of the price level.

Elementary Theory of Financial Markets 5
PART 2: THE PORTFOLIO BALANCE DECISION

The demand for wealth — the saving decision — is fundamental to household demands for financial assets. However, it is simply a decision about the *size* of total asset holdings, and must be accompanied by another decision about the *composition* of the collection of assets to be held.

It is convenient to term this collection of assets, an *asset portfolio* — or *portfolio*, for short. In selecting a portfolio the assetholder must be concerned with the balance between real assets and financial assets, and, of major concern to us at the moment, within the category of financial assets he must be concerned with the balance between the different types of financial instruments discussed in Chapter 3. He must make choices among the great variety of financial instruments available in the market. *The portfolio balance decision thus translates a general demand for assets into specific demands for specific assets.*

THE CHARACTERISTICS OF ASSETS _____

The asset holder has a wide set of assets from which to select a portfolio ranging from real assets such as land and paintings, through bonds and corporate stock, to deposits at financial institutions. Each of these assets provides its owner with a different set of characteristics. In this section we discuss some of the more important characteristics of assets which are relevant to people's portfolio choices.

Expected Yield

The central theoretical issue in any discussion of the portfolio balance decision is why any financial instrument should be chosen over any other as the form in which the household accumulates wealth. One important factor in this choice should be quite obvious. Other things being equal, a rational assetholder will always prefer an asset with a high expected yield to one with a low expected yield.

We have already encountered the concept of expected yield in our discussion of the saving decision. You will remember that it is the interest rate which is implicit in the relationship between the market price of the financial instrument and the expected stream of future payments associated with that instrument. We noted that the effect of expected yield on the total demand for wealth was ambiguous. A higher expected yield might lead to greater or less saving. However, no such ambiguity exists in the effect of expected yield on the demand for particular assets. Since all assets are substitutes for each other as forms in which wealth may be accumulated, other things being equal, the demand for any particular instrument will be greater the higher the expected yield.

Normally, discussions of the demand side of a market focus on market price, and yet so far in our exposition we have scarcely mentioned market price. Rather, we have implicitly developed an argument that expected yield plays the central role in financial markets that price plays in other markets (although we have found a positive relationship between demand and yield, rather than the normal negative relationship between demand and price).

This difference from the standard discussion of demand is more apparent than real, however. The fact is that *for any financial instrument, market price and expected yield are inversely related.* The validity of this statement should be obvious since, with the stream of future payments *fixed by contract*, the yield on the bond can only rise if the market price falls. This is implicit in the definition of expected yield.

For example, in 1979 the Government of Canada issued a bond with 10-year maturity. The coupon rate was fixed at 10%, so that the total annual interest payment on a $1000 (par value) bond is $100. These securities traded freely at prices determined in the open market. In mid-1980 the market price of a $1000 bond had fallen to $900. At this point the yield was 11.8%. Subsequently, bond prices fell even further. At the end of September 1981 the price of this bond was $665 implying a yield of 18.1%. As bond prices fell, the yield increased.

It follows, then, that the statement that the demand for a financial instrument is directly related to its expected yield is the same as the statement that the demand for the instrument is inversely related to its market price.

The whole subject of market prices and yields on assets is so important, not only for our analysis, but also in any decisions relating to fixed assets, that we have taken pains to develop and explore the concepts more carefully and systematically in the appendix to this chapter.

If expected yield were the only consideration in portfolio choices, then the rational assetholder, faced with alternatives of one security yielding 5% and one yielding 10%, would always choose the latter. In the market, attempts of individuals to sell the 5% securities to purchase the 10% securities should drive the price of the former down (and the yield up) and the price of the latter up (and the yield down). The end result should be a rough equalization of yields on the two securities. In fact, we observe in the market that the yields on different securities differ markedly and consistently. Why is this? The answer is that there are other factors which affect choices among assets, including credit risk, market risk, the risk of inflation, and differential taxation.

Certainty of Value and Risk

Financial instruments by their very nature involve payments that are to occur in the future. As a result the assetholder cannot be certain that his expectations as to the values he will receive in the future will in fact be realized. If his expectations are not realized, the actual yield on a security can turn out to be considerably different from its expected yield. We shall see that the degree of certainty attached to the future values of different securities differ markedly, and that differences in yield in the market are, in part, a reflection of differences in uncertainty.

Uncertainty as to the future value of any asset may arise from a variety of causes. The assetholder may not be certain of the value that he will realize from his asset at some definite time in the future when he plans to dispose of it. Since a financial asset is a claim to a stream of future payments, there will always be some uncertainty about whether the payments will in fact be made and, particularly in the case of variable-income securities, about the size of such payments. In Chapter 3, we defined this possibility as *credit risk*. Uncertainty also occurs with respect to the terms at which the asset can be sold at the future time when the assetholder wishes to convert his asset into money. This source of uncertainty is relevant only to marketable assets and will be referred to as *market risk*. Market risk remains relevant for a security even if all payments are made as promised. Market risk arises from uncertainty regarding the market conditions which may exist at the time the investor wishes to sell the security. We will refer to the combination of credit and market risk as overall risk, or, simply, risk.

As we will see later, an investor can protect himself from market risk at some definite date in the future by appropriately choosing the assets he holds. Often, however, the assetholder does not know with certainty the exact time at which he will want to convert his asset into money. He may, for example, have been saving to protect himself against uncertain contingencies such as sickness or unemployment, or for a once-in-a-lifetime holiday, or possibly retirement at some indefinite date in the future. In these cases, the investor is subject to market risk in some form or another whatever choice he makes. Thus, risk, to an investor, can result either from uncertainty with respect to an asset's value at a given date or from uncertainty on the investor's part as to the time at which he will need to dispose of his assets. We shall examine the first of these factors in some detail before turning to the second.

The Meaning of Risk.   We can formalize the concept of risk by assuming that for any given financial instrument there is a range of possible yields at the present market price. If large future payments are made, the yield will be high; if small future payments are made, the yield will be low. Indeed, if the future payments are very small or, in the extreme, non-existent, the yield will be negative. It must be stressed that we refer to the actual yield on the investment — what actually materializes.

The individual contemplating the purchase of this security cannot know what the outcome will be. However, if he is to make a rational decision, he must somehow assess the likelihood of alternative possible outcomes, and select *the outcome which seems most likely*. It is this value to which we refer when we use the expression *expected yield*. Note that the expected yield is not the only outcome regarded as possible nor is it necessarily the outcome which will materialize.

For purposes of theoretical discussions we can formalize these elements of the portfolio-selection process by assuming that the assetholder has in mind a subjective probability distribution of possible yields on the asset, such as that drawn in Figure 5-1.

FIGURE 5-1   Probability distribution of possible yields

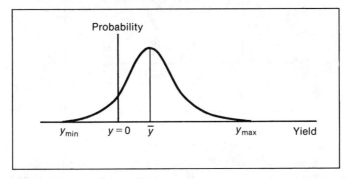

FIGURE 5-2   Two probability distributions: same expected yield, different risks

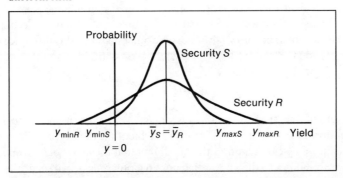

The area under the bell-shaped curve is equal to 1, indicating that in the judgment of the assetholder (but not necessarily in fact) one of the possible alternative yields listed along the base of the curve must occur. That is, he feels that there is a probability of 1 (perfect certainty) that the actual yield will be among those listed on the base. The probability that any particular one of these yields will materialize is significantly less than 1. The yield ($\bar{y}$ which he feels has the greatest probability of occurrence — the most likely outcome — is under the highest point of the probability distribution. In his judgment every other possible outcome has a lesser probability of occurrence.

What we mean by risk is the *dispersion of possible yield* around the *expected yield*. Consider Figure 5-2, which shows two probability distributions of the type plotted in Figure 5-1. Each of these distributions represents the assetholder's subjective judgments about the possible yields on two different securities. Each security has the same expected yield. However, they differ markedly in terms of the associated degree of risk. In the case of security S (for "safe") the alternative possible yields are clustered closely

FIGURE 5-3   Two probability distributions: same range, different risks

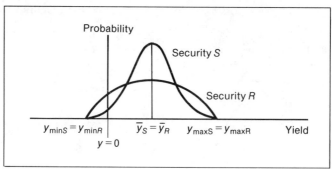

about the expected yield. In the case of security R (for "risky") the alternative possible yields are more dispersed. The assetholder has less confidence that that actual yield will be the expected yield in the latter case. He subjectively assigns a lower probability to the expected outcome, and is willing to admit the possibility of a wider range of alternative outcomes.

It is convenient for theoretical analysis to have a simple measure of risk in this probability sense. A number of possible measures are available. Perhaps the most simple measure would be the *range* of possible outcomes, i.e., the difference between the highest (y_{max}) and the lowest (y_{min}) yields which the assetholder would admit as possible outcomes. Formally, the range is

$$\text{RANGE} = y_{max} - y_{min}$$

As a measure of risk, the range is seriously defective because it takes into account only one dimension of risk. While it allows for the fact that the outcome may be different from the expected yield, it ignores the possibility that the assetholder implicitly assigns different probabilities to the alternative possible outcomes. Two securities might have the same range of possible yields, and yet one appears less risky than the other, because the assetholder assigns a lower probability to the extreme values, and hence has greater confidence in the accuracy of his estimate of the expected yield. This possibility is sketched in Figure 5-3.

We need as a measure of risk, then a number which takes account of both dimensions, i.e., of the range of possible outcome and of the probability of each outcome. This measure is provided by a statistic called *the standard deviation,* commonly represented by the Greek letter sigma (σ), a complicated measure both in its computation and meaning. For now, all we need know is that it is a measure of the dispersion of the probability distribution about the expected yield. The more dispersed the distribution, (i.e., the larger the standard deviation), the greater the probability that the actual yield will be different from the expected yield, and hence the greater the risk associated with that security.

Now that we have examined the meaning of risk, we are in a position to see why risk is important to the investor in making his choices among different assets. We will turn first to credit risk and its effects and then consider market risk.

Credit Risk.   As a first step in considering the effects of credit risk, we should make sure we understand what is the relevant yield to an investor in the presence of credit risk. The information found in the contract between lender and borrower and presented in financial pages in the newspapers permits us to determine only the *theoretical yield*. It is calculated on the presumption that all payments specified in the contract will be made in full and on time. The theoretical yield need not be the most likely, and indeed will not be, if there is some probability that all payments promised in the future will not be made as prescribed. Thus, we need to consider a concept of yield which depends on the investor's expectations of default by the borrower. The expected yield is calculated by taking into account the amount by which these payments are expected to fall short of the theoretical yield. The concept of expected yield refers to the most probable yield, based on the assetholder's expectations of the size and timing of future payments. In the case of a perfectly safe bond, expected yield and theoretical yield will be the same. It should be obvious that expected yield rather than theoretical yield is the relevant concept for investors making choices among assets.

We can best clarify this distinction between *theoretical* and *expected* yield by looking at a real example. Consider two securities that are roughly similar in all respects except for the identity of the debtor who is responsible for making the future payments. The one security is issued by the Government of Canada, has an 10.75% annual coupon and will mature in 1985. The other is issued by Chrysler Credit of Canada, has a 9.75% coupon and also matures in 1985. In mid-March, 1982, the Canada bond was selling for approximately $890 per $1000 par value, giving a theoretical yield of 15%, whereas the Chrysler bond was selling for $650 per $1000 par value, giving a theoretical yield of 30%. The identity of the borrower, in this case, explains much of the difference in these yields. Investors view the Government of Canada bonds as virtually riskless. In 1982, however, the future prospects of the Chrysler Corporation and its ability to meet its obligations for making payments were open to considerable doubt. If investors expected, for example, that there was one chance in 25 that the Chrysler Corporation would default, that is, make no further payments on these obligations, the expected value of this possibility would be 4% of the value of the Chrysler bonds held by the investor. With this belief, the investor would view the expected yield on Chrysler bonds to be 26% (the theoretical yield of 30% less than 4% expected cost of default). In general, then, differences in credit risk serve to explain some of the differences in theoretical yields among financial securities. The essential point to remember is that theoretical yields must be adjusted by the expected value of defaults on future payments in order to determine the expected yield to the investor.

We have seen in a general way how credit risk can explain differences in theoretical yields among different financial assets. While it would be nice if we could estimate the amount of credit risk for any security and, as a result, determine its expected yield, unfortunately we cannot. While such formal constructs as credit risk are indispensable for our analysis, we cannot realistically assume that each investor calculates the probability of default for each asset he might consider taking into his portfolio. And yet, each rational investor must form some impression of the degree of credit risk.

In truth, little is known about how this is done. Sometimes people rely on hunches, or moon phases, or "inside information," or just some "feeling" about each asset. For concerned wealth owners, however, there are group of professional investment counsel-

FIGURE 5-4 Yields of federal, provincial, and industrial bonds, 1978-82

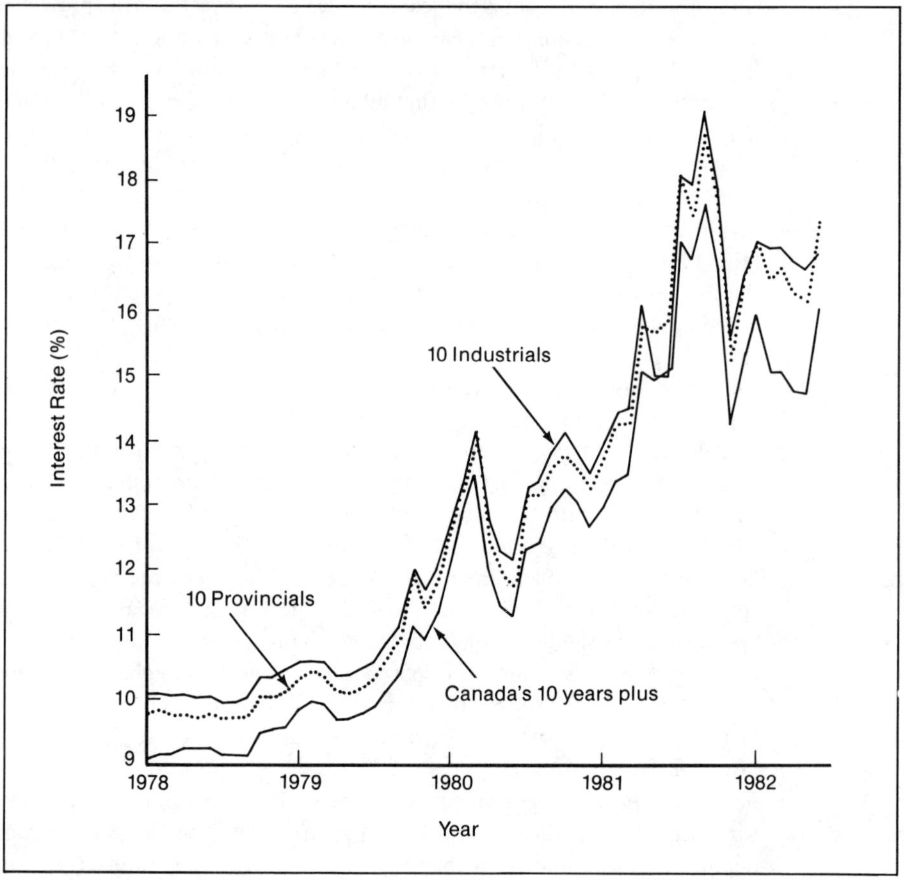

Source: *Bank of Canada Review.*

lors, whose advice is frequently sought, and presumably used. These counsellors employ any of a variety of techniques of "security analysis" and frequently provide ratings of securities.

Past performance generally weighs heavily in such analysis, although the past is frequently a very poor guide to future prospects and history must be tempered with a careful assessment of the implications of current and pending developments. In the market, and particularly in the market for bonds, certain more or less standard rules of thumb have emerged, and these are reflected in relatively standard differentials between yields on bonds of different types of borrowers. In Figure 5-4, we have plotted indices of yields on long-term bonds of several classes of borrowers over a number of years. Note that, in general, yields on Government of Canada bonds are less than those on bonds of all other borrowers. They are widely regarded as virtually riskless bonds. Yields on bonds of other borrowers range upward from those of the federal government. Of course, within each of the categories presented on this chart there will be a considerable range between individual borrowers of different "credit ratings," and the yields on many bonds will exceed those shown on the chart.

Market Risk.   Our analysis of credit risk has taken us a long way in understanding different yields on different instruments in the market at the same time. However, differences of credit risk cannot fully explain the differences in yields which can be observed. There are other factors which must be taken into account, one of which is the *market risk.*

As evidence for the proposition that credit risk alone will not be sufficient to explain observable and persistent differences in expected yields on financial instruments we need only consider yields on different financial instruments issued by the same debtor and for which credit risk is not a significant consideration. The one debtor which meets this requirement is the Government of Canada. Its bonds can be regarded as riskless securities in that there is almost no chance that the contractual payments will not be made. Not only are bonds backed by the general taxing powers of the government, but also the contract calls for payment in Canadian legal tender and the Government of Canada has the ultimate power to manufacture legal tender. If all else fails, the Government can "print" the money to meet its legal obligations. Thus, if credit risk is the only consideration, yields on all governments bonds should be approximately the same.

TABLE 5-1   **Yields on selected Government of Canada bonds, October 13, 1982**

Coupon rate	Date of maturity	Price	Yield to maturity
11¼%	March 15, 1983	$ 99.95	11.29%
10%	June 1, 1984	98.40	11.08%
11¼%	July 1, 1985	99.13	11.62%
15%	March 15, 1987	109.25	12.21%
10%	October 1, 1995	85.88	12.19%
13¾%	March 15, 2000	106.31	12.83%
10¼%	February 1, 2004	84.94	12.25%
Averages			
1-3 years			11.31%
3-5 years			11.51%
5-10 years			12.17%
over 10 years			12.40%

SOURCE: Bank of Canada, *Weekly Financial Statistics,* October 13, 1982.

This is seldom the case. A fairly "normal" situation is presented in Table 5-1 where we show the yields and prices on a selection of Government of Canada bonds outstanding on October 13, 1982. The yields shown in this table were calculated on the basis of prices quoted in the market on that day, and on the assumption that the promised future payments (interest and principal) would be paid. As can be seen, the yields on these government bonds tend to increase directly with the number of years to maturity.

If these bonds issued by the Government of Canada do not differ in terms of credit risk, we must ask in what way they do differ. One common view is that long-term bonds differ from shorter-term bonds because the investors' money is tied up for a longer period of time. While it is probably true that an asset holder may be concerned with the length of time his funds are tied up, this argument overlooks an essential feature of these bonds. They are *marketable*. A secondary market exists, and the holder of the bonds can sell them at the established market price any time he chooses. As long as he has this option, his money is not "tied up." What, then, is the source of the difference among these government securities?

One explanation for the differences among these securities is that shorter-term bonds have less market risk than longer-term bonds. We offered a general definition of a risk-free asset in Chapter 3. In short, an asset with low market risk is one whose market price is relatively stable. Thus, money, a financial instrument whose market price is fixed in terms of the unit of account, is considered to be a risk-free asset, at least when we are abstracting from price level changes. If short-term government bonds are to be considered to have low market risk, then prices must be relatively stable, although not necessarily fixed. In seeking the factors which govern the relative risk of instruments we must uncover those factors which tend to produce variations in market prices of instruments.

Two separate factors can be identified as affecting the market price of a financial instrument: the size of expected future payments, and the expected yield on alternative assets. A change in either one can be expected to produce a change in market price.

Clearly, a variable income security has considerable market risk. If the size of future payments is subject to change, then the market price of the instrument can be expected to change also, perhaps over a very wide range. Thus, common stock in corporations cannot be viewed as being free from market risk.

The second factor that can produce fluctuations in the market price of even riskless claims to fixed future payments is a change in the general level of yields on financial instruments, or, in other words, in the general level of interest rates. *The assertion that short-term government bonds are among the safest assets in terms of market risk is an assertion that their prices are not significantly affected as their yields rise or fall in sympathy with the general level of interest rates.* This is a property of short-term bonds not possessed by long-term bonds.

Price Stability and Term to Maturity. The basic mathematics of the relationship between yield term to maturity and market price are explored briefly in the Appendix to this chapter. The analysis in the Appendix shows that *as a general proposition* the market price and the yield on a bond will vary inversely, and that the decline in the market price for any given increase in yield will be greater the longer the term to maturity. That this general relationship is not just a theoretical construct, but also exists in fact, is illustrated in Figure 5-5.

Shown in this figure are the actual yields and market prices for two Government bonds during the period 1978-1981. The security on the upper panel was a bond which

FIGURE 5-5   Prices and yields: short term and long term
government bonds

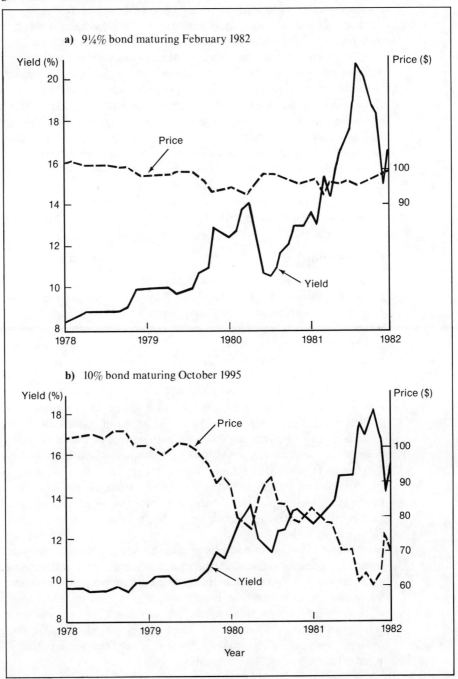

a) 9¼% bond maturing February 1982

b) 10% bond maturing October 1995

Source: *Bank of Canada Review.*

matured on February 1, 1982. At the beginning of the period it had a term to maturity of four years. By the end of the period it was on the verge of maturity. It was clearly a short-term bond, particularly in the latter part of the period. By contrast, the security on the bottom panel was long-term bond throughout. Maturing 1994, it had a term to maturity of 17 years at the outset and 13 years at the end of the period.

The contrast between the behavior of yields and prices on the two bonds is striking. Although the yield on the short-term bond actually moved over a much wider range than did the yield on the long-term bond, the market price of the short-term bond showed much greater stability than did the price of the long-term bond. Indeed, as the short-term bond approached maturity in the latter half of 1981, the sharp rise in yields was barely reflected in the market price of the bond. By contrast, a parallel, but smaller, rise in the yield on the long-term bond involved a sharp drop in its market price. From the end of January to the end of October, 1981, the market price of a $1000 (par value) bond dropped over 25% from $800 to $600. Since we have defined market risk in terms of stability of market price, it is clear that we must consider the short-term bond of the upper panel to be much less risky than the long-term bond of the lower panel.

Risk and Liquidity

In Chapter 3, we noted that economists often use the term "liquidity" to refer to the property of money that its value in terms of the unit of account is fixed. In fact, the word liquidity is a blanket term used by economists to accept a number of qualities of financial assets. It is useful for present purposes to discuss the relationship between the concepts of liquidity and risk, particularly since it may appear to the student that economists use the terms "liquid" and "riskless" almost interchangeably.

Our discussion of risk to this point has been by necessity simplified by abstracting from reality. Assets have differed only by the degree of certainty attached to their yield over a given period of investment. As we will see, however, the investor often is uncertain about or does not even know the period of investment. This complication requires us to consider a number of other qualities of financial assets. For present purposes we will identify *predictability of value, realizability,* and *reversibility* as different dimensions of liquidity.

An essential ingredient to the concept of liquidity is predictability of value. The term is almost self-explanatory and can be related to our analysis of risk. A predictable asset is riskless in the sense that we can predict its value in terms of the unit of account at various times in the future.

Money, of course, is perfectly predictable in this sense since it is denominated in terms of the unit of account. A marketable government bond, on the other hand, is predictable only at its time of maturity when the government is obligated to redeem it for its face value. As we have seen, the further in the future the maturity date of a marketable government bond is, the less predictable is its current price. Finally, for many assets, such as common stock and commodities such as gold, fine paintings, or postage stamps, there is no date in future at which their value in terms of the unit of account can be predicted with certainty.

A distinction should be made between predictability of value in terms of the unit of account and predictability in terms of real value. By the latter term we mean the predictability of value in terms of purchasing power with respect to goods and services. In the absence of inflation, the two types of predictability are the same. In times of inflation, money can offer predictability in terms of the unit of account but not predictability in terms of real purchasing power.

FIGURE 5-6   Realizability of assets

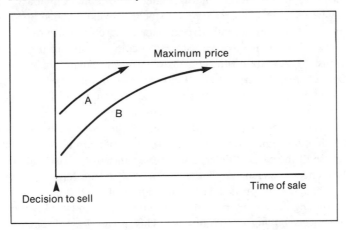

Realizability refers to the ability to sell an asset quickly at close to its current value. At any time, there is a variety of potential buyers, each of whom would pay a different maximum price for any given asset. In some circumstances, we may be able to contact many potential buyers quickly and find the one willing to pay the highest price; in others, it may be very costly to contact many buyers and, as a result, the probability that we will sell to the most eager buyer may be small. In the first case, the asset is more realizable than in the second. The concept of realizability may be illustrated more clearly by means of Figure 5-6. As we can see, assets A and B both have the same maximum realizable price. We see that once we make a decision to sell the asset A we can sell it for close to its maximum price quite quickly. Moreover, if we are willing to wait for only a short period of time, we will be able to realize its full value. In contrast, asset B can only be sold immediately for much less than its maximum value and, in addition, it takes quite a long time to search out a buyer who will pay its full value. Assets which are widely traded, such as stock in major corporations, are virtually perfectly realizable. The modern technology of stock trading permits us to offer our shares almost instantaneously to many buyers on several stock exchanges. In contrast, a seller of a rare Old Master painting will have to contact a number of art experts scattered throughout the world. In addition, the seller many not be aware of the various private collectors who might be interested in his painting if they knew it was available. Quite obviously, assets vary with respect to their realizability. Realizability will be important to any investor who cannot predict with certainty the time at which he will need his funds.

Reversibility, the other dimension of liquidity we consider, refers to the difference at any time between the buying and selling price of an asset. An asset with a small difference between buying and selling price is said to be reversible. This difference is composed of all the costs of selling and buying an asset and may include any commissions paid to agents or brokers, lawyers' fees when applicable, taxes and other fees paid to governments, and any difference between prices quoted to buyers relative to prices quoted to sellers. These costs include both the explicit payments made to others and the personal time and trouble involved in selling and buying. Assets vary substantially in terms of their reversibility. Some, such as savings deposits and Canada Savings Bonds, are virtually perfectly reversible. Common stocks or widely traded bonds many have transactions costs of only several percent depending on the size of the transaction. Selling a house is likely to involve real estate sales commissions of 5 to 6%, lawyers' fees, and land transfer taxes. Stamp and coin dealers appear to maintain buy-sell spreads of around 20%, whereas dealers in fine art have spreads of up to 50%. We would expect reversibility to be greater in assets that are commonly traded and are relatively homogeneous in that the quality of the asset can be determined readily. Again, shares in commonly traded corporations are quite reversible, in part because they are identical. On the other hand, a dealer in stamps or used cars must maintain a substantial buy-sell spread because of the costs of determining the quality of the assets offered to him by sellers. Differences between buy and sell prices affect the return for investors who acquire an asset at the buy price and can only dispose of it at the sell price which is below the current buying price. Any rate of return calculation must take into account the differences between buying and selling price. This spread clearly becomes more important the shorter the period over which the investor is expected to hold the asset.

There are assets that may do well with respect to some dimensions of liquidity, but not with others. As we have seen, shares in commonly traded corporations are realizable, reversible, but do not offer much predictability of value. Money, in contrast, scores well in all the characteristics we have mentioned. It is perfectly predictable, at least in terms of the limit of account, instantly realizable, and completely reversible. Money has a special place in economic analysis because it is the most liquid of financial instruments.

Inflation and Expected Yield

Inflation is a rise in the general level of prices consumable goods and services where prices are measured in terms of the unit of account. Since the price of money is fixed in terms of the unit of account, inflation can also be defined as *a decline in the purchasing power of money.* A unit of money will buy a smaller quantity of goods and services. Indeed, *inflation involves a decline in the real value of anything whose nominal value (in terms of the unit of account) is fixed.*

It should be evident from this statement that money is not the only financial instrument whose real value is affected by inflation. While there are few other financial instruments whose market prices are fixed, it must be remembered that bonds are claims to future payments which are fixed in terms of the unit of account. In a period of inflation, *the real value of these payments* will steadily decline. Thus the bondholder suffers a continuous erosion of his wealth.

Recognition of the possibility of inflation does not necessarily call for a radical revision of our analytical framework. It is significant because it is presumably the real rate of return on assets which is of concern to assetholders, both in their saving decisions and their portfolio balance decisions. But this means that the *expected rate of inflation must be allowed for in calculating the expected yields on financial assets,* and, by implication, *alternative possible rates of inflation must enter into the evaluation of the risks involved in holding bonds or money.* What we have done, then, in introducing the possibility of inflation, is to add another set of general considerations which must enter into the rational assetholder's calculations of expected yields and risks. Thus, to take a simple example, if an assetholder expects inflation at an annual rate of 1% per annum, then he must regard a bond with a nominal yield of 5% as having an expected *real* yield of 4% per annum. If he also considers, say, a 10% rate of inflation as a "possibility," then he must allow for this in evaluating the risks involved in holding bonds or money. Indeed, given the possibility of inflation, even government bonds and money cease to be riskless assets. *In making their portfolio, asset holders should be responsive to both the expected rate of inflation and the risk of inflation.*

Taxation and Expected Yield

There is one other important factor affecting the choice among financial instruments which requires at least passing comment. That is the effect of a taxation system which involves differential tax rates on income obtained in different forms. Some of the differential effects of the tax system, such as the depletion allowances for mining and petroleum firms, affect the relative earning capacity of firms in different industries. They thus affect the choice among financial instruments *indirectly* by affecting the relative profit rates in different industries, and hence the expected yields on their securities (and particularly their common stocks). Other provisions of the tax system —like the special tax treatment of capital gains — have a *direct* impact on portfolio choices.

Traditionally, in Canada, capital gains were exempt from taxation, but under a 1971 tax bill capital gains on financial assets became subject to taxation at half the normal progressive income tax rates. Although the effect is not as strong as earlier, the taxation system increases the expected yield (after tax) on securities which have the possibility of capital gains relative to all other securities (at least for individuals with high incomes and correspondingly high marginal tax rates). Of course, speculation on capital gains carries with it the *risk* of capital loss. However, because of differential taxation, the possibilities for capital gains must be given particular consideration in the portfolio choices of relatively wealthy people.

As in the case of anticipated inflation, the attempts of assetholders to adjust their portfolios to take advantage of differential tax rates should have the effect of adjusting the relative prices of securities to compensate for the tax differentials. Thus, the prices of securities which seem to promise capital gains should rise relative to the prices of other securities. However, only if everyone were in the same tax situation and had the same expectations for capital gains would the market price adjustment be complete.

RISK AND INVESTOR'S CHOICE

We are now in a position to provide a major element in our formal theoretical answer to the question of why yields on different securities can be continuously and consistently different in the market place. While there are some factors on the supply side to be considered, a major consideration on the demand side is assetholders' reactions to risk.

Suppose an assetholder were faced with the two securities represented by the probability distributions in Figure 5-2. Both securities have the same expected yield $(\bar{y}_S = \bar{y}_R)$. However, the distributions of possible alternative yields about the expected yield are notably different. Would the assetholder nevertheless be indifferent as to which security he took into his portfolio?

The answer is surely not. He cannot ignore the fact that security R is more risky. While the expected yields are the same on the two securities, he is *less confident* that this yield will materialize in the case of Security R than in the case of Security S. Is this not a factor which he should take into account in choosing between the two assets? That is, should he not react to the risk on each of the two securities quite independently of yield on each?

In deciding how he should react we must remember that the risk we are talking about has two sides. On the one hand, in the assetholder's judgment, there is a much greater probability that the yield on Security R will be less than the expected yield than is true in the case of the yield on Security S. On the other hand, there is also a greater probability that the yield on Security R will *exceed* the expected yield than is true in the case of the yield on Security S. *If the assetholder chooses the "safe" security he is also giving up the greater "risk" of a higher return.* Which will he choose?

Risk Aversion

In general, it is assumed that most assetholders are *risk averters*; that is, faced with the alternatives illustrated in Figure 5-2, the typical assetholder will always choose the less risky asset (S). A risk averter places a higher subjective value (or utility) on the avoidance of extremely small yields (including negative yields) than he does on the possibility of unusually large gains. *A risk averter would demand a larger expected yield on the more risky security before he would choose it over a less risky security.*

Not everyone is a risk averter. Some assetholders, although they appear to be in the minority, are better described as risk seekers, in the sense that they value the chance of larger returns more than the risk of smaller returns. Such individuals, faced with securities R and S under the circumstances of Figure 5-2, would choose security R.

Before we turn to examine the consequences of our assumption that investors are in general risk averse, we should examine the basis on which this assumption can be justified. The particular motives of individuals will be varied, of course, depending on individual situations. However, two major sources of a desire to avoid risk can be identified, one related to specific expenditure plans in the near future and one related to uncertainty as to the timing of expenditures.

Specific Expenditure Plans.
Part of the demand for financial assets is to create a bridge between the receipt of income and planned expenditures in the near future. An

individual householder might hold a personal savings deposit with a chartered bank into which he deposits his monthly paycheck, in anticipation of paying assorted bills over the forthcoming month. Similarly, corporations will accumulate liquid assets of various types in anticipation of future payrolls and other current expenditures. Risky assets, that is, assets with an unstable money value, would not be particularly appropriate to hold for the purpose of meeting expenditures anticipated during the next few weeks or months. When the time for making the expenditure arrives, the money proceeds from the sale of the assets might either fall short of or exceed the value of the expenditures the households planned to make. Households could avoid disruption of their expenditure plans by holding assets with low risk whose money value could be predicted with some certainty.

The timing of specific, planned expenditures will determine which asset allows the spender to avoid uncertainty with respect to the money value of his assets at the time at which his expenditures must be made. The asset most suitable for someone planning to purchase a car next month will be very different from the asset chosen by someone saving for planned retirement 10 years from now. The person purchasing a car next month will probably hold his funds in either a chequing account or possibly a savings account which pays interest on a daily basis. Any other asset, such as a common stock or government bond, would take too much time and trouble to make up for any interest that could be earned. Moreover, the investor would not be assured that his investment would maintain its value over the intervening month. The stock market might fall, or similarly, if interest rates went up sharply, the value of his marketable bond might also fall. In contrast someone planning to retire 10 years from now would be more likely to choose a longer-term asset. Investment in a 10-year government bond would give an assured money value 10 years from now, as it will be redeemed by the government for $1000 at that time. Moreover, the time pattern of interest payments is completely known for 10 years. If, instead, he invests in short-term government bonds or savings deposits, he will be assured that his $1000 capital remains stable over the 10 years but he cannot be assured of the interest rate he will earn over the period. If interest rates fall and remain low over the period, his accumulated interest and principal would be less than the amount assured by holding a 10-year bond. Thus, investors can be expected to avoid risk by "tailoring" their asset holdings to fit the pattern of expenditures they are planning to make in the future.

Uncertainty of Expenditure Plans.   A second source of risk aversion arises because an assetholder cannot anticipate the time when he will sell his assets. As time passes, he may encounter *unexpected* expenses, calls for payment of debts, interruptions to his employment and income, or unusual opportunities to purchase major real or financial assets, or simply a change in his desires to purchase goods and services now rather than in the future. Each of these contingencies involves unanticipated payments, calling for a sale of assets. If forced to sell when asset prices are low, he will incur substantial losses. However, if he holds short-term assets he can make the unanticipated payments without incurring these losses.

To illustrate this point, refer again to Figure 5-5. Consider the position of an individual who purchased a $1000 (par value) long-term bond at the end of 1980 for the then existing market price of $830. *If held to maturity,* the bond would have yielded

12.6% per annum. However, suppose the pressure of unanticipated expenditures forced him to sell the bond at the end of 1981. He, in fact, held the bond for one year, received interest payments from the government in the amount of $100, and then sold it into the market for $700 or $130 less than he paid for it. Instead of the expected yield of 12.6% per annum, his actual yield was negative, –6%.

Suppose that, instead, he held the short-term bond. He would have purchased it at the end of 1980 for $959, received interest payments from the government in the amount of $92.50, and sold it at the end of the year for $994, for an actual return on his investment of 13.2%. Although the expected yield (if held to maturity) of the long-term bond was greater than that on the short-term bond when purchased at the end of 1980, the actual yield on the long-term bond would have proven to be much less if the holder were forced to sell at the end of 1981.

In this sense, then, the demand for low risk assets is a reaction to a type of risk, that of having to make unexpected future payments. If we may be allowed a play on words, *the demand for assets with low risk exists because as time passes every assetholder must expect to have unexpected expenditures.* As we will see, this is of vital concern to certain types of financial institutions such as banks.

The Selection of a Portfolio

We have explored the characteristics of financial assets and have found risk to be among the important considerations for investors in making their choices. We have also examined investors' attitudes toward risk in choosing among different assets. The problem now is to draw these ideas together to see what they tell us about the nature of demands for financial assets.

The Concept of a Portfolio.   A basic concept, introduced early in the analysis, is that of a portfolio of assets. An assetholder's portfolio is simply the collection of assets which he chooses to hold.

We have already drawn certain strong conclusions about normal (i.e., risk averse) assetholders' preferences. We cast our analysis in terms of such abstract concepts as expected yield, and risk, which we considered to be attributes individual financial instruments. To complete our analysis we must consider the problem of choice among assets in the context of the selection of a complete portfolio. To that end, we must develop concepts of expected yield and risk as attributes of portfolios.

Expected Yield of a Portfolio.   Since he is only one among a great many participants in the market, each assetholder must take the expected yields on individual financial instruments as given. He cannot control them. He can only choose to hold or not hold the instrument. However, within limits set by the expected yields on instruments available in the market, each assetholder can control the expected yield on his portfolio through a careful selection of the instruments to be included in the portfolio.

The *expected yield on a portfolio* is simply the weighted average of the expected yields on the individual assets included in the portfolio — with the expected yield of each asset weighted by the proportion of the portfolio represented by that instrument.[1]

Any assetholder can increase the expected yield on his portfolio by increasing the proportion of his portfolio invested in relatively high-yielding assets, and he can reduce the yield on his portfolio by increasing the proportion invested in relatively low-yielding assets.

We have assumed that each assetholder has a strong *preference for yield.* The reason for this lies in our discussion of the saving decision (Chapter 4). Each household is presumably striving to maximize utility from its lifetime consumption potential. To accumulate wealth for the support of future consumption it must forego current consumption. The higher the expected yield on a portfolio the greater the future consumption which any given current wealth accumulation can be expected to support, i.e., the greater the lifetime consumption, and hence total utility, available to the household. A utility-maximizing household must therefore be attracted by higher yields. It must have a preference for yield. Faced with a choice between two financial instruments, other things being equal, it would choose the one with the highest yield.

But what is the import of the "other things being equal" assumption? What other things? Can we not assume that each assetholder simply maximizes expected yield without any qualifications?

We now know that the answer to this last question is no. If expected yield were the only consideration in the portfolio balance decision, assetholders would always choose instruments with high yields over those with low yields. Faced with assets with different expected yields, each assetholder would include only one asset in his portfolio — the one which appeared to promise the highest expected yield. It does not take a sophisticated statistical survey to show that few assetholders have portfolios consisting of only one asset.

There is another interesting implication of assetholders maximizing expected yield. If all assetholders had roughly the same expectations with respect to each asset, equilibrium in the market would require identical expected yields on all assets. As assetholders attempt to purchase those instruments promising high expected yields, they create excess demand in the market which tends to drive up the price of those instruments. At the same time, they will be selling those instruments promising low expected yields, tending to drive down the price of those instruments. Remember, the market price and the expected yield on any instrument vary inversely. When the price of high-yielding instruments increases, the yield correspondingly drops, and vice versa for the low-yielding instruments. The end result should be a rough equalization of expected yields on all securities. At that time, if yield were the only consideration, assetholders would be indifferent between financial instruments. The instruments would be perfect substitutes for each other as forms in which wealth can be accumulated.

In general, we cannot observe either an equalization of expected yields or single-asset portfolios. Assetholders must react to other attributes of financial instruments besides expected yield. One of these attributes is risk. The assetholder must be concerned not only with the expected yield on his portfolio, but also with the risk on his portfolio.

Riskiness of a Portfolio.   We developed the concept of risk as an attribute of individual financial instruments. Like expected yield, the riskiness of an instrument is something over which an assetholder has no control. However, within limits, he can control the degree of risk on his portfolio through a careful selection of assets to be included in it. What is the relationship between the degree of risk on individual assets and the degree of risk on the portfolio?

By the risk on a portfolio we mean the standard deviation of the expected yield on the portfolio. The concept is parallel to that developed for the risk on individual assets, and indeed the risk on the portfolio depends on the risk on the individual assets included in that portfolio. However, unlike the relationship between the expected yields on the portfolio and the assets which comprise it, in all but the simplest case, the risk on a portfolio is not a simple weighted average of the risks on the individual assets. The relationship is much more complex. Nonetheless, we can assume that in most cases an assetholder will increase the riskiness of his portfolio if he increases the proportion of relatively risky securities contained in that portfolio.[2]

Risk and Expected Yield.   An assetholder can vary the degree of risk and the expected yield through a careful selection of the assets to be included in his portfolio. However, he cannot choose the degree of risk and the expected yield independently of each other. Since risk and expected yield are both attributes of individual financial instruments, when the assetholder selects a particular group of assets to be included in his portfolio he not only obtains the expected yield provided by that combination of assets, he simultaneously obtains the degree of risk provided by those same assets. To obtain a different degree of risk on his portfolio he must select a different combination of assets, and that means he will obtain a different expected yield on his portfolio.

In general, higher degrees of risk are associated with higher expected yields. Thus, to obtain a higher expected yield on his portfolio, the assetholder must include a higher proportion of relatively risky assets, and that generally means a higher degree of risk in the portfolio as well.

We have assumed that assetholders in general are risk averters. Risk is something which they prefer to avoid, and they have to be bribed to take on higher degrees of risk through the expectation of a higher yield. In general, a risk averter will not select the portfolio of assets with the highest expected yield. That would provide too high a degree of risk. Similarly, in general a risk averter will not select the portfolio with the lowest degree of risk. That would provide too low an expected yield. Because there is a subjective "trade-off" between risk and expected yield in his system of preferences, he will normally select a portfolio consisting of more than one asset, and one which is somewhere between the two extremes of maximizing expected yield and minimizing risk.

The Equilibrium Portfolio.   We will demonstrate the nature of the choice between risk and yield in a particularly simple case in figures 5-7, 5-8, and 5-9. For this purpose we have assumed that there are only two assets. One, a government bond, is regarded as perfectly safe (zero risk). The other, a corporate bond, has a higher yield, but it also has a relatively high degree of risk. If these are the only instruments available, what combination of the two will the asset holder choose?

The Investor's Opportunities.   In these figures, the expected yield on the portfolio (y_p) is measured along the vertical axis. It is the weighted average of the expected yields on the safe (y_s) and the risky (y_r) securities, with the weights being the proportions (a_s, a_r), in which the two assets are included in the portfolio. That is,

$$a_s + a_r = 1 \tag{5.1}$$

and

$$y_p = a_s y_s + a_r y_r \tag{5.2}$$

The opportunities available to a typical investor are illustrated in figure 5-7. As can be seen, his return rises as he increases the proportion of risky assets held in his portfolio.

The risk on a portfolio depends on the risks on the individual securities in the portfolio and the proportions in which these two securities are included in the portfolio. In this particular case, the function linking the risks on the individual securities and the risk on the portfolio is simple. Since the risk on the government bond is zero ($\sigma_s = 0$), given the risk on the corporate bond, the risk on the portfolio depends simply on the proportion of the portfolio devoted to the relatively risky security. That is,

$$\sigma_p = a_r \sigma y_r \tag{5.3}$$

As a result, we can also use the horizontal axis of our diagrams to represent the risk of the portfolio, as is shown in Figure 5-7. This is a very special case. In general, the relationship is not that simple.

The line YR can now be interpreted as describing the combinations of expected yield and risk available to the assetholder by varying the proportions in which he divides his portfolio between the government bond and the corporate bond. At point Y the entire portfolio is invested in the government bond. The risk is minimized ($\sigma_p = 0$), and the expected yield on the portfolio is minimized ($y_p = y_s$). As we move out along the line YR, the proportion of the relatively risky security in the portfolio increases and, as a result, so do the expected yield and the risk on the portfolio. In the extreme, at point R, the entire portfolio consists of the relatively risky and high-yielding corporate bond. At that point, both risk ($\sigma_p = \sigma_r$) and expected yield ($y_p = y_r$) are maximized.

Each point along the line YR, then, represents a different possible portfolio with different degrees of risk and different expected yields. Which of the alternatives available to him will the assetholder choose?

The general answer is that he will select that portfolio — that combination of risk and expected yield — which will provide him with the highest possible level of utility. We can identify that portfolio in a theoretical sense through an application of indifference curve analysis.[3]

The curves labelled PP' in Figure 5-8 are indifference curves which describe the assetholder's preferences between expected yield and risk. They incorporate our assumption of risk aversion. Any one curve, say P_2P_2' identifies alternative combinations of expected yield and risk which the assetholder finds equally acceptable. He is indifferent between portfolios lying along this curve. Thus, he would find nothing to choose between the two portfolios represented by points E and F. While portfolio F involves a higher degree of risk, the assetholder would feel that he was fully compensated for assuming that higher degree of risk by the higher expected yield also associated with portfolio F.

While the assetholder would thus be indifferent between portfolios E or F, he would prefer either of these to the portfolio represented by the point G. This portfolio has the same degree of risk as portfolio F, but it also has a lower expected yield. There is a whole set of portfolios which the assetholder would regard as equivalent to portfolio G, including portfolio H. They all lie along the indifference curve P_1P_1', which then describes portfolios which are inferior to those lying along P_2P_2'.

FIGURE 5-7   Investor's opportunities

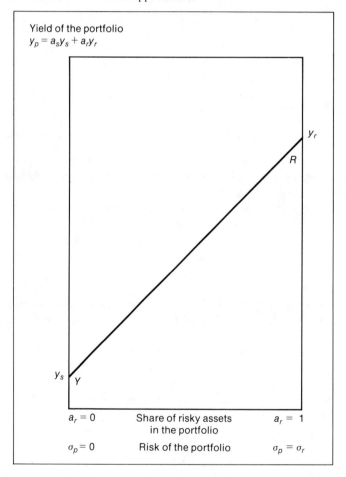

Yield of the portfolio
$y_p = a_s y_s + a_r y_r$

y_r

R

y_s

Y

$a_r = 0$ Share of risky assets $a_r = 1$
                 in the portfolio

$\sigma_p = 0$ Risk of the portfolio $\sigma_p = \sigma_r$

Similarly, the assetholder would prefer the portfolio represented by point J to either E or F. Portfolio J has the same risk as portfolio F, but a higher expected yield. There is a whole set of portfolios which the assetholder would regard as equivalent to portfolio J, all lying along the higher indifference curve P_3P_3'.

The investor's choice of a portfolio results from the interaction of the opportunities open to him, which are depicted in Figure 5-7, with his preferences, which in turn are depicted in Figure 5-8. To find the investor's choice, we must combine the analysis of opportunities and preferences, as in Figure 5-9.

If the assetholder is to maximize utility, he must select that portfolio available on the market (and hence lying along the line YR) which he prefers most. Thus, between portfolios E and H, both of which are available to him, he would always choose E. By

FIGURE 5-8 Investor's preferences

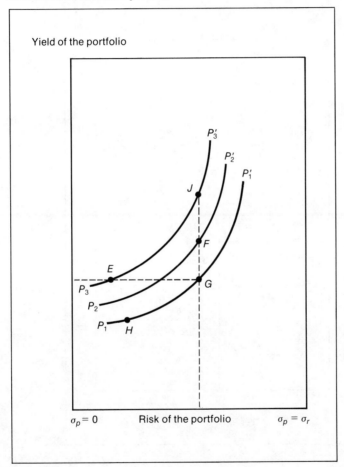

Yield of the portfolio

P_3'

P_2'

P_1'

J

F

E

P_3

G

P_2

P_1

H

$\sigma_p = 0$ Risk of the portfolio $\sigma_p = \sigma_r$

an extension of the same logic, between portfolios E and G, both of which are available, he would always choose E. (Why?) By contrast, he would much prefer portfolio J to any of these, including E. However, portfolio J is not available in the market. That combination of risk and expected yield cannot be obtained, given the risk and expected yield on the two securities from which he must construct his portfolio.

Portfolio E, then, is the portfolio which would be selected. It is the *equilibrium portfolio*. It does not provide the maximum expected yield. Portfolio R would do that. It does not provide the minimum risk. Portfolio Y would do that. However, it is on the highest indifference curve given the risk and expected yield on the financial instruments available in the market.

FIGURE 5-9   Investor's choice

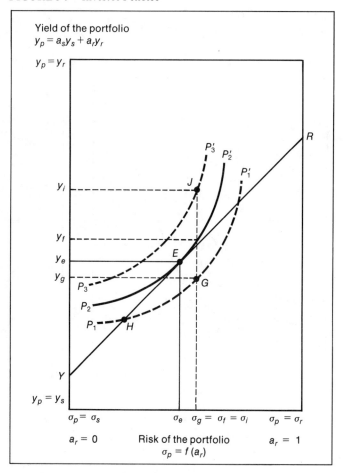

Conclusions: The Significance of Risk.   The existence of risk and risk aversion means that financial instruments are not all perfect substitutes in the minds of assetholders. An increase in the yield on one security will lead to some substitution of the higher-yielding security for the lower-yielding security (it will induce assetholders to take on more risk), but it will not lead to total replacement of the low-yielding security in asset portfolios. Figure 5-10 duplicates the essential feature of Figure 5-9 but allows for an increase in the yield on the corporate bond with no change in the yield on the government bond or in the risk on the corporate bond. The portfolio opportunity line thus becomes steeper. For any given degree of risk, the assetholder can now obtain a higher expected yield. The new equilibrium portfolio is now represented by point M on a higher indifference curve. The assetholder has assumed more risk and obtains a higher yield. As an

FIGURE 5-10   Effects of a high return on the risky asset

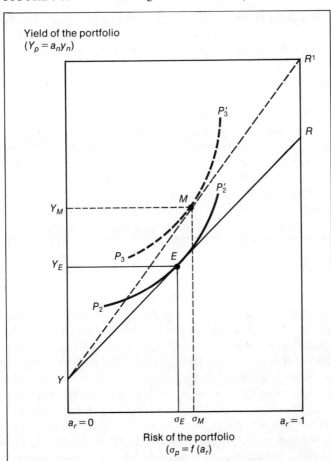

exercise, the student should demonstrate what happen when:

    a. the expected yield on the "safe" security is lowered;
    b. the riskiness of the "risky" security increases;
    c. the expected yields on both securities increase proportionately (remember: risk might be an "inferior good").

If we know the size of the assetholder's portfolio at that point in time, we can derive his demand for each type of security. Given the riskiness of each security, the demand for the risky security will be an increasing function of the differential between the expected yield on the risky and the "safe" securities. The opposite is true of the safe security. At wider and wider differentials the demand function probably becomes increasingly inelastic.

The market demand curve is the sum of individual assetholder's demand functions. The demand for risky securities, therefore, is presumably a function of the wealth of assetholders (and hence the size of portfolios) and the differential in yield between risky and safe securities.

In the same connection, we have assumed that the rate of return on assets does not depend on the size of the portfolio. For reasons which we will discuss in Chapter 9, this is not necessarily the case, particularly since there are "transactions costs" involved in purchases and sales of assets (and hence in all rearrangements of portfolios) which depend largely on the number rather than the value of transactions. To rearrange a large portfolio, where the value of each purchase or sale of a security is relatively large, will involve smaller transactions costs per dollar invested. For this reason, the return to the portfolio may be greater than for a small portfolio.

Finally, we have used the concept of expected yield in this discussion as yield to maturity and we have ignored the effects of inflation. The earlier discussions of liquidity and inflation should not be forgotten. There may be circumstances under which the yield for shorter holding periods is relevant, and all yields should be adjusted to a "real" basis (including the yield on money). Incorporating this in our analysis of the selection of a portfolio would make the whole matter impossibly complex.

GENERAL EQUILIBRIUM

Developing the demand for financial instruments in the context of the selection of a portfolio makes it clear that all financial instruments are substitutes, although imperfect substitutes. This means that a rise in the expected yield on a short-term government bond does not confine repercussions to the government bond market. It will produce general substitution effects, altering the demand for other short-term securities, but also reaching out in much diminished magnitude as far as the market for speculative stocks. As a result of substitution in portfolios, yields on all financial instruments should tend to increase. Furthermore, (and this will be of vital importance when we come to study monetary theory), substitutions may not be limited to financial assets. We earlier excluded consideration of choice between financial and real (or capital) assets. This was done primarily for convenience. But the reader should be aware that the change in the expected yield of one particular asset (be it real or financial) will in turn affect the demands for it and all other assets. Thus, if we can change the yields on financial assets relative to the yields on real assets we can expect thereby to affect the demand for real assets.

ENDNOTES

1. If the portfolio consisted of three assets, with expected yields of 0, 0.05, and 0.10, then the expected yield on the portfolio would depend on the proportion of each in the portfolio. If the proportions were 10%, 30%, and 60% respectively, then the expected yield on the portfolio would be

    $$\bar{y}_p = \frac{0.1 \times 0 + 0.3 \times 0.05 + 0.6 \times 0.1}{0.1 + 0.3 + 0.6}$$
    $$= \frac{0.015 + 0.06}{1}$$
    $$= \quad 0.075$$

    If, by contrast, the proportions were 60%, 30%, and 10%, respectively, the expected yield on the portfolio would be

    $$\bar{y}_p = \frac{0.6 \times 0 + 0.3 \times 0.05 + 0.1 \times 0.1}{1}$$
    $$= \frac{0.015 + 0.01}{1}$$
    $$= \quad 0.025$$

2. In fact, the relationship between the riskiness of the portfolio and the proportions of "risky" and "safe" assets in the portfolio is much more complicated than this. Full analysis of the topic — particularly if we admit the existence of a large number of different assets — requires relatively advanced mathematics. In a more advanced treatment of the subject it would be demonstrated that, *up to a point*, increasing the proportion of risky assets in the portfolio can reduce the riskiness of the portfolio as a whole. In other words, given the range of securities available in the market, there exists a combination of securities which is a *minimum risk portfolio*. In general, (although there are exceptions) that portfolio is a *diversified* portfolio. It does not consist of only the safest asset. Indeed, a portfolio consisting of several relatively risky securities *can* be less risky than a portfolio consisting of one relatively safe security. The main exception is when there is some security which is absolutely safe, i.e., there is no risk in holding it. Such a security might be money (although you should remember our discussion of the significance of inflation: If there is a risk of inflation, there is a risk of loss of real purchasing power — a risk of a negative yield — in holding money; perhaps in a more general framework, money is not a riskless security). If there is such a security, then a portfolio consisting only of it would be riskless, and hence, by definition, would be the minimum-risk portfolio.

    These issues involve the *theory of portfolio diversification* which is introduced in Chapter 9 and considered somewhat more systematically but still on an elementary level in the Appendix to that chapter. In all of this discussion we are using the standard deviation of the yield on each asset and on the portfolio as the measure of risk.

3. Students not familiar with such analysis should consult a good textbook on the principles of economics.

APPENDIX
CAPITAL VALUE AND YIELD: BASIC CONCEPTS
OF FINANCIAL MARKETS

This Appendix provides a more complete and systematic discussion of the relationship between prices and yields on financial instruments. We also require the concept of capital value (or present value). It is easiest to explore these concepts initially with respect to bonds. We will then turn to variable income securities.

Capital Value and Yield on a Bill

Consider first the simple type of bond which we previously called a bill. This is a financial instrument which calls for a single lump-sum payment at the end of a fixed period of time, which we will assume is one year. For simplicity we assume that the bill has no credit risk. There is no question but that the payment will be made.[1]

Capital Value of a Bill.   The basic question facing the potential purchaser of a bill is how much he should offer to pay for the bill (we assume that if he purchases it he will hold it until maturity). As with most questions in economics, the answer can only be given in terms of the alternatives open to him. Suppose he has the alternative of depositing the funds in the bank for one year (another riskless financial instrument) at a fixed rate of interest. If he chooses this alternative, by the end of the year he will have accumulated an amount equal to the amount deposited plus one year's interest on that sum. Then, since they are both riskless instruments, we can say that he should pay no more for the bill than the sum of money which he would have to deposit in the bank at the going rate of interest in order to accumulate, by the end of the year, an amount equal to the redemption value of the bill. That sum — the amount which he would have to deposit with the bank at the going interest rate — is the capital value of the bill.

We can define the capital value of the bill more precisely with the assistance of some basic financial mathematics. Suppose the going interest rates in riskless one year financial instruments is $100r\%$ per annum.[2] Then, $\$V$ lent now, at this interest rate, will accumulate to:

$$A_1 = V + Vr$$
$$= V(1 + r) \tag{5A.1}$$

by the end of the year. In other words, in order to accumulate the sum $\$A_1$ by the end of the year we would have to invest $\$V$ at the going interest rate of $100r\%$ per annum. If

---

[1] This assumption is important. Toward the end of this appendix we will distinguish between the expected yield and the theoretical yield on financial instruments. The theoretical yield is calculated from information in the contract between the borrower and the lender. It presumes that all contractual payments will be made in full and on time. The expected yield allows for the possibility of partial or total default, or delays in payment. If there is complete certainty that payments will be made there is no need to distinguish between these two concepts, and we can refer to either simply as the yield.

[2] It may seem strange to quote interest rates at $100r\%$ per annum. The interest rate "4% per annum" can be written in ratio form as ".04". If we want r to represent this ratio i.e., $r = .04$, then we must refer to the rate of interest at $100r\%$ per annum (i.e., $r = .04$).

A_1 is the redemption value of the bill, then $ V must be its present value. In general:

$$V = A_1 \left(\frac{1}{1+r} \right)$$

(5A.2)

Thus, if the bill called for a single payment of $1000 at the end of one year, and if the going rate of interest on riskless one year loans were 12% per annum, the present value of the bill would be:

$$V = 1000 \left(\frac{1}{1 + .12} \right)$$
$$= 893$$

Yield on a Bill.   Faced with the alternatives of a riskless bill and a riskless one-year bank deposit, an investor who has no other reason for preferring one instrument over the other should pay no more than $893 for the bill. If the market price of the bill (P) happened to be $893, a purchaser of the bill who held it to maturity and received the redemption payment of $1000 would effectively earn 12% per annum on his investment. The yield on the bill would be 12% per annum. If the market price exceeded $893 the yield would be less than 12% per annum. If the price were less than $893, the yield would exceed 12% per annum.

In interpreting these statements it must be remembered that we calculated the capital value of the bill using the rate of interest on a closely competitive financial instrument. Thus, what we mean by *the yield on the bill is the interest rate which is implicit in the relationship between the market price of the bill and its redemption value. It is the interest rate at which the present value of the bill would be equal to its market price.* Given that we know the market price (P) and the redemption value (A_1) we can find the yield by substituting these values in equation 5A.2 and solving for the interest rate. For a one year bill, the yield (y) will be:

$$y = \frac{A_1}{P} - 1$$

(5A.3)

If the market price of the $1000 bill were $909 the yield would be 10% per annum. If the market price were $877 the yield would be 14% per annum. Note that *for a given future payment, market price and yield vary inversely.*

Effect of Term to Maturity.   We have assumed that the bill has a one-year term to maturity. This is clearly a special case, one which we have assumed for convenience.

Suppose, instead, the bill had a two-year term to maturity. To find the present value we can ask what sum (V) we would have to invest in order to accumulate A_2 by the end of the second year, when the interest rate is $100r\%$ per annum.

From equation 5A.1 we know that $V will accumulate to $A_1 = V(1 + r)$ by the end of the first year. If this sum is then invested for a second year at the same interest rate, by the end of the second year will have accumulated:

$$\begin{aligned}
A_2 &= A_1 + A_1 r \\
&= V(1+r) + V(1+r)r \\
&= V(1+r)(1+r) \\
&= V(1+r)^2
\end{aligned}$$

(5A.4)

Or, dividing through by $(1 + r)^2$

$$V = \frac{A_2}{(1 + r)^2}$$

(5A.5)

It can be shown that in general the present value of a single payment of $\$A_n$ to be made at the end of n years, where the prevailing interest rate for loans of that duration is $100r\%$ per annum is:

$$V = \frac{A_n 2}{(1 + r)^n}$$

(5A.6)

The present value of a given payment thus varies inversely with the term to maturity. It also varies inversely with the interest rate, and there is a strong interaction between term to maturity and the interest rate. This is illustrated in Table 5A.1.

TABLE 5A-1   **Present value of a $1000 bill***

Term to maturity (years)	Interest rate (yield) (percent per annum and dollars)				
	10%	12%	14%	16%	18%
¼	976	971	966	962	957
½	952	943	935	926	917
1	909	893	877	862	867
2	826	797	769	743	718
5	621	567	519	476	437
10	386	322	270	227	191
20	149	104	73	51	37
50	9	3	1	½	¼
∞	0	0	0	0	0

* Rounded to the nearest dollar. The present values for maturities of ¼ year assume compounding four times per year; for ½ year, compounding twice per year; and for all other maturities compounding once per year.

Capital value and Yield on a Bond

Capital Value of a Bond.   The bill is a particularly simple type of bond which involves but a single future payment. In general a bond will involve a series of semi-annual payment (the coupon payments) and a final lump-sum payment (the par value or redemption value). If we assume for simplicity that the coupon payments are made once per year (rather than the usual twice per year) then what the purchaser is purchasing is a stream of payments of the order:

$$C_1 + C_2 + C_3 + \cdots\cdots\cdots C_n + A_n$$

where $C_1 \ldots C_n$ are the annual coupons and A_n is the final payment, made at the end of the nth year. What is the present value of such a stream of payments?

To eliminate a difficult complication we will again assume that we are talking about a bond on which there is no credit risk, e.g., a federal government bond. If we then assume that the interest rate is the same for riskless loans of all maturities, the present value of the stream of payments associated with the bond is simply the sum of the present values of each of its component parts. That is, the present value of the stream of payments is:

$$V = \frac{C_1}{(1+r)} + \frac{C_2}{(1+r)^2} + \frac{C_3}{(1+r)^3} + \cdots + \frac{C_n}{(1+r)^n} + \frac{A_n}{(1+r)^n}$$

This equation can be simplified to:

$$V = \frac{A_n}{(1+r)^n} + C \left[\frac{1}{r} - \frac{1}{r(1+r)^n} \right] \qquad (5A.7)$$

where $C_1 = C_2 = C_3 = \cdots C_n$.

In the case of a consol, a bond with a fixed annual payment in perpetuity and hence no redemption value, the formula can be further simplified to:[3]

$$V = \frac{C}{r} \qquad (5A.8)$$

The capital value of a bond thus depends in a rather complex fashion on the size of the annual coupon payments (C_1, C_2 ..... C_n), the redemption value (A_n), the term to maturity, (n) and the going level of interest rates (r). The capital value varies directly with the size of the coupon and redemption value, and what is important for our analysis, *inversely with the market interest rate.*

Yield on a Bond. The concept of the yield on a bond is analogous to the yield on a bill in that it is the interest rate which is implicit in the relationship between the market price of a bond and the stream of coupon payments and the redemption value. *The yield on a bond is the interest rate at which the present value of a bond would be equal to its market price.* If the price of the bond is greater than present value calculated at the going market interest rate, then the yield is less than the interest rate. If the price is less than the capital value then the yield is greater than the market interest rate.

We were able to offer a simple formula for the calculation of the yield on a one-year bill. No such simple formula can be derived for the more general case of the yield on a bond. However, comprehensive tables of bond prices and yields are published. For a bond with a given coupon and term to maturity, it is possible to read the yield off the table, if you are given the price (or the price, if you are given the yield).

---

[3] A Consol calls for annual payments through all future time, i.e., $n = \infty$. But, as n approaches ∞, $\frac{1}{(1+r)^n}$ approaches 0. Hence the terms $\frac{A_n}{(1+r)^n}$ and $\frac{C}{r(1+r)^n}$ both approach 0, and the capital value of the bond approaches $\frac{C}{r}$.

In Table 5A-2 we have presented a small sample of prices and yields on a bond with annual interest coupons totalling $130 and a redemption value of $1000. From this table we can see, for example, that a five-year bond selling for $844 will yield 18% per annum if held to maturity. Similarly, if it is to yield 18% per annum a 20-year bond must sell for $732 and a consol for $722.

TABLE 5A-2   **Price and yield on a 13% coupon bond***

Term to maturity (years)	Yield (percent and dollars)					
	10%	12%	13%	14%	16%	18%
1	1027.4	1008.6	1000	991.6	973.9	958.0
2	1052.6	1016.9	1000	984.0	952.4	922.3
5	1113.6	1035.4	1000	965.3	901.2	843.9
10	1183.7	1056.4	1000	948.3	854.6	774.8
20	1254.9	1074.8	1000	933.3	822.3	732.0
50	1296.8	1082.5	1000	928.7	813.0	722.3
∞	1300.0	1083.3	1000	928.6	812.5	722.2

* Assuming twice annual compounding.

The market price of a bond, then, can be regarded as the present value of the stream of coupon payments and the final redemption payment when the present value is calculated at a particular rate of interest, i.e., the rate of interest which is the yield on the bond. This is a true interest rate. It is the rate which a purchaser will earn on his investment if he buys the security at the market price. It is also the rate which a new borrower would have to pay if he borrowed money by issuing a comparable security. Thus, when we are considering the determination of the market price of a bond we are simultaneously considering the determination of an interest rate. As the price falls, the interest rate rises. They are linked mathematically.

The Yield on Variable Income Securities

In principle the same concepts can be applied to variable income securities (or real assets, for that matter). That is, it should be possible to calculate the yield on such a security on the basis of the existing market price. However, a complication arises since, unlike a bond, a fixed stream of future payments is not specified in the contract of a variable income security. Both the size and length of the stream of payments depend on future developments which can never be perfectly foreseen. As a result, we can only calculate the present value of a share of common stock, for example, on the basis of some *expected* stream of dividend payments which by its very nature must be conjectural. Individuals may disagree sharply on the most probable stream of future dividends, and individual opinions may be revised drastically from time to time as new information is forthcoming.

Risk on Fixed Income Securities.   In our discussion of the yield on fixed income securities we ignored the risk that the "fixed" interest and redemption payments will not be made. However, such risk exists with respect to most bonds. In this respect a "high risk" bond has some of the characteristics of a variable income security. The actual payments may be less than those specified in the contract, or they may be delayed beyond the time specified in the contract (of course, they cannot be more than specified in the contract). This is something which should be taken into account in calculating yield.

Theoretical versus Expected Yield.   We can refer to the yields calculated from information in the contract between borrower and lender as the *theoretical yield*. It is calculated on the presumption that the payments specified in the contract will all be made in full and on time. In the case of variable income securities no theoretical yield can be calculated, and in the case of high-risk bonds the theoretical yield may not be the most likely yield. We thus need the concept of *expected yield* to refer to the most probable yield, based on the assetholder's expectations of the size and timing of future payments. In the case of a perfectly safe bond, expected yield and theoretical yield will be the same.

By analogy with a consol, another security with no fixed maturity, the theoretical yield on common stock is sometimes measured by the ratio of current dividends to market price. This, however, could only be a valid calculation of the theoretical yield if the current dividend payments were expected to continue unchanged in perpetuity. Unlike the consol, for which the annual interest payment is fixed in perpetuity, in general there is no reason to expect the current dividend on common stock to continue indefinitely. As a result, the calculated dividend price ratio is not directly analogous to the yield on a consol, and indeed its meaning is not obvious.

Inflation and Taxes.   We would remind you of two points made in the text of the chapter. First, if the general level of commodity prices is expected to change, then it is important that "real" yields rather than "nominal" yields be calculated. The nominal yields calculated as discussed above should be adjusted for the expected rate of inflation. Second, it will generally be the after-tax yield which is relevant for investor decisions. Given the nature of our taxation system, the adjustment for expected taxes may affect not only the general level of yields but also the relationship between yields on different types of securities.

Summary

The concepts of capital value and expected yield are basic to all economic analysis involving intertemporal decisions, i.e., decision involving events which occur in more than one time period. These concepts are basic to the analysis of the determination of the market price of financial instruments because financial instruments are claims to payments to be made in future time periods. We will encounter the concepts again in discussing capital expenditure decisions of business firms since these are also decisions involving current expenditures (on plant and equipment) for the purpose of making profits in future time periods. The student is advised to review and master the concepts.

The main purpose of this Appendix has been to provide a more systematic definition of the concept of the expected yield on financial instruments, and a more careful development of the relationship between expected yield and the market price of the instrument. The important points to keep in mind are:

(1) If the stream of future payments is given, then the determination of the market price involves simultaneously the determination of the yield. Market price and yield are linked mathematically.

(2) Yield and market price vary inversely for any given stream of future payments.

(3) If the expected size of the future payments changes (as in a variable income security), then the price *or* the expected yield on that security must change in the same direction. Larger expected dividend payments on common stock in a corporation must mean either a higher price for the shares of stock, or a higher expected yield on the stock (or both).

(4) If the streams of payments on two financial instruments are different, then their market prices must be different if they are to give the same yield. Thus, if a 10%, twenty-year bond ($100 annual coupon) and a 12%, twenty-year bond ($120 annual coupon) are both to yield 11%, the price of the 10% bond must be $920 and the price of the 12% bond $1079.

This last point is important. It is the price of financial instruments which is determined in the market place. However, since the characteristics of financial instruments are so diverse, market price does not provide a useful basis for comparison of financial instruments. Expected yield is the most useful common denominator for purposes of comparison and decision-making.

Elementary Theory of Financial Markets 6
PART 3: THE BORROWING DECISION

To this point we have discussed the theory of financial markets only from the viewpoint of asset holders, the demand side of the market. We now turn our attention to the supply side, the decisions of households, business firms, and government to borrow in financial markets by issuing liabilities on themselves.

STOCKS AND FLOWS:
TWO CONCEPTS OF SUPPLY

The supply of financial instruments has its origins in acts of borrowing and lending — in the demands of deficit spending units for funds to finance their deficits. However, in discussing the supply side of the market, it is important to make a sharp distinction between two different concepts of supply. One is the *stock* of financial instruments outstanding at a particular *point in time*, and the other the *flow* of new borrowing over a particular *period of time*.

At any point in time there will be an outstanding stock of financial instruments already in the hands of assetholders. Both the size and the composition of this stock is a reflection of past history. It reflects previous borrowings by households, governments, and corporations. In our analysis of the financial system, this stock is something which must be taken as given — a predetermined variable.

The stock concept of supply is basic. However, we must recognize that over a period of time the outstanding stock is subject to change. Attempts of spending units to raise funds to finance deficits create a steady flow of new financial instruments onto the market which augment the basic stock. At the same time, partial or complete repayment of outstanding debts by some spending units work to reduce the outstanding stock. The difference between these two magnitudes — the flow of new borrowing and the flow of repayments —is the second concept of supply. It is supply as a *net flow: an addition to or subtraction from the basic stock over a period of time.*

Like the demand for financial instruments, the supply of financial instruments involves two fundamental decisions — a decision on the amount to be borrowed (the *borrowing decision*) and a decision on the types of financial instruments to be issued (the *liability balance decision.*) A complete analysis of the supply of financial instruments must simultaneously explain both decisions.

THE BORROWING DECISION

One major conclusion which will follow from our analysis of the borrowing decisions of households, governments, and corporations will be that, with certain important exceptions (including the borrowings of financial intermediaries, which fall into a class by themselves, and must be treated separately), the primary purpose of borrowing is to finance the purchase or construction of durable real assets. In the government sector these assets may consist of highways, schools, or sewage disposal plants; in the corporate sector, factory buildings, machinery, or equipment; and in the household sector, automobiles, household durables, or houses. The objects may be widely different, but they all have an extended life, and have value to their purchasers because they are expected to provide services either to be consumed directly or sold during future time periods. While the specific motivations of the individual sectors may differ widely, this aspect of the borrowing decision, which all sectors have in common, provides a convenient peg on which to hang our theoretical analysis.

The Consumer Sector

Since we have already made an extensive examination of the asset demands of households, it is convenient to begin our analysis with this sector. A simple adaptation of the balance sheet and accumulation identities of Chapter 4 provide a useful framework for the consideration of household borrowing decisions.

The Basic Identities Again.   Consider first the balance sheet identity, which we previously wrote as:

$$\text{WEALTH} = \text{ASSETS} - \text{LIABILITIES} \qquad (4.1)$$

By splitting assets into the two categories, financial assets and real assets, and rearranging the terms, we can rewrite this equation as:

$$\text{LIABILITIES} = \frac{\text{REAL}}{\text{ASSETS}} + \frac{\text{FINANCIAL}}{\text{ASSETS}} - \text{WEALTH} \qquad (6.1)$$

Or, expressing the same relationships in terms of flows over time,

$$\triangle \text{LIABILITIES} = \triangle \frac{\text{REAL}}{\text{ASSETS}} + \triangle \frac{\text{FINANCIAL}}{\text{ASSETS}} - \text{SAVING} \qquad (6.2)$$

(Remember, the symbol $\triangle$ means "the change in," and from equation 4.3, saving $= \triangle$ wealth).

Equation 6.1 simply states that the decision of a household to go into debt involves a desire to hold assets, real or financial, in excess of the household's wealth. Alternatively, equation 6.2, expressed in terms of flows, states that households turn to borrowing in financial markets when they desire to acquire additional real and financial assets in excess of their current savings. We have assumed that each household is striving to maximize the utility which it expects to derive from its lifetime income. Within the framework of the life cycle hypothesis, what reasons can we discover for household borrowing?

Categories of Borrowing.   The first category might be called *transitory borrowing*. A chance illness to the head of the household, which both interrupts the flow of income and creates medical bills, might be the occasion of borrowing, particularly in the case of households which do not have many marketable assets. In terms of the concepts which we developed earlier, this is a case in which income is temporarily depressed below its "permanent" level, and consumption is raised above its "permanent" level. Borrowing is a response to transitory or random factors — an alternative to making more fundamental adjustments to the household's "permanent" consumption plans.

In the second category we have borrowing which is part of a deliberate *plan to redistribute consumption over time* — a regular part of the life cycle of the household. A young family with good income prospects might borrow in order to support a level of present consumption in excess of its present income, planning to repay the accumulated debt out of its expected higher future income. This might well be the case of a married student, paying his way through university with the assistance of loans.

While it is difficult to marshall statistical evidence to support the proposition, it is clear that these two purposes (transitory borrowing and redistributing income over time), account for a relatively small part of the total indebtedness of a typical household. The third category is of much greater importance: *borrowing to finance the acquisition of specific assets.*

The typical household will presumably borrow to accumulate assets when the expected yield on those assets exceeds the expected interest cost on the debt. True, the desire for liquidity may be sufficiently strong that the household may borrow simply to create or maintain its stock of relatively liquid assets, even at some net interest cost to the household. However, the major rational for borrowing will be the excess of expected yield on assets over the interest cost on liabilities.

In some cases, these assets will be financial assets. Many households, particularly relatively high income households, borrow funds to purchase corporate stock upon which they expect to receive a relatively high return. Some of these funds will be borrowed from financial institutions, and some will be borrowed directly from stock brokerage firms. Still, borrowing for the acquisition of financial assets accounts for a small portion of the total indebtedness of the typical household.

The Expected Yield on Real Assets.   A rational householder will only borrow to finance the purchase of real assets — a house or household durable goods such as furniture or appliances — if the expected yield on these assets is greater than the interest cost incurred by borrowing. It makes little sense to acquire an illiquid real asset expected to yield 2% per annum, if to do so you have to borrow and pay an interest rate of 20% per annum. Are householders rational in their borrowing decisions?

This is a difficult question to answer empirically since the yield on most household real assets is not monetary. Rather, it is in the form of a stream of services consumed directly by the household. There is a market for many of these services (automobile rentals, coin laundries, movie theatres, and frozen food lockers are some familiar examples), and two Canadian economists have taken advantage of this fact to estimate the actual rate of return on selected consumer durables using the prices of equivalent services in the market place. They concluded that the implicit financial yield on the consumer durables owned by the typical household was very high indeed — frequently in excess of 25% per annum.[1] It must be noted that this result was found in a period when government bond yields were in the 5% to 6% range. In other words, the return on consumer durables was some four to five times that on financial assets. Moreover, this calculation ignores such intangible values as the convenience, independence, or security associated with owning rather than renting the object in question. Taking all things into consideration, the Royal Commission on Banking and Finance concluded

> Our studies indicate that by and large Canadians manage their finances with greater wisdom than appears to be popularly believed....Most households....have made sensible use of installment and other credit to acquire physical assets that yield them high returns, not only in financial terms but in terms of convenience and ease of household living.[2]

This statement sounds faintly like a comfortable platitude, and certainly, the Royal Commissioners notwithstanding, if one allows for such intangible elements in the returns on consumer durables as "convenience and ease of household living," the true

TABLE 6-1   The life cycle in household debt, assets, and net worth

Families, spring 1977 Average per family				
Age: head of household	Total debt	Consumer debt	Total assets	Net worth
under 25	$ 8 124	$2 807	$18 055	$ 9 931
25-34	16 434		44 335	27 901
35-44	14 221	2 676	76 323	62 102
45-54	10 211	2 848	95 720	85 505
55-64	4 348	1 451	83 396	79 048
65 and over	1 173	520	63 027	61 854
All families	9 989	—	66 111	56 122

SOURCE: Statistics Canada, *The Distribution of Income and Wealth in Canada, 1977* (Ottawa, 1979); and *Income, Assets and Indebtedness of Families in Canada, 1977* (Ottawa, 1980).

yield on such assets is impossible to measure. However, the point of relevance for us is that if households make some rough "calculation" of this sort, given the implicit yield on real assets, households should be less willing to borrow at higher interest rates. That is, *the supply of financial instruments from households should be an increasing function of the yield on consumer durable goods, and a decreasing function of the level of interest rates in financial markets* (i.e., of the yield on financial instruments).

Since the yield on consumer durables cannot be measured, this is a very difficult proposition to test. Numerous attempts have been made to identify the sensitivity of consumer borrowing to changes in the level of interest rates. The results of such tests are at best inconclusive. However, most economists feel that such a relationship does exist, although it may be relatively weak.

The pattern of debt, assets, and net worth for Canadian families in 1977 are shown in Table 6-1. The data appear to trace out a distinctive life cycle pattern similar to, but not identical with, that described in Chapter 4. This pattern of debt shown in Table 6-1 should not be too surprising in light of our discussion of household motives for going into debt. Total household debt peaks in the 25-35 age group and then falls off for older age groups. Households appear to go into debt during the stage of their life cycle when they are accumulating assets.

The Corporate Sector

Most business firms are engaged in the production of goods and services for sale in the marketplace with a primary objective of making profit. The exceptions to the profit-seeking characterization of businesses are sufficiently unimportant that we can ignore them. Why should a profit-seeking business borrow funds?

Financing Real Capital Formation. As in the case of households, the primary, but not exclusive, purpose of borrowing by business firms is to finance the purchase or construction of real assets, capital goods to be used in the process of production (including inventories of raw materials, goods in process of production, and finished goods awaiting sale). The issuance of financial instruments, whether stocks or bonds, is not the only method of financing capital formation. The firm could also use "internal" sources of funds by drawing down holdings of financial assets accumulated in the past or by financing out of current "business saving."

Interest Rates and the Yield on Capital Goods. Just as households cannot ignore the time dimension in planning consumption so as to maximize utility, business firms cannot take a static approach to the maximization of profits. The management must not only plan production with the production facilities presently at its disposal, it must also plan the expansion of those production facilities, at a rate and in directions which will maximize profits which the firm expects to receive in the future. This means that the management of the profit-maximizing firm must be continually alert for opportunities for capital expansion in which the expected yield will exceed the interest cost of the funds required to finance the expansion. Thus, the decision to invest in real capital formation should be directly dependent on the expected yield on real capital, and inversely dependent on the level of interest rates in the market. The higher the expected yield on real assets, the greater the volume of investment to be expected; the higher the level of interest rates (or expected yields on financial instruments), the smaller the volume of investment.

The Borrowing Decision.   The decision to borrow in financial markets depends on the interaction of the firm's internally generated funds with its desired level of capital formation. The firm must borrow in financial markets whenever its business saving is not sufficient to finance its current capital expenditures. To understand a firm's decision to borrow in financial markets, we must examine what determines the availability of internally-generated funds, or its *business saving.* By business saving we mean that portion of gross revenue of a firm which is not used to pay out-of-pocket costs such as wages, costs of raw materials purchased, interest on debt, taxes, etc., or is not paid out to shareholders in the form of dividends. It differs from the profits of the firm in two

FIGURE 6-1   Internally-generated funds available for investment: nonfinancial corporations, 1970-79

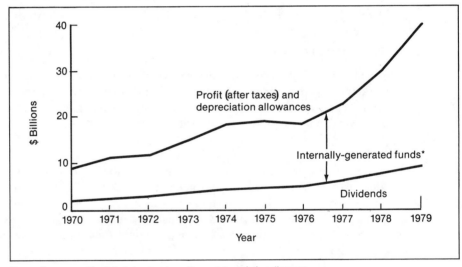

*Internally-generated funds include relaxed earnings and depreciation allowance.
Source: Statistics Canada, *Corporate Financial Statistics.* Ottawa, 1979.

respects. First, it includes only retained profits, those profits which remain after the payment of dividends. Second, it also includes the firm's capital consumption allowances, the accounting provisions made for the wearing out and obsolescence of the firm's capital stock.

The availability of internal sources of funds on a year-to-year basis depends primarily on the movements of profits and dividends. As can be seen from Figure 6-1, corporate profits after taxes fluctuate considerably from year to year. Firms, however, try to maintain relatively stable dividends. As a consequence, the yearly pattern of retained earnings tends to match that of net profits. If the firm's need for funds for capital formation were steady, the fluctuations of internally generated funds would lead

FIGURE 6-2   Financing of capital formation by nonfinancial corporations: 1970-79

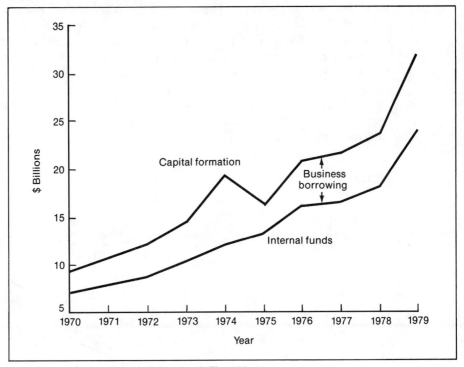

Note: The data are on a different basis from those in Figure 6-1.

Source: Statistics Canada, *Financial Flow Accounts, 1961-1969.* Ottawa, 1981.

to a changing supply of corporate securities. In fact, business capital expenditures fluctuate in response to economic conditions, expectations, and the general level of interest rates. We can see from Figure 6-2 that these fluctuations tend on the whole to add to the fluctuations in business borrowing caused by movements in internal funds. In other words, in years such as 1974, when business capital formation was high, internal funds were not relatively large, requiring firms to turn to the market to finance a larger portion of their investment than in other periods. Figure 6-2 also shows that internal funds historically have been more important than external funds as a source of capital expenditure.

The Government Sector

The borrowing decisions in the government sector have some points of similarity with those in the household and corporate sectors, and some notable differences, particularly at the federal government level.

Provincial and Municipal Borrowing.   Consider borrowing by junior governments in Canada. The stock of outstanding provincial and municipal bonds for the period 1970-80 is shown in Figure 6-3. The near equality between federal and provincial debt over the 1970s was a rather recent phenomenon. Borrowing by provincial and municipal governments is closely related to provincial and municipal capital expenditures. The remarkable rise of provincial government debt, which began in the 1950s and 1960s, reflected a corresponding sharp rise in expenditures for social capital — highways, bridges, hospitals, schools, and so on. The continuing rise in government debt in the 1970s reflects a further factor — inflation. Not only does inflation increase the price of everything purchased by government (as we will see in Chapter 7), it increases substantially the interest costs on government debt.

FIGURE 6-3   The stock of government bonds, 1970-80

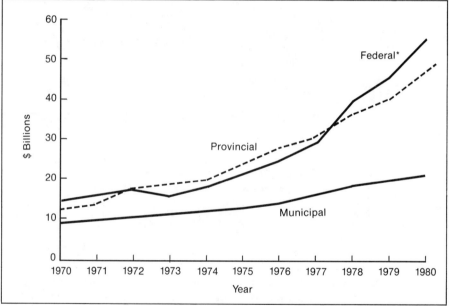

*Federal bonds outstanding net of bonds held by the Bank of Canada and federal government accounts.

Source: Department of Finance, *Economic Review.*

Expected Yield and Interest Rates.   It is possible to think of social capital providing a yield to society. The rational government official, then, will only borrow to finance a capital project when the yield on the real assets exceeds the interest cost of the funds required to finance the expenditure. As in the case of real assets in the consumer sector, however, the returns on social capital are mainly non-monetary. Although there are some exceptions, the returns take the form of a stream of services, consumed collectively by the members of the society, with no (or perhaps a nominal) charge. The calculation of the yield on these assets requires the imputation of value to these services.

In principle, the supply of financial instruments from junior governments should be responsive to the level of interest rates. Like borrowing in the consumer and corporate sectors, borrowing by junior governments is mainly to provide durable real assets which can be expected to provide a yield to the members of the society. The borrowing decision should involve a comparison of yield and interest cost: the higher the interest rate, the fewer the projects which will provide a yield in excess of interest cost, and the smaller the amount of borrowing.

The Federal Government.   Borrowing by the federal government has a radically different character. Like all other sectors, the federal government borrows when its revenues fall short of its expenditures. However, there is no clearly definable relationship between federal capital expenditures and federal borrowing (indeed if there is such a relationship, it is inverse).

The history of federal net borrowing prior to the period shown in Figure 6-3, indicates that much of the government's existing stock of debt had been accumulated during two periods, 1940-45 and 1958-63. The former was the period of World War II, and the latter a period of relative stagnation in the Canadian economy. Indeed, if we omit exceptional events such as major wars, the bulk of the borrowing by the federal government is related to the general state of the national economy. When unemployment is high, the government tends to run a deficit in its budget and hence must borrow. In periods of high levels of economic activity, the opposite is true. Now, however, the size of these increases in federal debt has been swamped by the effects of inflation in the 1970s. Still, these earlier periods of rapid growth of the federal government's debt would remain important as a source of growth if we corrected for inflation and considered the federal debt in real terms.

The Borrowing Decisions: Summary

In all but the federal government sector, the borrowing decision is primarily related to the decision to acquire real assets. Thus, the supply of financial instruments from the consumer, corporate, and junior government sectors is closely related to capital expenditures by these sectors (including the purchase of household durables as capital expenditures).

The capital expenditure decision can be considered as a process of comparing the yield on real assets with the interest cost of borrowed funds — i.e., with the expected yield on financial instruments. The higher the level of interest rates for any given level of expected yields on real assets, the less likely that any particular capital project will be undertaken. As a result, the supply of financial instruments from these sectors should be an inverse function of the level of interest rates.

The federal government is an exception to all of these generalizations. Peacetime borrowing by the federal government is more closely related to the level of economic activity than to the level of federal government capital expenditures.

THE LIABILITY BALANCE DECISION

Having decided to borrow, the household, corporation, or government agency must choose the type of financial instrument to be issued. For the most part this is a question of whether to issue a long-term or a short-term bond, but in the case of a corporation there is also the question of whether to issue bonds or stocks.

This subject is far too complex for us to explore here. However, it should be clear that there is a parallel set of considerations to those which we discussed in connection with the portfolio balance decision on the demand side of the market.

Relative Yields.   One consideration, clearly, must be the relative yields of financial instruments in the market. Other things being equal, the borrower will want to pay as low an effective interest rate as possible. As a result, he will be inclined to issue those financial instruments with the lowest effective yield.

Liquidity.   Relative interest costs are not the only considerations. Liquidity may also be important. However, from the point of view of the borrower, rather than being a desirable property of a financial instrument, liquidity will normally be an undesirable property. You will recall that liquid instruments are short-term instruments. A debtor with a major portion of his debt in liquid form faces the risk of having to redeem these securities on short notice. If his assets will only yield returns over a long period of time, this can cause severe financial difficulties.

There are exceptions, of course. Some of the assets financed through borrowing may yield their returns over a short period of time. This would be true of inventories, for example. Thus, a firm with a fluctuating level of inventories might find that short-term liabilities are the most appropriate types.

Speculation.   There are other exceptions to the general undesirability of liquidity as well. In particular, when interest rates are relatively high, borrowers may wish to speculate on a fall in interest rates in the future. Rather than contract for a long-term debt at relatively high interest rates, they may borrow on short term, planning to refinance the debt with long-term bonds when interest rates fall.

Borrower's Risk.   Borrowers also assume a risk, of course, in committing themselves to fixed future payments. The assets, which they count on to provide the income to meet these payments, may not return the expected yield. This will affect the choice between stocks and bonds as financial instruments to be issued. If it is financed through common stock, inadequate returns on the asset will not force the firm into bankruptcy court (although if the venture is successful beyond expectations, the additional returns must be shared with the new stockholders).

Borrower's risk may also affect the borrowing decision. Any risk-averting borrower will demand an expected return substantially in excess of the interest rate on borrowed funds to compensate for borrower's risk before he will undertake the venture.

Inflation and Taxation.   We saw earlier that both inflation and taxes are important influences on the portfolios choices made by individuals. These influences are equally important for borrowers. In the case of inflation, the effects are the opposite to those discussed previously in connection with the demand for securities. For example, any borrower who expects continued rapid inflation would need to adjust the market rate of interest to reflect the real cost of borrowing because future fixed-sum payments would be paid in "cheap" inflated dollars. The question of taxation is much more complex. The borrower must not only consider his taxation but also take into account the taxes which must be paid by lenders. Borrowers will attempt to minimize their cost of borrowing by adjusting their pattern of borrowing to take advantage of the tax treatment of different types of income payments.

A Note on the Federal Government

As in the case of the borrowing decision, the federal government should be (but is not always) an exception to all that we have said about the liability balance decision. The considerations governing the structure of the federal debt should be related to the general state of economic conditions rather than the range of considerations entering into the liability balance decisions of other spending units. This is a topic which we will consider in Chapters 20 and 23.

Conclusions

Just as the assetholder must choose among alternative assets to be held, so the debtor must choose among alternative types of instruments to be issued. In general, the considerations entering into the debtor's choices are the same as those entering into the assetholder's choices, but they work in the opposite direction. Thus, debtors tend to prefer low-yielding instruments (to them, the yield is a cost) and to avoid liquidity. Risk aversion would probably lead them to issue variable income rather than fixed income securities. The important point to note, however, is that just as all financial instruments are substitutes for each other in asset portfolios, so they are substitutes for each other as methods of borrowing funds. A change in the yield on one financial instrument will not only set in train adjustments in the composition of asset portfolios, it will also lead to changes in methods used by borrowers to finance their current deficits.

ENDNOTES

1. J.V. Poapst and W.R. Waters, "Rates of Return on Consumer Durables," *Journal of Finance*, Vol. XIX, No. 4 (Dec. 1964), pp. 673-77.
2. Royal Commission on Banking and Finance, *Report*, (Ottawa: Queen's Printer, 1964), p. 31.

Elementary Theory of 7
Financial Markets
PART 4: MARKET
EQUILIBRIUM

Until now, our discussion of the market for financial instruments has been concerned with the determinants of the behavior of the individual participants in the market — the households, business firms, and government agencies which are the ultimate lenders and borrowers. We examined how each participant might make decisions about the size and composition of his asset or liability portfolio by taking into account his reactions to liquidity and risk, and by taking the prices — or better, the expected yields — on the instruments as given. They are determined in the marketplace through the interaction of the demand and supply forces which result from the portfolio selection decision of all of the individual borrowers and lenders. It is one aspect of the process by which the market allocates credit among all alternative possible uses.

THE CONCEPT OF EQUILIBRIUM
IN FINANCIAL MARKETS

Equilibrium price is a familiar concept in economics: it is a price which, under existing conditions of demand and supply, has no tendency to change. Prices tend to rise under the pressure of excess demand, and to fall under the pressure of excess supply. An *equilibrium price,* therefore, *is a price at which there is neither excess demand nor excess supply: a price at which market demand and supply are in balance.* In the context of financial markets, this means a set of expected yields on financial instruments so that there is neither an excess demand for nor an excess supply of any category of financial instrument.

In a more advanced textbook the concept of equilibrium in financial markets would be the subject of very careful and extensive analysis. It is a difficult concept, because it involves two dimensions — stocks and flows. As we have seen, we can talk about supply both as a *stock* at a *point in time* (the stock of financial instruments outstanding) and as a *flow* over a *period of time* (the flow of net borrowing). Likewise, we can talk of the demand for financial instruments as a *stock* (the desired stock at a *point in time*) and a *flow* (the flow of net saving over a *period of time*). A thorough analysis of financial equilibrium, which is beyond the scope of the present discussion, would have to explore both dimensions and to examine the interrelationships between them. For now, certain elementary points should be kept in mind.

Stock Equilibrium.   If we could stop the clock and look at financial markets at a point in time, we would be faced with a situation in which the quantities of financial instruments outstanding are given. Given time, new securities can be issued, and existing securities retired. However, at any instant, the quantities are fixed by the cumulative effects of past history. In the immediate past, transactions in the market established a set of prices (and hence expected yields) for those securities. For this set of prices to be an equilibrium set in a stock sense, assetholders must have no incentive to alter the composition of their portfolios. *They must be content to hold the existing quantities of securities at the prevailing market prices for those securities.* This is the condition for stock equilibrium.

Suppose this is not the case and that there is a group of assetholders who feel that the market price for some of the securities which they are holding is too high (i.e., the expected yield is too low) relative to that on other assets (e.g. other securities, money, or physical assets). If we could somehow permit trading of securities without allowing time to pass (i.e., without changing the outstanding stocks of securities and other factors affecting demand and supply conditions), these assetholders would offer to sell what they consider to be the overpriced securities, and would submit bids for the underpriced securities. Since the quantities of these securities cannot change, the only effects of these transactions can be to rearrange portfolios (if the securities exist, some assetholder must have them in his portfolio) and to change prices. The price of the overvalued securities will be bid down, and the price of the underpriced securities bid up, the adjustments presumably continuing until stock equilibrium is established.

In one case, which will assume major importance in our later analysis, it may be that assetholders in general have more money in their portfolios than is consistent with portfolio balance at existing prices and expected yields on securities. They will attempt to dispose of money in exchange for securities. This attempt at shifting portfolios will lead to a bidding up of the prices of all securities (a lowering of interest rates). Neither the stock of money nor the stock of securities can change (remember, we assumed them to be fixed in number), yet the level (and perhaps the structure) of interest rates will change.

It is this change in interest rates which allows the public to achieve portfolio balance with the given stock of money. The opposite adjustment would occur if there were an excess demand for money.

Flow Equilibrium.   This analysis of the adjustment of prices and expected yields in the face of stock disequilibrium is highly artificial because it implies the passing of time without any changes in the external environment. However, time does pass, and as it does, the basic determinants of portfolio balance decisions change. The outlook for particular industries, and hence the expected returns on outstanding securities and the expected yield on new physical capital formation, changes. Physical capital can be created or depleted. Income is generated, and consumption and saving occur. Government policy can be implemented or changed. Commodity price levels may rise or fall, perhaps accompanied by changes in employment levels. Expectations with respect to any of a great variety of relevant developments — including future securities prices — may change slightly or drastically.

All of these considerations come to bear on two vital flows. First, as time passes borrowers can issue new securities and debtors can retire outstanding issues. Both the size and the structure of the stock of financial instruments available to be held will probably change. Second, the flow of saving during the period increases the size of asset holdings, thus increasing the demand for financial instruments. Dissaving has the opposite effect, of course. *Over that period of time, the prices* (and hence expected yield) *on financial instruments must adjust so that the increasing demands for financial instruments resulting from the flow of saving are just offset by the increasing stock of financial instruments resulting from borrowing to finance capital and other expenditures* (remember: both the saving decision and the borrowing decision should be sensitive to the level of interest rates, although perhaps in varying degrees). This, then, is the condition for flow equilibrium.

It should be evident from what has been said that what we mean by "flow" equilibrium is in fact "stock" equilibrium at successive points in time, with the basic determinants of equilibrium changing from instant to instant.

Market Equilibrium and Resource Allocation

Most microeconomic theory focuses attention on the determination of relative prices in equilibrium. However, the underlying concern is always the allocation of scarce resources among alternative possible uses. Whether in the markets for bread and bicycles, or the markets for financial instruments, the process of price determination takes on importance because it is at the core of the process by which production and employment decisions are made in a market economy.

The market for financial instruments allocates credit. Thus, the price of financial instruments not only determines the yield to assetholders, it also determines the cost of funds to borrowers. The yield to assetholders should affect savings decisions, thus also affecting the share of income devoted to consumption and the share available to finance capital formation. The interest cost to borrowers should influence their willingness to engage in deficit spending, whether for consumption or capital formation. *Thus, the determination of equilibrium prices in financial markets should influence choices between present and future consumption, as well as the pace and industrial composition of capital formation.*

Market Equilibrium and Government Policy

There is also another aspect of equilibrium in financial markets which must be noted. We have seen that all financial instruments are more or less close substitutes, both as assets which might be held by assetholders and as liabilities which might be issued by debtors. This means that the markets for the various types of financial instruments cannot be considered separately. They are tightly interconnected, so that a disturbance to equilibrium in one market will also involve disturbances in others. But, as we have just noted, the prices of financial instruments also enter into decisions on consumption and public and private capital formation. This opens up the possibility that the government can engage in operations in the financial markets — altering the size of the outstanding stock of certain financial instruments (e.g. government debt, money) — for the purpose of altering the level of expenditures on consumer goods and capital goods. It creates the possibility of a monetary policy to regulate the level of aggregate demand for goods and services.

This is the topic of the second half of the book.

Equilibrium and Security Yields

We have examined the concept of equilibrium in financial markets and are now in a position to examine the forces shaping the attainment of equilibrium in financial markets. In particular, we will consider the pricing of risky assets, the determinants of the structure of interest rates on government bonds, and the effects of inflation on market interest rates. In each of these cases, we will find that the outcome in any financial market is shaped by the forces of demand and supply in much the same way as in most other markets.

THE PRICING OF RISKY ASSETS

We have already seen that financial assets differ from each other with respect to the riskiness of their returns. In fact, risk is one of the most important elements that must be taken into account in any examination of the workings of financial markets. In this section we will analyse the way in which various assets have different rates of return which depend in large measure on their risk.

In Chapter 5, we examined the way in which investors react to risk and return in choosing their portfolios. In this chapter, we consider how the interaction of individual demands for assets leads to the "pricing" of risk in financial markets in terms of the relationship between risk and return on various assets.

The starting point for our analysis will be an economy consisting of identical, risk averse investors, each with a set of preferences which can be represented by an indifference curve such as I_1 as shown in Figures 7-1 to 7-3. We will also assume that the assets in the economy consist of a fixed amount of a perfectly safe asset and a fixed amount of a risky asset so that the level of risk for the whole collection of assets for the economy can be represented as $\bar{\sigma}$ in Figure 7-1. The problem then is to determine the pattern of yields between safe and risky assets which will make the assetholders willing just to hold the existing collection of assets.

Consider first the pattern of interest rates which gives the opportunity line AA shown in Figure 7-1 for the investors. This line indicates a return r_s on the safe asset and r_r on the risky asset. Under these conditions the investors would be willing to hold the

FIGURE 7-1   Risk and yield: Return to risk too low

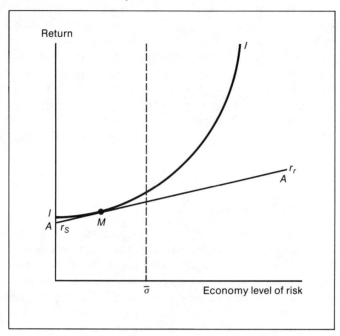

portfolio represented by the point *M*. As can be seen, the risky assets do not have a sufficiently high return for investors to hold the available supply as represented by $\bar{\sigma}$. Similarly if the opportunity line for investors were *BB*, shown in Figure 7-2, which indicates a higher return on the risky asset and a lower return on the safe asset, they would be willing to hold the combination *N*. At the relatively high return r'_r for risky assets and low return, r'_s for safe assets, investors would be willing to hold more than the available supply.

In other markets studied by economists, any difference between quantity demanded and supplied leads to adjustments in prices to eliminate this difference. In financial markets, such a difference leads to a change in the pattern of yields (and, as we know, security prices). If investors want to hold less than the available supply of risky assets, the rate of return on risky assets must rise to induce investors to hold more of these assets. Thus at any point such as *M*, the interest rate on risky assets must rise relative to the return on safe assets. Similarly, it could be shown that at points such as *N*, the return on risky assets must fall in order to reduce investors' demands for risky assets so as to be equal to the supply. The composition of the assetholders' desired portfolios would match the supplies of safe and risky assets only if interest rates adjust so as to give the market opportunity line *CC* shown in Figure 7-3, which is tangent to the indifference curve at *L*. An interest rate r''_r on risky assets together with an interest rate r''_s on safe assets is the only combination which would give such a line. We can see that unless this combination of interest rates existed the pattern of interest rates would have to adjust until equilibrium is reached.

FIGURE 7-2   Risk and yield: Return to risk too high

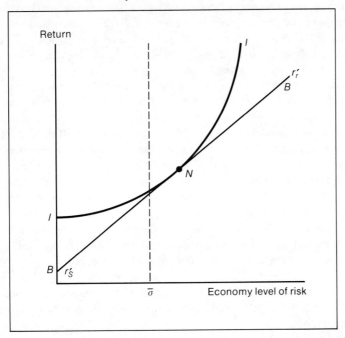

FIGURE 7-3   Risk and yield: Equilibrium

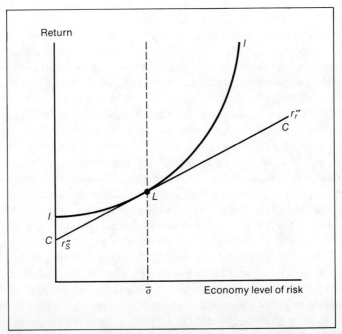

While our analysis has been oversimplified in a number of respects, we have still managed to capture a number of important features of financial markets. In particular, we can see that risky assets are likely to earn a higher return than safe assets. This higher return is required in order to persuade the risk averse investor to hold risky assets rather than holding only safe assets. In other words, risky assets must earn an expected risk premium over safe assets in a world where investors are risk averse.

This risk premium must be distinguished from the difference between the theoretical yield and expected yield for any asset which has credit risk (which we examined in an earlier chapter). This difference between theoretical and expected yield represents the value of any expected default expressed as a rate of return. It depends, then, on the probability of default and the amount expected to be defaulted. Every investor, whether risk averse or not, must adjust the theoretical yield by the value of expected default to give an expected yield. The risk premium that we have developed above is a completely separate concept. It indicates the amount by which the *expected* return on any risky asset must be higher than the expected return on a safe asset in order to persuade risk averse investors to hold this risky asset in their portfolios. The theoretical yield, as found in the bond quotations on the financial pages of the newspapers, thus includes both the risk premium and the expected value of any losses suffered through default. Thus, in our example of Chrysler Corporation, we would find that even after the adjustment of the theoretical yield to reflect expected default, the expected yield on Chrysler Corporation bonds might exceed the return on other safer assets because of the risk premium.

To this point we have looked at risk and return in financial markets in a very simplified way in order to abstract from the many complexities of the real world. While, in general, investors are probably risk averse, not all investors have the same preferences with respect to risk and return. In addition, suppliers of financial assets are likely to adjust the proportion of risky and safe assets that they issue in response to different patterns of interest rates. While incorporating each of these elements into the analysis would make it more complicated, the overall result would remain essentially unchanged.

A more significant limitation of the analysis was the assumption of only one risky asset. In reality, investors face a choice of many risky assets, each with a different degree of risk. When we recognize the presence of several, or even many, risky assets, we must ask whether some clear relationship can be established between the riskiness of an asset and its expected return. The answer turns out to be negative. With many assets to choose from, the investor is interested in the risk of his portfolio rather than the risk of any one asset. Thus, the relevant feature of any asset for the investor's decision is the degree to which it increases the risk of his portfolio. Two securities that have the same risk when considered separately may have very different effects when added to a portfolio. For example, one asset might consist of shares in a corporation which earns a high return when the economy is doing well in general but a very low return when the economy does poorly. If the other asset, though subject to similar fluctuations in return in terms of their size, manages to do well when the economy is faltering, the investor would be willing to add it to his portfolio at even a low return because the addition of this security would offset some of the risks of other securities. Thus, we would expect in general that the expected return on assets would increase as their level of risk increases. Nevertheless, the relationship would not be perfect: some assets with high risk would earn less than assets with lower risk.

THE EQUILIBRIUM PATTERN OF
INTEREST RATES

We have already seen in Chapter 5 that different securities issued by the same borrower can have different yields at any time according to their term to maturity. We are now in a position to try to explain the determinants of this pattern of yields. The explanation of how these different yields can arise provides another good example of the workings of financial markets.

In explaining the yields on different securities, we will concentrate on securities issued by the Government of Canada, the largest borrower in Canadian financial markets. Figure 7-4 shows the yields on all Government of Canada bonds outstanding on July 30, 1980, with the bonds arranged in ascending order of term to maturity. The yields plotted on this chart were calculated on the basis of prices quoted in the market on that day, and on the assumption that the promised future payments (interest and redemption value) would in fact be made. These yields are expressed in terms of *basis points* or one-hundredths of a percentage point. A line — commonly called a *yield curve* — has been drawn indicating the general relationship between yield and term to maturity on that date. Not all yields lie exactly on the yield curve, but the curve is broadly representative.

This is regarded as a fairly normal yield curve. The striking thing about it is that yields on very short-term bonds are lower than yields on longer-term issues. The curve initially rises sharply at the left. Thus, the yield on the shortest-term security plotted, a 91-day treasury bill, was approximately 10.06% per annum. The yield on a one-year bond was 60 basis points higher (10.66% per annum) and on a five-year bond 163 basis points higher (11.69% per annum). By contrast, beyond 10 years the curve is relatively

FIGURE 7-4   Yield curve: Government of Canada bonds, July 30, 1980

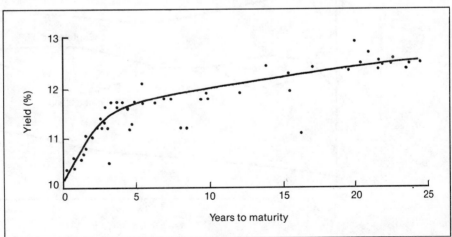

flat. A bond with 10 years to maturity had a yield of 11.85% per annum whereas the yield on one with over 25 years to maturity was 60 basis points higher at 12.45% per annum.

We should be aware that the pattern depicted in Figure 7-4 is not the only pattern that can be expected to occur. In other words, long-term bond yields are not always higher than short-term bond yields. As evidence we have plotted yield curves for four different dates in Figure 7-5. For both June 1980 and September 1980, the yields on very short-term securities are below the yields on long-term bonds. In the former case the yield rises steadily with years to maturity, whereas in the latter the yield curve has a pronounced "hump." The yields on three- to four-year maturities are higher than those on shorter bonds and also those on any bonds up to 10 years maturity. It is also possible for short-term bonds to have a higher yield than longer-term bonds, as is shown for March 1980 and December 1980. In the former case, the yield declined with years to maturity, whereas in the latter, the pattern almost defies description!

The shape of the yield curve thus changes from time to time. Indeed, there is a fairly regular cyclical pattern to these changes. When the general level of interest rates is relatively low, the yield curve tends to have the shape of that in Figure 7-4. As interest rates rise, however, short-term interest rates tend to rise more rapidly than long-term interest rates. Remember that we said earlier that short-term yields move over a wider range than long-term rates, although the market prices of short-term bonds tend to vary

FIGURE 7-5   Yield curves, Government of Canada bonds*

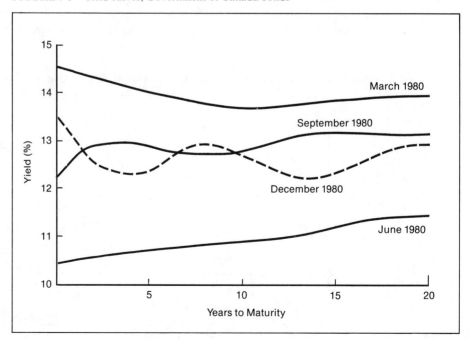

*The yield curves were drawn using the month-end observations for various maturities of Government of Canada bonds.

Source: Department of Finance, *Economic Review*, 1981.

over a narrower range. As a result, the yield curve becomes flatter. In periods of relatively high interest rates, the yield curve tends to develop a "hump"; and in extreme circumstances it may develop the consistent downward slope of March, 1980 in Figure 7-5.

Expectations and the Yield Curve

We cannot develop a complete analysis of changes in the shape of the yield curve without analysing both the demand and the supply sides of the market. Nevertheless, a major part of the explanation of these gyrations in the pattern of interest rates rests in what we might call the speculative demand for financial assets. This speculative demand arises from investors' expectations of future levels of the interest rate.

We can start to understand the role of expectations in shaping the yield curve by considering the choices available to an investor planning to hold an asset for some definite period of time. Consider, for example, an investor planning to lend funds for a period of one year. This investor can be said to have an *investment horizon* for one year. One obvious choice available to him is the purchase of a one-year security. It is less obvious that he has many more choices to consider. He can purchase marketable securities with maturity greater than one year and plan to sell them at the end of the year. Alternatively he could hold securities with a maturity of less than one year and invest the proceeds in other short-term securities at the maturity of the first. In other words, an investor may hold securities with maturity either longer or shorter than his investment horizon.

How does an investor decide which security he will hold over his investment horizon? We will see that the decision depends on his expectations of future interest rates. Consider an example in which an investor with a one-year horizon has the choice between a one-year security and a two-year security. The two-year security differs from a one-year security only in that it extends the loan for a second year at terms which are agreed upon in advance. In effect, a two-year bond can be thought of as two one-year bonds sold together with one of the bonds applying to the current year and the other to the next year.

The investor knows exactly in advance the yield he will receive on the one-year bond. If a bond selling for $1000 has a coupon rate of 12%, the investor is assured he will have exactly $1120 at the end of the year for each $1000 of bonds that he purchases today. If, instead, he purchases a two-year bond with the same 12% coupon rate, he cannot be assured of the amount he will earn over the year. Whether he earns 12% or more, or less, depends on the conditions in security markets when he sells the bond at the end of the first year. Suppose that at the end of the first year these markets have changed so that newly issued one-year bonds yield 14%. In other words, new investors in these bonds can be assured of $1140 at the end of year two for each $1000 invested in these bonds at the end of year one. The original investor's two-year bond has to compete with these newly issued one-year bonds over the second year of its life. As a consequence, its price must fall sufficiently below $1000 to $982 so that with its 12% coupon it gives the same 14% yield as the newly issued bonds. At a price of $982 the bond will give a new investor the principle of $1000 together with $120 interest at the end of the second year. The capital gain of $18 together with the interest of $120 are approximately 14% of the price of $982 at the end of year one. Similarly, if interest rates fell to 10% for the second year, it can be shown that the bond's price would rise to $1018 at the end of the first year.

The original investor's realized yield from holding a two-year bond purchased at $1000 with a 12% coupon over his one-year investment period depends on the level of interest rates at the start of the second year. If the interest rate at that time is above 12%, the investor earns less than 12% for the first year. If the interest rate moved to 14%, his return would be $120 in interest less the $18 loss suffered by selling the bond purchased at $1000 for $82, giving a yield of just 10.2%. Conversely if the interest rate for the second year had fallen to 10%, he would earn 14.2% ($120 interest plus $18 capital gain on his original $1000 bond purchase).

The investor's choice between the one-year bond and the two-year bond clearly depends on his expectations of future interest rates. If he expected interest rates to rise, he would choose the one-year bond to avoid the capital loss on the two-year bond implied by the higher interest rate. Conversely, if he expected interest rates to fall he would choose the two-year bond to earn the expected capital gain. Only if interest rates were expected to remain unchanged at 12% would he be indifferent between the one-year and the two-year bonds.

The final step in our analysis is to determine what would happen at the beginning of the first year if all investors felt the interest rate would be different from 12% for the second year. Suppose, first, all investors expect the interest rate on one-year bonds to move from 12% to 14% at the end of the first year. In this case, no one would want to buy the 12% two-year bond at $1000. In fact, its price would have to fall to $984. At this price, the first-year investor would earn 12% by selling this bond at $982 (interest of $120 less a capital loss of $2 over the original price of $984 gives a yield of 12%). As we have seen before, at a price of $982, over the second year the investor can earn 14%, the same return expected to prevail over that second year for one year bonds. By calculation, we would find that the apparent yield of the two-year bond at this price would be approximately 13%. Similarly, if interest rates were expected to fall to 10%, the two-year bond would be valued at $1016, giving an apparent yield to maturity of 11%.

The features of our simple example have a lesson which applies to the bond market in general. If investors' expectations of future interest rates were the only factor determining the shape of the yield curve, the yield to maturity of a long-term bond can be thought of as the average of the short-term rates expected to prevail over the life of the bond. Thus, when interest rates are expected to fall, the yield to maturity on short-term bonds exceeds that on long-term bonds. The reason for this difference is that the yield on the short-term bond is an average of the yields over only the period of high interest rates, whereas the yield on the longer-term bond would also include periods of lower interest rates. We can consider a specific example to make this clearer. Suppose investors expect the yield of one-year bonds to fit the following pattern:

Year	Expected one year rate for year
1	14
2	12
3	10
4	10
5	10

In this case the yield on a one-year bond would be 14% and the yield to maturity on a two-year bond 13% (the average of 12% and 14%). Similarly it can be shown that the yields on three-year, four-year and five-year bonds would be 12%, 11.5%, and 11.2% respectively. The yield curve corresponding to these data is shown in Figure 7-6.

FIGURE 7-6   Hypothetical term structure of interest rates

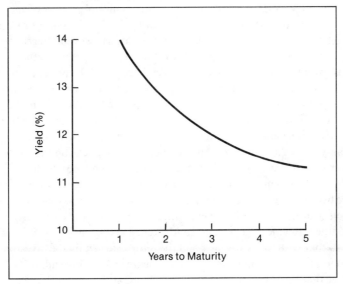

Our analysis gives us a basis for understanding the variety of shapes which are possible for the yield curve for securities of different maturities. Our example showed the case where future short-term rates are below current short-term rates, which gives a downward sloping yield curve. The reader should be able to work out that the "normal" pattern shown in Figures 7-4 would be caused by a pattern of short-term rates which are expected to be successively higher in each period in the future.

This analysis also helps us to understand the way in which changes in the economy can affect the shape and position of the yield curve. For example, we can distinguish between factors which cause the expectation of a permanent change in short-term interest rates and those which cause the expectation of only a temporary change in short-term interest rates. The former, by shifting all short-term interest rates upward, ends up by shifting the entire yield curve upward. In contrast, an expected change only in current short-term rates has the effect of twisting the curve. To see this effect, we should consider as a starting point a circumstance where short-term interest rates were expected to remain constant. Then the yield curve for different maturities would be perfectly flat in terms of expectations. Now let us assume that some change occurs that affects only the current short-term rate of interest but has a smaller impact on interest rates expected to prevail further in the future. This type of change raises the yield to maturity on short-term bonds by a greater amount than on long-term bonds and as a result twists the yield curve into downward sloping shape much as in Figure 7-6. The yield curve twists in this manner because the current short-term yields are a larger proportion of the total yield for short-term securities than for long-term.

Risk Aversion and the Normal Yield Curve

Some economists believe that factors other than expectations of future interest rates help to determine the shape of the yield curve. We can see their point by remembering that the normal yield curve (that is, the most common pattern of interest rates by maturity) has an upward slope, as is shown in Figure 7-4. If interest rate expectations alone explained the yield curve, this normal pattern would suggest that investors normally expect interest rates to rise in the future or, more precisely, they expect interest rates to rise more frequently than they expect them to fall. Experience over a long span of time does not reveal any continuing upward trend in interest rates that would bear out this expectation. So either investors must continually err in the direction of overestimating future interest rates (and never learn from their mistakes!), or something in addition to expectations is needed to explain the typical yield curve.

So far, we have assumed that the one-year and two-year bonds are identical as far as the investor is concerned and, as a result, that he will choose whichever has the higher expected return over his investment horizon. We need now to consider an important difference between the one-year bond and the two-year bond as options for the investor. The one-year bond provides its yield with complete certainty because the investor is assured of the repayment of principal and interest at the end of the year. We have seen, in contrast, that with the two-year bond the return earned by the investor for one year must be uncertain at the time that the investment is made. Instead, this return depends on the price that the investor receives for the bond at the end of the year he holds it. In other words, the two-year bond exposes the investor with a one-year horizon to market risk whereas the one-year bond does not.

Whether the greater market risk of the longer-term bond makes any difference depends on the investor's attitude toward risk. We saw earlier, in Chapter 5, that economists in general assume that investors are risk averse. In other words, the typical investor requires a higher return to hold risky assets than he does to hold safe assets. Risk averse investors thus would requires a higher return, or *risk premium*, in order to hold a two-year bond rather than a one-year bond for an investment planned for a period of only one year. In general, risk averse investors require a risk premium as an incentive to invest in securities with term to maturity longer than the investors' horizon.

The presence of a risk premium helps to explain why the normal yield structure is upward sloping. We can consider three possible patterns of yield structure (designated by the lines AA) based solely on expectations as shown in Figure 7-7. Figure 7-7(a) represents a yield structure where investors expect higher interest rates in the future, whereas Figure 7-7(c) represents the structure with lower expected interest rates. In Figure 7-7(b) investors expect interest rates to remain unchanged. If investors were risk-averse and viewed longer-term bonds as riskier than short-term bonds, the actual yield pattern would have to include a liquidity premium in order to persuade investors to hold the longer term securities. The effect of the liquidity premium would be to twist the yield curve in a counter-clockwise direction as shown in Figure 7-7. We can see that the yield curve reflecting investors' expectations of higher interest rates becomes

FIGURE 7-7   Liquidity premiums and the term structure of interest rates

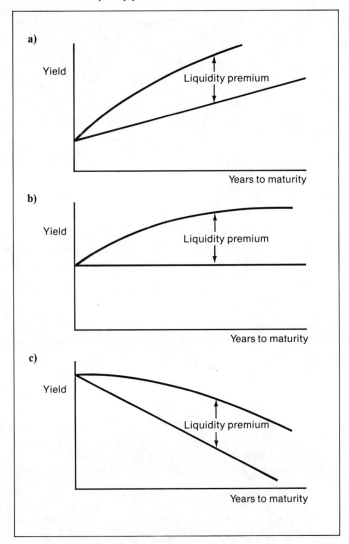

steeper, whereas the yield curve corresponding to expectations of lower interest rates becomes flatter. Finally, when the liquidity premium is added to the flat yield curve corresponding to the expectation of unchanging interest rates, the resulting yield curve becomes upward sloping. In each of these cases a further element has been added to the yield curve which reflects investors' expectations of future interest rates. Moreover, in each case the resulting yield curve combining expectations and this liquidity premium by itself appears to indicate that investors expect higher interest rates in the future than, in fact, they actually do. The recognition that longer-term bonds may have more uncertainty with respect to their yields and that investors are risk averse serves to give an explanation for the shape of the so-called "normal yield curve."

INFLATION AND INTEREST RATES

The final example of the working of financial markets to be considered is the impact of inflation on security yields. This issue is particularly interesting because the presence of persistent inflation distinguishes the 1970s and early 1980s from preceding years. At the same time, the most notable feature of financial markets over this period was the substantially higher interest rates in comparison to previous experience. The purpose of this section is to identify the channels by which inflation affects financial markets so as to determine the degree to which these higher interest rates can be explained by the higher rates of inflation.

Inflation and its Effects

While inflation gains much attention from the media, rarely is the meaning of the concept made clear. Economists define "inflation" as a general rise in the price level of goods and services. The definition abstracts from the changes in individual prices; increases in some prices by 15% per year and others by 5% per year are perfectly compatible with an inflation rate of 10%. An alternative and equivalent view of inflation which may be more useful for present purposes is to regard inflation as a fall in the general purchasing power of money.

Monetary and Real Assets.   We must start by asking whether inflation has any effects at all on the economy. Isn't money first a unit of account which serves as a measuring rod and isn't inflation then just a change in the measuring units? Our height clearly does not change when we measure in metres rather than feet, so why should changing the value of money affect the economy? To answer this question we must recognize some differences which exist among the various assets in which people can hold their wealth. Some assets, which we will call *real assets*, are claims on goods and services. A familiar real asset is common stock in a manufacturing company which represents ownership of the factories, equipment, and inventories of the company. As the price level increases through inflation, we would expect that the money value of these assets also increases and, as a consequence, so too the value of the stock which represents a share in ownership of the company. Other assets, which we will call *monetary assets,* are claims on a fixed amount of money. Examples of monetary assets are bonds, bank deposits, and currency. Unlike real assets, monetary assets lose some of their real value as a consequence of inflation. The rising price level, together with the fixed money value of these assets, means their purchasing power in terms of goods and services falls with inflation. Inflation, then, changes the relative value of financial assets; these assets denominated in money lose their value relative to real assets.

It is often said that inflation benefits borrowers and hurts lenders, but we can see that this statement is incomplete. Not all creditors must lose through inflation. An individual who makes a loan which requires repayment of 10 bushels of wheat can be assured of the real value of the loan in terms of wheat regardless of the rate of inflation. Any redistribution of purchasing power from lender to borrower which occurs as a result of inflation happens because the loan is expressed in terms of the measuring rod of money. Inflation decreases the real value of the lender's monetary asset which, of course, is the same thing as decreasing the real value of the borrower's monetary debt.

Thus, we must be careful to remember that *inflation leads to a redistribution towards monetary debtors and away from monetary creditors.*

Anticipated and Unanticipated Inflation.   Economists make the distinction between *anticipated inflation* and *unanticipated inflation* in sorting out the effects of inflation on financial markets. Common sense suggests that lenders would try to avoid the losses caused by inflation if they could. Often they cannot because they did not foresee the future inflation at the time they set the terms of the loan. When borrowers and lenders fail to react in advance to price increases, the inflation can be described as unanticipated. On the other hand, when lenders and borrowers forecast price increases correctly, and react on these forecasts, the inflation can be characterized as anticipated. Any actual inflation is unlikely to have been predicted exactly by lenders and borrowers, and as a result contains elements of both anticipated and unanticipated inflation. In addition, lenders and borrowers can sometimes overestimate future rates of inflation so that anticipated inflation exceeds actual inflation. Any actual inflation then consists of differing degrees of anticipated and unanticipated inflation.

Inflation and Interest Rates.   The effects of inflation on financial markets are the direct result of the reactions of lenders and borrowers to the inflation they expect to take place in the future. How then can lenders act so as to protect themselves from the decrease in the money value of their loans which results from inflation? In answering this question, we should remember that the lender has the choice of holding either monetary assets or real assets. With a given rate of interest, the real return expected by the investor on his monetary assets depends on his expectation of inflation. A higher rate of inflation means more of his asset is lost through its decreased purchasing power. We would expect investors to shift their holdings away from monetary assets toward real assets in response to any expectation of higher inflation.

Borrowers also adjust to expectations of higher inflation. They realize that higher inflation reduces the cost of borrowing at any interest rate because the inflation reduces the real value of their debt over time. We would expect borrowers to react to this lower cost of borrowing by trying to borrow more at each interest rate than if they had not expected higher inflation.

Both these responses by borrowers and lenders will affect the pattern of yields in financial markets. Lenders will be less willing to lend by means of monetary instruments such as bonds, whereas borrowers will be more willing to borrow through these means. We can see the effects of inflation more clearly by examining its influence on the demand for and supply of loans shown in Figure 7-8. In this analysis, the lender can be regarded as the supplier of loans; in effect, he lends funds by making loans to the borrower. Similarly, the borrower is the demander of loans. This diagram is different from the usual analysis in that the demand and supply are drawn to depend on the interest rates rather than prices. The supply curve for loans, S_L, slopes upward to the right, reflecting the greater willingness of lenders to make loans as the expected yield on these loans increases. The demand curve for loans slopes downward to the right indicating that borrowers are less willing to borrow as the expected interest cost rises. We will assume that interaction of the demand and supply in absence of any expectation of inflation gives an interest rate of i_0 (or 5%) in our example.

As we saw earlier, the expectation of inflation affects both the willingness of lenders to supply funds and borrowers to demand funds. For present purposes, we must go further and determine the size of these effects. Suppose both lenders and borrowers expect 10% inflation. Without expectation of inflation, lenders were just willing to supply the quantity Q_0 of loans at an interest rate of 5%. The lender now realizes that the real value of his loan will decrease by 10% as a result of inflation. To remain in the same real position, he will have to charge a higher interest rate of roughly 15%, of which 10% offsets the loss in real value of his assets and 5% represents the real return he requires in absence of inflation. Similarly, the borrower should realize that the real value of his debt will fall as inflation reduces the purchasing power of the money in which it is denominated. If he was willing to pay 5% for his borrowing in absence of expected inflation, he should be willing to pay 15% when he expects 10% inflation. The extra 10% offsets the decreased real value of his debt that results from inflation. In terms of Figure 7-8, the expectation of a 10% inflation shifts up both the demand and the supply curves by the amount of the expected inflation. In our example the resulting equilibrium interest rate increases from 5% to 15%. We see that in this simple example the market interest rate increases by an increase in the amount of inflation that lenders and borrowers expect over the future.

FIGURE 7-8   The effects of inflation on interest rates

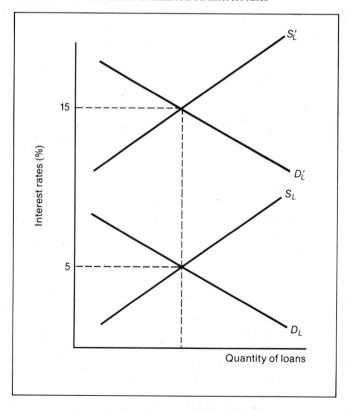

Nominal Rates and Real Rates.   Economists have paid close attention to studying the impact of inflation on financial markets ever since inflation emerged as a persistent problem in the late 1960s. These effects, however, were originally analyzed some 50 years earlier by Irving Fisher, an American economist. Because of Fisher's work, economists now distinguish between two elements of the rate of interest: the *nominal rate* which measures the actual rate we observe in financial markets, and the *real rate*, which corrects the nominal rate for any expected inflation. Our result concerning the effects of inflation on interest rates can be expressed in Fisher's terms by the following equation:[1]

$$i_n = i_r + \pi^e.$$

where i_n denotes the nominal rate i_r, the real rate, and π^e, the expected rate of inflation. We can see from this equation that any increase in expected inflation should raise the nominal interest rate by the amount of the increase of the expected inflation. Alternatively we can view any observed interest rate as consisting of two components: the real interest payment made by the borrower to the lender and a payment to offset the erosion of the purchasing power of the debt caused by inflation.

Index Bonds.   The adjustment of market interest rates is only one way in which the redistributions of wealth between lenders and borrowers that are caused by inflation can be offset by the workings of financial markets. In a number of countries, such as Israel and Brazil, where severe inflation has persisted over substantial periods, financial instruments have been developed which protect the lender against any reduction in the real value of his asset due to inflation. These instruments, called *index bonds,* have the value of both the principal, which must be repaid, and the interest rate payments continually revalued at the current level of prices. For example, if after the first year the price level increased from 100 to 110, an index bond with an initial value of $1000 would be revalued to $1100.

Similarly, if the bond had a 2½% coupon, the annual interest payment would be based on the bond's current value. This payment would be $27.50 at the end of the first year, or 10% higher than the $25 which would be paid if the price level had remained constant. In effect, the index bond is a financial instrument which has both its principal value and interest return fixed in real terms.

The process by which index bonds protect investors from inflation can be compared to the adjustment of market interest rates to expected inflation. We can compare the position of two investors, one who invests in a one-year index bond and the other who invests in a one-year conventional bond. If inflation turns out to be 10% over the year, the investor in the index bond ends up with $1127.50 ($1100 principal and $27.50 interest) at the end of the year. If the expectation of 10% inflation had been entirely reflected in financial markets, and also if the expected real return on conventional bonds was 2½%, the investor holding the conventional bond would have earned 12¾% (the 2½% real interest, 10% to offset the decreased real value of his $1000 principal and a further ¼% to offset the decreased real value of the interest.[2]) With his $1000 principal and his $127.50 in interest, he also would have $1127.50 at the end of the year. He has earned the same 2½% real return as the holder of the index bond. The adjustment in financial markets in response to expected inflation means the real return on the index bond and the conventional bond would be identical, if the inflation had been anticipated correctly. In other words, the market adjustment to expected inflation can be thought of as duplicating the adjustment which is built into the index bond.

The index bond and the conventional bond would give different returns from each other if the rate of inflation were incorrectly anticipated. The index bond gives the same real return regardless of the actual rate of inflation because the value of both the principal and the interest payment are adjusted to maintain their real value. In contrast, the real return on a conventional bond is affected by any difference between the expected rate of inflation and the rate which actually occurs. As we have seen, if the rate of inflation is higher than anticipated, the real return to the lender is lower than anticipated because of the unexpected decrease in the real value of his asset. Less obvious is the fact that if the rate of inflation is lower than anticipated, the real return to the lender is higher than expected because the decreased value of his asset is less than he judged it would be when he purchased the bond. Thus, although an index bond duplicates the adjustment processes which occur in financial markets in response to expected inflation, the index bond guarantees a real return in advance whereas the market adjustment is riskier in that the investor's expected real return is attained only if inflation is correctly anticipated. We should, therefore, not be surprised to find that index bonds have been used for lending and borrowing in economies which have persistently high and variable rates of inflation.

When Are Interest Rates High?   Our analysis of the effects of inflation raises an important economic question: when do we judge interest rates to be high? Interest rates for house mortgages were in the 5 to 7% range in the 1960s, but had risen to 18 to 20% by the early 1980s. (Mortgage rates were as high as 90% in Argentina in 1980, and the interest rate on bank loans reached 7300% per year in Germany in 1923.) What do these differences tell us about the cost of borrowing? Before answering this question we must first establish some bench mark for judging whether an interest rate is high. One criterion suggested by our earlier analysis is the effect of any interest rate on the incentives for lending and borrowing. An interest rate is high if it either discourages borrowers or unduly encourages lenders. In our numerical example, the interest rate rose from 5 to 15% without affecting the amount of lending and borrowing because the higher interest rate was the result of an expectation of higher inflation. On the other hand, had the interest rate risen from 5% to 20% we would find substantial real effects. Borrowers would be less willing to demand loans whereas lenders would be more eager to make loans available. The answer then demonstrates the usefulness of Fisher's equation. Our focus for determining whether interest rates are high or not should go beyond the nominal rate alone; we should also attempt to adjust market rates for expected inflation to derive an estimate of the real rate of interest. It is the real rate of interest which is relevant for the determination of economic behavior.

To return to our initial examples, the rate of inflation averaged only 4% in the late 1960s but had accelerated to 10% or more by the late 1970s; the inflation rate in Argentina was over 100% in 1980; and, by 1923, the German economy had succumbed to a hyperinflation which produced inflation rates of up to 300 000% on an annual basis over a short period of time. It is quite possible that the expected real cost of borrowing in Argentina in 1980, or in Germany in 1923, was less than the real cost of borrowing through a home mortgage in Canada in 1980 because borrowers and lenders both expected that the high interest rates would be offset by the depreciated real value of the loan.

Interest Rates and Inflation in Canada.   We have spoken continually of the concept of "expected inflation" throughout our analysis of the effects of inflation on financial markets. This concept raises a significant problem in terms of the usefulness of our analysis. If we are to judge whether interest rates are high, we need to be able to measure the expected inflation. Unfortunately, in practice, it is not possible to determine precisely what people's expectations of inflation are and how they are formed. Economists have tried a variety of methods for approximating expectations of inflation ranging from direct surveys of investors' views to statistical estimates based on past rates of inflation. Recent work involving a variety of approaches tends to support Fisher's initial insight that interest rates adjust on a one-for-one basis to changes in expected inflation. James Pesando, in his study of the impact of inflation on Canadian financial markets, summarizes the results of recent studies:

> Although precise estimates of the impact of price expectations vary, most estimates are in the vicinity of one — that is, an increase of X per cent in the expected rate of inflation produces an increase of X per cent on nominal or market interest rates. On the whole, especially since 1960, one can infer with a reasonable amount of confidence that increases in the expected rate of inflation are matched by approximately equal increases in market rates.[3]

In addition, the effects of changes in expectations of inflation have been one of the most important influences determining interest rate movements in recent years. Pesando concludes:

> One should also note in passing that the studies universally indicate that variations in the expected rate of inflation have been the source of most of the variations in market rates of interest in both Canada and the United States since the mid-1960's.[4]

We have now seen that financial markets react to inflation in such a way that nominal interest rates adjust to reflect the inflation. It may be asked how this conclusion fits in with our earlier result that inflation causes redistribution from monetary creditor to monetary debtor. In answering this question, we must remember the distinction that we made earlier between anticipated and unanticipated inflation. As long as the inflation remains unanticipated, lenders suffer losses because the real value of their holdings of debt decrease with inflation. Once the inflation is correctly anticipated, however, the nominal interest rate adjusts to reflect the higher inflation. The erosion in the real value of the debt continues year after year but it is offset by a higher nominal interest rate.

We must be careful to avoid making a false deduction from our analysis to this point. However tempting it may appear, we cannot conclude that the investor has no need to worry about future inflation. On the contrary, unanticipated inflation can create substantial losses for investors locked into long-term securities. To understand this point, we should note what happens in financial markets during the transition between unanticipated and anticipated inflation. The anticipation of inflation, as we have seen, causes nominal interest rates to rise, but, as we know from Chapter 5, higher interest rates lead to lower bond prices. Existing bonds must fall in price in order to compete with newly issued bonds which have terms that reflect the anticipated inflation. This fall in the price of bonds results because investors who anticipate inflation are unwilling to buy bonds whose terms do not reflect the inflation. In effect, the current holders of the bonds suffer a capital loss which reflects the expected value of all the future redistributions which are expected to result from the anticipated inflation. The change in bond prices will not be uniform; holders of long-term bonds will suffer larger capital losses than will holders of short-term bonds. Similarly, the issuers of long-term debt find the real value of these debts has decreased by more than the decrease in the value of short-term debt.

Some indication of the importance of this effect can be gained from examining the prices of Canadian government bonds. For example, on December 30, 1981 one issue of bonds due to mature in 1996 and originally issued at $100 had a market value of only $32. Our analysis which suggests that this bond must have been issued before the upsurge of inflation turns out to be correct. This bond was issued when its coupon rate of 3 was competitive with other current market rates. By December 1981, this bond had to compete with bonds of similar maturity with coupon rates as high as 13½%. The lesson from this analysis should be clear: even though anticipated inflation does not redistribute wealth from creditor to debtor, the transition to unanticipated inflation can import substantial losses to creditors, especially the holders of long-term debt.

Taxation, Inflation, and Interest Rates

So far we have analyzed the effects of inflation on interest rates in a very simplified way which abstracts from many features of the real world. We could justify such a simplification if the departures of our analysis from the real world were minor and if incorporating them did not alter our conclusions. Unfortunately, this is not the case. Someone once suggested that only two things are inevitable: taxes and death. As we will see, not only are taxes inevitable, they also affect the adjustment of interest rates in response to inflation. In this section, we will examine the effects on lenders, borrowers, and the equilibrium in the bond market.

The Effects on Lenders.   The first question is how the taxation of a lender's interest income alters his response to expected inflation. The first step toward finding the answer lies in the recognition that lenders are concerned with their real income *after taxes*. A higher interest rate does not benefit the lender if it is either offset or more than offset by higher taxes. Under Canadian tax law, all interest received by lenders is subject to income tax even if it is just compensating for the reduced real value of the lender's assets. The taxation of lender's interest income thus affects the amount by which nominal interest rates must rise to offset any erosion in the real value of the debt caused by inflation. Consider the simple example of a lender who earns a nominal return of 5% in absence of inflation and is subject to a marginal tax rate of 50%. As shown in Case 1 in Table 7-1, his after-tax return is 2½%. If inflation is instead expected to be 10% per annum, what rate of interest will this lender require? If the nominal interest increases by the amount of the expected inflation to 15%, would the lender earn the same real after tax return? As can be seen from Case 2, he would not. After payment of taxes at a 50%

rate, the lender's nominal return would only be 7½% and his real after tax return would be -2½% (the 7½% after tax return less 10% depreciation in the real value of his asset). As is shown in Case 3, to earn 2½% in real terms, the lender must earn a nominal return of 25%. His after-tax nominal return will be 2½% which, after adjustment for expected inflation of 10%, gives a real after-tax return of 2½%. Why does this result differ from that in which the interest return is not taxed? The reason is that under our tax system in Canada taxes are levied against nominal interest payments so that the lender must pay taxes against all interest payments including that portion required to offset the losses in real value resulting from inflation. Thus the nominal rate must adjust by enough so that

TABLE 7-1   **Calculation of real return after taxes**

Case 1: No inflation, 50% marginal tax rate

Nominal return	5 %
Less taxes	2½
Real return after taxes	2½%

Case 2: 10% inflation, 50% marginal tax rate, nominal rate rises by 10%

Nominal return	15 %
Less taxes	7½
Nominal return after taxes	7½
Less adjustment for inflation	−10
Real return after taxes	− 2½%

Case 3: 10% inflation, 50% marginal tax rate, nominal rate rises by 20%

Nominal return	25 %
Less taxes	12½
Nominal return after taxes	12½
Less adjustment for inflation	−10
Real return after taxes	2½%

Case 4: No inflation, 16⅔% marginal tax rate

Nominal rate	3 %
Less taxes	− ½
Real return after taxes	2½%

Case 5: 10% inflation, 16⅔% marginal rate, nominal rate rises by 12½%

Nominal rate	15 %
Less taxes	2½
Nominal return after taxes	12½
Less adjustment for inflation	10
Real return after taxes	2½%

the lender earns a nominal interest rate which is higher by an amount sufficient to offset the losses from inflation and also pay the additional taxes.

Our analysis shows that the amount by which the lender's return must adjust so as to maintain the same real return depends on the tax rate that the lender pays. The higher the tax rate the lender pays, the greater must be the increase in the nominal interest required to offset the lender's losses from any additional inflation. This suggestion can be confirmed by comparing Cases 4 and 5 with the earlier examples. As we saw from Cases 1 and 3, when the lender's marginal tax rate is 50%, the nominal rate must increase by 20% to offset the effects of a 10% greater inflation. As shown by comparing Case 4 with Case 5, when his marginal tax rate is only 16 2/3% the nominal rate needs to increase by only 12½%. The reason should be clear: a smaller portion of any increase in the nominal interest rate must go to the payment of taxes.

FIGURE 7-9   The effects of the interaction of inflation and taxation on the supply of loans

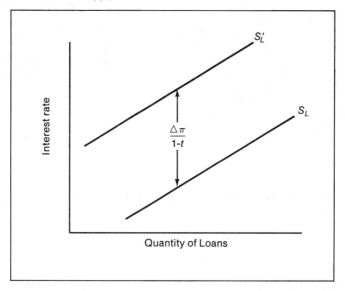

Our analysis of the effects on market interest rates of the interaction between expected inflation and the taxes paid by lenders can be made more general than the case-by-case approach taken so far. We have seen that for each dollar of bonds the lender receives i in interest and must pay taxes at a rate t on that interest. His after tax income from each dollar of bonds then is $(1-t)i$. If inflation increases by $\triangle \pi \%$ per year, the real value of the lender's assets will decrease by a further $\triangle \pi \%$ per year. The lender will require that his after tax return increase by $\triangle \pi \%$ in order for him to be willing to lend the same amount. In other words, the market interest rate must adjust by enough so that the change in after tax return equals $\triangle \pi$. Expressed as an equation, this condition becomes

$$(1-t)\triangle i = \triangle \pi.$$

By rearranging this equation we see that the change in market rate required to maintain the lender's real position is

$$\triangle i = \frac{\triangle \pi}{1-t}.$$

As can be easily checked, this equation formed the basis of the numerical examples in Table 7-1. In terms of our earlier demand and supply analysis, the lender's supply curve for loans moves upward by $\triangle \pi/(1-t)$ for each quantity of loans when the lender's interest income is taxed at a rate t, as shown in Figure 7-9.

The Effects on Borrowers.   We have seen how the presence of taxes affects the change of interest rate required to compensate lenders for inflation. We must now consider whether the presence of taxes affects the borrowers' response to inflation. Before doing so we should first summarize the features of the tax system which apply to borrowers. Some borrowers, such as corporations which are subject to corporate income tax, are able to include any interest payments they make as an expense against their taxable income. The corporate income tax is paid only on income in excess of allowable expenses so that every extra dollar of interest expense reduces the firm's taxable income by one dollar if everything else is held constant. With the reduction in taxable income, the corporation pays less corporate income tax and the amount of the reduction depends on the applicable tax rate. In other words, a firm does not bear all the cost of its higher interest payments to the extent that its required tax payments are reduced.

Let us turn to a specific example of a borrower who is able to use interest as an expense against his taxable income. How does inflation affect his willingness to pay a higher interest rate? As we have already seen, a 10% inflation reduces the real value of this debt by 10% per year. He would be willing, therefore, to incur a higher cost of borrowing of up to 10%; this higher interest cost of 10% would be exactly offset by the 10% depreciation in the real value of his debt. The question we now must answer is by how much can the interest rate rise and still leave him paying a 10% higher interest cost net of taxes? To answer this question, we will consider a firm which is subject to 50% corporate tax rate. For this firm, every dollar of additional interest expense reduces the firm's taxes by 50 cents; the cost to the firm of these higher interest payments, taking into account the reduced taxes, is half the increase. When the inflation rate is 10% per year, this firm would be willing to pay an interest rate of 20% higher than it would in absence of any inflation. As shown by comparing Cases 1 and 2 in table 7-2, the 20% higher interest payments would be offset by the reduction in the firm's taxes together with the reduction in the real value of the firm's debt. Similarly, we would be able to establish that had the borrower's tax rate been 16 2/3%, the interest rate would rise by only 12% in response to a 10% higher inflation and still leave the borrower in the same real position. In terms of our demand and supply analysis, the borrower's demand curve for loans shifts upward by $\triangle \pi/(1-t)$ for each quantity of loans when the borrower's interest income is taxed at a rate t. This shift is shown in Figure 7-10.

The effects of expected inflation on the borrower can also be expressed more analytically. For each dollar of debt, the borrower's after tax interest cost is $(1-t)i$, where t is the tax rate and i the market interest rate. If the rate of inflation expected by the borrower increases by $\triangle \pi$, he would be able to pay $\triangle \pi$ more on an after tax basis and

TABLE 7-2 **Inflation, Taxes, and the Real Returns**

Case 1: No inflation, 50% corporate income tax rate

Interest expense	5 % per annum
Reduced taxes resulting from interest expenses	2½
After tax interest expense to firm	2½%

Case2: 10% expected inflation, 50% corporate income tax rate

Interest expense	25 % per annum
Reduced taxes resulting from interest expense	12½
After tax interest expense to firm	12½
Reduced real value of debt	10
After tax real interest expense to firm	2½%

remain in the same real position; the higher interest costs are exactly offset by the decreased real value of his debt. This condition can be expressed by the following equation:

$$\triangle \pi = (1-t)\triangle i,$$

FIGURE 7-10 The effects of the interaction of inflation and taxation on the demand for loans

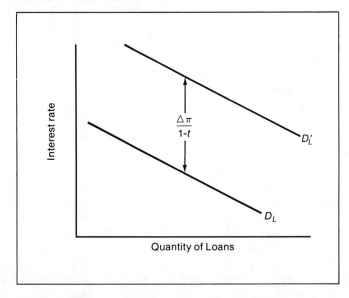

where the left side expresses the changed inflation and the right side expresses the higher interest cost to the borrower. As before, rearrangement shows the adjustment of the market rate required to leave the borrower in the same real position:

$$\triangle i = \frac{\pi}{1-t}.$$

This equation shows the adjustment in the market rate which is required to leave the borrower's cost of funds unchanged in response to a change in the expected rate of inflation. In terms of the demand and supply analysis, this equation states that the borrower's demand for funds, shown in Figure 7-10, shifts upwards by $\triangle \pi / (1-t)$ when the rate of inflation expected by the lender increases by $\triangle \pi$.

The Effects on Interest Rates.   We are now in a position to combine our analysis of lenders with our analysis of borrowers in order to determine how the presence of taxes modifies the response of market interest rates to inflation. We will given an example of the effects of an 10% increase in the expected rate of inflation (i.e., from 5% to 15% expected inflation) and, for the sake of avoiding undue complexity, we will consider only the case where the borrower and lender are subject to the same tax rate of 50%. As we already have seen, the lender's supply curve for loans can be expected to shift upward by 20% (i.e., $\triangle \pi / (1-t)$, where $\triangle \pi$ equals 10% and t equals 50%). In other words, the lender requires a 20% higher market rate to maintain his same real position. We have also seen that, as a result of the higher inflation, the borrower can pay a 20% higher interest rate and be no worse off. In other words, the borrower's demand for loans also shifts up by 20%. The equality of the two shifts results from our assumption that the borrower and lender are subject to the same tax rate and , just as important, they must both perceive the same change in expected inflation. From examining Figure 7-11, we can see that the market rate of interest goes up by 20% and also that the volume of lending and borrowing remains unchanged. While this last result may be somewhat surprising, the reason for it is quite clear. The change in the market rate was just sufficient to maintain the real after tax cost of funds to the borrower and also the real after tax return to the lender. Without any change in the real after tax interest rate, neither the lender nor the borrower has any incentive to change his behavior in the market for funds.

So far in our analysis of the interaction of inflation with the tax system and their combined effects on market interest rates, we have examined only one aspect of the tax system: the tax treatment of interest expense for borrowers and interest receipts for lenders. We have also considered only the case where lenders and borrowers are subject to the same tax rate. In reality, both lenders and borrowers are subject to a variety of different tax rates. Moreover, inflation interacts with many other aspects of the tax system in determining its overall effect on financial markets. Among these other features of the tax system affected by inflation are the treatment of allowable depreciation expense on real assets such as buildings and equipment, machinery, and the valuation of inventories used in producing the final product. In times of inflation, the allowable expenses for these items, which are based on amounts paid when they were purchased, may not correspond to the present amount that would have to be spent for replacement. Given the many ways in which inflation interacts with the tax system, our

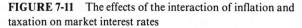

FIGURE 7-11   The effects of the interaction of inflation and
taxation on market interest rates

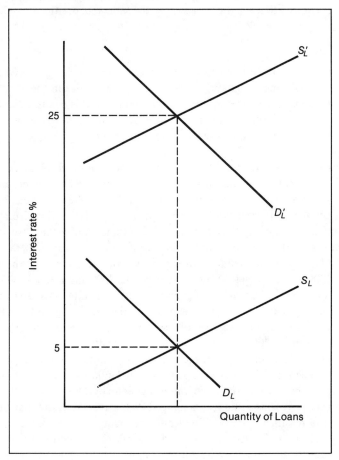

present purpose cannot be to give a comprehensive analysis of the topic. If we have
learned that the effects of inflation on financial markets cannot be studied without an
appreciation of the features of the tax system, our analysis will have fulfilled its purpose.

Summary.   In this section we have analyzed the effects of inflation on market interest
rates for the purpose of illustrating the equilibrium process at work in financial
markets. Because of the apparent persistence of inflation in our economy, the topic has
interest in its own right. Whether inflation accelerates or abates, any investor would be
wise to understand how changes in inflation affect market interest rates. We must
recognize, however, that our analysis has been incomplete in that we have only touched
on the effects of the tax system and have ignored other influences such as the international linkages among financial markets, the possible effects of inflation on the real rate
of interest itself, and a host of other complications. Nevertheless, our results remain

valid in general when these other factors are taken into account. Unanticipated inflation redistributes wealth from monetary creditors to monetary debtors. Lenders and borrowers will, however, eventually become aware of persistent inflation and adjust their behavior accordingly. Their response causes interest rates to rise so as to offset any changes in the real values of debts which would otherwise be caused by inflation. Empirical investigations tend to support the proposition that any increase in expected inflation leads to roughly an equal increase in market interest rates. Our investigation suggests that many of the changes that have occurred in financial markets in recent years can be attributed to the emergence of persistent inflation in our economy.

ENDNOTES

1. Fisher's equation as shown in the text is really an approximation. The π^e term takes into account the decreased real value of the principal but does not reflect the decreased real value of interest payments. The correct form would be $i_n = i_r + \pi^e + \pi^e i_r$. We have chosen to use the approximation so as to keep the analysis as simple as possible.
2. Our numerical example is one instance where we must take into account Fisher's exact equation shown in Footnote 1.
3. James E. Pesando, *The Impact of Inflation on Financial Markets in Canada* (Montreal: C.D. Howe Research Institute, 1977), p. 21.
4. *Ibid.*, p. 7.

Elementary Theory of Financial Markets **8**
PART 5: INTERNATIONAL ASPECTS OF MARKET EQUILIBRIUM

To this point our analysis of the microeconomics of the Canadian financial system has largely ignored the important fact that Canadian financial markets and many Canadian financial institutions are international in scope. The international connection broadens the range of alternatives open to assetholders and borrowers in Canada. Canadians can purchase the stocks and bonds of corporations and governments in the United States and other countries almost as easily as they can purchase Canadian securities; and major Canadian borrowers can borrow in financial markets throughout the world as well as in Canadian markets. The existence of these options has a powerful effect on the equilibrium of Canadian financial markets.

INTERNATIONAL YIELD DIFFERENTIALS

The widening of the field of choice for Canadian assetholders and debtors is important in itself. It permits a closer matching of asset holdings with asset preferences than would be possible with a narrower range of choice. However, it also imposes a powerful constraint on yields on Canadian securities, i.e., on Canadian interest rates.

Portfolio Selection and Borrowing. This constraint arises because expected yield is a major consideration in the selection of assets to be included in a portfolio, and expected interest cost is a major consideration in the borrowing decision.

    If expected yield was the only consideration in portfolio management, Canadian assetholders would switch between Canadian and foreign securities to obtain the maximum yield. They would sell Canadian securities from their portfolios and purchase foreign securities if the expected yield in Canada was below that on foreign securities, and vice versa. Similarly, if interest cost was the only consideration in the borrowing decision, Canadian borrowers would switch between Canadian and foreign sources of funds to minimize the expected interest cost. They would borrow abroad if interest rates were lower there, and in Canada if interest rates were lower here. Foreign assetholders and borrowers would presumably behave in like fashion, buying Canadian securities if their expected yields were relatively high and borrowing in Canada if the interest cost was relatively low.

The Convergence of Interest Rates.   Such behavior on the part of Canadian and world borrowers and assetholders means that Canadian and world interest rates will be drawn together. To illustrate this point, consider what would happen if Canadian interest rates were substantially higher than those in the rest of the world. Both Canadian and foreign assetholders would sell foreign securities and purchase Canadian securities, putting upward pressure on the prices of Canadian securities and hence downward pressure on Canadian interest rates. The opposite pressures would be present in foreign capital markets. Correspondingly, Canadian and foreign borrowers would avoid borrowing in the Canadian market, and would borrow instead in foreign markets, reducing the flow of new securities to the Canadian market, and adding to the upward pressure on security prices and to the downward pressure on interest rates in Canada. The opposite pressures would develop in foreign security markets. In this manner, Canadian and foreign interest rates would be drawn together.

The Magnet of World Interest Rates.   But we can draw an even stronger conclusion. It is likely that Canadian interest rates will do all of the adjusting; world and particularly United States interest rates will act like a magnet, drawing Canadian interest rates toward them. We must remember that Canada is a small country in a large world, and that our financial system is small by comparison to that of the United States let alone the rest of the world. Canadian demands for foreign securities and Canadian borrowing in foreign markets are unlikely to have a major impact on foreign security yields. However, foreign demands for Canadian securities will have a major impact in this country.

What will be the relationship between equilibrium yields on Canadian securities and yields on securities in the United States? If Canadian and American securities were *perfect substitutes* for each other in the minds of both Canadian and American assetholders, in equilibrium the yields on comparable Canadian and American securities would be *identical*. Any departure of yields from equality would induce a shift of demand or supply between the markets, until equality was reestablished. Canada and the United States would be part of a single, fully integrated North American capital market.

Some Evidence.   Is it true that yields on comparable Canadian and U.S. securities tend to be equal? The evidence provided by Figure 8-1 is interesting. While yields on the long-term bonds of the governments of Canada and the United States tend to move up and down together, they are far from equal. Although they are both the highest quality securities in the respective capital markets (and in this sense "comparable") in recent years, with minor aberrations, the yield on Canadian government bonds has been persistently higher than the yield on U.S. government bonds. What other factors are at work to explain this result?

FIGURE 8-1   Yield on long-term government bonds, Canada and the United States, 1966-1980

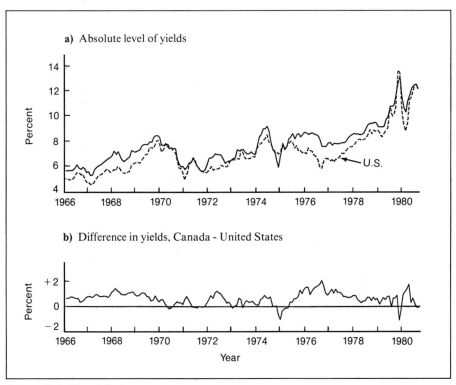

Source: *Bank of Canada Review.*

THE FOREIGN EXCHANGE MARKET

A major part of the answer lies in the existence of a type of risk which we have not yet discussed. This is a risk, peculiar to international transactions, which arises because two different currencies are involved, the currency of the lender and that of the borrower. The rate of exchange between the two currencies may change during the life of the financial instrument. We call this risk the *foreign exchange risk*. To understand it, we must first examine the foreign exchange market and the forces which determine the foreign exchange rate.

The Foreign Exchange Rate

As far as residents of Canada are concerned, foreign monies are just so many other financial instruments, instruments which we can call *foreign exchange*. These monies are useful for making payments outside Canada. There is a market — the foreign exchange market — in which foreign monies are bought and sold, and the prices established in this market — prices of foreign monies — are called foreign exchange rates. There are as many foreign exchange rates as there are foreign monies. However, in practice, the U.S. dollar plays the key role in the Canadian foreign exchange market. For this reason, we will adopt the convention of referring to *the foreign exchange rate* as *the Canadian dollar price of one U.S. dollar.*

It is important to keep this convention in mind. There are few terms in economics which generate as much confusion as "the foreign exchange rate." The confusion arises because one can quote the foreign exchange rate from either the Canadian point of view (the Canadian price of foreign money) or the foreign point of view (the foreign price of Canadian money). Mathematically, these prices are reciprocals. That is, if the foreign exchange rate, from the Canadian point of view, is Can. $1.20, the price of the Canadian dollar from the American point of view is U.S. $0.833. Many Canadians, nonetheless, cite the latter number as the foreign exchange rate. In order to minimize confusions, we will call the former (Can. $1.20) the *foreign exchange rate,* and the latter (U.S. $0.833) the *external value of the Canadian dollar.* When the foreign exchange rate rises (e.g., to Can. $1.25) the external value of the Canadian dollar falls (in this case to U.S. $0.80). This is commonly referred to as a *devaluation* or *depreciation* of the Canadian dollar. When the exchange rate falls (e.g., to Can. $1.15) the external value of the Canadian dollar rises (in this case to U.S. $0.87). This is commonly referred to as an *appreciation* of the Canadian dollar.

The Foreign Exchange Market

We mean by the foreign exchange market an international market in which Canadian dollars are exchanged for foreign monies, particularly U.S. dollars. Transactions occur on three levels: in the retail market, in the interbank market, and in the international market.

The Canadian Retail Market.   The chartered banks are the heart of the foreign exchange market in Canada. As a part of their function of providing payments facilities for the economy, the banks "deal" in foreign exchange. That is, they buy and sell foreign exchange to meet the needs of their customers, be they businesses, households, or governments.

If the banks are to satisfy the requirements of their customers immediately and without question, they must hold an inventory of foreign exchange. To this end, the banks hold some foreign currency in the vaults of their branches, and maintain deposits with foreign correspondents. These are the banks' "working balances." Foreign exchange purchased through the branch network is added to the working balances, and foreign exchange sold through the branch network is drawn out of the working balances.

However, both profit maximization and the ever-present foreign exchange risk dictate that working balances should be no larger than is necessary for efficiency in foreign exchange operations. This means that the banks must have an efficient mechanism for the quick disposal of excess foreign exchange acquired through their branches, and for the quick acquisition of foreign exchange to replenish working balances should they be depleted as a result of the activities of the branches. Such a mechanism is provided by the interbank market.

The Interbank Market.   Physically, the interbank market in Canada is primarily located in Toronto where there is a foreign exchange brokerage office which is owned and operated by the Canadian Bankers' Association and to which only members of the Association and the Bank of Canada have access. This broker dominates the interbank business in Canada, although in recent years a number of private brokerage firms have also opened for business. Banks with excess foreign exchange offer it for sale to other banks through the broker. Similarly, banks which are deficient in foreign exchange submit bids through the broker for the required amounts. When a transaction is arranged — when the broker manages to find a buyer and a seller who can agree on an amount and a price — both the amount and the price (but not the identities of the principals) are reported to all participants in the market, thus providing them with continuous, current information on the state of the market.

The foreign exchange rate established in the interbank market — shall we call it the "wholesale rate"? — is the key rate. It is the one reported in official statistics of the foreign exchange rate. To the banks it represents the cost of acquiring foreign exchange for their retail operations. Accordingly, they use it, with an appropriate mark-up, as the basis for setting their "retail" rate.

Changes in the exchange rate established in the interbank market reflect the balance of supply and demand pressures in the whole Canadian banking system. However, the foreign exchange rate is not established in the Canadian interbank market in isolation. There is a necessary international dimension to interbank foreign exchange transactions, and hence to the foreign exchange market.

International Arbitrage.   When the foreign exchange rate is determined by trading on the interbank market in Toronto, its reciprocal, the external value of the Canadian dollar, is also determined. However, an interbank foreign exchange market also exists in New York (and in other financial centers around the world), where Canadian dollars as well as other currencies are bought and sold. Clearly, the price of a Canadian dollar in the New York market must be the same as the external value of the Canadian dollar in the Toronto market (making due allowance for the cost of transactions between the markets, of course), or it would be profitable to purchase Canadian dollars in one market for sale in the other.

For example, suppose the price of one U.S. dollar established in the Toronto market was $1.20, implying an external value of the Canadian dollar of U.S. $0.833. If the price of the Canadian dollar in New York was U.S. $0.84, it would be profitable to exchange Canadian dollars for U.S. dollars in New York, and then to sell the U.S. dollars in Toronto. The gross profit (from which we must deduct transactions costs) would be U.S. $0.007 per dollar transferred. On a large volume of funds, this would be a very attractive proposition.

Transactions of this type, involving buying in one market and simultaneously selling in another, are called *arbitrage*. Arbitrage may involve more than two foreign exchange markets, and it may be conducted by professional arbitrageurs who are alert "disorderly cross-rates" of exchange, or by the normal participants in the market. Perhaps most important as a continuing force in the market are the operations of banks, buying foreign exchange in the cheapest market, and selling their excess foreign exchange in the dearest market. The banks are well organized to do this, being in instantaneous contact with their agencies in New York and other major international financial centers.

An International Market.   The important point is that arbitrage will bring foreign exchange rates in different markets into line with each other, almost instantaneously. In this way, arbitrage ties the foreign exchange markets in all countries together into a single international foreign exchange market. In this market what appears to Canadians as a demand for foreign exchange appears to the rest of the world as a supply of Canadian dollars. Similarly, what is from the Canadian point of view a supply of foreign exchange, is, from the non-resident's point of view, a demand for Canadian dollars. It does not matter whether a given exchange of Canadian dollars for U.S. dollars occurs in Toronto or in New York; arbitrage will ensure that it has the same effect on the foreign exchange rate in both markets.

Supply and Demand in the Foreign Exchange Market.   So much for the institutions of the foreign exchange market. They simply provide the framework within which the forces of supply and demand work themselves out. If we are to understand the significance of the foreign exchange market and the foreign exchange rate for the functioning of the Canadian financial system, we must reach behind the institutions of the market and explore the underlying demand and supply forces.

Demands to exchange Canadian dollars for foreign exchange can originate either inside Canada or abroad, and can be for many different purposes, including a simple desire to hold foreign money in place of Canadian money as an asset, perhaps for speculation on changes in the exchange rate. However, in general we can think of the demand for foreign exchange as arising out of the desires of Canadian residents to make payments abroad, for the purchase of goods and services from non-residents, to make gifts, to purchase equities or bonds from non-residents, or to make other investments abroad. Similarly, the supply of foreign exchange arises out of the desires of non-residents to make payments in Canada, either for the purchase of goods and services from residents of Canada, to make gifts to Canadian residents, for the purchase of equities or bonds, or to make other types of investments in Canada.

The analysis of supply and demand in the foreign exchange market must start with these flows of international payments — with Canada's balance of international payments.

TABLE 8-1   **Canada's balance of international payments, 1981 ($ Millions)**

I. CURRENT ACCOUNT

Merchandise exports	$ 84 221	Merchandise imports	$76 870
Non-merchandise exports		Non-merchandise imports	
Travel	3 760	Travel	4 876
Freight and shipping	4 279	Freight and shipping	3 792
Interest and dividends	3 321	Interest and dividends	13 635
Other services	3 887	Other services	6 092
		Withholding tax	1 110
Total: goods and services	$99 468	Total: goods and services	$106 375
International transfers:		International transfers:	
Inheritances, immigrants' funds and other private remittances	3 075	Inheritances, emigrants' funds and other private remittances	796
TOTAL: Current receipts	$102 543	Official contributions	718
		TOTAL: Current payments	$107 889
		Net balance on current account	−5 346

II. CAPITAL ACCOUNT*

Direct investment	
Foreign direct investment in Canada	−$4 600
Canadian direct investment abroad	− 5 900
Portfolio investment: long-term forms	
Canadian securities	
Trade in outstanding issues (net)	86
New issues	13 493
Retirements	− 2 953
Foreign securities	− 95
Other long term capital flows	527
Portfolio investment: short-term forms	
Resident holdings of foreign currency bank balances	11 229
Non-resident holdings of Canadian:	
Bank deposits	1 401
Money market instruments	1 850
Other short term capital transactions (net)	592
Net balance on capital account	$15 630

III. OFFICIAL MONETARY MOVEMENTS*

Official international reserve assets†	− $172
Official monetary liabilities	− 1 044
Net official monetary movement	−$1 216

TABLE 8-1   (continued)

IV. RECONCILIATION

Net balance on:

Current account	−$5 346
Capital account	15 630
Official monetary movements	− 1 216
Errors and omissions	− 9 068

* A minus sign indicates an increase in foreign assets or a decrease in foreign liabilities (a net capital outflow).

† Excluding a new allocation of special drawing rights with the International Monetary Fund, which did not reflect transactions affecting the Canadian balance of international payments.

SOURCE: Statistics Canada, *Quarterly Estimates of the Canadian Balance of International Payments.* Second Quarter, 1982 (Ottawa, 1982).

THE BALANCE OF
INTERNATIONAL PAYMENTS

The balance of international payments is a statistical summary of the actual flow of economic transactions between residents of Canada and residents of the rest of the world during a given period of time. Statistics on Canada's balance of international payments for the year 1981 are presented in Table 8-1.

The Accounts

For purposes of balance of payments accounting, international transactions are commonly divided into three major categories: current account, capital account, and official monetary movements. For our purposes, the distinctions are important because they suggest the variety of economic forces which affect demand and supply in the foreign exchange market and hence the foreign exchange rate.

Current Account.   Recorded in the current account are transactions involving receipts and payments for goods (merchandise exports and imports), services (travel, freight and shipping, etc.), and recurring international transfer payments (public and private gifts). Receipts give rise to a supply of foreign exchange in the foreign exchange market; payments give rise to a demand for foreign exchange.

Clearly, the forces which determine the flow of transactions recorded in the current account are complex. Some are non-economic. Thus, political, personal, and humanitarian motives affect international gifts, although the income of potential donors, for example, may also be important. Some reflect history. Thus, payments of interest and dividends involve contractual arrangements made in the past in connection with international investments made then (although, again, current profits may well affect the international flow of dividends). The important principle to keep in mind, however, is that current account transactions involve either a use of income (imports of goods and services, gifts), a payment for the services of factors of production (interest and dividends), or a source of income (exports of goods and services). It should not be surprising, therefore, that the forces which affect the flow of aggregate demand, income, and output in Canada and abroad are also the forces which affect the current account, including those factors which affect choices between Canadian-produced and foreign-produced goods and services (i.e., product characteristics, relative prices, and the foreign exchange rate). These are all matters which we will explore in more detail in Chapter 22. Suffice it to say here that any disturbance to income levels, relative prices in Canada and abroad, or the foreign exchange rate will affect the flow of current account transactions and hence supply and demand in the foreign exchange market.

Capital Account.   Recorded in the capital account are international transactions involving the purchase and sale of financial assets and liabilities — international borrowing and lending. Whereas current account transactions are an aspect of income and expenditure flows, capital account transactions are an aspect of the accumulation of wealth, including portfolio balance decisions.

The capital account reports the *flow* of international transactions in financial instruments during a given period of time (in Table 8-1, the year 1981). This should not be confused with the *stock* of international indebtedness outstanding at any point in time. The magnitudes are related, of course, in the same way that saving and wealth are related. The capital account of the balance of international payments shows the international transactions which produce a change in the size and composition of the balance of international indebtedness.[1] It should not be surprising that the annual capital flows are small relative to the stock of outstanding debt. For purposes of comparison, Canada's balance of international indebtedness as of December 31, 1977 (the most recent date for which data are available), is shown in Table 8-2.

International investments can be classified in as many ways as there are characteristics of assets and liabilities and of borrowers and lenders, and the publications of Statistics Canada provide much detailed information. Table 8-1 shows three basic classifications: by residency of borrower or lender (resident/non-resident); by term to maturity (long-term/short-term); and by ownership and control (direct/portfolio). Direct investment is associated with non-resident control of corporations: non-residents invest in business firms which are operating in Canada but which are controlled by non-residents, or Canadians invest in business firms which are operating abroad but which are controlled by Canadians. The incentive for such investment is presumably expected profits. Portfolio investment, by contrast, implies international investment in securities without any implication of foreign control. It may involve transactions in Canadian or foreign stocks or bonds, including securities issued by business firms, financial intermediaries, local and national governments, and international organizations; and the securities may be long-term or short-term, new issues or outstanding issues. The incentive to such investment is presumably expected yield, but the possibilities for portfolio diversification may also be important.

It is through the capital account, then, that the Canadian financial system is linked to the international financial system. But it is also through the capital account that all disturbances in Canadian and major world financial systems are transmitted to the Canadian foreign exchange market, and hence to the foreign exchange rate. A rise in

TABLE 8-2   **Canada's balance of international indebtedness, December 31, 1977 ($ Billions)**

I. ASSETS

Direct investment	$13.4
Portfolio investment	
Long-term securities (stocks, bonds)	5.3
Miscellaneous private assets	1.8
Bank deposits (private holdings)	3.5
Other short-term instruments	6.4
Government of Canada, loans etc.	6.9
Net official monetary assets	4.7
Recorded assets	42.0
Errors and omissions (assumed to be assets)	12.7
TOTAL: Gross assets	$54.7

II. LIABILITIES

Direct investment	$47.0
Portfolio investment	
Government bonds (all levels)	23.7
Corporate securities	15.4
Miscellaneous (mortgages, real estate, etc.)	9.6
Bank deposits of non-residents	3.9
Other short-term instruments (money market, receivables, etc.)	9.2
TOTAL: Gross liabilities	108.8
Balance of international indebtedness (Gross assets — gross liabilities)	$54.00

SOURCE: Statistics Canada, *Canada's International Investment Position, 1977* (Ottawa, 1981).

rates of return on investments abroad will attract funds from Canada, creating a demand for foreign exchange, and putting upward pressure on the foreign exchange rate. The opposite will happen if there is a decline in rates of return abroad. The foreign exchange rate will be very sensitive to the multitude of factors that may affect international investment decisions.

Official International Monetary Movements.   There is a third major account in the balance of international payments, which is also a capital account, a record of transactions in assets and liabilities. However, because of the special role of these transactions, they are recorded separately. In the monetary account are recorded transactions involving Canada's official external reserves — a pool of gold, foreign exchange, and drawing rights at the International Monetary Fund (an international bank which advances foreign exchange to member governments) owned by the government and used for intervention in the foreign exchange market. The government will sell foreign exchange (reducing a Canadian asset = a *capital inflow*) to prevent a rise in the foreign exchange rate (= a depreciation of the Canadian dollar); and it will purchase foreign exchange (increasing a Canadian asset = a *capital outflow*) to prevent a fall in the exchange rate (an appreciation of the Canadian dollar).

The separate identification of the monetary account makes a very important point about the determination of the foreign exchange rate. Not only is the rate subject to market forces coming through the current account and the capital account, it is also subject to government policy coming through the monetary account. Anticipation of the behavior of the exchange rate involves predicting not only market developments but also government policy.

The Balance of Payments Identity

A basic principle of balance of payments accounting is that the sum of the net balance on current account and the net balance on capital account must equal the net change in official reserves. We can express this as an identity:

$$
\begin{array}{c}
\begin{array}{ccccc}
\text{EXPORTS OF} & & \text{IMPORTS OF} & & \text{CAPITAL} \text{CAPITAL} \\
\text{GOODS AND} & - & \text{GOODS AND} & + & \text{IMPORTS} \text{EXPORTS} \\
\text{SERVICES} & & \text{SERVICES} & &
\end{array} \\[2ex]
\begin{array}{cl}
= & \begin{array}{c} \text{NET OFFICIAL} \\ \text{MONETARY} \\ \text{MOVEMENT} \end{array}
\end{array}
\end{array}
\qquad (8.1)
$$

In this equation the expression "capital imports" refers to the inflow of funds in payment for securities sold to non-residents (including the inflow of funds for direct investment in Canada). *A capital import involves either an increase in Canada's external liabilities* (in any form, including non-resident equity in Canadian firms), *or a reduction in Canada's external assets.* Similarly, the expression "capital export" refers to the outflow of funds in payment for securities purchased from non-residents. *A capital export involves either a reduction in Canada's external liabilities or an increase in Canada's external assets.*

The validity of the balance of payments identity should be intuitively obvious. However, to demonstrate the point, consider the situation in which there is a negative balance of $100 000 in the current account (i.e., imports of goods and services exceed exports of goods and services by $100 000). One way of looking at the current account is to say that the export of goods and services provides the foreign exchange to finance the import of goods and services. In the present case, exports will not pay for the full value of imports. How is the deficit to be financed?

If you think about it, there are a strictly limited number of possibilities. It is possible that residents of Canada will draw down their holdings of foreign exchange, or perhaps will sell foreign securities, providing foreign exchange through the foreign exchange market to importers, permitting them to pay for the extra $100 000 worth of goods and services. But this reduction in Canada's external assets is a capital import. The current account deficit is financed by a capital import, and the balance of payments identity holds.

Alternatively, the foreign vendors of the goods and services might extend credit, or non-residents might decide to purchase Canadian securities or, indeed, to increase their holdings of Canadian money, thus making the necessary foreign exchange available through the foreign exchange market. However, any of these occurrences imply an increase in Canada's external liabilities, and hence a capital import. Again, the current account deficit is financed by a capital import, and the balance of payments identity holds.

All of these capital account transactions depend on a fortuitous coincidence of circumstances. Suppose that under the existing conditions in Canadian and foreign financial markets no Canadian holder of foreign currency assets chooses to dispose of part of his holdings and no foreign assetholder is willing to take additional Canadian dollar assets into his portfolio. Then, *either the government must provide the foreign exchange out of its holdings, or the current account deficit cannot occur.* There are no other possibilities. *A current account deficit must be financed either by a private capital inflow or an official capital inflow.*

Exactly the opposite propositions hold true for a current account surplus.

Errors and Omissions.   While the balance of payments identity *must* hold at all times, the balance of payments statistics seldom confirm it. Difficult problems of measurement face the balance of payments accountant. Some items are based on official reports (e.g., for import tax purposes); some are obtained through the cooperation of private bodies; some are estimated from related data; and some are missed completely. As a result, the reconciliation statement at the bottom of Table 8-1 contains an "errors and omissions" item, which shows the net difference between the two sides of the equation. Historically, this item has been relatively small (which does not mean that the errors were necessarily small; there may have been offsetting errors). In the 1970s, the errors increased in size, and in 1981, as shown in the table, they reached the astounding total of $9 billion.

External Aspects of Financial Equilibrium

As a statement of Canada's external transactions, the balance of international payments is also a summary of the demand and supply forces in the foreign exchange market, and, together with the balance of international indebtedness, it gives us a quantitative perspective on the importance of international factors in the determination of equilibrium in Canadian financial markets. Without going into a more detailed analysis of the balance of payments, two points should be emphasized.

First, it should be obvious from the size of the capital account and the balance of international indebtedness that external factors cannot be trivial in the determination of equilibrium in Canadian financial markets. International capital *flows* are large, both in and out of Canada; and the *stock* of international assets and liabilities, built up as a result of flows over many years, is even larger. An equilibrium set of yields in Canadian financial markets must be one which leaves foreign (as well as Canadian) assetholders content with both their current holdings of Canadian assets and the rate of increase in these assets. Otherwise, they will make adjustments which cannot help affecting Canadian financial markets. In thinking about the economics of the Canadian financial system, this is a relationship which we neglect at our peril.

Second, the determination of the foreign exchange rate is of basic importance. It is determined in the foreign exchange market, and it must be set so that demand and supply (as reflected in the balance of payments accounts) balance. But lurking behind the accounts are many complex economic forces. All of the forces which affect incomes and prices in Canada and the rest of the world will funnel into the market through the current account; and all of the forces affecting interest rates and profit opportunities in Canada and the rest of the world will funnel into the market through the capital account. And, of course, we must not ignore government policy, as reflected in official monetary movements. Given the multitude of complex forces at work, it should not be surprising that *the foreign exchange rate is subject to unanticipated changes,* of both small and large magnitude (particularly if the government does not have a policy of maintaining a "fixed" exchange rate). The outcome of most international transactions — particularly the return on assets and the cost of borrowing — will be affected by changes in the exchange rate. Thus, in analyzing equilibrium in Canadian financial markets, we must take into account a *pervasive foreign exchange risk.*

FOREIGN EXCHANGE RISK AND MARKET EQUILIBRIUM

A foreign exchange risk exists whenever an assetholder owns a financial instrument calling for fixed future payments in a foreign money, or whenever a debtor has an obligation to make fixed future payments in a foreign money. It is possible that, before the payment date, the foreign exchange rate will change, so that the fixed amount of foreign money will represent a different amount of domestic money than was expected when the asset was purchased or the obligation entered into. To the Canadian asset-holder, the risk is that the foreign exchange rate will drop. The fixed sums of foreign money he will receive as interest and principal on his foreign assets will produce fewer Canadian dollars than expected, and the yield on the asset will correspondingly be less than expected. By contrast, to the Canadian borrower the risk is that the exchange rate will rise. If this happens, the fixed future payments of foreign money which he is obligated to make will cost him more Canadian dollars than expected, and the actual interest cost of the loan will be correspondingly greater than expected.

Fixed and Flexible Exchange Rates

Many economists have advocated a policy of *fixed exchange rates* and, from time to time, governments have adopted such a policy. In general, the exchange rate is not rigidly fixed, but rather its fluctuations are confined within narrow limits. Thus, from 1946 through mid-1971, by an international agreement (the Bretton Woods Agreement) almost all Western nations pledged to intervene in the foreign exchange market to keep the foreign exchange rate within 1% of a declared par value. This system collapsed in the early 1970s, for reasons which will be explored later (Chapter 23), and the world went on a regime of *flexible exchange rates*, without any explicit commitments from governments about par rates of exchange.

With a flexible exchange rate the risks of exchange rate changes are obvious. The rate can vary from day to day, or from month to month, by large or small amounts. However, we should not think that the system of fixed exchange rates was devoid of foreign exchange risk, for two reasons. First, par values could be adjusted without notice, and occasionally were. Such discrete changes tended to be relatively large. Hence, while the probability of a change in the par value occurring during the term of a foreign investment might be very small, the potential loss (or gain) from such a change might be very large. There was a major foreign exchange risk even though the foreign exchange rate was "fixed." Second, for short-term international investments, even very small changes in the exchange rate, say within the Bretton Woods range of 1% on either side of par, could have serious consequences.

Foreign Exchange Risk and Term of Investment

This point is illustrated in Example 8-1, in which we have assumed that the yield on U.S. treasury bills is 12% per annum whereas the yield on Canadian treasury bills is 11% per annum. If yield was the only consideration and if the foreign exchange rate was firmly fixed at $1.20, the Canadian investor would choose a U.S. treasury bill in preference to a Canadian treasury bill (ignoring transactions costs and any differential in the taxation of interest earned abroad).

However, as the example makes clear, this yield advantage in investing in the U.S. treasury bill would disappear if the exchange rate dropped by as little as one quarter of 1% in the 90-day period. Any larger drop in the exchange rate would make it advantageous to have invested in Canadian treasury bills, even though the raw yield is smaller. A drop in the exchange rate greater than 2.9% in the 90-day period would mean that the yield to a Canadian investing in the U.S. treasury bill was actually negative. Of course, if the exchange rate increased, the Canadian investor would receive an unexpected bonus. We leave it to you to work out an appropriate example.

For an even shorter-term investment, the drop in the exchange rate which would eliminate the relative gain from investing in U.S. treasury bills would be much smaller. Thus, if the Canadian and U.S. treasury bills in Example 8-1 were for 30 days, the drop in the exchange rate which would eliminate the advantage of investing in the U.S. bills would be less than one-tenth of 1% — from $1.20 to $1.199. Such fluctuations are commonplace. For long-term bonds, the calculation is more complicated, and we will not provide an example. However, the basic principal stands. A drop in the exchange rate will reduce the gains from investing in foreign securities; but the drop required to eliminate the relative gains from long-term investments is much larger than for short-term investments. In this very restricted sense, the foreign exchange risk is larger for short-term than for long-term international investments.

A parallel argument applies to a Canadian borrower considering the options of borrowing in Canada or abroad. Presumably, he would be attracted to foreign sources of funds if the interest rate abroad was lower than in Canada. In this case, the risk which he faces is that the exchange rate will rise. If the exchange rate rises between the time at which the foreign debt is contracted and the date of repayment, the effective cost of funds will be higher than expected. Of course, if the exchange rate falls, the effective cost of funds will be less than expected.

Thus, exchange risk permeates all international asset and liability transactions; and like all risks it is two-sided. There is a possibility of losing through unfavorable movements in the exchange rage, and the possibility of gaining through favorable movements (and the favorable and unfavorable movements are opposite for borrowers and lenders). It is also important to note that the potential losses (or gains), measured in terms of the effective yield on the foreign asset (or the effective interest cost on the

EXAMPLE 8-1   **The foreign exchange risk on short-term foreign investments**

Initial conditions

(1)	United States dollar price of U.S. Treasury Bill yielding 12% per annum, par value U.S. $1000*	= U.S.$	971
(2)	Spot exchange rate	= Can.$	1.20
(3)	Canadian dollar price of U.S. treasury bill (1) × (2)	= Can.$	1165

Case 1
Spot exchange rate constant at $1.20

(4)	Return at the end of 90 days (U.S.$ 1000 × 1.2)		= Can.$	1200
(5)	Gross gain (4) − (3) or 3% for 90 days	= 12% per annum	= Can.$	35
(6)	Yield on Canadian treasury bills	= 11% per annum		
(7)	Net gain (5) − (6)	= 1% per annum		

Case 2
Spot exchange rate falls by 0.25% to $1.197

(8)	Return at the end of 90 days (U.S.$ 1000 × 1.197)		= Can.$	1197
(9)	Gross gain (8) − (3) or 2.7% for 90 days =	11% per annum	= Can.$	32
(10)	Yield on Canadian treasury bills	= 11% per annum		
(11)	Net gain	= 0% per annum		

Case 3
Spot exchange rate falls by 1% to $1.88

(12)	Return at the end of 90 days (U.S.$ 1000 × 1.188)		= Can.$	1188
(13)	Gross gain (12) − (3) or 2% for 90 days =	8% per annum	= Can.$	23
(14)	Yield on Canadian treasury bills	= 11% per annum		
(15)	Net loss	= −3% per annum		

Case 4
Spot exchange rate falls by 2.9% to $1.165

(16)	Return at the end of 90 days (U.S.$ 1000 × 1.165)		= Can.$	1165
(17)	Gross gain (16) − (3) or 0% for 90 days =	0% per annum	= Can.$	0
(18)	Yield on Canadian treasury bills	= 11% per annum		
(19)	Net loss	= 11% per annum		

NOTE: Some computations may not work out exactly because of rounding.
* See Table 1, Appendix to Chapter 5, p. 102.

foreign liability), from a given change in the exchange rate, are much greater for short-term investments (or debts) than for long-term ones.

So much for the nature of the foreign exchange risk. The important question is: what are the implications of this risk for equilibrium in Canadian financial markets? In particular, why does this factor help explain the persistent and relatively stable divergence between yields on Canadian and U.S. securities shown in Figure 8-1?

Risk Aversion Once More

The answer can be found in the general assumption that assetholders are risk averters. That is, other things being equal, they will demand a higher yield before they will take the relatively more risky security into their portfolios.

It should be obvious that what we have said about the exchange risk facing Canadian assetholders who purchase foreign securities applies also to foreign assetholders who purchase Canadian securities. Other things being equal, they will demand a relatively higher yield before they will choose a Canadian security over a comparable security denominated in their own currency.

It is also important to remember that during the period covered by Figure 8-1, Canada was almost continuously a net importer of capital. That is, foreign assetholders were steadily accumulating claims on Canadian governments, corporations and households much in excess of the corresponding Canadian claims on non-residents. From 1960 through 1977, Canada's net international indebtedness increased from $17 billion to $54 billion. In this book, we cannot explore the underlying "real" economic forces inducing this heavy net international borrowing. However, it is useful to consider what was happening in financial markets to product this result.

In terms of the analytical concepts developed earlier, at the prevailing level of yields on financial instruments the aggregate flow of funds demanded as a result of the borrowing decisions of Canadian spending units was continuously and significantly in excess of the supply of funds made available as a result of the simultaneous saving decisions of Canadian households. If an inflow of capital, in the form of foreign purchases of Canadian financial instruments, had not been possible, the excess demand for funds in Canadian capital markets would have forced Canadian security yields to higher levels. This would have resulted in a smaller accumulation of real assets in all sectors of the Canadian economy, i.e., by governments, consumers, and particularly businesses. In other words, foreign assetholders were bribed to finance part of the capital formation which occurred in Canada during this period through the offer of an attractive yield on Canadian financial instruments. That yield had to be sufficiently in excess of yields in U.S. capital markets to compensate for all risks, including the foreign exchange risk.

THE AVOIDANCE OF RISK

It would be inappropriate to leave the discussion of foreign exchange risk without some consideration of techniques of avoiding this risk. The basic principle, called *hedging,* is quite straightforward. It simply involves the assumption of one risk to offset an equal and opposite risk.

Hedging

In our discussion of the nature of foreign exchange risk we noted that the situations of assetholders and debtors were opposite. While the holder of a foreign currency asset *loses* if the exchange rate falls, the holder of a foreign currency liability *gains*. If the exchange rate rises the assetholder gains while the debtor loses. As a result, if someone holds simultaneously a foreign currency asset *and* a foreign currency liability of the same magnitude, he will have no foreign exchange risk. Whatever he loses on the assets as a result of a fall of the exchange rate he will automatically gain on the liability, and vice versa if the exchange rate rises. In other words, he has a *hedge* against exchange rates changes. *Foreign exchange rate risk exists only when one has an open position — when foreign exchange assets and liabilities are not equal.*

This principle is of vital importance to financial intermediaries, particularly chartered banks, which are heavily engaged in foreign exchange transactions but which do not which to assume any significant foreign exchange risk. It also helps explain some borrowing in foreign financial markets. Thus, some business firms, which have substantial continuing foreign exchange earnings as a result of their export business, feel that this provides a natural hedge against foreign borrowing. However, the important application of the principle from our point of view involves the use of *forward exchange contracts* to eliminate the risk on short-term foreign currency investments.

Forward Exchange

In our discussion of the foreign exchange rate we did not recognize that at any time there may be several different prices in the foreign exchange market for the same foreign money, depending upon the *time of delivery*. The basic distinction of importance to us is the one between *spot exchange,* involving immediate delivery, and *forward exchange,* involving delivery on some specified future date.[2]

Forward Exchange Contracts.   A forward exchange contract is an agreement for the purchase or sale of a specified amount of foreign money on a specified future date *at a price agreed upon at the time the contract is signed regardless of the actual spot exchange rate prevailing in the market on that future date.* A forward contract fixes the exchange rate for a particular transaction which will take place at a particular time in the future, and thus serves to *eliminate the foreign exchange risk for that transaction.*

We tend to think of the foreign exchange market in terms of transactions in spot exchange. However, an active market also exists in forward exchange contracts, although the market is largely confined to contracts of 180 days or less. Very long-term contracts are rare. Thus, on any given day in the foreign exchange market there will be a structure of foreign rates, not just a single spot exchange rate. There will be a set of forward exchange rates, i.e., rates at which contracts can be negotiated for the purchase or sale of forward exchange 30 days, 60 days, 90 days, etc., in the future.

Commercial Transactions in Forward Exchange.   Forward exchange contracts are important to many firms engaged in foreign trade in goods and services where there is a delay between the time a contract is signed for the delivery of merchandise and the time at which payment is to be made. If payment is to be made in foreign currency, the profitability of the transaction may well depend on the level of the exchange rate. A rise in the exchange rate would increase the cost of goods and services to an importer, and a fall in the exchange rate would reduce the returns from sales of goods and services by exporters. Each can fix the foreign exchange rate for any given contract by means of a forward exchange contract —and since their interests are opposite (the importer wants to buy in the forward market, the exporter wants to sell) there is a basis for a market. The institutional arrangements are provided by the banking system. Banks will enter contracts to sell forward exchange to the importer and to buy it from the exporter. Of course, the bank's selling price will be slightly higher than its buying price, the difference being its implicit "fee" for services rendered.

"Covered" Foreign Investments

Most transactions in forward exchange are related to attempts to avoid the foreign exchange risk on commercial transactions. However, forward exchange contracts also have obvious advantages for short-term international investors. They permit the purchaser of a foreign currency asset to fix the rate of exchange at which he will convert the proceeds of his investment back to his own currency, and thus eliminate the potential foreign exchange risk on his investment.

In Example 8-1, we assumed that the yield on 90-day Canadian treasury bills was substantially lower than the yield on comparable U.S. securities. The example made it abundantly clear that any Canadian assetholder who was tempted by this yield differential into investing in the U.S. security would assume a serious foreign exchange risk. A very small change in the exchange rate could not only eliminate the underlying yield advantage to investing in the United States, but also turn a potential net gain into an actual loss. However, at the time he purchases the U.S. security the Canadian assetholder can avoid this risk by simultaneously entering into a forward exchange contract with his bank in which the bank agrees to purchase U.S. dollars in the amount of the redemption value of the U.S. treasury bills (i.e., U.S. $1000 in the example) at an exchange rate agreed upon now.

Note carefully that two foreign exchange transactions are involved. The Canadian assetholder *simultaneously* purchases spot exchange and "sells" forward exchange. Such a pairing of spot and forward exchange transactions is commonly called a *swap*. When an assetholder makes a foreign investment in this way we say that the investment is *covered*. That is, the forward exchange contract serves to "cover" any potential foreign exchange risk.

A *covered foreign investment, thus, will be riskless* (assuming the foreign security is also riskless). The important question facing the Canadian assetholder is whether such an investment can also be *profitable*. Obviously, this depends not only on the level of yields in the two countries, but also on the relationship between the forward and the spot exchange rates.

The Yield on Covered Foreign Investments.   Again, an example may be useful in order to develop this point. Example 8-2 uses the same assumptions about the spot exchange rate and relative yields on treasury bills as were used in Example 8-1.

EXAMPLE 8-2   **The forward exchange rate and the net yield on covered short-term foreign investments**

Initial conditions

(1)	United States dollar price of U.S. treasury bill yielding 12% per annum, par value U.S. $1000*	= U.S.$	971
(2)	Spot exchange rate	= Can.$	1.20
(3)	Canadian dollar price of U.S. treasury bill (1) × (2)	= Can.$	1165

Case 1
90-day forward exchange rate = $1.20

(4)	Return at the end of 90 days (U.S.$ 1000 × $1.20)		= Can.$	1200
(5)	Gross gain (4) − (3) or 3% for 90 days	= 12% per annum	= Can.$	35
(6)	Yield on Canadian treasury bills	= 11% per annum		
(7)	Net gain (5) − (6)	= 1% per annum		

Case 2
90-day forward exchange rate = $1.197

(8)	Return at the end of 90 days (U.S.$ 1000 × 1.197)		= Can.$	1197
(9)	Gross gain (8) − (3) or 2.75% for 90 days	= 11% per annum	= Can.$	32
(10)	Yield on Canadian treasury bills	= 11% per annum		
(11)	Net gain (9) −(10)	= 0% per annum		

Case 3
90-day forward exchange rate = $1.212

(12)	Return at the end of 90 days (U.S.$ 1000 × 1.212)		= Can.$	1212
(13)	Gross gain (12) − (3) or 4% for 90 days	= 16% per annum	= Can.$	47
(14)	Yield on Canadian treasury bills	= 11% per annum		
(15)	Net gain (13) − (14)	= 5% per annum		

* See Table 1, Appendix to Chapter 5.

However, in the present case we assume that the funds invested in U.S. treasury bills are returned to Canada at the 90-day forward exchange rate prevailing in the market *now* rather than at the spot exchange rate which may prevail in the market at the end of 90 days. This makes the forward exchange rate a crucial factor in the investment decision.

Clearly, if the forward exchange rate is equal to the spot exchange rate (as in Case 1), there will be a strong advantage to the Canadian assetholder in investing in U.S. treasury bills rather than in Canadian treasury bills. Through the forward exchange market, the international investor can arrange to sell his U.S. dollars for the same price which he paid for them, and he will thus gain the full international differential in security yields, in this case 1% per annum. In the world of short-term investments, that is a very large differential — and, what is important, it is one which the purchaser of the U.S. treasury bill can obtain *with no additional risk*.

The difference that the level of the forward exchange rate can make is illustrated in Cases 2 and 3. The first of these cases demonstrates that if the forward exchange rate is as little as one-quarter of 1% below the spot exchange rate, it eliminates any advantage to investing in the U.S. treasury bills on a fully hedged basis, in spite of the 1% yield differential. Any lower forward exchange rate would reduce the covered yield on U.S. treasury bills below that on Canadian treasury bills. Case 2 illustrates the proposition that *if the forward exchange rate is lower than the spot exchange rate it will reduce the net yield on covered foreign investments.*

Case 3 illustrates the opposite proposition. *If the forward exchange rate is above the spot exchange rate it will increase the net yield on covered foreign investments above the raw yield.* In the case cited, a forward rate 1% above the spot rate increased the yield to Canadian investors in U.S. treasury bills by 4% per annum.

The Interest Parity Theory

We have so far skirted around the question of how the forward exchange rate is determined.

The forward exchange rate is simply a price — a price negotiated now for a transaction that will occur at a specified time in the future. As a price it is set by the interaction of the forces of supply and demand in the marketplace. What can we say about supply and demand in the forward exchange market?

If you pause and think about it, we have, in fact, already said quite a bit. At the very least, we have identified two major classes of demand and supply, what we might call on the one hand *commercial demand and supply,* and on the other hand *assetholder demand and supply* (later we will consider a *speculative demand and supply* as well). But we have also suggested the basic determinants of these demand and supply forces. We now need to draw these observations together.

Commercial Demand and Supply.   Commercial demands and supplies of forward exchange reflect attempts to hedge against normal foreign exchange risks on short-term commercial transactions. The commercial demand for forward exchange must, therefore, be related to the flow of Canadian imports since it results from attempts by importers to fix the foreign exchange rate on future payments for import which they are presently contracting to purchase. Either because the level of the exchange rate will affect the demand for imports or because at relatively high forward exchange rates the importer may elect to "take the risk," we expect that this demand curve will slope downward to the right. That is, we expect that the higher the forward exchange rate, the smaller the quantity of forward exchange which will be demanded for commercial reasons.

Similarly, the commercial supply of forward exchange must be closely related to the flow of Canadian exports since it reflects the attempt of exporters to fix the exchange rate on payments which they expect to receive in the future for exports which they are presently contracting to sell. We would expect that this supply curve will rise to the right (like a normal supply curve). This in part reflects the fact that exports will be more profitable at higher exchange rates (and hence more will be offered for sale), and in part the fact that at relatively low forward exchange rates the exporter may be inclined to "take the risk" of not selling his foreign exchange earnings in the forward market.

We thus expect that commercial demand and supply in the forward exchange market can be described by curves of the "normal" shape, but assetholder's demands and supplies are a different story.

Asset Demand and Supply.   Return again to Example 8-2. It tells us that, given the difference on yields on short-term securities between Canada and the United States, and given the level of the spot exchange rate, there is a critical level of the forward exchange rate above which it is profitable for Canadian assetholders to rearrange their portfolios, selling their short-term Canadian securities, and replacing them with fully covered short-term U.S. securities. Moreover, because this can be done without altering the riskiness or the liquidity of their portfolios, assetholders should be prepared to move very substantial sums of money across the national border in response to such an incentive. All such transactions will create a supply of forward exchange because the Canadian assetholders will in each case be selling U.S. dollars in the forward market in the amount of the redemption value of their purchases of U.S. securities. At this point — determined by the level of the spot exchange rate and the difference between yields on short-term securities in the two markets — *the supply curve for forward exchange should become virtually perfectly elastic.* A small rise in the forward exchange rate above this point should induce large-scale readjustments in portfolios and hence large-scale supplies of forward exchange.

What is true of Canadian assetholders should be equally true in reverse for U.S. assetholders. A *rise* in the forward exchange rate for whatever cause should induce Canadians to make covered investments in the United States: a *fall* in the forward exchange rate should induce Americans to make covered investments in Canada.

To appreciate this point you must remember that the external value of the Canadian dollar and the foreign exchange rate move in opposite directions. As the spot exchange rate falls, the external value of the Canadian dollar rises. Similarly, if the forward exchange rate falls, the forward price of the Canadian dollar rises, and if the forward exchange rate is substantially below the spot exchange rate, the external value of the Canadian dollar is greater in the forward market than in the spot market. Thus, at low levels of the forward exchange rate, the American investor in Canada will gain any differential in interest rates plus the excess of the forward value of the Canadian dollar over its spot value. He will be that much more tempted to invest in Canada. He can do so with no risk, and with a higher yield than could be obtained in the United States on a corresponding short-term investment. As a result, if the forward exchange rate is driven down for any reason, there will come a critical point at which it becomes profitable for American assetholders to rearrange their portfolios, selling U.S. treasury bills and buying Canadian treasury bills on a fully covered basis. At this point — which again is determined by the level of the spot exchange rate and the difference between yields on short-term securities in the two financial markets — the demand curve for forward exchange should become virtually perfectly elastic. The supply of U.S. dollars in the forward exchange market is the American demand for forward Canadian dollars.

The Interest Parity Theory.   These points are illustrated in Figure 8-2. The demand for forward exchange is depicted as having the shape normally associated with a demand curve through most of its length. However, it is shown as becoming perfectly elastic at some point, and thus establishing a lower limit for the forward exchange rate. Similarly, the supply of forward exchange is depicted as having the shape normally associated with a supply curve through most of its length, but becoming perfectly elastic at some point and thus establishing an upper limit for the forward exchange rate. It is perhaps paradoxical that while the bulk of the transactions in the market are "commercial" transactions, the forward exchange rate will in effect be set by the possibly small flow of transactions on "assetholder" account. Regardless of the balance of supply and demand pressures in the forward market resulting from normal commercial transactions, the reactions of Canadian and American assetholders should hold the forward exchange rate within narrow limits — limits which are set by the level of short-term security yields in the two countries. The forward exchange rate is free to fluctuate, but only within these limits.

FIGURE 8-2   Demand and supply for forward exchange (given the level of the spot exchange rate and short-term security yields in Canada and the United States)

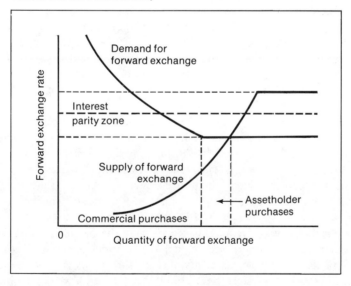

The range between the upper and the lower limits of the forward exchange rate might be called the *interest parity zone*. This range reflects the fact that assetholders incur costs in adjusting their portfolios and in buying or selling forward exchange. In part these are brokerage costs in the respective short-term money markets, and in part the "fee" which the bank charges for its services in the form of a spread between the buying price and the selling price for forward exchange (the bank sells forward exchange at a higher price than it will buy it). In many expositions of the theory of forward exchange these transaction costs are neglected. As a result, the interest parity theory is presented as though it determined a precise forward exchange rate, rather than upper and lower limits to the rate. If we made this assumption, the interest parity rate would be the mid-point of the interval. It is marked with a dotted line on Figure 8-2.

Forward Exchange and Financial Market Equilibrium

Having explored the mechanics of forward exchange and of covered foreign investment, we must ask the significance of all of this for the things in which we are interested, and particularly for the determination of equilibrium in Canadian financial markets.

Interest Rate Differentials.   Before we introduced the topic of forward exchange contracts we had established that there is an important international dimension to equilibrium in Canadian financial markets. As long as assetholders and borrowers are free to deal in either domestic or foreign financial markets, there should be a general tendency for yields on Canadian securities to be pulled toward yields in the relatively much larger foreign capital markets. Indeed, we have shown that in the Canadian case, there seems to be a relatively stable and persistent differential between security yields in Canada and those in the United States.

Now, however, our analysis of forward exchange seems to overthrow all of these propositions, at least for short-term securities. Forward exchange contracts eliminate the foreign exchange risk. Thus, as far as a Canadian assetholder is concerned, a covered investment in a U.S. treasury bill should be in all relevant respects the same as any investment in a Canadian treasury bill. In neither case is there any foreign exchange risk. Moreover, they are of the same term of maturity, and thus have essentially the same degree of liquidity. They should be perfect substitutes for each other and, thus, forces in the market place should dictate that the yields on the instruments will be driven to equality with each other, in equilibrium. Note, however, that the U.S. yield relevant to this discussion is the U.S. treasury bill yield, *adjusted for the cost or gain on forward exchange contracts* (i.e., adjusted for the difference between the forward and the spot exchange rate). *It is this adjusted yield to which the Canadian treasury bill yield will be equated by market forces.* Except in the peculiar circumstance of the forward exchange rate and the spot exchange rate being equal, there is no reason why the "raw" yields on treasury bills in the two markets will be equal. Indeed, we can say that the forward exchange market drives a wedge between yields in the Canadian short-term security market and the U.S. short-term security market. In principle, this wedge should permit the "raw" yields to move independently of each other, with the forward exchange rate adjusting to keep the "adjusted" yields equal to each other. If we allow for transactions costs, of course, perfect equality cannot be expected. Rather, fluctuations in the adjusted yields should be confined to relatively narrow limits.

Some Evidence.   Do these theoretical conclusions bear any relationship to the facts? Some evidence is presented in Figure 8-3, which shows the differential in yields on prime money market paper in Canada and the United States, and that differential adjusted for the spread between the forward and the spot rates of exchange. In the bottom panel we have also plotted the spread between the forward and spot rates, expressed in percent per annum.

FIGURE 8-3 Yields and yield differentials: 90-day finance paper, Canada and the United States, 1966-1980

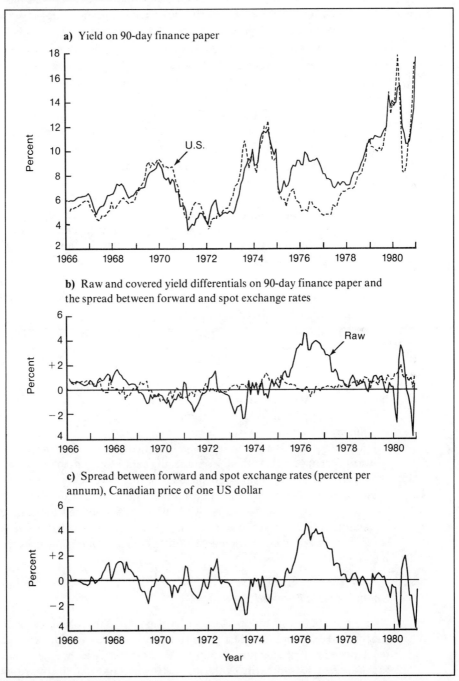

a) Yield on 90-day finance paper

b) Raw and covered yield differentials on 90-day finance paper and the spread between forward and spot exchange rates

c) Spread between forward and spot exchange rates (percent per annum), Canadian price of one US dollar

Source: *Bank of Canada Review* data.

Several conclusions seem to stand out from this chart.

(1) The "raw" differential between yields in the Canadian and the U.S. money markets fluctuates widely. In the period in question, the range of fluctuation was between 5% per annum and - 2% per annum.

It is instructive to compare the fluctuations in the "raw" yield differentials for short-term securities shown on this chart with those for longer-term securities shown on Figure 8-1. While there is a basic similarity in the pattern, the range of fluctuation at the short end is much wider.

(2) Fluctuations in the spread between the spot exchange rate and the forward exchange rate almost parallel the fluctuations in the "raw" yield differential.

Although it is quite clear that the correlation between these two series is less than perfect, a strong association is very evident. Remember that when the yield on Canadian bills is substantially in excess of the yield on U.S. bills, U.S. assetholders will attempt to buy Canadian securities. To cover the foreign exchange risk, they will sell Canadian dollars in the forward market, or, what is the same thing, to buy U.S. dollars in the forward market. As a result, the forward exchange rate will be driven up relative to the spot rate, thus eliminating the advantage to Americans of investing in Canada on a covered (or riskless) basis.

(3) As a result, fluctuations in the covered yield differential were generally confined to a much narrower range than fluctuations in the "raw" differential.

This is what the interest arbitrage theory would predict.

(4) However, on several occasions fluctuations in the covered yield differential were outside the range which would seem reasonable under the interest abritrage theory.

We do not have an independent measure of transactions costs in arbitrage transactions, but costs as great as the equivalent of 1.5 or 2% per annum (which are implied on some dates if we interpret the covered yield differential on Figure 8-3 as reflecting the market in equilibrium) seem implausibly large.

We interpret this evidence as suggesting that the interest arbitrage theory of the forward exchange rate, with appropriate allowance for transactions costs, is substantially correct, but that it cannot explain all of the movements of the forward rate. In drawing Figure 8-2 we assumed that both the demand and the supply curves in the forward market would be perfectly elastic at limits defined by transactions costs. Apparently, this is not a valid assumption; it would seem Canadian assetholders are less sensitive to risk-free international yield differentials than this theory implies. What is missing from the analysis?

Speculation in Forward Exchange

One important consideration which we have ignored is the role of speculation in setting the forward exchange rate. This is a serious omission because forward exchange is the ideal medium for speculation, and many economists argue that the forward exchange rate is determined primarily by the market's expectations of the future spot exchange rate.

Methods of Speculation.   To explore these ideas, consider a situation in which an individual expects a rise in the foreign exchange rate in the near future, say in 90 days. That is, he expects the spot rate 90 days from now to be higher than the spot (and forward) rate today. To profit by the expected rise in the exchange rate, he has two options:

(1)   He can purchase U.S. dollars in the spot market, and hold the U.S. funds for 90 days, then sell them at the (hopefully) higher price prevailing in the spot market. The cost of the speculation will be the interest income foregone on his Canadian funds invested in U.S. dollars (or the interest cost of borrowing the Canadian funds), net of the interest earned on the U.S. funds, which will presumably be invested in short-term U.S. securities for the duration of the speculation, *plus* the transactions costs involved in both the foreign exchange and the securities transactions.

(2)   He can "purchase" U.S. dollars in the forward market, to be sold 90 days hence in the spot market. Remember: the "purchase" of forward exchange involves a *contract* to make a purchase at a given price 90 days from now; no transaction occurs until that date. The speculator does not have to invest his capital (or borrow money) to make the speculation (except to the extent that the institution on the other side of the contract requires a "margin" deposit, in effect a partial down payment). At the maturity of the forward contract, the simultaneous sale of the U.S. dollars in the spot market provides the funds to pay for the purchase agreed to under the forward contract. If the spot price is now higher than the 90-day forward rate was 90 days ago, the speculator profits. (Of course, if it is not, he loses).

You should note that the first method of speculation implies higher costs, both in terms of interest costs on the capital invested and in terms of transactions costs (there are more transactions to be effected). Speculation through the forward market only requires the speculator to invest capital to the extent of margin requirements on forward contracts. It is in this sense that forward exchange is the ideal medium for speculation. It is also worth noting that in recent years the development of a "futures" market in Canadian dollars (among other currencies) as an adjunct of the Chicago Commodity Exchange has greatly increased the facilities available to exchange rate speculators.

The argument with respect to speculation on a *fall* in the foreign exchange rate is similar. You should note, however, that a contract to sell forward exchange permits a speculator to "sell" something which he does not own (and does not have a contract to receive). He hopes to profit by purchasing the foreign exchange in the spot market to meet his forward contract obligations when the forward contract matures, and to profit from a spot rate which is lower than the rate specified in the maturing forward contract.

Expectations and the Forward Exchange Rate.   Our example considered only an isolated speculator. Suppose, however, that the expectation of a rise in the foreign exchange rate were more general, i.e., was held by the "market" at large.

In this situation, there would be many speculators. Their activities would have a powerful impact on the foreign exchange market. In particular, a concentration of speculative activity in the forward market, increasing the demand for forward exchange, will drive up the forward exchange rate until there is no further advantage to speculative purchases of forward exchange. That is, the 90-day forward rate will be driven up close to the spot rate which "the market" expects will prevail 90 days hence.

A similar argument applies if the exchange rate is expected to fall.

It is reasoning of this sort which leads to the conclusion that the forward exchange rate reflects market expectations of the future spot rate. How can we reconcile this analysis with the interest parity theory of the forward exchange rate?

Interaction Between Speculation and Interest Arbitrage.   If all speculative activity is concentrated in the forward market, the effect will be not only to drive up the forward exchange rate but also to widen the spread between the forward exchange rate and the spot exchange rate. Given short-term interest rates in Canada and abroad, this will create profitable opportunities for riskless interest arbitrage. Arbitrageurs will purchase exchange in the spot market to effect their investment transactions and simultaneously will sell forward exchange in the forward market. Thus, the arbitrageurs are indirectly providing the forward exchange which the speculators are demanding.

Of course, speculation may occur in the spot market — speculators may purchase foreign exchange to hold until the expected rise in the foreign exchange rate occurs. Such speculation will increase the demand for spot exchange, and directly increase the spot exchange rate. The above analysis suggest, however, that even if all of the speculation is concentrated in the forward market, interest arbitrage will transfer the pressure of speculation to the spot market. Indirectly, through the intermediary of risk-free arbitrage, speculation in the forward market will increase the spot exchange rate.

This argument suggests that while expectations may have a decisive impact on the *level* of the forward exchange rate from time to time, if the market is working well, interest arbitrage should regulate the *spread* between the forward rate and the spot rate. The expectations theory of the forward exchange rate and the interest arbitrage theory are thus not inconsistent. Indeed, they are complementary.

It should also be remembered that as a theory of the adjustment of exchange rates to each other, the interest arbitrage theory takes short-term interest rates as given. In fact, the arbitrage transactions which we are describing should have some effect on interest rates, in Canada if not in the United States. The interest arbitrage theory, then, is an explanation of the mutual adjustment of four variables: two exchange rates and two interest rates.

Imperfect Capital Markets

If the interest arbitrage theory does not fully explain the behavior of the spread between the forward and the spot exchange rates, riskless opportunities for profit making are being ignored in the market. Why?

One possibility is that capital markets are imperfect. It is unlikely that the imperfections are in the availability of information. The profit opportunities must be widely known. It is more likely that restrictions on the availability of funds (to meet margin requirements) prevent potential arbitrageurs from taking full advantage of the arbitrage opportunities.

PORTFOLIO DIVERSIFICATION

Our analysis of international investment transactions suggests that Canadian asset-holders will purchase foreign securities when the expected yield on those securities is sufficiently in excess of the expected yield on comparable Canadian securities to compensate for the additional (foreign exchange) risk of having foreign securities in the portfolio. In the special case of short-term securities, this risk can be avoided through a forward exchange contract, but for such "covered" investments to be worthwhile the forward exchange rates has to be outside a particular limit. We have also noted the possibility of capital flows induced by expectations of a change in the exchange rate. However, these propositions are not sufficient to explain all international transactions in financial instruments, and particularly the large volume of transactions in similar securities flowing *both ways* across the national boundary, often in defiance of apparent yield differentials. We cannot explore the subject fully in this brief discussion. However, there is at least one other consideration which we must note in passing — portfolio diversification.

In our discussion of the economics of selecting a portfolio of assets in Chapter 5, we noted that, in general, a diversified portfolio is less risky than a portfolio containing a single asset. A crucial consideration is the degree to which the risks on the various assets in the portfolio are "independent." This consideration may lead many assetholders to include some foreign currency assets in their portfolios, even when there is no obvious yield incentive to do so. The fact that the securities are drawn from another economy, with a different government and different macroeconomic policies, should result in some independence in risks (although you should remember that the business cycle is an international phenomenon). Probably more important from a Canadian perspective is the fact that foreign economies contain a much wider range of firms, with independent managements, and frequently in industries which are not represented in the Canadian economy.

CONCLUSIONS

That Canadian capital markets have strong links with international, and particularly U.S. capital markets is a fact of fundamental importance in understanding the functioning of the Canadian financial system and of the macroeconomics of the Canadian economy, a theme to which we will return repeatedly throughout this book. The discussion in this chapter has been of necessity brief and hence incomplete (the topic is large enough for a book in itself). However, perhaps we have said enough to establish several important points.

First, we must extend the concept of equilibrium in financial markets which we developed earlier. Recall that we used this concept to describe a set of yields on financial instruments at which there is neither excess supply nor excess demand in the markets for those instruments. Our discussion of equilibrium focused on domestic demands and supplies, in both stock and flow dimensions. It should be apparent from the analysis in this chapter, however, that we cannot ignore international capital flows in considering equilibrium in Canadian financial markets. Indeed, we conclude that full equilibrium in Canadian financial markets implies a set of yields at which there is neither excess demand nor excess supply from either *domestic* or *international* sources. In effect,

Canadian financial markets are but a part of a larger international capital market, in which it is the demand and supply from all sources combined which determine the equilibrium set of yields.

This implies a second, stronger conclusion. From Canada's perspective, the foreign capital market of most immediate importance is that of the United States (although transactions with European markets have increased substantially in importance in recent years). Given the relative size of the markets in Canada and the United States, it follows that, in equilibrium, yields on Canadian securities will be substantially determined by yields established in the United States. Canadian demands and supplies will contribute to the determination of equilibrium yields, but their impact is on the larger international market, and is not peculiar to Canada. An increase in the supply of financial instruments in Canada will tend to increase yields, but the amount of the increase which actually occurs will be limited by an inflow of funds from abroad. A widening of the international yield differential will attract foreign assetholders to Canadian securities (or will induce Canadian borrowers to approach foreign capital markets).

Without diminishing the importance of the second conclusion, our analysis suggests a third conclusion which is also important. While strong, the link between Canadian yields and U.S. yields on similar securities is far from rigid. An important factor which weakens the link is the presence of foreign exchange risk — the risk of a change in the foreign exchange rate during the period that the foreign security is held. With respect to very short-term securities, the foreign exchange risk is of overwhelming importance. As a result, yields on very short-term securities in Canada and the United States display considerable independence, and most international transactions are made on a "covered" basis. It is only when adjusted to take account of the spread between forward and spot exchange rates that the yields on short-term securities in the two countries appear to be tied together. Even with respect to long-term securities, however, the link between Canada and the United States is far from perfect.

However, all things considered, the dominant impact of international financial markets on Canadian financial markets is both obvious and of profound importance. We must keep it in mind throughout the rest of our analysis.

ENDNOTES

1. However, the capital account of the balance of international payments excludes an important factor in the change in international indebtedness — the re-investment of retained earnings by non-resident controlled corporations. Many economists would argue that the re-investment of profits ought to be recorded in the balance of payments, both as an additional outflow of dividends in the current account and as an inflow of capital in the capital account. While in a sense this creates two artificial transactions, it does serve to remind us of the understatement of the investment of foreign-owned funds in Canada during any given year.
2. Transactions in "spot" exchange involve the purchase or sale of claims to bank deposits in foreign financial centers. Thus, Canadian banks sell claims to their deposits with foreign correspondent banks, and they buy claims on foreign banks to be transferred to their accounts with these foreign correspondents. The actual delivery of the funds in the foreign center normally will not occur until the next business day.

APPENDIX
SOME MATHEMATICS OF FORWARD EXCHANGE

In order to facilitate the exposition we have adopted the convention of identifying variables which are demoninated in U.S. dollars or which refer specifically to the U.S. financial market with the subscript u. Variables which are denominated in Canadian dollars, or which relate to Canadian financial markets (with one exception) have no subscripts. In general we assume that the U.S. financial markets are the only ones relevant for Canadians.

In the Canadian market:

S = the spot exchange rate (the Canadian dollar price of one U.S. dollar for immediate delivery).

F = the 90-day forward exchange rate (the Canadian dollar price of one U.S. dollar for delivery in 90 days).

r = the yield on 90-day Canadian government treasury bills, in percent per annum.

In the U.S. Market:

r_u = the yield on 90-day U.S. government treasury bills, in percent per annum.

M_u = the market price of one U.S. treasury bill, priced to yield r_u percent per annum.

R_u = the redemption value of that treasury bill.

From the analysis in the Appendix to Chapter 5, we know that:

$$R_u = M_u \left(1 + \frac{r_u}{4} \right) \tag{8 A.1}$$

It is important to note that the yield on the treasury bill, r_u, has been quoted in percent per annum. In equation 8 A.1 this yield has been divided by four to make it percent per 90 days.

The Canadian Assetholder's Investment Decision

The Amount of the Investment. At the prevailing spot exchange rate, the Canadian dollar price of one U.S. treasury bill, M, will be:

$$M = SM_u \tag{8 A.2}$$

This is the sum which we will assume may be invested.

The Canadian Dollar Return on the Investment. In order to avoid any foreign exchange risk, the Canadian purchaser of a U.S. treasury bill must simultaneously enter into a forward exchange contract to sell U.S. dollars in an amount equal to the redemption value of the bill. The bill will mature in 90 days. Under the terms of his forward contract, the Canadian assetholder will be required to sell his U.S. dollars for Canadian dollars at the agreed price, F, regardless of the spot exchange rate prevailing in the market at that time. Thus, the Canadian dollar return on the investment in U.S. treasury bills is:

$$FR_u = F \, M_u \left(1 + \frac{r_u}{4} \right) \tag{8 A.3}$$

The Yield on a Covered Investment

Define a new variable, r_c, which is the yield in percent per annum to the Canadian assetholder on a covered investment in U.S. treasury bills. From 8A.2 and 8A.3 we know that:

$$SM_u \left(1 + \frac{r_c}{4} \right) = F \; M_u \left(1 + \frac{r_u}{4} \right)$$

$$S \; (4 + r_c) = F \; (4 + r_u)$$

$$r_c = \frac{F}{S} \; (4 + r_u) - 4$$

$$= \frac{4F}{S} - 4 + \frac{F}{S} \; r_u$$

$$= 4 \left(\frac{F-S}{S} \right) + \frac{F}{S} \; r_u \tag{8A.4}$$

The first term on the right hand side of this equation, $4(F-S)/S$, is the gain or loss on the foreign exchange "swap" on the purchase price of the U.S. treasury bill, expressed in percent per annum. If the forward exchange rate is less than the spot rate, this term will be negative. The cost of the swap will reduce the net yield on the covered investment.

The second term on the right hand side, $F/S(r_u)$, is the gain resulting from the yield on the treasury bill in the U.S. Note that this yield is either augmented or reduced depending on whether the forward rate exceeds or falls short of the spot rate. In general, F/S will be close to 1. Therefore, equation 8A.4 is commonly simplified to:

$$r_c \cong 4 \frac{(F-S)}{S} + r_u \tag{8A.5}$$

The Investment Decision.   If the Canadian assetholder is to find covered investment in U.S. treasury bills a profitable transaction it must be true that:

$$r_c > r$$

that is:

$$4 \frac{(F-S)}{S} + \frac{F}{S} \; r_u > r \tag{8A.6}$$

If the opposite is true, that is, if:

$$4 \frac{(F-S)}{S} + \frac{F}{S} \; r_u < r \tag{8A.7}$$

then U.S. investors will find it profitable to make covered investments in Canadian treasury bills. The yield on these investments will exceed the yield obtainable on U.S. treasury bills.

Market Equilibrium: The Interest Arbitrage Theory

The interest arbitrage theory assumes that assetholders in both countries will regard investments in domestic securities and fully covered investments in foreign securities as perfect substitutes for each other. As a result, the only condition compatable with equilibrium is:

$$r = r_c$$

$$= 4\,\frac{(F-S)}{S} + \frac{F}{S}\,r_u \qquad\qquad \textbf{(8A.8)}$$

If we take short-term security yields as given in the two markets, this becomes a theory of the determination of the forward exchange rate.

By manipulation of equation 8A.8 we obtain as the equilibrium forward exchange rate:

$$F = S\left(\frac{r+4}{r_u+4}\right) \qquad\qquad \textbf{(8A.9)}$$

In other words, the equilibrium forward exchange rate depends on the level of the spot exchange rate and the relationship between short-term security yields in the two countries.

Some Qualifications

Term to Maturity.   In all of these calculations we have assumed a 90-day term, with all security yields quoted in percent per annum. If we assumed a different term to maturity, the equations would be slightly different. Thus, for a 30-day investment, equation 8A.9 would become:

$$F = S\left(\frac{r+12}{r_u+12}\right) \qquad\qquad \textbf{(8A.10)}$$

The number 12 replaces the number 4 in the equation because we are now dealing with an investment for 1/12 of a year rather than ¼ of a year. In general:

$$F = S\left(\frac{r+q}{r_u+q}\right) \qquad\qquad \textbf{(8A.11)}$$

where $1/q$ is the fraction of one year for which the investment will be outstanding.

Transactions Costs.   Like most expositions of the interest arbitrage theory, this discussion ignores transactions costs (i.e., brokerage fees for the several transactions in foreign exchange and in the security markets). If we allow for such costs, equations 8A-6 and 8A-7 do not hold precisely. The difference between yields must be great enough to cover transactions costs before the investment will occur.

Flexible Interest Rates.   This statement of the interest arbitrage theory also assumes that yields on short-term securities are fixed, whereas the forward exchange rate is free to move. It is not clear that all of the adjustment will be taken up by movements in the forward exchange rate, however.

Suppose equation 8A-6 holds. That is, suppose there is some advantage to Canadian assetholders to make short-term covered investments in the United States. Their attempts to do so should simultaneously increase short-term security yields in Canada (as they sell, or refrain from buying, short-term securities), increase the spot exchange rate (as they attempt to purchase U.S. dollars), reduce short-term security yields in the United States (as they attempt to purchase U.S. securities), and reduce the forward exchange rate (as they arrange forward contracts to sell the U.S. dollars). Obviously, it is an oversimplification to assume that only the forward exchange rate adjusts.

ELEMENTARY THEORY OF FINANCIAL INTERMEDIATION 9

In addition to the analysis of financial markets, the economics of the financial system is largely an analysis of the nature, operations, and impact of a group of business firms which we call financial intermediaries. They loom so large in the financial system that their activities can have a decisive impact on the effectiveness of the system as a mechanism for the allocation of credit, and hence they can have a significant effect on both the composition and the level of economic activity. Moreover, government monetary policy is largely effected through financial intermediaries. Their economic importance is pervasive.

In Chapter 1 we made passing reference to financial intermediaries, their nature, function, and importance. In this chapter we propose to examine them in greater detail and, in the process, to develop an elementary theory of financial intermediation. In the following three chapters we will consider the specific characteristics of various types of financial intermediaries.

THE CONCEPT OF FINANCIAL INTERMEDIATION

A Borrower — Lender Conduit

In our earlier discussion of financial intermediaries we noted that financial intermediaries stand between the ultimate lenders (surplus spending units) and the ultimate borrowers (deficit spending units). They borrow from one group and lend to the other.

However, many economic units simultaneously borrow and lend: indeed, we might go so far as to say that at some time or other *most* (if not all) economic units do so. Thus, if we adopted a catholic definition of a financial intermediary we would have to include other economic units in addition to those firms, such as banks, trust companies, and insurance companies, which we normally consider to be financial intermediaries. Many individuals or families are simultaneously creditors and debtors. They hold such things as bank deposits and saving bonds while at the same time they have outstanding consumer loans or mortgage debt. Similarly, many corporations extend trade credit and make long-term investments in other corporations while at the same time they have outstanding bank loans or long-term debt. Moreover, and especially in recent years, many corporations have become increasingly aware of the opportunity costs (in terms of income foregone) of holding large amounts of cash for lengthy periods. Therefore, they frequently invest their funds for short periods in various money market instruments. Indeed, corporations have become major suppliers of funds to the money market. Should we consider all such individuals and corporations to be financial intermediaries?

A More Specialized Concept

In one sense, all of these individuals and corporations are financial intermediaries. Perhaps we could call them *ad hoc* intermediaries. Their financial activities have an important place in the overall functioning of the financial system. Our concept of financial intermediation must be more specialized than this, however. We are concerned with a group of firms which make this type of financial activity their *primary business.* That is, their activities in simultaneously borrowing and lending are not an adjunct of some other activity, but rather are the essential reason for their existence. They are *continuously* engaged in the business of borrowing and lending (not just on an *ad hoc* basis) and, in general (with a few exceptions), they stand ready and willing to accept any and all funds placed with them at the posted interest rate.

Most financial intermediaries are private *profit-seeking firms.* There are exceptions. Two rapidly growing groups of intermediaries, *caisses populaires* and *credit unions,* are "cooperative banks." However, even these "cooperative banks" seek to make a return over and above costs, and in that sense they are profit-seeking institutions. Clearly, in order to earn profits *financial intermediaries must be able to borrow at a lower rate of interest than that at which they lend.* How can they do this? Why should any spending unit lend to a financial intermediary at a lower rate of interest than he could lend to the ultimate borrower (and to whom the intermediary will in fact lend the same money)?

Transmutation of Assets.   The answer must be that depositors regard claims on financial intermediaries as in some sense superior to claims on ultimate borrowers. This means that, if given the choice between a claim on an ultimate borrower and a claim on a financial intermediary *bearing the same effective yield,* these wealth owners would always choose the claim on the intermediary, and would only choose the claim on the ultimate borrower if it bore a significantly higher effective yield.

It is for this reason that many economists argue that the essence of financial intermediation is the transmutation of assets. Transmutation means literally the transformation of something from one nature, substance, or form into another. The financial intermediary accepts claims on ultimate borrowers which the ultimate lenders would not accept, and issues claims to be held by the ultimate lenders which have characteristics which the ultimate borrowers could not duplicate. The intermediary does not create real wealth, but *merely changes the form of the claims on real wealth held by the assetholders of the economy.* In this act of transmutation the financial intermediary creates an asset form with unique characteristics.

The ways in which financial intermediaries can transform financial assets are numerous and varied. Among the types of transformation of assets carried on by financial intermediaries are *payments intermediation, maturity-risk intermediation,* and *denomination intermediation.* Not all financial institutions, however, carry on all these forms of intermediation.

In performing *payments intermediation,* a financial institution holds a collection of assets which do not serve as a means of payment, but issues claims which can be used by their holders for making payments for goods and services. In essence, these liabilities serve as part of the money supply. As we saw in Chapter 2, the liabilities of chartered banks comprise the major component of the money supply in Canada. Nevertheless, credit unions, caisses populaires, and trust companies all issue liabilities which can be used for making payments. Moreover, experience suggests that it would be unwise to draw a hard and fast line between intermediaries performing payments intermediation and other intermediaries. Over time, the range of claims used for payments purposes has been extended from the claims of governments, or government banks such as the Bank of England, to commercial banks, and then on to the claims of other financial institutions. Even in the 1980s, we are witnessing the extension of the payments system in the United States to include claims on savings and loan associations, which were previously excluded, and now even balances held with stockbrokers.

Maturity-risk intermediation is probably the most complex form of asset transformation conducted by a financial institution. We use the term *maturity-risk intermediation* to refer to the supplying of funds on terms which are not matched by the terms of the financial institution's source of funds. In fact, maturity-risk intermediation can occur in a number of different forms such as *term intermediation, capital value intermediation,* and *interest rate intermediation.*

Perhaps the simplest of these is *term intermediation* by which a financial institution commits funds for a longer period than that for which funds have been borrowed. By carrying out term intermediation, a financial institution is able to meed the borrower's need to have an assured source of funds at the same time as assuring the ultimate lender's ability to have ready access to his funds as needed. A financial institution is able to provide this term intermediation by its expectation that it will be able to find a lender to replace the original depositor when he decides to withdraw his funds. Almost every intermediary supplies term intermediation to some degree. The major exception might be mutual funds which just channel the lender's resources into marketable securities such as stocks and bonds. Even here, the mutual fund can avoid the need to buy or sell securities to the extent that its inflow of new funds offsets its outflow of withdrawals.

Capital value intermediation.   This requires the financial institution to issue claims against itself which have a fixed money value even though the assets acquired by the institution do not. By performing capital value intermediation, the intermediary may protect its liability holders against the risk of default by its borrowers. In addition, we have seen that the current value of many securities such as stocks and marketable bonds depends on present market conditions. By offering claims which have a fixed money value, a financial institution allows its depositors to be assured of the value of their funds regardless of market conditions. The significance of capital value intermediation can be appreciated by comparing the claims issued by a mutual fund with those issued by a bank. The holder of a mutual fund unit has a share of the collection of assets held by the fund. When he acquires his claim he pays the current unit value established for the fund. When he withdraws his funds from the mutual fund he receives the current value established for the fund units, which may be greater or less than the value at the time he acquired the units. In contrast, when he makes his deposit, the depositor at a bank is assured of the terms at which he can withdraw the funds in the future. These terms are independent of the actual experience by the bank on its portfolio of assets.

A financial institution carries out *interest rate intermediation* either when it lends at fixed interest rates, even though the interest paid on its sources of funds is not fixed or, alternatively, when it borrows at a fixed rate when its lending rate is variable. Interest rate intermediation occurs because some borrowers and lenders prefer the certainty of a fixed rate of interest established in advance. Obviously, households and businesses may find their planning easier if they can be assured definitely of the rate of interest they are required to pay as a result of purchasing a house or a piece of new equipment. On the other hand, the financial institution may be financing its lending by a succession of overlapping borrowings from lenders who do not wish to commit their funds for the same period for which the loan is made to the borrower. Some lenders, however, may prefer to be assured of a fixed return on their funds. For example, pensioners may wish to be assured of steady monthly income rather than being dependent on the fluctuations of market interest rates.

In some cases, financial institutions try to match the period of commitment with respect to the interest rate on loans to the period they are committed to on the funds they have borrowed. For example, many mortgage lenders in Canada attempt to balance their lending on five-year mortgages with the funds that they borrow through issuing five-year term deposits. These institutions could not be regarded as supplying interest rate intermediation. Financial institutions which do engage in interest rate intermediation will find that their profitability depends on the movement of market interest rates. Institutions which lend on fixed interest rates over long periods while borrowing on a short-term basis will suffer when market rates rise and benefit when market interest rates fall.

It is interesting to note that the higher and more volatile interest rates in the 1970s and early 1980s have led many financial institutions to change the amount of risk they undertake through interest rate intermediation. In the late 1960s and early 1970s, the standard residential mortgage in Canada was a renewable five-year term mortgage under which the borrower was assured of a fixed interest rate for a five-year period. Some residential mortgages, most notably the government-guaranteed mortgages issued under the National Housing Act, had as much as a 20-year term with a fixed interest rate. As interest rates rose through the 1970s, those financial institutions which had borrowed short-term money to finance their long-term investments suffered a severe squeeze on their profits. Many institutions reconsidered at this time the amount of risk they would expose themselves to by making long-term loans at fixed interest rates. Some institutions reacted by attempting to match their long-term lending more closely with long-term borrowing. This reaction was also reflected in the terms offered in their mortgage loans. By the early 1980s, many mortgage lenders were only supplying mortgage funds with terms as short as one or two years. In effect, the higher and more volatile interest rates of the 1970s led to a reduction in the degree of interest rate intermediation performed by mortgage lenders and left more of the risk of interest rate fluctuations in the hands of the borrowers.

The final form of intermediation carried on by financial institutions is perhaps obvious but still important in terms of its contribution to the economy. *Denomination intermediation* refers to the process by which a financial institution supplies funds to borrowers in amounts different from the funds collected from lenders. The most common sort of denomination intermediation involves the financial institution's making a large loan to a borrower which is beyond the resources of any one lender but which instead is based on borrowings from a large number of lenders. The advantage to the borrower from denomination intermediation is quite clear: it can avoid the costs of dealing with a large number of lenders, each of which has a different preference with respect to the terms of the loan. In effect, the financial institution specializes by packaging the terms of the loan to suit both large borrowers and small lenders.

Underlying all these different types of intermediation is the central principle of *portfolio diversification*. A claim on a financial intermediary is, in fact, a claim on a diversified portfolio of assets and is but one claim in a diversified portfolio of liabilities. It is the fact of diversification — primarily on the asset side, but also on the liability side — which permits the intermediary to create financial instruments with all of these specific and valuable properties.

A THEORY OF PORTFOLIO DIVERSIFICATION

The essential effect of portfolio diversification is that it reduces risk. Diversification of asset holdings reduces the risk of loss of the total value of asset holdings (and also the "risk" of unexpected gains in the total value of asset holdings). Diversification on the liability side reduces the risk of having to make payment simultaneously on all liabilities (and also the "risk" of unexpected increases in liabilities).

Diversification of Asset Holdings

A more precise statement of the theory of portfolio diversification is reserved for the Appendix to this chapter. That exposition is necessarily mathematical since the fundamental proposition is basically mathematical, being derived from a primary proposition of probability theory. However, on an intuitive level, this basic principle underlying diversification of asset holdings can be succinctly stated in the old adage, "Don't put all your eggs in one basket." In the present context, it might better be restated as, "Don't put all your wealth in one asset." In the case of the eggs in one basket, it only takes a single misstep, a single fall, to break them all. In the case of investing all of your wealth in one asset, it only takes the failure of one debtor to cause complete financial ruin.

In Chapter 5, we defined "risk" as the probability of significant variations in the actual yield on an asset around the expected or most likely yield. We also extended this concept and talked about the yield and the risk on a portfolio of assets. The yield on the portfolio will be the average yield on the assets which comprise the portfolio. The theory of portfolio diversification tells us, however, that the risk on the portfolio — the probability of significant variations in the actual yield about the expected or most likely yield on the portfolio — will be less than the average of the risks on the separate assets comprising the portfolio. Indeed, the risk on the portfolio will vary inversely with the number of independent assets comprising the portfolio. As the number of independent assets in the portfolio increases to a very large number (in the extreme, to infinity), the risk on the portfolio approaches zero. This is true even though each of the constituent assets of the portfolio has a significant risk attached to it.

This means that an assetholder faced with two assets equal in all relevant respects (i.e., same risk, same expected yield), should, if he has any aversion to risk at all, hold some of both assets rather than investing all of his funds in only one of them. By doing so he will have the same expected yield on his portfolio (the average of the two identical expected yields is the same as either of them) and at the same time have a lower degree of risk.

In general (as was shown in Chapter 5), assets with high risks normally have high expected yields. As a result, diversification involving assets of high and low risk normally involves a reduction in the expected yield on the portfolio as a whole.

Independent and Dependent Assets

There is one vitally important qualification which must be made to these conclusions on portfolio diversification. In order to reduce risk, the assets in the portfolio must be at least partially *independent*. By independent assets we mean that the outcome of one asset is not directly associated with the outcome of any other in the portfolio.

Under what conditions might assets be dependently related? Suppose that between two assets, A and B, there existed a relationship such that if A (for example, an automobile company) failed, the B (a steel plant selling its entire output to A) would fail, we would say they were *dependently* related. Holding a portfolio of dependently related assets would not reduce risk.[1]

Remember, however, that while in a micro sense investments may be independent (e.g., a loan to a shoe store and a provincial bond), in a macro sense most assets are mutually dependent. If some calamity struck the entire economy, such as a major depression, most ventures would incur losses and many would collapse, with corresponding declines in the market values of most financial assets. Even in the ordinary course of business fluctuations, most industries tend to prosper or want together, and as a consequence their common stocks tend to rise and fall together. In this sense, then, there may be some limit to the reduction in risk that can be achieved through portfolio diversification.

Diversification of Liabilities

Since financial intermediaries borrow as well as lend, the risk of fluctuations in asset values are not the only serious risks that they face. They also face the possibility that their creditors may not extend their loans. That is, the holders of claims on financial intermediaries may all demand payment at the maturity of the loan. For easy reference we shall call this form of risk "banker's risk." For many financial intermediaries — for example, banks — this risk is particularly acute because a substantial portion of their liabilities are payable on demand. Under extreme circumstances, virtually the entire set of claims against the intermediary could be presented for payment in cash simultaneously, forcing total liquidation of the intermediary. This is a contingency which the management of the intermediary cannot ignore. The probability of a mass withdrawal of funds (a "run" of the intermediary) may be extremely low, but certainly there is always a risk of significant withdrawals of funds in a short period of time.

In the earlier part of this century runs were rather common; in more recent times they have been rare but not unheard of. Indeed, one of Canada's most recent experiences with a run involved one of the savings banks in the city of Montreal and took place in the mid-1960s. A rumor spread through one district of the city that the bank had suffered some serious losses on its loans and would shortly be forced to close. Within 48 hours worried depositors withdrew more than half of the bank's deposits. The run was stopped only after the Minister of Finance announced in the House of Commons that the government had every faith in the management and would stand behind it to ensure its continued operation.

It may well be that the run on the bank in Montreal will be one of the last to occur in Canada. In 1967, the federal government established the Canadian Deposit Insurance Corporation which insures the deposit liabilities of banks, other federally chartered financial institutions, and most provincially incorporated trust and mortgage loan companies up to an amount of $20,000 per depositor at each institution. In Quebec, deposits at caisses populaires and at branches of trust and mortgage loan companies incorporated in that province are similarly insured. Since the $20,000 limit would cover the majority of deposits in banks, most depositors need have no fear of suffering a loss should the banks fail.

Some indication of the effects of deposit insurance in instilling confidence in the financial system can be illustrated by an episode in the early 1980s. One trust company with a shareholders' equity of $15 million in 1980 reported losses of $11 million during 1981, which led management to concede "that the company might not be able to meet its liabilities as they fall due." As a result of intervention by the Canada Deposit Insurance Corporation, another trust company agreed to manage the affairs of the first trust company, with the deposit insurer agreeing to advance the funds to meet the troubled trust company's liabilities. For our purposes, the most relevant lesson of this story is not that depositors were protected from losses (such protection up to the $20,000 limit is provided for all depositors at insured institutions), but rather that an institution could be on the verge of failure without generating a panic of withdrawals. Depositors have become complacent about the safety of their deposits in the presence of deposit insurance. Yet, while runs may be a thing of the past, intermediaries cannot ignore the possibility of sizeable fluctuations in the total level of their liabilities. As intermediaries gain experience with the changes in the levels of their liabilities, they are able to determine with some certainty what a normal degree of variation will be. More important, they will be able to fix what portion of their total liabilities they can expect to have outstanding at all times. With the knowledge that, even though most or all of their liabilities are payable on demand, only a certain portion is likely to be withdrawn at one time, they, in turn, can invest a portion of their total portfolio in the higher-yielding longer-term assets such as mortgages and government bonds. In effect, they can borrow short-term and lend long-term.

It is important to remember, however, that no intermediary will have complete certainty as to what proportion of its liabilities will be outstanding at any given time. The fact that these calculations are approximate, and not exact, creates a problem. Should the intermediary invest a large portion of its portfolio in long-term assets and then suffer a redemption of its liabilities larger than expected, it might be forced to sell these assets at a loss in an effort to raise cash. Similarly, excessive pessimism about the possible withdrawal of liabilities may lead the intermediary to hold large amounts of short-term, low-yielding assets when it might well increase its return to the portfolio by holding more long-term assets.

The primary determinants of banker's risk are very complicated and are only now beginning to be explored fully. Recent empirical work, concerned with the nature of bank liabilities in particular, found that the level of banker's risk varied directly with the average liquidity of the deposits. Thus, the greater the percentage of total deposits not subject to chequing (i.e., payable on demand *de jure* or *de facto*), the larger was the portion of total deposits likely to remain with the firm at all times.

More importantly, given the risks of withdrawal by any one creditor of the intermediary, it is quite clear that the risk to the total portfolio is significantly reduced by diversification. Where there may be significant risk that any one creditor will demand his money on any given day, the risk that all creditors will demand their funds at the same time is very small indeed.

But this proposition applies only if the creditors can be described as independent. Thus, if the depositors in a small bank in a small town are all employed in the same industry, the probability that they will all deposit and withdraw funds together may be very high. They could not be described as independent. Similarly, if all creditors heard and believed the same rumor of impending failure of an intermediary, as in the Montreal case, the probability that they would all attempt to withdraw their funds again is high indeed. They could not be described as independent. As will become evident when we examine the various intermediaries in detail, the nationwide branch bank networks in Canada, each with as many as several million or more separate depositors, have a high degree of independence with their liabilities. Indeed, many people claim that the high degree of diversification both of liabilities and assets which results from nationwide branching in large part accounts for Canada's freedom from bank failures for almost 50 years.

In summary, the essential point is obvious. The asset portfolio of the intermediary must be managed with an eye to the risks involved on the liability side as well as the risks involved on particular assets. As we will see in our discussion of specific types of intermediaries in later chapters, the risks assumed on the liability side leave a decided imprint on the asset portfolio of the institution.

ECONOMIES OF SCALE IN PORTFOLIO MANAGEMENT

The reduction of risk on asset holdings through portfolio diversification is a general phenomenon. What a financial intermediary does in this way, any individual could, in principle, do for himself. Moreover, by lending directly to the ultimate borrowers the individual could avoid the costs of intermediation. (Remember: financial intermediaries are profit-seeking firms. In order to cover their operating costs and make a profit they must pay to their creditors a lower rate of interest than they earn on their diversified portfolios of assets.) While portfolio diversification is fundamental to financial intermediation, by itself it does not seem sufficient to explain the fact that intermediaries exist and flourish.

Part of the explanation is that in the long run financial intermediaries are able to earn a substantially higher net return on their assets than could most individuals holding a similar range of financial assets. The essential difference between individual portfolio diversification and a claim on a financial intermediary is that the latter is a proportionate claim on a much larger total portfolio. The superior earnings position of the financial intermediary derives from economies of large-scale operations.

The concept of economies of scale should be a familiar one to all students of economics. Where economies of scale exist (and they are neither universal nor continuous through all scales of operations) a firm can achieve a lower level of costs per unit of output by increasing the scale of its operations, and making adjustments in techniques of production and organization appropriate to the larger scale.

All attempts to apply this concept to financial intermediaries have encountered the same problem: how do you identify and measure the output of financial intermediaries? The measurement of costs is relatively straightforward, but, as discussed in Chapter 1, the problem of measuring output in the sense of the value of the services performed by financial intermediaries has not been solved to the satisfaction of many economists. Without a fairly accurate measure of output, how can we measure and discuss variations in costs per unit of output as the level of output changes?

Fortunately, in the present context we can beg the question. We are not immediately interested in costs in relation to the level of output of the intermediary (unless we take the size of the intermediary's portfolio of assets as an indicator of output, as many studies have done), but rather in the impact of costs on the net return per dollar invested in diversified portfolios of different sizes. It is in this unorthodox sense that we refer to economies of scale. The student should be aware that it is not exactly the same concept as that employed in the theory of the firm.

Why should there be economies of scale in portfolio management? We can divide the relevant considerations into three categories. In part, the economies arise because of indivisibilities in financial assets. Perhaps more obvious are economies which arise in connection with the decision-making processes relating to the management of the portfolio. To some extent, economies also arise in connection with transactions in financial markets, and hence are dependent only indirectly on the size of the asset portfolio.

Indivisibility of Financial Assets

Not all financial assets are available in small denominations. For example, treasury bills only come in multiples of $1000 and a number of stocks sell for more than $100 per share. Moreover, higher commissions must be paid on so-called odd lot transactions which for many stocks include any transactions of less than 100 shares. These minimum unit sizes are beyond the financial capacity of many wealth owners and, because of this, the range of alternative investment forms is limited. Could an individual with total assets of $5000 invest in a diversified portfolio including several mortgages on residential property? Obviously not. However, a deposit in a trust and loan company effectively buys him a share of a portfolio including many such mortgages. The financial intermediary is able to hold a broader range of assets, including some higher-yielding assets, simply because of the larger total size of its portfolio.

Economies in Management

The management of an investment portfolio involves choices among alternatives. The essential inputs are prompt, accurate information on current and prospective developments in a broad range of economic activities, and technical expertise in interpreting the financial implications of these developments. Each potential investment (including those already in the portfolio) must be assessed in terms of probable return and risk, and its merits considered relative to all possible alternative uses of funds. A large investment portfolio will be able to support a group of individuals who will devote their full time to supervising the investment of funds. By working full time rather than part time on the problems of investment they frequently become specialists in particular industries, regions, or groups of securities. They acquire an expertise and knowledge that frequently allows them to evaluate a particular investment opportunity quickly and shrewdly. It is almost impossible to imagine such expertise in a wide range of markets being possessed by any one individual.

It is true that such technical expertise is itself a marketable commodity. Individuals can hire the services of professional investment counsellors, and indeed many brokerage houses will offer advice of this sort as a part of their services to their customers. However, the fees of independent investment counsellors tend to bear more heavily on small portfolios than on large portfolios. Thus, suppose the fee of an independent counsellor is $100 per day or any fraction of a day. The larger the amount of wealth involved the lower will be the cost per each dollar of having this expert advice. For example, if the portfolio was worth $5000 the cost per dollar of assets for the one day's advice would be 2¢ while if the portfolio was worth only $500 the cost would be 20¢ per dollar of assets. The larger portfolio is better able to combine expert, specialized advice with low cost per dollar of assets.

Economies in Market Transactions

The optimum portfolio for a wealth owner or an intermediary will normally not be constant in size and composition over time. As wealth increases or the yields and risks associated with various investment alternatives change so will the composition or structure of the portfolio. But changes in the size and composition of the portfolio imply transactions in financial markets, and these transactions are far from costless. As we saw in Chapter 3, there are "transactions costs" in the form of fees and commissions of brokers and dealers as well as miscellaneous other costs involved in purchasing and selling securities in the market (and corresponding costs in making loans and handling deposit accounts). With few exceptions transactions costs are stated either as a flat sum per transaction or as a declining percentage of the value of the transaction. As a consequence, in most transactions, the larger the total amount involved the lower will be the transaction cost per dollar exchanged.

Clearly, if two equally diversified portfolios, one large and one small, were to involve the same number of market transactions in a given period of time, the burden of transactions costs would be heavier on the smaller portfolio than on the larger one. As a result, the net return on the smaller portfolio would be less than on the larger portfolio. The smaller one cannot get the benefits of the same degree of diversification, adapt to all market developments, and get the same return on the portfolio as can the larger.

Economies of Scale and the Role of Financial Intermediaries

If we regard the primary characteristic of the financial intermediary as the provision of a claim on a diversified portfolio of financial assets, this analysis suggests on *a priori* grounds one reason why such intermediaries should exist and flourish. Economies of scale in the management of investment portfolios, including economies in market transactions, permit the intermediary to obtain a higher net return on a diversified portfolio for any given degree of risk than could an investor with a relatively small sum to invest.

This also suggests that financial intermediaries should be relatively more important to investors with relatively small portfolios than to those with relatively large portfolios. There is some direct evidence that this is the case. Thus, successive surveys of consumer finances undertaken in Canada have shown, among other things, an inverse correlation between total assets held and the percentage of earning assets held in the form of deposits with financial institutions.

OTHER ASPECTS OF THE MARKET
POSITION OF FINANCIAL INTERMEDIARIES ⎯⎯⎯⎯⎯⎯⎯⎯⎯

Clearly, the analysis of portfolio diversification, including the analysis of economies of scale in portfolio management, is only a partial explanation of why financial intermediaries exist and flourish. We have neglected another minor element in the determination of the riskiness of claims on financial intermediaries. More important, we have not given due consideration to a point introduced earlier, but not fully developed, relating to the diversity of products offered by intermediaries.

Risk and the Capital Accounts

We should not forget that financial intermediaries are generally corporations, with stockholders who have subscribed capital to the corporation, and which have normally retained earnings over a period of time so as to accumulate surpluses and reserves. We can group all of these items together as the capital accounts of the intermediary. These accounts are, in fact, the excess of the value of the assets of the corporation over the value of the fixed dollar claims against that corporation. This excess of the value of assets over liabilities provides an additional margin of safety to the depositors since they have a prior claim on the earnings and assets of the corporation; that is, the claims of the depositors must be met before the claims of the stockholders can be considered. Some intermediaries will use their reserves to stabilize payments of interest to depositors in spite of fluctuations in earnings on the assets held by the intermediary. This analysis suggests that not only do financial institutions reduce risk through diversification, they also transfer some risk from depositors to the owners of shares in the financial institution.

Product Differentiation

We must reemphasize, in explaining the growth of financial intermediaries, that they have succeeded in creating financial instruments with characteristics which could not be created by many ultimate borrowers. We need only think of the liquidity and convenience of demand deposits, or the special features of insurance or the diversified portfolio of stocks obtainable from a mutual fund to realise this.

As long as wealth owners, or surplus spending units as we called them in Chapter 1, cannot obtain directly or by personal diversification a particular type of asset that they desire, there exists the possibility of an intermediary being created to provide the missing form. This is one of the primary reasons why we have such wide diversity in the types of intermediaries operating in Canada.

In a very general sense, these institutions are basically similar in that they all perform the function of financial intermediation. Thus, the theoretical analysis of this chapter applies to all of them. However, in a more specific sense, each group plays a different role in the financial system. These differences are reflected in the types of liabilities which they issue as they collect funds, and in the types of assets which they acquire as they allocate those funds among the many investment alternatives. The main point of the next three chapters is to bring out the unique characteristics of each group of institutions, and hence to explore the role which each plays in the financial system. It should not be surprising, therefore, that our analysis focuses on the characteristic of the institutions' assets and liabilities.

FINANCIAL INTERMEDIARIES IN CANADA

Our discussion of financial intermediation to this point has been abstract and theoretical. In the chapters that follow, we will be describing the business of the many varied types

TABLE 9-1   Domestic assets of major financial intermediaries, June 1982

A. *Deposit institutions*	*$ Billions*	*Percent*
Chartered banks	211	53
Trust and mortgage loan companies	71	18
Credit unions and *caisses populaires*	33*	8
Total: major deposit institutions	315	80
B. *Other intermediaries*		
Life insurance companies	60	15
Sales finance and consumer loan companies	14	4
Mutual funds, real estate investment trusts and other investment companies	7	2
Total: Other major intermediaries	81	20
TOTAL: Major financial intermediaries	396	100

* March 31, 1982

SOURCE: *Bank of Canada Review,* November 1982; Statistics Canada, *Financial Institutions,* Second Quarter, 1982.

of intermediaries that operate in the Canadian financial system. Before dealing with the individual financial institutions, we should gain some perspective of their relative significance in terms of financial institutions as a whole. Table 9-1 provides a profile of the Canadian financial system of 1981. Note that the institutions have been grouped according to those that offer deposit liabilities and those that do not. These data show that the deposit institutions account for over three-quarters of the total assets of intermediaries and that the chartered banks account for over half of the total by themselves. As might be expected, we will be devoting much of our attention to a careful study of the banking system.

ENDNOTES

1. There is one additional relationship which, for completeness, should be mentioned. Some assets might inversely related; that is, if one is successful the other will fail by an equal amount. An example might involve an umbrella manufacturer and a brewery. If we have a sunny, hot summer the brewery prospers at the expense of the umbrella maker, whereas the tables are turned if the summer is wet and cold. Diversification with such inversely dependent assets would reduce risk to zero.

APPENDIX
PORTFOLIO DIVERSIFICATION AND RISK

The Concepts of Expected Yield and Risk

The concepts of expected yield and risk on an asset were introduced in Chapter 5. We noted that the yield on an asset is always uncertain. A number of alternative outcomes are possible, but some are less likely to occur than others. We represented this situation by a probability distribution of alternative possible yields, with the expected yield being the most likely of the alternative possible outcomes, and the risk being represented by the standard deviation of the probability distribution of these outcomes.

Expected Yield   What we mean by the expected yield is what the mathematicians refer to as the mathematical expectation of the probability distribution. It is simply the average of the alternative possible yields when each possible yield is weighted by the probability that it will occur. The formula for calculating the expected yield is:

$$\bar{y} = \sum_{i=1}^{\eta} p_i y_i \tag{9A.1}$$

where η represents the number of alternative possible yields in the probability distribution, y_i represents each of the alternative possible yields, and p_i represents the probability

that that particular yield (the ith yield) will occur (remember that $\sum_{i=1}^{\eta} p_i = 1$).

Standard Deviation.   The standard deviation, a complex measure of the distribution of the alternative possible yields around the expected yield, is a much more difficult concept. Its derivation and properties are explored in any basic textbook in statistics.[1] In brief, it is the square root of the average of the squared deviations of the alternative possible yields from the expected yield. The mathematical formula is:

$$\sigma = \sqrt{\frac{\sum_{i=1}^{\eta}(y_i - \bar{y})^2}{n}} \tag{9A.2}$$

where the symbol σ (the Greek letter sigma) represents the standard deviation.

In the discussion of these problems another concept, the variance of the distribution, is sometimes used. The variance is simply the standard deviation squared. That is,

$$V = \sigma^2 = \frac{\sum_{i=1}^{\eta}(y_i - \bar{y})^2}{n} \tag{9A.3}$$

---

[1]   See for example: Edwin Mansfield, *Statistics for Business and Economics* (New York: W.W. Norton, 1980), pp. 41-47.

Expected Yield and Risk on a Portfolio

By a portfolio we mean a collection of assets. A portfolio is diversified if it includes more than one asset (providing the assets are independent to some degree).

Expected Yield of a Portfolio.   The expected yield of a portfolio is simply a weighted average of the expected yields of the individual assets which comprise the portfolio. Thus,

$$\bar{y}_P = \sum_{i=1}^{m} \chi_i \bar{y}_i \qquad\qquad \textbf{(9A.4)}$$

where m represents the number of assets in the portfolio, y_p represents the expected yield on the portfolio, y_i represents the expected yield on each asset comprising the portfolio, and x_i the proportion of the portfolio represented by that asset $\Sigma \chi_i = 1$. Thus, for a portfolio consisting of two assets, A and B, the expected yield would be:

$$\bar{y}_P = \chi_A \bar{y}_A + \chi_B \bar{y}_B \qquad\qquad \textbf{(9A.5)}$$

Risk of a Portfolio.[2]   The risk of a portfolio is the standard deviation of a probability distribution of the alternative possible yields on that portfolio. The risk of the portfolio depends on the composition of the portfolio (the relative shares of each asset in the portfolio), the risk on each asset in the portfolio, and the relationship between the yields on the assets included in that portfolio. In the comparatively simple case of a two-asset portfolio, it can be shown that:

$$\sigma_P^2 = \chi_A^2 \sigma_A^2 + \chi_B^2 \sigma_B^2 + 2\chi_A \chi_B R \sigma_A \sigma_B \qquad\qquad \textbf{(9A.6)}$$

where σ_p is the standard deviation of the portfolio (σ_p^2 is the variance of the portfolio) and R is the coefficient of correlation between the yields on the two assets.

  The coefficient of correlation is a new concept which requires brief explanation. (For a full exposition of its derivation and properties the student is referred to any basic textbook in statistics.[3]) For our purposes, suffice it to say that it is a measure of the extent to which the yields on the two assets tend to move together. If $R = 1$, then every time the yield on asset A increased, the yield on asset B would also increase by a predictable amount. This is a case of perfect positive correlation. Similarly, if $R = -1$, then every time the yield on asset A increased, the yield on asset B would decrease by a predictable amount. In the terminology used in the chapter, the assets are inversely dependent and there is perfect negative correlation between their yields. If $R = 0$, then the yields on the two assets move quite independently of each other. Knowing the yield on asset A does not permit you to say anything definite about the yield on asset B. Of course R can have any of these three polar values or some value in between. But let us examine the three polar cases in detail, leaving it to the reader to work out the conditions for other values.

---

[2] See for example: Harry Markowitz, *Portfolio Selection,* Monograph 16 for the Cowles Foundation for Economic Analysis at Yale University (New York: John Wiley & Sons, 1959), pp. 72-101.

[3] Mansfield, *op. cit.,* pp. 381-87.

Perfect Positive Correlation

If the yields on the individual assets are perfectly correlated, ($R = 1$), then the variance of the portfolio becomes:

$$\sigma_P^2 = \chi_A^2\sigma_A^2 + \chi_B^2\sigma_B^2 + 2\chi_A\chi_B\sigma_A\sigma_B \tag{9A.7}$$

This is a familiar quadratic equation.

If we take the square root of this equation to obtain the standard deviation of the distribution of possible yields on the portfolio, we find that:

$$\sigma_P = (\chi_A\sigma_A + \chi_B\sigma_B) \tag{9A.8}$$

The risk on the portfolio is the weighted average of the risks on the individual assets. Since the expected yield on the portfolio is also the weighted average of the expected yields on the portfolio, diversification does not reduce risk for any given level of expected yield.

Independent Assets

In the case of independent assets, ($R = 0$), the term $2\chi_A\chi_B R\sigma_A\sigma_B$ in equation 9A.6 drops out. In this case, the *variance* of the portfolio is a weighted average of the variances on the individual assets. That is,

$$\sigma^2_P = \chi_A^2\sigma_A^2 + \chi_B^2\sigma_B^2 \tag{9A.9}$$

However, the risk on the portfolio, represented by the standard deviation, is:

$$\sigma_P = \sqrt{\chi_A^2\sigma_A^2 + \chi_B^2\sigma_B^2} \tag{9A.10}$$

From equations 9A.7 and 9A.8, we already know that $\chi_A\sigma_A + \chi_B\sigma_B$ is the square root of an expression larger than that in equation 9A.10. Therefore,

$$\sigma_P < \chi_A\sigma_A + \chi_B\sigma_B \tag{9A.10a}$$

Perfect Negative Correlation

Finally in the case of perfect negative correlation, ($R = -1$). Equation 9A.6 becomes:

$$\sigma^2_P = \chi_A^2\sigma_A^2 + \chi_B^2\sigma_B^2 - 2\chi_A\chi_B\sigma_A\sigma_B \tag{9A.11}$$

Again, this is a familiar quadratic equation, the square root of which is:

$$\sigma_P = (\chi_A\sigma_A - \chi_B\sigma_B) \tag{9A.12}$$

The significant thing about this portfolio is that there is some combination of the two assets in the portfolio $\chi_A/\chi_B = \sigma_B/\sigma_A$ in which the risk on the portfolio is zero.

Conclusions

The important results are those represented by equation 9A.4 and 9A.6. They tell us that the expected yield on a portfolio is the weighted average of the expected yields on the assets comprising the portfolio. It can be shown, however, that if assets are wholly or partially independent of each other in a statistical sense $(0 < R < 1)$, then the risk on the portfolio will be less than the weighted average of the risks on the assets comprising that portfolio. The results of portfolio diversification have been explored for portfolios consisting of two assets — it can be shown that they apply to assets consisting of more than two assets. The analysis can also be extended to determine the composition of the portfolio which provides the minimum risk. In general (contrary to the example developed in Chapter 5), this is a portfolio which includes some of each asset, with the proportion of each asset inversely proportional to the variance of its yield.

An Example.   A simple example, for the case of a two-asset portfolio, can be developed using the data presented in Table 9A-1. If we assume $R = 0$ and the portion of the portfolio held in asset $A = .8$ and the portion held in asset $B = .2$.

The expected value of the portfolio equals

$.8 \times .05 + .2 \times .05 = .05$

TABLE 9A-1   **Example of a two-asset portfolio**

Asset		Outcome		
	Rate of return	*Estimated probability*	*Expected value*	*Standard deviation*
A	0.10	0.33	—	—
	0.05	0.33	0.05	0.041
	0.00	0.33	—	—
B	0.0605	0.99	0.05	0.105
	−1.00	0.01	—	—

Similarly the *variance* for such a portfolio is equal to

$(.8)^2 (.041)^2 + (.2)^2 (.105)^2$

$= .00152 = \sigma_P^2$

Therefore, the standard deviation of the portfolio equals .039.

Thus, the portfolio of 80% asset A and 20% asset B has the same expected yield as an entire portfolio of either A or B and yet has a lower standard deviation (risk) than either of these alternative portfolios. We therefore say that such a portfolio is a more *efficient* portfolio.

THE CHARTERED BANKS 10

The most familiar, most pervasive, and perhaps most important type of financial institution is the bank. It has been the subject of more theoretical speculations and empirical studies by economists than any other type of financial institution and its name is enshrined in innumerable university courses and textbooks on money and banking. In basic economics textbooks it is identified as having unique, almost quasi-magical powers to "create money." Perhaps as a result, it has been the principal target of monetary reformers, crank and otherwise, and certainly the banking industry is regulated and supervised to a more intense degree than almost any other class of business.

THE CONCEPT OF A BANK

Several definitions of a bank are possible. Indeed, in the most general sense, all financial institutions which accept relatively short-term deposits from the general public might be classified as banks. All such institutions have some degree of what we called in Chapter 9 "banker's risk." That is, they all face the possibility that a substantial portion of their liabilities may be presented for payment over a short period of time.

The Commercial Bank Concept.   Economists customarily distinguish between *commercial* banks and *savings* banks, primarily because of differences in the nature of their deposit liabilities and corresponding differences in the characteristics of their assets. A "pure" commercial bank (if it ever existed) would have short-term, highly volatile deposit liabilities which would be used as money in the normal course of events. It would have a relatively high degree of banker's risk, and as a result it would hold mainly short-term assets, including large quantities of short-term "commercial loans" (i.e., loans to businesses for working capital purposes). By contrast, a pure savings bank would have longer-term, lower-volatility savings deposits, and a correspondingly lower degree of banker's risk. As a result, it would mainly hold longer-term assets such as bonds, equities, and mortgages (and hence would be involved primarily in financing the formation of fixed capital, assets with a long working life calling for long-term financing). The unmodified term "bank" would normally be applied to commercial banks.

The "Money/Money Substitutes" Concept.   Despite the merits of classifying pure types of banking institutions for theoretical analysis, it is impossible to apply this dichotomy in practice. The important existing banking institutions are hybrids. Thus, in our discussion of the payments system in Chapter 2 we saw that a number of intermediaries issue liabilities which are used as money in the economy. Moreover, many financial institutions issue liabilities which are a close substitute for money as liquid assets, which led the Royal Commission on Banking and Finance to include in the concept of a bank:

> all private financial institutions issuing banking claims: that is, claims which serve as means of payment or close substitutes for them...We would include among banking liabilities all term deposits, whatever their formal name, and other claims on institutions maturing, or redeemable at a fixed price, within 100 days of the time of original issue or of the time at which notice of withdrawal is given by the customer.[1]

As the Commission notes, this is a very broad definition, which straddles the "pure" types discussed above, and encompasses

> the present chartered and savings banks, many trust and loan companies, some other deposit-taking institutions and [some] sales finance companies...It would also include the caisses populaires and credit unions...[2]

Such a definition makes an important point about the essential similarity and close competitiveness of institutions which bear different names and are regulated under different legislation. However, it does tend to obscure very real and important differences among institutions which can be included within this omnibus definition of a bank. As a result, neither the "pure" concepts of economic theory nor this broad definition by the Royal Commission provides a very useful basis for organizing a discussion of Canadian financial intermediaries.

A "Legal Status" Concept.   In the absence of any more fundamental principle, we must fall back on the essentially arbitrary categories established through the legislative treatment of financial institutions. In this sense *a bank is simply an institution considered as such in the laws of the land* — an institution issued a charter under the terms of the *Bank Act*. At the beginning of 1981, there were only 11 such institutions in Canada.[3]

THE CHARTERED BANKS IN
THE FINANCIAL SYSTEM _____

The chartered banks' claim to primacy of treatment in any discussion of the Canadian financial system is on several counts.

The Money Issuing Function

One of the primary reasons why economists take an intense interest in the activities of financial institutions is their underlying concern with the causes and implications of changes in the size of the money supply. While our discussion of the payments system in Chapter 2 showed that other private financial intermediaries also issue claims which are used as money, it also showed that the deposit liabilities of chartered banks are of overwhelming importance in this regard. If the money supply is the focal point for our interest in financial intermediaries, then we must be primarily interested in the chartered banks. Indeed, if, as the Royal Commission on Banking and Finance (among others) argued, "...issuing of claims which serve as a means of payment..."[4] is the central principle for identifying a bank, then the chartered banks must be taken as banks *par excellence.*

Nature of Asset Holdings

The money-issuing function of the chartered banks is of vital importance, and that alone would be sufficient to demand that we pay close attention to them. However, financial intermediaries are also a vital part of the mechanism whereby the savings of society are allocated among alternative possible uses. The selection of assets by these intermediaries can have significant microeconomic consequences. The size and composition of their asset holdings set the chartered banks apart from other financial intermediaries. The next largest concentration of assets is in the hands of the trust and mortgage loan companies, which have total assets approximately equal to 30% of the domestic assets of the chartered banks.

Concentration in Lending Activities

Like other financial intermediaries, part of the chartered banks' portfolios consists of *cash* and *marketable securities* (5% and 10% respectively of Canadian dollar assets). While these assets have particular importance to the banks (and while the banks are major holders of certain types of securities), we are more interested at present in the other major portion of their assets, loans.[5] The chartered banks' lending activities are highly concentrated in a few categories of loans, with the result that they tend to dominate (although seldom fully control) certain types of lending.

This is particularly true and important in the case of short-term commercial loans to business firms and to farmers to finance inventories of raw materials, goods in process of production, and finished products waiting to be sold.

In mid-1981 over $110 billion (or 58%) of their Canadian dollar assets were in the form of such commercial loans. In this sense the chartered banks were "commercial banks." Although there are, of course, other commercial lenders, they are not nearly as important as the chartered banks. In mid-1981, there was about $23 billion of "commercial paper" outstanding in the money market and approximately $8 billion in commercial loans outstanding from sales finance companies.

The chartered banks are not exclusively commercial lenders. We should not forget that they are also a major factor in the provision of consumer credit. Thus, of an estimated total of just over $47 billion consumer credit in mid-1981, personal loans from banks accounted for more than 68%, much of it in the form of longer-term installment credit to finance the purchase of automobiles and other consumer durable goods. In mid-1981, the banks also held $17 billion worth of *mortgages* on residential property. The banks also engage in some longer-term lending to businesses. Thus, a significant and growing portion of chartered banks' business loans are "term" loans (i.e., over two years to maturity), generally to smaller businesses for capital expansion purposes. Moreover, some portion of chartered banks' holdings of securities, particularly municipal and corporate bonds (but also some provincial bonds) might also be regarded as longer-term loans to these debtors, in the sense that an active secondary market for these issues does not exist and the banks acquire them in large blocks through direct negotiation with the issuer.

International Intermediation

There is another important dimension to the chartered banks' activities which merits at least passing mention in any discussion of their role in the financial system. While we customarily think of them in terms of their impact on the economy of Canada, we must remember that these banks are not simply domestic financial intermediaries. Of their total assets, 40 are foreign currency assets. As noted in our analysis of the payments system, the chartered banks provide the link between the Canadian payments system and payments systems in the rest of the world. They buy and sell foreign exchange, and through their trade association they jointly operate the Canadian foreign exchange market. Dealing in foreign exchange, however, accounts for a small portion of their total holdings of foreign currency assets. In addition to the essentially mechanical activity of providing international payments facilities, the chartered banks are important *international financial intermediaries*. That is, not only do they borrow from one set of individuals to lend to another within Canada, they engage in such activities in other national financial systems and across national boundaries.

What is a Chartered Bank?

Chartered banks are not simply an example of a commercial bank. They are the department stores of the financial industry, not specialty shops. It is true that their lending activities are highly concentrated in short-term loans to business financial institutions, governments, and consumers, and that in each area the chartered banks have a major and frequently a dominant share of the market. However, they also hold large portfolios of marketable securities, and they also engage in longer-term lending. From whatever vantage point you examine them, these are very complex institutions. Since we cannot hope to capture the full scope of their activities it is necessary to focus on a few essential features.

TABLE 10-1   **Chartered banks: consolidated balance sheet, June 30, 1982 ($ Millions)**

I. DOMESTIC INTERMEDIATION

Assets				Liabilities			
Cash				*Deposits*			
Currency and Bank of Canada deposits		$ 6 105		Demand deposits:			
Liquid assets				General public	$18 130		
Treasury bills	$ 6 891			Government of Canada	4 918	$ 23 048	
Short-term government bonds	570			Personal savings deposits		99 436	
Day, call and short loans	1 695	9 156		Other notice deposits		48 473	$170 957
Loans				*Other liabilities*			
Mortgages	31 484			Bank of Canada advances	42		
Other loans	128 652	160 136		Acceptances, letters of credit and guarantees (contingency)	12 284		
Securities				Debentures	2 610		
Long-term government bonds	696			All other liabilities	7 560	22 496	
Other securities	10 345	11 041					
Other assets							
Canadian dollar items in transit (float)	2 261						
Acceptances, guarantees and letters of credit	12 284						
All other assets	9 833	24 378					
Canadian dollar assets		210 818		*Canadian dollar liabilities*		193 453	
Foreign currency claims on residents of Canada		30 464		*Foreign currency deposits of Canadian residents*		10 589	
Total: domestic assets		241 282		*Total: domestic liabilities*		204 042	

II. FOREIGN AND INTERNATIONAL INTERMEDIATION

Foreign branch assets	89 464	Foreign branch liabilities	89 734
Foreign currency claims at Canadian head offices of non-residents of Canada	47 421	Foreign currency deposits at Canadian head offices of non-residents of Canada	72 181
	136 885		161 915

III. CAPITAL ACCOUNTS

		Reserves for losses and shareholders' equity	12 200
Total: domestic and international assets	$378 159	Total: domestic and international liabilities and capital accounts	$378 159

* Details may not add to totals because of rounding.

SOURCE: *Bank of Canada Review*, November 1982

THE BALANCE SHEET OF
THE CHARTERED BANKS _____

We have already encountered the concept of the balance sheet identity in Chapter 4. A balance sheet is simply an elaboration of that identity. It is a formal statement of the assets, liabilities, and net worth of a firm, household, or other institution, as of a particular date. In a balance sheet, the assets and liabilities will be shown in more or less detail depending on the purpose of the balance sheet, and will be organized into categories thought to reveal important characteristics of the business.

Table 10-1 presents a "consolidated" balance sheet for all of the chartered banks considered together as of June 30, 1982. Since it is in effect a balance sheet for the chartered banking industry, it conceals important differences among the several firms which comprise the industry. However, perhaps we can examine the structure of this balance sheet as though it were the balance sheet of a "typical" chartered bank.

The assets and liabilities in Table 10-1 are grouped into categories designed to highlight certain important features of the banking business. Perhaps the basic division to be emphasized is that between domestic intermediation on the one hand, and international or foreign intermediation on the other. Within the domestic component of the balance sheet, note on the one hand the relative importance of deposits payable on demand among the liabilities and, on the other hand, the high degree of liquidity possessed by the asset portfolio. One of our major concerns will be to explore the relationship between these facts.

DOMESTIC INTERMEDIATION:
THE COLLECTION OF FUNDS _____

We have defined a financial intermediary as a firm whose primary business involves simultaneously borrowing from one set of spending units and lending to another, normally at a profit to the intermediary. In our discussion of financial intermediation in Chapter 9 we argued that this posed a paradox. To make a profit, the intermediary must lend at a higher interest than it borrows. Why, then, do not the ultimate lenders and borrowers by-pass the intermediary completely, with gains to both of them? Considering only the domestic aspects of the banks' operations initially, we must answer these questions: From whom do the banks borrow? Why are Canadian assetholders willing to hold claims on the chartered banks rather than potentially higher-yielding claims on ultimate borrowers? What are the characteristics of claims on chartered banks which make them attractive to these assetholders?

The Instruments of Intermediation: Deposits

Even if one includes the capital (or net worth) accounts as a domestic source of funds, over 80% of the funds which the banks have raised from domestic sources are in the form of deposits, of which more than two-thirds are in fact, if not always in law, payable on demand. This suggests at least part of the answer to our questions. To a large extent chartered banks raise funds by appealing to the assetholders' demands for liquidity, a basic factor which we identified in Chapter 5 as entering into the portfolio balance decision.

The liquidity of most bank liabilities is a basic reality which pervades all aspects of the banking business. Every bank must so manage its affairs that it is able to meet all demands for the withdrawal of funds from demand deposits, and must always allow for the possibility of a very substantial withdrawal in a short period of time.

Liquidity is thus the key concept in exploring the place of banking liabilities in assetholders' portfolios. However, that is not the whole story. The chartered banks do not simply offer assetholders a single type of deposit with a single uniform characteristic — a high degree of liquidity. The chartered banks offer several types of deposits, each with particular and distinct characteristics designed to appeal to assetholders' multifarious asset preferences. While most chartered bank deposits are payable on demand, some can only be withdrawn at the end of a fixed term or after a specified period of notice. Some are transferable by cheque, others are not. Some pay no interest, others pay interest at substantially different annual rates. Why do banks offer so many different types of deposits?

Demand Deposits.   As we saw in Chapter 2, demand deposits — or *current accounts* as they are sometimes called — must be considered to be money. They are almost perfect substitutes for currency in many uses, and indeed in some aspects of the payments process demand deposits must be regarded as superior to currency. Demand deposits are perfectly liquid, pay no interest, and are transferable by cheque. The regular current account is designed primarily for the use of business firms — or more generally for spending units which regularly make a large volume of payments. However, there is also a special form of demand deposit which is designed for the use of individuals, the so-called personal chequing account. Normally, banks levy a fee for each cheque written on a demand deposit and, in addition, normally a monthly fee for servicing the account which will depend on the size of the balance maintained in the account. If the minimum balance is sufficiently large, the banks may waive service charges, and thus in a sense pay interest on the account.

It should be noted that not all demand deposits are held by individuals and business firms. The Government of Canada maintains very large balances with the chartered banks, as do provincial and municipal governments. There is also a significant amount of deposits by other banks. The latter are primarily deposits of foreign commercial banks who hold Canadian dollar balances so that they can effectively handle their customers' demands for Canadian dollars. These balances confirm the existence of a correspondent banking system (be it domestic or international) that we discussed in Chapter 2.

The Demand for Demand Deposits.   In providing this type of deposit, then, the chartered banks are reacting to assetholders' demands for assets which can be stored cheaply and safely and which can be transferred from person to person, often over long distances, quickly and at low cost. They are satisfying the demand for an efficient medium of exchange.

If it is primarily a demand for a medium of exchange, the demand for this type of deposit should depend on the flow of transactions in the economy, and hence on the

FIGURE 10-1   Relationship between demand deposits, cheques
cashed and gross national product

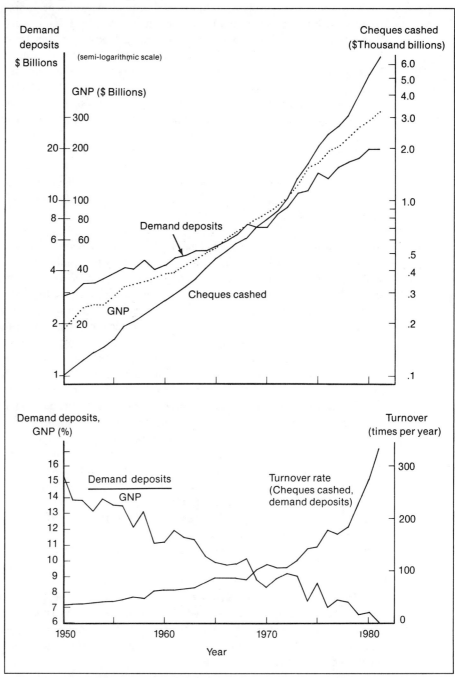

Source: *Bank of Canada Review.*

level of economic activity. Thus, as the value of the gross national product increases over time, the quantity of demand deposits demanded should similarly increase. If the rate of increase in the gross national product should falter, or indeed if the gross national product should fall, a corresponding change should occur in the demand for demand deposits.

However, recent developments in economic theory suggest that the relationship between the level of economic activity and the quantity of the medium of exchange demanded should be neither rigid nor simple. The validity of this conclusion should be obvious from the information plotted in Figure 10-1. The upper panel of this chart shows the gross national product, the average stock of demand deposits, and the value of cheques cashed against demand deposits for the years 1950-1981. You should note the roughly parallel movements in the lines describing the behavior of the gross national product (which can be taken as a measure of the level of economic activity) and the value of cheques cashed against demand deposits (which can be taken as a measure of the flow of expenditures effected using demand deposits). The behavior of the stock of demand deposits over this period of time was also broadly similar. However, the relationship was much less close, and in particular there was a much smaller relative increase in the stock of demand deposits than in either of the other two series. As a result, the ratio of demand deposits to the gross national product declined substantially (but not continuously) over this period, and the rate of turnover (or velocity of circulation) increased approximately ninefold.

We will have occasion to explore the demand for money in greater detail in Chapter 20. At this point, we can conclude that a basic determinant is the value of transactions to be effected, or the level of economic activity. However, over time, the spending units in the economy have found methods of economizing on their cash balances, so that the ratio of demand deposits to gross national product has been cut by almost 70% in a little over 30 years.

Personal Savings Deposits.   Table 10-1 shows that the largest single source of funds for the chartered banks is personal savings deposits. In fact, this is not a homogeneous category of deposits. As shown in Table 10-2, there are several kinds of personal savings deposits, with subtly different characteristics. However, all are designed as a safe, relatively liquid asset to be held in small or large amount by individual assetholders.

In mid-1982, approximately 46% of all personal savings deposits were in a form which had a *fixed term* to maturity. This includes funds invested in savings certificates, issued by some of the banks, which have similar characteristics to Canada Savings Bonds. They are cashable at any time at a specified price, but offer a significantly higher yield if held to maturity.

Most of the funds in personal savings deposits are not in fixed term accounts, however. Almost 50% of the funds are in what, for want of a better name, we might call *no-fixed-term* accounts. Such accounts are available in two forms, one subject to transfer by cheque and the other not directly transferable by cheque. Although the bank can legally require notice before any withdrawals, funds in these accounts are in fact withdrawable on demand.

Unlike the holder of a demand deposit, the holder of a chequable personal savings deposit receives interest on the funds left in the bank. However, he also generally pays a

TABLE 10-2   **Distribution of personal savings deposits, 1967-82**

Type of deposit	September 1967	June 1972	June 1982
	($ Millions)		
Fixed term	$ 1 040	$ 4 697	$45 143
No fixed term			
Non-chequable	2 285	8 355	46 889
Chequable	8 148	6 024	6 594
Total	$11 474	$19 076	$98 626
	(percent)		
Fixed term	9%	25%	46%
No fixed term	—	—	—
Non-chequable	20	44	48
Chequable	71	32	7
	100	100	100

SOURCE: *Bank of Canada Review*, various issues

higher service charge per cheque written and very active use of the account is discouraged. The holder of a non-chequable personal savings deposit receives a still higher rate of interest on the funds left with the bank.

The Demand for Personal Savings Deposits. The personal savings account in chartered banks must be one of the most widely held of financial assets. Thus, on April 30, 1981, there were some 36 million accounts on the books of the banking system, a figure which might be compared with the population of Canada which was then estimated at 24 million. (Of course, many individuals hold more than one account, and some accounts are held by clubs and similar organizations.) Moreover, while the average balance in a personal savings account has been increasing over the years, it remains relatively small. On April 30, 1981, it was approximately $2900 (as compared to $960 in 1969 and $675 in 1957). It is also worth noting that one-third of these accounts had a balance of less than $100, and 60% had a balance of less than $1000.

A variety of studies have examined the factors determining the demand for personal savings deposits at the chartered banks in relation to alternative forms of saving. One variable suggested by economic theory is the relative return on savings deposits and other assets. Interestingly enough, two recent studies suggest that holdings of deposits at trust and loan companies and caisses populaires are only slightly sensitive to the interest rates paid on savings deposits at chartered banks.[6] To an extent, this result is not too surprising for it suggests that the typical savings deposit is sufficiently small that it is not worth the depositor's time and effort to shop around for small differences in interest rates.

Although this type of account thus appears to have a particular appeal to the relatively small assetholder, we must not overlook the fact that there are some very large personal savings deposits as well. Thus, on April 30, 1981, there were some two million accounts with a balance of $10 000 or more, including about 50 000 with a balance of $100 000 or more. While accounts in excess of $10 000 make up only 7% of the number of personal savings accounts, their relatively large size means that they provide a much higher proportion of the funds which banks raise through personal savings accounts.

The demand for personal savings deposits is thus primarily, but not exclusively, a demand on the part of assetholders with relatively small portfolios for a safe, highly liquid asset, bearing a modest but virtually guaranteed rate of return. We must not forget that in some part it is also a demand for a medium of exchange, a demand for a chequing account suitable for handling a relatively small number of monthly payments. As we have already noted, in June 1982 about 7% of the funds in personal savings deposits were in chequable accounts. However, this percentage has fallen sharply over time (it was as high as 70% in 1967) as individual assetholders are induced by higher interest rates to hold the non-chequable accounts and by lower service charges to hold personal chequing accounts.

People presumably hold chequable personal savings accounts partly as a medium of exchange, but the overall significance of such accounts in the payments process should not be exaggerated. There are no separate statistics for turnover rates on chequable and non-chequable savings accounts. However, in 1980 the rate of turnover of all personal savings accounts was 1.19 times per year. Since approximately 7% of all personal savings deposits were in chequable form in 1982, this implies a turnover rate for the "active" accounts of about 17 times per year. By contrast, the turnover rate of demand deposits was 284 times per year.

Not only are chequable savings accounts much less active than demand deposits, cheques drawn on personal savings accounts are relatively unimportant in the total flow of payments through the economy. Such cheques accounted for less than 3% of all cheques cashed by chartered banks in 1980. A measure of the money supply held for transactions purposes which excluded personal savings accounts would not be grossly misleading. The primary economic significance of personal savings accounts, whether chequable or not, is as a safe, highly liquid asset bearing a moderate yield which is particularly attractive to individual assetholders with relatively little wealth.

Other Notice Deposits.   The primary difference between fixed-term personal savings deposits and other notice deposits is a matter of size. Both represent funds deposited with the banks for fixed periods of time at pre-determined rates of interest. However, deposit receipts, the major form of other notice deposits, are normally sold in denominations of $100 000 or more. Whereas personal savings accounts are directed at individual assetholders, other notice deposits are designed as temporary repositories of the excess cash balances of corporations, governments, and other organizations.

The relatively high interest rate which banks pay for corporate notice deposits reflects the intense competition for these funds, both domestically (from other financial institutions and from the money market) and internationally. Indeed, for very large blocks of funds the rates are negotiated individually for each customer. However, the fact that these rates are much higher than those paid on personal savings deposits, let alone demand deposits, does not necessarily mean that the corporate notice deposit business is less profitable. The fact that funds are attracted in large blocks, and that they are for a fixed term, means that the administrative costs associated with them are relatively low per dollar of deposit.

It is also worth noting that corporate notice deposits carry with them a relatively high degree of banker's risk, even through each deposit is for a fixed term and hence is relatively illiquid. Since each deposit is relatively large, the bank cannot achieve the same degree of diversification of its liabilities with corporate notice deposits as it could, for example, with an equal value of personal savings deposits. As a result, corporate notice deposits tend to be more volatile in the *aggregate* than personal savings deposits.

Foreign Currency Deposits.   It may be surprising to discover than not all deposits owned by Canadians in Canadian chartered banks are denominated in Canadian dollars. Indeed, in mid-1982, Canadian residents held almost $10 billion in deposits denominated in foreign currencies — almost 6% of the domestic deposits of the chartered banks. These foreign currency deposits are almost exclusively in U.S. dollars.

The Demand for Foreign Currency Deposits.   What accounts for the willingness of Canadian residents to hold U.S. dollar deposits with Canadian chartered banks?

A part of the U.S. dollar deposits grows out of the normal international commercial activities of Canadian business firms. Just as business firms find it important to maintain working balances of Canadian dollars to facilitate their activities in Canadian markets, so firms which conduct a major portion of their transactions in international markets may find it very convenient to maintain working balances of U.S. dollars. Since these firms are resident in Canada, it is logical that they would prefer to hold some or all of these balances with their regular Canadian bankers. According to the Canadian Bankers' Association, the principal users of this facility have traditionally been:

> Canadian exporters, Canadian companies operating plants in the United States, and customers requiring a depository for investment capital awaiting exchange into Canadian dollars or repatriation to the United States.[7]

To this extent, the presence of U.S. dollar deposits does not raise any new issues in our analysis of the banking system. They are just another example of the role of bank money in the exchange process.

However, this explains only part of the holdings of foreign currency deposits in chartered banks by residents of Canada. To a very large extent foreign currency deposits are held by residents of Canada as a substitute for Canadian dollar time deposits, i.e., as a short-term liquid investment.

This fact again raises the issue which occupied so much of our attention in Chapter 8. Other things being equal, a Canadian assetholder is exposed to *foreign exchange risk* whenever he invests in a foreign currency asset, regardless of whether that asset is a claim on a non-resident or on a Canadian bank. It is the currency in which the claim is to be paid which creates the risk, not the country in which the debtor resides. You should also remember that this risk can be most devastating for relatively short-term securities, including short-term deposits.

Under these circumstances, why do Canadian assetholders purchase foreign currency term deposits with Canadian banks?

In some degree, Canadians invest in foreign currency deposits in spite of foreign exchange risk. Perhaps they are speculating on favorable movements in the exchange rate; perhaps they regard the risk as justifiable; perhaps they are diversifying their portfolios; perhaps because of offsetting risks elsewhere in their total financial situation (i.e., the presence of foreign currency liabilities) they have no net risk. However, to some degree they avoid the foreign exchange risk through the now familiar device of the forward exchange contract. At the beginning of 1981, over $700 million of the resident-owned foreign currency deposits with Canadian banks were in the form of "swapped deposits," i.e., foreign currency deposits accompanied by a forward exchange contract under which the bank agrees to repurchase U.S. dollars on maturity of the deposit at an agreed exchange rate. The yield to the depositor depends on the interest rate paid on the deposit and on the difference between the spot exchange rate (at which he purchases the U.S. dollars) and the forward exchange rate (at which he resells the U.S. dollars), as in the examples worked out in Chapter 8.

Why do Canadian investors invest in foreign currency deposits? Aside from the myriad of individual motives unique to the investor in question, the answer is simply that he can obtain a more attractive yield by so doing, often (through the "swapped" deposit) without any additional risk.

Trends in Domestic Deposit Liabilities

It should be evident by now that the various types of deposits issued by chartered banks are close but not perfect substitutes for each other. At one end of the spectrum are demand deposits which are highly liquid and non-interest bearing, and at the other are long-term deposit certificates which are relatively illiquid and pay a premium interest rate.

If we examine behavior of bank deposits in the recent past (see Figure 10-2) we can see that the composition of deposit liabilities has been undergoing dramatic changes in recent years.[8] The relatively slow rate of growth of public demand deposits (9% per annum for 1970-1980) stands in contrast to the somewhat more rapid rate of growth of personal savings deposits (15% per annum) and the very rapid rate of growth of other notice deposits (20%).

What accounts for these different trends in the four main types of chartered bank deposits? The answer lies in the banks' response to the competitive environment of the 1960s and onward.

Perhaps the crucial element in the new situation was the development of an active money market which was both domestic and international in scope. Corporate treasurers became increasingly aware of opportunities for investing excess cash balances in short-term assets such as treasury bills, finance company paper, and repurchase agreements with bond dealers. Holding large balances in demand accounts which paid no interest was, in terms of income foregone, an expensive proposition that offered few, if any, benefits.

The banks responded by offering interest rates on relatively large term deposits — whether denominated in Canadian currency or "swapped" into U.S. dollars — which were competitive with rates offered on money market instruments. The result of this attempt to recapture short-term corporate funds has been very successful, if somewhat costly, in terms of rates paid. For example, at the beginning of 1981 notice deposits amounted to more than $34 billion, and rates paid were 17% or more for money deposited for as little as 30 days.

FIGURE 10-2   Trends in chartered bank deposit liabilities

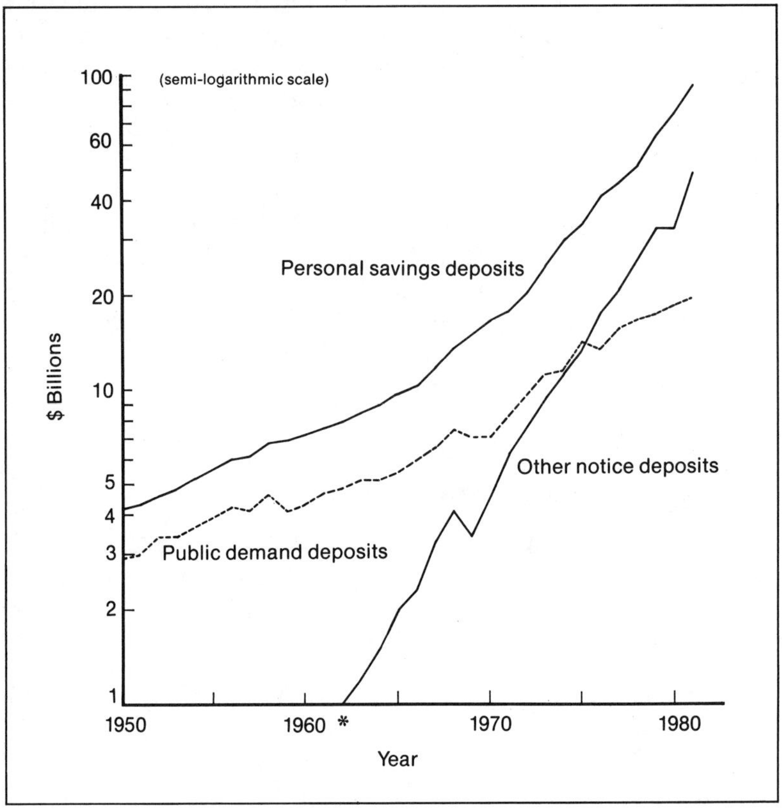

*Prior to 1962 notice deposits were less than $1 billion.
Source: *Bank of Canada Review.*

A similar situation developed in the market for personal savings deposits. In this case, competition from near banks made large inroads into the relative positions of the chartered banks (see Table 10-3). In response, the banks have made strong efforts to maintain their position in this market through such means as more competitive interest rates, more flexible banking hours, and interest paid on daily balances, though many of these devices were in response to prior innovations by their competitors.

Non-Deposit Sources of Funds

The balance sheet presented in Table 10-1 shows several other categories of domestic liabilities and the capital account as non-deposit sources of funds. Of these only the capital account has any major significance.

Acceptances, Guarantees, and Letters of Credit.   The account, *Acceptances, Guarantees, and Letters of Credit* cannot really be described as a "source of funds" for bank

TABLE 10-3   Personal savings deposits held in various financial intermediaries

	1955		1965		1970		1982	
	$Millions	%	$Millions	%	$Millions	%	$Millions	%
Intermediary								
Chartered banks	5 633	54	9 725	43	15 030	46	98 625	47
Credit unions and *caisses populaires* (deposits & shares)	598	6	2 275	10	3 778	11	30 235*	14
Trust and mortgage loan companies	1 066	10	5 078	22	7 586	23	56 486	27
Canada Savings Bonds	3 137	30	5 552	25	6 579	20	24 613	12
Total	10 434	100	22 630	100	32 973	100	209 959	100

* March 31, 1982

SOURCES: Royal Commission on Banking and Finance, *Report* (Ottawa, 1964); *Bank of Canada Review,* various issues.

operations. Unlike the other entries on the balance sheet, this represents a "contingent" liability. Although there are several different types of items recorded in this account, in general the bank has simply undertaken to guarantee certain liabilities of some of its customers (and hence there is an exactly offsetting asset account, *Customers' Liability under Acceptances, Guarantees, and Letters of Credit)* in order to make those liabilities more acceptable in the market place. The bank could only be called upon to make payment in full out of its own resources if the customer failed to meet his obligation. In this sense it is a contingent liability. For this service, the bank charges a fee, and as a result it is useful to include such items in the balance sheet.

Other Liabilities   The other liabilities of the banks include such things as dividends payable but not yet collected by the shareholders, accrued tax liabilities, mortgages on bank property, and other petty debts. This category also includes debentures which are long-term debts issued by the chartered banks. In mid-1981 debentures issued totaled $2.3 billion. The supposed advantage to the banks of raising funds via debentures is their relatively long term (usually five years or more) coupled with their exemption from any reserve requirements. Banks were first permitted to issue debentures as a result of the revision of the *Bank Act* in 1967. While initially the banks were slow to make use of their power to issue debentures, in recent years their interest in this form of finance has increased considerably. Nevertheless, debentures are still only a minor source of funds and will likely remain so because of the limitation on their issue to an amount no more than one-half of bank's equity and reserves.

Another liability which is important, although its magnitude is generally very small (and most often zero), is *Advances from the Bank of Canada.* These are short-term loans made by the central bank to the chartered banks. When a bank, for reasons of a sudden and adverse clearing against it or because of a sudden deposit withdrawal, finds itself short of the legally required amounts of vault cash and/or deposits with the central bank, it can borrow the needed funds for a short period of time from the central bank. This loan, or *advance*, gives the chartered bank time to liquidate some of its assets and then use the proceeds to repay the loan from the central bank. Later in this chapter, when we consider the position of the banks in the money market, and again in Chapter 19 when we discuss the functions of the central bank, we shall discuss various aspects of these advances in greater detail.

The Capital Account.   What we are calling the capital account of the banks is simply the difference between the reported values of the banks' assets and liabilities. The sums recorded in this account derive from two sources — the capital subscribed by the original purchasers of shares of the banks' stock, and appropriations from the earnings of the banks over the years. They thus represent a source of operating funds for the banks, funds which can be ascribed directly or indirectly to the banks' shareholders.

In fact, the capital account has two separable components — *accumulated reserves for losses* and *shareholders' equity.* The distinction between these two components is important to the accountant concerned with measuring the profitability of the bank, or to the government concerned with assessing corporate income taxes (the banks are allowed to make limited additions to reserves for losses in most years without treating these funds as taxable profits). However, from our present point of view the distinction is not important. They serve essentially the same function by providing a margin of safety for the bank's depositors and other creditors. This margin of safety is provided by the fact that the value of assets exceeds the value of creditors' claims by the magnitude of the capital accounts, and by the fact that the creditors' claims must be satisfied before any distribution of assets can be made to shareholders should the corporation be wound up. Thus, the capital accounts provide an estimate of the value of the residual claim of the shareholders to the assets of the bank: a claim which is legally "subordinated" to the claims of the bank's creditors, including depositors.

DOMESTIC INTERMEDIATION: THE ALLOCATION OF FUNDS

We have discovered that the liability side of the balance sheet of the chartered banks has a relatively unique structure, but that in recent years that structure has been undergoing rather dramatic changes. The same things can be said about the asset side of the balance sheet. There is a standard, historical mould, but the pattern of chartered bank involvement in the flow of credit to the economy has been changing significantly in recent years, and as a result the structure of the banks' asset holding has been changing too.

If we want to analyze the banks' activities in the credit field, we must take account of four groups of factors: (1) the classic or historical pattern of chartered bank activities; (2) the incentives to change created by attempts to maximize profits in a changing economy; (3) the ever-present necessity of coping with the high degree of banker's risk inherent in the structure of bank liabilities; and (4) a number of overriding legal constraints on what the banks are permitted to do.

The Allocation of Funds: Bank Loans

In a book which was for many years the standard exposition of Canadian chartered bank policies and practices, A. B. Jamieson asserted that:

> The chartered banks give two main functions: (1) to provide a safe depository for the funds of individuals and business concerns throughout Canada, and (2) within the limits of prudent banking to make these funds available to facilitate production and trade.[9]

Ten years later, in their brief to the Royal Commission on Banking and Finance, the Canadian Bankers' Association echoed agreement. Asserting that one of the primary functions of the chartered banks must be "…to make loans," they argued that

> the first priority in back lending must still be given to short term business borrowing for working capital purposes.[10]

The management of all other aspects of the banks' asset portfolios, including the banks' investment activities, must normally be "…subsidiary to bank lending activities."

This is the traditional view of the role of the chartered banks in the flow of credit to the economy. Is it a valid description of the contemporary activities of the chartered banks?

We provided part of the answer to this question in the introduction to this chapter. The chartered banks today remain the primary source of short-term credit for businesses in Canada. But perhaps that should not be too surprising. The Canadian banking system developed over the years with the commercial lending function foremost in mind. As the Canadian Bankers' Association like to emphasize, "there appears to be no other source similarly qualified to provide, administer and supervise this type of loan."[11] The business of making loans involves face-to-face negotiations between the lender and the borrower. The organization of the banking system facilitates this process. Thus, the banks have networks of branch offices, and in the case of the five largest banks these networks are nationwide in scope. In early 1979, the 11 banks in operation had between them 7457 offices in Canada, with the five largest banks accounting for almost 87% of them. These branch offices are in part deposit collection and administration points, but they are also loan offices, strategically located to service loan accounts. The business of making loans also involves a degree of skill in judging credit-worthiness. As the Canadian Bankers' Association again emphasizes:

> The training of branch managers is aimed at the development of officers who can seek out lending opportunities and make good loans. The manager's recognition and advancement depends to a significant degree on his abilities in making loans.[12]

Such, then, is the bankers' self-image. They consider themselves to be particularly well-adapted to make loans, especially commercial loans, and they consider commercial lending to have first priority in their credit activities. Are these assertions borne out by the facts?

Loans versus Securities.   In mid-1982, the outstanding loans of the banks included $31 billion in mortgages, $129 billion in Canadian dollar loans and $25 billion in foreign

FIGURE 10-3   Relationship between loans, securities and total assets

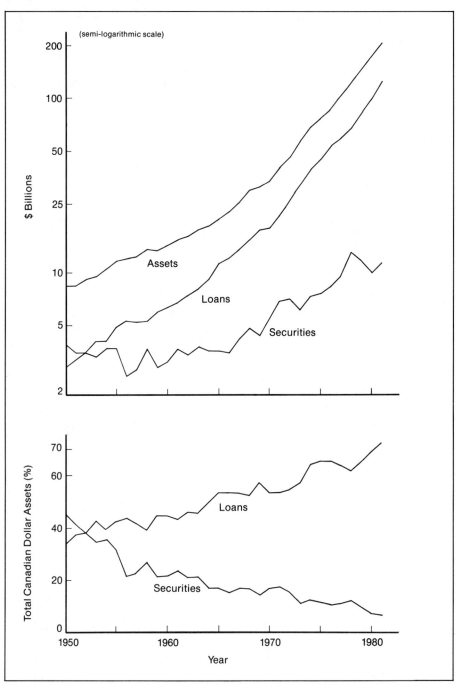

Source: *Bank of Canada Review.*

currency loans to residents. In contrast, the banks held $8 in government bonds (including treasury bills) together with $10 billion in other securities. Overall, the value of loans was almost eight times the value of domestic securities held by the banks. Figure 10-3 shows how the importance of domestic loans has increased relative to the total domestic assets of the banks. From a minority position at the beginning of 1950 (31% of assets), loans had increased to a dominant position of 60% by 1965. This growth continued at a slow pace to the point where loans accounted for over 68% of assets by the start of 1981. The relative importance of loans among the assets of chartered banks has now surpassed their levels in the late 1920s.[13] At the same time, there has been a corresponding decrease in the relative importance of securities from 50% in 1950 to 23% in 1965. This trend has also continued so that securities are now less than 10% of assets. In fact, the banks' holdings of government bonds (excluding treasury bills) are now no more than they were in 1950. What Jamieson said about the nature of the banking business in 1952, and what the Canadian Bankers' Association said in 1962, was even more true in 1980. The story of the growth of the chartered banks from the 1950s onward has been a story of the growth of their lending business.

The Composition of the Loan Portfolio. The assertion that the main thrust in the banks' credit activities takes the form of "making loans" is clearly correct. Security holdings are of much smaller relative importance. What about the additional assertion that bank loans are primarily "commercial" loans?

Evidence on trends in the composition of the banks' loan portfolio is presented in Table 10-4. It is clear from these data that the "traditional" commercial lending business is still the dominant activity of the chartered banks, although it has been declining in relative importance. Perhaps the most notable change which is evident in Table 10-4 is the increased relative importance of personal loans. Almost 40% of the loan portfolio is in the form of mortgages and other loans to individuals and, moreover, this component of the loan portfolio has increased steadily over time. Through the medium of credit and other marketing arrangements, the banks have been pursuing the personal loan business with increasing vigor.

The Commercial Loan Theory. We have seen that in contemporary practice, the chartered banks are primarily, but far from exclusively, providers of short-term credit to finance "production and trade." In an earlier day, banking theory made concentration on such loans a matter of high principle, and indeed it was argued that "any departure from this principle is bound to prove eventually disastrous."[14] The essential argument was that if the loans of chartered banks were used to finance the production and distribution of goods, the loans would be safe because they were "supported continually during their currency by the existence of the goods," and the loans would be "self-liquidating" because the goods when sold would provide the means to repay the loans.[15] This was an argument that the volume of bank credit would automatically be adjusted to the needs of trade, and therefore could be neither excessive nor deficient; and it was also an argument that the banks would never have liquidity problems because of the revolving, short-term nature of their assets.

This is not the place to assess the merits of what has variously been called the "commercial loan" theory of banking or the "real bills" doctrine (commercial loans are

TABLE 10-4   **The chartered banks' Canadian dollar loan portfolio**

	1950	*1960*	*1970*	*1981*
Commercial loans				
Farmers	243	420	1 135	7 841
Other industries	1 566	3 683	9 808	66 202
Total commercial	1 809	4 103	10 943	74 042
Financial loans	351	681	997	1 147
Commercial and financial	2 160	4 784	11 940	75 190
Government and institutional	186	538	1 222	3 873
Personal loans				
Mortgages	—	971	1 324	17 148
Other personal loans	597	1 385	5 019	30 307
Total personal	597	2 356	6 333	47 855
TOTAL CANADIAN DOLLAR LOANS	2 943	7 678	19 495	126 918
Percentage Distribution				
Commercial and financial	74	62	61	59
Government and institutional	6	7	6	3
Personal:				
Mortgages	0	12	7	14
Other personal loans	20	18	26	24
TOTAL	100	100	100	100

SOURCE: *Bank of Canada Review*, various issues

"real bills" because they are backed by a corresponding value of real goods in the final stages of production). Suffice it to say that it was proven deficient both from the point of view of regulating the volume of credit and from the point of view of safeguarding the liquidity of banks. Indeed, institutional arrangements have been developed to supplant reliance on the commercial loan principle. As we will see, in contemporary banking practice, reliance is placed on the central bank to regulate the overall volume of credit, and on individual bank holdings of short-term financial instruments which can be sold in the money market and the reserve lending power of the central bank to safeguard the liquidity of the banking system.

Earlier versions of the *Bank Act* were firmly rooted in the commercial loan theory of banking. However, just as institutional arrangements for controlling the supply of credit and safeguarding the liquidity of the banking system have developed away from the real bills principle, so the lending powers conferred on the chartered banks in successive revisions of the *Bank Act* in recent years have embodied widening departures from the spirit of the commercial loan theory.

Early versions of the *Bank Act* contained a blanket prohibition against lending money:

> upon the security, mortgage or hypothecation of any lands, tenements or immovable property, or of any ships or other vessels, or upon the security of any goods, wares or merchandise...except as authorized by this Act.

The crucial question, then, was what type of loans secured directly or indirectly by merchandise were explicitly authorized by the *Bank Act*.

The permissible scope of bank lending activities were spelled out in several sections of the *Bank Act*, including what have become the most famous sections of the *Act*, Sections 86 and 88. In general, these sections permitted the banks to make loans on the security of natural resources or manufactured goods in the process of distribution or production. Section 86 was primarily concerned with the distribution phase. It permitted loans secured by warehouse receipts or bills of lading for such products, i.e., on the security of evidence that such products had been placed in the custody of an independent warehouseman or a transportation company and could not be released without the bank's agreement. Section 88, by contrast, was of primary concern in the production phase. It permitted loans on the direct security of specified goods still in the hands of farmers, manufacturers, and wholesalers.

In other words, Section 86 and 88 of the *Bank Act* specifically permitted — perhaps we should say encouraged — the chartered banks to make the type of loan called for by the real bills doctrine: short-term, "self-liquidating" loans to facilitate production and distribution. By contrast, other sections of the *Act* specifically prohibited the chartered banks from making loans of a type which would violate the real bills doctrine: loans secured by long-lived capital equipment, buildings, or land. It should be noted, however, that the banks were permitted wide latitude to hold stocks and bonds, to make loans on the security of stocks and bonds, or to make loans "without security".

The essential provisions of Sections 86 and 88, modified, sharpened, and somewhat broadened, remain in the *Bank Act* today (but now combined together under Section 178). However, the impact of the blanket prohibitions on other types of loans secured by real goods has been blunted or removed in special legislation and in successive revision of the *Bank Act* since the late 1930s. In 1937, the banks were encouraged to make unsecured Home Improvement Loans, subject to a partial government guarantee. In the 1944 revision of the *Bank Act*, the banks were permitted to make loans on the security of ships and ship equipment, fishing vessels and agricultural equipment, and under the *Farm Improvement Loans Act* of the same year they were permitted and, indeed, encouraged by a partial government guarantee to make longer-term loans for farm improvement on various types of security, including a mortgage on the farm. Similar provisions were made for longer-term loans to help establish veterans in a business or in a profession under the 1946 *Veterans' Business and Professional Loans Act*. (In 1960, the same type of guarantees were offered on longer-term capital loans to small businesses under the *Small Business Loans Act*).

These special provision violated the spirit of the real bills doctrine, but in strictly limited amount and with most important cases subject to governmental guarantee. The more significant changes were yet to come. One of these changes, which had a profound effect on the character of the chartered banks' business, was a provision of the 1954 *Bank Act* which permitted the chartered banks to make loans to individuals who were neither farmers, manufacturers, or wholesalers, on the security of chattel mortgage, that is:

> upon the security…of household property, that is to say, motor vehicles and any personal or movable property for use in or about dwellings and lands and buildings appurtenant thereto…

The banks had long made personal loans, largely on the security of stocks and bonds, or unsecured loans. This new provision opened the whole field of consumer installment credit in a fashion which was a complete violation of the real bills principle. At the time of the 1954 revision of the *Bank Act*, Parliament was not yet ready to extend similar blanket permission to enter the one major field of credit still closed to the banks, i.e., mortgage lending on the security of land and buildings. However, by the provisions of the *National Housing Act* of 1954 the banks were permitted to acquire mortgages which had been insured by the Government of Canada. The final step was taken in the 1967 revision of the *Bank Act*, when the prohibition against mortgage lending was removed, and the banks were given blanket permission to take as security for loans "...any real or personal, immovable or movable property," although a ceiling of 10% of Canadian dollar deposits was placed on total holdings of non-insured mortgages.

Our earlier discussions of the banks' loan portfolios shows that commercial lending remains the core of their credit activities, and so Section 178 (the successor to Sections 86 and 88) retains a prominent and important place in the *Bank Act*. However, successive revisions of the *Bank Act* have relaxed the constraints imposed by the real bills doctrine, and the chartered banks have diversified their lending activities to a degree that they now deserve the sobriquet "the department stores of the financial system."

Safeguarding Liquidity

We must now turn our attention to an aspect of the banks' management of their asset portfolios that we have so far glossed over, their techniques of coping with the banker's risk which is inherent in the structure of their liabilities. How are the banks able to guarantee payment of such an overwhelming portion of their liabilities on demand?

Cash Reserves.   A bank is required to be continuously willing and able to pay out cash when cash is demanded by its depositors. To a limited extent, normal cash drains will involve actual payments of currency over the counter in some or all of 7457 bank offices across the country. To meet these potential over-the-counter cash drains each bank needs currency in the vaults of each of its offices across Canada. Primarily, however, cash drains will result from inter-bank settlements of net clearing balances. Since the clearing process is centralized, this implies that each bank needs funds at the Bank of Canada in Ottawa to meet potential clearing house drains (any reader who does not recall the nature of the cheque clearing process should review Section 2 of Chapter 2).

One obvious solution to the problem posed by possible cash drains would be for each bank to keep on hand at all times, both in its vaults and on deposit at the Bank of Canada, sufficient cash to meet all conceivable short-term demands for funds on the part of its depositors. As we have already pointed out, the bankers know that under normal circumstances it is highly unlikely that a large portion of deposits will be called for payment in a short period of time. As a result, the cash which they would have to hold to be "safe" would only be a fraction of their deposit liabilities — with the size of that fraction depending on the bankers' assessments of the probable volatility of their deposits and the degree of safety which they desire.

An examination of Table 10-1 reveals that the banks do in fact hold substantial amounts of cash, both in the form of currency in the vaults of their many banking offices and in the form of deposits with the Bank of Canada (and to a lesser extent with other banks). Is this, then, the bankers' primary method of hedging against banker's risk?

The Cash Reserve Requirement and Bank Liquidity.   We have to be very cautious in placing such a construction on the relatively large holdings of cash by the chartered banks. The banks do not hold all of this cash voluntarily. Under the terms of the Bank Act they are required to hold cash, either in their vaults or in their deposits with the Bank of Canada, in the amount of 10% of all Canadian dollar demand deposits, 2% on the first $500 million saving and notice deposits and 3% on all saving and notice deposits beyond $500 million.[16] In addition, for the first time, the *Bank Act* of 1980 specified that the banks hold reserves against foreign currency deposits of residents of Canada at offices in Canada, the level being 3% of these deposits. Prior to March 1981, the applicable reserve ratios were 12% against Canadian demand deposits and 4% against Canadian savings and notice deposits. Given the composition of deposits at the beginning of 1981, the reserve ratio was approximately 5.42% of total Canadian dollar deposits.

One might argue that if the banks are required to hold this cash, then it cannot serve as a hedge against bankers' risk, because by definition the cash is not available to be paid out to depositors. Of course, this is not true of any excess reserves of cash, that is, holdings of currency and deposits at the Bank of Canada over and above those required by the Bank Act. Excess reserves are clearly available to be paid out to depositors. However, excess cash reserves tend to be very small. Only rarely have they exceeded 0.1% in any reserve averaging period. Surely, excess reserves of that magnitude do not give banks a significant margin of safety. However, the apparent conclusion that the bulk of the banks' holdings of cash cannot be counted as a liquid asset must be modified somewhat because the legal cash reserve requirement is neither as simple nor as rigid as the above discussion implies. The actual cash reserve requirement, expressed as an equation, is as follows:

$$
\begin{array}{l}
\text{Required} \\
\text{Deposit} \\
\text{at the} \\
\text{Bank of} \\
\text{Canada}
\end{array}
= .10 \begin{bmatrix} \text{Demand} \\ \text{deposits} \end{bmatrix} + .02 \begin{bmatrix} \text{First \$500} \\ \text{million of} \\ \text{saving and} \\ \text{notice} \\ \text{deposits} \end{bmatrix} + .03 \begin{bmatrix} \text{Saving and} \\ \text{Notice} \\ \text{deposits} \\ \text{beyond} \\ \text{first \$500} \\ \text{million} \end{bmatrix} + \begin{bmatrix} \text{Foreign} \\ \text{currency} \\ \text{deposits} \\ \text{of} \\ \text{residents} \end{bmatrix} - \begin{array}{l}\text{Vault} \\ \text{cash}\end{array}
$$

| Daily average required over current averaging period | Measured by average of four consecutive Wednesdays ending with second Wednesday in month prior to the averaging period |

Take particular note of the time periods involved. Only the required deposit at the Bank of Canada refers to the present time period. All other elements in the equation relate to an earlier period.

From the point of view of the liquidity of the banks' cash holdings, there are two important elements of flexibility in the reserve requirement: (1) the fact that the reserve requirement need only be satisfied on a *daily average* over a set period of time; and (2) the fact that the vault cash (currency) which is to be counted in calculating the cash reserve was that held by the bank *last month*.

The significance of the first point should be obvious. Since the banks do not have to satisfy the reserve requirement every business day, they can draw their reserve deposits below the required level on some days as long as they exceed the requirement on other days by an amount sufficient to provide a daily average which satisfies the requirement. This introduces an important element of flexibility, making the banks' reserve deposits at the Bank of Canada more liquid than might appear at first glance.

Clearly, in assessing the liquidity of these deposits, an important question is how far the banks are willing to draw down their deposits below the required level on any given day. Since daily statistics are not published, we do not know. However, it undoubtedly depends in part on the *length of the averaging period*. The longer the averaging period, the easier it will be for a bank to make up reserve deficiencies and hence the less reluctant it will be to fall substantially below its requirement on any given day. In Canada, the reserve averaging period has been 15 days from January 1969 onwards.

The significance of the second point — the fact that it is last month's vault cash which enters the calculation of reserve holdings — may not be as obvious. However, it means that there is no legal impediment to a bank paying out currency which it has in its vaults. The entire holdings of currency could, in principle, be paid out without affecting the bank's legal reserve position. It is true that it will affect the reserve deposit which the bank must hold at the Bank of Canada on a daily average the *next month*.[17] However, paying out currency cannot create a reserve deficiency *this month*.[18] For this reason, cash in the vaults of bank offices across the country can be regarded as a perfectly liquid asset, at least for meeting over-the-counter drains.

The Demand for Excess Cash Reserves.   We can conclude that bank holdings of cash provide only a *partial* hedge against banker's risk. Vault cash is available to satisfy over-the-counter demands for currency, and adverse clearing balances can be satisfied out of excess reserves or out of very temporary reductions in reserve deposits below the legal requirement. Clearly, the magnitude of the excess cash reserve is a crucial determinant of liquidity. However, we have seen that the banks in fact hold very small excess cash reserves. Given the banks' ever-present liquidity problem, is this not surprising? Should we not expect the banks to have a strong demand for liquidity, and hence to hold large sums of their most liquid asset, excess cash reserves?

The explanation for the low level of excess reserves among Canadian chartered banks is simple. The banks require sufficient stocks of liquid assets to meet possible clearinghouse drains. However, these liquid assets need not be excess cash reserves. They can be *any short-term asset which is virtually risk free and which can be converted into cash on very short notice*. While excess cash reserves do have the desirable property of immediate availability, they have the undesirable property of being sterile. By law, the Bank of Canada cannot pay interest on the chartered banks' reserve deposits. By contrast, other liquid assets which the banks might hold do bear interest. As a result, a profit-maximizing banker will attempt to keep his excess cash reserves to a minimum, holding instead short-term liquid securities, as long as he can be confident that the securities can be converted into cash, on very short notice, and at a relatively small cost. This requires an active, efficient short-term money market (the nature of which was discussed in Chapter 3.)

Refer again to Table 10-1 and note the very substantial bank holdings of short-term, liquid securities. Over 5% of Canadian dollar assets were in the form of day, call or short-loans, treasury bills, and other short-term Government of Canada bonds on June 30, 1981. These short-term, liquid instruments are normally referred to as the banks' *secondary reserves*.

The Secondary Reserve Requirements.   As in the case of cash reserves, not all of the banks' holdings of secondary reserves are voluntary. Under a 1956 agreement sponsored by the Bank of Canada, the chartered banks were obliged to hold cash, treasury bills, or day-to-day loans in the amount of 7% of their Canadian dollar deposit liabilities over and above the cash reserve required by the *Bank Act*, making a combined reserve requirement of cash and liquid assets of 15% of Canadian dollar deposits.[19] In the 1967 revision of the *Bank of Canada Act*, the Bank of Canada was given the statutory authority to formally establish such a secondary reserve requirement, and to change it from time to time subject to a maximum rate of 12%. The required ratio was initially established in March 1968 at 6%. From then until 1977 it was changed nine times, reaching a peak of 9% during 1970. More recently, the Bank of Canada has abstained from using the secondary reserve ratio as an instrument of policy. From February 1977, the rate remained unchanged at 5% until November 1981, at which time it was lowered to 4%. With the cash reserve ratio in the neighborhood of 5%, this makes the combined cash and liquid asset reserve requirement roughly 9% of Canadian dollar deposits. The combined ratio will change from time to time as the changing composition of bank deposits changes the cash ratio, or it the Bank of Canada elects to use the secondary reserve ratio once again as an active instrument of monetary policy.

Applying the same argument as we developed in the case of the cash reserve requirement, the existence of the secondary reserve requirement means that the banks' holdings of treasury bills and day-to-day loans are not fully liquid. To the extent that the banks are obliged to hold these securities, they cannot be sold into the market to satisfy cash drains except on a very temporary basis. However, as in the case of primary reserves, typically the banks have held excess reserves of treasury bills and day-to-day loans. Over time, the size of these excess reserves has steadily diminished from the levels of 2% maintained in the early 1970s, so that by 1981 these excess reserves averaged approximately 1.2% of deposits over the year and reached a level as low as 0.8% during the year. Like the very small average excess cash reserve, this excess secondary reserve does not provide a substantial margin of safety for the banks. Surely this is not the full extent of their hedge against their banker's risk.

Other Liquid Assets.   The assets which may be held to satisfy the statutory secondary reserve requirement are very precisely defined. They are cash, treasury bills, and

Calculating Required Reserves:
An Example

The approach used to determine the primary reserve requirements for chartred banks may seem complicated at first reading and it is. The matter can be clarified by use of the example of the (fictitious) Bank of Northern Yukon and the determination of its cash reserves for one of the reserve averaging periods in the month of August 1985.

Reference Dates. As a first step in determining these reserve requirements, we must settle on the reference dates for calculating deposits and vault cash. The regulations governing these reserves state these values are to be calculated for "Wednesdays in each of the four consecutive weeks ending with the second Wednesday in the month preceding that period." The second Wednesday in July is July 10. This Wednesday and the three preceding Wednesdays, July 3, June 26, and June 19 are the reference dates for calculating reserves.

Measurement of Deposits. The records of the Bank of Northern Yukon reveal that deposits on the relevant dates are as summarized in the table.

Total deposits in Canadian dollars or with residents averaged $4450 million over the reference dates which apply for the first averaging period in August 1985

Determination of Required Primary Reserves. The primary reserve requirement for the Bank of Northern Yukon can be calculated by use of formula (10.B1) below.

The legal reserve requirements together with the composition of its own deposits mean the Bank of Northern Yukon must maintain a cash reserve of $230 million or 5.17% of total domestic deposits.

The calculations at this point do not include the vault cash which was held by the bank on the reference dates and which can be counted as part of its cash reserve. We deduct this average of $125 million vault cash from the cash reserve requirement and find that the Bank of Northern Yukon must maintain average deposits of $105 million at the Bank of Canada over the two reserve averaging periods in August 1985.

Reserve Management. The first reserve averaging period in August consists of the first 11 weekdays of the month. The managers of the Bank of Northern Yukon do not, of course, have to maintain the $105-million deposit with the Bank of Canada on a day-to-day basis. In fact, the management very likely has a strategy for reserve management which takes into account things such as expected deposit inflows and outflows, money market conditions, their perception of the current

$$.10 \begin{bmatrix} \text{Demand} \\ \text{deposits} \end{bmatrix} + .02 \begin{bmatrix} \text{First \$500} \\ \text{million of} \\ \text{savings and} \\ \text{notice} \\ \text{deposits} \end{bmatrix} + .03 \begin{bmatrix} \text{Savings and} & + \text{Foreign} \\ \text{notice deposits} & \text{currency} \\ \text{beyond first} & \text{deposits} \\ \text{\$500 million} & \text{held by} \\ & \text{residents} \end{bmatrix} = \begin{matrix} \text{Required} \\ \text{cash} \\ \text{reserves} \end{matrix}$$

$$.10 \times 1450 \quad + .02 \times 500 \quad + .03 \, [1900 \quad + 600] \quad = 230$$

(10.B1)

Bank of Northern Yukon: Deposits and Vault Cash
(Millions of dollars)

Date	Demand deposits	Savings and notice deposits	Foreign currency deposits held by residents	Vault cash
June 19, 1985	$1 300	$2 400	$500	$120
June 26, 1985	1 450	2 350	600	135
July 3, 1985	1 500	2 450	625	115
July 10, 1985	1 500	2 400	675	130
Average	$1 450	$2 400	$600	$125

monetary policy of the Bank of Canada, and even their reaction to any surprises in the movement of their cash assets to date in the reserve averaging period.

Suppose we are in charge of the Bank of Northern Yukon's cash reserve management, and our staff has informed us that we have maintained only an average of $103 million the first eight days of the reserve averaging period. This means we *must* have fallen short of our required reserve by $16 million on a cumulative basis and must make up this amount over the next three business days. What do we do? The answer depends on many factors.

One possibility is that we have been worried that we would have difficulties in meeting our reserves in this averaging period. Possibly, the Bank of Canada has been acting to create a shortage of reserves and that its policies are reflected in money markets where funds are in short supply. In this case, we would take fairly drastic action either by selling securities, or by raising interest rates paid on deposits, especially wholesale deposits, so as to attract more funds. We may also consider shifting funds from vault cash to deposits at the Bank of Canada to ease the reserve position for this period. This latter action, of course, may only delay the reserve shortage, for the vault cash would have been counted as part of cash reserves for the next month. Finally, as a last resort, we may resign ourselves reluctantly to borrowing from the Bank of Canada.

This preceding sketch is not the only possibility. We may, instead, have anticipated that cash reserves would be easily obtained later in the reserve averaging period. Maybe we know of a large deposit inflow or possibly some of our government security holdings are due to mature. Indeed, we may have been planning on having a $20-million cumulative reserve deficiency at this point which would be easily made up during the remainder of the period. In this case, we may react exactly opposite to the way we did before. We may not compete as hard for new deposits as we had been, at least not in terms of adjusting interest rates paid. Moreover, we may hold back on selling securities on the money market and may even be inclined to buy. The lesson of this last example is that the ease or tightness of a bank's reserve position can only be judged in a broad perspective which includes many factors beyond the cumulative reserve position to date.

day-to-day loans to investment dealers who have lines of credit with the Bank of Canada. No other assets can be included. However, there are other equally, or almost equally, liquid assets which form part of the total hedge against banker's risk. In this latter category we would have to include all short-term government securities, call and short loans to other investment dealers, and some foreign currency assets — with longer-term government bonds and other marketable securities standing in a second rank of defense.

The Bank of Canada and Bank Liquidity.   The analysis to this point shows that the banks' primary hedge against banker's risk consists of substantial holdings of liquid assets. This requires an active, stable money market which the banks can rely on to guarantee the liquidity of their secondary reserves. We have ignored the role of the Bank of Canada in safeguarding the liquidity of the banking system.

In fact, the Bank of Canada enters the picture in two ways. In the first instance, the Bank of Canada will make short-term advances to the chartered banks. Such advances are for a minimum of seven days, and are made at an interest rate, called the bank rate. Since March 1980 this rate has been set at a level 0.25% above the 90-day treasury bill rate established by tender for these bills on the preceding Thursday. If a second advance is granted to a bank during any averaging period, it may be at a higher rate. This accentuates the idea that borrowing from the central bank should only a a last resort. In general, the banks prefer not to borrow from the Bank of Canada and, as a result, the average amount of such outstanding advance is very small. For example, the maximum average level of advances in any reserve averaging period during 1981 was $34 million, an amount under 1% of total required reserves for chartered banks at that time. In fact, chartered banks had outstanding advances from the Bank of Canada on only 34 days during 1981.

The second contribution of the Bank of Canada to the overall problem of maintaining bank liquidity is to effectively underwrite the stability of the money market. It will be recalled that the Bank of Canada will also make advances to a selected list of government security dealers — the same dealers to whom the chartered banks may make day-to-day loans which can be counted as part of their secondary reserve requirement. This facility is used more actively than is the provision for direct advances to the chartered banks. Advances to the security dealers will be made at what we might call the *dealer rate* which under current arrangements equals the bank rate.

In addition to providing these lender-of-last-resort facilities, the Bank of Canada keeps a close eye on the money market with a view to maintaining "orderly" conditions. If necessary, the Bank will intervene in the market, buying or selling short-term government securities if it detects developments which might disrupt the functioning of the market.

The purpose of the reserve lending power and timely interventions of the Bank of Canada is to provide a broad, stable market which the banking system can rely upon for reserve adjustments. Thus, banks with sizable cash drains have several options open to them: (1) They can temporarily draw down their cash reserves in the expectation of a reversal of the drain in the near future. (2) They can call day loans, i.e., assets which they have accumulated, confident that the security dealers will always be able to pay on demand. (3) They can sell into the money market any of a variety of short-term securities. Which technique they choose presumably depends on which one costs them least (i.e., in selling securities, which security produces the least income for them). Similarly, banks with cash inflows have several adjustment techniques, and they will choose among the alternatives on the basis of maximizing their returns. In general, we can expect most banks to be in the money market daily adjusting their cash holdings.

Other Assets

We have not specifically discussed several categories of assets which appear on the domestic portion of the banks' balance sheet (Table 10-1). The account, *Items in Transit*, or bank *float* as it is sometimes called, includes such things as cheques which have been deposited with a bank but not yet collected from the bank on which they were drawn. The account, *Acceptances, Guarantees,* and *Letters of Credit* is simply the asset counterpart of the contingent liability account of the same name which we discussed earlier. It appears as an asset because this is the liability of the banks' customers under the letters of credit or guarantees issued by the banks. *All Other Assets* is a grab bag of miscellaneous assets, including the banks' premises.

That leaves *foreign currency loans* to Canadian residents. Aside from drawing attention to the fact that the banks make such loans in sizable magnitude, little need be added to our earlier discussions of the foreign currency business of the banks in Canada. Just as corporations find it desirable to maintain U.S. dollar bank accounts, so many find it desirable to have their loans denominated in U.S. dollars.

THE ROLE OF THE BRANCH SYSTEM

The most prominent feature of the Canadian banking system is its organization around the branch network. As we have seen that there are 7457 bank branches in Canada. Moreover, each of the five largest banks has over 1000 branches. This system can be contrasted with that in the United States, where there are some 15 000 separate banks which in total have only 39 000 branches or no more than 2.6 branches each.

In the Canadian banking system, many functions are performed by the same institution which in other countries are performed by different institutions. In the United States, for example, the largest banks in New York City carry on for the most part of wholesale banking business bidding for large deposit balances from investors throughout the country and financing the largest corporations in the United States. In these activities they are competing with the largest banks in Chicago, San Francisco, and other financial centers. They also are competing with large international banks from abroad. The smallest banks in the United States, on the other hand, can be viewed as mainly retail banks, serving only customers from their local community, in many cases only a very small town. Indeed, the total deposits of any of the smallest banks may even be less than a small deposit or loan transaction of one of the largest banks.

Even though Canadian banks perform both the retail and wholesale banking functions, individual branches can be identified as fulfilling primarily a retail role whereas others may be more important on the wholesale side. The widespread branch system provides the means by which the banks service their customers in the primary retail functions of collecting personal savings deposits and the granting of personal loans. In contrast, non-personal term deposits and commercial loans are concentrated in a few large branches in the financial centers such as Toronto, Montreal, and Vancouver.

The specialization functions of branches in the Canadian banks can be seen from examining balance sheet data of a 10% sample of all chartered bank branches, supplied by the banks to the Economic Council. These data shown in Table 10-5 reveal a wide range of sizes. The largest 1% of the branches held more than $100 million in deposits each. In contrast, almost one half of the branches in the sample held less than $500 000 in deposits. Moreover, the largest 10% of branches accounted for over 25% of total deposits and 30% of all loans.

As might be expected, the role of different-size branches differed according to activity. The largest branches with over $100 million in deposits made over 35% of the commercial loans and accounted for 58% of non-personal term deposits. At the other end of the scale, the smallest branches with less than $500 000 in deposits held only 4% of non-personal term deposits and made only 6% on industrial loans even though they comprised almost 50% of all branches in the system. In contrast, the largest branches were not as dominant with respect to retail functions such as personal savings deposits and personal loans. The branches with over $100 million in deposits held only 6% personal savings accounts and advanced 9% of consumer loans. The smallest branches were more significant in these retail functions. These small branches accounted for over 20% of personal savings deposits (compared with their 4% of non-personal term deposits) and 28% of personal loans (compared with 6% of commercial loans).

INTERNATIONAL INTERMEDIATION

Aside from their size and nationwide structure, perhaps the most distinctive feature of the chartered banks is the role which they play in international finance. There are, in fact, three aspects to the banks involvement in international finance.

As we have already seen, the banks provide part of the apparatus of the *international payments system*, i.e., the foreign exchange market and an international network of correspondent banks. Secondly, in areas such as the Caribbean, they provide *commercial banking services*. In many of the countries in the Caribbean, Canadian banks, sometimes in partnership with local enterprise or government, are among the most important financial intermediaries. This commercial banking activity in the Caribbean, Latin America, and parts of the western United States is primarily concerned with "retail" or consumer and small and intermediate business accounts. The major source of foreign business, however, and the one that truly involves the banks as intermediaries in international financing markets, can be termed *"international wholesale" banking*. By this is meant the transacting of business in large multiples of funds (frequently $1 million or more) involving corporations, governments, and other banking or financial firms. This market is truly international in scope. Funds borrowed in one country are lent in others. With very rare exceptions the typical consumer is excluded from this highly competitive global market.

We have already considered the international payments system extensively in Chapter 2. Our remarks in this section can be confined to the second and third aspects of the international business.

TABLE 10-5   **Activities of bank branches**

Sample distribution of bank deposits by branch size, 1974

	Number of branches	Percent	Personal savings deposits		Other term deposits		Demand deposits		All deposits	
			$ Millions	Percent	$ Millions	Percent	$ Millions	Percent	$ Millions	Percent
Branch deposits ($ Million)										
100 and over	6	1.0	188.8	6.5	946.9	57.6	329.5	22.1	1 465.3	24.2
50-99.9	7	1.1	97.3	3.3	212.9	13.0	120.7	8.1	430.9	7.1
40-49.9	2	0.3	46.6	1.6	15.6	0.9	25.9	1.7	88.1	1.5
30-39.9	2	0.3	13.6	0.5	12.5	0.8	39.8	2.7	65.9	1.1
20-29.9	16	2.5	182.7	6.3	84.7	5.2	108.5	7.3	375.8	6.2
15-19.9	40	6.4	356.0	12.2	117.6	7.2	158.7	10.7	632.3	10.5
10-14.9	60	9.5	476.1	16.3	79.1	4.8	175.5	11.8	730.6	12.1
5- 9.9	192	30.5	924.1	31.7	108.4	6.6	301.7	20.3	1 334.2	22.1
Less than 5	304	48.3	626.7	21.5	65.3	4.0	227.8	15.3	919.7	15.2
TOTAL*	629	100.0	2 911.9	100.0	1 642.9	100.0	1 488.1	100.0	6 042.9	100.0

* Details may not add up to totals because of rounding
SOURCE: Sample survey of bank branch data from individual banks

Sample distribution of bank loans by branch size, 1974

	Number of branches	Percent	Industrial loans		Personal loans		Other loans, excluding agricultural and government		All loans*	
			$ Millions	Percent	$ Millions	Percent	$ Millions	Percent	$ Millions	Percent
Branch deposits ($ Million)										
100 and over	6	1.0	507.4	36.6	113.3	9.4	802.1	41.0	1 585.2	30.9
50-99.9	7	1.1	356.4	25.7	52.4	4.4	373.6	19.1	797.2	15.5
40-49.9	2	0.3	51.8	3.7	10.1	0.8	25.3	1.3	88.4	1.7
30-39.9	2	0.3	9.4	0.7	7.8	0.7	5.1	0.3	22.3	0.4
20-29.9	16	2.5	38.3	2.8	71.5	5.9	62.7	3.2	258.0	5.0
15-19.9	40	6.4	138.1	10.0	122.9	10.2	168.7	8.6	469.1	9.1
10-14.9	60	9.5	97.4	7.0	156.7	13.0	202.8	10.4	531.2	10.3
5- 9.9	192	30.5	106.2	7.7	326.9	27.2	171.7	8.8	729.9	14.2
Less than 5	304	48.3	81.5	5.9	341.8	28.4	144.5	7.4	656.6	12.8
TOTAL†	629	100.0	1 386.3	100.0	1 203.5	100.0	1 956.5	100.0	5 138.0	100.0

* Includes industrial, personal, agricultural, government, and other loans
† Details may not add up to totals because of rounding
SOURCE: Sample survey of bank branch data from individual banks supplied to Economic Council. See Economic Council of Canada, *Efficiency and Regulation* (Ottawa, Supply and Services Canada, 1976), p. 13.

Foreign Commercial Banking Operations.   The foreign branch business of the banks has a long history. The Maritime-based Bank of Nova Scotia was the first to venture abroad in 1889 and was subsequently followed by the Royal and Bank of Commerce. The main stimulant to this type of expansion was the obvious dependence of Canada on international trade and the particular role this trade played in the Caribbean and Latin America. On the west coast the first Bank of British Columbia (later absorbed by the Commerce) developed a branch network in Oregon and California.

The growth of deposits in these foreign branches has been uneven. Political events (such as the Cuban Revolution) resulted in some offices being closed. In some nations of the West Indies, governments have set up indigenous banks to compete with the foreign Canadian operations. More recently the Canadian operations in the western United States have been expanded by mergers with smaller banking firms. It can be expected that as trade increases in importance, especially with South America, the banks will continue to expand their overseas branch networks.

International "Wholesale" Banking.   Almost all Canadian chartered banks maintain *agencies* in New York and other financial centers such as London and Paris. These offices function as branches, with the one notable exception that those in New York cannot directly accept deposits, but rather act as agents for the head office. For example, if an American corporation with a temporary excess of cash was encouraged to deposit some funds with a Canadian bank, these funds, although solicited by the agency, would be recorded as being carried in U.S. funds on the books of the head office in Canada. Since the chartered banks are forbidden by American law to directly solicit deposits to be held at their agencies they are effectively excluded from the local "retail" market. Given the nature of the wholesale market that they operate in, most of their deposits are closely akin to deposit receipts or certificates, i.e., they are left with the bank for stated periods of time at negotiated rates of interest.

Almost from their very beginning the Canadian chartered banks have held sizable amounts of their assets in forms denominated in foreign currencies. In part this was to be expected, given the importance of trade to the economy. Banks held balances with American and British banks as well as currency of the two nations to be able to meet the demands of their customers.

Some foreign currency assets still represent the counterpart of the liabilities obtained in their foreign branch networks. The Canadian banks that act as domestic banks in other countries, for example, not only collect deposits but make loans to consumers and businesses in their host country.

Yet the holdings of foreign assets throughout the history of banking in Canada have been the result of more than foreign exchange transactions and overseas branching operations. Of key importance has been the continuing substantial investment by Canadian banks in the New York money market. Prior to the establishment of a central bank and the consequent development of a truly effective domestic money market, the banks held a substantial portion of their liquid assets in New York. The most common form was short-term loans to stockbrokers and security dealers and U.S. treasury bills. When a bank in Canada was faced with a liquidity problem these assets could be quickly sold and converted into gold for return to Canada.

Even with the growth of the domestic money market, the Canadian banks have not abandoned their investments in New York. It is here that the banks invest a large portion of the proceeds of their swap deposits and a portion of the deposits obtained through their agencies. Indeed, the Canadian banks play a dominant role in financing Wall Street. At various times in the past, loans from Canadian banks have been equal to as much as 50% of the total financing received by New York brokers and dealers.

In the past 25 years there has developed a large international financial market that deals in the lending and borrowing of large sums of U.S. dollar balances. While it is called the *Euro-dollar Market*, it is not strictly a European market. It accounts for a major part of the rapid expansion of foreign currency business done by the Canadian banks. A large part of the funds obtained by the banks' agencies in New York are invested in this market, as are some of the foreign currency deposits of Canadian residents.[20]

The typical lenders of dollar balances to the Canadian banks are major corporations. The banks in turn lend these funds to European or Asian banks, corporations, and occasionally governments. For the borrower, the market offers several attractions. It may be that domestic sources of credit are either unable or unwilling to extend credit to the borrower. Frequently, interest rates are lower in the Euro-dollar Market than in domestic markets. In some cases foreign currency, and especially U.S. dollars, cannot otherwise be obtained because of quotas or exchange controls.

For the lender of funds in the market (the Canadian banks among others), the attractions are also tempting. While competition among banks for Euro-dollar deposits frequently reduces the margin between the interest rate received and the interest paid to a fraction of 1%, on a large volume of transactions the revenue can be substantial. Moreover, the large size of each transaction, and the international reputations of most borrowers, make both the costs of intermediation and the credit risks extremely low per dollar of deposits. In addition, the banks may attract other business in this way. For example, they may gain the Canadian business of international corporations.

Why is it that corporations with excess funds do not participate directly in the market rather than using banks? The answer for the most part was given in Chapter 9 where we discussed intermediation. The banks, with their wide network of international correspondents, are able to obtain a more precise picture of demand conditions in the market. But more important, even though these corporations may have several millions to invest, it is unlikely that they could obtain the degree of diversification and consequent reduction in risk that they enjoy when they put their funds with a bank. In essence, Canadian banks operating in the Euro-dollar market perform the same service for giant corporations that they do in the domestic market for individual savers, i.e., provide a means for asset diversification. It would be the rare, though not inconceivable, corporation that would find it worthwhile to participate directly in such a large financial market.

FOREIGN BANKS IN CANADA

Just as the Canadian banks have offices and operate in other countries, foreign banks in turn carry on an extensive business in Canada. At one time the *Bank Act* did not distinguish between foreign-owned and Canadian-owned banks. At various times, banks which were completely foreign owned operated in Canada. In the early 1960s, however, the First National City Bank, one of the largest New York banks, took steps to take over the Mercantile Bank, a small, specialized bank owned by Dutch interests. The Canadian government reacted by introducing a clause into the 1967 revision that limited foreign ownership of any chartered bank to less than 25% of the outstanding shares. At the same time, a transitional arrangement was established which restricted the size of the Mercantile Bank until it conformed with the new provision.

The prohibition on foreign ownership of banks did not succeed in excluding all activity for foreign banks in Canada. Many foreign banks entered the Canadian markets indirectly through subsidiaries operating in a variety of forms such as trust companies, leasing companies, and in other less formal ways. By the time of the 1980 revision to the *Bank Act*, opposition to the restriction on foreign ownership of banks developed from a variety of sources. Some Canadian banks complained that foreign banks were able to avoid the restrictions of the *Bank Act* in establishing Canadian operations. Other Canadian banks found that their own foreign operations were to be constrained by authorities in other countries who demand reciprocity of treatment for their banks from Canadian authorities in order to permit the entry of Canadian banks into their country. In addition, the Economic Council of Canada argued "that the prospect of foreign bank entry in both the wholesale and retail banking markets would be beneficial to Canadian consumers of banking services."[21] The 1980 revision of the *Bank Act* provided for the chartering of foreign banks in Canada, with these banks subject to a limit of eight per share of the total domestic assets of the banking system and a limit of two to the number of offices of each subsidiary. Moreover, foreign banks which do not wish to establish subsidiaries are permitted to have representative offices which must be registered with the Inspector General of Banks.

By February 1982, 47 foreign bank subsidiaries had been authorized under the *Bank Act* , and it was anticipated that a further group of banks would be established in early 1982, bringing the total to 60. About half of these were conversions of existing subsidiaries that had been already operating in Canada in one form or another, whereas the other half were newly created entities. Most observers anticipate that the foreign banks will emphasize wholesale business in both their lending and fund raising. The constraint on the expansion of branches will likely discourage their active entry into retail markets such as consumer loans and savings deposits.

CONCLUSIONS

In their domestic operations, the chartered banks provide one classic stereotype of a financial intermediary. The banks collect funds by appealing to assetholders' demands for highly liquid assets, including assets which can be used as a medium of exchange. The banks have become increasingly successfully in developing different types of deposits to appeal to many different specific asset preferences. On the other side of their operations, the use of the funds collected, the banks have primarily been short-term commercial lenders. This pattern of activities is also changing, as the banks extend more term loans and consumer loans, and acquire more residential mortgages.

The banks also hold very sizable portfolios of marketable securities, some long-term but most short-term. As we have seen, the main purpose of these securities is to provide a hedge against banker's risk, and to transfer lending power over time. As a result, bank holdings of securities fluctuate fairly widely, from day to day, week to week, month to month, and year to year.

We must also not forget that the chartered banks are not simply domestic intermediaries. They have vast international operations, as commercial banks in several countries and as true international intermediaries. The banks also carry on a significant foreign currency business with residents of Canada.

ENDNOTES

1. Royal Commission on Banking and Finance, *Report* (Ottawa; 1964), p. 378.
2. *Ibid.*, p. 363.
3. The 1980 revision of the *Bank Act* provided for the chartering of foreign-owned banks to do business in Canada. As February 1982, 47 foreign banks had been granted limited charters as foreign-owned banks.
4. The Royal Commission added "or as close substitutes for such money claims." *Report*, p. 377.
5. In Chapter 3, we distinguished between loan transactions and investment transactions as follows:

   In the former category we place all transactions involving face-to-face negotiations between borrowers and lenders....In the second category we place all transactions in "public issues," financial instruments designed to be sold on an impersonal basis to any and all buyers.

6. The studies on the demand for savings deposits at different types of financial institutions include J. P. Chateau, "The Demand for and Supply of Deposits by Credit Unions," *Journal of Banking and Finance* 4 (1980), pp. 151-73 and Kevin Clinton, "The Demand for Liabilities of Trust and Mortgage Loan Companies," *Canadian Journal of Economics*, 7 (May, 1974), pp. 191-204.
7. Canadian Bankers' Association, *Submission to the Royal Commission on Banking and Finance*, July 1962, p. 101).
8. The vertical axis on Figure 10-2 is a logarithmic scale. As a result, equal changes on any of the lines on the chart represent equal percentage rates of change.
9. A.B. Jamieson, *Chartered Banking in Canada* (Toronto: The Ryerson Press, 1953), p. 205.
10. Canadian Bankers' Association, *Submission to the Royal Commission on Banking and Finance* (1962), p.13.
11. *Ibid.*, p. 13.
12. *Ibid.*, p. 43.
13. In the later 1920s loans accounted for between 55% and 60% of the banks' Canadian assets. During the depression of the 1930s this proportion fell to the neighborhood of 30%, as bank loans to businesses and financial institutions fell off sharply. During World War II, total bank assets increased sharply, from approximately $3.3 billion in 1939 to $7.2 billion in 1946. However, a large part of the increase in assets took the form of purchases of Government of Canada securities, issued to finance the war effort. As a result, the share of loans in the total portfolio continued to fall. In 1946, loans accounted for only 20% of Canadian dollar assets, whereas securities accounted for 58%, and well over 90% of those securities were Government

of Canada bonds. In part, the long-run trend so evident in Figure 10-3 is a prolonged adjustment to the very abnormal situation produced by the depression and the war.

14. E.L.S. Patterson, *Canadian Banking*, rev. ed. (Toronto: The Ryerson Press, 1941), p. 193.
15. *Ibid.*
16. The purpose of the two levels of reserves on saving and notice deposits is to encourage the development of small banks. These new reserve requirements are to be phased in over four years, beginning March 1981.
17. You should note that there are two effects on next month's reserves. The fact that cash holdings this month are lower, increases the amount which must be held on deposit with the Bank of Canada next month. However, the reduction in cash holdings also reduces deposits this month, and that reduces the level of reserves which must be held next month. If all of the cash drain were a result of a reduction in demand deposits, every dollar of cash lost this month would increase the required reserve deposit next month by $0.90 ($1 − 0.10 × $1).
18. It should be noted that if the banks attempt to replenish the currency withdrawn by depositors by withdrawing currency from the Bank of Canada to be placed in branch vaults, that action will tend to create a reserve deficiency. However, it is the banks' attempt to keep their vault cash constant in the face of cash withdrawals by depositors, not the cash drain itself, which creates the dollar for dollar reduction in reserves with the Bank of Canada.
19. The 1956 agreement served two purposes. It helped create a captive market for treasury bills and day-to-day loans to government security dealers, thus facilitating the rapid development of the money market. In addition, it served to impound large quantities of liquidity which the banks might attempt to use to increase bank loans at times when the Bank of Canada is attempting to restrict cash. It is presumably for the latter reason that the Bank of Canada reported in its 1967 Annual Report that "the present circumstances have not been regarded as appropriate ones in which to do away with the secondary reserve requirement." Bank of Canada, *Annual Report*, 1967, p. 49. We will have occasion to explore some of the economics of adjustments in the banks' asset portfolios later in the book.
20. A good description of the Euro-dollar market activities of the Canadian banks can be found in E. Wayne Clendenning, *The Euro-Currency Markets and the International Activities of Canadian Banks* (Ottawa: Economic Council of Canada, 1976).
21. Economic Council of Canada, *Efficiency and Regulation*, p. 97

THE NEAR BANKS AS FINANCIAL INTERMEDIARIES 11

In the previous chapter we considered a group of financial intermediaries which, by any definition, must be classified as banks. The chartered banks hold the largest and most diversified portfolio of assets held by any group of financial intermediaries in Canada. However, as we saw in Chapter 9, the relative position of the chartered banks *vis-à-vis* other financial intermediaries has been declining in recent years. Particularly important in contributing to the erosion of the relative position of the chartered banks has been intense competition from a large number of generally smaller intermediaries which, though in many ways different from each other, can be readily grouped together in the general category of "near banks."

THE CONCEPT OF A NEAR BANK

Our definition of a near bank is quite simple. *It is a financial intermediary which raises a major portion of its operating funds by issuing liabilities which are close, if not perfect, substitutes for the major liability of the chartered banks — personal savings deposits.* In this sense, the bulk of near bank liabilities are close substitutes for money as liquid assets, and hence near banks belong in the category of financial intermediaries which both the Royal Commission on Banking and Finance and the Economic Council argued ought to be grouped together with the chartered banks for regulatory purposes.

The primary difference between the banks and the near banks lies in their respective involvements in the payments system. Both banks and some near banks issue demand deposits, but those issued by the chartered banks are the primary medium of exchange in the economy. The role of chequable savings deposits in the payment system, whether issued by banks or the near banks, is much less important. As a result, although near banks issue liabilities which are equivalent to bank deposits in chartered banks, their involvement in the payments system is comparatively minor.

There are other differences between the banks and the near banks. The near banks do not have the massive involvement in international finance that is characteristic of the banks. The near banks are essentially domestic, personal savings banks. Given the dominant importance of personal savings deposits among their liabilities, in general, the average volatility of their liabilities is lower than that of the banks, and hence, the degree of banker's risk faced by these institutions is not as great as that facing the banks. Not surprisingly, as we shall see upon detailed examination, the structure of their asset portfolios is markedly different from those of the banks. It is also worth noting that for the most part, these institutions, unlike the banks, are under the jurisdiction of the provincial rather than the federal governments, though *de facto* the federal government is playing an increasingly important role in their inspection and supervision. The reader should bear in mind that while we emphasize these differences to permit us to obtain, for purposes of subsequent analysis, some sort of classification system, these firms all are engaged essentially in the same activity, financial intermediation. Their liabilities provide wealth-owners with asset forms that are preferable to the direct holdings of claims on borrowers and at the same time provide borrowers with a lower cost source of finance than if they borrowed directly from wealth-owners. Thus the *essential differences between banks and near banks are in form and not in substance.*

CO-OPERATIVE BANKS:
THE CREDIT UNIONS AND *CAISSES POPULAIRES* _____

The Nature and Organization of Cooperative Banks

In organizational form, if not in substance, the next group of intermediaries which we want to consider are the very antithesis of the chartered banks. Whereas the chartered banks are privately owned, profit-seeking firms with centrally controlled, nationwide branch operations, accepting deposits from and lending to the general public, the credit unions and *caisses populaires* are cooperative, non-profit seeking firms, with autonomous local, normally (but not exclusively) single-office operations, accepting deposits from and lending money to members only. In the case of the chartered banks, there is a clear distinction between borrowers and depositors on the one hand and the shareholders (or owners) on the other (although shareholders can be depositors and can borrow from the bank, of course). In the case of the cooperative banks, both borrowers and depositors must be members and, as members, all have equal voting rights. In keeping with their local character, each credit union or *caisse populaire* is independent in its operating policies (although there are centralizing arrangements which we will examine shortly).

Local autonomy also brings with it diversity in character and organization, diversity which is accentuated by the tangled historical roots of the movement in Canada. Cooperative banking movements with somewhat different philosophies developed in Quebec at the turn of the century (the *Desjardins Caisses Populaires Movement*), in Ontario, and in the Maritimes in the 1930s (the *Antigonish Movement*). The latter movement subsequently spread to the prairie provinces as well. In the 1940s a major new thrust came from the United States when the *Credit Union National Association* (now called CUNA International) began organizing efforts in Canada. The indigenous Canadian cooperative banking movements were predominantly rural, organized on community lines (including neighborhood associations in cities) with membership open to all residents of the community, and stressed the savings aspect of the cooperative bank more than the lending aspect (much of the lending was for "productive" purposes, i.e., loans to small enterprises, farmers, and fishermen). This was particularly true of the *caisses populaires* (which developed primarily, but not exclusively, in the Province of Quebec). As a result, cooperative banks in Quebec are normally organized on parish lines, and the largest number are rural. However, in recent years the urban *caisses populaires* have been growing much more rapidly than their rural counterparts, both in number and in size, and the majority of *caisses populaires* assets are now in urban associations. However, the conservative nature of the lending policy and the emphasis on the stimulation of thrift among members has not disappeared from the movement. The CUNA-inspired credit unions, by contrast, tend to be organized on an industrial or occupational basis with membership open to all persons sharing the common industrial or occupational bond, and are much more deeply committed to a "liberal" policy of personal lending for a variety of purposes, including consumption. In some provinces, the requirement of a common bond among members has been effectively waived so that membership in any credit union is open to all who desire it. Some would characterize these credit unions as being "consumer banks" which just happen to be owned by their customers.

The Cooperative Bank Movement.   Prior to the late 1930s, cooperative banking in Canada had a firm, broad base only in Quebec. Of the 277 local cooperative banks reported to be in existence in 1935, 239 were in Quebec, and 47 000 of an estimated 52 000 members of cooperative banks in Canada belonged to Quebec local societies. The total assets of all cooperative banks were approximately $10.5 million, most of which was held by Quebec *caisses populaires*. Over the next three decades the growth of the movement was spectacular. Thus, by 1950, there were almost 3000 local societies, with over one million members and total assets of $312 million. By 1968, there were more than 4860 locals, with 4.6 million members and $3.7 billion in assets. Ten years later, in 1978, although the number of credit union locals had fallen to 3868, total membership reached 8.9 million and total assets were over $22 billion. Over the 10-year period, membership grew by 93% and total assets increased by an amazing 500%.

The growth of cooperative banks has been significant in shaping the development of financial intermediation in Canada in recent years. Moreover, while many of the individual operations are extremely small, their combined resources ($32 billion) are sufficiently large to make them an important factor in the functioning of the total financial system.

Considerable diversity exists among the credit unions and *caisses populaires*. In 1978, some 355 locals had less than $100 000 in total assets. Many of these small locals are operated on a part-time basis by predominantly volunteer workers. At the other extreme are the 131 locals which each had assets of over $25 million. The very largest of these, Vancity in British Columbia, had as much as $1000 million total assets at the end of 1981. As can be seen from Table 11-1, considerable differences exist in the strength of credit unions among provinces. Credit unions are particularly strong in Saskatchewan, Quebec, British Columbia, and Manitoba where in each case the proportion of credit union members to population exceeds 30% and credit union assets are more than $1000 per head. The locals appear to be substantially larger in B.C. than in the rest of Canada. Finally, it is interesting to note the differences in emphasis in credit union business. Credit unions in B.C., and to a lesser degree in Quebec and Saskatchewan, hold a high ratio of mortgages to assets, whereas the locals in provinces where the credit union movement is less strong appear to emphasize personal loans to a greater degree. Such diversity makes it both difficult and potentially misleading to derive simple generalizations about the operations of cooperative banks in Canada.

Centralizing Organizations.   While local autonomy is a vigorously maintained basic principle of the cooperative bank movement, the local credit unions or *caisses* do not remain as islands unto themselves. There are several centralizing organizations. Thus, the *caisses populaires* in Quebec belong to one of two provincial *federations,* and credit unions inside and outside of Quebec belong to one of several *leagues.* While attempting to avoid interference with the autonomy of the local credit unions and *caisses,* the leagues and federations provide technical assistance to the locals, particularly in the organizational stages of new locals and in maintaining and supervising accurate bookkeeping and accounting.

The leagues and federations also provide educational services for local officers and members, and carry on lobbying and public relations activities for the cooperative banking movement. In Quebec, the federations are also involved in the formal inspection and supervision of the activities of the local *caisses* to see that all legal conditions are satisfied and to ensure the soundness of the management practices in the interest of protecting depositors. In other provinces, the formal supervisory function is performed by agencies of the provincial government.

Of more direct interest to us than the federations and leagues themselves, are their financial arms, the *central credit societies* (or centrals, for short). Although the federations and leagues involve loose, joint affiliations of autonomous credit societies, the centrals take on some of the characteristics of central banks for groups of cooperative banks. They provide financial advice, do much of the systems' investing in stocks, bonds, and other marketable securities, and act as lenders of last resort. They are credit unions for credit unions.

Most credit unions and *caisses populaires* hold deposits with a central credit society. In part, these deposits are surplus funds at the disposal of local societies. By lending such funds to individuals and to other credit unions with excess demands for funds, or by investing them in any of a variety of securities, the central provides a mechanism for the more effective utilization of the funds available within the cooperative banking system. But the role of the central credit societies goes well beyond arrangements for inter-credit union mobility of funds. By arrangements with the chartered banks, the centrals act as agents of the locals in the clearing and collection of cheques, and they hold and manage the liquid secondary reserves of the locals. Thus, the deposits with the central credit societies are in part clearing balances (out of which the central will pay cheques drawn on the local and to which it will credit the proceeds of cheques

TABLE 11-1 Characteristics of credit unions and caisses populaires by province, 1978

	New foundland	Prince Edward Island	Nova Scotia	New Brunswick	Quebec	Ontario	Manitoba	Saskat- chewan	Alberta	British Columbia	Canada
Number of members	11 079	22 480	161 513	198 559	4 598 516	1 716 000	351 926	518 085	432 990	894 325	8 905 173
Number of locals	21	13	118	136	1 557	1 245	196	238	180	164	3 868
Membership per local	528	1 729	1 369	1 458	2 953	1 378	1 795	2 177	2 405	5 453	2 302
Members as a percentage of population	1.9%	18.3%	19.1%	28.4%	73.3%	20.2%	34.1%	54.3%	21.8%	35.0%	37.7%
Total assets ($ Millions)	$24.3	$28.5	$189.9	$281.9	$10 130.0	$4 227.0	$1 142.4	$2 081.0	$1 427.4	$3 691.0	$23 223.4
Assets per member	$2 195	$1 268	$1 176	$1 422	$2 203	$2 463	$3 246	$4 107	$3 297	$4 127	$2 608
Assets per capita	$42	$235	$225	$403	$1 615	$498	$1 108	$2 181	$171	$1 443	$948
Personal loans as a percentage of assets	69%	84%	69%	48%	17%	40%	19%	12%	50%	9%	—
Mortgage as a percentage of assets	12%	—	8%	28%	48%	36%	32%	44%	32%	72%	47%

SOURCE: Statistics Canada, Credit Unions 1978. (Ottawa, 1981).

presented for collection on behalf of the local), and in part a pool of funds which can be drawn upon in time of need.

If the centrals are to serve effectively as a "mutual aid fund" for local credit unions, the centrals must pay careful attention to the liquidity of their own asset portfolios. To this end the centrals hold substantial quantities of cash on deposit with chartered banks, and substantial portfolios of short-term securities. In addition, in 1953 a federal charter was obtained for what was planned as a nationwide central credit society, the *Canadian Cooperative Credit Society* (CCCS). A major purpose of the CCCS is to provide funds for liquidity purposes through the provincial centrals to local credit unions. To meet this need the CCCS is empowered to borrow on a short-term basis from the money market. The CCCS also serves as a national coordinating body on matters of common concern to credit unions and their members.

The Balance Sheet of the Cooperative Banks

A balance sheet for local credit unions and *caisses populaires* is presented in Table 11-2.

TABLE 11-2 **Local credit unions and *caisses populaires: balance sheet,* June 30, 1982**

	$ Millions	Percent		$ Millions	Percent
Cash and demand deposits	3 455	11	Deposits:		
			Term	13 985	43
			Demand	13 672	42
Loans	7 951	24	Total	27 657	84
Mortgages	15 667	48	Shares	2 578	8
Investments	4 636	14	Reserves and surplus	680	2
Other assets	1 114		Other liabilities	1 968	6
TOTAL	32 202	100		32 202	100

SOURCE: Statistics Canada, *Financial Institutions,* second quarter, 1982 (Ottawa, 1982).

Sources of Funds.   The bulk of cooperative banks' funds are derived from members' deposits which are split fairly evenly between demand deposits and term deposits. Members' shares, which were more important in the past, now account for 8% of the total funds available to cooperative banks.

We should not make too much of the role of share capital in providing funds to cooperative banks, however. Like deposits, shares are in fact redeemable on demand (though technically subject to notice.) However, they are not transferable by cheque, and as a result they are much less volatile than deposits. Cooperative bank shares are held more as intermediate or long-term assets than for liquidity. Deposits, by contrast, are more widely used for transactions purposes, with almost 30% of demand deposits transferable by cheque.

Uses of Funds.   The primary uses of the funds of cooperative banks are for loans to members, either in the form of mortgages or other loans. Some surplus funds are invested in securities, normally through the centrals, but most of the "investments" of the cooperative banks are short-term securities held (generally by the centrals) as secondary reserves. Cash, both in the form of till money and in the form of deposits with chartered banks, is held for the usual transactions reasons.

The Demand for Cooperative Bank Liabilities

It should be clear from what we have said that deposits and shares in a credit union must be regarded as substitutes for personal savings deposits in chartered banks. Why do some wealth-owners choose to hold a portion of their assets in the form of claims on credit unions or *caisses populaires?*

As with all aspects of the cooperative movement, ideology is probably an important factor. The cooperative banks cannot be regarded simply as another differentiated group of financial intermediaries. They represent a movement with a particular philosophy which values voluntary co-operation and mutual assistance in economic affairs. In the words of one spokesman:

> the whole idea of the Credit Union Movement is to get people to work together locally, to handle their own finances, to work (out) economic problems which beset them as a particular group and to determine their own financial matters as much as possible to within the structure which has been created.[1]

Undoubtedly, many members hold funds in credit unions or *caisses populaires* simply because they subscribe to this philosophy (and many non-members refuse to join because they object to this philosophy).

Beyond this there are some important economic reasons. As we have already pointed out, one is the possibility of relatively easy access to low-cost credit associated with membership in the credit society.[2] In other instances there may be advantages associated with the location of the credit society's offices. For example, in many industrial based credit unions, the union office is located within the plant and it maintains hours which coincide with work schedules. In some areas, particularly in rural Quebec, the cooperative bank may be the only intermediary in the community.

It is doubtful that all of these considerations are sufficient to explain the remarkable growth of cooperative banks in the postwar period. The yields on shares and deposits in the cooperative banks relative to that on personal savings deposits in the chartered banks must also be a vital factor. Local autonomy complicates the picture. The cooperative banks do not all pay the same interest and dividend rates. The dividend rate depends on the "profitability" of the operations during the year. Not unexpectedly, according to one careful study, relatively new institutions tend to have lower dividend rates than do older, well-established institutions. Similar diversity is to be noted in the rates paid on deposits. In spite of this wide diversity, it is nonetheless true that throughout the postwar period both the interest and dividend rates paid by the established cooperative banks have been somewhat above the rate paid on personal savings deposits by the chartered banks.

How can the cooperative banks simultaneously pay higher rates of interest and dividends on borrowed funds, and lend to members at lower rates of interest than competitive institutions? In many instances the office staff is minimal or entirely voluntary, so that administrative costs are low per dollar of assets. This is particularly important in small credit unions and *caisses populaires* where the diseconomies of small-scale operations would otherwise be a serious impediment to profitable operation. Secondly, since most loans are made to members who are known on a personal basis by the officers of the institution the rate of default is extremely low.

TRUST COMPANIES

Canadian trust companies are in a sense simultaneously two businesses within the same organization. On the one hand they act as trustees, managing or administering estates and other trust funds, and on the other hand they are true financial intermediaries, collecting funds through deposits and investing those funds in the hopes of making a profit.

The Estate, Trust, and Agency Business

Our primary concern will be with trust companies' activities as financial intermediaries, but we should briefly review the other side of their operations, referred to as the *Estate, Trust, and Agency* business.

When a trust company is acting as a financial intermediary, it is a principal in the financial transaction. It collects money by issuing claims on itself, and it then purchases assets for its own account. Profits, if any, are a result of differences between the yield on the assets and the interest paid on liabilities. When the trust company is acting as a trustee, by contrast, it is not a principal in the transaction (although it may legally "own" the assets). Rather, it acts as an *agent*, administering trust funds for a set fee for services rendered. Under some arrangements the trust company has no discretion in the investments to be made; the company merely acts as an agent for the owner of the funds, carrying out his explicit instructions (although perhaps offering him advice). Under other arrangements the trust company has a wide range of discretion with respect to the investments to be made; the company is a trustee in the true sense. However, even in the case of these trusts, the company's discretion may be limited by the agreement under which the trust was created, or by applicable provincial trusteeship laws. The range of activities encompassed by the ETA accounts is broad. For example, the companies act as administrators of estates and personal trust funds, they manage pension funds, and they administer funds set aside by corporations for the repayment of bonded debt.

Over the years the ETA business has increased rapidly. From $3.9 billion in 1952, the book value of assets under administration increased to $7.4 billion in 1960, $18.8 billion in 1969, and to $80.7 billion in mid-1982. These accounts represent a very sizeable concentration of assets: in 1982 they were almost twice the value of assets held by trust companies as the result of their business as intermediaries. Data covering the deployment of funds entrusted to the administration of trust companies are shown in

Table 11-3. As can be seen, these funds are primarily concentrated in bonds, shares and, to a lesser degree, mortgages. While the trust companies have complete discretion with respect to the employment of very few of these funds, the policies pursued by the trust companies in administering the ETA funds over which they do have control can have a profound effect on the flow of credit through financial markets. Therefore, to consider only their activities as financial intermediaries would be to vastly understate their importance in the financial system.

TABLE 11-3   **Trust companies: distribution of assets of E.T.A. accounts, June 30, 1982**

	$ Millions	*Percent*
Mortgages	10 709	13
Bonds and debentures	33 848	42
Preferred and common shares	24 395	30
Other investments	11 734	15
TOTAL	80 686	100

SOURCE: Statistics Canada, *Financial Institutions*, second quarter, 1982 (Ottawa, 1982).

Trust Companies as Financial Intermediaries

The trust companies' business as financial intermediaries has grown even more rapidly than their business as trustees. In 1952, the book value of assets held in ETA accounts was more than eight times the value of assets held on an intermediation basis. By 1969, that ratio had fallen to three times and by 1982 it had fallen to less than twice. As financial intermediaries, the trust companies are the single most important group of near banks and are strong competitors of the chartered banks in the market for personal savings deposits. They also offer the banks effective competition in some aspects of what has been called the "wholesale" deposit market (i.e., the market for relatively large blocks of funds on short-term deposit). Indeed, many observers believe that the rapid growth of the trust companies intermediary business in recent years has been largely at the expense of the chartered banks.

Not all trust companies operate an intermediary business. Those that do must operate under a charter issued by either the federal government or one of the provincial governments. However, all trust companies must register with the appropriate authorities in the provinces in which they do business, and must conform to the regulations of those provinces regardless of the province in which they are chartered. Most of the large trust companies have operations in Ontario, and hence must abide by Ontario regulations. As a result, there is less diversity in the applicable regulations than might otherwise be the case. These regulations restrict the types of assets in which trust companies can invest funds derived from deposits (so-called "guaranteed" funds). However, the range of permissible investments is wide enough to allow broad latitude to the trust companies in deciding on investment policies.

Sources of Funds.   Like the chartered banks, the trust companies offer both chequable and non-chequable personal savings deposits which are nominally subject to notice but which are in fact payable on demand. But their most important source of funds is term deposits (including guaranteed investment certificates), which are generally non-transferable and are to be left with the company for a prescribed period of time at a predetermined interest rate. By paying competitive interest rates and "tailoring" the deposits to the customers' needs in terms of both size and maturity, they have been successful in attracting corporate as well as individual funds. The preponderance of term deposits are in the one- to five-year maturity range when initially deposited.

Uses of Funds.   Like other banks and near banks, the trust companies must manage their asset portfolios with one eye on the ever-present banker's risk. However, this risk is probably less pressing on trust companies than on banks because they do not participate in the same central way in the payments system. Nonetheless, they must hold substantial quantities of liquid assets, including cash and marketable short-term securities. They are not required by law to hold cash reserves in any specified ratio, and as a result they can keep sterile cash to a working minimum. In mid-1982 their cash reserves amounted to less than 1.5% of total deposits but almost 6% of personal savings deposits, which are payable on demand (Table 11-4). Their holdings of marketable short-term securities and short-term deposits with banks and other financial institutions were much larger (in part reflecting provincial, particularly Ontario, laws which require them to hold sizeable amounts of broadly defined "liquid" assets).[3] Thus, at mid-1982, their holdings of cash and liquid assets amounted to almost 16% of total deposits.

In this respect the trust companies are not significantly different from banks. What is strikingly different in their asset portfolios is the very large holdings of mortgages, at mid-1982 over 60% of their total assets. This concentration of asset holdings in mortgages corresponds to the concentration of liabilities in fixed term deposits. As a "savings bank" a trust company does not have to be as concerned as a bank must be about holding a high proportion of its assets in quite illiquid forms. In recent years, laws restricting the acquisition of other assets by trust companies, particularly unsecured loans and equities, have been relaxed somewhat, and these categories of assets have been increasing in importance (although they remain a very minor factor in the balance sheet).

Summary   In their financial intermediation operations, the trust companies are classic examples of savings banks. They offer the public a range of deposit forms, but heavily emphasize term deposits. They are involved in the payments system only peripherally, as a convenience to their personal savings depositors. There has been no "banking principle" to cause them to refrain from mortgage lending, and provincial laws have permitted (indeed, encouraged) them to make mortgage loans. Over the years, trust companies have been a primary source of mortgage funds, and the housing boom associated with Canadian population growth has provided a powerful spur to the growth of trust companies as financial intermediaries. We will examine some of the consequences of the very rapid growth of trust companies in Chapter 16.

TABLE 11-4 **Trust companies as financial intermediaries: consolidated balance sheet, June 30, 1982**

Assets	$ Millions	Percent	Liabilities	$ Millions	Percent
Liquid assets			Personal savings deposits		
Cash and demand deposits	601	1	Chequable	2 063	4
Term deposits	2 590	6	Other	8 064	17
Treasury bills	290	1		10 127	22
Short-term paper	2 961	6	Term deposits		
Liquid assets	6 442	14	Less than 1 year	5 506	12
Securities			1-5 years	18 145	39
Government of Canada	1 052	2	Over 5 years	7 339	16
Other Canadian bonds	3 437	7		30 990	67
Equities	1 964	4	Bank and other loans	302	1
Other investments	586	1	Other liabilities	2 629	6
Securities	7 039	15	Shareholders' equity	2 101	5
Loans: personal and other	3 023	7			
Mortgages	27 872	60			
Other assets	1 774	4			
TOTAL	46 150	100	TOTAL	46 150	100

SOURCE: Statistics Canada, *Financial Institutions*, second quarter, 1982 (Ottawa, 1982).

MORTGAGE LOAN COMPANIES

In their activities as financial intermediaries, mortgage loan companies are almost indistinguishable from trust companies. They operate under similar legal provisions, particularly in Ontario, and several mortgage loan companies own trust companies, or vice versa, and operate their businesses essentially as a single unit. Of course, mortgage loan companies do not have the estate, trust and agency accounts which are characteristic of trust companies; and their balance sheets show considerably greater concentration on mortgages among their assets and debentures and term deposits among their liabilities (Table 11-5). However, they represent the same type of "savings bank" operation as the trust companies.

Sources of Funds.   Like the banks and trust companies, mortgage loan companies issue both chequable and non-chequable personal savings deposits, which are effectively payable on demand. However, as a source of funds, these deposits are very much less important to mortgage loan companies than to either banks or trust companies — 2% of total liabilities in mid-1982 (Table 11-5) as compared to 22% for trust companies (Table 11-4), and over 45% of Canadian liabilities for chartered banks. Most of their funds are raised by issuing longer-term financial instruments, particularly debentures and term deposits with original maturities in the range 1-5 years. They also borrow substantial sums from banks, trust companies, and other institutional lenders.

Uses of Funds.   Given the minor importance of deposits payable on demand among their liabilities, it is not surprising that mortgage loan companies have found it unnecessary to hold a large share of their assets in highly liquid form. In mid-1982, cash amounted to less than 1% of total deposits (but 24% of deposits payable on demand), and highly liquid assets to 6% of total deposits. By contrast, mortgages accounted for over 83% of total assets! Again, a classic "savings bank" — the contrast with a chartered bank could not be more extreme.

QUEBEC SAVINGS BANKS

Of all the near banks which we examine in this chapter, one category, the Quebec Savings Banks, is an exception to the general rule of the primacy of provincial responsibility for the chartering, regulation, and supervision of near banks. The *Quebec Savings Bank Act* is a federal law which, like the *Bank Act,* is subject to revision every 10 years. However, the category is very small. For many years there were two Quebec Savings Banks, but in late 1969 one of them (La Banque d'Economie de Québec) converted into a chartered bank, leaving only one, the Montreal and District Savings Bank, with total assets (including all subsidiaries) of $4 billion.

Regulation of Quebec Savings Banks

Traditionally, Quebec Savings Banks had a reputation for conservative investment policies — in substantial part, a reflection of the restrictive provisions of the law under which they operated. Most important in this regard were restrictions on investments in mortgages, which were first permitted in a small way in 1948. Subsequently, the

TABLE 11-5   Mortgage loan companies: consolidated balance sheet, June 30, 1982

Assets	$ Millions		Percent	Liabilities	$ Millions		Percent
Liquid assets				Personal savings deposits:			
Cash and demand deposits	135		1	Chequable	69		
Term deposits	387		2	Non-chequable	478	547	2
Treasury bills	192		1	Term deposits			
Short-term paper	281		1	Less than 1 year	1 280		
Liquid assets		994	4	1-5 years	12 478		
Securities				Over 6 years	796		
Government of Canada	196		1	Debentures and other	1 325	15 879	66
Other Canadian bonds	689		3				
Equities	313		1	Bank and other loans		4 528	19
Other investments	796		3	Other liabilities		1 756	7
Securities	1 994	1 994	8	Shareholders' equity		1 321	5
Loans: personal and other		382	2				
Mortgages		20 035	83				
Other assets		621	3				
TOTAL		24 029	100	TOTAL		24 029	100

SOURCE: Statistics Canada, *Financial Institutions*, second quarter, 1982 (Ottawa, 1982).

proportion of assets which could be invested in mortgages has been progressively increased (in the 1980 Act it was set at 65% of deposits), but as late as 1959 more than half of their assets were in cash or federal and provincial bonds. The severity of these and other restrictions undoubtedly explains why all of the near banks established in the postwar period have been in other categories. Indeed, the history of the Quebec Savings Banks may contain a significant moral. When the original legislation was passed, the government anticipated the development of a nationwide network of sound, federally supervised savings banks to parallel the network of chartered banks. However, the portfolio restrictions enacted to guarantee their soundness also stifled their growth when the competition for savings became intense and their provincially chartered competitors were not similarly encumbered.

As is evident in Table 11-6, the balance sheet of the Quebec Savings Banks is beginning to look much like the balance sheets of other near banks.

TABLE 11-6   Quebec savings banks: balance sheet, June 30, 1982

Assets	$ Millions	Percent	Liabilities	$ Millions	Percent
Cash:	360	8	Deposits:		
Securities:			Personal term	2 750	63
Gov't of Canada	101	2	Other personal	758	17
Provincial	286	7	Other	526	12
Municipal	57	1	Other liabilities	325	7
Other	330	8			
Mortgages	2 729	62			
Loans	178	4			
Other assets	318	7			
TOTAL	4 360	100	TOTAL	4 360	100

SOURCE: *Bank of Canada Review*, (November, 1982).

The Balance Sheet of Quebec Savings Banks

The liability side of the balance sheet is notably simple. Virtually all of the funds are obtained from personal savings deposits, which are like similar deposits with banks and other near banks. The structure of the asset portfolio reflects the regulations under which a Quebec Savings Bank operates. There is a cash reserve requirement which, at 5% of deposits, is relatively heavy, even compared to chartered banks. It may be satisfied by holdings of currency or deposits with the Bank of Canada or a chartered bank. There is also a 15% secondary reserve requirement, which may be satisfied with cash or securities of the Government of Canada or of one of the provinces.

The bulk of the assets consists of secured and unsecured loans (mainly to individuals) and mortgages. The ability to extend both mortgage and unsecured personal loans is one advantage which a savings bank has over most other near banks. A savings bank can now provide individual wealth owners with virtually all of the services offered by the chartered banks except those involved in large-scale domestic and international payments.

GOVERNMENT SAVINGS
DEPOSITORIES

In addition to all these various near bank competitors of the chartered banks, there exists a group of institutions which compete for the same pool of savings, but which are generally not true intermediaries. Most of these government-owned institutions only perform *half* of the intermediation function: they collect funds by issuing savings deposits, but they do not lend funds to other spending units (unless one wishes to argue

TABLE 11-7   **Deposits with government savings institutions, March 30, 1981**

	($ Millions)
Post Office Savings Bank	3
Province of Ontario Savings Office	623
Alberta Treasury Branches	
Public deposits	
Not bearing interest	230
Bearing interest	1 972
Provincial government deposits	79
TOTAL	2 907
Canada Savings Bonds	15 966

SOURCE: *Bank of Canada Review,* (February, 1982).

that they lend the funds to the government). The only exceptions are the Alberta Treasury branches which engage in some lending to the general public.

Government savings institutions are in a sense vestiges of the past when they were relatively important as storehouses of wealth (e.g., the government post office savings accounts in the late 19th and early 20th centuries) or when they were considered to be a source of funds for provincial treasuries (e.g., Ontario Savings offices and the Alberta Treasury branches). In recent times, with the exception of the Alberta Treasury branches, their growth rates have been quite low. In fact, in late 1969 the federal Post Office Savings Bank stopped accepting deposits. Their combined assets of $1.8 billion do not make them an important factor in the financial sector.

In many ways, Canada Savings Bonds and similar securities issued by provincial governments, perform similar functions as deposits with government depository institutions. That is, they provide a safe, and by virtue of their instant convertibility to cash, perfectly liquid asset offering a relatively high rate of return. Data on total issues of savings bonds by provincial governments are not available. However, as is noted in Table 11-7, the total value of Canada Savings Bonds outstanding is 5½ times as great as total deposits in government depositories. These bonds do provide strong competition for funds with private depositories.

THE BANKS AND THE NEAR BANKS ────────────────────────────

In this chapter we have examined a diverse group of institutions, ranging from cooperatives like *caisses populaires* which have virtually displaced chartered banks in many small communities, to government-operated depositories which are not complete financial intermediaries. The unifying feature of these institutions is that they offer deposit liabilities that are close substitutes for liabilities of chartered banks, both personal savings deposits and term deposits. However, the balance of liabilities payable on demand and payable after a fixed term is very different from that of chartered banks, as are the legislative provisions under which they operate. The asset portfolios are correspondingly very different. A heavy concentration in mortgage lending, financed through term deposits, makes most near banks effectively "savings banks."

The near banks have competed vigorously with the chartered banks over the postwar period, frequently offering more attractive interest rates and more convenient office locations, business hours, and banking services, forcing the banks to respond in kind. Until the 1967 revision of the *Bank Act,* which removed some of the constraints on chartered bank operations in the "savings banking" field, the near banks grew much more rapidly than the chartered banks. Many factors contributed to the divergence in growth rates. Undoubtedly, the growth of trust and loan companies was directly linked to the strong demand for housing in Canada; and to some extent the growth of cooperative banks reflected ideological commitments and relatively low operating costs through essentially volunteer labor. However, in a positive way, aggressive business policies, reflected in vigorous and imaginative competitive efforts, were vital to the success of the rapid-growth institutions. But we must not forget, in a negative way, that many restrictive government regulations contributed directly to the performance of the slow-growth institutions. It is significant that in the years since the 1967 revision of the *Bank Act,* the growth of the chartered banks has been much closer to that of its major competitors. We will return to this theme in Chapter 16.

ENDNOTES

1. Royal Commission on Banking and Finance, *Hearings* (Toronto: F.J. Nethercut and R.J. Young, 1962), p. 3066.
2. This view was bolstered recently by evidence in a study of the *caisses populaires.* See J.P. Chateau, "The Demand for and Supply of Deposits by Credit Unions: The Caisses Populaires Case," *Journal of Banking and Finance* 4 (1980), pp. 151-73.
3. Ontario law, which as noted earlier is of dominant importance, specifies a 20% reserve requirement for trust companies and mortgage loan companies; but it is only applicable to deposits payable in less than 100 days, and it can be satisfied with cash, bank deposits, bonds, or loans secured by bonds, of the government of Canada or of any province, or a line of credit from a chartered bank.

OTHER FINANCIAL INTERMEDIARIES 12

In the previous two chapters we examined financial institutions whose liabilities are either money or near substitutes for money. To round out our discussion of Canadian financial intermediaries we must now turn our attention to a heterogeneous collection of intermediaries whose liabilities do not have this characteristic. That is not to say that these institutions have little economic significance, for a major portion of the savings of society are channeled through them. They now hold total assets in excess of $140 billion. Moreover, they offer specialized investment or lending opportunities to individuals and enterprises which may not fit the established patterns of business or even the legal powers of banks and near banks.

The range of activities of firms in this residual group is extensive. At one extreme we have the mutual fund, a type of intermediary which simply provides portfolio diversification and professional selection of securities for the assetholder. The liabilities of the mutual fund do not have the special property of liquidity like those of deposit-type institutions. At the other extreme are insurance companies, a set of institutions whose liabilities have very specialized characteristics, the special nature of which makes it easy to forget to include the companies in a list of intermediaries. One tends to forget that they borrow or lend, and to regard them simply as firms selling a service, insurance.

Between these two extremes are several other, more or less specialized intermediaries, which seek out sources of funds to be borrowed on a wide variety of terms, lend for specialized purposes, and, by holding a diversified portfolio of securities, perform the essential function of risk spreading. These specialized intermediaries are so numerous and so varied that they almost defy systematic cataloguing, and the list is continually changing as firms are established to take advantage of new opportunities for profitable intermediation.

PURE INTERMEDIATION:
THE MUTUAL FUND

The Nature of a Mutual Fund

The concept of a mutual fund is relatively simple. Individuals contribute funds to a central investment pool by purchasing shares or "units" in the fund. This pool is used to purchase a portfolio of securities. Part of the income earned on the portfolio is used to cover management expense, with the residual income either paid out to the members as dividends or added to the pool of funds available to purchase securities. Members' claims on the fund are proportionate to the *number* of units which they own. Over time, the value of any given portfolio of securities will change as a result of changes in the market prices of the securities comprising the portfolio. As a result, the value of each unit will change. Furthermore, an "open-ended" fund will sell additional units to old or new members, thus acquiring additional funds for investment, and producing a further change in the total value of the portfolio. The cost of each new unit will depend on the value of the portfolio of securities at the time the new unit is issued. This may be higher or lower than the costs of the original units, and earlier subscribers will correspondingly earn capital gains or capital losses on their units. Open-ended funds will also cash in the units of their members for their unit value at that point in time (less certain charges), selling securities out of the portfolio for this purpose if necessary.

In principle, any group of individuals could organize such a "fund". For example, you and nine other friends could decide to form a mutual fund. You might decide that the value of the initial units will be $10. Each purchases one unit, providing an investment fund of $100.

As the value of the assets purchased with the original subscribed capital rises or falls so does the value of the units. But since it is an open-ended fund, the number of units is not limited to the original number, and the value of a unit is not fixed at the original value. Thus, if after one month the value of the portfolio has increased so that the unit value is $12, (i.e., the total fund is now worth $120) additional units would cost $12 each. Similarly if, in the following month, because of an adverse turn in the market, the total portfolio falls in value so that the unit value is but $8, then additional units can be purchased at that price, and existing units can be cashed in for that price. Why? Because that is the value of the assets which must be sold out of the fund so that a unit can be cashed in.

Such a mutual fund is more likely to be called an "investment club." Unlike a true mutual fund it does not sell units to the general public, but rather confines its membership to a specified group of individuals. Such clubs are increasingly common, and the arrangements normally call for fixed monthly subscriptions by each member of the club. Given the small scale of the typical club's investment portfolio, the opportunities for portfolio diversification are limited, as are the possibilities for expert management (see the discussion of economies of scale in financial intermediation in Chapter 9.) People frequently join such clubs to learn about the stock market and to gain experience in making investment decisions while pooling the limited time which each can devote to research on securities. On a small scale, the basic principle is the same as that involved in a true mutual fund (although the operations of true mutual funds are supervised by government agencies).

Originally, mutual funds tended to concentrate only on holding common shares in the portfolios. One interesting development over the last decade has been the development of special purpose mutual funds which offer the investor the chance to participate in holdings of bonds and mortgages. In mid-1981, $3.8 billion (69% of total mutual fund portfolios) were held by equity funds, $1.2 billion (22%) by mortgage funds, and $.5 billion (9%) by income (or bond) funds. Thus, despite the growth of alternatives, the equity fund remains the predominant component of the mutual fund industry.

Asset Portfolios of Mutual Funds

A consolidated statement of the assets of Canadian mutual funds is shown in Table 12-1. The contrasts between the portfolio of this intermediary and those of most of the other financial intermediaries which we have examined so far are very pronounced.

TABLE 12-1 Open-ended mutual funds: assets valued at market value, June 30, 1982

	$ Millions		Percent
Liquid assets			
Cash and demand deposits	106		2
Term deposits	130		3
Short-term paper	280		6
Total Liquid assets		516	11
Fixed income securities			
Government of Canada bonds	254		5
Other Canadian bonds	203		4
Preferred stock and other	274		6
Foreign fixed income securities	95		2
Mortgages	1 088		23
Fixed income securities		1 914	41
Variable income securities			
Canadian common stocks	1 272		27
Foreign stocks	1 138		24
Variable income securities		2 410	52
Other assets (including unrealized losses on securities)		– 162	– 3
TOTAL		4 678	100

SOURCE: Statistics Canada, *Financial Institutions*, second quarter, 1982 (Ottawa, 1982).

Liquidity.   You should particularly note the relatively small holdings of cash and other liquid assets characteristic of mutual funds. Unlike intermediaries such as banks or trust companies, mutual funds do not face a high degree of banker's risk, and hence they do not have a strong liquidity preference, but, like banks, their liabilities are payable on demand (the units can be cashed in at any time). Unlike in banks, the dollar value of the claims is not fixed, but fluctuates in value with changes in the market value of the asset portfolio.

Less Liquid Assets.   Traditionally, mutual funds have been a means by which small investors have been able to participate in a diversified portfolio of equities. As recently as 1970, common stock accounted for over 80% of the market value of mutual funds. Since then, because of the relatively poor performance of the stock market and the development of specialized mutual funds which concentrate their holdings on mortgages and bonds, the share of equities in mutual fund portfolios has decreased. Nevertheless, common stocks still account for over 50% of the market value of mutual fund holdings.

Foreign Securities.   It is also interesting to note the proportion of the assets of mutual funds which are foreign, primarily U.S., equities. Most funds hold some foreign securities, and some hold them exclusively. The overall proportion of foreign securities now stands at 25% of the fund portfolios and is considerably lower than the 41% of 1970 value mainly because of changes in Canadian tax laws which have made foreign securities less attractive. Still, mutual funds remain a means by which Canadians, especially those with small portfolios, can make investments abroad.

The Demand for Mutual Fund Shares

Growth Rate.   Unlike the growth of other intermediaries, the growth rate of mutual funds has been quite erratic. In the period 1959-1972, the market value of total assets of mutual funds increased almost 400%. By 1974, the value of mutual fund assets, after some increase early in the decade, had fallen to just two-thirds of its value in 1972. While much of the decrease in value reflected movements in the market value of the assets held, some withdrawal of funds also occurred. Only in the latter part of the 1970s have mutual funds once again experienced strong growth so that, at the end of 1980, the market value of assets was approximately 220% of the low value of 1974. This growth was caused almost equally by appreciation in the value of security holdings and the inflow of new funds. What accounts for this demand for mutual funds shares?

Risk Spreading.   In Chapter 5 we analyzed the demand for financial instruments in terms of a choice at the margin between expected yield, and risk with inflation and taxation as important considerations entering into the calculation of the "real" yield on the instruments. Although shares of mutual funds are more liquid than many assets, it is clear that, unlike banks and trust companies, mutual funds do not appeal to assetholders' demands for liquidity. Rather, it is in the realm of risk and expected yield that we must find the answer to our question.

The essential characteristics of common stock as a financial instrument were discussed in Chapter 3. The point stressed was that these securities involved a residual claim to the potentially highly variable profits of a business enterprise. Considered individually, therefore, common stocks are relatively *risky assets.* Assetholders with a strong aversion to risk might be expected to eschew heavy investment in stocks unless their asset portfolios were large enough to permit substantial portfolio diversification and to generate sufficient income to permit the purchase of professional investment advice. A mutual fund, by pooling the funds of many small assetholders, can achieve the necessary scale of operations to afford professional selection of securities and to achieve substantial portfolio diversification.

You will recall from Chapter 9 that the expected yield on a diversified portfolio of securities is the weighted average of the yields on the individual securities included in the portfolio. In this sense, the mutual fund does not alter the yields available in the market place. What the fund does is to reduce the risk associated with any given level of expected yield. Thus, *the mutual fund effectively improves the trade-off between risk and expected yield available to assetholders,* particularly to those with relatively small asset portfolios.

Are Mutual Fund Shares Riskless?   It is worth noting that although a mutual fund effectively reduces risk through portfolio diversification, even a mutual fund which invests in a broad range of corporate stocks cannot render negligible the total risk to its shareholders. As noted in Chapter 5, portfolio diversification is only effective in reducing risk if the yields on the assets included in the portfolio are *independent.* To some extent this is true of the yields on common stocks. Individual companies may prosper or fail regardless of the fates of other companies. However, because of broad cyclical movements in the economy as a whole, the profits of all companies have a tendency to rise and fall together. Thus, the yields on common stocks are not completely independent, but have some degree of positive correlation. The shares of even a widely diversified mutual fund cannot be riskless.

Specialization Among Mutual Funds.   Note also that the degree of portfolio diversification varies widely among funds. Thus, there are funds which invest almost exclusively in companies with new mining properties, or in companies engaged in the production, transmission, or distribution of oil, gas, or electricity, or in insurance companies, and there are even funds which invest exclusively in other mutual funds. Clearly, while all funds achieve some risk spreading through diversification among companies, the degree of risk spreading may vary between funds.

This fact reflects the different investment objectives of mutual funds. For example, many funds assert that they are "growth" oriented. That is to say, the investment policies of the fund are aimed at maximizing capital gains with little if any concern for income in the form of dividends. Other funds, however, stress a regular flow of income. Such funds usually consist primarily of bonds, and they appeal most to persons who are retired or are about to retire, and to whom a regular flow of income is important. Other funds aim at a "balance" between income and capital gains, and their portfolios contain both bonds and equities. Finally, there is a group of funds that are "fully managed." This means that the management of the fund is not restricted to any particular investment policy, but will adjust the composition of the portfolio from time to time, and perhaps quite radically, in response to anticipated developments in securities markets.

Inflation and Taxes.   At one time, the belief that common stocks, unlike bonds and other fixed income securities, would not necessarily be eroded as a result of inflation contributed to the appeal of mutual funds for small investors. Through portfolio diversification, mutual funds consisting of common stock could reduce some of the risk attached to holdings of common stock, while at the same time they were thought to provide a hedge against the risk of inflation. In the past, this argument was a significant consideration leading to the investment in mutual fund shares. The disappointing performance of the stock market during the inflationary periods of the late 1960s and 1970s contributed, however, to the slow growth of mutual fund investment as investors questioned the ability of stocks to protect them against inflation.

In Chapter 5 we also noted that the taxation system may affect choices among financial instruments. A particularly important consideration in this regard is that capital gains are taxed in Canada at half the rate applied to other forms of income. This adds to the attractiveness of specialized stock funds which offer the possibility of capital gains to the investor.

Mutual Funds: A Pure Intermediary

We can summarize the essential contribution of mutual funds to the structure of the financial system by saying that the mutual fund provides the individual assetholder with a better trade-off between risk and yield on corporate securities (and particularly common stock) than he could obtain in the market place. In part, this is accomplished by taking advantage of economies of scale in portfolio management: through professional appraisal, selection, and trading of securities. Indeed, the performance of the mutual fund depends directly on the abilities of the management firm. The integrity and abilities of management are another source of risk to the individual investor. However, the fundamental principle through which the mutual fund alters the risk-yield trade-off is portfolio diversification. Indeed, if we regard portfolio diversification as the *sine qua non* of financial intermediation, perhaps we could say that mutual funds are "pure intermediaries." They are an important and growing factor in financial markets, and have come to represent one of the more important forms in which wealth-owners hold wealth.

CLOSED-END INVESTMENT FUNDS

The mutual funds which we have been discussing are all open-ended funds, in that they involve unlimited provision for the issuance of new shares or units. In one sense they are a comparatively recent innovation in the Canadian financial system. The first funds were established in the early 1930s, but widespread recognition and rapid expansion did not occur until the mid-1950s and early 1960s. Indeed, by far the largest number of funds now in operation have charters that date no earlier than the mid-1950s.

However, the basic principle upon which the mutual funds operate — improving the trade-off between risk and yield for individual assetholders by spreading risks over a diversified portfolio of securities — is very simple, and in this respect mutual funds were long anticipated by the operations of investment companies or closed-end investment funds.

Like a mutual fund, a closed-end investment fund is a pool of funds for investment in a diversified portfolio of securities. As is apparent from Table 12-2, by far the most important assets of these funds are common stocks of Canadian corporations. Thus, again like mutual funds, they perform the function of risk spreading for individual investors wanting to hold corporate shares. However, unlike mutual funds, at any time a closed-end fund has a fixed ceiling to the number of its shares outstanding. New issues of shares are possible, of course, in much the same way as new issues of any corporate shares are possible. However, the closed-end fund does not stand ready to cash in its shares for the prevailing pro rata value of its assets, nor does it stand ready to issue new shares on demand at that same price. Instead, the fixed number of shares outstanding are traded in the stock markets just like other equities. Moreover, closed-end funds generally issue both preferred and common shares, and some have a limited amount of bonded indebtedness outstanding as well.

TABLE 12-2   Close-end investment funds: assets valued at market value, June 30, 1982

	$ Millions	$ Millions	Percent
Liquid assets			
Cash and demand deposits	4		—
Term deposits	64		8
Short-term paper	5		—
Liquid assets		73	9
Fixed income securities			
Government of Canada bonds	13		2
Other Canadian bonds	13		2
Preferred stock and other	76		9
Foreign fixed income securities	12		1
Mortgages	—		—
Fixed income securities		114	14
Variable income securities			
Canadian common stocks	352		42
Foreign stocks	94		11
Variable income securities		446	53
Other assets (including unrealized gains on securities)		216	25
TOTAL		844	100

SOURCE: Statistics Canada, *Financial Institutions*, second quarter, 1982 (Ottawa, 1982).

Most mutual funds have strict limits to the amount of their investment in any particular firm, particularly in voting shares. Such rules are in part designed to ensure diversification, but they also have the effect of ruling out the possibility of the fund exerting effective control over the operations of the enterprise. While some closed-end investment funds have a similar limitation, others take an active role in the management of enterprises in which they have a large financial interest. If an investment fund does take an active role in management of enterprises, it is problematic whether we should continue to consider it to be a financial intermediary. There is a subtle, ill-defined line across which the fund becomes in effect a holding company, controlling and operating a diversified, conglomerate industrial empire.

SPECIALIZED INTERMEDIATION:
CONSUMER LOAN AND SALES FINANCE COMPANIES

In Chapter 10, when we discussed the portfolio changes that had occurred in the banking industry, we pointed out the growth in their personal loans. By the end of 1981, these loans stood at over $300 billion. A large part of this growth was in loans secured by chattel mortgages, i.e., term loans for the purchase of consumer durables and, more recently, consumer services such as vacations. The banks, however, are not the sole lenders in this field. The *caisse populaires* and credit unions and, more recently, trust companies are increasingly important participants in this market. These other participants in the consumer loan market accounted for only 16% of the outstanding consumer debt in 1981. One final group of institutions which traditionally specialized in this market consists of consumer loan companies and sales finance companies. While at one time the dominant lenders in this market, these institutions have seen their share of total consumer debt outstanding decline to just 6% in 1981.

Consumer Loan Companies

The consumer loan companies specialize in direct cash lending to individuals. There are a large number of firms in this business. Most of them are small local operations with one or two offices, but several have large-scale, nationwide chains of branches. At the end of 1979, there were four small loan companies and a further 23 consumer loan companies operating under the federal *Small Loans Act*. These companies together have over 1750 offices and almost $1.5 billion of total assets.

At one time, these companies concentrated their business on small cash loans (legally defined as being under $1500), but now these loans are only a small portion, less than 10%, of the companies' assets. Part of the reduced importance of these small loans is the expected consequence of inflation which has made this legal definition less relevant to many borrowers. The companies still remain committed to cash lending and larger loans account for almost two-thirds of the total assets of small loan companies.

The vast bulk of loan applicants are wage earners with low incomes and many have previously borrowed from similar companies. Many of the applications for loans are refused because the applicant is considered to be an unworthy risk given past experience, because it is felt that he is currently overextended in his debt commitments, or because security, if required, is not deemed to be adequate. In spite of this high refusal rate, a fifth of all loans balances outstanding at the end of 1979 were in "delinquent" accounts. Indeed, 10% of the balances were in accounts which were at that time delinquent over three months. Actual losses are very much less than this, of course, partly because many delinquent accounts are subsequently repaid, and partly because loan companies ultimately must resort to calling the security offered for the loan. (The most common security is a chattel mortgage. In the event of default, the loan company will take possession of the chattels.) Most loans are granted either for purposes of debt consolidation or for essential purchases such as food, housing, and clothing. In recent years, however, the companies have begun lending to people for other reasons such as financing vacations or automobile purchases. However, the consumer loan companies are primarily engaged in cash lending to a relatively risky clientele, a clientele who, for the most part, turn to these companies because they are unable to find credit accommodation elsewhere.

Sales Finance Companies

Unlike consumer loan companies, sales finance companies have little if any direct contact with the public. Rather than actively solicit business from the public, as the loan companies do, almost all of their business in consumer lending originates with some other business firm. For example, an automobile dealer will sell a car to a customer with a time purchase plan. The customer signs a contract agreeing to pay a certain sum each week or month for a specified period of time. The dealer in turn takes this contract to a sales finance company which purchases or *discounts* the contract. The dealer by this method receives the proceeds (or more accurately the proceeds less the discount charged by the finance company for taking over the contract) of the sale at once rather than receiving the funds over an extended period of time.

While the financing of consumer purchases of durable goods is the most familiar aspect of the sales finance companies' operations, a major part of their lending involves the financing of dealer inventories, particularly for automobile dealers (dealers in other durables are most commonly financed directly by manufacturers or by bank loans). In this respect the sales finance companies compete directly with the chartered banks. Finance companies find that dealers whose inventories they finance bring most, if not all, of their term purchase contracts to them, so the tie-in becomes quite strong. Two of the largest firms in the business are in fact subsidiaries of automobile manufacturers and are considered to be an integral part of the total marketing approach of these companies.

Finally, sales finance companies have diversified their lending activities even further. As the banks and near banks began to make inroads into the field of consumer finance, the sales finance companies responded by reversing the process. They began lending on a term basis to companies that, because of the risk or term demanded for loans, were unable to find accommodation at chartered banks.

In summary, as in the case of consumer loan companies, a large part of the lending activity of the sales finance companies is concentrated in a relatively risky sector of the economy. Many of their indirect consumer loans are to people who have been refused accommodation at some other financial intermediary. This high risk is in part evidenced in the relatively high rates they charge on loans. In addition, however, the sales finance companies are important in financing dealer inventories of certain durable consumer goods, and they compete with the chartered banks in this field.

Source and Use of Funds

As is evident in Table 12-3, 90% of the assets of consumer loan and sales finance companies are in accounts and notes receivable. Only 1% of their assets are in liquid forms. The deliberate assumption of high-risk, relatively small personal and commercial loans is the hallmark of these institutions. How can they do this, and not only survive, but actually thrive?

Part of the answer lies in the much-repeated statement —through portfolio diversification they spread the risk and hence somewhat reduce the significance of risk in their overall operations. Another part of the answer lies in the fact that most of their loans are secured either by merchandise which can be repossessed, or by other security. Indeed, when sales finance companies discount paper for dealers, part of the risk is frequently borne by the dealer. Another factor is their interest rates, which are commensurate with the risks assumed, and at times the level of these rates is the subject of public concern and opprobrium. Equally important, however, is the nature of their liabilities. Clearly, sales finance or consumer loan companies could not pursue their present patterns of activities if they faced the degree of banker's risk associated with the liabilities of banks or trust companies.

Because of consolidation, the data in Table 12-3 conceal major differences between consumer loan and sales finance companies. As we have seen, the consumer loan companies carry the riskier, least liquid assets. Correspondingly, their sources of finance tend to be relatively more secure, long-term arrangements. Thus, for the smaller, independent consumer loan company, the major source of funds is capital subscribed by the shareholders (including retained earnings). Larger, independent firms also issue long-term debt and sometimes borrow on shorter-term on the open market. Many of the larger firms are owned either by American firms or by larger Canadian sales finance companies. In these cases, long-term loans from the parent firms provide the bulk of the operating funds.

The sales finance companies are larger, more diversified borrowers than are the consumer loan companies. A major portion of their funds is obtained on long or medium-term bases, either through the issuance of longer-term bonds, or through retained earnings and capital subscribed by shareholders. This provides an element of stability to their financial position. However, in an industry which has substantial cyclical and seasonal swings in demand, reliable short-term accommodation is also essential. As in the case of the consumer loan companies, the traditional source of such funds has been bank loans, particularly for the smaller finance companies. However, on various occasions the finance companies found that excessive reliance on bank borrowing had some disadvantages. In periods of general credit restraint, which coincided with periods of relatively strong demand for finance company loans, the chartered banks reduced their lines of credit to the finance companies. These restrictions were particularly severe in 1956-57 and 1959-60. Although short-term borrowing outside the banking system had already developed as an important source of finance, these episodes induced the finance companies to actively cultivate such resources. As a result, finance companies played a major role in the development of the short-term money market in Canada (see Chapter 3). Finance paper became one of the major instruments traded in that market, and short-term borrowing in the money market by finance companies is now more than their short-term borrowing from banks. At times in the recent past, open-market borrowing has had even greater relative importance.

Conclusions

Although their operations are somewhat different, the consumer loan companies and sales finance companies are commonly grouped together: in both cases, loans are

TABLE 12-3 **Consumer loan and sales finance companies: consolidated balance sheet, June 30, 1982**

Assets	$ Millions	Percent	Liabilities	$ Millions	Percent
Liquid assets			*Short-term liabilities*		
Cash and demand deposits	56	—	Bank loans	1 501	11
Term deposits	7	—	Canadian notes	3 420	25
Short-term paper	46	—	Foreign notes	430	3
Liquid assets	109	1	Receivables	420	3
			Short-term	5 351	42
Accounts and notes receivable			*Long-term liabilities*		
Retail sales financing:			Canadian bonds	3 320	24
Consumer	3 207	24	Foreign bonds	541	4
Industrial and commercial	3 714	27	Owing affiliated companies	2 024	15
Retail sales	6 921	51	Long-term	5 885	43
Wholesale financing	2 212	16	Other liabilities	162	1
Business loans	1 123	8	Capital accounts	1 859	14
Personal loans	1 112	8			
Residential mortgages	957	7			
Lease contracts	767	6			
Receivables	13 092	96			
Other assets (including allowance for uncollectable debts)	64	1			
TOTAL	13 264	100	TOTAL	13 264	100

SOURCE: Statistics Canada, *Financial Institutions*, second quarter, 1982 (Ottawa, 1982).

largely made directly or indirectly to persons, and their loans are relatively risky. Inevitably, their operations impinge on those of other financial intermediaries. They compete with various lending institutions in the consumer loan field, and they compete with the chartered banks in some aspects of the commercial loan field. However, they are primarily specialized intermediaries which have developed skills in intermediating a particular type of risk, associated with relatively small personal loans. They have sought out sources of finance to meet their needs, and in the process have played a major role in the development of the short-term money market in Canada.

SPECIALIZED INTERMEDIATION: INSURANCE COMPANIES

The combined assets in Canada of the general insurance companies (i.e., those specializing in insurance against fire, theft, automobile accidents, disability, etc.), and the life insurance companies totaled $60 billion at mid-1982. Clearly, the insurance companies represent a major concentration of financial resources. But is it legitimate to refer to them as financial intermediaries? Selling insurance seems to have little in common with commercial banking.

Insurance as an Asset

Before attempting to answer this question, we should first explore the nature of insurance as an asset.

"Pure" Insurance.   In its "pure" form, insurance simply involves a pooling of risks. Life insurance is probably the most familiar type of insurance, hence an example involving life insurance may help make the point.

Imagine that you are one of 100 people all of the same age and sex who decide to insure each other's lives for the forthcoming year. The agreement is that if anyone of the group dies during the year his estate will be paid $1000. By consulting an actuary — a person trained, among other things, to derive probabilities of people of specified characteristics dying over a specified time period on the basis of mortality tables (historical records of the incidence of death) — you discover that it is most probable that one of the 100 people will die during the course of the year. This means that each member of the group must expect to contribute $10 during the year. Of course, the incidence of death is uncertain. It may be greater or less than the most probable number, and the necessary individual contribution may be higher or lower than $10. However, actuarial estimates of the death rate are surprisingly accurate, at least for large groups. For a small group — and 100 is a small group — the risk to the insurers will be relatively great.

In order to avoid the risk that some member will not pay their share when called upon, you may agree to form a mutual insurance company, with each paying his contribution — his premium — in advance. In order to cover the expected payments from the fund during the year, each member's premium would have to be $10. The higher the probability of death within the specified time period, or the larger the payment to be made upon death, the higher the premium would have to be. The insurance company must also recognize that the death rate may be higher than predicted, and it must make financial provision for such a contingency — it must maintain "reserves." In order to accumulate funds for this purpose, and in order to cover the costs of administering the company (collecting the premiums, keeping the company's books, managing its funds, dealing with policyholder's claims, selling insurance, etc.), the premium will have to be substantially higher than $10 — perhaps $12 to $15.

A life insurance policy is an asset to each policyholder: a claim on the insurance company. But it is a very unusual asset. Unlike a bond, for example, the date of future payment is not fixed, and indeed the fact of payment is not certain. Payment will only be made if a specified event (in this case a death) occurs during a specified time period (the term of the policy, in this case the following year). If that event does not occur during that time period, and it may not, then no payment at all will be made and *the policyholder has no further legal claim on the insurance company.*

The Present Value and Expected Yield on "Pure" Insurance.   If pure life insurance is an asset which can be purchased in varying quantities in the market place, then rational choice presumably calls for a comparison of the present value of the insurance with its market price, or alternately of the expected yield on insurance with the yields on other assets which might be purchased with the same funds.

Consider again the earlier example of an insurance policy calling for a payment of $1000 should the insured die during the forthcoming year. Since the amount of the payment is uncertain — it may be either $1000 or $0 — we can only calculate the present value of the asset on the basis of the expected value of the payment (i.e., taking account of the probability that a payment of $1000 will be made). In the present case, given that there are two possibilities, a payment of $1000 with a probability of .01, or a payment of $0, with a probability of 0.99, the present value of the insurance payment is:

$$\bar{v} = (0.01) \times (\$1000) + (0.99) \times (0)$$
$$= \$10$$

In other words, the purchaser of this insurance policy must pay perhaps $15 for a claim to a possible future payment, when the present value of that claim is only $10! Clearly, *the expected yield on such an asset is negative.* The same basic principles can be applied to pure insurance policies written for contingencies other than death, and, while the calculations are more complicated for terms longer than one year, always with the same result. *If insurance companies are to cover all administrative and selling costs and to make a profit, the expected yield on pure term insurance must be negative.*

There is always a wide variety of assets available in the market place having expected yields which are greater than zero. Why, then, would anyone purchase pure insurance as an asset?

The Demand for "Pure" Insurance.   Our analysis of the problem of asset selection in Chapter 5 stressed that expected yield was not the sole criterion governing such choices. Rather, the problem is that of choice, at the margin, between expected yield, and risk. Purchasers of pure insurance are acquiring an asset designed as *a hedge against the risk of financial loss,* and they are doing it at some expected net cost in the sense that the expected yield on the asset is negative. In general, insurance is purchased to hedge against the risk of destruction or impairment of other assets, such as the risk that fire may destroy a house or factory, or that illness or death of the major bread-winner might impair the future income of the household. However, it may also be taken out as a hedge against a great variety of other financial contingencies, including very commonly the risk of legal liability for automobile accidents.

Insurance Policies as a Vehicle for Systematic Saving

Not all insurance policies sold by life insurance companies are of this "pure" or "term" variety. A "pure" insurance policy cannot be used as a vehicle for the accumulation of savings since at the end of the specified term, if the event against which insurance was taken out (death, fire, accident) has not occurred, the policyholder has no further claim on the company. However, life insurance companies also offer a variety of policies which permit the systematic accumulation of savings. The periodic "premiums" paid to the insurance company include the cost of insurance *per se* (plus the administration costs, of course) plus an additional sum which constitutes a periodic payment into a cumulating fund. At the end of a fixed term, the policyholder has a claim to a specified lump sum payment from the company (whether he dies within the period or not), and during its life the policy has a cumulating cash value which the policyholder can claim (by surrendering his policy) or frequently borrow against. Such a policy involves the principle of co-insurance. In the early years of the policy the insurance is primarily provided by the insurance company, whereas in the later years of the policy the insurance element declines sharply, with protection provided primarily by the policy-holder's own savings accumulated with the company.

It is difficult to calculate the rate of return on such savings-type life insurance policies. However, most calculations that have been made suggest that the rate of return is generally low relative to yields available on alternative assets. Nevertheless, such insurance policies have been popular with the result that life insurance historically has provided a major vehicle for saving in Canada. Indeed, in the early 1960s it was estimated that approximately one-quarter of personal saving each year was accomplished through life insurance. By the 1980s this rate had fallen to one-eighth of personal saving. Still, despite its decline in importance, saving through life insurance has been and remains a significant asset in household wealth. Why has insurance been such an apparently attractive vehicle for savings?

In part, the answer may be that the policyholders do not know the rate of return on their savings accumulated with life insurance companies. In part, they may be attracted by the very fact that insurance is combined with saving. They may also be impressed with the apparent safety of their funds with insurance companies. Also, policyholders are clearly attracted by the systematic nature of the savings process.

Insurance Companies as Financial Intermediaries

At the end of 1980 there were 402 insurance companies registered with the federal government, of which 160 were incorporated in Canada. In addition, insurance was also written by 40 fraternal benefit societies and by a number of smaller provincially-incorporated insurance companies. Considered as an industry, the insurance business is more international in scope than any of the other groups of financial intermediaries which we have examined. Thus, although Canadian fire and casualty insurance companies do relatively little business outside of Canada, over one-fifth of the life insurance policies of Canadian life insurance are written outside Canada. For several of the larger life insurance companies, foreign policies account for well in excess of 40% of their total life insurance business. At the same time, many foreign insurance companies are active in Canada. Thus, at the end of 1980, more than one-quarter of the life insurance policies and more than three-quarters of other insurance policies in effect in Canada had been written by foreign-controlled insurance companies. Foreign insurance companies doing business in Canada must register with the federal Superintendent of Insurance, and must maintain assets in Canada equal to their Canadian liabilities (calculated on an actuarial basis). These funds are included in the asset data reported in Table 12-4.

Such, in crude outline, is the insurance industry. However, we have left hanging the question raised earlier. Can we legitimately consider insurance companies to be financial intermediaries?

Are Insurance Companies Financial Intermediaries?   When we explored the concept of financial intermediation we saw that it has two important aspects. On the one hand a financial intermediary issues financial instruments, claims on itself, and uses the funds

TABLE 12-4   **Insurance companies: Canadian assets, June 30, 1982**

	LIFE INSURERS		GENERAL INSURERS	
	$ Millions	*Percent*	*$ Millions*	*Percent*
Liquid assets				
Cash and demand deposits	197	—	338	2
Term deposits	404	1	501	3
Short-term paper	1 524	3	859	6
Total Liquid assets	2 125	5	1 698	11
Fixed income securities				
Government of Canada bonds	2 664	6	2 970	19
Other bonds	12 600	28	4 546	30
Preferred shares	699	2	870	6
Fixed income securities	15 963	36	8 386	54
Variable income securities				
Common shares	2 156	5	857	6
Mortgages				
Residential	9 305	21		
Non-residential	7 636	17		
Mortgages	16 941	38	1 002	7
Other assets	7 613	17	3 447	22
TOTAL	44 795	100	15 390	100

SOURCE: Statistics Canada, *Financial Institutions*, second quarter, 1982 (Ottawa, 1982).

so collected to make loans and acquire a variety of financial assets. On the other hand, by holding a large, diversified portfolio of assets, a financial intermediary takes advantage of economies of scale and spreads risk, permitting it to offer a class of financial instruments with a better trade-off between risk, expected yield and/or liquidity than would otherwise be available in the market.

Many economists would argue that, given this concept of a financial intermediary, insurance companies can only be considered to be financial intermediaries to the extent that they issue life insurance policies with a savings feature attached. Financial intermediation involves the holding of a diversified portfolio of assets in order to spread risks. Pure insurance is different. It simply involves a pooling of risks. For pure insurance there need be no necessary accumulation of assets, and hence no lending activities. By this criterion, companies which do not issue savings-type life insurance policies (e.g., most general insurance companies) should not be classified as financial intermediaries.

However, the business of an insurance company does not simply involve its acting as an agent to effect a pooling of risks among its policyholders. The company stands as a true intermediary in the process. An insurance policy is a claim on the insurance company, just as a bank deposit is a claim on the bank. And just as the bank cannot know with certainty the portion of its deposits which will be called for payment in any given period of time, so an insurance company cannot know with certainty the claims for payment which will be made under outstanding policies during any period of time. Accordingly, the insurance company, like the bank, must make provision for the possibility that its estimates are wrong. It must accumulate a pool of assets — contingency reserves — to guarantee its ability to make the contractual payments. And the composition of the portfolio of assets must be adapted to the degree of risk which the insurance company has assumed. While it is true that the major accumulation of funds administered by insurance companies is the savings of life insurance policyholders, there would seem to be little merit in the argument that general insurance companies (or life insurance companies with respect to their "term" insurance business) are not financial intermediaries. Moreover, as is apparent in Table 12-4, we are talking about a sizeable concentration of financial assets.

The Deployment of Insurance Company Funds. The degree of risk assumed by general insurance companies is greater than that assumed by life insurance companies. The accidental destruction of real property like railroad rolling stock, a house, or an automobile is much less predictable than death or retirement. Since the requirements for funds to make payments on policies are correspondingly less predictable, the general insurance companies find that they must keep relatively more liquid asset portfolios than do the life insurance companies. This is illustrated in Table 12-4 which shows the assets held in Canada by both groups of companies. You should note the relatively small holdings by life insurance companies of both cash and short-term notes and deposits.

Another important difference in their asset portfolios is the life insurance companies' relatively heavy concentration on mortgages. As a long-term asset, mortgages are a particularly suitable asset to match against the long-term liabilities of life insurance companies. At one time, life insurance companies were the largest private institutional lenders in the residential mortgage market. In recent years, the shorter terms to maturity of residential mortgages has caused the life insurance companies to turn more to non-residential mortgages with longer terms.

Competition Between Financial Intermediaries

While insurance is clearly a rather unique type of financial instrument, we should not assume that insurance companies and other financial intermediaries do not compete for funds. While the competition may be more remote than that between banks and trust companies for term deposits, it *is* there, particularly in regards to life insurance with a savings feature.

During the past two decades there have been significant changes in the market for long-term consumer savings. Whereas life insurance was at one time virtually the only form of long-term contractual savings available, there have developed in recent years a number of substitutes, the most important of which are the mutual funds and pension funds. The life insurance companies also faced renewed attacks from other longer-established forms of saving, such as time deposits with chartered banks and Canada Savings Bonds. Rates paid on these forms of saving rose steadily throughout the past two decades and the low rates paid on life insurance savings served to reduce the relative appeal of this form of saving. The life insurance companies responded to these competitive challenges in various ways. First, there has been a gradual increase in the rates paid on savings held by the life companies. Second, they have increased their efforts to sell combined packages of group term, health, and disability insurance along with pension fund administration. By this scheme, an insurance company agrees to provide low-cost group term and other insurance and at the same time undertakes to administer the pension fund of the employer. Finally, the insurance companies have in recent years attempted to increase the attractiveness to individual savers of their own insurance policies by embellishing them with additional services such as medical coverage, and occasionally disability insurance. Despite these efforts, the growth of insurance companies has not managed to keep pace with that of other financial intermediaries. From the end of 1970 to the end of 1981, the insurance companies have increased their assets from $15 billion to $51.9 billion, an increase of 11% per year. As a basis for comparison, the personal disposable income grew from $54 billion to $222 billion, or at 13.7% per year.

During this period, the insurance companies faced added competition from the Canadian Pension Plan introduced in 1966, which by mid-1981 had accumulated assets of almost $20 billion. In its fiscal year ending April 1981, the plan's contributions exceeded the benefits it paid out by over $680 million. It appears, therefore, that the accumulation of long-term savings is changing away from insurance companies in favor of pension plans and, more importantly, pension plans administered by the public and not the private sector.

SPECIALIZED INTERMEDIATION:
PENSION FUNDS

We must consider pension funds like insurance companies, to be one group of financial intermediaries offering a highly specialized product — a retirement income. In our discussion of the demand for financial instruments in Chapter 4, we argued that the underlying demand for wealth reflected a desire to redistribute income and consumption over time. A pension plan does this explicitly. It collects a portion of each member's income during his working life and returns it (plus interest) in the form of an annual pension following retirement. Most pension plans involve an element of insurance as well. That is, members of the plan who live unusually long will continue to receive their pension in spite of the fact that their lifetime contributions by themselves would not have been adequate to purchase such a stream of retirement income. At the end of 1980 in addition to the Canadian Pension Plan operated by the Government of Canada, there were more than 3200 other trusteed pension plans with total assets of $52 billion administered by trust companies and another 10 000 plans administered by insurance companies with total assets of $14 billion. In the years to mid-1981, the increase in assets held by these funds was $8.5 billion, so that they are a major collector and investor of long-term consumer savings.

Investment of Pension Funds

Since the managers of funds can predict with great certainty both the inflow of funds and, more importantly, the outflow (they know when each member will retire and have some experience with early withdrawals due to death) the funds have little need for liquidity. As is evident in Table 12-5, their assets are primarily concentrated in long-term forms with only minimal amounts of cash or short-term assets. Perhaps because most pension plans promise a *fixed income* during retirement, the bulk of the assets are fixed income securities, and particularly provincial, municipal, and corporate bonds.

TABLE 12-5   **Assets of trusteed pension funds, December 31, 1980**

	$ Millions	Percent
Liquid assets		
Cash	1 910	4
Fixed income securities		
Government of Canada bonds	5 510	11
Provincial and municipal bonds	14 001	28
Other bonds	5 888	12
Variable income securities		
Canadian stocks	8 480	17
Foreign stocks	2 080	4
Investments in pooled and mutual funds	2 527	5
Loans		
Mortgages	5 757	11
Other assets	4 600	9
	50 753	100

SOURCE: *Bank of Canada Review*, (January, 1982).

There is one further aspect of pension funds which merits mention. Table 12-5 shows a relatively heavy concentration of investments in provincial and municipal bonds. Closer examination of detailed data reveals that this concentration is particularly heavy among pension plans for employees of provincial, municipal, and educational institutions. Thus, provincial and educational employee funds respectively held 41% and 67% of their assets in the form of provincial bonds, and municipal employee funds held 58% in provincial and municipal bonds. In short, apparently the administrators of many pension funds, and particularly those administered by provincial and municipal governments, use the funds as a source of self-financing.

These proportions are considerably lower than they were a decade earlier. Yet, still relevant today is the observation of the Royal Commission on Banking and Finance:

> Clearly pension fund investment decisions — particularly in plans at each level of government — are not made exclusively in terms of yields available on different assets. At the extreme, some funded plans administered by provincial governments held non-marketable long-term obligations of the government concerned — which is virtually equivalent to operating an unfunded plan. Given the size of the flows involved, this tendency to disregard market considerations on the part of many funds, particularly some of the large ones, can lower both the returns to the members on their pension savings and the efficiency of capital allocation in the market.[1]

We can legitimately question whether such pension funds can be regarded as financial intermediaries.

OTHER SPECIALIZED LENDERS

In addition to the various types of intermediaries we have discussed, there exist many other firms which specialize in supplying finance to industry. These include venture capital firms which both lend and participate directly via equity holdings and/or management in small and new enterprises. To a large extent they provide venture capital to firms that cannot raise funds through bank loans or are too small or closely held to warrant bond or equity issues. Venture capital firms often operate under special legislation which provides them advantages but at the same time restricts their investment in any one enterprise. Also included among the specialized lenders are so-called merchant banks which engage in commercial lending, wholesale financing, commercial mortgages, and export trade financing. The final group which we include among specialized lenders, financial leasing corporations, are not strictly lenders. Rather, they lease equipment to corporations which have to finance the purchase of capital assets. A financial lessor, unlike a conventional lessor, pays for and takes title to equipment chosen by the enterprise using the asset. The financial lessor does not hold any inventory. Moreover, the financial lessor plans the payment under the lease so that he can cover the cost of the asset plus his profit over the life of the lease. Financial lease contracts are clearly an alternative to loan finance and usually arise for reasons related to tax advantages.

[1] Royal Commission on Banking and Finance, *Report*, p. 260.

In mid-1981, specialized business lenders and financial leasing corporations had total assets of approximately $14.9 billion. Generally, they are financed through the short-term money market and the issuance of bonds by parent companies and associates. While quantitatively small in relation to the total financial sector, these specialized firms do play an important role in supplying funds to smaller and riskier enterprises that might otherwise have difficulties in raising funds.

GOVERNMENT LENDING INSTITUTIONS

There are a number of government-operated lending institutions which are important participants in the financial system, although, like the governmental savings institutions discussed in Chapter 11, they are not true financial intermediaries. Some provide insurance — such as the Export Development Corporation which insures loans taken out by exporters and also provides finance for exports by direct loans. Other agencies insure farm crops, and provide loans to veterans, small businesses, and students. While these various insurance programs are important in some contexts, the two institutions operated by the federal government that are of most direct and immediate importance to the financial sector are the Federal Business Development Bank and the Canada Mortgage and Housing Corporation.

The Federal Business Development Bank is wholly owned by the Government of Canada. Founded as the Industrial Development Bank in 1944 by an act of Parliament, it was established to provide medium and long-term financing for business firms unable to obtain financing on reasonable terms and conditions elsewhere. At first the Bank was restricted to lending to manufacturing enterprises but this constraint was removed in 1961, and now the institution lends to almost any business enterprise.

Loans are normally for relatively small amounts (the average is about $45 000), which highlights the fact that the primary customers of the bank are relatively small, high-risk business ventures. By mid-1981, total loans outstanding amounted to $2061 million.

Originally the Central Mortgage and Housing Corporation, the predecessor to the Canada Mortgage and Housing Corporation, was established to administer the *National Housing Act*. Since its creation in 1945, the Corporation has undergone several transformations so that at present it has several major fields of activity. First, it insures mortgages under the NHA. By that we mean that it guarantees the loans made by private investors to individuals for the building of new homes and for the purchase and rehabilitation of existing residences. Second, the Corporation lends directly to individuals for housing construction, to nonprofit organizations for the construction of low-cost, low-income rental housing, and to local governments for major water and sewage projects. Finally, the Corporation tries to promote uniform building standards and codes throughout the nation.

The insuring of mortgages by the Corporation helps to reduce the cost of mortgages and provides a high-yield, low-risk, but still relatively illiquid, asset to the borrower. Normally, the difference in rates paid on an insured mortgage and a "conventional" or non-insured mortgage is between one half and one full percent. Furthermore, insured mortgages can be granted for up to 90% of the value of the house while conventional first mortgages are normally limited to 75% of the value of the purchase.

The program of direct lending has been instrumental in providing low-cost, low-income rental housing in major urban areas. At the beginning of 1982, the Corporation had loans outstanding of $9 billion. In 1981 alone it lent more than $400 million. Thus, in terms of its direct lending and insuring of mortgages, the Corporation plays a major role in the mortgage market.

At the same time, the Corporation undertook a major effort to establish an active secondary mortgage market in Canada. The efforts of the Corporation on this initiative have had only limited success. Mortgages by their very nature are non-homogenous even when sheltered under the protection of NHA insurance. Normal purchasers of mortgages frequently prefer to deal directly with the lender in an effort to tie in other business. Firms that might deal in the secondary market, therefore, are either already in the market or can find equally long-term substitutes which are more homogenous and which have less risk associated with them. Nevertheless, several private institutions do sell packages or mortgages that are guaranteed by the selling institution. These firms, however, provide the bulk of the secondary market.

COMPETITION AMONG
TYPES OF INTERMEDIARIES

We have now completed our detailed survey of Canadian financial intermediaries. For purposes of description we have divided the intermediaries into groups or categories. While most of these groupings have roots in federal or provincial laws, we also discovered that each group had a rather distinctive pattern of assets and liabilities. On this basis we could say that each group represented firms engaged in a particular field of financial intermediation. However, it should also be obvious that from an economic point of view the various categories of financial intermediaries are largely — but not completely — arbitrary. The activities of firms in each group impinge directly on those of some, if not all, other groups.

Consider, for example, the chartered banks. While the banks are unique in that part of their liabilities constitute a substantial portion of the money supply, they will face strong competition in other sectors. Thus, the trust companies, the mortgage loan companies, and the *caisses populaires* and credit unions all compete with the banks for personal savings deposits. In assets, the banks face competition with the sales finance companies for consumer loans, with the trust companies, mortgage loan companies, credit unions, *caisses populaires,* and insurance companies for mortgages.

While the banks are much less specialized in their intermediation than is the case with some other intermediaries, their example should make the major point. *The activities of intermediaries do not fit into tight, specialized compartments. The patterns of overlapping activities among groups of intermediaries are both complex and quantitatively important.* Moreover, as the discussion in the previous chapters suggests, *these patterns are not static; they are continually changing.*

These are points which should be kept in mind as we turn our attention to questions of public policy with respect to competition and soundness in the financial system.

PART II

Public Policy and the Financial System

Our purpose in exploring the microeconomics of the Canadian financial system in detail was to develop a basis for reviewing and assessing *public policy* with respect to financial institutions and financial markets. So far, however, our discussion has been almost entirely in *positive* terms. We have described the important features of the system and have developed basic theories of the functioning of financial markets and financial intermediaries. Such analysis is important in considering public policy. The analysis of the functioning of the system with and without governmental intervention, and hence the identification of the implications of intervention, are exercises in positive economics. However, that is not all that has to be considered. We must also address such important normative issues as the objectives of policy and the assessment of the performance of the system against some qualitative standard of "goodness" or "badness." Moreover, in the study of public policy, some understanding of the history of the interaction between policy and the development of the financial system is important, if only to show how we got to where we are now and to suggest what has been successful and unsuccessful in the past. Equally valuable is the study of public policy in other institutional contexts. For Canadians, the development of public policy in the United States provides both comparisons and contrasts, study of which can clarify our understanding of our own problems.

The purpose of the four chapters in this part of the book is to consider the major issues of Canadian public policy against the background of the preceding analysis, in historical context, and by comparison with policies and developments in the United States. In Chapter 13, we discuss the purpose and objectives of policy and their expression in Canadian laws and regulations. Normative questions about objectives of policy do not lend themselves to crisp, decisive analysis and answers. However, we do identify the various objectives pursued by governments, discuss their rationales, and suggest the potential for conflicts among them — and particularly, potential conflicts between policies for financial stability and policies for competition. In the history of public policy in both Canada and the United States, the tension between these concerns has been a major theme. Perhaps as a result of the devastating consequences of the depression of the 1930s for the financial affairs of a whole generation, concern about stability assumed a dominant position in both countries through the 1960s — themes developed and explored in Chapters 14 and 15. However, as stability and prosperity became the norm, increased attention was focused on competition in financial industries. The result has been a significant reorientation of public policy in both countries. The nature and implications of this reorientation are considered in Chapter 16.

THE SOCIAL INTEREST IN THE FINANCIAL SYSTEM: ISSUES IN MICROECONOMIC POLICY

13

While the degree of regulation of financial institutions falls short of that of the telecommunications and transportation industries, chartered banks and other financial institutions are among the more heavily regulated businesses in Canada. The high degree of regulation raises a number of important questions. Why are banks and other financial institutions so heavily regulated? What forms of regulation are most appropriate to achieve the goals of regulation? How appropriate is the existing framework for the regulation of financial institutions?

In the following sections, we first examine the arguments put forward to justify the regulation of the financial system and then consider the specific types of regulation which have been used in Canada to meet the goals of regulation.

WHY REGULATE FINANCIAL INSTITUTIONS?

The Economic Council of Canada, in its review of the goals of the regulation of financial institutions stated:

> The existing regulations governing deposit institutions in Canada have been justified on the grounds that they protect depositors, assist in the workings of monetary policy, encourage competition and efficiency in financial markets, influence the composition of economic activity, preserve the separation of financial and nonfinancial activities and foster the Canadian ownership of the financial sector.[1]

While we accept the Economic Council's view that these are indeed the goals which motivate existing regulations in Canada, we need to assess the underlying rationale of each goal to determine the costs and benefits of different types of regulation.

Depositor Safety

From one standpoint, the liabilities of financial institutions are essentially the same as the liabilities of any other corporations in our economy. Both are promises to stated amounts (principal and interest) at specified dates. Why then do we subject financial institutions to much more stringent regulations in relation to their liabilities than we do other corporations? In particular, why do we devote so much effort to ensure the safety of deposits at financial institutions?

The answers to these questions lie in our analysis of financial institutions as "financial intermediaries" in Chapter 9. There we saw that financial intermediaries are able to transform the characteristics of assets in such a way that the depositors view the intermediary's liabilities as more desirable than the collection of assets which is held by the institution. Most importantly, the deposits of financial intermediaries are among the most liquid assets in the economy. However, financial institutions are only able to supply liquid deposits to their customers to the extent that these customers are confident that the financial institution will honor the commitment to make future payments.

Confidence   Confidence in a financial institution's ability to meet its obligations to its customers can be fostered in a variety of ways. Historically, financial institutions evolved as offshoots from other economic activities in which entrepreneurs had developed a reputation for trust. With a fully operative legal system, we could imagine financial institutions and their customers reaching private contracts which would constrain the activities of the financial institutions so as to limit the risks faced by their depositors. Individual financial institutions would make information available to consumers as to the range of activities they would undertake in order to enable depositors to decide whether that financial institution would meet their needs. Such a system would be very unwieldy. The types of contracts which evolve would be complex and difficult for the average depositor to understand. In any case, it might make little sense for the customer to digest the contents of a 20-page contract just to make a deposit of $100 or less. From this perspective, we can view government regulation as establishing categories of financial institutions of differing risk classes. For example, the depositor at a chartered bank can be assured that the bank's commitment to repay the face value of the deposit will be met. In contrast, the holder of a mutual fund share typically knows that he is entitled only to a share of a portfolio which may fluctuate in price. In effect, government regulation can be viewed as a substitute for private contracts in informing the customer of the likely risks he faces in holding the liabilities of a financial institution. This argument for regulation suggests that the benefit from such regulation arises from the savings of costs in seeking information and making transactions which result from the establishment by the authorities of common rules for similar financial institutions.

Interdependence.   Another argument for regulation directed toward the assurance of depositor safety arises because of a particular type of interdependence among financial institutions. The acceptability to the general public of the liabilities of any given financial institution depends on the public's confidence in its ability to honor the terms of its liability. Failure of even a single financial institution to meet its commitment with respect to its deposits can impair the public's confidence in other financial institutions which will find themselves facing increased withdrawals of deposits by their customers. The liquid component of the portfolios of financial institutions which are adequate for meeting normal outflows may be exhausted by unpredicted outflows, spreading failure further through the financial system.

Canada has been fortunate in that confidence runs on financial institutions have been short-lived and isolated to single institutions rather than spreading through the system. In the United States, in contrast, thousands of banks were caught up in the crisis of confidence and contagion of runs that led to the suspension of over 9000 banks in the early 1930s. Our point on the interdependence of financial institutions is well illustrated by the events of this period. The total losses to depositors at the failed banks were probably no more than $1.5 billion. On the other hand, the accompanying decline in the money supply caused by withdrawals of currency from banks which remained in business was $18 billion — or over 12 times the direct losses suffered by the depositors at failed banks.

Thus, the interdependence among similar financial institutions leads to a further argument for regulation of financial institutions to enhance depositor safety. The regulation and control of financial institutions from the point of view of interdependence attempts to enforce a common standard on all financial institutions so as to prevent the costs of unsound practices of some financial institutions from falling on other financial institutions and their customers.

Payments Media.   A final argument for regulation directed toward bank safety arises from the role of financial institutions as suppliers of a major part of the media of payment essential for the working of a market economy. In Chapter 2, we saw that although the banks are the predominant provider of the deposit component of the money supply, other financial institutions, notably trust companies, credit unions, and *caisses populaires* also offer deposits which can be used for making payments. As we have seen, an effective medium of payment must be generally acceptable as payment for goods and services. Failure of any financial institution issuing part of the money supply then jeopardizes the general acceptability of the deposit component of money. The less acceptable the medium of exchange, the more frequently will individuals have to resort to other more costly means of carrying out transactions. Thus, the integral role of a financial institution in supplying the means of payment in the economy is the source of a further argument in favor of regulating financial institutions.

Regulation and Monetary Policy

The government in Canada, as in most industrialized countries, has undertaken responsibility for attaining certain macroeconomic objectives such as high and stable employment and price stability. While much debate continues as to the setting of reasonable standards for these goals and the choices to be made when the goals conflict, general agreement exists that monetary policy is an important instrument available to the government for attaining these goals. Keynesians, as we will see in more detail later, stress the effects of monetary policy in determining interest rates and the flow of credit to different sectors in the economy. Monetarists, in contrast, argue that monetary policy works through the direct effects of changes in the money supply on expenditure.

According to either view, the impact of monetary policy on financial institutions and, in turn, their reactions to the policy, are an essential element in the workings of monetary policy. In the words of the Economic Council:

> If it is to manage the money supply, the central bank must have the power to vary either the amount of cash available or the reserve requirements that must be met by the banks. If the Bank of Canada is to control the cost and availability of credit, then it needs certain other powers that will enable it to influence lending by deposit institutions.[2]

The bank of Canada's monetary policy, whether directed at the money supply or at interest rates, works initially by changing the reserves available to financial institutions, and among these primarily the banks. The effectiveness of this measure depends on the reactions of the banks to changes in their reserve holdings. If banks attempt to maintain a stable relationship between their cash holdings and their deposits, any change in available cash will force the bank to readjust its portfolio in an attempt to reestablish its previous balance between cash and deposits. On the other hand, if banks tolerate flexibility in their ratio of cash to deposits, the response to a change in cash reserves cannot be assured and the response of the economy to monetary policy would be less predictable. Some economists, as a result, argue that regulation of financial institutions, and especially the banks, is required in order to make monetary policy an effective instrument for controlling the economy.

Social Goals of Policy

The regulation of financial institutions goes beyond the narrow economic objectives such as depositor safety and the workings of monetary policy. The prominent role of the financial system in any developed economy may lead the government to try to attain what can be characterized as social goals through manipulating the flow of credit so as to encourage certain types of activity and discourage others. In addition, the government may also have views on ownership of major financial institutions both in terms of their nationality and their relationship with the rest of the economy.

Credit Allocation.   The government may be concerned with the flow of credit among various users for a variety of reasons. The government may desire more finance for some sectors, such as housing, exports, or small business, than they would receive in the absence of special measures because it believes that these activities by their very nature should be encouraged. In other cases, the government may encourage the flow of credit to depressed regions or to cooperative housing because it feels such measures will lead to a more desirable distribution of income. Similarly a government may wish to discourage lending to certain types of activities which it regards as socially wasteful and against the social interest. In the early 1980s, for example, the Canadian government expressed concern about the role of the chartered banks financing corporate takeovers as distinct from other forms of investment.

Separation of Financial Activity.   An additional concern which has influenced the regulation of financial institutions in Canada is the appropriate relationship between the financial system and other sectors of the economy. Some would argue that ownership and control of the financial system should be kept separate from the ownership and control of the nonfinancial sector. The reasons for this separation are several. It has been suggested that financial institutions may not be as critical in assessing risks, or they may even be willing to accept greater risks when the request for the loan comes from an associated enterprise. This greater tendency to undertake risk would be incompatible with assuring an adequate level of safety for depositors.

The second argument for the separation of financial and nonfinancial activity may be more fundamental. It suggests that failure to maintain separation of the financial and nonfinancial sectors may lead to an excessive concentration of power in one set of institutions. As the Economic Council stated in its report on financial institutions:

> Many view the concern about the sheer size of the larger banks as a more important reason for the separation of financial and nonfinancial sectors. While the activities of deposit institutions in any specific market are now subject to competition legislation, the overall accumulation of power across many markets is a separate question. The separation of financial and nonfinancial sectors is, at best, an indirect means of dealing with this issue, but it should at least limit the size of these institutions and their pervasiveness throughout the economy.[3]

Canadian Ownership.   The final concern which we will consider with respect to the regulation of financial institutions is the degree of foreign ownership. Prior to 1967, foreign ownership of Canadian financial institutions was not limited in any way. The Porter Commission in its review of the Canadian financial system as background for the 1967 revision of the *Bank Act,* examined the question of foreign ownership and concluded that "a high degree of Canadian ownership of financial institutions is in itself healthy and desirable, and that the balance of advantage is against foreign control of Canadian banks."[4] Among the disadvantages of foreign ownership identified by the Commission were the allocation of lending for noneconomic reasons and a lack of compliance with the objectives of Canadian monetary policy.

Competition as a Policy Objective

At the time of both the 1967 and the 1980 revisions of the *Bank Act,* the government emphasized that an important objective of its proposals was to increase the degree of effective competition in the financial system. It is true that economists commonly advocate a high degree of competition as an objective of public policy towards most industries in the economy, but should we treat the financial system in the same manner in which we treat other industries? Is not the financial system different in an important sense which makes competition an *inappropriate* objective of public policy with respect to it?

Competition and Economic Efficiency.   At the root of public policy designed to stimulate competition is a concern for *economic efficiency* — a concern that society obtain the maximum possible benefit from the limited real productive resources at its disposal. Economic efficiency has two basic dimensions. The first is that excessive resources not be absorbed in the production of any product. That is, each good or service which is produced must be produced at the *least attainable cost.* If the quantity of output of every product were predetermined, that would be all that there was to economic efficiency. However, all resources have alternative possible uses. The range of products produced and the quantity of each product produced can be altered. Therefore, the second condition for economic efficiency is that all resources must be allocated to their most valuable uses. That is, *optimum quantity* of each good or service must be produced. One of the important conclusions of elementary economic theory is that, if we accept relative valuations of goods and services implicit in consumer demand curves, then, with certain exceptions, *highly competitive markets provide the most reliable mechanism for achieving economic efficiency in both senses.*

Competition and Efficiency.   As was argued in Chapter 1, the financial system can be considered an industry — a collection of firms producing financial services. The production of these services absorbs part of the scarce resources of the economy. As in any other industry, then, it is important that the appropriate quantity of financial services be provided, and that they be provided at least attainable cost.

However, to rest the case for a high degree of competition in the financial system on such an analogy with other industries is to miss an important dimension of the matter. The significance of the financial system cannot be assessed simply in terms of the resources absorbed in producing financial services — in terms of value added in banking and finance. The financial system is, above all, a mechanism for allocating credit to alternative possible uses, and a mechanism for providing assetholders with convenient forms in which they may accumulate wealth. The allocation of credit affects the structure of economic activity; it determines, among other things, what lines of activity will expand and what new ventures will get off the ground. The range of financial instruments available, and the yield on each instrument, affects the welfare of all assetholders. The fundamental case for a policy of stimulating competition in the financial system must rest on the importance of competition in *ensuring that credit is allocated to its most valuable uses* (i.e., to the uses promising the highest rates of return) *at the minimum attainable cost,* and in *ensuring that a broad range of financial instruments is made available to assetholders on the best possible terms* (i.e., offering the most favorable combinations of risk, liquidity and expected yield).

REGULATION IN CANADA

We are now prepared to assess the actual regulation of Canadian financial institutions so as to determine how the goals of regulation are realized in practice. In examining the regulation of financial institutions, we will find it useful to make a distinction between two broad classes of regulation. Portfolio regulation refers to rules which govern the composition of portfolios held by financial institutions. These rules take the form of ratios, in some cases in the form of ceilings and in others floors, between certain assets and certain liabilities in the balance sheets of the institutions to which they apply. An extreme form of portfolio regulation is an absolute prohibition on certain types of activities by financial institutions. *Structural regulation,* in contrast, refers to the terms and conditions which must be satisfied in order either to become incorporated as a given type of financial institution or to participate in a particular type of financial business. These two groupings are not mutually exclusive. An absolute prohibition on certain types of business, for example, not only limits the portfolios of the affected institutions, it also limits the group of participants permitted to engage in that activity.

Any comprehensive evaluation of the regulations applying to financial institutions in Canada is far beyond the scope of our present purpose. Instead, we will concentrate on the major regulations which apply to the chartered banks. On occasion, however, we shall note where significant differences arise in the treatment of the banks and other financial institutions. Our objective will be to determine the relationship between the existing regulations and the goals of regulation. Our ultimate objective in this chapter is to be able to evaluate the appropriateness of the system for regulation of financial institutions in Canada for meeting the apparent objectives of the regulators. In order to fulfill this task, we must understand the constraints facing the regulators of banks and other financial institutions. Therefore, we turn first in this chapter to review one of the major constraints facing regulators in Canada — the division of powers between the federal and provincial governments.

Division of Responsibility

At present, the system of regulation of major institutions in Canada can be described as one of "mixed jurisdictions." As we can see from Table 13-1, the banks are exclusively under federal authority while, in contrast, credit unions and *caisses populaires* are primarily under provincial jurisdiction. Finally, trust and mortgage loan companies can be incorporated either by federal or provincial authorities, in each case with the power to operate throughout the country.

The presence of 11 centers of policy makers with overlapping jurisdiction has been a source of dismay to some observers. Nevertheless, some areas of cooperation and uniformity can be identified. Even in the absence of direct cooperation, there is considerable similarity among provincial laws governing provincially incorporated financial systems. Moreover, as we have seen, a system of deposit insurance covering the chartered banks and trust and mortgage loan companies (both federally and provincially incorporated) was achieved through cooperation among federal and provincial authorities. Still, the constitutional division of powers places a major obstacle in the way of a unified national policy. While both the Royal Commission on Banking and Finance and the Economic Council have identified the key role of this issue in any approach to reform of the regulation of financial institutions, and have made recommendations concerning the division of powers, the authorities have not taken major initiatives in this direction.

Regulation and Depositor Safety

The last bank failure in Canada occurred with the collapse in 1923 of the Home Bank, one of the smaller banks at the time. A number of trust and mortgage loan companies have failed more recently, but their depositors have not suffered any losses from these failures since the establishment of the Canada Deposit Insurance Corporation in 1967. Depositor safety has been protected by a combination of both portfolio regulation and structural regulation.

TABLE 13-1 **Functions and responsibilities of the regulators of deposit institutions, 1975**

	Federally incorporated		Provincially incorporated		
	Chartered banks	*Trust & mortgage loan companies*	*Trust & mortgage loan companies*	*Credit unions*	*Caisses populaires*
Federal					
Bank of Canada	Lender of last resort; regulator of liquidity				
Inspector General of Banks	Inspector; administrator of Bank Act				
Canada Deposit Insurance Corporation (CDIC)	Insurer of deposits; lender of last resort	Insurer of deposits; lender of last resort	Insurer of deposits (outside Quebec); lender of last resort	Lender of last resort	
Superintendent of Insurance		Inspector; administrator of Trust & Loan Act, administrator of Small Loans Act	Administrator of Small Loans Act	Administrator of Small Loans Act	Administrator of Small Loans Act
Minister of Consumer & Corporate Affairs	Administrator of Interest Act	Administrator of Interest Act	Administrator of Interest Act	Administrator of Interest Act	Administrator of Interest Act

Provincial

Quebec Deposit Insurance Board (QDIB)		Insurer of deposits (in Quebec); lender of last resort		Insurer of deposits; lender of last resort
Registrar of Trust and Loan Companies	Licenser of business in provinces	Inspector; administrator of Trust & Loan Act; licenser of business in province		
Ministry of Financial Institutions (Quebec)				Inspector (delegated to centrals); administrator of Caisses Populaires Act
Supervisor of Credit Unions			Inspector; administrator of Credit Union Act	
Credit Union Reserve Board (some provinces only)			Insurer of deposits; lender of last resort	

SOURCE: Economic Council, *Efficiency and Regulation.*

Portfolio Regulation and Depositor Safety.   Portfolio constraints have been traditionally viewed as the main measures by which the goal of depositor safety has been
assured. Nevertheless, can we legitimately ask how the various forms of portfolio
regulation can be expected to contribute to depositor safety? For some regulations,
such as the borrowing limits and liquidity rules for trust and mortgage loan companies,
the justification is quite clear. Borrowing limits, which set a maximum ratio of
borrowing to shareholders' equity, do serve to ensure that depositors are protected by
assets beyond the value of borrowed funds. In other words, the borrowing limits
establish the amount of losses which can be sustained before the value of assets falls
below the value of outstanding liabilities. Similarly, the liquidity ratios ensure that a
major proportion of the trust and loan company assets are held in assets which have
relatively low risk. The ceiling on bank holdings of residential mortgages is more
difficult to understand from the perspective of depositor safety. Traditionally, it was
argued that residential mortgages, as an illiquid long-term asset, were inappropriate
investments for financial institutions such as chartered banks which issued liabilities in
the form of deposits that were essentially withdrawable on demand. Now this rationale
is less clear with the reduction of the term of most mortgages from twenty years and
longer to less than five years, with many having a maturity of only one or two years.
Moreover, while the chartered banks were limited in the participation in the mortgage
market, their major competitors in the market for deposits — trust and loan companies,
the *caisses populaires* and the credit unions — all were virtually unconstrained in their
mortgage holdings and indeed treated residential mortgages as one of their most
important investment outlets. Finally, the contribution of cash and liquidity ratios as
applied to the banks to depositor safety must be regarded as minimal at best. While
such ratios do ensure that the banks hold a proportion of their portfolios in the form of
liquid assets, they also mean that because these liquid assets must be used to satisfy the
reserve requirements, they are of limited help in meeting large-scale deposit drains.
Although some flexibility is provided by the fact that reserve requirements need only be
met over the reserve averaging period, the reserve averaging period of one-half month
means that any deposit drain must be made up in no more than 10 business days, or
even less if the drain occurs in the midst or at the end of any reserve averaging period.
Some critics of cash ratios and liquid asset ratios maintain that the need they create for
banks to hold a portion of their portfolio in assets which yield either no or only low
returns means that the reduced earning power of the banks makes them, in fact, less
certain to be able to meet their depositors' claims.

Deposit Insurance and Regulation.   The existence of deposit insurance, which protects
the typical depositor from losses resulting from the failure of insured financial institutions, raises a number of questions. Does deposit insurance reduce the need for
regulation designed to assure depositor safety? What implications does the presence of
deposit insurance have for the regulation of financial institutions? With respect to the
first question, we should recognize that deposit insurance does not eliminate the risk
that financial institutions cannot meet their obligations; rather, it shifts the risk away
from the depositor to the deposit insurer. The role of regulation, then, becomes that of
limiting the risk of the deposit insurer.

The answer to the second question depends on whether the deposit insurer faces the same risk as depositors would in its absence. In one respect, the deposit insurer probably faces lower risks than the depositors would have. As we have seen earlier, the threatened failure of a bank in absence of deposit insurance was likely to precipitate a run as depositors attempted to protect their funds. Moreover, the run caused by one questionable bank might even spread to other banks which are fundamentally sound. In contrast, with deposit insurance, bank customers are more likely to maintain their deposits with the knowledge that their funds are protected. There are, however, forces that make the risks to the deposit insurer greater. In absence of deposit insurance, many depositors, especially depositors of large amounts, will attempt to assess the risks of different institutions so as to either hold their funds only at safe institutions or to ensure that the return they earn at other institutions is commensurate with the greater risks. Thus, the decisions of informed customers can serve to discipline the management of financial institutions: if they take greater risks than deemed appropriate by those customers, they must face either a withdrawal of funds or the necessity of paying higher rates of interest to maintain their deposits. The coverage of deposit insurance thus reduces both the incentives for depositors to assess the risks of different financial institutions and the reluctance of the management of financial institutions to undertake risks.

The deposit insurer can choose between two approaches for limiting the risks to which he is subject. Under one approach, he defines the maximum degree of risk he will accept by establishing rules with respect to acceptable assets and liabilities for institutions he insures. Any institution which is covered by deposit insurance must abide by these rules in conducting its business. In essence, these rules would take a similar form to the portfolio regulations applied to financial institutions in the absence of deposit insurance. This approach is the one which has been followed in Canada; the creation of deposit insurance did little to alter the set of portfolio regulations applied to insured institutions. The alternative approach to limiting risks resembles the techniques used for other types of insurance where the costs of insurance are related to risks involved. The use of variable rate charges for deposit insurance would permit the deposit insurer to charge higher rates to those financial institutions which are subject to greater risk. The rates charged would depend on such factors as the composition of an institution's assets, the imbalance between the maturity of an institution's assets and liabilities, past loss experience, the concentration of its loans with a single borrower or even a single type of activity, and the size of its deposit liabilities in relation to its shareholders' equity. A number of economists have argued that a deposit insurance scheme with a variable premium could serve as a substitute for much of our present system of regulation. One advantage of the scheme would be that it would provide greater flexibility to insured institutions which would be able to change their emphasis among lines of business more easily in response to changing demands and would also be able to experiment in different types of lending, subject, of course, to paying the appropriate premium. The argument for such an approach to regulation persuaded the Economic Council to:

> recommend…a system of variable premium rates for deposit insurance, according to established criteria reflecting differences among institutions with regard to potential claims on the insurer.[5]

In our discussion of deposit insurance, we need to consider one final issue. Should the regulators permit a bank or other financial institution to fail? In answering this question, a distinction should be drawn between the stability of the financial system and the solvency of individual financial institutions. While financial instability does involve the failure of financial institutions, the failure of selected institutions need not imply general financial instability as long as the failure of one institution does not set off a chain reaction. Now that we have a system of deposit insurance for underwriting the stability of the financial system, the question then becomes whether the government must create an environment in which it is virtually impossible for *any* financial institution to go bankrupt.

We should recognize that the possibility of bankruptcy performs an important economic function. It forces the owners and managers of a business to accept ultimate financial responsibility for their actions (although, given limited liability provisions, their responsibility is limited to the value of their investment). Such responsibility is presumably an incentive to efficiency, responsiveness to market developments, and competitive innovation. Strong arguments can be made that banks and other financial institutions ought not to be an exception to the general rule that bad management results in either bankruptcy or takeover by other interests. One advantage, then, of deposit insurance over simple regulation is that it permits the failure of financial institutions without jeopardizing the financial system. It enables the authorities to protect depositors without at the same time protecting the managers of financial institutions from the consequences of their actions.

Structural Regulation and Depositor Safety.   As we will show more clearly in Chapter 14, structural regulation has been a major means by which Canadian banking authorities have attempted to assure the soundness of the banking system. Both high capital requirements and the need to obtain a special act of Parliament, with its attendant delays, made entry into banking especially difficult. The importance of the restriction of entry into banking cannot be considered in isolation; its significance depends on whether banking is strictly differentiated from other activities.

In the past, regulation in Canada served to differentiate the chartered banks sharply from other financial institutions. On the asset side, this differentiation appears with respect to the types of lending each class of financial institution is permitted to undertake. As we have seen, the chartered banks were prohibited for many years from holding residential mortgages which, in contrast, is a major part of the lending business of trust and loan companies. At the same time, the trust and mortgage loan companies have been restricted from commercial lending, the major activity of the chartered banks. In each case, there may be good reason for the exclusion of one financial institution or the other. As we have discussed already, the long-term mortgage instrument was judged too illiquid to be held by banks because of the short-term nature of their liabilities. Similarly, trust companies were restrained from corporate lending because of belief that such lending was incompatible with their estate, trust, and agency business in that the companies would be exposed to conflicts of interest to the extent that they loaned funds to corporations whose securities they held in trust accounts. For our purpose, however, the reasons for these prescriptions are less important than the fact that they created distinctly segmented markets which remain, only slightly modified, to this day.

The main differentiation on the liability side arises from the use of an institution's liabilities as a means of payment. Demand deposits at banks have traditionally served as the major means of payment in the Canadian economy. Moreover, the cheque-clearing system, prior to the 1980 *Bank Act* revision, has been operated by the Canadian Bankers' Association in which membership was limited to chartered banks. While this limitation did not prevent other deposit-taking institutions, such as trust and loan companies and credit unions, from supplying chequable deposits, each of these institutions had to arrange for a chartered bank to serve as its clearing agent. While this limitation on providing means of payment may not have been explicitly motivated on the grounds of depositor safety, it was a direct consequence of the federal government's concern for restricting entry into banking and its actions in making the clearing system a monopoly of the Canadian Bankers' Association.

Regulation and Monetary Policy

Economists disagree on the degree and types of regulation of financial institutions needed because of their central role in the transmission of monetary policy. The central bank controls the money supply, as we will see in detail later on, through changing the amount of reserves available to the chartered banks for meeting their reserve requirements. An inadequacy of reserves forces the banks to contract their outstanding deposits in order to meet their required reserve levels, whereas a surplus of reserves permits them to expand deposits. Many economists argue that a legal reserve requirement is necessary in order to ensure that the banks react to their loss of reserves. In the absence of reserve requirements, it is suggested that banks may just allow their ratio of reserves to deposits to decline, rendering the monetary policy ineffective. Other economists suggest such fears may be groundless, in that few bankers, out of business prudence and experience, would be willing to let their reserve ratios decline very far in face of a loss of reserves. While the response of the bankers may not be as predictable in the absence of reserve requirements, the effect of their absence on the workings of monetary policy would be an inconvenience at most, requiring central banks to monitor more closely the responses of the banks to monetary policy in order to gain the overall effect they desire.

The other regulation which is commonly justified on the basis of monetary policy, is the secondary reserve requirement which the chartered banks may be obliged to hold in the form of treasury bills, day-to-day loans, and excess cash. Their purpose in terms of monetary policy is to inhibit shifts by banks out of government securities and into commercial lending in periods of credit restraint. In fact, since the *Bank Act* of 1967, the secondary reserve ratio has been variable so that upon notice the Bank of Canada can require the chartered banks to increase their holdings of assets eligible for the secondary reserve at the expense of other assets. As in the case of primary reserves, economists are split with respect to the usefulness of the secondary reserve requirement. Some would argue that the ability to control the volume of commercial lending is an important element of monetary policy and, as a result, the variable secondary reserve requirement is a useful instrument of monetary policy. Others, who believe the control of the money supply is the appropriate goal of monetary policy, argue that since such secondary reserve requirements contribute nothing to the control of money they are unnecessary and serve only to provide a sheltered market for government debt by constraining the portfolio choices of the chartered banks. We should note that the practical importance of the secondary reserve requirement has decreased steadily in recent years. Since reaching a peak of 8.5% at the end of 1971, the secondary reserve requirement has been reduced steadily to a level of 4% in early 1982.

Regulation and Social Goals

Earlier, we saw that the government may use regulation of the financial system to pursue such not strictly economic goals as allocating credit toward areas of social priority, maintaining separation between financial and nonfinancial economic activity, and ensuring substantial Canadian ownership of the financial system. While we have grouped these noneconomic goals together to this point, we should recognize that they are substantially different. Therefore, we will treat the means for attaining these objectives separately.

Credit Allocation. The means available to the regulators of financial institutions for achieving a desired allocation of credit toward social objectives are quite varied but, as a group, can be described as selective credit policies. Direct measures include restrictions, either ceilings or floors, on the proportion of a financial institution's portfolio which may be held in certain types of assets. Such direct measures are quite rare in terms of the Canadian experience. From 1954 on, Canadian banks have been required to maintain certain minimum proportions of their portfolios primarily in treasury bills for the purpose of either fostering a short-term money market or providing finance to the federal government on favorable terms.

More common in Canada has been the use of moral suasion by which the authorities indicate to financial institutions the types of behavior that they, the authorities, think would be desirable in particular circumstances. During the 1950s, the Governor of the Bank of Canada frequently requested the chartered banks to maintain or reduce their level of consumer lending during times of credit restraint. In addition, during the 1950s and 1960s the government made requests to the banks to favor certain sectors such as small business and firms in depressed regions during tight monetary policy. Such requests appear to have been less frequent throughout the 1970s than previously, in part, no doubt, because of the Bank of Canada's emphasis on monetary aggregates as distinct from credit conditions in the conduct of its monetary policy.

Many economists question the effectiveness of measures to direct credit allocation in fulfilling the objective of encouraging or discouraging various types of expenditure. One objection to these measures is that they may not be very effective in attaining their apparent goals. Expenditures are not always tied closely to specific forms of finance. Favorable financing arrangements may just cause people to use these arrangements to finance activities which they would have undertaken anyway or even to undertake other activities than those toward which the favorable finance was directed. In the face of cheap mortgage credit, households may borrow more than they would have needed for housing purposes in order to finance something else such as a second car or a vacation. Even if the finance is used for its intended purpose, the only effect may be to provide favorable terms for projects which would have been carried out anyway rather than to encourage greater investment.

A further objection to the use of selective credit policies concerns the impact on the financial institutions to which they apply. These institutions are required to shift their portfolios toward the types of lending favored by government and away from the business they would have chosen on their own at the expense of their return. If the group of financial institutions subject to selective credit controls is only part of the financial system, its share of the total business of financial institutions can be expected to differ from those institutions not subject to the same policies.

The development of the chartered banks in relation to other financial institutions immediately prior to the *Bank Act* of 1967 serves as an illustration of the impact of selective credit controls on one set of institutions. While the banks were not forced to provide finance to any particular sector, they were prohibited from charging any more than 6% on their loans under a longstanding provision of the *Bank Act*. In periods of low interest rates, the ceiling was of little consequence. During the early 1960s, as interest rates rose, the cost of funds for the banks increased relative to the 6% ceiling, making it increasingly difficult for banks to compete with other financial institutions. As we will see in Chapter 16, in the years immediately prior to the removal of the 6% ceiling in 1967, the relative position of the chartered banks in the financial system continually deteriorated. Subsequently, the growth of the chartered banks has been much nearer to that of the rest of the system.

Canadian Ownership.   The goal of domestic ownership of financial institutions was acted upon for the first time in the *Bank Act* of 1967, which, as we will see in Chapter 16, imposed restrictions on the foreign ownership of any chartered banks. A similar provision was introduced in subsequent revisions of the federal legislation governing trust companies and mortgage loan companies. It is interesting to note that none of the provinces have followed the federal government in restricting the degree of foreign ownership of financial institutions under their jurisdiction. Indeed, a committee reporting to the provincial government in Quebec declared:

> We cannot see why Quebec should block a foreign group —American say — from taking control of an institution chartered in Quebec when an Ontario or Western Canadian group could have access to it. If our aim is to maintain control of financial institutions in Quebec hands, we do not see why a New York group should be treated differently from Toronto or Winnipeg groups. This would be answered by saying that Quebec legislation should be adapted in such a way as to prevent groups outside Quebec — rather than foreign groups — from gaining control of financial institutions.[6]

Subsequent governments in Quebec have been attracted to this principle of encouraging Quebec ownership of financial institutions and have taken active (and successful) steps to discourage takeover bids for Quebec-based financial institutions from interests outside the province. In one case, the government threatened legislative action to block such a takeover attempt. The foreign ownership issue provides a good illustration of the potential for federal-provincial conflicts in the regulation of financial institutions. Despite the federal government's goal to avoid foreign control of financial institutions, the implementation of this objective has been complicated by the differing views on the issue held by provincial authorities.

Separation of Financial Activity.   The separation of financial activity from nonfinancial business has been achieved by a variety of measures, some of which have limited the banks from nonfinancial activities and others which have prohibited other business from controlling banks. Historically, the former type of regulation has been the more important instrument for maintaining this goal. The longstanding section 86 of successive *Bank Acts* (now section 174 after the 1980 revision) has a blanket prohibition which prescribes that:

> A bank shall not, directly or indirectly a) deal in goods, wares and merchandise or engage in any trade or business...[7]

In the same spirit, section 193 prescribes:

> A bank shall not own shares in a Canadian corporation in any number that would, under the voting rights attached to the shares owned by the bank, permit the bank to vote more than ten per cent of the votes...[8]

There are exceptions to this clause which relate to subsidiaries performing essentially financial services and to established shareholding positions in nonfinancial business which exceed the provisions in section 193 but which must be disposed of over the next few years. The ownership of banks by other businesses is precluded by a subsection of section 174 which limits the assets of any bank to less than 20 times its authorized capital if more than 10% of its issued shares are held by any one shareholder and his associates.

Regulation and Competition in Financial Markets

We have saved our discussion of the relationship between regulation and competition in financial markets to the end for good reason. A high degree of competition is an objective in which the general public, as we have seen, has a vital interest. But is competition consistent with the other objectives of regulation? As a first step to answering this question, we should review the Canadian experience in order to determine the degree to which competition has been constrained by the regulators' pursuit of the other objectives. More important, however, is the question whether it is necessary to constrain competition in the general interests of financial stability.

The Conflict Between Competition and Other Objectives.   We have seen that the goals of depositor safety, effective working of monetary policy, and the so-called social objectives of policy have been met by a variety of different measures. What may have been less obvious is that most of these measures affect the degree of competition in financial markets. We recall that the chartered banks' participation in the mortgage market has historically been prohibited and even now is strictly limited, whereas the trust and mortgage loan companies are effectively precluded from commercial lending.

Moreover, we have seen that the entry restrictions for chartered banking have been extremely stringent and during the 1967-1980 period precluded the entry of any new banks with greater than 25% foreign ownership. Moreover, the banks' ability to move into other lines of business has been curtailed as has until recently the ability of other businesses to own or control banks. When policy goals appear in conflict, as they do in the case of depositor safety and a competitive financial system, it can be asked whether the authorities have excessively emphasized one goal at the expense of the other.

In the Canadian case, there is some evidence that the goal of stability has been emphasized at the expense of competition and efficiency. After their respective reviews of Canadian financial institutions, both the Royal Commission Banking and Finance (1964) and the Economic Council (1976) put forward recommendations designed to increase the degree of competition in financial markets. We will review both studies and the resulting *Bank Act* revisions (1967 and 1980) in Chapter 16. As we will see, some of the major recommendations were not enacted, but some significant proposals for increasing competition were. It is too early to assess the impact of the 1980 *Bank Act*, but it is useful to ask: What has happened since 1967? Has the historical pattern been broken?

We find some evidence that price competition among banks is more prevalent than before the 1967 *Bank Act*. Several differences stand out. Many banks now offer customers the choice between savings deposits which pay interest on the average daily balance and those which pay a higher rate on minimum monthly balance. Similarly, customers are able to choose among chequing accounts with charges based on services used, others with flat rate charges, and still others without any charge if a sufficient balance is maintained. While not all banks offer the whole range of options with respect to chequing and savings deposits to their customers, certainly the variety of options is much greater than in the 1960s and permits customers to choose the arrangements that will be most beneficial. Moreover, while many of the rates and charges of different banks still tend to move together, it is no longer as a result of interbank agreements but more likely as a result of common responses to market forces.

We should recognize, however, that all these changes should not be attributed solely to changes in banking legislation. At least three other forces which we have noted at one time or another have influenced the degree of competition in banking since the 1967 *Bank Act*.

First, the decade of the 1970s was one of rapid and increasing inflation compared to previous years. The generally higher level of interest rates forced consumers and businesses to manage their resources more carefully so as to minimize their costs of borrowing and maximize the returns on their assets. Financial institutions which responded to these needs could attract business away from others, and force them to respond in turn. Second, computer technology provided a variety of new means through which financial institutions could compete. Daily interest accounts would likely have been prohibitively expensive through conventional bookkeeping techniques and only became feasible as banks adopted on-line deposits at branches. Finally, many of the innovations among financial institutions were initiated by the near banks rather than the chartered banks themselves. Even though the so-called package accounts with fixed monthly charges originated with commercial banks in the United States, they were introduced to Canada by a trust company. Sorting out the relative contributions of inflation, computer technology, and competitive pressures from near banks, as compared to that of changed banking legislation, is surely an impossible task. Still, we note the marked differences in banking in the 1980s compared to the 1960s and have some awareness of the sources of change.

ENDNOTES

1. Economic Council of Canada, *Efficiency and Regulation: A Study of Deposit Institutions* (Ottawa, 1976), p. 49.
2. *Ibid.,* p. 51.
3. *Ibid.,* p. 54.
4. Royal Commission on Banking and Finance, *Report,* p. 374.
5. Economic Council, *Efficiency and Regulation,* p. 66.
6. Government of Quebec, *Report of the Study Committee on Financial Institutions* (Quebec, 1969), pp. 203-4.
7. *Banks and Banking Law Revision Act,* 1980, p. 170.
8. *Ibid.,* p. 213.

THE DEVELOPMENT OF THE CANADIAN FINANCIAL SYSTEM TO 1970
The Quest for Stability

14

This chapter discusses the evolution of the Canadian financial system through the 1950s, with emphasis on the impact of changing concepts of governmental regulation. Together with the following chapter on the financial system of the United States, it is an essential prelude to the discussion of current issues in public policy in Chapter 16.

DOMINANT THEMES

From relatively uncomplicated beginnings in the colonies of British North America, the growth and increased complexity of the Canadian economy called for the parallel development of a network of financial institutions and markets, providing specialized financial services and specialized forms for the accumulation of wealth. Simultaneously, technological progress changed the capacity of financial institutions to provide financial services. These included the channeling of funds to finance production and capital formation and the provision of more efficient methods of making payments, thus contributing directly to the process of economic growth. Frequent business crises posed challenges to the stability and vitality of financial institutions and to government policy. The system had to adapt continuously to the changing economic environment. As we shall see more clearly in the next chapter, however, the product of this historical process is a financial system which is very different from that of the United States, although the two systems developed under similar economic conditions. It is clear that there is something else which is important in explaining the development of the Canadian system.

The Impact of Public Policy

The mold for the Canadian banking system was cast at the outset. Unlike their counterparts in the United States, the authorities in what was to become Canada adopted a system of commercial banking involving a few very large-scale banking firms. These firms developed substantial economic and political power, and the vested interests of the established banks emerged as a very powerful conservative force in the evolutionary process.

Beyond these first steps, *public policy* continued to be a powerful factor shaping the development of the system. Deliberations surrounding successive revision of banking legislation became the arena for struggles between opposing interests. In part, changes in public policy related directly to *the structure of the industry,* as, for example, government measures affecting the ease of establishing new banks or the ease of merging existing firms into an even smaller number of large firms. The process continues today. Thus, the most recent revision of the *Bank Act,* in 1980, will alter the structure of the system, opening the way for the chartering of foreign-controlled banks.

Other concerns of public policy related to the *development of effective institutions for the regulation of the money supply in the public interest,* and the *continuing search for institutions and policies which would guarantee the stability of banks* and other financial institutions (individually and in the aggregate), and which would protect unsuspecting creditors from severe financial loss. As we shall see, the struggle began with the government's casting envious eyes on the banks' right to issue notes for circulation as currency. At various stages it involved a) proposals to lodge part of the public debt in the banking system, b) compulsory governmental inspection of financial institutions, c) the establishment of a central bank, d) federal supervision and control of provincially chartered institutions, and e) compulsory deposit insurance. The debate involved a conflict between the public's concern for safety and the bankers' desires for freedom from cumbersome and perhaps costly restrictions.

The Impact of the United States

The development of Canadian public policy toward the financial system was not simply a groping for solutions to internal Canadian financial problems. It was also heavily influenced from time to time by developments in the financial system and the financial policies of the United States. At times, the Canadian reaction was one of imitation. Thus, the model for the original Canadian bank charters was an early American bank (although the fundamental concepts had deeper British roots). At other times, the Canadian reaction was one of revulsion. On balance, the latter reaction has dominated. As a result, the Canadian financial system, and particularly the banks, developed along radically different lines from the American counterpart.

THE ORIGINS OF CANADIAN BANKING

Banking, or at least efforts to establish banks, began almost simultaneously in the three colonies of Upper Canada, Lower Canada, and Nova Scotia. In these three areas, where the problems of economic survival and growth were formidable, there were neither organized financial markets nor formal financial intermediaries. While private financing could be obtained, normally from merchants who acted as primitive private bankers, the supply was irregular and interest rates were frequently very high. Capital was scarce, risks were high, and financial markets were imperfect. Moreover, there was no official provision of a stable, uniform currency which would expand with the growth of the colonies. In the absence of such a currency, the money supply consisted of a polyglot mixture of private script issued by merchants, the remains of some *ad hoc* government issues, some French coins left over from the old regime, and an infinite variety of foreign coins and notes (which circulated at varying rates of exchange). In the words of one student of Canadian banking history:

> During the second quarter of the nineteenth century the office of a Canadian currency broker was a veritable curiosity shop, exhibiting the remnants of several national currencies in the last stages of demoralization. There, from a currency point of view, the halt, the blind and the disowned of many mints foregathered in shabby company. Their thin, worn and battered faces mutely witnessed to a long and busy life with much travel and hard usage. Only the chronic scarcity of coinage in times of peace enabled this motley crew to occupy the market-place and brazen their way into fairly respectable company.[1]

In such an environment, banks were sometimes regarded as panacea. To the merchant they held out the promise of a reliable source of commercial credit at reasonable rates. To individuals, they offered a convenient method for the safekeeping of wealth. To the economy as a whole, they promised an elastic supply of a uniform currency: bank notes.

Bank Notes as Currency.   It may seem strange to think of privately owned banks as issuers of currency. We are accustomed to currency being issued by governments or central banks; private banks offer demand deposits transferable by cheque. In the early 19th century, however, the use of cheques to effect transactions was little developed, so that the right to operate a bank was almost by definition the right to issue notes. Bank notes were the major liability of early banks, and it is doubtful whether without this power a bank could have survived and developed. To illustrate the very different nature of early banking in Canada, Table 14-1 traces the balance sheet of one bank, the Bank of Nova Scotia, from 1833 to the present. Note the decline in the importance of notes in circulation and the capital accounts (funds provided by the owners of the bank) and the rise in the importance of deposits as a source of funds. Note also the change in the relative importance of gold and silver among the assets of the bank. By law, all bank notes were convertible into specie on demand, a fact which made it necessary for note-issuing banks to hold very substantial gold and silver reserves. In the early days these were foreign coins, some of which had formal status as legal tender.

Contrary Political Forces.   While the obvious need for greater uniformity in the currency and for improved credit facilities seemed to argue strongly for the establishment of banks, this view was not unanimous. Sad experiences in the United States with paper currencies, coupled with comparable experiences in Canada with various private and public issues, had soured many individuals on any form of paper money. Moreover, many believed that banks would soon establish a stranglehold on farmers, the economy,

TABLE 14-1   **The Bank of Nova Scotia, 1933-1980: composition of liability and asset portfolios**

	1833	1863	1892	1931	1980
Liabilities		(Percent)			
Notes in circulation	19.4	28.0	11.2	4.9	—
Deposits	22.0	34.6	61.6	78.9	88.1
Other liabilities	—	4.7	1.3	1.9	9.4
Capital accounts	58.6	32.7	26.0	14.2	2.5
TOTAL	100.0	100.0	100.0	100.0	100.0
Assets					
Gold and silver	32.3	12.7	3.7	0.8	1.6
Coin and legal tender	2.0	—	4.8	8.6	2.3
Other bank notes	0.3	0.8	3.4	0.3	—
Foreign currency	—	—	—	0.6	0.1
Correspondent balances	0.2	—	3.0	5.8	28.0*
Securities	65.3	85.4	16.7	24.1	6.1
Loans	—	—	66.6	53.5	54.2
Other assets	—	1.2	1.7	6.2	7.6
TOTAL	100.0	100.0	100.0	100.0	100.0

* Includes Euro-dollar deposits.

SOURCE: The Bank of Nova Scotia, 1832-1932 (Toronto: Bank of Nova Scotia, 1932); *Canada Gazette* (Ottawa: Queen's Printer, February, 1980).

and the government. The rivalry between the rising wealthy merchant class, with their limited political power, who favored the establishment of banking, against the agrarian aristocracy of the Family Compact and Chateau Clique who favored banking only on their terms (i.e., that they own them) may explain why it was not until 1822 that banks were chartered in Lower Canada (Bank of Montreal) and Upper Canada (Bank of Upper Canada). The Bank of Montreal began business as a "private bank," without a government charter, in 1817 after repeated attempts to secure a charter had been bogged down in the political infighting of the day, but it did not obtain a charter until 1822. In Nova Scotia, the Bank of Nova Scotia received its charter in 1820.

The First Bank Charters

The first bank charters set the pattern in which the Canadian banking system developed. It is striking that, even down to detailed wording, they were based upon the charter which Alexander Hamilton, the first Secretary of the Treasury of the United States, drew up for the first Bank of the United States. However, it is also important to note that Hamilton's charter was based on concepts of banking developed in Great Britain, and particularly in Scotland. Although this concept of banking was eventually discarded in the United States, the Imperial connection served to strengthen the concept in Canada.

Hamilton envisaged the first Bank of the United States as an embryonic central bank which would regulate and bring order to the American banking industry, and would provide a pattern for the orderly future development of that industry. At the time the First Bank of the United States was established (1792), the American banking system was a disparate collection of state-chartered and private banks, many of which followed questionable, often fraudulent, banking practices with the result that some banks failed, bank notes were frequently worthless, and many unsuspecting individuals lost heavily. Hamilton's charter gave the first Bank of the United States wide powers to open branches, to issue currency, and to compete with, and hence discipline and supplant, shaky local banks. By wholesale adoption of this charter, the early Canadian banks obtained the same rights, and the Canadian banking system developed along Hamilton's lines.

Principles Established by the Early Bank Charters

Legislative Chartering.   Like all limited liability companies at that time, banks were chartered by a special act of the relevant legislature (a few private banks emerged which had no charters — they were in effect partnerships with unlimited liability — and a few banks for a time held charters from the Imperial government). This principle of legislative chartering of banks was subsequently rejected in the United States in favor of chartering through executive action. In Canada, aside from a short period to be discussed subsequently, the principle of legislative chartering for fixed terms subject to extension by subsequent legislation was retained.

"Commercial" Banking.   In the early bank charters, the scope of the business of banks was defined by prohibitions against certain activities, prohibitions which made Canadian banks classic "commercial banks." Thus, they were prohibited from dealing in goods and services or real estate and from lending on the security of mortgages or real estate. Their activities were effectively confined to short-term commercial and personal lending, and international finance.

Bank Notes.   The banks were permitted to issue bank notes designed to circulate as currency, with certain limitations on the total amount outstanding at any one time, and subject to the requirement that they be convertible into gold or silver on demand.

Branching.   It is also significant that the first bank charters did not contain prohibitions against the opening of branches. They thus permitted Canadian banks to develop networks of branch offices, including offices in colonies other than the one in which the bank was initially chartered. This laid the groundwork for the most striking difference between banking systems in Canada and the United States: the nation-wide branch banking system.

Protection of the Public.   Perhaps reflecting the acrimonious debates surrounding the initial chartering of banks, the early charters also contained primitive arrangements for "the better security of the public," i.e., the depositors and note holders who were the creditors of the banks. Thus, a ceiling was established on total bank debts, the directors of each bank were made personally responsible for bank debts in excess of the legal limit, and the government was given the power to call for periodic reports from the banks on their paid-in capital, total debts, deposits, notes in circulation, and cash on hand.

"POPULIST" PRESSURES

With the formation and early success of the first banking corporations, several groups emerged who wanted to enter what appeared to be a profitable venture. But, as the clamor for new bank charters increased, the Imperial authorities became concerned lest charters be granted to individuals more intent on quick speculative gains via extensive note issue than on long-term profits through "sound banking practice," and they sent to the colonial legislatures "suggestions" on how existing and future charters might be improved to minimize the risk of failure and hence of loss to depositors and note holders — early examples of the importance of security as an objective of public policy. In several cases, the British authorities disallowed charters which had been granted by Canadian governments, strengthening the general concepts of banking set out in the original bank charters.

In spite of this external intervention, both the number of banks and their total assets continued to grow. In 1830, there were six banks in Canada (with unknown total assets). Between 1830 and the end of 1867, 50 new banks were successively established. Taking into account mergers, repealed charters and failures (17 banks failed between 1830 and 1867, or almost one out of every three banks in operation at some time during this period), only 35 banks, with total assets of $84 million, remained active at the end of 1867. Over the same period, the number of active banks in the United States increased by 1579, from 329 to 1908.

"Populism" and "Free Banking"

The growth of the banking system, and particularly the concentration of that growth in the hands of a few firms, did not meet with universal acclaim. An essentially agrarian "populist" reaction emerged, rooted in a fear of the "money trust" and drawing much of its inspiration from opinions which were widely held and politically very influential in the United States.

"Populism" in the United States.   Hamilton's First Bank of the United States was successful in disciplining the more adventurous local banks in the United States. However, its very success earned it lasting enemies. When its charter came up for renewal in 1811, it was allowed to lapse by a hostile Congress. The financial problems which the American government encountered by relying on the fragmented banking system for financing the War of 1812 led them to charter a second Bank of the United States in 1816. However, it met the fate of its predecessor, this time at the hands of Andrew Jackson and his populist supporters.

The Banks of the United States served as a focal point for agrarian discontent. The populists were suspicious of the banks' dominant position in the financial system, and resented the conservative banking policies which the Banks attempted to enforce throughout the country. The populists believed that the banks were in league with other money interests in the financial centers of Philadelphia, New York, and Boston to exploit the rural areas. It was argued that conservative commercial banking principles discriminated against them —an allegation which had some substance, in that land or mortgages on land were not considered bankable assets on conservative commercial banking principles. Moreover, the instability of agricultural crops and markets made any loans to farmers a risky asset, and called for premium interest rates (if indeed credit would be extended at all).

The populists favored "free banking," that is, they wanted banking legislation making it easy to establish small banks under local control, using local funds and, most importantly, making local loans (primarily to farmers). The free banking principle involved the granting of a bank charter by executive action to any group which met the minimum requirements set out in the legislation. In general, these minimum requirements — and particularly the minimum amount of capital which had to be subscribed to the new bank — were kept low, for the express purpose of facilitating the entry of small banks. Restrictions were normally placed on the opening of branch offices to encourage retention of local control.

The free banking principle was rooted in a concern for ready access to credit rather than a concern for the protection of depositors and note holders. However, state free banking acts generally included provisions requiring specified collateral (typically government bonds) against bank notes outstanding. While not widely successful as a device for protecting the note holder, this did have the incidental effect of creating a captive market for government securities.

The Free Banking Movement in Canada.   In Canada, populist fears of a bank conspiracy against the farmer and little merchant throughout the 1830s and 1840s brought about recurrent agitation, particularly in the legislature of Upper Canada, to permit free banking. The legislature eventually did pass a free banking statute and its provisions reflected the populists' philosophy. Bank charters could be issued by executive decision, capital requirements were low, and free banks were precluded from branching. Furthermore, the amount of notes which could be issued was limited to the amount of government debt held by the banks, and the banks were required to maintain redemption centers for their notes at various points throughout the colony. This final feature was included to prevent the notes of the bank being discounted in places distant from the bank's office. (Discounting was a common feature when information as to the soundness of the bank and its ability to redeem its notes in gold was lacking. To offset the possible risks of holding the notes, individuals and businesses would only accept them at less than their face value.)

To some extent, the free banking movement failed to obtain widespread acceptance in Canada because legislative charters could still be obtained. In those states where free banking was established the provision for legislative charters was simultaneously abolished, so that new banks had to conform to the free banking principle. In Upper Canada, however, the option of a legislative charter proved to have strong attractions, particularly in the right to open branch offices and more liberal provisions for note issue. Only six banks were established under the *Free Banking Act,* one of which had previously been operating under an Imperial charter. Two of these failed quickly, and the others soon converted to legislative charters.

While the principle of free banking was not established in Canada, populist suspicions of an eastern "money trust" which would discriminate against rural and western interests did not die. Indeed, it persists in some sectors of the country today.

The Banks and Governmental Finance

The controversies surrounding the banking system in this period brought to the fore another important issue: the financial relations between government and the banks.

The period was marked by several attempts on the part of the colonial governments to encroach on the traditional rights of the banks to issue bank notes. Some of the proposals simply involved requiring banks to hold government securities as collateral behind bank notes outstanding. Others, pushed more vigorously, involved the substitution of a government-issued paper money for bank notes. The motivations underlying these proposals were undoubtedly complex, but two themes stand out clearly from the debates: a desire to protect the public from the consequences of the competitive over-issuance of bank notes by the banks, and a desire to augment the financial resources of the government.

The attractiveness to the government of a governmental monopoly over the issuance of paper money should be obvious. It permitted the creation of *interest-free* public debt. Its unattractiveness to the banks is equally obvious. Interest-free government debt was being substituted for interest-free bank debt. Moreover, the sums involved were significant. In 1861, notes in circulation accounted for over 21% of the total funds (liabilities plus capital stock) of the banks in the Province of Canada, and they were substantially more important as a source of funds than interest-free deposits.[2] It is not surprising that the banks opposed such schemes vigorously (and, during this period, quite successfully).

The regulatory significance of such schemes is not as obvious. The proposed governmental issue of paper money was to have a fixed gold reserve. It is true that the banks were required by their charters to convert their notes in gold and silver on demand, but they were not required to maintain any fixed minimum relationship between their notes and their holdings of gold and silver. The bankers argued that the absence of such restraints on the issuance of paper money was essential if the money supply was to have adequate "elasticity" to meet seasonal and secular demands for money. The government argued that elasticity created the danger of over-issue.

Formal proposals for a government monopoly in Canada over paper money were defeated in 1841 and 1860. In the midst of a minor financial crisis in 1865, a partial measure was enacted, permitting a limited issue of government paper money. In the following year, the first issue occurred, with the cooperation of the government's fiscal agent, the Bank of Montreal, which restricted its bank notes outstanding. The new government notes were used to a limited extent as bank reserves, partially replacing specie for that purpose. While it was a limited measure, with limited effect, the *Provincial Notes Act* of 1866 was important in that it ended the chartered banks' monopoly of note issue.

The Beginnings of Diversified Financial Intermediation

Although the chartered banks continued to totally dominate the financial system, the seeds of various other types of financial intermediation were planted in this period.

As we have seen, the chartered banks were conceived as "commercial banks." They were discouraged from making long-term loans, and were prohibited from lending on the security of real estate. This left major gaps in the financial system. In response, several financial intermediaries specializing in longer-term, particularly mortgage, financing made their appearance. A number of "building societies," precursors of the modern mortgage loan company, were established in Upper and Lower Canada as early as 1845, and two Quebec savings banks were established in 1846 and 1848. The early building societies were heavily involved in farm mortgages. Insurance companies also began to emerge as important financial intermediaries in this period. The first insurance written in Canada was by agencies of British companies (fire insurance in 1801 and life insurance in 1846), but by the end of the period a number of Canadian companies were well established.

CODIFICATION OF THE BASIC PRINCIPLES: CONFEDERATION TO 1891

The first two decades following Confederation was a period of rapid growth in the banking system. From 1867 to 1890 total bank assets increased three-fold, from $84 million to $260 million. Initially, the growth in total assets was accompanied by an increase in the number of firms.

In the seven years 1868 - 1874, 20 new banks were established, and after several failures and mergers the total number of active banks increased from 35 to the all-time peak of 51. In the following 17 years, six more banks were established, but four mergers and 12 failures gradually reduced the number of active firms to 41 by the end of 1890. The number of bank offices rose from 123 in 1867, to 230 in 1874, and 426 in 1890. Chartered banks were not the only financial intermediaries to experience substantial growth during the period. Previously established savings banks, building societies, and insurance companies continued to expand, and several new types of intermediaries were established. Consolidation in the banking system was accompanied by increased diversification in financial intermediation considered as a whole.

The Legal Framework

The British North America Act assigned responsibility for the regulation of currency and banking to the federal government. As a result, one of the first orders of business for the first Government of Canada was to formalize arrangements in these areas.

Monetary Legislation.   The first problem to be tackled was the issuance of paper money. Following temporary legislation in 1868, resolutions were introduced into the Parliament by the Minister of Finance calling for a restructuring of Canadian banking and monetary legislation on the model of the *National Bank Act* of the United States (1864). The resolutions incorporated both the principle of linking paper money to government financing, and populist concepts of the appropriate banking structure. The banks were to be deprived of the right to issue bank notes on the security of their general credit and restricted to issuing government printed notes on the security of an equal value of government bonds deposited with the Minister of Finance (such notes would be legal tender, would be convertible into gold on demand, and would be backed in addition by fixed gold reserves held by the banks). The plan also called for the creation of small local banks, with small capital requirements, so as to achieve greater "diffusion of banking interests in different localities." This reemergence of populist concepts was again decisively rejected in a one day debate in the House of Commons.

The monetary legislation which was passed, the *Dominion Notes Act* of 1870, was a compromise. The concepts of a government monopoly over paper money, and of government bond-secured bank notes were rejected. The right of the banks to issue bank notes on their own security was confirmed, but restricted to notes with a denomination of $4 or greater. Thus, the government established a monopoly over small-denomination ($1 and $2) notes. As a further measure to increase governmental participation in the profits from note issuance, the banks were required to hold at least half of their cash reserves in Dominion notes. The Dominion notes themselves had fractional gold reserves behind them, and in this sense the Act confirmed that the new nation would be on the gold standard. Aside from periodic increases in the ceiling on the amount of Dominion notes which could be outstanding and changes in the gold backing for these notes, no major changes in the principles underlying the issuance of currency occurred until Canada abandoned the gold standard (1914). Dominion notes gradually increased in importance, but not until 1908 did the total value of Dominion notes outstanding exceed the total value of bank notes, and even then almost 85% of the outstanding Dominion notes were lodged in bank vaults. At no time, until they were superseded by Bank of Canada notes, did Dominion notes account for a major fraction of currency in circulation.

The First Bank Act.   If the monetary legislation of 1868-1870 represented a compromise with the concepts of American populism, no such compromise was evident in the *Bank Act* of 1871. Although provisions for the security of depositors and note holders were extended, the Act codified the principles which had been set out in the first charters and firmly established through practice.

The rejection of populist ideology is most clearly marked in the provisions for establishing new banks and for branching. The Act continued the principle of legislative chartering of banks, with each charter subject to review and renewal every 10 years, and potential new banks faced a substantial financial hurdle in the form of a minimum capital requirement of $500 000. In the United States at that time, a National Bank, i.e., one chartered by the federal government, could be established in a small town with capital of $50 000 and charters could be obtained from most states for banks with even less capital. Clearly, the framers of the first *Bank Act* intended to have no truck with American-style "free banking."

Once established, a bank could open branches "at any place or places in the

Dominion." With respect to the business of the banks, there were no significant innovations. The "commercial" character of banking was reinforced by provisions which evolved into the familiar Section 88 and by the continuation of prohibitions against mortgage lending and dealing in real estate. The provisions of the *Dominion Notes Act* of 1870 with respect to bank notes and bank reserves were also incorporated in the *Bank Act,* and extended somewhat. For the greater security of the public, shareholders of banks were subjected to double liability, and the banks were required to submit more detailed periodic reports to the government.

Unsettled Issues.   In the two subsequent revisions, 1880 and 1890, only minor changes were made in the *Bank Act.* A redemption fund was established to guarantee the redemption of the notes of failed banks, the share of Dominion notes in bank reserves was increased, bank notes were confined to denominations in multiples of $5, and the scope of commercial loans (Section 88) was expanded. As a harbinger of future developments, the minimum capital requirement for new banks was altered so that $250 000 had to be paid in before the bank could commence business, and the bank had only one year from the time it obtained its charter to raise this capital.

The central concern underlying most of these adjustments to the *Bank Act* was the security of bank creditors. Between 1871 and 1890 13 banks failed, including four in 1878 and five in 1887. The failure of a few others was averted through amalgamation with other sound institutions. In general, it was the smaller banks which failed, and frequently they were relatively new institutions. The measures which were taken were designed to protect the note holders (the "unsuspecting creditors") of failed banks, who accepted the notes in good faith as currency, and to make it more difficult for small, new banks to be established.

Even more radical solutions to the problem of bank instability were proposed. The concept of a government monopoly over the currency supply, through the creation of a government bank of issue — a prototype central bank — was in the air, but gained little support. Direct attempts to impose governmental inspection on the banks and to require fixed-percentage cash reserve requirements were advanced by the government, but successfully warded off by the political pressures mounted by the banks. Indeed, in the case of the fixed-reserve requirement, the bankers were permitted to argue their case before the cabinet — a highly irregular procedure. These reforms remained "unfinished business" for some time.

Profile of the Financial System in 1890

The elaboration of the financial system continued, as new intermediaries were established and existing ones grew. Two of the new ones were government savings banks: the Post Office Savings Bank and the Dominion Government Savings Bank. Of more lasting importance was the appearance of the first trust company in Ontario in 1882. Insurance and mortgage loan companies continued to grow, both in total assets and in numbers. As a result, by 1890 non-bank financial intermediaries — and particularly intermediaries specializing in long-term mortgage financing — were emerging as significant factors in the financial system.

TABLE 14-2   **The Canadian financial system, 1890**

I. THE MONEY SUPPLY

	$ Millions	Percent
Dominion notes (held outside banks)	5.9*	6.2
Bank notes	35.0	37.0
Public demand deposits with chartered banks	53.7	56.8
TOTAL	94.6	100.0

* The banks held $9.7 million of Dominion notes

II. THE ASSETS OF FINANCIAL INTERMEDIARIES

Chartered banks	260	54
Other deposit-taking intermediaries		
Quebec savings banks	11*	2
Government savings banks	43*	9
Mortgage loan companies (building societies)	123	26
Total	177	37
Other financial intermediaries		
Life insurance companies	43	9
General insurance companies	n.a.	—
Total	43	9
TOTAL (available data)	480	100

* Deposits

SOURCE: Urquhart and Buckley, *Historical Statistics of Canada*
(Toronto: Macmillan, 1965); *Statistical Year Book of Canada,*
1891 (Ottawa: Department of Agriculture, 1891).

Table 14-2 presents a profile of financial intermediation in Canada in 1890 based on the limited statistical information available.

CONSOLIDATION AND GROWTH: 1890-1914

In the 25 years between 1890 and the outbreak of World War I, both the Canadian economy and the banking industry experienced a fundamental change in structure and size. In the economy, agriculture declined in relative importance, the industrial base continued to grow, and international trade expanded rapidly. In the banking system, growth and consolidation were the order of the day. In less than 25 years, bank assets increased from $260 million to more than $1.55 billion and the number of branches rose from 426 to over 3000, but the *number* of banks declined from 41 in 1890 to 22 in 1914.

The Merger Movement

Various factors contributed to the consolidation of the banking system.

Legislation   One factor was changes in the *Bank Act*. The increase in capital requirements in 1890 restrained entry. In the 24-year period 1890-1913 only 11 new banks were
established as compared to 28 in the previous 21 years, although the rate of growth of
bank offices and bank assets in the second period was almost double that in the first.

While entry was restrained, mergers were facilitated. In 1900, the *Bank Act* was
changed to permit a bank to purchase the assets of any other bank. Prior to this change,
all mergers required a special Act of Parliament. Following this simplification of
merger procedures, 17 mergers were consummated before the end of 1914. In the
previous 33 years there had only been six mergers.

Economic Factors.   The legislative changes of 1900 facilitated mergers, but the incentive for these amalgamations had to rest elsewhere. The owners of one bank had to have
an incentive to sell, and the owners of another to buy. That is, the assets of the absorbed
bank had to be worth more to the buyer than to the seller. What might cause such a
divergence in valuations? Little substantive research has been done on bank mergers in
this period, so we do not know the answer to this question. However, some hypotheses
have been advanced.

Impending insolvency is frequently suggested as the common reason for selling a
bank. Relatively *high costs* appear also to have plagued some banks, whether through
inefficiency in management or through the inability of very small banks to exploit
economies of scale. It is also important to note that small localized banks could not
achieve the degree of *diversification in asset holdings* common to very large institutions.

For some purchasing institutions, merger may have provided a relatively cheap
method of *penetrating markets* where they previously had little or no representation.
For example, certain regions of the Maritimes were regarded as areas suitable for
expansion, not so much because the demand for loans would be heavy but rather
because the supply of deposits would be in excess of local needs. Here then was a steady
source of finance for the expanding markets in the west.

For the bank desiring to enter a new market the choice was either to buy an existing
bank or to start from scratch. The first alternative had great value because it provided
the purchaser with offices and personnel as well as established accounts and deposits,
and it eliminated a potential competitor.

Even in the absence of significant penetration of new market areas, the existence of
economies of scale would create an incentive to merge. The merged banks would have
lower costs than either of the original firms. In some cases a drive to be the largest bank
seems to have been operative, and the simple desire to reduce the degree of competition
in the market place may have been a powerful consideration.

Bank Failures

Limitations on entry and bank mergers were only two of the three elements in the
consolidation process. The third was the failure of banks. In this period 11 banks
disappeared through failure (and two others had their charters suspended).

Bank failures more often than not were the result of poor management. Excessively
risky loans were made which subsequently proved to be worthless and this meant the
financial position of the bank was impaired. The inability of some smaller banks to

achieve a high degree of diversification in asset holdings also left them in an exposed position. In several cases, however, the failure was the direct result of the fraudulent practices of the general manager or directors who had used the funds of the bank for private investment schemes or similar dubious ventures. As a result the bank would find it had few tangible assets and therefore would be forced to end business.

In two cases, the manner in which the failures were handled was rather unusual. Normally, because of the double liability provision, a failure implied the loss to the shareholders of their equity plus that sum again. Not infrequently these amounts plus what could be covered from the sale of the bank's assets were not sufficient to cover the bank's liabilities and as a result depositors also suffered losses. The failure of a large bank could affect the entire banking community. To avoid such repercussions, the Bank of Montreal agreed to take over the failing Ontario Bank in 1906. The other remaining banks agreed to participate in losses suffered by the Bank of Montreal as a result. Because of this action the loss to the depositors was zero and the financial disaster that would have followed had the bank failed was avoided. In 1908, when the Sovereign Bank failed, 12 chartered banks divided the existing branch network of the Sovereign Bank among them and agreed to share losses in proportion to the value of the deposits that each had assumed.

These arrangements amounted to a primitive *ad hoc* deposit insurance scheme. It could not be relied upon in all cases, however, as the failure of the Home Bank in 1923 was to demonstrate.

In summary, the structure of the chartered banking industry underwent a major transformation between 1890 and 1913. This transformation was facilitated by legislation permitting mergers and restricting entry, and was partly effected through mergers and partly through bank failures. At the end of 1914 there were only 22 banks remaining in active operation in Canada.

A Tentative Experiment in Central Banking

An episode occurred in 1907 which, while minor in terms of the long-run development of Canadian banking, foreshadowed the creation of the *Finance Act* in 1914 and represented a tentative beginning for central banking in Canada. A financial crisis in New York in the fall of 1907, which involved the closure of major banks, threatened the availability of funds to finance the movement of the western Canadian wheat crop to market. The government took emergency measures, including the provision of a discount facility through the Royal Trust Company, making available to banks additional reserves in the form of Dominion notes against the pledge of grain or securities. These Dominion notes were issued without regard to the legal requirement for gold reserves. The arrangement was short-lived (5½ months), but it was effective. The lesson was remembered when the government had apprehensions of a monetary crisis at the outbreak of war in Europe in 1914.

Profile of the Financial System: 1914

The growth of non-bank financial intermediaries continued during this period, but not at as rapid a rate as the growth of the chartered banks. Thus, as Table 14-3 shows, the chartered banks actually increased their share of the total assets of Canadian financial intermediaries. This increase in asset holdings was financed by a sharp increase in total deposits in banks, and particularly interest-bearing savings and notice deposits. Both notes in circulation and capital accounts declined in importance as sources of funds. The banks were not passively yielding the savings banking business to non-bank intermediaries.

TABLE 14-3   **The Canadian financial system, 1914**

I. THE MONEY SUPPLY

	$ Millions	Percent
Subsidiary coin	19.7	4.0
Dominion notes (outside banks)*	19.2*	3.9
Demand deposits with chartered banks	350.0	70.7
Bank notes	106.0	21.4
TOTAL	494.9	100.0

* The banks held $143 million of Dominion notes

II. THE ASSETS OF FINANCIAL INTERMEDIARIES

Chartered banks	1 556	60
Other deposit-taking intermediaries		
Quebec savings banks	42	2
Government savings banks	56	2
Mortgage loan companies	479*	19
Trust companies	19†	1
Caisses populaires	2	—
Total	598	23
Other financial intermediaries		
Life insurance companies	370	14
General insurance companies	48	2
Total	418	16
TOTAL (available data)	2 572	100

* 1913.

† Federal trust companies only. Provincial companies probably had assets several times as great as federal companies. E. T. & A. account of federal companies as $30 million in 1914.

SOURCE: Urquhart and Buckley, *Historical Statistics of Canada* (Toronto: Macmillan, 1965); *The Canada Year Book; Statistical Year Book of Quebec.*

An important new type of near bank was introduced in this period when the first *caisse populaire* was organized in Levis, Quebec, in 1900. By 1915, there were 91 societies with 23 614 members and total assets in excess of $2 million.

WAR FINANCE: 1914-1920

The Bank Act of 1913

In 1913, parliament undertook the revision of the *Bank Act* that had been delayed for three years. The changes that were enacted did not constitute a major overhaul of the legislation, but nevertheless, some of these alterations were important.

The battle over outside inspection which had occupied so much of the debate from 1880 onwards was partially resolved by the institution of a shareholders' audit. Each year the shareholders were to elect a firm to carry out a complete audit of the bank and the results were to be distributed to the shareholders and the Minister of Finance. The aim was to reduce the possibility of fraud which had been found to be the cause of several recent spectacular failures.

The demands from the West for increased credit facilities had been partially solved by the enactment in 1908 of a temporary provision whereby the banks during certain portions of the year, could issue notes in excess of the legal limit (provided that such excess issue was backed by gold or Dominion notes of a like amount). In 1913, this temporary provision was made permanent and, as an additional measure, banks were authorized to make loans secured by threshed grain grown upon the borrower's land.

Finally, because of growing agitation on the part of many who believed that mergers were threatening the country with a money trust and a consequent diminution of competition, all subsequent mergers required the approval of the Minister of Finance.

The Finance Act

Less than a year after the revision of the *Bank Act*, Canada was at war. The rules so carefully reviewed and redrawn just 12 months earlier, now appeared inadequate. The immediate problem was to preserve the liquidity and stability of the financial system. Canadian money was convertible into gold on demand, but gold held by the government and the banks was only a fraction of their combined monetary liabilities. Under normal circumstances the banks could also draw on their assets in New York (primarily call loans in the securities markets), and transfer the proceeds in the form of gold to Canada. However, if the demand was large and continuing, these foreign assets would also be quickly exhausted. Concerned that the Canadian monetary system was vulnerable to the panic withdrawal of gold (it is reported that some runs on banks did occur), the government made two important institutional changes.

Suspension of the Gold Standard.   In early August 1914, the government, by Order-in-Council (subsequently ratified through legislation), suspended the gold standard. That is, it "temporarily" revoked the requirement that Dominion notes and bank notes be convertible into a fixed amount of gold on demand. Gold's role as the "standard" money into which all other monies were legally convertible was assumed by paper money, Dominion notes and bank notes, and the Canadian dollar was left to fluctuate in the foreign exchange market.[4] The gold standard was not reestablished until July 1926, and was suspended again informally in early 1929 and legally in 1931. Through most of the inter-war period — and indeed through most of its post-1914 history — Canada had a flexible foreign exchange rate.

Lender of Last Resort.   The second major change involved the creation of a "discount window," patterned on the brief experiment in 1907, through which the banks could obtain additional cash reserves on demand. Under the *Dominion Notes Act* the issuance of new Dominion notes was strictly limited. Under the *Finance Act,* these controls were virtually removed. The Minister of Finance was authorized to advance Dominion notes to the banks upon the pledge of securities approved by the Treasury Board including the banks' own promissory notes. This means that the Minister of Finance was acting as lender of last resort where the banks could always find accommodation in times of need, one of the major functions of a central bank.

Wartime Inflation.   These provisions permitted a major wartime expansion of the money supply as an aspect of the financing of the war effort, and, particularly in the last years of the war and in the immediate post-war period, a very sharp inflation of prices (Table 14-4). Consumer prices almost doubled. However, as dramatic as were the monetary expansion and the inflation, the lasting significance of the *Finance Act* of 1914 rested elsewhere. It set the nation's monetary system on a course which culminated in the establishment of a true central bank in 1935.

TABLE 14-4   **The Canadian money supply, 1913-1920 ($ Millions)**

	1913	1920	Increase
Subsidiary coinage	$ 19	$ 30	$ 11
Dominion notes			
Total outstanding	131	312	181
Held by banks	111	279	168
Held by others	20	32	12
Bank notes outstanding	109	229	120
Total currency in circulation	148	292	144
Bank demand deposit liabilities	381	657	276
TOTAL MONEY SUPPLY	529	949	420
Cost of living index	100	190	90%

SOURCE: Urquhart and Buckley, *Historical Statistics of Canada* (Toronto: Macmillan of Canada, 1965).

Profile of the Financial System: 1920

As is evident in Table 14-5, one of the important effects of war finance was to temporarily increase the relative importance of the chartered banks in the financial system (a phenomenon which was repeated during World War II). Indeed, this marked a watershed in the dominance of the chartered banks over the financial system. From this date on their relative position *vis-à-vis* other financial intermediaries declined. While the banks continued to grow in size (and diminish in number by mergers and failures), both new and existing non-bank intermediaries enjoyed even faster rates of expansion.

TABLE 14-5   The Canadian financial system, 1920

I. THE MONEY SUPPLY

	$ Millions	Percent
Subsidiary coin	30	3.2
Dominion notes (outside banks)	32	3.4
Bank notes	229	24.1
Demand deposits with chartered banks	657	69.3
TOTAL	949	100.0

II. THE ASSETS OF FINANCIAL INTERMEDIARIES

Chartered banks	3 057	75
Other deposit-taking intermediaries		
Quebec savings banks	63	1
Government savings banks	43	1
Mortgage loan companies	189*	5
Trust companies	83†	2
Caisses populaires	6	—
Total	384	9
Other financial intermediaries		
Life insurance companies	590	14
General insurance companies	125	3
Total	715	17
TOTAL (available data)	4 066	100

* 1922.

† Excluding E. T. & A. accounts of $722 million.

SOURCE: Urquhart and Buckley, *Historical Statistics of Canada
(Toronto: Macmillan, 1965); Canada Year Book; Statistical
Yearbook of Quebec.*

Neufeld has argued that the relative decline of the banks was an inevitable result of their failure to innovate. The banks did not develop new types of financial instruments which would be attractive forms in which the nation could accumulate its savings. In Canada, as elsewhere, as the wealth of the community increased, money declined in relative importance as a form in which claims to wealth were held. This affected the banks, particularly since they were the major issuers of money, and the retardation of their growth was particularly noticeable in their monetary liabilities — demand deposits and notes in circulation — as is evident in Figure 14-1. If the banks were to continue to outstrip the rising demand for money (which depended roughly on the rate of growth of aggregate output) they had to attract a substantial portion of the savings of the nation to their savings and notice deposits. In the competition for these savings the banks lost ground both to near banks, offering comparable instruments at somewhat higher yields, and to other intermediaries particularly life insurance companies, offering very different types of instruments. They also began to face greater competition from the attractions of direct investment in stocks and bonds.

FIGURE 14-1   Chartered banks: Major liabilities, 1867-1940

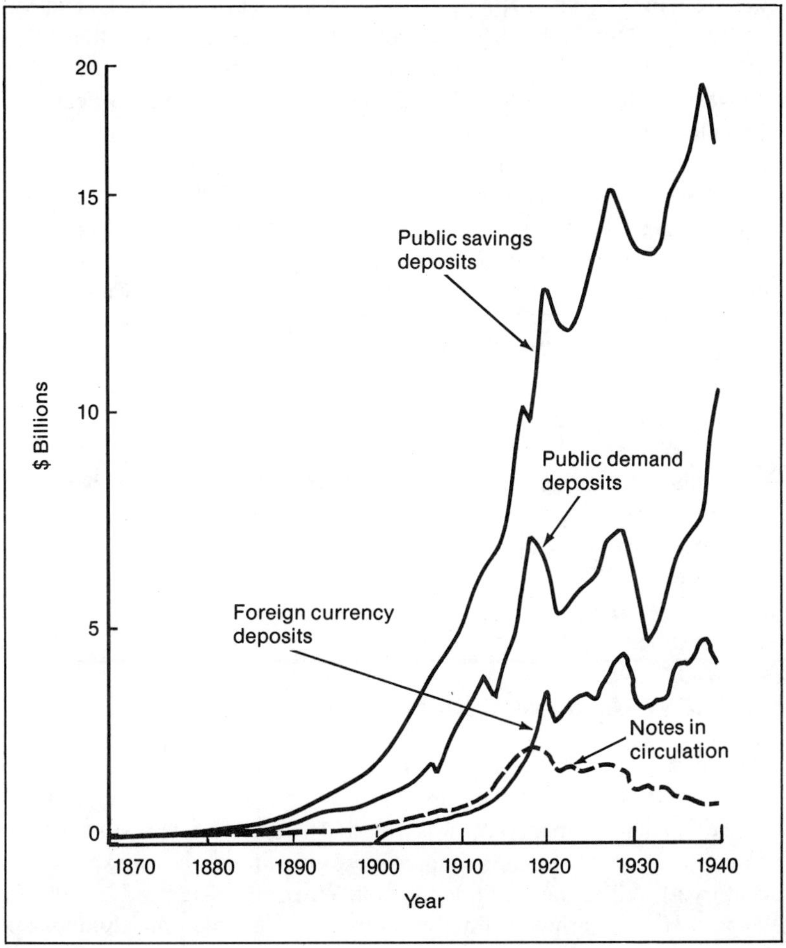

Development of the Capital Market.   The war period did not produce any fundamental changes in the structure of financial intermediation, but merely postponed the gradual erosion of the position of the chartered banks. However, the war did have a major direct impact on the development of the capital market and its institutions in Canada.

Such markets predated the war, of course. Stock exchanges had been organized in Montreal and Toronto long before Confederation. Thus, the Montreal Stock Exchange traces itself back to an informal arrangement of 1832, and the Toronto Stock Exchange to 1852. Several exchanges were incorporated formally in the years following Confederation and a number of bond-underwriting and distributing houses were established. However, these were satellite organizations. For the financing of Canadian development, the relevant capital markets were not in Canada but in London, England, and in New York. For example, it is estimated that between 1904 and 1914 some $2186 million worth of Canadian government and corporate bonds were issued of which almost 70% were sold in the United Kingdom and an additional 9% in the United States. Between 1900 and 1914 total foreign investments in Canada are estimated to have increased from $1232 million to $3837 million, with over 70% of the latter owned in the United Kingdom and 23% in the United States. Although estimates of capital formation in Canada at this time are at best rough, the increase in foreign capital invested in Canada in this period appears to have accounted for over 40% of total capital formation![6]

One of the direct effects of the war was to drastically curtail Canada's access to the London capital market at a time when financing requirements — particularly of the federal government — were increasing markedly. New York replaced London as the dominant external source of capital funds. At the same time, Canadian capital market institutions became firmly established. Thus, in the years 1915-1920, new Canadian bond issues amounted to $3428, more than double the previous six-year period, of which 67% were sold in Canada with most of the balance sold in the United States. The Bond Dealers' Association of Canada was established in 1916 with 32 members. By 1921 it had expanded to 103 members.[7]

Although foreign capital markets continued to loom large in Canadian financial affairs, and although an important volume of activity already existed in Canadian markets, we can roughly date the emergence of a viable Canadian capital market from this period.

THE FINANCE ACT AND
THE CENTRAL BANK ISSUE: 1920-1935

The two decades between the wars marked the transition of the government's role from that of an almost passive participant to a potentially strong though immature manager of the financial system. This was a period of great stress upon the financial system, containing one of the most impressive waves of expansion experienced in the 20th century as well as the worst depression. When the system was found weak in certain respects, the government finally assumed a role which, partly under pressure from bankers, it had earlier avoided. Two developments are of particular importance.

Government Inspection of Chartered Banks

The first major development was a direct result of Canada's latest and perhaps most spectacular bank failure. In the spring of 1923, the Home Bank failed. The relatively young (chartered in 1905), middle-sized bank, which was thought to be sound, was discovered by new management to be insolvent. A Royal Commission appointed to examine the reasons for the failure found evidence of misconduct on the part of several officers of the firm. As a result of the Commission's report, and the associated public demands for better guarantees of responsibility and safety, the office of the Inspector General of Banks was established within the Department of Finance, with the power and responsibility to inspect each bank annually, reporting irregularities to the Minister.

The question of external inspection, as we have seen, dated back to the 1880s. From the very beginning, the banks had fought successfully to avoid what they considered would be an unwarranted invasion of their privacy and a costly and time-consuming nuisance. Only under great pressure, associated with an earlier suspicious bank failure (the Farmer's Bank), had they accepted the external shareholder's audit in 1913. When that procedure was proven deficient in protecting the broader public interest, the banks' ability to resist governmental inspection evaporated. The principle was firmly established that the integrity and stability of banking institutions are "public goods," transcending the private interests of banks and their owners, and calling for special governmental attention.

A Central Bank

The second major change in the interwar period involved a broader application of this principle. A central bank was established to manage the nation's monetary affairs and to promote the stability of the banking system as a whole.

At the turn of the century, neither Canada nor the United States had a central bank, although the concept recurred in discussions in both countries. In the United States, Congress appointed a National Monetary Commission in 1908 to study the structure and performance of the American financial system. The Commission recommended the establishment of a central bank, and, although it did not conform fully to the Commission's proposal, the Federal Reserve System was established in 1913. In Canada, successive proposals for a central bank were rejected, including a 1918 proposal which had the support of the President of the Canadian Bankers' Association and the interest of the Minister of Finance. It was argued that a central bank was not necessary in the Canadian context and, after 1914, that the lender of last resort facilities provided by the *Finance Act* were an adequate substitute for a central bank. In 1923, the *Finance Act* was revised, making the discount facilities which had been created as a temporary wartime arrangement a permanent feature of the banking system.

Was the *Finance Act* an adequate substitute for a central bank?

Deficiencies of the Finance Act

Lender of Last Resort.   One of the traditional functions of a central bank is to act as a "banker's bank" — a lender of last resort for the financial system. In this function it can be said that the *Finance Act* did for the Canadian financial system what the Federal Reserve System did for the U.S. financial system, and did it more simply. In place of the network of 12 Federal Reserve Banks and their branches was the already existing administrative machinery of the Department of Finance. The arrangement was inexpensive, and it apparently worked without political intervention. Its effectiveness might be judged by the fact that whereas in the United States the failure of thousands of banks during the monetary turmoil of the early 1930s led to the temporary closure of the entire banking system, in Canada not a single bank failed. The effectiveness of the *Finance Act* in underwriting the liquidity of the banking system was one of the strong points in the argument of many bankers that a central bank was not necessary.

Monetary Management.   Such a conclusion, however, implies a very narrow concept of the role of the central bank in the financial system. While we have not yet explored this aspect of central banking, the management of the money supply is an essential function of a modern central bank, and in this respect the *Finance Act* cannot be considered to have been a substitute.

The *Finance Act,* it will be recalled, was adopted simultaneously with the suspension of the gold standard. The pre-1914 gold standard left little scope for governmental management of the money supply. Indeed, such monetary management was unnecessary, and, in principle, contrary to the spirit of the gold standard. While gold directly constituted a very small fraction of circulating money, both the money which the government directly issued (Dominion notes) and the total money supply were supposed to be regulated by the gold reserves of the government. As Figure 14-2 illustrates, there was a very close relationship between official gold reserves and Dominion notes outstanding before the enactment of the *Finance Act* in 1914.

FIGURE 14-2   Gold reserves, Finance Act advances and outstanding Dominion Notes, 1890-1935

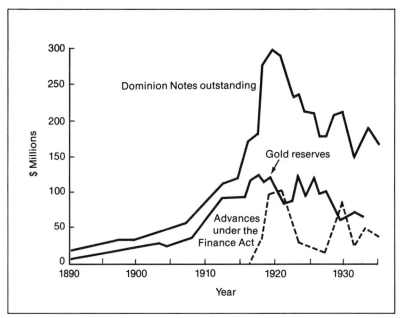

The *Finance Act* broke the strong link to gold. As Figure 14-2 illustrates clearly, major changes in the supply of Dominion notes outstanding after 1914 were dominated by advances under the *Finance Act* rather than changes in gold reserves. Indeed, large changes in the supply of Dominion notes occurred during World War I and again in the late 1920s in spite of opposite changes in gold reserves.

However, the significant thing is that the *Finance Act* was not designed (and was certainly not used) to give the government the *initiative* in controlling the money supply. The *government was a passive participant. The initiative for bringing the mechanism into play rested solely with the chartered banks.* They had to want advances under the *Finance Act* for monetary expansion to occur, and could choose to repay advances at any time, thus effecting monetary contraction. The government could alter the interest rate charged on such advances (the discount rate), but there is no evidence that they even considered using this power to systematically encourage or discourage borrowing in the interests of steady monetary expansion. Indeed, it was forcefully argued that the *Finance Act* contained no authority to use the discount rate in this way.

The Finance Act and the Gold Standard.   The gold standard was reestablished in Canada on July 1, 1926, when convertibility of Dominion notes into gold was resumed. Gold was money internationally. It could be used to make international payments. Thus, when in 1928-29 a deficit emerged in the Canadian balance of international payments (in the sense that exports and net sales of securities were not sufficient to pay for imports), gold was drained out of the Canadian financial system. However, contrary to the gold standard principle, the money supply was not allowed to contract. Indeed, the very economic expansion which produced the balance of payments deficit also produced increased demands for money and credit which were accommodated by advances under the *Finance Act*. The combined expansion of the money supply and precipitous decline in gold reserves (Figure 14-2) led to a second suspension of gold convertibility and the termination of the gold standard in Canada.

The *Finance Act* was enacted in 1914 because the government was unwilling to accept the discipline of the gold standard in wartime. In the late 1920s, the *Act* permitted monetary expansion independently of gold reserves and, in 1929, the gold standard was again suspended because the government was unwilling to accept the gold standard discipline which called for monetary contraction. During the following years, sharp monetary contraction occurred anyway. Just as the *Finance Act,* as administered, provided no method of regulating monetary expansion, it now provided no method of moderating monetary contraction. The great depression that followed provided the definitive demonstration that the *Finance Act* had not given Canada a complete central bank.

The Great Depression.   The great depression was worldwide in scope. The Canadian economy, exposed as it was to developments in world markets, was severely hit. Thus, the value of exports of goods and services was cut in half between 1929 and 1932, net sales of new Canadian securities in world capital markets stopped (indeed, retirements slightly exceeded new issues by 1932), and what had been a substantial inflow of capital for direct investment in Canada turned into a large net outflow. Inside Canada, economic activity ground to a standstill. By 1933, capital expenditures by business were only 20% of what they had been in 1929, and the gross national product 58% of its 1929 market value. Of course, a substantial part of the drop in each case was accounted for by the precipitous decline in the price level. However, the *real* gross national product (adjusted for changes in prices) fell by almost 30% in four years, and by 1933 official estimates show 20% of the labor force unemployed (and these are widely regarded as conservative estimates).

Monetary contraction paralleled and reinforced the decline in output. Thus from

FIGURE 14-3   The money supply and aggregate output, 1900-1934

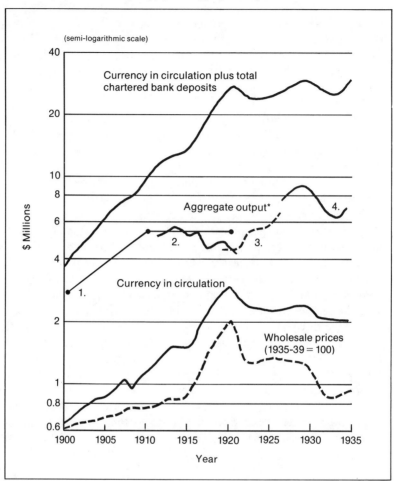

*There is no continuous series for aggregate output back to 1900. The four series used
are those of (1) Firestone, (2) Deutsch, (3) Jones, (4) D.B.S. Cf. M.C. Urquhart and
K.A. Buckley, *Historical Statistics of Canada* (Toronto: Macmillan, 1965). pp. 112-138.
The early estimates have been deflated by the wholesale price index.

1929 to 1933, chartered bank deposits and currency in circulation fell by 12.5% (Figure
14-3). Even more dramatic declines occurred in total bank assets (20%) and bank loans
in Canada (36%). Although no banks failed in Canada, and thus a collapse of the
banking system did not aggravate the depression, the government found itself without
the means to actively manage the money supply, either to alleviate its own financial
problems or to counteract the forces of depression.

The Macmillan Commission and the Central Bank.   As the economic situation grew

TABLE 14-6   The Canadian financial system, 1934

I. THE MONEY SUPPLY

	$ Millions	Percent
Subsidiary coin	27	4
Dominion notes (outside banks)	34	4
Bank notes	123	16
Demand deposits with chartered banks	575	76
TOTAL	759	100

II. ASSETS OF FINANCIAL INTERMEDIARIES

	$ Millions	Percent
Chartered banks	2 919	49
Other deposit-taking intermediaries		
Quebec savings banks	75	1
Government savings banks	45	1
Caisses populaires and credit unions	9*	—
Mortgage loan companies	207	3
Trust companies	228†	4
Caisses populaires and credit unions	9*	—
Total	564	9
Other financial intermediaries		
Life insurance companies	2 340	39
General insurance companies	171	3
Small loan companies	2	—
Sales finance companies	n.a.	—
Mutual funds and investment companies	n.a.	—
Total	2 513	42
TOTAL (available data)	5 996	100

* Loans.

† Excludes E. T. & A. accounts of $2436 million.

SOURCE: Urquhart and Buckley, *Historical Statistics of Canada* (Toronto: Macmillan, 1965); *Canada Year Book; Statistical Yearbook of Quebec.*

worse and the banks continued their contraction, criticisms of the financial system intensified. The government finally yielded to the pressure for some type of reform by appointing a Royal Commission chaired by Lord Macmillan to study the desirability of establishing a central bank in Canada. Its major recommendation was that a central bank be established, which, to minimize possible political interference, would be privately owned, with its liabilities limited to four times its holdings of gold. It was to be given a monopoly over the issuance of currency (i.e., replacing both Dominion notes and bank notes with Bank of Canada notes). The recommendation was followed, and the Bank of Canada began operations in March, 1935.

REFINEMENT OF CENTRAL
BANKING INSTITUTIONS: 1935-1967 _____

The Bank of Canada

When the Bank of Canada opened its doors in March 1935, it was a privately owned bank with approximately 12 000 individual shareholders. Following the election of 1936, the government assumed majority ownership of the bank (through the expedient of issuing new shares), and appointed a majority of the Board of Directors. Complete nationalization was achieved in 1938 when the Government purchased all privately held shares. The Bank of Canada is now a crown corporation, with the Minister of Finance, on behalf of the Government of Canada, the sole shareholder. All profits from the Bank's operations accrue to the Government.

The Bank's management is nominally in the hands of a government-appointed Board of Directors, including 12 directors "from diversified occupations" appointed for three-year terms, a Governor and a Deputy Governor, appointed for seven-year terms. The Deputy Minister of Finance also sits on the Board as an *ex officio* member. An Executive Committee comprised of the Governor, the Deputy Governor, two directors and the Deputy Minister of Finance (without vote) meets weekly, with the full Board meeting a few times a year to review developments and ratify the decisions of the Executive Committee. Although the Minister of Finance is kept fully informed, in practice, the continuing operations of the Bank are in the hands of the Governor and his professional staff.

Monopoly of Currency.   Under the original Bank of Canada Act, the chartered banks were required to gradually reduce their notes outstanding over a 10 year period to approximately one-quarter of their 1934 value. In 1944, however, the banks' right to issue notes was revoked, and by 1950 chartered bank notes were formally retired from circulation. The Bank of Canada was given a monopoly over paper money. Thus, the banks finally lost a right which they had fought a long hard battle to maintain. However, as Figure 14-1 confirms, by the early 1930s the relative importance of banks' notes in circulation as a source of funds for the banks had declined substantially.

Fiscal Agent of the Government.   The Bank of Canada also assumed a role which had historically been the prerogative of the Bank of Montreal, that of fiscal agent for the Government of Canada. In this capacity the bank manages the Government's cash position, operates its chequing account, makes arrangements for the issuance and retirement of government debt, and handles the Government's foreign exchange transactions. In these respects the Bank's role is that of banker, not policy maker.

Cash Reserves of the Banks.   When the Bank of Canada was established, the chartered banks were compelled to sell their gold held in Canada to the Bank of Canada, and were required to hold cash reserves in the amount of 5% of their Canadian deposits in the form of either Bank of Canada notes or deposits at the Bank of Canada. A long battle against required reserves had been lost, although the reserve requirement as established was less onerous than most banks had been accustomed to maintaining. These requirements were eventually increased and made more effective.

It is also interesting to note that a vestige of the gold standard was maintained. The Bank of Canada was required to hold gold reserves in the amount of 25% of its note and deposit liabilities, but the requirement was immediately suspended and was eventually removed from the Act.

Lender of Last Resort.   The Bank of Canada replaced the Department of Finance as lender of last resort for the chartered banking system. Unlike experience under the *Finance Act,* this facility was in fact little used until the late 1950s when monetary policy became effectively more restrictive, the money market was more highly developed, and the nature of the discounting arrangements altered substantially. The Bank of Canada was also empowered to make advances to the Government of Canada and to the provincial governments, although the Bank has declined to become involved in provincial government finances.

Monetary Manager.   The primary function of the Bank of Canada is to formulate and execute monetary policy, i.e., to manage the supply of money and credit and hence influence the level of interest rates in Canada. We will analyze this aspect of the Bank of Canada's operations in considerable detail later. The important point is that the combination of a fixed cash reserve requirement, which eventually became an effective constraint on the banks, and the ability of the Bank of Canada to control the quantity of reserves available *made it possible for the Bank of Canada to take the initiative in changing the Canadian money supply*. This represented the major change from the arrangements under the *Finance Act.*

The Development of the Central Banking Apparatus

We do not intend to examine the history of monetary policy under the Bank of Canada in this chapter. However, in order to bring to a close the analysis of the evolution of the financial system, it is useful to point out a few milestones in the development of the central banking apparatus from 1935 on.

Institutional Gaps.   With the passage of the central banking legislation, management of the money supply became a direct responsibility of a government agency. But the simple conferring of power did not imply that the Bank of Canada was immediately capable of taking a confident, independent stance and able to impose its will upon the system. Central banking skills had to be learned, and operating techniques, appropriate to the Canadian situation, developed. The Bank's task was complicated because certain crucial institutions, like a short-term money market, did not really exist in Canada. Partly as a result of this the chartered banks were reluctant to operate with cash reserves close to the legal requirements, and developed the habit of keeping large excess reserves. Thus, whereas the banks were required to hold reserves equal to 5% of their Canadian deposit liabilities, in the early years of the Bank of Canada they actually held more than twice that amount. This provided a cushion which partially insulated the banks from the Bank of Canada's monetary policies, and complicated the problem of monetary management.

In any case, the Bank of Canada soon became totally immersed in the problems of war finance and postwar readjustment, during which time the concept of a central bank pursuing an active, periodically restrictive and independent monetary policy was deliberately suppressed. Indeed, almost from its inception until the early 1950s, the Bank of Canada was preoccupied with problems of government finance and the stability of the government bond market at low levels of bond yields. As long as it was committed to operations to peg the price of government bonds it could not simultaneously restrict the money supply since such restriction would have implied higher bond yields. As a result, the problem of adapting the structure of the financial system to better facilitate active, independent central banking operations was postponed until the revision of the *Bank Act* in 1954.

Bank Act of 1954.   A few changes were made in the chartered banks lending authority in 1944 (e.g., for intermediate term credit to farmers and fishermen) and 1954 (e.g., loans on insured mortgages and chattel mortgages), most of which were discussed in Chapter 10. However, the main change of concern to us is the revision in the cash reserve requirement. In place of a daily requirement of 5% of Canadian deposits the banks were now required to maintain a monthly average reserve equal to 8% of deposits. In addition, the Bank of Canada was given the authority to increase this requirement by no more than 1% per month to a maximum of 12%.

The banks responded by bringing their actual cash reserves into line with required reserves, reducing their average cash reserve from 10.24% in 1953 to 8.29% in 1956. This meant that the banks no longer had a cushion of "excess reserves." The availability of cash was a highly effective constraint and, given the Bank of Canada's ability to control the supply of cash, this gave it effective control over the supply of money and credit.

The Money Market.   The second major change involved the development of a broad, active short-term money market. This market was discussed in detail in Chapter 3. In the mid-1950s, the Bank of Canada deliberately fostered its development, particularly by underwriting the liquidity of the market with lines of credit to major dealers. The development of the market was important in making it feasible for the banks to operate very small excess reserves, and it provided a solid market in which the Bank of Canada could buy and sell securities to affect the availability of cash to the banking system.

These two measures completed the development of the central banking apparatus as we have it today. The only other important consideration was the status of the Bank of Canada within the government heirarchy, and particularly the status of the Governor of the Bank of Canada.

Status of the Bank of Canada.   As we have noted, from 1938 the Bank of Canada has been wholly owned by the Government of Canada. However, until the revision of the *Bank Acts* in 1967 there was no clear, legal definition of the degree of independence possessed by the Bank of Canada in formulating monetary policy. Can the Governor and his Board of Directors make major policy decisions independently or are they directly responsible to the Government of the day, so that the Bank is simply responsible for implementing the Government's monetary policy?

The tradition of an independent central bank which can, among other things, impose a measure of monetary discipline on the government of the day is of long standing. It was again endorsed to a limited degree by the 1964 Report of the Royal Commission on Banking and Finance on grounds of:

> the historical tendency of governments of all forms to develop the habit of inflating the currency. Since the process of inflation is understood by relatively few people and since it has few organized opponents in our society, a special responsibility is imposed on the central bank to see that the objective of price level stability is not forgotten by government merely because other goals have more political popularity in the short run.[8]

Governments can be trusted with taxation, conscription, and capital punishment, but not with management of the money supply.

As we saw, the Macmillan Commission proposal dealt with this problem by creating a privately owned central bank. By definition it was "independent." While the degree of autonomy of the nationalized institution was not defined, it was generally understood that the Governor was responsible to the Minister of Finance in the sense that the Bank could not legitimately pursue a line of policy which was contrary to that of the government. At the same time, the first Governor of the Bank made it abundantly clear that since the *Bank of Canada Act* gave the Bank responsibility for monetary policy he would not implement a policy with which he was in fundamental disagreement. He reserved the ultimate right to resign in protest.

In fact, conflict between the Bank and the government on matters of policy never became an issue until the late 1950s and early 1960s. At that time the "sound" money policies of the second Governor of the Bank, James Coyne, came into sharp conflict with the expansionary policies of the government. Moreover, the Governor effectively challenged the implicit supremacy of the government in determining the course of monetary policy, and went so far as to publicly criticize government fiscal policy. The conflict was resolved in mid-1961 when the House of Commons passed a bill declaring the office of Governor of the Bank of Canada vacant. While the Senate refused to accede to the bill, the Governor resigned immediately after the Senate vote. On taking office, the third Governor of the Bank of Canada, Louis Rasminsky, formally accepted the principle of joint responsibility, with the government having the ultimate right "to direct the Bank as to the policy which the Bank is to carry out." This principle was formally incorporated in the *Bank of Canada Act* in the revision of 1967.

Profile of the Financial System in 1967

Table 14-7 provides a profile of the Canadian financial system in the mid-1960s. The increasing complexity of the system is only partially reflected in this table. It shows the continuing primary position of the chartered banks, and suggests the increasing importance of a number of other institutions, such as trust companies and credit unions. But each of the categories of institutions hides within it a proliferation of specialized firms. The appropriate scope of competition among financial intermediaries became the primary concern of public policy in the next stage in the development of the system.

TABLE 14-7   **The Canadian financial system, 1967**

I. THE MONEY SUPPLY

	$ Millions	*Percent*
Subsidiary coin	328	2
Bank of Canada notes	2 408	14
Demand deposits with chartered banks	6 330	36
Other chequable deposits	8 314	48
TOTAL	17 380	100

II. ASSETS OF FINANCIAL INTERMEDIARIES

Chartered banks	31 649	48
Other deposit-taking intermediaries		
Quebec savings banks	506	1
Government savings banks	254	—
Mortgage loan companies	2 751	4
Trust companies	4 311*	7
Caisses populaires and credit unions	3 367	5
Total	11 189	17
Other financial intermediaries		
Life insurance companies	12 912	20
General insurance companies	2 307	4
Consumer loan and sales finance companies	4 500	7
Mutual funds and investment companies	2 762	4
Total	22 481	34
TOTAL (available data)	65 319	100

* Excluding E.T. & A. accounts.

SOURCE: Bank of Canada, *Statistical Summary, 1969 Supplement* (Ottawa, 1970).

THE QUEST FOR STABILITY

The search for dominant themes and stages in the development of the financial system carries with it a serious risk of oversimplification. It should be clear from the brief discussion in this chapter that there were many crosscurrents in the development process, and the stages which we have identified were seldom clearly defined in practice. Nonetheless, it is possible to see in the development of public policy through the 1950s a dominant concern for the stability of the financial system, with less concern for competition. In the 1960s and subsequently, the relative emphasis placed on competition in the system changed significantly. However, before we discuss this change in the thrust of public policy, it is useful to review the parallel developments in the United States through the 1950s.

ENDNOTES

1. Adam Shortt, "The Early History of Canadian Banking," *Journal of the Canadian Bankers' Association,* Vol. V., pp. 13-14.
2. R. M. Breckenridge, *The History of Banking in Canada* (Washington: Government Printing Office, 1910, for the National Monetary Commission), p. 85.
3. *Ibid.,* p. 95.
4. It is interesting to note that bank notes were given an unusual legal status. The banks were empowered to meet all depositors' demands for payment by issuing their own bank notes. Depositors could not insist on withdrawing their deposits in gold or Dominion notes. The banks could legally pay off one liability by issuing another — a prvilege normally reserved to governments.
5. E. Neufeld, "The Relative Growth of Commercial Banks," *Essays in Money and Banking in Honour of R. S. Sayers,* C. R. Whittlesey and J. S. G. Wilson, eds., (Oxford: Clarendon Press, 1968), pp. 130-150.
6. J. Viner, *Canada's Balance of International Indebtedness, 1900-1913* (Cambridge, Mass.: Harvard University Press, 1924).
7. *Submission of the Investment Dealers Association of Canada to the Royal Commission on Banking and Finance,* p. 2.
8. Royal Commission on Banking and Finance, *Report,* (Ottawa: Queen's Printer, 1964), p. 541.
9. Bank of Canada, "Statement of the Governor of the Bank of Canada issued August 1, 1961," *Evidence of the Governor before the Royal Commission on Banking and Finance* (Ottawa: Bank of Canada, 1964), pp. 131-132.

THE FINANCIAL SYSTEM OF THE UNITED STATES
The Quest for Stability

15

The themes which we emphasized in our review of the development of the Canadian financial system through the 1950s have parallels in the United States — but also very important contrasts. At an early stage, greater emphasis was placed on decentralization and competition within the financial system, so that the U.S. financial system developed in a very different pattern. The problems faced by the policy makers reflected the fragmented structure of the system, and the problem of instability appeared in a much more acute form than in Canada. Indeed, the American experience is frequently used to highlight the potential conflict between stability and competition. For this reason alone, the development of the U.S. financial system and U.S. financial policies merit close study by Canadian students. This is part of the purpose of this chapter.

There is a second reason for Canadian students to study the American financial system. Given the importance of the U.S. economy to Canadian economic activity and the strong links between the financial systems of the two countries, an understanding of the American financial system is basic to a complete understanding of the Canadian system. Unfortunately, both the structure of the banking system and the arrangements for its regulation appear to be so different in the United States (and so complex) that many Canadian students find them perplexing. Another part of our purpose in this chapter is to help bridge this gap in understanding, by discussing the American financial system from a Canadian perspective.

We begin with a review of the American financial system as we find it today.

COMMERCIAL BANKING

The American counterparts of Canadian chartered banks are called, simply, commercial banks. In some ways they are very different from Canadian banks, but they perform essentially the same functions in the financial system.

The Balance Sheet of Commercial Banks

One method of highlighting the similarities and differences between American and Canadian banks is by comparing their balance sheets. Relevant asset and liability data are presented in Table 15-1. It is apparent from these data that the nature of financial intermediation by the two sets of banks is broadly comparable, but that there are some interesting differences. First consider the asset side of the balance sheet.

Loan and Security Holdings.   In discussing the business of Canadian chartered banks in Chapter 10, we noted that according to the bankers' self-image, the main focus of their attention is loans, and particularly short-term business loans. Although personal loans have been increasing in importance, business loans remain the core of the Canadian banks' asset portfolios. Security holdings perform the secondary functions of safeguarding liquidity, transferring lending capacity over time, and permitting broader portfolio diversification.

Table 15-1 suggests a similar emphasis in American commercial banking. Although loans account for a much smaller proportion of total assets than in Canada (particularly if mortgages are considered separately from the loan portfolio), they are clearly the dominant earning asset. The bulk of the loan portfolio consists of business loans, but personal loans are also of major importance (they account for a smaller portion of total assets than in Canada, but a larger proportion of total loans apart from mortgages).

The composition of the security holdings of American commercial banks is also different from that of Canadian banks. Whereas the American banks have very large holdings of state and local government bonds, the Canadian banks hold relatively more federal government securities. However, the Canadian banks' holdings of federal bonds have fallen sharply in recent years (in 1969 they accounted for 16.5% of total assets), and we should remember that their choice of securities is constrained by the secondary reserve requirement. Indeed, treasury bills, held primarily to satisfy this requirement, accounted for almost 75% of all federal government securities held at the end of 1980. There is no general requirement of this type in the United States, but many state chartered banks are permitted to satisfy part of their legal reserve requirement with holdings of federal or state bonds. In considering the American banks' large holdings of state and local government securities, it is also relevant to note that interest on these securities is tax exempt and, in a sense which is not true in Canada, American banks are locally oriented institutions. We will return to this point later.

Before going on, we should note an important caveat with respect to data like those presented in Table 15-1. These data are *averages* for the banking system as a whole. The U.S. banking system, however, has many banks and great diversity in such characteristics as asset holdings — much greater diversity than in Canada, with its relatively few

TABLE 15-1   **Comparative balance sheets of commercial banks in Canada and the United States, December 1980 ($ Billions)**

| | UNITED STATES | | CANADA | |
	U.S. Dollars	Percent	Canadian Dollars	Percent
Cash assets	$(331.9)	(17.6)%	$(57.5)	(20.4)%
Currency and coin	20.2	1.1	3.1	1.1
Deposits with central bank	30.4	1.6	5.5	2.0
Deposits with other banks				
Domestic	68.5	3.6	0.8	0.3
Foreign	129.8	6.9	45.4	16.1
Items in process of collection	83.1	4.4	2.7	1.0
Money market loans				
Federal funds sold	70.3	3.7	—	—
Day-to-day loans	—	—	0.1	—
Securities	(334.4)	(17.7)	(23.1)	(8.2)
Federal government bonds	163.6	8.7.	9.8	3.5
Other domestic governments	146.3	7.8	0.6	0.2
Other domestic securities	15.3	0.8	6.9	2.5
Other foreign securities	9.3	0.4	5.8	2.1
Loans	(1 023.5)	(54.2)	(173.6)	(61.7)
Real estate (incl. mortgages)	269.1	14.3	18.5	6.6
Agriculture	32.3	1.7	8.2	2.9
Commerce and industry	287.8	15.2	55.4	19.7
Financial institutions				
Domestic	44.1	2.3	1.9	0.7
Foreign	37.1	2.0	1.0	0.4
Individuals	187.4	9.9	30.6	10.9
Other loans				
Domestic	35.2	1.9	3.2	1.1
Foreign	27.4	1.5	54.8	19.5
Other assets	(126.6)	(6.7)	(26.9)	(9.6)
Total	1 886.7	100.0	281.2	100.0
Deposits at domestic offices	(1 189.8)	(63.1)	(195.2)	(69.4)
Public deposits:				
Demand	333.7	17.7	18.5	6.6
Savings	197.3	10.5	74.9	26.6
Time	476.7	25.3	34.0	12.1
Government deposits	85.0	4.5	4.1	1.5
Other bank deposits	68.9	3.7	1.7	0.6
Other deposits	28.1	1.4	0.8	0.3
Foreign currency deposits				
Banks	n/a		30.5	10.8
Others	n/a		30.6	10.9
Deposits at foreign offices	(291.3)	(15.4)	(51.9)	(18.5)
Banks	147.7	7.8	34.8	12.4
Others	143.6	7.6	17.1	6.1
Other liabilities	(297.9)	(15.8)	(25.7)	(9.1)
Capital accounts	(107.6)	(5.7)	(8.4)	(3.0)

SOURCES: *Canada Gazette*, 1981; Federal Deposit Insurance Corporation, *Annual Report*, 1980.

large banks. Small rural banks tend to have very different balance sheets from large city banks, and the large banks, because of their size, tend to have relatively heavy weight in the aggregate statistics. Thus, for example, in 1980 there were almost 300 banks with over 35% of their total assets in federal government securities. These were primarily small, rural banks, with limited lending opportunities. In Canada, similar institutions would be branches of large nationwide banks, with an excess of deposits over loans, the balance of the funds made available to head office for use elsewhere in the bank. By contrast, at the other end of the scale, there were almost 2000 banks in the United States with holdings of federal securities of less than 3% of total assets.

Mortgages.   The relatively smaller holdings of business and personal loans on the part of American commercial banks is largely offset by much greater relative holdings of mortgages. As we saw in Chapter 14, traditional banking theory in Canada held that mortgages were not appropriate assets for commerical banks. This principle was incorporated in the *Bank Act*, and it was not until 1954 that Canadian banks were permitted to hold mortgages which had been insured by the federal government (although, as we saw earlier, the ceiling on interest rates which banks could charge on loans deterred the banks from acquiring insured mortgages after 1959), and it was not until 1967 that they were permitted to hold uninsured mortgages.

American banks have not been subject to such a blanket proscription of mortgage loans. Historically, it is true that the proposition that mortgages were not appropriate assets for commercial banks had considerable support in the United States. Indeed, in the *National Bank Act* of 1864, national banks were prohibited from holding mortgages. However, this provision did not affect the asset holdings of state chartered banks, a fact which helped these institutions to survive and prosper in the face of competition from the national banks which were supposed to replace them, and in spite of punitive measures taken against them by the federal government. Moreover, when the Federal Reserve System was established in 1913, the prohibition on national bank mortgage investments was relaxed, and permissible mortgage holdings were tied to the stock-holders equity or the savings and time deposits of the bank.[1] It is widely argued that the importance of loans directly or indirectly linked to real estate among the assets of commercial banks, and particularly of small, rural, state-chartered banks, was one of the factors contributing to the high rate of bank failures in the United States, and general instability of the system in the 1920s and 1930s.

Interbank Deposits.   One of the interesting characteristics of the American banking system is the importance of correspondent relationships among banks, reflected in Table 15-1 in deposits with other banks, which appear among both assets and liabilities. Correspondent banks in regional and national financial centers provide many services to banks in smaller centers, including the clearing and collecting of cheques and other financial instruments as described in Chapter 2. They do much more, however, including arrangements for participation in the national money market and the foreign exchange market, provision of management advice and technical services, and partici-pation in major loans and investments which are too large for the local bank alone. In Canada, Canadian currency interbank deposits are very small, and mainly reflect the activities of Canadian banks as correspondents for foreign banks. Domestic corres-pondent relationships are not important to the operation of the payments system, except with respect to near banks (whose deposits with banks are not classified as interbank deposits). The functions which are performed by correspondent banks in the United States are internal to branch-banking firms in Canada, with national and regional head office implicitly providing correspondent facilities for local branches. In the United States, therefore, correspondent relationships are, to some extent, a substitute for nationwide branch banking.

While domestic interbank deposits are relatively unimportant in Canada, foreign currency interbank deposits are another matter.

Foreign Currency Business.   The much greater importance of assets and liabilities denominated in foreign currencies held by Canadian banks is another difference between the balance sheets of the banking system of Canada and the United States. It shows up among deposit liabilities, loans (and to a lesser degree securities), and interbank deposits held as assets. As we noted earlier, the growth of the foreign currency business reflects the development of Canadian banks as international banking institutions, which are very active and important participants in the Euro-dollar market.

We should not conclude from these data that U.S. banks are not deeply involved in international banking. Again we must emphasize the diversity of banking institutions in the United States. While most small banks conduct a strictly local banking business, the very large banks carry on a worldwide business. However, reflecting the role of the U.S. dollar in international finance, most of that business tends to be conducted in U.S. dollars, not in foreign currencies. At the end of 1980, a network of foreign branches and subsidiaries of U.S. banks reported assets of U.S.$320 billion or 17% of total assets (and U.S. banks reported liabilities to non-residents of a similar magnitude).

Cash Reserves.   Like Canadian banks, American banks must satisfy minimum legal cash reserve requirements. If we ignore the situation of near banks, cash reserve requirements in Canada have been centralized in administration, uniform in application among banks, and, at least until recent years, simple in structure. In the United States, by contrast, cash reserve requirements have been fragmented in administration, differential in application among banks, and, as a result, complicated in structure. This reflects a complex regulatory system, rooted in constitutional principles, with diverse policy objectives (more about these issues later). However, the American system is changing to a relatively simple, centralized one, which will be even more comprehensive than the Canadian arrangements.

Because the transition to the new arrangements is in a very early stage, the data on cash reserves in Table 15-1 substantially reflect the old system of reserve requirements. Under this system, by choosing to be or not to be a member of the Federal Reserve System, a bank could, in effect, choose between two sets of reserve requirements, those imposed by the state in which it was operating (a nationally chartered bank would have to obtain a state charter to avoid the national requirements) and those imposed by the Federal Reserve System. For members of the Federal Reserve System, the reserve requirements depended on the size and composition of deposits (and, prior to 1979, on the location of the bank: requirements were higher for banks in major cities). The

requirements for August 31, 1980, just prior to the implementation of the new requirements, are shown on the upper section of Table 15-2. As can be seen, the requirements
were higher for demand deposits (bearing no interest but transferable by cheque) than
for savings and time deposits (bearing interest but not transferable by cheque). Within
the demand deposit category, the requirements were higher for banks with large
amounts on deposit, and within the time deposit category, they were higher for deposits
with short maturities.

TABLE 15-2 **Cash reserve requirements for**
depository institutions in the
United States, December 31, 1980

I. MEMBER BANKS
Before implementation of the Monetary Control Act

Net demand deposits

$0-2 million	7%
2-10 million	9½%
10-100 million	11¾%
100-400 million	12¾%
over 400 million	16¼%

Savings deposits 3%

Time deposits
$0-5 million

30-179 days to maturity	3%
180 days to 4 years	2½%
4 years or more	1%

Over $5 million

30-179 days to maturity	6%
180 days to 4 years	2½%
4 years or more	1%

II. DEPOSITORY INSTITUTIONS
After implementation of the Monetary Control Act

Net transactions accounts

$0-26 million	3%
Over $26 million	12%

Non-personal time deposits

Less than 4 years to maturity	3%
4 years or more to maturity	0%

Eurocurrency liabilities 3%

SOURCE: *Federal Reserve Bulletin*, July 1981.

State-chartered banks which did not join the Federal Reserve System (non-member
banks) had to satisfy the reserve requirements established by the state authorities. These
differed from state to state, and so are not easily summarized. However, in general they
were considerably less onerous than the federal requirements.[2] One result was a steady

erosion of membership in the Federal Reserve System, as banks opted for state charters and lower reserve requirements.

The *Monetary Control Act* of 1980, enacted after many years of controversy, established legal cash reserve requirements for deposits in all depository institutions which have federal deposit insurance, whether or not they are commercial banks. The reserve requirements thus apply to federally-insured commercial banks and near banks (mutual savings banks, savings and loan associations, and credit unions). The reserve requirements which will be in effect when the *Act* is fully implemented are set out in the bottom half of Table 15-2. There is a long transition period between the existing requirements and the new requirements — up to eight years in the case of non-member institutions.

The Banks and the Money Market. In our discussion of the Canadian banking system we emphasized the importance of the money market as the place where banks make day-by-day adjustments in their cash reserve positions. These adjustments can be made by buying or selling short-term securities in the market, or by varying the amount of credit extended to dealers in government securities, particularly credit in the form of day-to-day loans.

The money market performs the same function in the American banking system, but on a much larger scale and with somewhat different institutional arrangements. As in Canada, the basic money market instruments are short-term government securities, particularly treasury bills, and selected short-term commercial and finance paper. The banks can make adjustments to their cash positions daily, by purchasing or selling short-term financial instruments, either outright or on purchase-and-resale agreements, by varying the credit which they extend to security houses, or by borrowing from the central bank.

However, the American money market has an important adjunct not found in Canada on a significant scale, a market in bank reserves *per se*, called the *federal funds market*. Federal funds are deposits with Federal Reserve Banks. They are funds which member banks can use to satisfy their legal reserve requirements. Through the agency of a federal funds broker, banks with temporarily excess reserves can lend them to banks with deficient reserves, normally for an overnight period. The interest rate on such loans is set competitively, and is highly sensitive to shifts in demand and supply pressures.

Transactions in the federal funds market are for relatively large sums of money, so that only the larger banks can effectively participate in the market. As a result, while the American banking system as a whole normally has a significant volume of "excess reserves," i.e., cash reserves over and above those required to satisfy the minimum legal requirements, these excess reserves tend to be held mainly by smaller country banks. The federal funds market provides an efficient mechanism by which the large city banks can keep their actual cash holdings very close to the legal requirement.

The amount of federal funds indebtedness outstanding varies widely from time to time. The amount outstanding at the end of 1980 is shown on Table 15-1 as an asset item, "Federal Funds Sold." Because these are interbank transactions there is a corresponding liability, included in this table in the account "other liabilities."

In recent years, banks have also developed techniques of managing their liabilities in order to adjust their cash positions. One method involves variations in their own negotiable certificates of deposit outstanding. Certificates of deposit are short-term money market instruments, issued in denominations of $100 000 or more. Unlike regular time deposits, they can be traded in a secondary market. They have become a major liability of American banks. Thus, at the end of 1980 negotiable certificates of deposit amounted to over 37% of the time and savings deposit liabilities of large commercial banks. The fact that they are traded in a competitive market makes it possible for a bank to take the initiative in changing the volume of its certificates outstanding, at least within limits, and hence to use these certificates to adjust its cash reserve position. By issuing certificates at competitive rates a bank can attract reserves from other banks, and by retiring maturing issues can reduce excess reserves.

Another technique of cash adjustment involves borrowing in the Euro-dollar market, an international market in U.S. dollars. By borrowing in that market, typically through the agency of its own foreign branches, a large American bank can bolster its own cash reserve position.[3] In this way, purely domestic money market transactions take on an international dimension.

Deposit Liabilities.   There are also interesting differences in the composition of the deposit liabilities of Canadian and American banks, and particularly in the relationship between demand, personal savings and time deposits as sources of funds. Canadian banks appear much more like personal savings banks than do banks in the United States, which are relatively more dependent on demand deposits and time deposits as sources of funds.

In this connection, it should be noted that traditionally a much sharper distinction has been drawn between savings and demand deposits in the United States, although recent developments are weakening the distinction. In principle, savings deposits are not chequable and can only be withdrawn by presenting a passbook. In recent years, however, a system of automatic transfers from savings to demand deposits has developed, which has made many savings deposits *de facto* chequable.

Conclusion: Balance Sheet Differences.   Viewed through a comparative analysis of their balance sheets, banks in Canada and the United States display some interesting differences, but by and large they have common characteristics. The most striking contrasts between the two banking systems are not in the nature of their assets and liabilities, but in the numbers and sizes of commercial banks — in the structure of the commercial banking industry.

The Industrial Structure

We should perhaps expect that a nation which has 10 times our population and almost 13 time our gross national product will also have many more banks. However, the actual difference in the number of firms in the commercial banking business is far greater than can be explained by these scale factors alone. Whereas Canada had 11 chartered banks at the end of 1980, the United States had over 14 700. Even making allowance for the new foreign-controlled banks chartered under the 1980 *Bank Act*, the relative numbers do not reflect the relative sizes of the economies.

Banking Firms versus Banking Offices. While the United States has many more *banking firms* than we might expect on the basis of the relative sizes of the two economies, it has relatively fewer banking *offices*. In the United States, there are 53 000 commercial bank offices, one for every 4100 people. In Canada, there are 7400 offices, one for every 3200 people. A few banks in the United States have very extensive branch networks. For example, in the state of California, the Bank of America alone operates 1100 offices, more than all but the largest three Canadian banks, and four other banks each operate between 300 and 600 offices. However, over half of American commercial banks are *unit banks*, operating only one office. Indeed, in 11 states (mainly in the Midwest and South) branch banking is prohibited. Sixteen states permit branch banking in limited areas, generally the same county or contiguous counties to that containing head office. The rest of the states permit statewide branch banking, but branch banking across state boundaries is prohibited under the so-called *McFadden Act* (1927) (although, as we will note below, bank holding companies provide a way around this law). Nationwide branch banking networks, comparable to the major Canadian banks, are unknown. On average, the 6800 branch banking firms operate only six branches each. Among Canadian banks, by contrast, the average number of offices is 674, and the five largest banks each have more than 1000 offices in Canada.

Size Distribution of Banks. One direct consequence of the prevalence of unit banking in the United States is a proliferation of commercial banks with very small financial resources, as is evident in Table 15-3.[4] Thus, at the end of 1980, 88% of American banks had total domestic assets of less than $100 million — less than half the size of the smallest Canadian bank at that time. These very small banks typically have only one office, and solicit deposits and make loans in a very limited local market, usually a small town and its immediate hinterland. A high proportion of their loans are for agricultural purposes, and they are little involved in commercial and industrial finance. They do not participate actively in the national money market, have almost no dealings in foreign exchange, and rely heavily on their big city correspondents for assistance and advice, and for the provision of specialized banking services for their customers.

Not all American banks are small local institutions. There are many medium-sized firms which carry on a normal range of commercial banking activities in cities throughout the nation. In addition, the large metropolitan areas contain some of the world's major banks, including the world's largest bank, the California-based Bank of America. This means that there is an extreme range between large and small banks. While there are almost 900 banks with assets less than $5 million, there are 29 banks with assets in excess of $5 billion. In contrast to the tiny local banks, the giant institutions carry on banking activities which are national and international in scope. Most of them have representatives (but not branches) in major cities throughout the country in order to service their large industrial customers, and like the major Canadian banks, they generally have branches or agencies in the world's financial centers. Some of the major American banks also operate networks of branch offices carrying out a normal commercial banking business in other countries, particularly in South and Central America.

In terms of the magnitude of the financial resources at their disposal, the very large banks dominate the American banking system. As we saw in Table 15-3, the 350 banks

TABLE 15-3 The distribution of commercial banks by size, 1980

Size of bank (Domestic Assets) ($ Millions)	Number of Banks		Domestic Assets	
	Number	Cumulative Percentage	Amount ($ Billions)	Cumulative Percentage
less than 5	874	5.9	2.6	—
5-9.9	1 937	13.2	14.7	1.1
10-24.9	4 662	50.8	78.1	6.2
25-49.9	3 553	75.0	126.1	14.4
50- 99.9	1 972	88.4	135.7	23.3
100-299.9	1 159	96.3	184.0	35.2
300-499.9	197	97.6	77.0	40.2
500-999.9	161	98.7	109.1	47.2
1 000-4 900	160	99.8	335.0	69.0
5 000 or more	29	100.0	476.8	100.0
	14 704		1 539.0	

SOURCE: Federal Deposit Insurance Corporation, *Annual Report,* 1980.

with domestic assets of $500 million or more (2.4% of the banks) held over half of the domestic assets of commercial banks in 1980 —and the 29 giant banks held over 30% of domestic assets.

Group and Chain Banking. The figure of 14 700 incorporated banks somewhat exaggerates the number of *independent* banking firms in the United States. Many banks belong to either banking groups or banking chains.

A banking group exists when two or more banks are controlled by a holding company. This type of bank organization has increased significantly in importance in recent years. Thus, in 1969, there were 86 multibank holding companies controlling 723 banks with 19% of commercial bank domestic assets; in 1980, this had increased to 361 holding companies controlling 2426 banks with 35.7% of domestic banking assets.[5] Many of these groups are relatively small, involving a few unit banks in a single state. However, several are very large, with hundreds of offices and billions of dollars in assets, making them among the largest banks in the country.

Group banking has a significant impact on the banking structure in some areas, weakening the effects of restrictions on branch banking. In unit banking states, holding companies, in effect, create branch banking organizations. Thus, in the unit banking states of Montana, Wyoming, Colorado, and Texas, over half (in Colorado 66%) of banks deposits are held by group banks. Interstate branch banking is prohibited in the United States, but group banking permits a holding company to own banks in more than one state, effectively sidestepping the prohibition. Thus, the largest multibank holding company, based in California, controls 21 banks with 900 offices in 11 western states (and 33 offices abroad, including Canada), and total assets in excess of $32 billion. It advertises itself as though it were a large branch bank; indeed, all of the banks in the group have adopted the same name.[6]

Chain banking differs from group banking only in that no holding company is involved. Rather, control of two or more banks is in the hands of an individual or a partnership. Unlike banking groups, chains do not have to register with the federal banking authorities, and hence there are no data on them. One study, which covered only banks which were members of the Federal Reserve System, identified 431 chains involving 1169 banks in 1962.[7] Most chains involved only two banks but some involved more, and one involved 21 banks. A more recent study of the seventh Federal Reserve District (Illinois, Iowa, Wisconsin, Indiana, and Michigan) found 86 chains controlling 332 banks (only half were members of the Federal Reserve System) and 11% of the deposits in the district.[8] The effects on concentration in banking in the district were substantial, particularly in those states which prohibited either branch banking or multibank holding companies.

Even taking chain and group banking organizations into account, there are probably between 10 000 and 12 000 independent banking firms in the United States. Does this mean that the American banking industry approximates the economists' idealized concept of a "purely competitive" industry?

Banking Markets and Banking Competition.   It would be a mistake to think that all 12 000 independent banking firms compete in the same market. Banks are multi-product firms. They provide a variety of services for, accept deposits from, and extend credit to, customers who differ greatly in their access to alternative sources, partly because of the cost and inconvenience involved in dealing with relatively remote banks (another case of the importance of transactions costs), and partly because of the importance of information on credit worthiness in the functioning of loan markets.[9] Thus, it is generally argued that the market for services provided to households (chequing accounts, personal savings accounts, safety deposit boxes, mortgage credit, consumer credit, etc.) is largely local in scope. In the case of business firms, small, local firms in the distributive trades are primarily dependent on local banks, while larger firms with more established regional reputations may have ready access, with little or no additional costs or inconvenience, to banks over a much wider area, and very large firms, with established nationwide reputations, have access to the large banks in all parts of the country. Many of the very large firms have regular dealings with several banks, sometimes because of a provision in American banking laws which limits the amount of credit which can be extended to any single borrower to 10% of the bank's capital.

It is important to keep this hierarchy of markets in mind in interpreting the structure of the American banking system. While the national banking market may be highly competitive in many respects, local banking markets are much more concentrated and apparently less competitive, particularly outside the larger urban areas, and in spite of the fragmentation of the banking system into small unit banks. Thus, a study for 1959 revealed that 55% of all unit banks were in towns with only one banking office, and 92% were in communities with no more than two banking offices.[10] Including both branch banking and unit banking states, there were over 10 000 communities in the United States which had only one banking office, and 15 400 which had no more than two offices. They were almost exclusively communities with less than 25 000 inhabitants, but among them they accounted for two-thirds of the banking offices in the United States. For these communities, the fragmentation of the banking system does not mean the absence of monopoly in local banking markets.[11] The same study also revealed a high degree of concentration of bank deposits in larger urban areas. Indeed, in all but the largest metropolitan areas in unit banking states, the degree of concentration in deposit holdings is approximately the same as it is in Canada on a nationwide basis.

It has been argued that modern developments in transportation and communication reduces the significance of local banking monopolies defined in this geographic sense. Customers can now deal with banks in a broader area with little additional cost or inconvenience. However, several studies have produced evidence showing that concentration in this sense has a decided impact on interest rates charged and paid by banks. In general, interest rates on loans and service charges on accounts tend to be higher, and interest rates paid on deposits to be lower, the higher the degree of concentration in the banking market. The most competitive rates are those set in the national market for big business accounts.

Evolution of the Banking Structure

We have described the structure of the commercial banking system of the United States as it was on December 31, 1980. The structure is not static, but is undergoing rather fundamental changes. It is perhaps useful, at this point, to briefly consider the structure of the system in historical perspective.

Figures 15-1 and 15-2 trace the numbers of banks and of banking offices in the United States at five-year intervals since 1900. These charts show a history of wide fluctuations.

1900-1929: Expansion and Retrenchment.   During the first two decades of this century, there was a strong, virtually uncontrolled upsurge in the number of banks, almost all of which were unit banks, and many of which were heavily involved in agricultural development. From 8700 in 1900, the number of banks increased more than threefold to 29 000 in 1921.

The decade of the 1920s, by contrast, was a period of retrenchment in numbers of banks and offices. The forces of expansion (opening of new banks and branches) were gradually overwhelmed by the forces of contraction (mergers, voluntary liquidations, and failures). Many of the new banks proved to be unsound, and a relatively large number of bank failures had become almost commonplace in the American banking system. Thus, an average of 85 banks closed each year from 1900 through 1919 because of financial difficulties. This figure rose ominously to 505 in the troubled year of 1921, and in spite of general prosperity continued to rise to 775 in 1924 and to a temporary peak of 976 in 1926. In effect, the banking system was painfully purging itself of the chartering excesses of the pre-World War I era. To Canadian observers, accustomered to only occasional failures, the apparent instability of the American system was astounding (and, many said, instructive).

The Banking Crisis of 1933.   The onset of the depression of the 1930s was accompanied by a violent contraction of the banking system. Between 1928 and the end of 1933, the number of commercial banks dropped from 25 000 to under 14 000. Over 4000 banks failed in 1933 alone, and some 9100 failed in the four years 1929-1933. Total collapse of the system was only narrowly averted through emergency measures, including a bank

FIGURE 15-1   Number of commercial banks in the United States, 1900-1980

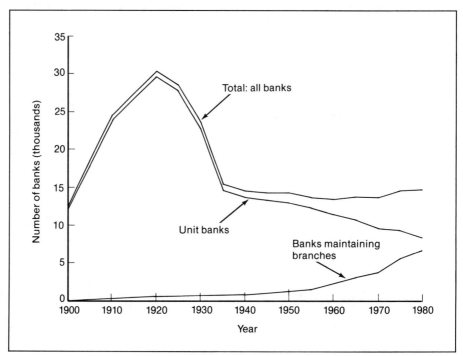

Source: *The Statistical History of the United States from Colonial Times to the Present* (New York: Basic Books, 1976); Federal Deposit Insurance Corporation, *Annual Report*, 1975, 1980.

"holiday" in 1933, following which only demonstrably sound banks were allowed to open for business. This cathartic experience engendered a continuing fear that a banking system based on virtually free entry, open competition and limited controls over asset holdings was inherently unstable. As we shall see, this argument still has a profound effect on the content of public policy with respect to the structure of the banking system.

In response to the banking crisis of 1933, the federal government extended its authority over the banking system. Bank failures dropped immediately to their pre-1920 level, and from 1942 on became comparatively rare. There followed a prolonged period of stability. Indeed, by 1950 there were roughly the same number of commercial banks and only 11% more banking offices than there had been in 1933.

Expansion through Branch Banking.   The 1950s and 1960s saw a new upsurge in the banking system. With the exception of the years 1963-65, the number of *banks* continued to decline, at an average rate of about 50 banks per year, the net result of the

FIGURE 15-2   Number of banking offices in the United States, 1900-1980

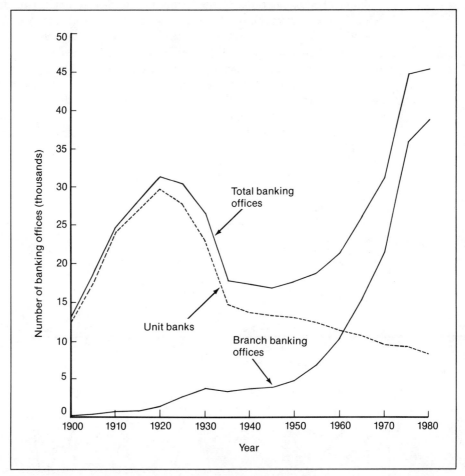

Source: *The Statistical History of the United States from Colonial Times to the Present* (New York: Basic Books, 1976); Federal Deposit Insurance Corporation, *Annual Report,* 1975, 1980.

chartering of about 100 banks per year and the disappearance through mergers of about 150 (bank failures played an insignificant role.) However, the number of banking *offices* increased rapidly, at an average rate of 860 offices per year. Although unit banks remained more numerous than branch banks, the branch banking form of organization was rapidly taking over the system. The picture would be even more dramatic if we could include bank holding companies in the analysis as branch banks.

This pattern of development was a result of the interaction between market forces and governmental regulation, at both federal and state levels. Indeed, during this period, it seems clear that the structure of the banking system was kept in a chronic condition of disequilibrium by the authorities as they responded to two types of pressures. The first was external to the banks, a rapid growth and shift in location of demands for new banking facilities, resulting from both the overall growth of the economy and of population and changes in the geographic structure of the population (both inter-state movements and movements to the suburbs). The regulatory authorities applied strict tests for the admission of new banks and the opening of new offices, somewhat retarding the system's adaptation to these shifts in demand. The second was internal to the banks. Economies of scale in banking created strong pressures to increase the size of banking firms. In some instances, this was accomplished through

FIGURE 15-3   Components of the changing structure of the banking system of the United States: New banks, bank mergers and banks closed, 1950-1980

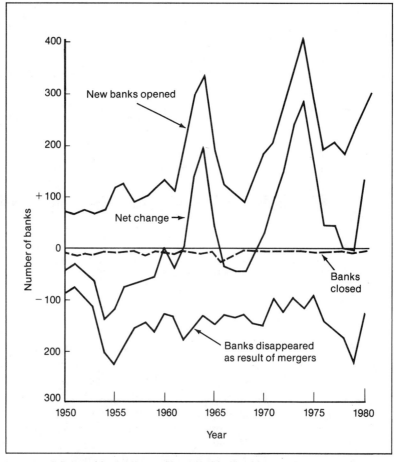

Source: U.S. Bureau of Census, *Historical Statistics of the United States, Colonial Times to 1957* (Washington: 1960); *Federal Reserve Bulletin.*

branch banking, and in some cases through bank mergers. However, both state laws limiting branch banking and federal policies with respect to bank mergers restricted the pace of these adjustments.

A New Spirit of Regulation.   In the 1970s, as Figures 15-1, 15-2, and 15-3 show clearly, the pattern again changed. The admission of new banks increased, from an annual average of 129 per annum in the years 1950-1969 to 250 per annum in 1970-1980. With mergers and closures following their historical patterns, the number of banks in the system again increased. However, the number of unit banks continued to fall (and increasing numbers of the unit banks became members of banking groups), while the number of branch banking firms increased sharply. The number of banking *offices* increased even more sharply.

To a significant degree, the developments of the 1970s reflect a new thrust in banking regulation, with more emphasis on the encouragement of competition. We will consider this further in Chapter 16.

Branch and Group Banking: A Convergence of the Systems?   In short, it might be argued that while it started with a very different structure, the American banking system has been moving slowly and tentatively in the direction of a structure like that of the Canadian banking system. That is, the branch banking form of organization has been growing at the expense of unit banking. However, the extent of this movement has been restricted by both federal and state policies, and the present structure of the system still stands in stark contrast to the structure of the Canadian system. Public policy had profound effects on the development of both the Canadian and the American banking systems; and to a significant degree, it is differences in public policy which explain the remarkably different structures of the two systems. Before turning to an analysis of the development of public policy in the United States and the lessons which it may have for Canadians, however, it is useful to review briefly the structure of the near banking system in the United States. Like the banking system, it also has some features which are unfamiliar to Canadians.

NEAR BANKS

The United States has a rich variety of specialized financial intermediaries in addition to commercial banks. Many of these — insurance companies, pension funds, mutual funds, finance companies — are the direct counterparts of institutions found in Canada and discussed in earlier chapters. Although there are differences in detail, the operations of these intermediaries are sufficiently similar in both countries that we need not discuss them further. Indeed, many insurance and finance companies have operations on both sides of the border.

Moreover, as is apparent in Table 15-4, while near banks have a slightly greater relative importance in the United States, and life insurance companies in Canada, the structure of the financial system is almost identical in the two countries, except within the near bank sector. In the case of near banks, the United States has institutions which have no exact counterpart in Canada.

TABLE 15-4   **Comparison of the structures of the financial systems of Canada and the United States: total assets of major financial intermediaries, December 31, 1980**

	United States		Canada	
	$ Billions	*Percent*	*$ Billions*	*Percent*
Commercial banks	1 887	43	171	44
Near banks	873	20	91	23
Savings and loan	630	14	—	—
Mutual savings banks	172	4	—	—
Credit unions	72	2	32	8
Trust and loan companies	—	—	55	14
Quebec savings banks	—	—	2	—
Government depositories	—	—	2	1
Other intermediaries	1 626	37	127	33
Life insurance companies	476	11	38	10
Other insurance companies	187	4	20	5
Pension funds	729	17	50	13
Mutual funds	58	1	5	1
Finance companies	175	4	14	4
Total	4 385	100	389	100

SOURCES: *Federal Reserve Bulletin,* July, 1981; *Statistical Abstract of the United States, 1981* (Washington: Government Printing Office, 1981); Statistics Canada, *Financial Flow Accounts,* fourth quarter, 1981; *Bank of Canada Review,* January, 1982.

Types of Near Banks

Savings and Loan Associations.   The most important type of near bank in the United States is the savings and loan association. The consolidated balance sheet for all savings and loan associations is summarized in Table 15-5.

Savings and loan associations play the same role in the financial system of the United States as do trust and mortgage loan companies in Canada. They intermediate between individual savers and the mortgage market. Their major liabilities are savings deposits, highly liquid, relatively safe financial instruments which are attractive substitutes for money in the portfolios of individual assetholders. The major use of funds is to make mortgage loans, and they hold about the same proportion of their assets in mortgages as do Canadian mortgage loan companies (82%).

Like commerical banks, savings and loan associations may be incorporated by either the federal government or state governments. All federal associations must be "mutual," i.e., owned by their depositors, like a cooperative bank or a mutual insurance company. The "deposits" in a mutual association are actually "shares" on which dividends are paid. Some states permit "stock" associations to be incorporated as well. A stock association is like a regular commercial corporation. It has a separate set of stockholders who own the business and share in its profits. (At the end of 1978 about 15% of the 4700 savings and loan associations in the United States were stock associations.)

TABLE 15-5 **Near banks in the United States, December 31, 1980 ($ Billions)**

	Savings and loan associations	Mutual savings banks	Credit unions
Cash	57.6*	4.3	
Mortgages	502.8	99.9	
Other loans		11.7	47.8
Securities		50.6	
Other assets	69.4	5.0	23.9
Total assets	629.8	171.6	71.7
Deposits	511.0	154.8	64.4
Other liabilities	84.8	5.4	7.3
Net worth and reserves	33.3	11.4	

* Includes "investment securities."
SOURCE: *Federal Reserve Bulletin,* July, 1981.

Mutual Savings Banks.   Next in importance to savings and loan associations are mutual savings banks. The consolidated balance sheet of mutual savings banks is also summarized in Table 15-5.

As their name implies, these banks are also mutual associations, owned by their depositors. They operate under charters issued by 17 states, primarily in the Northeast (and particularly in New York, Massachusetts, and Pennsylvania). At the end of 1979, there were approximately 460 mutual savings banks in the United States.

As can be seen in Table 15-5, the primary business of the mutual savings banks is also intermediation between households and the mortgage market. Their main source of funds are savings deposits, and their main use of funds mortgage loans. Thus, both in their organization and in the nature of their financial intermediation they are much like savings and loan associations. However, they operate under charters which permit them to follow a much more flexible investment policy than savings and loan associations.

Credit Unions.   American credit unions are essentially the same as Canadian credit unions (as distinguished from *caisses populaires*). This should not be surprising, because the credit union movement is international and the Canadian credit union movement drew a major stimulus from the American movement in the early 1940s. Credit unions are local mutual associations, normally organized on industrial or occupational lines. They accumulate funds in savings "shares" or deposits, and make personal loans to members for a variety of purposes. They may have federal or state charters. Federal credit unions are supervised and examined by the National Credit Union Administration. State credit unions are supervised by the state authorities, although those which have joined the deposit insurance fund of the National Credit Union Administration are also supervised and examined by the federal agency.

Credit unions are relatively less important in the financial system of the United States than they are in Canada (but remember that the Canadian figures include *caisses populaires* which have a somewhat different character). At the end of 1979, there were about 22 000 credit unions (12 700 with federal charters and 9300 with state charters) with total assets of $66 billion (about 11% of the total assets of savings and loan associations).

Characteristics of Near Banks

This very brief survey suggests that the major differences between the near banking sectors in Canada and the United States are in the names of the institutions rather than in the substance of their business. This is essentially correct and, in recent years, near banks in the two countries have become more alike, as both have invaded some of the traditional preserves of commercial banks. However, there are some respects in which the American near bank sector differs from its Canadian counterpart.

Trusteeship Function.   In Canada, chartered banks have not been permitted to assume trusteeship functions. A separate group of institutions, trust companies, exist for this purpose, and they have developed into the country's largest and most important near banks. Given the close connection between commercial banking activities and the trusteeship business, the chartered banks developed working arrangements with trust companies, and indeed some chartered banks have close ownership affiliations with trust companies. In the United States, by contrast, the trusteeship function can be freely assumed by commercial banks. As a result, there are few trust companies which are not commerical banks, and those that do exist are not deposit-accepting institutions. The peculiar Canadian near bank, the non-bank trust company, does not exist in the United States.

Dualism: Fragmentation and Compartmentalization.   The system of dual control, federal and state, which we noted earlier in connection with commercial banks, is also characteristic of the near banking system. A division of authority between federal and provincial governments is also present in Canada, but here it has not prevented the development of nationwide networks of branch offices by major trust and loan companies. Savings and loan associations and mutual savings banks are permitted to operate branches in most states, but large, nationwide firms cannot exist. There are some interstate holding companies which control several stock savings and loan associations, but legislation in 1959 prohibited the formation of additional holding companies or the acquisition of new associations by existing holding companies. There are no restrictions on interstate branching by federally-chartered credit unions (a fact which has induced some state-chartered credit unions to take out federal charters).

The consequences of relatively rigid dualism are not simply the fragmentation of banks and near banks into many small firms. It has also tended to put each category of financial intermediary into a separate compartment, with its own regulatory authorities and support facilities (deposit insurance and lender of last resort facilities).

Deposit Insurance. In 1967, Canada established a system of deposit insurance for banks and certain near banks. In the United States, a system of federal insurance for mutual savings banks and savings and loan associations is of longer standing, dating from the banking reforms of the early 1930s.

Mutual savings banks are eligible for insurance by the Federal Deposit Insurance Corporation, the agency which insures deposits in commercial banks. Two-thirds of the mutual savings banks, holding over 90% of the assets of mutual savings banks, are so insured. In addition, the State of Massachusetts operates its own deposit insurance plan for mutual savings banks. Savings and loan associations can obtain similar insurance from another federal agency, the Federal Savings and Loan Insurance Corporation. All federal associations must take out this insurance, but it is optional for state-chartered associations. Almost three-quarters of all associations are so insured. Some states have their own insurance plans. Since 1970, federally-guaranteed insurance is also available to credit unions through the National Credit Union Administration. Insurance is compulsory for federally-chartered credit unions and is available to state-chartered credit unions which meet the Administration's financial and management standards. All members are subject to regular examination and supervision by the Administration, so that, as with the other types of deposit insurance, a side effect has been to extend federal control to state chartered institutions.

Lender-of-Last-Resort Facilities. Most near banks do not have direct access to central bank credit in the United States.[12] However, unlike Canada, the United States developed a special lender of last resort for savings and loan associations and mutual savings banks — the Federal Home Loan Bank System.

The Federal Home Loan Bank System was established in 1932 to provide lender-of-last-resort facilities to institutions involved in residential mortgage lending. In structure it is similar to the Federal Reserve System. Thus, there are 12 regional Federal Home Loan Banks, under the supervision of the Federal Home Loan Bank Board. Like the Federal Reserve Banks, the Home Loan Banks make short-term emergency loans to members faced with unexpected withdrawals of deposits (called withdrawal advances), but, unlike Federal Reserve Banks, they also make longer-term loans to members as a more or less permanent addition to the borrowing association's resources (called expansion advances). The Banks finance their advances with deposits by member associations, including interest-bearing time deposits, and with funds raised on the open market. The System also has a line of credit with the Federal Treasury which can be drawn upon in an emergency.[13]

The presence of a lender of last resort of this type undoubtedly helps explain why savings and loan associations hold such a large portion of their assets in otherwise illiquid mortgages in spite of the fact that their deposit liabilities are effectively payable on demand. The banker's risk is, in effect, shifted to the Federal Home Loan Banks. However, the Federal Home Loan Banks also serve another purpose. They mobilize funds, largely in the open market but partly from members in areas where there are surplus savings, for investment in areas of the country where the supply of mortgage money is relatively less adequate and mortgage rates relatively high. To a limited extent, they thus substitute for nationwide branch organizations and help surmount the imperfections of the national capital market. In recent years, advances from Federal Home Loan Banks have amounted to less than 4% of the assets of savings and loan association, but their importance is increasing.

To a limited extent, the Federal Home Loan Bank System can also operate like a central bank, deliberately manipulating the volume of funds available to member institutions. On occasion, by restricting the availability of "expansion advances" to members, the System has helped reinforce the policies of the Federal Reserve System.

Membership in the Federal Home Loan Bank System is compulsory for all federal savings and loan associations, and is optional for mutual savings banks and state savings and loan associations.

Under very recent legislation (1979), the Central Liquidity Facility of the National Credit Union Administration now stands as a lender of last resort for credit unions, both federal and state.

GOVERNMENT REGULATION OF BANKING: PRINCIPLES OF PUBLIC POLICY TO 1970

To a Canadian observer, the arrangements for the chartering, regulation, and supervision of banks and near banks in the United States are of bewildering complexity. This is not a product of a conscious design. Rather, it reflects a long and contentious history of interaction between state and federal governments, and among agencies within the federal government. The unique product has been labelled the "dual banking system."

The Dual Banking System

The Constitutional Issue.   The issues between the federal and state authorities have their roots in the interpretation of the Constitution of the United States. Like Canada, the United States has a federal form of government, with governmental responsibilities constitutionally divided between the federal and the state authorities. The Constitution explicitly assigns to the federal government the power to "coin money and regulate its value", but, in contrast to the *British North America Act*, it makes no mention of the regulation of banking. Since powers not specifically granted to the federal government were reserved to the states, the states claimed the right to incorporate and regulate banks.

First and Second Bank of the United States.   The right of the individual states to charter and regulate banks thus has a firm constitutional basis. However, the federal government also claimed this right. In 1791, the federal government chartered the First

Bank of the United States, and following its demise, chartered the Second Bank of the United States in 1816. These banks carried on a commercial banking business through branches in various parts of the country (providing the model for the Canadian banking system), but they were also incipient central banks, striving to bring order and stability to a banking system populated by state-chartered institutions, many of which were small, unreliable, "wildcat" banks. In the face of strong political pressures, the charters of the federal banks were revoked, although their constitutionality was affirmed by the Supreme Court. This not only delayed the establishment of a true central bank, but also meant that the principle of nationwide branch banking under the supervision of the federal government was never established in the United States.

The National Bank Act.   The *National Bank Act* of 1863 created a permanent federal presence in the field of commercial banking. This Act provided for the chartering of a new class of commercial banks, to be called national banks. In general, the federal requirements for a bank charter were more restrictive than state requirements. Cash reserves and minimum capital requirements were higher, there were stricter controls over loans and investments (e.g., mortgage loans were prohibited initially), and there were superior provisions for the security of banknote holders. Significantly, the legislation left the status of branch banking ambiguous, neither granting nor explicitly denying the right to operate branches. However, the lack of explicit authority to open branches was interpreted as denying permission. It was not until 1927 that national banks were permitted to open branches, and then only in the city in which their head office was located. In 1933, this restriction was removed. National banks were permitted to open branches providing they abided by whatever restrictions the state in question had imposed on branch banking by its state banks. In this way the principle of state precedence in the matter of branch banking was accepted, and *nationwide* branch banking by national banks effectively prohibited (except through interstate group banks).

It was hoped that the strict controls over national banks would give them an appearance of greater security and stability which would provide a competitive advantage over state banks, so that state-chartered institutions would be driven from the industry. However, the demise of state banks did not materialize, in spite of a discriminatory tax imposed on bank notes issued by state banks. As a result, the United States ended up with a "dual banking system" — a system under which there are two parallel sets of laws, regulations, and regulatory authorities governing banks and banking. Indeed, since each state has its own laws and regulations, there are, in effect, 51 banking systems. As we have seen, the same principle was extended to near banks.

It could be argued that the existence of 51 chartering authorities does not necessarily imply the high degree of fragmentation of the banking system which we observe in the United States. Indeed, if all 51 governments had similar banking statutes, put no limits on branch banking, and allowed full rights to banks chartered in other states on a reciprocal basis, the structure of the American system might only marginally different from our own. However, the fact is that the states did not develop a uniform approach to banking regulation and do not grant reciprocal rights to banks chartered in other states.

Principles of Public Policy

It is difficult to account for the extreme diversity of banking policies among states and between the state and federal governments without a searching examination of American banking and political history. However, there are at least four themes which stand out in the historical record: "populism," the search for stability through a central bank, the avoidance of "overbanking," and the preservation of competition. Their interaction has produced an amazing tangle of regulatory authorities with differing, and often conflicting, objectives.

"Populism" and the Banking Structure

Fragmentation of the banking system occurred as a matter of deliberate design in many states, particularly in the Midwest and South. During the formative period in banking legislation, what we earlier called "populism" was the dominant political force in these areas (as, in some respects, it still is). Basic to this doctrine was the belief that local affairs (very broadly defined) should be locally controlled. This manifests itself partly in pressure for the decentralization of political authority (local authority versus the state, states rights versus the federal government), and partly in a fear of centralization of economic power through ubiquitous industrial and financial "trusts."

Unit Banking.   Banking was obviously of critical importance from the populist point of view, and decentralization of banking could be best achieved through unit banking. Branch banking was prohibited or severely restricted in most states in this area, and the "populist" forces fought bitterly against the First and Second Banks of the United States, and against all subsequent moves to create uniformity and to expand federal authority. Even the central bank, when it was eventually established in 1913, was decentralized. It was a system of 12 regional central banks, owned by the commercial banks themselves, and with only limited centralized co-ordination.

Although state banking laws have been changing, and many exceptions to once rigid legal restrictions have been allowed, there are still 11 states in the South and Midwest which are generally considered "unit banking" states. In another 16 states, predominantly in the same area but including some of the major eastern states (i.e., Massachusetts, New Jersey, and New York), branch banking is severely restricted, in some cases to the county in which the head office is located and in other cases to that and contiguous counties. Only 23 states, and the District of Columbia, permit unlimited statewide branch banking. These states are predominantly in the East and the Far West. Interstate branch banking is prohibited, except, as we have seen, through the device of group banks. As we noted earlier, national banks are required to abide by the relevant state banking regulations with respect to branch banking.

Free Banking.   In addition to restrictions on branch banking, populist banking policy involved "free banking." Pioneered in New York in 1838, the free banking principle for the granting of bank charters soon spread to all states, and was incorporated into the *National Bank Act* of 1863. This principle required the banking authority to grant a charter to any individual or group which satisfied certain minimum requirements set down in the statute. It allowed no administrative discretion. The purpose was to prevent the granting of monopolistic privileges by opening the industry to all who thought they could make a profit. The effect was a rapid proliferation of small banks.

The Search For Stability: The Central Bank

If populist banking policies meant free entry to the banking industry, and banks which were small, locally owned, and sensitive to local credit requirements, it all too often also meant banks which had weak management and insufficiently diversified portfolios, and which were peculiarly vulnerable to bankruptcy. As we have already seen, the American banking system had a history of devastating instability. The search for methods to eliminate this instability provided a second theme in American public policy, and, since it was inevitably centralizing in its effects, this search came into sharp conflict with the populist principle.

There were several early attempts to bring discipline and stability to the banking system, some by state governments and some by the federal government. We have already seen that the First and Second Banks of the United States and the *National Bank Act* were both unsuccessful attempts on a national level. The same might be said of the eventual establishment of a central bank in 1913.

The Federal Reserve System: A Compromise With Populism.   In principle, a central bank should be able to underwrite the stability of the banking system. While it may not be able to prevent the failure of selected individual banks which have been the victims of fraud, bad management, or an unfortunate combination of circumstances, by standing as a lender of last resort it should be able to prevent the failure of some banks from bringing down other banks in their train. However, the Federal Reserve System proved incapable of saving the system in the 1929-1933 debacle. Part of the problem was the nature of the central bank. While the National Monetary Commission had recommended the establishment of a strong central bank with broad powers, what was enacted was a compromise with populism.

The pre-eminence of states' rights meant that membership in the Federal Reserve System could only be made compulsory for national banks. Membership was voluntary for state banks. On the eve of the crisis in 1929, two-thirds of the commercial banks in the United States (holding, however, only one-third of bank assets) were not members of the Federal Reserve System. Although the financial troubles of the 1930s sharply increased the importance of the Federal Reserve System, by the mid-1960s almost 60% of all commercial banks were non-members (although they held less than 20% of bank assets), and this proportion was rising as banks gave up their membership. Voluntarism was a serious limitation to the extension of federal control over the banking system. It meant not only that most banks did not have access to the central bank as a lender of last resort, but also that the Federal Reserve System could not impose strict standards on its members without inducing many of them to forsake membership (including, perhaps, a national bank charter) for non-membership.

In its internal organization, the Federal Reserve System was decentralized. It was not to be a monolithic national central bank, but a federation of 12 regional reserve banks. Moreover, the individual Federal Reserve Banks were not to be owned by the federal government, but by the member banks, with elaborate controls to ensure that the boards of directors could not be dominated by the larger banks in the district. The national body that was also created, the Federal Reserve Board, with members appointed by the President of the United States, had very little power.

The Federal Reserve Banks were to hold the cash reserves of member banks, and, within limits, they could issue notes to be used as currency. However, their main activity was to make advances to member banks, as necessary. A crucial restriction was that all such advances had to take the form of "rediscounts" of "eligible paper" — short-term promissory notes which the member banks had taken in security for normal commercial loans to farmers, merchants, or industrial firms. That is, the Federal Reserve Banks were not given full discretion in managing the supply of money and credit, but had their actions tied to the real bills principle. The extension of credit by the Federal Reserve Banks was to be dictated by the "need of trade," as interpreted by member banks. The Federal Reserve System was not designed as a vehicle for a vigorous, centralized national monetary policy.

Reform of 1933-34: Moves to Centralization.   The crisis of 1933 produced a fundamental change in the Federal Reserve System. The appearance of a decentralized service organization for member banks was maintained, but the substance of it was revoked. Two interrelated centralizing institutions were created. First, the weak Federal Reserve Board was transformed into a strong Board of Governors of the Federal Reserve System, with statutory independence from political pressures (each governor is appointed by the President of the United States for a 14-year term, with only one governor retiring every other year). Second, an *ad hoc* co-ordinating committee for transactions in government securities which had emerged in the 1920s was given legislative status as the Open Market Committee. It is a 12-man body, including the seven Governors and five representatives of the 12 Federal Reserve Banks. The Open Market Committee has sole authority over Federal Reserve transactions in U.S. government securities.

On the operational side, the link to the real bills doctrine was discarded, and along with it the notion that the Federal Reserve System should play a passive role in the financial system. In spite of the relaxation of the rules governing advances, quantitatively, discounts and advances declined to insignificance. Transactions in government securities became the primary vehicle for the extension of credit to the banking system. This placed the initiative for credit policy in the hands of the centralized Open Market Committee, not the individual Federal Reserve Banks or the discounting member banks. Moreover, the Board of Governors was given the power to vary the cash reserve requirements of member banks, a powerful, if blunt, instrument of monetary control.

The transformation of the Federal Reserve System into a centralized agency for monetary policy was not the only significant change in government policy toward the banking structure in the period 1933-35. Perhaps more important in terms of extending federal control over the commercial banking system was the creation of the Federal Deposit Insurance Corporation. For near banks, parallel institutions were created in the Federal Home Loan Bank Board and the associated Federal Savings and Loan Insurance Corporation. A Federal Bureau of Credit Unions was also established, but it was not until the 1970s, which it was superseded by the National Credit Union Administration, that effective central control was extended to state-chartered credit unions.

The Avoidance of "Overbanking"

While not the primary purpose of the plan, as it turned out, the establishment of the Federal Deposit Insurance Corporation made it possible for the federal government to exert considerable control over the subsequent evolution of the structure of the banking system.

The Federal Deposit Insurance Corporation.   The F.D.I.C. provides insurance to bank depositors, guaranteeing the safety of their deposits in insured banks. Membership in this plan was made compulsory for all members of the Federal Reserve System, but was also made available to non-member banks who could qualify under the F.D.I.C.'s strict standards. The plan proved to be immensely popular. By the end of the first year of operation, 85% of all non-member banks had been admitted to the insurance plan. Now, almost all banks are insured by the F.D.I.C.

New Banking Policies.   With federal deposit insurance virtually a *since qua non* of banking, the federal government was placed in a strong position to impose new policies on the whole banking system. A new pattern of banking policies emerged, emphasizing the soundness of assets and management policies, limitations on "destructive competition," and the avoidance of "overbanking."

In order to improve the quality of assets and management policies, federal supervision was extended to all state banks which joined the F.D.I.C. This involved new, conservative criteria for the valuation of bank assets, and regular inspection by federal officials. Federal bank examiners not only assess and report on the quality of the bank's assets, but also on the quality of the bank's management.

Both competition for deposits among established banks and the entry of new banks were restricted. Thus, the payment of interest on demand deposits was prohibited, and the Federal Reserve System and the F.D.I.C. were required to set ceilings on interest rates which could be paid on savings and time deposits. It was argued that free competition via interest rates had contributed to the instability of the banking system. Badly managed and irresponsible banks were said to have paid excessive interest, forcing otherwise sound institutions into financial difficulties. Initially, the ceiling was accepted with enthusiasm by many bankers, but in the 1960s it became an object of controversy. In the face of rising interest rates, the ceiling established under the Federal Reserve's "Regulation Q" limited the banks' flexibility in meeting competition from near banks, foreign banks, and the money market, and as a result there was considerable agitation to eliminate or modify it.[14]

Entry was regulated on all sides. A new bank not only had to obtain a charter from the state or national authorities, but also a certificate of insurance from the F.D.I.C.[15] Both the Comptroller of the Currency, in issuing new bank charters, and the F.D.I.C., in issuing new insurance certificates, were required to consider such things as the bank's "future earnings prospects," "the general character of its management," and "the convenience and needs of the community to be served." A bank similarly had to obtain approval for an increase in its capital or for the opening of new branches, with the same criteria to be applied by the regulatory authorities.

We saw earlier how the new policies affected the development of the banking structure. Bank failures became relatively rare, and losses to depositors even rarer, the number of banks in the system declined steadily, and until the early 1950s, the number of bank offices increased slowly. Branch banking became the dominant form for the expansion of banking facilities.

The Preservation of Competition as a Policy Objective

The reforms of the 1930s were designed to rationalize and stabilize the banking system, in large part by extending federal regulation and by restricting competition. In the 1950s and 1960s, as stability seemed to have been achieved, renewed emphasis was gradually placed on the preservation of competition in banking markets, particularly where competition was threatened by a proliferation of bank holding companies or by bank mergers. Thus, under the *Bank Holding Company Act* of 1956, bank holding companies were required to register with the Board of Governors of the Federal Reserve System, and the Board's approval was required for all acquisitions of banks by holding companies. In addition to various factors relating to the management and financial condition of the banks and the "needs and convenience" of the community, the Board was required to consider the impact on competition in assessing such applications. Similarly, under the *Bank Merger Act* of 1960, all bank mergers involving banks under federal jurisdiction required prior approval, and again the impact on competition was one of the factors which had to be considered in assessing applications. Moreover, Supreme Court decisions held that banks were subject to the antitrust laws, which in effect made the impact on competition the primary consideration in considering mergers.

In spite of the new emphasis on competition, however, the dominant themes in banking policy through the 1960s were centralization and regulation, in the interest of stability.

Public Policy and the Banking Structure

The banking system of the United States has developed under the often conflicting pressures of public policies administered by state governments and several agencies of the federal government. Indeed, the very complexities of the banking structure which are so perplexing to Canadian observers are themselves a direct product of complex and conflicting public policies. The role of "the authorities" is ubiquitous. Thus:

> Private entrepreneurs are not permitted to enter the banking industry without the consent of the public authorities. Where they are allowed to enter, they may branch or merge only with the approval of the public authorities. While private entrepreneurs are left the choice whether to seek entry or to seek expansion of their banking operations, the ultimate decisions on bank entry and bank expansion through branching or merger is assigned to the public authorities.[16]

This represents a degree of governmental control over the banking system which is unknown in Canada. Perhaps it is not surprising that a major drive for deregulation began in the 1970s.

ENDNOTES

1. Banks are permitted to hold uninsured mortgages to the extent of their stockholder's equity or 70% of their combined time and savings deposits, whichever is greater. There is no limit on holdings of federally insured mortgages.
2. The actual reserve ratios were not always lower (although in most cases they were). However, the requirements could frequently be met by holding interest-bearing assets, certain securities or deposits with correspondent banks.
3. The American banks' involvement in the Euro-dollar market as a technique for domestic cash adjustments is discussed briefly in "Euro-dollars: A Changing Market," in *Federal Reserve Bulletin*, Vol. 55 (Oct. 1969), pp. 765-84.
4. The data in Table 15-3 are different from those in Table 15-1. The latter includes all assets, domestic and foreign. The former includes only domestic assets. If foreign assets were included, the range of the size distribution would be even more extreme because the foreign assets are concentrated among the larger banks.
5. "Developments in Banking Structure, 1970-1981," *Federal Reserve Bulletin 68* (February 1982), pp. 77-85. It should be noted that there are many more bank holding companies than this. Many bank holding companies own only one bank (single bank holding companies), a form of organization adopted for taxation purposes.
6. *Moody's Bank and Finance Manual*, Vol. 3 (1981), pp. 396-97.
7. J. C. Darnell, "Chain Banking," *National Banking Review*, Vol. 3 (Mar. 1966), pp. 307-31.
8. "Chain Banking in the District," Federal Reserve Bank of Chicago, *Economic Perspectives* (Sept/Oct., 1977), pp. 15-20.
9. The classic discussion of these issues is D. Alhadeff, *Monopoly and Competition in Banking* (Berkeley, California: University of California Press, 1954). See also C. H. Kreps, Jr., "Characteristics of Local Banking Competition," in D. Carson, ed., *Banking and Monetary Studies* (Homewood, Illinois: R. Irwin, 1963), pp. 319-332; Guttentag and Herman, *op. cit.*, pp. 34-38.
10. J. M. Guttentag and E. S. Herman, "Banking Structure and Performance," in *The Bulletin*, New York University, Graduate School of Business Administration, Institute of Finance, No. 41/43 (Feb. 1967), pp. 47-50. Similar data are reported in C. H. Kreps, Jr., *op. cit.*, and "Changes in Banking Structure, 1953-62," in *Federal Reserve Bulletin*, Vol. 49 (Sept. 1963), pp. 1191-98.
11. The presence of group and chain banking also increases the degree of concentration in local banking markets. We noted some aspects of this in our discussion of group banks. There is little comparable information for chain banks, but the study referred to earlier found that in 1962 over half of all chains had their affiliated banks in one county, suggesting that chains did increase concentration in certain local markets in a significant degree. Darnell, "Chain Banking."
12. Mutual Savings Banks are eligible for membership in the Federal Reserve System, but none have chosen to join. However, mutual savings banks in New York have organized their own "central bank," the Savings Bank Trust Company, which is a member of the Federal Reserve System.

13. The Federal Home Loan Bank Board is also responsible for the Federal Savings and Loan Insurance Corporation, which also has a line of credit with the Treasury. Under recent legislation, the Federal Reserve System was given the authority to purchase bonds of agencies like the Federal Home Loan Bank Board, and has used this power to a limited extent. This also provides a residual source of liquidity for the system.

14. Regulation Q applies to member banks, but the F.D.I.C. adopts the same ceilings for non-member insured banks. In 1966, a similar ceiling was imposed on rates paid by savings institutions, administered by the Federal Home Loan Bank Board.

15. Unless, of course, it chooses to operate without F.D.I.C. insurance. It has been reported, however, that many state banking authorities refuse to issue a charter unless the F.D.I.C. will issue a certificate of insurance (see Comptroller of the Currency, *Annual Report*, 1964, p. 242).

16. A. Brimmer, "Market Structure, Public Convenience and the Regulation of Bank Mergers," *The Banking Law Journal*, Vol. 86 (Sept. 1964), pp. 773-93.

TWO PATHS TO A COMPETITIVE FINANCIAL SYSTEM 16

Starting with very different financial structures and very different traditions of regulation of financial institutions, both Canada and the United States set new courses for the regulation of the financial system in the late 1960s and the 1970s. The paths differ, in part because the starting points differ, but the objective is the same — a more competitive financial system. Changes in direction in policy seldom happen abruptly. This was no exception. In both countries there was a long period of transition, in which new developments in the financial system were studied intensively by committees and legislators. However, there were important legislative focal points: in Canada, the *Bank Acts* of 1967 and 1980, and in the United States, the *Depository Institutions Deregulation and Monetary Control Act* of 1980.

CANADA: THE ROYAL COMMISSION ON BANKING AND FINANCE

The starting point for the study of the new course of public policy in Canada must be the Royal Commission on Banking and Finance (commonly called the Porter Commission, after its chairman, Dana Porter). Appointed in 1962, with a broad mandate "to enquire into and report upon the structure and methods of operation of the Canadian financial system,"[1] the commission reported in 1964 with broad sweeping recommendations for revisions to banking policy. Much of the *Report* was devoted to a review and assessment of the performance of financial institutions; and the recommendations showed a deep concern for competition in the financial system. While not all of the Commission's major recommendations were accepted, the *Report* had a powerful impact on banking legislation in 1967 (and again in 1980).

The Porter Commission's studies must be seen in the context of a major change in the Canadian financial system, in effect the development of an alternative banking system.

An Alternative Banking System

The 1950s and early 1960s saw the emergence and vigorous growth of an alternative banking system, at least for a range of banking activities. Credit unions, *caisses populaires*, mortgage loan companies, and trust companies competed imaginatively and effectively with chartered banks for the savings deposit and term deposit business of Canadian households and firms, and for some lending business, particularly mortgages and personal loans (cooperative banks). New firms were established and new offices were opened at convenient locations in cities across Canada; new services were offered to customers, including chequing facilities and more flexible opening hours; and relatively attractive interest rates were offered on deposits and loans. Over the 15-year period 1951-1966, the total Canadian deposits of the chartered banks increased 2.5 times, from $8 billion to $20 billion. At the same time, the liabilities of *caisses populaires* and credit unions increased 8.2 times, from $359 million to $2.9 billion, and deposits with trust and mortgage loan companies 8.6 times, from $630 million to $5.4 billion. From minor factors in the financial system, by the mid-1960s the near banks could no longer be ignored. Their total deposits had grown to about 40% of the total Canadian deposits of the chartered banks.

To some extent, the differential growth of the near banks was fostered by the differential regulation of the two banking systems. Almost all of the near banks operated under provincial jurisdictions, whereas the chartered banks were a federal responsibility; and, in general, the provincial regulations were less burdensome on the near banks than were the federal regulations on the chartered banks. It is difficult to generalize about the regulation of the near banks because provinces had different rules for the various categories of near banks, and for any given category the rules varied among provinces. However, three restrictions on the activities of the chartered banks seem to have been particularly important in fostering the expansion of near banks: relatively heavy cash and secondary reserve requirements; a 6% ceiling on interest rates on loans; and restrictions on mortgage lending, particularly on uninsured mortgages. For the near banks, reserve requirements were more flexible, and did not force them to hold large amounts of sterile cash; there were no effective ceilings on interest rates on loans; and the field of mortgage credit was wide open. Their almost unrestricted ability to make mortgage loans provided a powerful impetus for their remarkable spurt of growth.

The appropriate nature and scope of competition between the two banking systems was one of the top items on the agenda for banking reform in the mid-1960s, along with the question of competition within the banking system more narrowly defined.

In this context, the Porter Commission made two central proposals: *unification and centralization of regulation* of financial institutions, and emphasis on *increased competition* among such institutions.

Uniform Regulation of Financial Institutions

Canada is a federal state, with a constitutional division of powers and responsibilities between federal and provincial governments. The *British North America Act* assigned to the federal government exclusive responsibility for many aspects of the financial system, including interest rates, bills of exchange and promissory notes, currency and coinage, the incorporation of banks, savings banks, and "banking" in general. If we accept a comprehensive definition of the concept of "banking" this would seem to give the federal government broad powers over most financial intermediaries. However, neither the constitution nor the courts has provided a definition of "banking," and the effective definition is limited to those institutions specifically enumerated in the *Bank Act* or the *Quebec Savings Bank Act*. Only those institutions are permitted to use the words "bank," "banker," or "banking" to describe their business.

The *B.N.A. Act* assigned to the provinces exclusive jurisdiction over "property and civil rights" and the incorporation of companies "with provincial objects." This has meant that the responsibility for regulating markets in securities is provincial, and the provincial governments have the right to charter and supervise all types of financial institutions except "banks." Even the requirements that provincial companies must have "provincial objects" has proven to be of little significance. Simply by registering in other provinces as extra-provincial companies, many provincially incorporated financial institutions are able to carry on a nationwide business.

Because we have 11 centers of policy making with overlapping jurisdictions, it is not surprising that the Royal Commission on Banking and Finance found "a mixed and sometimes confused pattern of regulation."[2] The constitutional division of powers places a major obstacle in the way of a unified national policy. To obtain such a policy would require federal-provincial and interprovincial cooperation, or definitive legal interpretations (e.g., of the scope of "banking") permitting the assertion of federal supremacy in the regulation of financial affairs. Substantial progress has in fact been made through provincial government cooperation to develop uniform regulations for security trading. Furthermore, there is considerable similarity among provincial laws governing provincially incorporated financial institutions. (Provincial arrangements for continuing inspection and supervision in both fields, however, differ significantly.)

The Royal Commission, in an effort to achieve a uniform policy, urged the more radical approach of unilateral federal assertion of jurisdiction over all private financial institutions engaged in the "business of banking," broadly defined to include the issuing of all

> ...claims which may be transferred immediately or on short notice by cheques or on customers orders..., other demand liabilities..., [and] term deposits, whatever their formal name, and other claims...maturing or redeemable at a fixed price within 100 days of the time of original issue or of the time at which notice of withdrawal is given by the customer...[3]

Such a definition would include all provincially-incorporated near banks. Furthermore, since the Commission recommended that all other institutions should be "prohibited unequivocally from operating as banks,"[4] the result would have been a substantial reduction in provincial responsibility for and power over financial institutions.

Parliament chose not to act on this central proposal of the Porter Commission for a truly comprehensive banking law in the 1967 revision of the *Bank Act*. Many authorities doubted that it was constitutional, or, if constitutional, that it was politic in view of contemporary federal-provincial relations. A similar provision became the centerpiece of the American reform of 1980. In Canada, the issue reemerged 10 years later, in the next major study of the financial system, but, as we shall see, while some progress was made in the 1980 *Bank Act*, the concept remains an item of unfinished business.

Competition as an Objective of Policy

Whether uniformity of regulation was achieved or not, the Porter Commission strongly urged that increased competition become a primary objective of governmental policy — both competition among banks and between banks and other financial institutions. The Commission's research provided the first comprehensive and thorough analysis of concentration and competition in the Canadian financial system. We will not explore their analysis of competition in other financial markets, but rather will focus on the banking system, the main object of the reforms introduced in the *Bank Acts* of 1967.[5]

Concentration in Banking.   By the mid-1960s there were only eight chartered banks in Canada. As can be seen in Table 16-1, only five of these could be said to be nationwide "retail" banking firms, with significant branch banking operations in most, if not all provinces. These five banks among them held over 93% of the total assets of chartered banks (the three largest accounted for over two-thirds of total assets). Two smaller banks were primarily regional, with most of their offices concentrated in Quebec and contiguous areas (generally in French-speaking communities), the largest of which had less than half the assets of the smallest of the big five. The smallest bank had only seven offices in major cities across Canada and was relatively specialized in international finance (although it was rapidly expanding its Canadian business).

In other branches of financial intermediation, while a relatively high degree of concentration of assets in the hands of a few large firms was typical (except in the case of cooperative banks), there were many more firms and the degree of concentration was not as extreme as in the case of chartered banks. Thus, at the end of 1966 there were almost 4800 cooperative banks, 135 life insurance companies, over 300 general insurance companies, over 100 trust and loan companies, over 80 consumer loan companies, and over 60 mutual funds. The percentages of assets held by the five largest firms in some of these categories were as follows: trust companies, 53%; mortgage loan companies, 75%; life insurance companies, 48%; consumer loan companies, 68%; and mutual funds, 69%.

Concentration and Competition.   Chartered banking in Canada in the mid-1960s was an industry which obviously fell into the analytical category of "oligopoly" — an industry in which there are a few dominant firms, each of which is acutely conscious that its market position depends directly on the competitive actions of the other firms.

TABLE 16-1 Concentration in the Canadian chartered banking system, December 31, 1966

	Total assets		Canadian Assets		Offices					
	$ Millions	Percent	$ Millions	Percent	B.C.*	Prairie Prov.	Ont.	Que.	Atlant. Prov.	Canada
Royal Bank of Canada	6 958	25.0	5 837	24.6	124	262	401	174	135	1 096
Canadian Imperial Bank of Commerce	6 708	24.2	5 696	24.0	203	303	615	180	62	1 363
Bank of Montreal	5 487	19.8	4 869	20.5	135	231	350	188	84	988
Bank of Nova Scotia	3 653	13.2	2 737	11.5	75	117	282	66	144	684
Toronto Dominion Bank	3 071	11.1	2 765	11.6	67	143	387	71	11	679
Banque Canadienne Nationale	1 107	4.0	1 104	4.7	—	4	19	598	—	621
La Banque Provinciale du Canada	551	2.0	551	2.3	—	—	23	325	20	368
The Mercantile Bank of Canada	234	0.8	161	0.7	1	2	1	2	1	7
Total	27 773	100.0	23 719	100.0	605	1 062	2 078	1 604	457	5 806

* Includes Yukon and Northwest Territories

SOURCE: *Canada Gazette; Canada Year Book.*

Oligopolists are normally reluctant to use price aggressively as a competitive weapon. There is a general fear that price cutting will degenerate into a mutually destructive "price war." As a result, there are strong pressures inherent in the market structure to induce firms to agree on prices. Carried to the extreme, such agreements transform the oligopoly into a *cartel* — a monopoly by agreement. Even in the absense of formal cartel arrangements, the market structure induces firms to be very cautious about price cutting, and perhaps to implicitly acknowledge one firm as the "price leader," effectively setting the price for the whole industry. Competitive energies are then directed to other "non-price" strategies. Rivalry for market shares takes the form of competitive variations in the nature and quality of the product, or in ancillary services rendered to customers. Many economists argue that, carried to the extreme and without the safeguard of price-cutting competition, such non-price competition can involve substantial economic waste in the sense that excessive resources are absorbed in the production of the output which is produced. Because the price is higher than necessary, an inappropriate amount of the product is produced.

Concentration, then, does not necessarily imply an absence of competition among firms in the industry, but it is inimical to aggressive competition, and particularly to the use of price as a competitive weapon. The research of the Porter Commission suggested that the Canadian banking industry was almost a textbook case of oligopoly.

Competition in Banking.[6]   The Commission concluded that while "banking is in many ways a highly competitive business," "there is a strictly limited amount of *price competition* among banks," either in their lending or their deposit-taking activities. Their rates are subject to agreed minimum levels. Price competition has been further restricted in periods of credit restraint by agreements among the banks to the effect that no banks will take over an account from another by offering a better rate or a larger line of credit.

Active price competition was discovered only in the market for very large-size term deposits (primarily deposits by corporations), including large-size foreign currency deposits. This is an aspect of the high degree of competition in the short-term money markets.

Interest rates paid on deposits and charged on loans are not the only significant "prices" charged by banks for their services. Other charges, such as service charges on deposit accounts, can be of equal importance to many customers. Historically, these charges have also been the subject of "discussions" and "understandings" between banks.

The bankers appear to have regarded such discussions and understandings as a necessary method of avoiding a form of competition which they felt was likely to give rise to "unsound" banking practices. Thus, for example, in testimony before the Standing Committee of the House of Commons in 1954 the then president of the Canadian Bankers' Association concluded that:

> the competition between banks is keener today than I have ever seen it...Basically we compete on the question of service, reputation and general ability to convince people that we are as good or better than our competitors... *I hope that there is no price cutting competition...because I regard that as being poor competition* [our italics].[7]

Similarly, in commenting on "price competition" in their brief to the Royal Commission on Banking and Finance the Canadian Bankers' Association argued that "Among the chartered banks themselves...competition *must* take a different form," i.e., it must take the form of competition in the quality of the services provided.[8]

The Royal Commission concluded, however, that exclusive emphasis on the quality of service in the competitive process had led to "a wasteful form of competition," particularly through excessive proliferation of bank branches. Increased price competition would lead to more concern with efficiency, the more careful tailoring of the "quality" (and also the price) of banking services to customers' demands and a reduction in the proliferation of bank branches.

Entry.   There is another important dimension to the interaction between industrial structure and competition. Studies of oligopoly suggest that interfirm agreements on prices will only be effective in the longer run if there are substantial barriers to the entry of new firms. If entry is easy, high profits will attract new competitors, which will limit the willingness and ability of the oligopolists to agree on high prices.

TABLE 16-2   The changing structure of the banking system: new banks, mergers, and failures, 1867-1966

Year end	Number of active banks	New bank charters		Banks closed		No. of bank offices
		Not used	New active banks	Mergers	Failures	
1867	35	—	—	—	—	123*
1900	35	(20)	26	7	19	708
1925	11	(15)	11	26	9	3 840
1950	10	(1)	1	2	0	3 679
1960	9	—	1	2	0	5 051
1966	8	(1)	0	1	0	5 806
Net Change						
1867-1925	−24	(35)	+37	−35	−28	
1925-1966	−3	(2)	+ 2	− 5	0	

* 1868.

SOURCE: Buckley and Urquhart, *Historical Statistics of Canada* (Toronto: Macmillan, 1966).

Table 16-2 provides an historical perspective on the structure of the banking system through the mid-1960s. In the 100 years covered by the table, the industrial structure changed significantly, from a system comprised of 35 banks with an average of 3.5 offices per bank, to one comprised of eight banks with an average of 725 offices per bank. However, it is important to note that the major transformation was basically completed by 1925. Thus, in spite of the entry of 37 new banks between 1867 and 1925, the total number of active banks declined from 35 to 11, partly as a result of bank failures and partly as a result of bank mergers. Since 1925, the process of consolidation through merger has continued, although on a much diminished scale. However, it is significant that between 1925 and the end of 1966, only two new banks were successfully established, both organized by large, well established foreign banks (one English and one Dutch). Neither grew to be a significant factor in the Canadian banking system. Neither established a nationwide chain of branches to compete directly with the "big five" in offering a full range of banking facilities. Indeed, one — Barclay's Bank of Canada — was eventually absorbed by another of the larger Canadian banks. In the years before the Porter Commission, entry in the chartered banking business in Canada was not easy, and the entry of new banks did not provide a powerful external source of competitive pressure. What were the important barriers to entry?

Legislative Barriers to Entry.   Some of the major barriers to entry were inherent in the technology and structure of the industry. Thus, substantial economies of scale in banking would have made it difficult for small new firms to compete on the same low cost basis as large established banks; or the established market position of the large existing banks may have been intimidating to potential entrants. Of interest to us in this context are the barriers to entry which were embedded in the laws regulating banks. These are barriers which were directly amenable to change through deliberate public policy.

One was a formidable *incorporation barrier*; for, unlike most companies, the incorporation of a chartered bank required a special act of Parliament. Because the bill had to be introduced as a Private Members' bill and passed in the limited time provided for Private Members' bills, it was easy for a few Members of Parliament to delay it substantially. Once it has passed second reading, it was referred to a standing committee. Here the sponsors of the bill were cross-examined and asked to "show their capacity, their financial position, and their intent…to demonstrate their capacity to carry on the banking business"[9] before the bill was reported to the House for third reading. Once the act of incorporation was passed and the charter granted, a certificate had to be issued by the government, entitling the new bank to commence business. Before issuing the certificate, the government had to satisfy itself that all legal requirements had been met.

The delays, and associated costs, could be substantial. Thus, while the first version of the bill involved some very contentious issues relating to provincial government participation in a chartered bank, it is interesting to note the case of the Bank of British Columbia, the chartering of which began during this period. The total time elapsed between the initial petition (May 4, 1964) and the opening for business (July 17, 1968) was *over four years*.

In addition to these qualitative controls, the *Bank Act* also erected a *financial barrier* to entry in the form of a minimum capital requirement. A new bank had to have at least $1 million of capital subscribed before it could be allowed to commence business. Of this, $500 000 had to be deposited with the Minister of Finance before the certificate could be issued to commence business, and the balance had to be raised within one year of incorporation. By way of contrast, in the United States, minimum capital requirements for national banks ranged between $50 000 and $200 000. State requirements were similar, although in several states they were even lower.

A Broader Concept of Entry and Competition.   In this discussion of concentration, entry, and competition in the Canadian banking industry in the mid-1960s, we have focused almost exclusively on the chartered banks. This is a legal category of firms — those regulated under the *Bank Act*. However, it is not clear that this legal category is an "industry" in an economic sense.

The concept of an industry is one of the most widely used concepts in economics, but in a world in which the goods and services produced by different firms are seldom identical but frequently similar, the concept of an industry is somewhat vague, and the groupings of firms used for statistical analysis are generally quite arbitrary. This is clearly true in the case of financial intermediaries. For example, considered as financial intermediaries (i.e., ignoring the E.T. and A. business) the operations of many trust companies and mortgage loan companies are virtually indistinguishable, although they operate under different laws. They draw on the same sources of funds (term and savings deposits) and use these funds to acquire the same types of assets (primarily mortgages). Indeed, there are sharper differences in operations among firms within each of the categories "trust companies" and "loan companies" than between "typical" firms in each category. And what is true of trust and loan companies is true of many other categories of intermediaries. Thus, trust and loan companies are faced with competition from cooperative banks. Quebec savings banks, chartered banks and governmental depositories in the market for funds, and in addition, from life insurance companies in the market for assets.

This suggests that in analyzing concentration and competition in financial intermediation, we ought not to look at legal categories, but ought to examine separately each line of financial activity (e.g., savings deposits, demand deposits, commercial lending, mortgage lending, consumer lending, etc.). Moreover, various studies show that frequently it is a mistake to think of a single national market. Many borrowers, particularly individuals and small firms, cannot compete for funds on a nationwide basis, but are effectively confined to local lenders. A truly comprehensive analysis of concentration and competition ought to take this into account.

Such a study has not been undertaken for Canada. As a result there are few strong conclusions which can be drawn. However, it is clear that the activities of financial intermediaries overlap in a very complex pattern, that competition has impinged in varying degrees and at various points on the activities of the chartered banks, and that in the period under study, this was a primary factor eroding the banks' dominant position in the financial system.

It is important to note that, unlike chartered banking, entry into most categories of non-bank financial intermediation was comparatively easy. This in part reflects the fact that most types of non-bank financial intermediaries were chartered by provincial governments which were in competition for new businesses. In each of the categories referred to above there was a major expansion in numbers between 1950 and 1966: on the order of 50% in the case of cooperative banks, 100% in the case of trust and loan companies, and 90% in the case of life insurance companies. Although there continues to be a high degree of concentration of asset holdings among non-bank financial intermediaries, *the relatively easy entry of new firms provided a vital source of competitive pressures.*

Active competition among non-bank financial intermediaries and between these institutions and the chartered banks was *a major dynamic force in the Canadian financial system.* Presumably, a policy of enhancing competition in banking would also strive to improve competition among types of financial intermediaries. This was one of the strong messages of the Porter Commission.

CANADA: THE BANK ACT OF 1967

The long delayed revision of the *Bank Act* finally occurred in 1967. Although many recommendations of the Porter Commission, such as the comprehensive concept of banking, were not adopted, the Commission's objective of increasing the degree of competition in the financial system was reflected in important provisions of the Act.

Anti-Combines Provisions

All interbank agreements to set interest rates or other charges on loans or deposits were prohibited (Section 138), striking directly at the agreements which the Royal Commission found to be commonplace in banking and which they considered to be a primary restraint on active price competition. In the same spirit, the Act also prohibited certain interlocking directorates (Section 18). Thus, a person could not be a director of a chartered bank if he was simultaneously the director of another chartered bank, a Quebec savings bank, or a trust or mortgage loan company which accepts deposits from the public, and the directors of any one bank could not constitute more than one-fifth of the directors of any corporation incorporated in Canada.

The Act also introduced rules designed to maintain a clear separation between banks and their customers. Banks were not to control important customers; and important customers were not to control banks.[10] Thus, chartered banks were prohibited from owning, directly or indirectly more than 10% of the voting shares of any relatively large Canadian corporation or more than 50% of the shares of a smaller corporation, with certain specified exceptions (essentially corporations providing ancillary services directly to the bank). Similarly, the transfer of bank shares to any individual, or closely associated group of individuals, was prohibited if the transfer would increase his holdings to more than 10% of the outstanding shares of stock. The transfer of any shares to the federal government or to any provincial or foreign government was also prohibited.

Competition with Near Banks

Although the Porter Commission's comprehensive concept of banking was not adopted for regulatory purposes, the Act relaxed traditional restrictions on the business of chartered banks which affected the banks' ability to meet competition from other financial institutions, particularly in attracting savings deposits and in extending mortgage credit. The intent was to increase competition between banks and near banks, although many economists argue that the overall effect was to enhance the market position of the chartered banks.

One major change broadened the lending authority of the banks. Thus, for the first time the chartered banks were permitted to make "conventional" mortgage loans (i.e., mortgage loans which had not been guaranteed by any agency of the federal government). An upper limit on mortgage holdings was established, with a provision for this limit to be gradually increased to 10% of each bank's total Canadian dollar deposits and debentures. At the same time, the 6% ceiling on the interest rate which could be charged by banks on loans was raised initially to 7.25% per annum, and was removed entirely on January 1, 1968.

Also important to the competitive position of the banks was a major change in their cash reserve requirements. In place of the former 8% cash reserves behind all Canadian dollar deposits, banks were required to hold 4% cash reserves against deposits "payable after notice" and 12% against deposits "payable on demand." By early 1980, given the composition of deposits, this had the effect of lowering the average required cash reserve ratio from 8% of Canadian dollar deposits to 5.3%. The right of the Bank of Canada to vary this reserve ratio was rescinded. However, a secondary reserve ratio was enacted, which could be varied by the Bank of Canada between the limits of 0 and 12%. Initially set at 6%, it was subsequently raised in three steps to 9% (July 1970), then lowered steadily until, at the end of 1980, it was 5%. The lagged form of reserve accounting (discussed in Chapter 8) was retained, and applied to required secondary reserves. The Bank of Canada was given the authority to reduce the averaging period from one month to one-half month, which it did in January 1969.

The reduction in the level of the cash reserve requirement, like the removal of the interest rate ceiling and the broadening of lending authority, permitted the banks to increase the average earnings on their assets, thus removing the basis for the common argument that the banks could not pay competitive interest rates on savings deposits (remember: the Bank of Canada pays no interest on the reserve deposits of the banks). From the point of view of competition between the banks and the near banks, the new *structure* of the reserve requirement was particularly important. Although the required reserve ratio was higher for demand deposits, the near banks did not compete for this business. For savings and term deposits, the business for which the banks and near banks competed directly, the reserve requirement was much lower. For one category of deposit, that denominated in foreign currency, there was no reserve requirement. In subsequent years, the relative importance of Canadian dollar demand deposits declined very sharply, and the relative importance of low reserve requirement savings, time and foreign currency deposits increased.

As an alternative to deposits as a source of funds, the banks were also given the authority to issue debentures. These are marketable securities, representing a general claim on the assets of the bank which is subordinated to that of depositors. Under the Act, bank debentures must have a minimum term to maturity of five years, and unlike regular term deposits the banks are specifically prohibited from cashing the debentures before the expiration of the minimum five-year period. This gave the banks greater flexibility in competing for funds in the market.

Foreign Banks

Apart from deposit insurance, there was nothing in the *Bank Act* of 1967 to encourage the entry of new chartered banks. Indeed, one set of provisions had the opposite effect. Foreign-controlled banks — a potential source of new entrants — were prohibited.

The legal provision (affecting chartered banks, Quebec savings banks and federally incorporated trust, loan and life insurance companies) was a prohibition against the transfer of shares to non-residents if the transfer would increase non-resident holdings to more than 25% of the outstanding shares. The *Bank Act* also required that three-quarters of a bank's directors had to be citizens of Canada ordinarily resident in Canada.

The provisions relating to trust, loan and insurance companies were designed to prevent institutions presently controlled by Canadians from falling under foreign control. The provisions were not retroactive. Institutions controlled by non-residents at the time the law was introduced in Parliament were specifically exempted from these regulations. This principle was not carried forward in the *Bank Act*. Rather, another new rule relating to existing non-resident ownership was introduced which was retroactive. Any chartered bank which was already controlled by non-residents had its total size (liabilities plus capital accounts) limited to 20 times the capital which was authorized by the Minister of Finance unless its non-resident share holdings fell below 25%. This provision applied to only one bank, the Mercantile Bank, which was owned by the First National City Bank of New York. Subsequently, First National City Bank reduced its ownership to permit the Mercantile Bank to expand.

Deposit Insurance

The primary effects of the provisions of the *Bank Act* of 1967 discussed so far were to improve the competitive position of chartered banks. The 1967 *Bank Acts* made one important step in the direction of strengthening near banks and encouraging new banks. The *Canada Deposit Insurance Act*, and the parallel *Quebec Deposit Insurance Act*, represent significant new departures in public policy in Canada. For the first time, Canadian governments *guaranteed* the safety of deposits with certain financial institutions.[11]

The *Canada Deposit Insurance Act* required all federally incorporated financial intermediaries which accept deposits from the public in Canada — banks and trust and loan companies — to take out deposit insurance with the Canada Deposit Insurance Corporation. Provincially incorporated trust and mortgage loan companies are permitted to join the insurance plan if they meet certain minimum qualifications, obtain permission from their provincial government, and agree to conduct their business in accordance with the provisions of the Federal *Trust Companies Act* or *Loan Companies Act*, whichever is relevant. In fact, most provinces have passed legislation requiring provincially chartered trust and loan companies to join C.D.I.C., and the Corporation now insures deposits in trust and loan companies chartered by all provinces outside Quebec.

While formally the Corporation can only guarantee a single deposit up to a maximum of $60 000, in fact the broad powers of the Corporation are designed to provide protection to all depositors. Thus, the Corporation is required to ensure that each member institution is *inspected* at least once each year, to satisfy itself that the institution is in sound financial condition and is conducting its operations in accordance with sound business and financial practices. The Corporation also has important *lender of last resort* powers, which extend well beyond insured institutions. In this regard, the CDIC provides facilities to much of the non-bank financial system which are similar to those traditionally provided to chartered banks and the money market by the central bank. The CDIC thus contributes to the underwriting of the liquidity of the financial system. The CDIC is empowered to purchase assets from any member institution, to make loans to a member or guarantee loans made by others, or to deposit funds with a member, if such actions seem appropriate to maintain the liquidity of the institution and hence to guarantee the safety of public deposits in it. In the event of insolvency of a member, the Corporation will make payment to each depositor in cash or will provide him with a deposit in another sound institution, in the amount of his deposit up to the legal maximum of $60 000. Under later legislation the Corporation is also empowered to provide lender of last resort facilities to Canadian-controlled sales finance companies, cooperative credit societies, and provincial corporations which in turn provide lender of last resort facilities to credit unions.

The Corporation's funds are derived from two sources. At the outset, the federal government subscribed $10 million capital funds and advanced an additional $15 million. These funds have been repaid, although the Corporation retains the right to borrow from the federal treasury if necessary. Each member institution pays an annual insurance premium, in proportion to the value of insured deposits. By the end of 1980, the Deposit Insurance Fund aggregated $196 million, against insured deposits of $96 billion.[12]

The *Quebec Deposit Insurance Plan* has wider coverage than the federal plan. While the maximum insurance per deposit is the same, deposits in a broader class of financial institutions are covered, including most importantly the *caisses populaires* and credit unions. Indeed *every* deposit-accepting institution in the province of Quebec (aside from the federally chartered banks) is required to register with the Quebec Deposit Insurance Board, which has broad powers to supervise each institution's operations (including the power to cancel its registration). Since only registered institutions are allowed to accept deposits, the power to cancel a firm's registration gives the Board a powerful basis for regulating the provincial financial system.

Arrangements have been made to avoid duplication in insurance coverage and to coordinate the activities of the Canada Deposit Insurance Corporation and the Quebec Deposit Insurance Board. Trust and loan companies incorporated outside Quebec are to insure their Quebec deposits with the Q.D.I.B., and trust and loan companies incorporated in Quebec can choose to insure their deposits outside Quebec with the C.D.I.C. Where it is relevant, provision is made for the join inspection of trust and loan companies. Also, under a revision of the Canada Deposit Insurance Act, the C.D.I.C. is empowered to lend money to the Q.D.I.C. if necessary.

Increasing competition was only a subsidiary theme in the decision to institute deposit insurance. Nevertheless, the existence of deposit insurance should have a significant impact on the competitive environment. By removing part of the risk to depositors — both through the formal guarantee of part of each intermediary's deposits and through the requirement of consistent and rigorous inspection procedures — it should have the effect of improving the competitive positions of new banks and other financial institutions. The established chartered banks argued strongly that they did not require deposit insurance; that their record for depositor safety spoke for itself. It was also argued that if the established institutions were required to join the insurance plan, then, since their deposits involved a lesser risk, the insurance principle should dictate that they pay lower premiums. The fact that they were nonetheless required to pay the same premiums as new or more risky institutions suggests that the insurance premiums in part a "competition tax," the proceeds of which are implicitly used to promote the competitive position of less well-established institutions.

It is interesting to note, in this context, that the CDIC has not been called upon to make insurance payments to any depositors in chartered banks — none have failed. However, the Corporation had been in business for less than a year when it was called upon to make payments to depositors in a trust company which went into receivership. Subsequently, two other trust companies failed, one in 1970 and another in 1980. The Corporation's losses from the latter cannot be ascertained yet, but the losses from the first two were small.[13]

CANADA: THE AFTERMATH OF THE 1967 *BANK ACT*

Although many of the radical changes proposed by the Porter Commission were not implemented, the *Bank Act* revisions of 1967 rank among the most substantial in the history of Canadian banking. They were followed in 1980 by further revisions, which were equally fundamental. Before considering the 1980 *Bank Act*, we should ask: What happened in the intervening years?

Competition

One of the major purposes of the 1967 revisions was to increase competition in the financial system. Given the major issues identified by the Porter Commission, the reform was incomplete and the effects were mixed, leaving an agenda of "unfinished business."

Interbank Price Competition. The 1967 *Bank Act* appears to have eliminated explicit interbank agreements on interest rates and other charges. New types of loans and deposits have proliferated, with diverse conditions and terms. Interest rates have become much more differentiated and much more flexible, and they have become an important vehicle for interfirm competition. The banks, of course, are still faced with the uncertainties which are inherent in the oligopolistic structure of the market. In one area, decisions on the timing and magnitude of changes in basic interest rates on loans and deposits, an interesting solution to the oligopolistic problem appears to have emerged. Changes in the Bank of Canada's bank rate seem to be the signal for adjustments to bank interest rates. In effect, the Bank of Canada has become the price leader for the banking system.

Competitive Positions of Banks and Near Banks.   In some important respects, the competitive position of the chartered banks appears to have been strengthened by the relaxation of constraints on their activities in the 1967 *Bank Act.*

The banks moved quickly to take advantage of their new lending authority. Thus, from 3.5% of Canadian assets at the end of 1966, bank mortgage holdings increased to almost 11% by the end of 1980. Over the same period, the average cash reserve ratio fell from 8.1% of Canadian dollar deposits to 5.3%. Studies for the Economic Council of Canada show that the profitability of the chartered banks increased after 1967, both absolutely and in relation to trust and loan Companies.[14] Although the rapid growth of the alternative banking system continued, the gap between the growth rates of banks and near banks narrowed considerably, particularly with respect to that part of the deposit business for which the banks and the near banks competed directly. Thus, over the decade 1970-1980, the average of growth of balances in savings and time deposits with banks was similar to the rate of growth of deposits in near banks (Table 16-3). The rate of growth of business demand deposits was much lower.

TABLE 16-3 **Growth rates: banks and near banks, 1954-1980**

Average annual rates of growth of deposits at chartered banks, trust and loan companies, and credit unions.

	1954-1970	1970-1980
Trust and loan companies	14	16
Credit unions and *caisses populaires*	13	22
Chartered banks:		
Total deposits	9	18
Canadian dollar deposits	7	15
Business demand deposits	3	9
Personal chequing deposits	—	15
Savings and time deposits	8	16
Foreign currency deposits	16	21

SOURCE: *Bank of Canada Review,* various issues.

The Clearing System.   There were also a number of developments which improved the business environment for near banks, including the relaxations (by federal and provincial governments) of some restrictions on their lending authority. A continuing source of concern, however, was access to the cheque clearing system, which, historically, was controlled by the Canadian Bankers' Association. As part of its proposal for uniformity of treatment of banks and near banks, the Porter Commission had recommended formation of a private association with membership open to banks and near banks to handle cheque clearing, with all members of the association required to hold reserve deposits with the Bank of Canada. Neither part of this proposal was implemented in the 1967 Act.

During the early 1970s, however, several significant changes did occur in the clearing arrangements for near banks. In 1971, it was agreed that a near bank would be free to negotiate mutually acceptable arrangements with the bank acting as its clearing agent without reference to rules set by the Canadian Bankers' Association. In 1972, near banks were granted their own transit numbers rather than having to be identified with a particular branch of their clearing bank. This change permitted a near bank to change its clearing agent without changing the clearing instructions imprinted on its cheques. While giving the near banks more bargaining power, these changes did not resolve all of the near banks' misgivings about the clearing system. After reviewing the issue, the Economic Council identified this as an item of "unfinished business," and recommended that:

> direct access to the clearing system and participation in its management, on a basis equal to that of the chartered banks, be extended to suitably qualified near banks willing to accept the responsibilities implied by such participation.[15]

Entry and the Industrial Structure.   Although the first version of the 1967 *Bank Act* (Bill C-102), introduced in May 1965, contained a radically different procedure for incorporation, it was withdrawn, and the final version of the Act made no changes to the legislative barriers to the incorporation of chartered banks. The capital requirements also remained the same, although, of course, inflation meant that the real financial barrier was lower.

TABLE 16-4   **The changing structure of the banking system: new banks, mergers, and failures, 1966-1980**

Year end	Number of active banks	New bank charters		Banks closed		No. of bank offices
		Not used	New active banks	Mergers	Failures	
1966		0	6	−3	0	5 806
1980	11					7 414
Net Change						
1966-1980	+3		+6	−3		

SOURCE: *Canada Year Book*, 1968 (Ottawa: Queen's Printer, 1968); Canadian Bankers' Association, *Bank Directory of Canada*, 1981 (Toronto: Canadian Bankers' Association, 1981).

Six new chartered banks opened for business in the period 1966-80 (Table 16-4). However, two of them merged with existing banks and another merger between two well-established banks meant that the net increase in the number of banks was only three, from eight in 1966 to eleven in 1980, and there was little change in the degree of concentration in the banking system. Thus, the five largest banks held almost 91% of the total assets of all banks at the end of 1980, only slightly down from 93% in 1966 (Table 16-5). Conditions of entry remained an item of "unfinished business."

TABLE 16-5   Concentration in the Canadian chartered banking system, December 31, 1980

	Total assets		Canadian assets		Offices					
	$ Millions	Percent	$ Millions	Percent	British Columbia*	Prairie Provinces†	Ontario	Quebec	Atlantic Provinces	Canada
Royal Bank of Canada	66 879	24	42 182	24	207	362	581	217	141	1 509
Canadian Imperial Bank of Canada	57 738	21	40 435	23	236	405	762	211	92	1 703
Bank of Montreal	50 748	18	33 138	19	168	286	503	225	110	1 292
Bank of Nova Scotia	44 507	16	21 891	12	110	202	412	95	193	1 012
Toronto Dominion Bank	35 819	13	21 921	12	116	227	543	97	30	1 013
Banque Nationale du Canada	16 245	6	11 657	7	4	10	65	669	38	786
Mercantile Bank of Canada	3 959	1	2 580	1	1	4	6	2	2	15
Bank of British Columbia	2 413	1	1 964	1	35	12	—	—	—	47
Continental Bank of Canada	1 686	1	1 584	1	1	4	8	6	3	22
Canadian Commercial and Industrial Bank	971	—	777	—	1	4	1	1	1	8
Northland Bank	280	—	225	—	2	5	—	—	—	7
TOTAL	281 244	100	178 294	100	879	1 523	2 878	1 524	617	7 414

* Includes Yukon

† Includes Northwest Territories

SOURCES: *Canada Gazette*; Canadian Bankers' Association, *Bank Directory of Canada* (Toronto: Canadian Bankers' Association, 1981).

Internationalization of the Banking System

Perhaps the most remarkable development in the financial system in the aftermath of the 1967 *Bank Act* was the internationalization of banking. This had two dimensions: the continued rapid development of the foreign currency business of Canadian banks, and the rapid growth of foreign banking activity in Canada, outside the purview of the *Bank Act*.

Foreign Currency Business of Canadian Banks.   Even more striking than the change in the relative competitive position of the chartered banks in the market for Canadian deposits, shown by Table 16-3, was the rapid growth of bank deposits and assets denominated in foreign currencies. In 1954, foreign currency deposits totalled only $1 billion, approximately 10% of Canadian dollar deposits. By 1970, foreign currency deposits had increased to 45% of Canadian dollar deposits, and by 1980 to 84%. If the differential rates of growth of foreign and Canadian currency deposits continue, foreign currency deposits will be more important than Canadian dollar deposits as a source of funds by 1984. About 12% of the foreign currency deposits are owned by residents of Canada; the balance is owned by banks, corporations, and individuals resident in other countries, collected through the worldwide network of bank branches, agencies, and representative offices. The growth of the foreign currency business was largely responsible for the banks' ability to sustain, and indeed increase, their relative importance among Canadian financial institutions, but it also brought with it potential problems for public policy.

The *Bank Act* of 1967 had no legislative constraints on the international banking activities of Canadian banks. Indeed, the lack of a reserve requirement against foreign currency deposits could be interpreted as official encouragement of that business. At the same time, however, foreign currency deposits were not covered by deposit insurance. A major study done for the Economic Council of Canada in 1976 suggested that while Canadian banks have not encountered any "unusual difficulties" with their international banking activities, the size of the unregulated foreign currency portfolio exposes the banks to considerable additional risk.[16] The Economic Council further concluded that the Canadian Deposit Insurance Corporation is also exposed to larger risks because of the magnitude of foreign currency deposits: and, even though the foreign currency deposits are not insured, the incentive to Canadian depositors not to withdraw deposits in panic at the threat of financial difficulties means that the risk of bank failure is reduced by deposit insurance, giving the foreign depositors a margin of protection for which no insurance premium is paid.[17]

Foreign Banking Activity in Canada.   As we have seen, the 1967 *Bank Act* prohibited the establishment of foreign-controlled chartered banks in Canada, and related legislation restricted foreign ownership of other federally-chartered institutions. However, provincial regulators of trust and mortgage loan companies did not follow the federal government's lead. A number of provincial trust and loan companies, for example, had substantial foreign ownership. Moreover, many enterprises were able to compete with banks in some activities even though they were not formally incorporated as financial institutions. Important in this regard were the representative offices of foreign banks, sometimes referred to as "suitcase bankers," who negotiated deposits or loans on behalf of their foreign parents. While competing with the chartered banks, it could be debated whether, in any legal sense, they were doing a banking business *in Canada*. The federal authorities were able to control who could become a "bank," and advertise themselves as such, but they could not control entry into all banking activities.

In the aftermath of the 1967 *Bank Act*, there was an explosion of foreign banking activity in Canada. Estimates of the numbers of foreign banks operating in Canada ranged between 50 and 100.[18] From 1974 to 1980 reported assets of Canadian financial institutions affiliated with foreign banks increased from $1.8 billion to $10.3 billion, a total which does not include deposits or loans of Canadian institutions with foreign banks arranged through representative offices in Canada but carried on the books of banks abroad. The Economic Council, after its review of foreign bank activities in Canada, concluded that

> Whatever the intent of Parliament in the last [1967] *Bank Act* revision, foreign banking firms have expanded their role in Canada, largely beyond regulatory control.[19]

In spite of the provisions of the 1967 *Bank Act*, the appropriate role of foreign banks in Canada remained an item of "unfinished business."

Reciprocity in Banking Policy.   The question of the appropriate treatment of foreign banks in Canada involved another issue, which, interestingly, made some of the Canadian banks strong supporters of a policy of incorporating foreign-controlled banks in Canada. This was the issue of "reciprocity" between Canada and other countries in the treatment of foreign banks.

During the 1970s, some Canadian banks were finding that various aspects of their foreign operations were being hampered, or at least threatened indirectly by the Canadian prohibition on foreign banks. A number of foreign banking authorities were threatening to require reciprocity of treatment for their banks in Canada as a condition for the continued operation of Canadian banks in their jurisdiction. Perhaps the greatest threat came from the United States, where some Canadian banks had large and active subsidiaries. There, the authorities were proposing a system of mutual reciprocity whereby foreign banks would be granted the same powers as domestic banks on the condition that American banks were not discriminated against in the foreign bank's country.

The commitment to foreign business differs substantially among Canadian banks. Perhaps not surprisingly, therefore, the chartered banks were not unanimous in their desire to permit foreign banks entry into Canada so as to gain reciprocal treatment in other countries.

Profile of the Banking System, 1980

By the end of 1980, the Canadian financial system had become even more complex, with the proliferation of specialized financial institutions, some of them under government control or sponsorship. At the same time, the data available to describe the structure of the system have become much more complete and detailed. A summary of the system in 1980 is presented in Table 16-6.

TABLE 16-6   **The Canadian financial system, 1980**

I. The money supply

	$ Millions	Percent
Subsidiary coin	1 024	2
Bank of Canada notes	9 377	22
Demand deposits at chartered banks	18 513	43
Other chequable deposits	13 901	33
Total (payments money)	42 815	100

II. Assets of financial intermediaries

	$ Millions	Percent
Chartered Banks:		
Canadian dollar assets	171 296	30
Foreign currency assets	109 948	19
Total assets	281 244	49
Other deposit-taking intermediaries		
Quebec savings banks	1 747	—
Government savings banks	2 446	—
Mortgage loan companies	16 075	3
Trust companies*	38 968	7
Caisses populaires and credit unions	31 610	6
Total	90 846	16
Other intermediaries		
Affiliates of foreign banks	10 279	2
Sales finance and consumer loan companies	14 295	3
Investment dealers	6 673	1
Life insurance companies	37 629	6
Other insurance companies	20 091	4
Pension funds	49 723	9
Mutual funds and investment companies	5 166	1
Other private intermediaries	24 337	4
Other government intermediaries	34 754	6
Total	202 947	35
TOTAL	575 037	100

* Excluding E.T.& A. Accounts.

SOURCE: Statistics Canada, *Financial Flow Accounts,* fourth quarter, 1981 *Bank of Canada Review.*

CANADA: THE *BANK ACT* OF 1980

Although the 1967 revision of the *Bank Act* involved many fundamental reforms, there remained a sizeable agenda of "unfinished business" from the Porter Commission's recommendations, and the 1970s saw a number of developments in financial markets which called some existing regulations into question. In the mid-1970s, the Economic Council of Canada undertook a major study of the financial system, analyzed the impact of the earlier reforms and recent developments,and confirmed the importance of many of the outstanding Porter recommendations. As a result, the 1980 revision of the *Bank Act* was almost as sweeping as the 1967 revision.

The Powers of the Chartered Banks

A number of changes in financial markets in the 1970s were based on technological advances, particularly the use of the computer. Others were a reaction to features of the taxation system or to the emergence of rapid inflation. The banks began to offer new services to their customers or modified existing services; but in some cases the actions of the banks were checked by directives from the Minister of Finance who declared certain lines of business to be outside the powers of chartered banks. The revision of the *Bank Act* offered an opportunity to review the powers of the banks in relation to the changing patterns of business appearing in financial markets. Among the important issues treated in the 1980 *Bank Act* were the banks' offerings of computer services to customers and their participation in leasing and factoring.

Data Processing.   The fact that many aspects of banking involve an immense number of identical transactions made banking particularly suitable for the application of computer technology. The banks first used computers to carry out their "backroom" bookkeeping, and then gradually placed many banking services "on-line." As a consequence, the banks developed both the computer facilities and the expertise to offer data processing services to their customers. In supplying these services, the banks competed with independent computer service firms which were, typically, quite small, Canadian-owned, and operating on a regional or local basis. There were loud cries of unfairness. Out of concern for "the possibility of unfair competition, concentration of economic power and conflict of interest" the Minister of Finance halted further expansion of the banks into data processing by issuing a directive which:

> limited banks to offering automated payments, that is, data processing services related to the making of payments; and wholesale banking services, that is, the provision to other financial institutions of computer services integral to banking operations.[20].

The provisions of the 1980 *Bank Act* essentially duplicated the terms of the Minister's directive by prohibiting the banks from providing "other than...banking-related data processing services."[21] Regulations, pursuant to the Bank Act, which can be changed from time to time, define the scope of bank-related data processing and currently permit such activities as payroll processing for nonfinancial business and a wide range of businesses.

The limitation of the banks' participation in data processing illustrates the conflict among the policy goals which we discussed in Chapter 13. The unrestrained involvement of banks might have led to greater competition in data processing, which might have meant that data processing services were provided at least cost. On the other hand, full participation by the banks would have been a breach of the principle of separation of financial and nonfinancial activities. In this case, the authorities made a clear choice to maintain the separation rather than to encourage competition in data processing.

Factoring and Leasing.   Another issue in the *Bank Act* revision was the treatment of bank powers with respect to factoring and leasing. Each of these activities can be viewed as a close substitute for bank lending in many circumstances. Carrying out factoring, the banks purchase accounts receivable from sellers of goods and services. In effect, the banks are financing the buyers' purchases of goods and services, extending credit indirectly. Leasing, in contrast, refers to transactions in which the bank purchases capital equipment to be used by an industrial firm, and leases the equipment to the firm on a medium- to long-term basis.

It is easy to dismiss factoring and leasing as needless complications of simple lending arrangements. However, the development of these activities brought considerable benefits to the leasing and factoring customers. In both cases, small and medium-sized businesses, which were short of capital, were able to avoid the necessity of financing their accounts receivable and their equipment by turning instead to a factoring or leasing company. In the case of leasing, there also was a tax consideration that made leasing attractive to some firms with low levels of profits which, as a result, would be unable to take advantage of the depreciation allowances resulting from capital expenses. Under a lease arrangement, the leasing firm gains the benefit of the depreciation allowance and can pass some of the benefit on to its customers.

In the years leading up to the *Bank Act*, both leasing and factoring activity expanded substantially in Canada, but to a large degree through subsidiaries of American and other foreign banks. The chartered banks had not been specifically empowered to carry on leasing and factoring. Some banks did enter these activities through subsidiaries and joint ventures, while others did not because they feared such activities might be declared outside the scope of banking.

The extension of bank powers to the activities of leasing and factoring seemed to be a logical step in the *Bank Act* revision because they are essentially the equivalent of financial transactions. The tax issue did pose a dilemma for the policy makers; the application of the capital cost allowances to the banks would reduce their tax liability. The dilemma was eliminated in the May 1976 budget which specified "tax-payers will not be allowed to claim capital cost allowance on leased equipment in excess of their net rental income from that type of property."

The 1980 *Bank Act* permitted the banks to participate in both factoring and leasing indirectly through subsidiaries. The leasing and factoring episode was instructive in at least one respect. The pace of change in financial markets can easily make the rules governing chartered banks or other financial institutions inappropriate for current conditions. Neither factoring nor leasing were involved in the 1967 revision of the *Bank Act*. The emergence of these activities on a large scale was very rapid; by the time of the 1980 revision, the exclusion of the banks appeared patently inappropriate. Possibly, it was anticipation of the rapid rate of technical and institutional change that led the framers of Canadian banking legislation to require decennial review and renewal of the legislation.

Reserve Requirements.   The ability of the banks to compete with other financial institutions was also improved somewhat by a further reduction in cash reserve requirements: from 12% to 10% against demand deposits, from 4% to 2% on the first $500 million, and 3% on the balance of savings and term deposits. However, for the first time, a reserve of 3% was required behind foreign currency deposits, partially offsetting the benefits of the reduction in the requirement applicable to Canadian dollar deposits.

The Clearing System

As we have seen, direct access of near banks to the cheque clearing system was a source of controversy which was not resolved by the 1967 *Bank Act* or subsequent developments. In the *Bank Act* of 1967, the government finally adopted the recommendations of the Porter Commission and the Economic Council, replacing the clearing system operated by the Canadian Bankers' Association with the Canadian Payments Association in which membership is open to any financial institution offering chequable deposits. Membership is required for all chartered banks, but is optional for other financial institutions. The Association will be run by a board composed of four directors from the chartered banks, two from the credit unions, one from the trust and loan companies and one representing other institutions such as the Montreal City and District Savings Bank and government savings institutions.

The establishment of the Canadian Payments Association places the near banks on the same footing as the chartered banks with respect to the cheque clearing system. This step eliminated what many people perceived as a significant obstacle to the ability of near banks to compete with chartered banks in offering payment services. The effect of creating the Canadian Payments Association may, however, be more substantial than just allowing participation in the cheque clearing system. We have already seen that the payments system is undergoing considerable change that is likely to continue. The federal government has given a mandate to the Canadian Payments Association to devise the payment system of the future. Thus, by joining the Association, near banks can participate in planning and setting standards.

One final aspect of the opening of the clearing system to the near banks needs to be mentioned. In the federal government's initial proposals, any near bank participants in the clearing system were to be required to hold reserves of the Bank of Canada on a similar basis to the chartered banks. This step was interpreted by many as part of a federal government initiative to gain some degree of control over provincially-regulated financial institutions. Certainly, several provincial governments interpreted the step in this way and protested most strongly to the federal government. The proposal was ultimately dropped from the legislation. The episode does serve to illustrate, however, that both the Porter Commission and the Economic Council were overly optimistic about the prospects for a unified system of regulation for financial institutions.

Entry Into Banking

While retaining incorporation through a special Act of Parliament as an option, the 1980 *Bank Act* fundamentally changed conditions of entry into chartered banking in two respects.

Incorporation by Letters Patent.   First, the Act provided a way around the legislative barrier, permitting a much simpler method of incorporation for a new bank — application to the Minister of Finance who has the authority to issue a charter ("letters patent") when he is satisfied that all of the other provisions of the *Bank Act* for incorporation have been satisfied. A notice of intention to apply for a charter must be published in the *Canada Gazette* for four weeks, and the Inspector General of Banks must make a public enquiry into any objections received within 30 days. However, the potentially long legislative procedure is circumvented, although the financial barrier to incorporation remains intact, and for some new entrants is increased; that is, the minimum paid-up capital remains at $1 million, except for "Schedule B" banks for which it is $2.5 million.

"Schedule A" and "Schedule B" Banks.   The second fundamental change was a relaxation of the 10% ownership law introduced in the 1967 Act. Instead of a prohibition against ownership of more than 10% of a bank's voting shares by a single "interest," this criterion was used to divide banks into two categories. Schedule A banks meet this criterion, Schedule B banks do not. Schedule B banks have higher minimum capital requirements to commence business and are subject to other restrictions. In particular, a Schedule B bank may not have domestic assets in excess of 20 times its "authorized capital" (a sum which has been approved by the Minister of Finance), and initially may open only a head office and one other branch in Canada. Additional branches in Canada are subject to the approval of the Minister of Finance. No branches may be opened outside Canada. There are no such restrictions on Schedule A banks.

Conversion of Near Banks into Banks.   The powers of any financial institution can be changed either through a legislated extension of the powers of the class of financial institution to which it belongs, or through the institution's changing itself into another type by switching its basis of incorporation. The first approach was the one advocated by both the Porter Commission and the Economic Council after their study of Canadian institutions. The alternative approach may be just as satisfactory for any institution which finds itself constrained by its existing powers.

The 1980 *Bank Act* facilitates such conversions. By making provision for Schedule B banks, the Act makes it possible for a trust company, for example, to incorporate a chartered bank without surrendering ownership and control. Beyond this, there are a number of transitional arrangements relating to activities which are not permitted to banks under the *Bank Act* (e.g., trusteeship activities). Under the new regime, a near bank can carry out a staged transition, creating a Schedule B bank as a subsidiary. Any of the near bank's activities which fall within the scope of chartered banking can be transferred to the banking subsidiary, with the parent continuing the business which is not permitted under the *Bank Act*. Over time, the near bank has two choices. It can dispose of the parts of its business which are not permitted under the *Bank Act* and, if its ownership is not concentrated, gradually combine with the banking subsidiary to become a Schedule A bank. Alternatively, it can continue its own business while owning a Schedule B bank.

Implications.   The 1980 *Bank Act* thus involved a very fundamental conceptual change with respect to the regulation of entry into banking. It remains to be seen whether it will elicit a large number of new, indigenous Canadian banks. Initially, the main effect was to permit the entry of a number of banks who were poised to enter the industry, i.e., subsidiaries of foreign banks.

Foreign Banks

The 1980 *Bank Act* reversed the 1967 prohibition on foreign-controlled banks, however, the Act did not permit unrestricted entry of foreign banks. On the one hand, subsidiaries of foreign banks were obviously Schedule B banks, which meant that the restrictions on size and branches applied to them. On the one hand, special provisions applied to banks which had more than 25% foreign ownership.

Schedule B Restrictions. The Schedule B limitation on the opening of branch offices in Canada effectively precludes a foreign bank from developing a substantial retail banking business which requires a chain of branches. Most foreign banks indicate plans to concentrate on "wholesale" banking, dealing in the money market and with large business customers. Moreover, the effects of the limitation of total assets to 20 times authorized capital may be substantial in light of the fact that at the end of 1981 the actual asset-to-capital ratio of domestic banks averaged over 30.

Foreign Ownership Restrictions. A subsidiary of a foreign bank is permitted to incorporate as a Schedule B bank providing its home country provides reciprocal treatment for Canadian banks and providing

> ...the Minister is satisfied that it has the potential to make a contribution to competitive banking in Canada.[23]

However, the total share of the Canadian banking market which may be held by foreign subsidiaries is also limited by the Act. Thus, the Minister cannot incorporate new foreign bank subsidiaries or increase the authorized capital of existing subsidiaries

> where, in the opinion of the Minister, the effect thereof would be to increase the average outstanding total domestic assets of all foreign bank subsidiaries to an amount that would exceed eight per cent of the total domestic assets of all banks in Canada...[24]

The ceiling on the total size of foreign banks in Canada is probably the most restrictive element of the provisions which permit foreign banks into Canada. This restriction will discourage vigorous growth by foreign bank subsidiaries. Any foreign-controlled bank planning to expand rapidly in competition with other banks must eventually apply to the Inspector General of Banks for an increase in its authorized capital. It cannot be assured that additional capital will be authorized, depending on the total market share of foreign-controlled banks. If the Minister concludes that the increase in authorized capital may lead to a market share for foreign-controlled banks in excess of the 8% limit, he is required to deny the application. Then, the combination of the authorized capital and the 20-times authorized capital rule will be binding, restricting the competitive potential of the foreign-controlled bank.

In summary, the *Bank Act* revision of 1980 reversed the prohibition on foreign banks in Canada instituted under the 1967 revision. The changes have probably met the

Canadian chartered banks' desire to gain reciprocal treatment in foreign countries. They also ensured that foreign banks were no longer permitted to carry on activities in Canada that are denied to Canadian banks. Still, foreign banks are limited in their borrowing powers, their ability to open branches, and in their overall size. The total assets of all foreign banks operating in Canada have been restricted to be smaller than any one of the "big five" banks. Given these constraints, it is unlikely that the changed treatment of foreign banks will alter the force of competition among Canadian financial institutions.

The Scope of Regulation

There is one other feature of the 1980 Bank Act which merits emphasis. Rather than reducing the scope of regulation of the financial system, it has probably increased it — for example, bringing unregulated activities of foreign banks within the purview of the *Bank Act*. It has also introduced a new element into Canadian banking policy, *discretionary regulation* by the Minister of Finance.

Unlike much legislation, the *Bank Act* had traditionally been self-contained. Any provision governing the banks was spelled out, both in principle and in detail in the Act. In contrast, some other pieces of legislation state the general principle and leave the detailed statement of the principle to so-called "regulations." A major difference between legislation and these regulations is that legislation can only be changed by an act of Parliament whereas a regulation can be changed by Order-in-Council.

For the first time, the *Bank Act* in 1980 left the details of a number of provisions to be spelled out by accompanying regulation. In particular, the regulations appended to the Act govern the terms of the participation of bank subsidiaries in activities such as leasing and factoring, establish the basis for calculating primary and secondary reserves, and prescribe the calculation and required disclosure of interest rates on loans and deposits. The use of regulations will permit the authorities to alter the rules governing the chartered banks without having to wait for the decennial revision of the *Bank Act*. On the other hand, the movement to the use of regulations removes one of the advantages of the older system. No longer do the chartered banks and their customers have the assurance that the framework in which the banks operate will remain unchanged between *Bank Act* revisions. It remains to be seen whether this change signals the move to a more active and interventionist approach to the regulation of banks or whether it is merely a means for responding to the pace of change in financial markets.

1980 Bank Act: Conclusions

The regulation of financial institutions must be directed at a variety of conflicting goals ranging from depositor safety and effective monetary control to competition and efficiency in the workings of the financial system. The legacy of past regulation has been a segmented financial system consisting of a variety of institutions each operating under a different authority and a different set of rules. Both the Porter Commission and the Economic Council recommended legislative changes which were designed to increase competition in the financial system by enhancing the powers of the near banks relative to the chartered banks. Some of the changes in the 1980 *Bank Act* enhanced the powers of the chartered banks by approving their presence in activities such as leasing and factoring. The competitive position of the near banks was improved by the transfer of clearing arrangements to the Canadian payments system and by permitting them to own Schedule B banks. On the other hand, one potential source of competition, the foreign banks, while permitted formal recognition, were constrained to have a minor role in the Canadian financial system. Also, in early 1983, in the midst of a financial problem involving several trust and loan companies, the government announced that deposit insurance coverage was being increased from $20 000 to $60 000.

THE UNITED STATES:
THE CHANGING FINANCIAL ENVIRONMENT

As in Canada — indeed, both earlier and in heightened degree — the financial environment in the United States changed markedly in the 1970s. Policy gradually adapted. At the beginning of the decade, the concepts underlying the purpose and approach, and the administrative structure for the regulation of financial institutions, remained virtually unchanged from those established in the reforms of the mid-1930s. Competition was restrained in favor of financial stability, with particular restraints on interest rates on deposits, on the entry of new firms, and on the opening of new offices. Financial institutions were placed in regulatory compartments, which were partly defined on functional lines (banks vs. near banks) and partly on constitutional lines (federal vs. state authority). A particularly sharp division was made between commercial banking (commercial loans, chequable deposits) and near banking (mortgage loans, time and savings deposits).

The New Environment

The regulatory reforms of 1980 were foreshadowed by two developments in the 1960s.

An Experiment in Deregulation. One of the early developments is reflected in the bulge in the number of new banks opening in the years 1963-65, which we noted earlier (Figure 15-3). The new banks chartered in this period were predominantly national banks, in contrast to preceding experience.[25] This can be directly attributed to the appointment of a new Comptroller of the Currency, James Saxon, the federal officer responsible for the chartering and supervision of national banks. Among other things, Saxon drastically altered existing policies governing the granting of national bank charters in the interest of stimulating competition, thus contradicting a basic tenet of postdepression banking policy.[26] The new policy was short-lived. At the end of Saxon's short term of office, the old pattern of change in the population of commercial banks reasserted itself. However, the bulge in new bank charters in 1963-65 seemed to indicate that there was a substantial number of potential bankers, who thought they saw profitable opportunities for new banks (which may in part have been a product of restrictions on the expansion of branch banking), but who were kept out of the market by federal regulations. One statistical study estimated that the cumulative effect of restrictions on entry between 1936 and 1962 was to reduce the total number of banks in the industry by 1500.[27] The Saxon interlude demonstrated the potential for regulatory reform in one aspect of policy.

The Money Market and "Disintermediation."   The second early development was the demonstration of the competitive power and inventiveness of the open market, as the money market — including the very important Euro-dollar market — developed instruments and institutions to challenge both banks and near banks for short-term funds, undermining, and to some extent reversing, the effects of regulation. Rather than ensuring stability, the regulations were creating some instability. In periods of high interest rates, a problem emerged which is commonly called "disintermediation" in the banking literature of the United States. Funds were drawn out of time and savings deposits with banks and near banks, and placed directly in the money market, bypassing the financial intermediary sector, and creating serious financial problems for institutions with long-term, fixed interest rates, and relatively illiquid assets (mortgages). The initial response was an extension of the existing system of regulation (e.g., in 1966 Regulation Q-type ceilings on interest rates were extended to savings and loan associations and mutual savings banks to prevent them from engaging in interest rate competition which might be destructive to their financial positions)[28] and a strengthening of the lender-of-last-resort facilities available to near banks to make their asset portfolios more liquid. However, when the problem intensified in the 1970s, it became apparent that a new approach to regulation was necessary.

Developments in the 1970s.   Several developments in the 1970s converged to precipitate regulatory reform.

The first was an intensification of the problem of disintermediation. The decade, as compared to its predecessors, was one of high inflation. As we saw in Chapter 7, the anticipation of inflation will normally induce high interest rates; and the decade of the 1970s saw both inflation rates and interest rates at almost unprecedented levels. Although the Regulation Q ceilings were adjusted from time to time, both the banks and the near banks faced intensified competition from the open money market whose institutions continued to adapt to the new environment. Many near banks, with their relatively inflexible assets, found their solvency in jeopardy.

One particularly interesting, and in this context important, money market innovation was the creation of a new financial intermediary, the *money market fund.* This is a mutual fund which holds only short-term money market instruments, the returns from which, less a management fee, are returned to shareholders as dividends (which are often declared daily). Such funds have highly liquid asset portfolios, and offer the same liquidity to holders of their shares in that they may be purchased or redeemed on demand, and normally without fee. Thus, they offer an alternative to time or savings deposits with banks or near banks, offering a market-determined (and hence fluctuating) rate of interest which is not restrained by Regulation Q. In the environment of the 1970s, this innovation developed rapidly. It was introduced in 1972; by 1974, there were four funds; by 1978, 50 funds; and by mid-1980 over 80 funds with total assets of $80 billion.[29]

A second development was the intensification of incentives for banks to escape from federal regulation in favor of state regulation in an undermining of the centralized regulatory structure. Because no interest is paid on cash reserves, the holding of such reserves entails an opportunity cost in terms of foregone interest earnings, a cost which increases with higher levels of interest rates. In Canada, banks are limited in their responses to the costs of regulation. There is no alternative to a federal bank charter. In the United States, the dual banking system does provide an alternative. When the costs of regulation under one system, in general the federal system, becomes excessive, a bank has the option of switching to the other system. During the 1970s, the federal authorities became acutely concerned about the impact of such switching on their ability to maintain effective control over the financial system, including control over the money supply.

A third development was the erosion of the separation of financial institutions into segmented markets, a process which intensified in the 1970s. Of particular importance in this regard was another innovation, the *negotiable order of withdrawal (NOW) account*.[30] A NOW account is an interest-bearing savings deposit on which negotiable orders of withdrawal payable to a third party (in effect, cheques) can be written — a clear violation of the spirit of regulations designed to sharply differentiate between chequable deposits and savings deposits, and to prohibit the payment of interest on chequable deposits. Introduced by mutual savings banks in Massachusetts following a favorable court decision in 1972, this type of account was rapidly adopted by other mutual savings banks, initially in New England but eventually in other states. Regulatory changes extended the issuance of NOW or similar accounts to savings and loan associations, commercial banks, and credit unions ("share drafts") in many states. In 1975 the federal authorities responded by permitting commercial banks to transfer funds from a customers' savings deposit to his time deposit on telephone request or by pre-authorization, in effect making savings deposits chequable.

As a fourth important element in the situation, in late 1971 a special Presidential Commission on Financial Structure and Regulation (the Hunt Commission) submitted a report which recommended sweeping changes in the regulation of financial institutions for the purpose of lessening the compartmentalization of the financial system and increasing competition among financial institutions.[31] Included in the Commission's recommendations were the phasing out of Regulation-Q-type ceilings on interest rates on deposits, permission for near banks to issue chequable deposits, common reserve requirements for all banks and near banks, broader lending and investment powers for near banks, and easier entry for new banks and new branches. Beginning in 1973, the recommendations of the Hunt Commission provoked many legislative proposals, which were debated intensively, and which culminated in the *Depository Institutions Deregulation and Monetary Control Act* of 1980.

THE UNITED STATES:
DEREGULATION AND MONETARY CONTROL ACT, 1980

The new legislation profoundly affects, directly or indirectly, the operations of every type of deposit-taking institution in the united States.[32] The law is divided into several "Titles." Title I, the *Monetary Control Act*, effectively extends Federal Reserve authority over all deposit-taking institutions; Title II, the *Depository Institutions Deregulation Act*, provides for the gradual elimination of all interest rate ceilings; Titles III and IV extend the business powers of near banks; Titles V-VII provide for related changes in other legislation, including state usury laws; and Title VIII provides for the regulation of foreign takeovers of U.S. financial institutions. In the following sections, we focus only on the major provisions.

Uniform Reserve Requirements

The *Monetary Control Act* makes a further big stride in the direction of uniformity of treatment of all institutions involved in the banking business. It is designed to ensure the Federal Reserve System's power to implement monetary policy in spite of the attrition in Federal Reserve membership among commercial banks and the compartmentalization of regulatory authority over near banks, by extending uniform cash reserve requirements to almost all deposit-taking institutions. The basis for this action is federal deposit insurance which, as we have seen, is now available to almost all commercial banks, mutual savings banks, savings and loan associations, and credit unions.

The act specifies uniform cash reserve requirements for the *same type of deposit* in all institutions which have or are eligible for federal deposit insurance, regardless of the type of institution (bank or near bank) or the source of its charter (federal or state). These requirements were summarized in Table 15-2 (Chapter 15). The basic distinction is between "transactions accounts" and "nonpersonal time deposits." The former includes all deposits which can be used to make payments, demand deposits, NOW accounts, and other accounts which can be transferred by telephone or pre-arrangement — deposits which would be included in a payments concept of the money supply. For transactions accounts, the reserve requirement was initially set at 12% but it is adjustable by the Board of Governors of the Federal Reserve System, within the range 8% to 14%. A special provision was made for smaller institutions, in that a lower reserve requirement (3%) was set for the first $25 million of transactions deposits, with the limit to be adjusted in the future by the Board of Governors in accordance with the growth of transactions balances.

In the case of nonpersonal time deposits, a reserve requirement of 3% was set initially, adjustable over the range 0% to 9%, with the possibility of different requirements by maturity (initially the requirement was set at 0% for deposits of four years or more to maturity). Adjustment to the new requirements is to be gradual. An eight-year transition period was specified for the extension of reserve requirements to institutions not presently covered, and a four-year transition period in cases where existing reserve requirements exceeded those prescribed in the Act.

As a counterpart to the application of centralized reserve requirements, all institutions subject to those requirements are granted borrowing privileges at Federal Reserve Banks on the same basis as member banks.

The Regulation of Interest Rates

The second major element in the reform represents a sharp change in the approach to the regulation of financial institutions. As we have seen, ceilings on interest rates on deposits had been a central instrument of public policy since the 1930s. Title II of the Act prescribes that all interest rate ceilings be phased out in an orderly way so that they will be eliminated by 1986. Other than setting the target date for the elimination of ceilings on interest rates, the Act left the implementation at the discretion of a committee consisting of the heads of major regulatory agencies.

Removal of the ceilings will not be easy because it threatens the traditional patterns established among financial institutions. Some indication of the difficulties was revealed by the fact that the implementation committee was sued by one group of financial institutions on the announcement of the first set of adjustments to the ceiling. The advocates of the change, however, predict they will result in an environment in which competition among deposit-taking institutions will ensure that their customers are able to earn a market rate of return on their savings.

Many institutions which were subject to rate ceilings on their deposits were also subject to state-imposed limitations on the interest rates they could charge on their loans. In general, Title V of the Act either removed state-imposed interest ceilings or replaced them with flexible ceilings based on market rates. Interestingly enough, Title V was not the final step with respect to state-imposed interest ceilings on lending by financial institutions; states were given up to three years to opt out of this provision and reinstate their interest ceilings.

The Powers of Financial Institutions

Titles III and IV of the Act represent another major step toward uniformity of treatment in the regulation of deposit-taking institutions in the United States. Title II permits, or in some cases legitimizes, the issue by near banks of deposits which serve as payments money, an activity which at one time was the sole preserve of the commercial banks. Moreover, Title III combined with the provisions of other titles allows the payment of interest on transactions balances held by individuals. Title IV extends the range of assets that can be held by deposit-taking institutions which compete with commercial banks. Savings and loan associations have their powers increased to permit them to hold a limited amount of corporate debt either through direct lending or investment, to issue credit cards and make consumer loans through their use, and to carry on trust and fiduciary powers on a similar basis to the banks. While the effect of these changes still restricts the near banks to a narrower range of lending and investment powers, it reduces substantially their dependence on residential mortgages as a major outlet for investment.

The Effects of the Reforms

While it is still too early to judge the ultimate effects of these wholesale changes in the regulations governing financial institutions, a number of predictions can be safely made. Before the changes, savers with small amounts of funds were restricted to savings instruments with returns set by regulation, whereas those with larger amounts of funds were able to choose among instruments with rates set by the market. Holders of small deposits have been put on a more comparable footing and for the first time since the depression will earn interest rates set by market forces. In addition, individuals will be able to choose to hold their chequing accounts at any of a variety of deposit-taking institutions. Moreover, all restrictions on interest payments they can receive on a chequing account have been eliminated.

Less easy to predict is the effect of the changes on the segmentation of activities among financial institutions. The opportunity has been given to savings institutions to move away from their concentration on mortgages. Whether the institutions respond to the opportunities to move into new fields of lending and investment remains to be seen. In some cases, the development of expertise for the new activities may be judged as too expensive; on the other hand, the greater possibilities for diversification may be an adequate incentive.

Such extensive change does not come without loss to some market participants. The deregulation of interest rates has caused substantial deposit outflows from savings institutions. In some cases, the regulators have had to arrange mergers, at times made possible only with the assistance of funds from deposit insurance. As might be expected with such major changes, the committee of regulators empowered to implement them has been proceeding with some caution and restraint and even then has been criticized for moving too quickly. Nevertheless, the changes in regulatory structure may not be at an end. Further expansion of powers for banks and near banks and the lifting of legal barriers to interstate banking are among the possible future changes which are now being proposed.

TWO PATHS TO A
COMPETITIVE FINANCIAL SYSTEM

In the 1970s, traditional patterns of regulation of financial institutions were severely tested by the reactions of financial institutions and financial markets to the combined forces of technical change, taxation, high and variable interest rates, and inflation. The responses of the Canadian and American authorities differ in important respects, although both seek a more competitive, more flexible financial system. The U.S. reforms emphasize deregulation and uniformity of treatment of financial institutions engaged in similar activities. The Canadian reforms involve only a small step in the direction of uniformity, and deregulation *per se* is not an important theme. It must be noted, however, that while other measures are involved, an important aspect of deregulation is the elimination of ceilings on interest rates on deposits, a type of regulation not present in Canada.

Students of Canadian banking should be following developments in the United States with intense interest, if only to speculate on the effects of similar policies if implemented in Canada.

ENDNOTES

1. Royal Commission on Banking and Finance, *Report*, p. 569
2. *Ibid.*, p. 362
3. *Ibid.*, p. 378
4. *Ibid.*, p. 364

5. Several pieces of legislation are involved, which we refer to collectively as the Bank Acts of 1967. They include, the *Bank Act*, the *Quebec Savings Bank Act*, the *Bank of Canada Act*, and the *Canada Deposit Insurance Act*.

6. Royal Commission on Banking and Finance, *Report*, pp. 117-29, 369-73.

7. Canada, House of Commons, Standing Committee on Banking and Commerce, *Proceedings, Decennial Revision of the Bank Act* (Twenty-Second Parliament, First Session, 1954), p. 234.

8. The Canadian Bankers' Association. *Submission to the Royal Commission on Banking and Finance* (July 1962), p. 157.

9. Canada, House of Commons, Standing Committee on Finance. Trade and Economic Affairs, *Proceedings, Decennial Revision of the Bank Acts*, (February 7, 1967), p. 1739.

10. It is not clear that the concept of maintaining the independence of banks from domination by single groups of economic interests if fully consistent with the basic policy of stimulating competition. The provision virtually prohibits the "takeover" of an existing bank except through amalgamation with an existing bank. A "takeover" can be an effective device for installing a new, more effective management team in a firm which is not achieving its full market potential, i.e., to improve efficiency, the fundamental purpose of a policy of stimulating competition. It is not obvious, therefore, that the 10% rule is perfectly consistent with the rest of the pro-competitive policy.

11. Following the introduction of the *Canada Deposit Insurance Act* in Parliament in January 1967, and in the face of a run on a trust company, the government of Ontario introduced and quickly passed an almost identical bill in the Ontario Legislative Assembly. Thus, the government of Ontario has the honor of establishing the first deposit insurance scheme in Canada. Shortly after the federal act was passed, the *Ontario Act* was revised to require trust and loan companies incorporated or registered in Ontario to insure deposits with the Canada Deposit Insurance Corporation.

12. Canada Deposit Insurance Corporation, *Annual Report*, 1980.

13. The losses of the Corporation in the first case were reimbursed by a provincial government under a special agreement. In the second case, the loss was estimated in 1980 to have been $440 thousand. Canada Deposit Insurance Corporation, *Annual Report*, 1974; 1980.

14. J. Mintz, *The Measure of Rates of Return in Canadian Banking*. (Ottawa: Ministry of Supply and Services, 1979). More recent data on net revenue as a percentage of revenue and of equity for chartered banks, trust and loan companies and credit unions are published quarterly in Statistics Canada, *Financial Institutions*. These data are consistent with Mintz' conclusions.

15. Economic Council of Canada, *Efficiency and Regulation*, (Ottawa, 1976), p. 104.

16. E. W. Clendenning, *The Euro-Currency Markets and the International Activities of Canadian Banks* (Ottawa: Ministry of Supply and Services, 1976).

17. *Efficiency and Regulation*, p. 65.

18. It is difficult to know how many foreign banks were active in Canada at this time. In instances where a foreign bank controlled a Canadian trust company or other financial institution, there is reasonably good information, including estimates of assets and liabilities. In the case of representative offices, which were not required to register until the 1980 *Bank Act*, there is less information. These offices acted on behalf of their parent firms, collecting deposits and engaging in activities prohibited for Canadian banks, such as factoring and leasing.

19. *Efficiency and Regulation*, p. 23.

20. Minister of Finance, *White Paper on the Revision of Canadian Banking Legislation* (Ottawa, 1976), p. 33.

21. *Banking and Banking Law Revision Act*, 1980. Section 174(2)j, p. 173.

22. Cited in the *White Paper on the Revision of Canadian Banking Legislation*, p. 30.

23. *Banking and Banking Law Revision Act, 1980*, Section 8(d), p. 14.

24. *Ibid.*, Section 302(7), p. 310.

25. In the years 1947 through 1962 some 351 national and 1225 state banks were chartered, an average of 22 national and 76 state banks per year. In every year new state charters were several times as numerous as new national charters. In the years 1963 through 1965 some 457 national and 382 state charters were issued, an average of 152 new national and 127 new state banks per year. The preceding relationship between new national and state charters was reversed. From 1966 on, the old pattern reemerged, as new national charters fell to 25, 14, and 16 in 1966, 1967, and 1968 respectively. Cf., Comptroller of the Currency, *Annual Report*, 1964; *Federal Reserve Bulletin*, various issues.

26. The whole issue is discussed in the Comptrollers' *Annual Report*, 1964.

27. S. Peltzman, "Bank Entry Regulation: Its Impact and Purpose," *National Banking Review* Volume 2 (Dec. 1965), reprinted in *Studies in Banking Competition and the Banking Structure* (Washington: The Administrator of National Banks, 1966), pp. 285-99.

28. The Board attempted to implement such controls a year earlier without legislative authority, by the expedient of denying advances to associations which violated Board-established interest rate ceilings. This experiment was not successful. The 1966 legislation was justified on the now familiar grounds that while a limited amount of competition in the financial system is desirable, "it could be carried beyond reasonable limits". See Federal Home Loan Bank Board, *34th Annual Report, 1966* (Washington: 1967), pp. 45-56.

29. Dunham, C., "The Growth of Money Market funds," *New England Economic Review* (Sept/Oct., 1980), pp. 20-34.

30. A very useful summary of developments through 1977 is in J.M. Lovati, "The Growing Similarity Among Financial Institutions," Federal Reserve Bank of St. Louis, *Review*, 59 (October 1977), pp. 2-11. See also K. Gibson, "The Early History and Initial Impact of NOW Accounts," *New England Economic Review* (Jan./Feb. 1975), pp. 17-26; R.C. Kimball, "Variations in the New England NOW Account Experiment," *(New England Economic Review* (Nov./Dec. 1980), pp. 23-39.

31. *The Report of the President's Commission on Financial Structure and Regulation* (Washington, 1971). The Report is intensively discussed in Federal Reserve Bank of Boston *Policies for a More Competitive Financial System.* (Boston, 1972).

32. The act is summarized in "The Depository Institutions Deregulation and Monetary Control Act of 1980," *Federal Reserve Bulletin*, 66 (June 19lat-
ing competition. It is not obvious, therefore, that the 10% rule is perfectly consistent with the rest of the pro-competitive policy.

PART III

Macroeconomics of the Canadian Financial System

The preceding sections of the book were concerned with the micro-economics of the financial system. We now turn to macroeconomic problems.

Macroeconomics versus Microeconomics

Microeconomics is concerned with the *composition* of economic activity. Applied to the financial system, it is an analysis of the behavior of individual decision-making units (households, firms, and governments in their roles as assetholders and debtors) and of the process by which their interaction in the market place determines a set of prices for financial instruments and the allocation of credit among alternative uses. By contrast, macroeconomics is concerned with issues relating to the *stability* of economic activity. The basic units of analysis are broad aggregates like "the money supply," "consumption," or "investment," and the analysis focuses on such variables as the general level of prices or the general level of employment. Monetary theory, as a branch of macroeconomics, is concerned primarily with the implications of the size of the stock of money for economic stability.

The Historical Roots of Monetary Theory

Monetary theory has had a long and contentious history including many diversions into the search for monetary panaceas for deep-seated social ills, and for a monetary constitution appropriate to fundamental reform of the social structure. However, modern monetary theory can be regarded as having two primary roots in the history of economic analysis.

385

The first root is the *classical quantity theory of money*, a proposition that in a fully employed economy there is a direct and proportional relationship between the supply of money and the general level of prices. Of particular significance are two building blocks of the quantity theory: the assumption that there is sufficient flexibility in wage rates and prices that in the long run the economy will automatically adjust to full employment, and the assumption that there is a stable demand for money function. As we will see, these are central propositions of some branches of modern monetary theory, and many of the debates and much of the empirical research in monetary economics in recent years have been concerned with the validity and implications of these assumptions.

The second major root of modern monetary theory is John Maynard Keynes' *General Theory of Employment, Interest and Money*. Published in 1936, in the midst of the most devastating depression the industrialized world had ever experienced, this book was an attempt to develop a consistent theoretical explanation of why the self-regulating mechanisms of a market economy are insufficient to guarantee continuous full employment of the nation's productive resources. As a theory of how an economy could be in stable equilibrium at less than full employment, *The General Theory* has been subjected to increasingly effective theoretical criticisms in the five decades since its publication. Nonetheless, it has had a profound and lasting impact on economics. While it would be stretching a point to say that it created modern macroeconomics, it did produce a reorientation of theoretical macroeconomics away from preoccupation with the general level of prices and the general "business cycle" in favor of the determination of an equilibrium level of employment. The central analytical concept became the level of aggregate demand, and with it came a whole new set of theoretical concepts with which to explore macroeconomic problems. As one of the most effective critics of Keynesian theory noted:

> In one sense, we are all Keynesians now; in another sense no one is a Keynesian any longer. We all use the Keynesian apparatus; none of us any longer accepts the initial Keynesian conclusions.[1]

The impact of Keynesianism on monetary economics is difficult to summarize. In part it was theoretical. Keynes took over the Classicists' concept of the demand for money, explored and extended it, and drew conclusions which had profound new implications for the effectiveness of monetary policy in regulating the level of aggregate demand. In major part, however, the impact was empirical. The controversies over the theoretical implications of Keynes' assumptions about the demand for money produced a spate of increasingly refined attempts to quantify the demand for money function. Similarly, Keynesian pessimism over the general effectiveness of monetary policy in influencing aggregate demand has stimulated many empirical studies of the impact of monetary variables on economic activity. Macroeconomic model building and testing

1. Milton Friedman, *Dollars and Deficits: Inflation, Monetary Policy and the Balance of Payments* (Englewood Cliffs: Prentice-Hall, 1968), p. 15.

have become major preoccupations of monetary economists. Equally important, however, has been the impact on attitudes of economists and governments
toward the role of government in the economy. The Keynesian analysis suggested that the management of aggregate demand was an effective method of
relieving large-scale unemployment, and that monetary and fiscal policies
could be used to manage aggregate demand. This implied an active role for the
government in the stabilization of the economy. This is in stark contrast to the
prescriptions of more classical monetary economics.

Objectives of Our Analysis

The modern macroeconomics of economies like Canada's is a large and
complicated subject. At even an intermediate level, it provides material for a
substantial book in itself. In this book, we do not attempt to provide a complete
course in the macroeconomics of the Canadian economy. Many important
topics are neglected; and many are given very cursory treatment. We focus on
money and on the impact of monetary variables on the level of aggregate
demand and hence on certain crucial macroeconomic variables like the general
level of prices and the general level of employment. However, one of the things
which has been learned from the endless controversies over the Keynesian
treatment of monetary factors is that they cannot be considered in isolation. We
cannot avoid exploring general macroeconomic models. It is a question of
emphasis. Because our concern is with monetary phenomena, we will concentrate our analysis on the monetary sectors of such models.

The money supply is the central variable in our analysis, partly as an
exploratory variable, and partly as an instrument of policy. If it is to be an
instrument of policy, our first concern must be with the ability of the government
to control the money supply. This is the subject of the first three chapters of
Part III. Chapter 17 examines the roles of the banks and the near banks in the
determination of the size of the money supply. It turns out that the important
variable is the monetary base. Chapters 18 and 19 demonstrate that the Bank
of Canada, a government-owned institution charged with responsibility for
monetary policy, can control the monetary base, and explore the use of several
policy instruments which the Bank has at its disposal for this purpose.

Control of the monetary base gives the Bank of Canada control over the
money supply. Control over the supply of money is only useful if we understand
the nature of the demand for money. Indeed, in the history of monetary theory
(and in current controversies over monetary policy) many of the bitter divisions
resolve, at least in part, into deep disagreements about the nature and stability
of the demand for money. This is the subject of Chapter 20.

Although the demand for and supply of money are basic, there is much
more to a working understanding of the effects of monetary policy on the
economy. We must first consider the impact on aggregate expenditures, an
effect which largely works through the sensitivity of expenditures to interest
rates and the availability of credit. But the change in expenditures is only part of
the story. Will it lead to a change in production and employment or prices or

both? The sensitivity of prices, and particularly wage rates, to excess demand in the market place becomes a central issue, which is also the basis of deep disagreements among monetary economists. However, it also turns out that the effects of monetary policy — indeed, the very *possibility* of monetary policy — depends on the arrangements with respect to the foreign exchange rate. Is it fixed, as under the gold standard? Or, is it flexible, the common arrangement since the early 1970s? These are the topics of Chapters 21 and 22, which are, of necessity, long, complicated, and difficult.

Perhaps the overall conclusion of our analysis is that the power to regulate the money supply is a power with very profound consequences. It has been argued by many economists that rational management of the money supply by the government can very significantly improve the performance of the economy, with benefits to all. It has been as vigorously argued by a growing number of economists that the effects of monetary policy are so powerful but so difficult to predict in timing and in detail that discretion with respect to the money supply cannot safely be vested in anyone, let alone a government which may have a direct incentive to abuse that power. Rather, it is argued, the money supply ought to be governed by a monetary constitution, which eliminates discretion. Exploration of this issue, in both domestic and international contexts, is the subject of the final chapter.

The Money Supply Process PART 1: THE BANKS AND NEAR BANKS

17

Our first task in analyzing the macroeconomics of the financial system is to examine how the supply of money is expanded and contracted.

THE MONEY SUPPLY

We discussed the nature and composition of the Canadian money supply in Chapter 2. You will recall that the appropriate scope of the concept of money is a matter of some controversy among economists. While all definitions have as common components *currency in circulation* and *demand deposits* with chartered banks (i.e., what is commonly called M1), alternative definitions include other types of deposits with chartered banks and with other financial institutions.

This controversy is important for the analysis of the demand for money and hence for the analysis of monetary policy. To analyze the *principles* of the money supply process, however, we can sidestep the issue, exploring the process with alternative definitions of money. In this chapter, we consider first a monetary system in which demand deposits are the only form of money; then explore the implications of adding currency; then time deposits with chartered banks; and finally deposits with other types of financial institutions.

THE BASIC PRINCIPLE OF DEPOSIT CREATION

To set the process of deposit-creation in clear relief, assume that we have a financial system with only one chartered bank, that this bank issues only demand deposits, and that these demand deposits are the only type of money used in the economy.

The basic principle by which this monopoly bank can expand the money supply follows directly from the concept of money and the nature of financial intermediation. You will recall that a financial intermediary finances its portfolio of earning assets by issuing liabilities, claims upon itself which have valued characteristics like liquidity, relatively low risk, etc. Normally, in order to acquire more earning assets, a financial intermediary must first *sell* its own liabilities. It must exchange its liabilities for money, offering them at a sufficiently attractive yield that assetholders will be willing to take them into their portfolios. However, the liabilities of our financial intermediary, a bank, have the peculiar characteristic that *they are money*. When the bank purchases earning assets, it pays for them by issuing its own liabilities. There is no question of the public's accepting the bank's liabilities in exchange for the promissory notes acquired by the bank. The public will accept them because they are recognized as money. As a result, by increasing its earning assets, the bank adds to the supply of money. This is the basic principle of money creation.

Credit Creation.   It is important to keep in mind that both sides of the balance sheet are involved in this process. *When a bank creates deposits, it simultaneously creates credit.* Indeed, the creation of deposits is not the primary objective. Rather, it is to add to the portfolio of earning assets, and thereby to increase the profits of the bank (it follows that credit creation will only occur when a bank finds profitable loans or securities to add to its portfolio). The creation of deposits occurs as a by-product. It is the method by which the banks finance the net addition to the stock of credit extended directly or indirectly to businessmen, consumers, and governments.

Money Creation and Wealth.   Note that the money created in this way will be an asset to whoever receives it, but in the aggregate *it does not increase the wealth of the community directly.* In the books of the bank there has been an equal increase in assets and liabilities. The bank's net worth has not increased. Similarly, in the books of the community at large there has been an equal increase in assets (money) and liabilities (debts to the bank). The public's net worth has not increased. In the technical jargon of the economist, money created in this way has come to be called "inside money." It is money offset by an equal value of private debt.

An Example.   To make these points quite clear and explicit consider Example 17-1. The initial balance sheet of the bank is simple. We have assumed that the assets consist of equal proportions of loans and securities, and that the sources of funds are either demand deposits or capital subscribed by shareholders. You should note that this bank has no cash reserves among its assets. By assumption, there is no other type of money besides its demand deposits. There is nothing to hold as cash reserves, nor is there need for such reserves.

The bank makes a loan for $10 000 to a businessman, crediting the businessman's demand deposit with that sum of money. The transaction is simply an exchange of assets and liabilities. The bank gains a claim on the businessman; the businessman gains a claim on the bank. Neither the net worth of the bank nor the businessman have changed; the assets and liabilities of both have increased by like amount. However, the

EXAMPLE 17-1   **Deposit creation by a monopoly bank ($ Thousands)**

A. Initial balance sheet

Assets		*Liabilities*	
Loans	5 000	Demand deposits	9 000
Securities	5 000	Capital accounts	1 000
	10 000		10 000

B. Deposit creation

Transaction: The bank makes a loan to a business.

Bank				Businessman			
Loans	+10	Deposits	+10	Deposits	+10	Loans	+10

C. Final balance sheet

Loans	5 010	Demand deposits	9 010
Securities	5 000	Capital accounts	1 000
	10 010		10 010

Net Change:

Money supply	+10
Credit	+10

businessman now has in his possession money which previously did not exist. The businessman is free to spend the funds he has borrowed to meet his payroll, purchase raw materials, pay for capital equipment, etc. As he makes those payments, the money created by his act of borrowing from the bank enters into general circulation. The money supply has expanded by $10 000. When the loan is repaid, a corresponding contraction of the money supply will occur, unless the bank replaces the loan with another of equal value.[1]

It should be obvious that the bank does not have to wait for someone to approach it for a loan in order to expand the money supply. If the bank enters the open market and purchases government bonds (or any securities), making payment by crediting the sellers' demand deposit, the same effect will occur. The money supply will expand by an equal amount. Indeed, whenever the bank purchases any asset this will happen (or even whenever the bank pays for goods or services rendered to it).

CONSTRAINTS ON DEPOSIT CREATION

The context in which we have developed the basic principle of deposit creation is highly artificial. Given our unrealistic assumptions, there is no effective constraint on the ability of the bank to create money other than its ability to find acceptable assets to purchase. By relaxing these assumptions we can identify the constraints which actually exist.

Cash Reserves and "Excess Reserves"

Banker's Risk.   We have so far assumed that there is only one type of money: demand deposits. Relaxation of this assumption reveals an important constraint on the bank, imposed by what we can call "banker's risk."

It does not matter what we assume to be the other money, providing only that it is not issued by the bank itself. If we take a historical perspective, it might be gold or silver coin; in the contemporary world it is likely to be paper money, issued by a central bank or other governmental agency, and endowed with legal-tender status. The important point is that *the bank is required to convert its deposit liabilities into legal tender, at par, and on demand.* Therefore, the bank's portfolio must be managed with one eye on its ability to meet possible demands for payment in legal tender.

The Demand for Cash Reserves.   This means that the banks will have a demand for legal tender to be held as cash reserves, and this demand will depend, among other things, on the size and potential instability of its deposit liabilities. The smaller the bank's cash reserves relative to its deposits the greater the risk that it will not be able to meet all depositors' demands for cash. However, it is highly unlikely that all, or even a large portion, of total deposit liabilities will be presented for payment in a short period of time. As a result, the bank does not have to hold cash equal in value to its deposit liabilities, or even nearly equal in value, to have a high degree of safety. The bank must hold cash reserves, but these can be but a fraction of total deposit liabilities.

What fraction of deposits should be held in reserves? There is one important point to remember about cash reserves — they are a *sterile asset.* Loans and securities yield interest to the bank; cash reserves provide safety, but they do not yield interest income. The higher the ratio of cash reserves to deposits, the greater the hedge against banker's risk, but the lower the interest income of the bank, the smaller the potential profits. In the extreme, of course, 100% cash reserves would provide absolute safety, but no interest income. We should also remember that in the presence of an active open money market there is a range of interest-bearing assets which bankers can hold as a hedge against banker's risk, permitting them to economize on cash reserves. If he is free to choose his cash reserve ratio, the banker will balance, at the margin, his concern for safety and his concern for profits.

It is sometimes assumed that, given free choice, bankers would tend to maintain a fixed ratio of cash reserves to deposits. It should be obvious, however, that the appropriate ratio will depend on the circumstances. By providing alternative hedges against banker's risk, an active money market encourages banks to reduce the ratio. The greater the banker's perception of risk, the higher the ratio; the higher the level of interest rates, and hence the greater the opportunity cost of holding sterile cash, the lower the ratio. Historical experience, in periods when bankers had free choice regarding cash reserves, reveals highly variable cash reserve ratios, as for example in Figure 17-1, which shows Canadian experience, 1892-1934. The range of fluctuation is wide. From 1902-1915 the average ratio was almost doubled, while from 1915-1929 it was more than cut in half again. Moreover, an aggregate ratio, such as that plotted on this chart, conceals the behavior of many individual banks which had widely different reserve

FIGURE 17-1   Bank cash reserve ratios, 1892-1934*

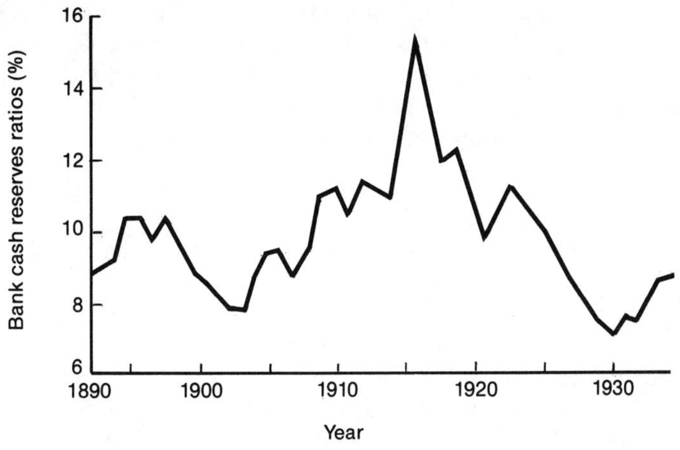

*Ratio of cash on hand to net liabilities.

Source: *Canada Year Book*, 1927-28; *Canada Year Book*, 1934-35.

policies, and the fact that annual averages are plotted conceals shorter-term fluctuations in the aggregate ratio.

Legal Reserve Requirements.   But bankers in the modern world do not have free choice with respect to cash reserves. As we saw in Chapter 14, the system in which the bank themselves decided on the appropriate level of their cash reserves eventually gave way to a system in which the government specified *minimum* acceptable ratios of cash reserves to deposits. At times (e.g., 1935-1954) the legal requirement was not an effective constraint on the banks. They chose to hold cash reserves substantially in excess of those required by law. At other times (e.g., 1954 to date) the cash reserve requirement was effective. The minimum cash reserve ratio specified by law was at least equal to, and apparently substantially greater than, that which the banks would have chosen to hold voluntarily. As a result, the cash reserve requirement introduced an important rigidity into the management of the banks' asset portfolios, and the cash reserve ratio became relatively stable.

"Excess" Reserves.   It is customary to refer to the difference between the cash reserves actually held by a bank ("actual" reserves) and those which the bank is required to hold by law ("required" reserves) as *"excess" cash reserves*. It should be obvious, however, that such reserves may be "excess" only in a formal legal sense. The bank is not *required* to hold them. However, given that there are penalties for failing to meet the legal cash reserve requirement, a bank will have an inducement to hold excess cash reserves even if the level of required reserves is more than adequate to meet all possible demands for payment. The bank faces another type of banker's risk — the risk that an unanticipated cash drain may reduce actual reserves below required reserves, exposing the bank to embarrassment and additional costs in the form of legal penalties.[2] This risk is an inducement to hold some excess reserves, an inducement which must be balanced, at the margin, against the opportunity cost of holding additional sterile cash. In other words, reserves which appear to be "excess" in a *legal sense* may not be "excess" in an *economic sense*. They may be reserves which the bank desires to hold, under the circumstances.

The Second Principle of Deposit Creation.   In Canada, the banks' demand for excess reserves is very small (in recent years excess cash reserves have averaged less than 0.05% of deposits). To simplify our analysis, we can assume that the monopoly bank wishes to hold no excess reserves. Then the profit motive dictates that whenever the bank has excess cash reserves it will acquire more earning assets. Deposits will expand. Conversely, if the bank has deficient cash reserves, it will dispose of earning assets. Deposits will contract.

This is a very important point. It is the second principle of deposit expansion: *Deposit expansion will only occur when banks have excess cash reserves, and it will continue until the excess reserves are exhausted.* A reserve deficiency (negative excess reserves) will correspondingly produce a contraction of deposits which will continue until the reserve deficiency is eliminated.

An Example.   This principle can best be explored by way of an example. For the purposes of Example 17-2 we have modified the initial balance sheet of the Monopoly Bank to allow for a 10% cash reserve requirement (as specified in the 1980 *Bank Act* for demand deposits).

At the outset, the bank has no excess reserves. It is required to hold cash in the amount of 10% of deposits, and it chooses not to hold more. In the next two chapters we will explore various ways in which the *supply* of cash reserves for the banks may increase or decrease. For our immediate purposes, assume that the government prints $10 000 of new currency which it deposits in its account with the bank. This is new money. From the government's perspective, its liabilities have increased (legal tender currency outstanding, held by the bank), but its assets have increased correspondingly, and in the form of a demand deposit which is more convenient for making payments. The government can now pay its bills by writing cheques on its demand deposit, putting the new deposit money into general circulation. From the bank's perspective, its deposit liabilities have increased by $10 000, but its cash assets have increased by the same amount. Its *actual reserves* have increased by $10 000, but its *required reserves* have increased by only 10% of that sum, i.e., $1000. The bank now has *excess reserves* of $9000.

The bank's portfolio is not in equilibrium. The profit motive dictates that it dispose of its excess cash reserves and acquire more earning assets. In the example, the bank makes new loans although it might well acquire additional securities. In either case, the

EXAMPLE 17-2   Deposit creation by a monopoly bank with a 10% reserve ratio ($ Thousands)

A. Initial balance sheet

Assets		Liabilities	
Cash reserves	900	Demand deposits	9 000
Loans	5 000	Capital accounts	1 000
Securities	4 100		
	10 000		10 000

B. Deposit expansion

STAGE I: (a) The government deposits $10 thousand of newly printed currency, and (b) then makes equivalent payments by cheque to the general public.

Bank		Government		Public	
(a) Cash +10	Deposits Gov't +10	Deposits +10	Currency +10		
(b)	Deposits Gov't −10 Public +10	Deposits −10		Deposits +10	
Net: Cash +10	Deposits +10	Deposits 0	Currency +10	Deposits +10	

Bank reserve position (end of Stage I)			*The money supply* (net change)	
Total deposits	9 010			Demand deposits
Required reserves	901	Stage I		+10
Actual reserves	910	Cumulative		+10
Excess reserves	9	(to the end of Stage I)		

STAGE II: The bank makes loans in the amount of its excess cash reserves, crediting $9 thousand to the deposits of businesses.

Bank		Public	
Loans +9	Deposits Public +9	Deposits +9	Loans +9

Bank reserve position (end of Stage II)			*The money supply* (net change)	
Total deposits	9 019			Demand deposits
Required reserves	901.9	Stage I		10
Actual reserves	910	Stage II		9
Excess reserves	8.1	Cumulative		19
		(to the end of Stage II)		

STAGE III: The bank makes loans in the amount of its excess cash reserves, crediting $8.1 thousand to the deposits of businesses.

Bank			Public		
Loans +8.1	Deposits		Deposits+8.1	Loans	+8.1
	Public +8.1				

<table>
<tr><td colspan="2" align="center">Bank reserve position
(end of Stage III)</td><td colspan="2" align="center">The money supply
(net change)</td></tr>
<tr><td>Total deposits</td><td>9 027.1</td><td></td><td>Demand deposits</td></tr>
<tr><td>Required reserves</td><td>902.71</td><td>Stage I</td><td>10.00</td></tr>
<tr><td>Actual reserves</td><td>910.0</td><td>Stage II</td><td>9.00</td></tr>
<tr><td>Excess reserves</td><td>7.29</td><td>Stage III</td><td>8.10</td></tr>
<tr><td></td><td></td><td>Cumulative</td><td>27.10</td></tr>
<tr><td></td><td></td><td>(to the end of
Stage III)</td><td></td></tr>
</table>

C. Final balance sheet

STAGE *n:*   This process continues until the bank no longer has excess reserves to lend.

Assets		Liabilities	
Cash reserves	910	Demand deposits	9 100
Loans	5 090	Capital accounts	1 000.00
Securities	4 100		
	10 100		10 100

<table>
<tr><td colspan="2" align="center">Bank reserve position</td><td colspan="2" align="center">The money supply
(net change)</td></tr>
<tr><td>Total deposits</td><td>9 100</td><td></td><td>Demand deposits</td></tr>
<tr><td>Required reserves</td><td>910</td><td>Stage I</td><td>10.00</td></tr>
<tr><td>Actual reserves</td><td>910</td><td>Stage II</td><td>9.00</td></tr>
<tr><td>Excess reserves</td><td>0</td><td>Stage III</td><td>8.10</td></tr>
<tr><td></td><td></td><td>Stage IV</td><td>7.29</td></tr>
<tr><td></td><td></td><td>...</td><td>...</td></tr>
<tr><td colspan="2" align="center">Multiplier</td><td>Stage n</td><td>0</td></tr>
<tr><td colspan="2">Deposit multiplier $= \dfrac{\Delta D}{\Delta R} = \dfrac{1}{r} = 10$</td><td>Cumulative
(to the end of
process)</td><td>100.00</td></tr>
</table>

proceeds are credited to someone's demand deposit, providing a net addition to the money supply.

    This is far from the end of the story, however. The extension of $9000 of loans will not re-establish portfolio balance, as is evident from the fact that excess reserves of $8100 remain at the end of Stage II in the example. Given the fractional reserve requirement, the increase in deposits has impounded as required reserves only a fraction of the excess reserve. thus, when deposits increase by $9000 required reserves increase by only $900 leaving excess reserves of $8100. Again, the profit motive dictates the extension of loans in the amount of the excess reserves, and an additional $8100 is credited to the public's deposits with the bank.

This process will go on until all excess reserves have been converted into required reserves. As is shown on the final balance sheet, that will be when total deposits have increased by $100 000, or 10 times the initial deposit of currency.

Algebraic Representation.   Using very elementary mathematics, it is possible to derive a general expression for the deposit expansion multiplier implied by our very simple assumptions. Let R represent cash reserves, D deposits, and r the reserve ratio (which has a value greater than zero but less than one).

For equilibrium in the bank's portfolio, there must be no excess reserves: actual reserves must equal what the bank feels it is required to hold (to satisfy legal requirements plus any extra which it requires for safety). That is, in equilibrium:

$$R = rD \tag{17.1}$$

or

$$D = R(1/r) \tag{17.2}$$

It follows that if equilibrium is to be maintained in the face of an increase in cash reserves:

$$\Delta D = \Delta R(1/r) \tag{17.3}$$

That is, given an increase in reserves, to maintain equilibrium in the bank's portfolio, deposits must expand by the factor, $(1/r)$. We call this the deposit expansion multiplier. Given a reserve ratio of .10 the multiplier is 10. The higher the ratio the smaller the multiplier. Thus, if the ratio were .2, the multiplier would be 5. By contrast, if the ratio were .04, the multiplier would be 25.

Currency Drain

Our development of the deposit expansion multiplier ignores the effects of the public's demand for currency as a medium of exchange. However, in discussing the composition of the money supply in Chapter 2 we noted that currency was more efficient than demand deposits for certain types of transactions. As a result, as the money supply expands, the amount of currency in circulation is likely to rise as well.

This increase in currency in circulation is significant because every dollar of currency in circulation is a potential dollar of bank cash reserves which, if it were lodged in the bank's vaults, would serve to support several dollars' worth of bank deposits (depending on the reserve ratio). In this sense, currency in circulation and bank cash reserves are both what economists call *high-powered money*. Given the total supply of high-powered money, an increase of currency in circulation will reduce bank reserves and will reduce the total money supply by a multiple of the cash drain. Correspondingly, a reverse drain from currency in circulation into bank reserves will expand the total money supply by a multiple of the increased in bank reserves.

In the example explored in the previous section we assumed an increase in bank reserves resulting from an increase in the total amount of high-powered money in existence. Clearly, if a drain of currency into circulation accompanies the expansion of the money supply, the total expansion will be less than that shown in Example 17-2. In order to see this, consider Example 17-3.

An Example.   In this example we assume that the public normally holds currency equal to 50% of deposits. Otherwise, the figures used in the example are the same as those in Example 17-2. However, there is a crucial difference in the process of monetary expansion. As the bank creates deposits, excess reserves are reduced by *two* factors:

(1) the increased deposits convert some of the excess reserves into required reserves (as in Example 17-2); and

(2) the public's demand for currency drains some of the excess reserves out of the banks and into general circulation.

The effect of the currency drain is to reduce the monetary expansion resulting from the injection of a given amount of new high-powered money into the banking system. In the example, the money supply multiplier is reduced from 10 to 2.4, and the deposit expansion multiplier from 10 to 1.67.

Algebraic Representation: When there are two types of money, currency and demand deposits, the money multiplier is somewhat more complicated, although the process is essentially the same. The money supply expands as the bank attempts to reestablish equilibrium in its asset portfolio, substituting earning assets for sterile cash assets; but the expansion is constrained by the public's attempts to maintain equilibrium between currency and demand deposits in its money holdings.

While in practice the demand for currency is much more complicated, as a first approximation we can assume that it takes the form:

$$C = cD \tag{17.4}$$

From our definition of high-powered money (H), we know that:

$$\begin{aligned} H &= C + R \\ &= cD + R \end{aligned} \tag{17.5}$$

Or,

$$R = H - cD \tag{17.6}$$

But we also know that:

$$D = R(1/r) \tag{17.2}$$

Therefore,

$$D = (H - cD)\, 1/r \tag{17.7}$$

Reorganizing, we get

$$D = H\, 1/(r + c) \tag{17.8}$$

In other words, in order to maintain equilibrium in the face of an increase in high-powered money (which may be used either for bank reserves or currency for circulation) total deposits must increase by a factor of $1/(r + c)$. This is the *deposit expansion multiplier*, allowing for an increase in currency in circulation as the money supply expands.

EXAMPLE 17-3   Deposit creation with cash drain monopoly bank with a 10% cash reserve ratio ($ Thousands)

A. Initial balance sheet

Assets		Liabilities	
Cash reserves	900	Demand deposits	9 000
Loans	5 000	Capital accounts	1 000
Securities	4 100		
	10 000		10 000

B. Deposit creation

STAGE I: (a) The government deposits $10 thousand of newly printed currency, and (b) makes equivalent payments by cheque to the general public. The public's demand for currency can be described by the equation $C = 0.5 D$. (c) The public divides its increased money holdings between currency and deposits on this basis, taking $3.33 thousand in currency and holding $6.67 thousand in deposits.

(a)

Bank		Government		Public	
Cash +10	Deposits Gov't +10	Deposits +10	High- powered money +10		

(b)

	Deposits Gov't −10 Public +10	Deposits −10		Deposits +10	

(c)

Cash −3.33	Deposits Public−3.33			Currency +3.33 Deposits −3.33	

Net change: Cash +6.67	Deposits +6.67		High- powered money +10	Currency +3.33 Deposits +6.67	

Bank reserve position (end of Stage I)			*The money supply* (net change)		
Total deposits	9 006.67			Deposits	Currency	Total
Required reserves	900.67	Stage I	+6.67	+3.33	+10.00
Actual reserves	906.67				
Excess reserves	6.00				

STAGE II: The bank makes loans in the amount of its excess reserves from Stage I ($6 thousand). The public takes the proceeds partly in currency ($2 thousand) and partly in deposits ($4 thousand), according to the demand for currency function.

Bank			
Cash	−2	Deposits	
Loans	+6	Public	+4
Net:		Deposits	+4
Assets	+4		

Public			
Currency	+2	Loans	+6
Deposits	+4		
Money	+6	Loans	+6

<table>
<tr><td colspan="2">Bank reserve position
(end of Stage II)</td></tr>
<tr><td>Total deposits</td><td>9 010.67</td></tr>
<tr><td>Required reserves</td><td>901.07</td></tr>
<tr><td>Actual reserves</td><td>904.67</td></tr>
<tr><td>Excess reserves</td><td>3.60</td></tr>
</table>

The money supply
(net change)

	Deposits	Currency	Total
Stage I	+6.67	+3.33	+10.00
Stage II	+4.00	+2.00	+6.00
Cumulative (to end of Stage II)	+10.67	+5.33	+16.00

STAGE III: The bank makes loans in the amount of its excess reserves from Stage II ($3.6 thousand). The public takes the proceeds partly in currency ($1.2 thousand) and partly in deposits ($2.4 thousand), according to the demand for currency function.

Bank			
Cash	−1.2	Deposits	+2.4
Loans	+3.6		
Net:		Deposits	+2.4
Assets	+2.4		

Public			
Cash	+1.2	Loans	+3.6
Deposits	+2.4		
Money	+3.6	Loans	+3.6

<table>
<tr><td colspan="2">Bank reserve position
(end of Stage III)</td></tr>
<tr><td>Total deposits</td><td>9 013.07</td></tr>
<tr><td>Required reserves</td><td>901.31</td></tr>
<tr><td>Actual reserves</td><td>903.47</td></tr>
<tr><td>Excess reserves</td><td>2.16</td></tr>
</table>

The money supply
(net change)

	Deposits	Currency	Total
Stage I	+ 6.67	+3.33	+10.00
Stage II	+ 4.00	+2.00	+ 6.00
Stage III	+ 2.40	+1.20	+ 3.60
Cumulative (to end of Stage III)	+13.07	+6.53	+19.60

C. Financial balance sheet

STAGE n: The process continues until the bank no longer has excess reserves to lend:

Assets		Liabilities	
Cash reserves	901.67	Demand deposits	9 016.67
Loans	5 015.00	Capital accounts	1 000.00
Securities	4 100.00		
	10 016.67		10 016.67

<table>
<tr><td colspan="2">Bank reserve position
(end of process)</td></tr>
</table>

Total deposits	9 016.67
Required reserves	901.67
Actual reserves	901.67
Excess reserves	0

The money supply
(net change)

	Deposits	Currency	Total
Stage I	+ 6.67	+3.33	+10.00
Stage II	+ 4.00	+2.00	+ 6.00
Stage III	+ 2.40	+1.20	+ 3.60
Stage IV	+ 1.44	+0.72	+ 2.16
...		...	
Cumulative	+16.67	+3.33	+24.00

Note:

High-powered money outstanding	+10.00
Currency in circulation	+8.33
Bank cash reserves	+1.67

Multipliers

$$\text{Money supply multiplier} = \frac{\triangle M}{\triangle H} = \frac{24.00}{10.00} = 2.4$$

$$\text{Deposit multiplier} = \frac{\triangle D}{\triangle H} = \frac{16.67}{10.00} = 1.67$$

It should be noted, however, that the total expansion of the *money supply* is somewhat *greater* than the expansion of deposits. The money supply (M) is composed of both deposits and currency in circulation. That is,

$$M = C + D \tag{17.9}$$

On the assumption of proportionality between currency in circulation and demand deposits,

$$M = cD + D$$
$$= D(1 + c) \tag{17.10}$$

Substituting 16A.15 in 16A.17:

$$M = \left(\frac{H}{r+c}\right)(1+c)$$

$$= H\left[\frac{1+c}{r+c}\right] \tag{17.11}$$

The expression in square brackets is the equilibrium *money supply multiplier*, allowing for currency drain.

We can work out examples to satisfy ourselves that the higher the currency drain coefficient, the smaller the money supply multiplier and the smaller the participation of the banking system in the total expansion of the money supply. With the same cash reserve ratio as in Example 17-2 (0.1), a currency drain coefficient of 0.8 produces a money supply multiplier of 2 and a deposit multiplier of 1.11; if the currency drain coefficient is 0.2, the multipliers are 4 and 3.33 respectively. Currency drain has a powerful impact on the monetary expansion process.

Other Banks: Clearinghouse Drain

An additional source of artificiality in our analysis of the deposit expansion process is the assumption that there is only one bank with a monopoly of the demand deposit business. In modern Canada, there have never been fewer than eight banks, and at times more than 35. In the United States, there are more than 13 000. Does this make a difference to the deposit expansion process? *The presence of more than one bank alters the details of the deposit expansion process but not the basic principles.*

The complication which arises from the existence of other banks is that any bank engaging in monetary expansion will likely experience a *clearinghouse drain.* That is, as cheques are written against its deposits, and payments are made, *some or all of the funds will be deposited in other banks in the system.* Thus, a bank which makes loans in the amount of its excess reserves, creating an equal amount of new deposits, is exposed to the risk that the entire sum will be withdrawn and deposited in other banks. This forces the first bank to pay over an equal value of reserves. Its excess reserves disappear. The important point, however, is that unlike a cash drain, the clearinghouse drain does not eliminate excess reserves from the banking system. *It merely transfers them to other banks.* These banks, impelled by the same profit motive, will make loans or purchase securities, initiating the second round of deposit expansion. They will also likely experience a clearinghouse drain, moving the reserves, the base of deposit expansion, throughout the banking system. Eventually most banks will probably have had some share of the increased deposits. The process of expansion will stop when all excess reserves have been purged from the system. Unless the risk of clearinghouse drain induces banks to hold larger cash reserves than would a monopoly bank, the total expansion of deposits will be the same with many banks as with one bank.

Will the reserve ratio be higher in a banking system with several banks? On *a priori* grounds one would think so, although the development of an efficient, active short-term money market has reduced the need to hold cash reserves by making it possible to make reserve adjustments in the money market. Secondary reserves may substitute for cash reserves as a hedge against clearinghouse drains. In any case, it is clear that in Canada in recent years, the required cash reserve ratio has been at least as high as, and probably considerably higher than, that which the banks would hold voluntarily. Canadian banks normally hold virtually no excess cash reserves. We can assume, therefore, that the existence of several banks does not increase the effective cash reserve ratio.

An Example.   Deposit expansion with more than one bank (but ignoring the cash drain) is illustrated in Example 17-4. We have assumed a very simple pattern of clearinghouse drain. The initial deposit stays with the bank in each case, but any deposits created by the bank are withdrawn almost immediately and deposited in some other bank. We do not know what a "realistic" pattern of drains would be (in Canada, with so few banks, it is generally assumed that each bank would retain its proportionate share of any deposits created). However, regardless of the pattern, the basic point is the same. *Even if the deposit-creating bank loses all of its excess reserves at each stage in the expansion process, those excess reserves immediately reappear in some other bank. For the system as a whole, the total expansion of deposits through all stages is not affected by the presence of several banks.* Each bank presumably shares proportionately in the total expansion.

EXAMPLE 17-4 Deposit creation with more than one bank ($ Thousands)

STAGE I: As in Example 17-2. (It is assumed that the deposits are initially held at Bank A.)

Bank A		Bank B		Bank C		Public	
Cash +10	Deposits +10	Cash 0	Deposits 0	Cash 0	Deposits 0	Deposits +10	

Bank reserve position
(cumulative change to the end of Stage I)

Cash reserves

	Deposits	Actual	Required	Excess
Bank A	+10	+10	+1	+9
Bank B	0	0	0	0
Bank C	0	0	0	0
System	+10	+10	+1.2	+9

The money supply
(cumulative change to the end of Stage I)

	Deposits
Stage I	+10
Total	+10

STAGE II: (a) Bank A makes loans in the amount of its excess reserves, crediting $9 thousand to demand deposits. (b) These deposits are withdrawn almost immediately and deposited in accounts with Bank B.

(a)

Bank A		Bank B		Bank C		Public	
Loans +9	Deposits +9					Deposits +9	Loans +9

(b)

Bank A		Bank B		Bank C		Public	
Cash −9	Deposits −9	Cash +9	Deposits +9				

Net change:

Bank A		Bank B		Bank C		Public	
Deposits 0	Cash 0	Cash +9	Deposits +9			Deposits +9	Loans +9

Bank reserve positions
(cumulative change to the end of Stage II)

Cash reserves

	Deposits	Actual	Required	Excess
Bank A	+10	+1	+1	0
Bank B	+9	+9	+0.9	+8.1
Bank C	0	0	0	0
System	+19	+10	+1.9	+8.1

The money supply
(cumulative change to the end of Stage II)

	Deposits
Stage I	+10
Stage II	+ 9
Total	+19

STAGE III: (a) Bank B makes loans in the amount of its excess reserves, crediting $8.1 thousand to demand deposits. (b) These deposits are almost immediately withdrawn and deposited in accounts with Bank C.

(a)

Bank A		Bank B		Bank C		Public	
		Loans +8.1	Deposits +8.1			Deposits +8.1	Loans +8.1

(b)

Bank A		Bank B		Bank C		Public	
		Cash −8.1	Deposits −8.1	Cash +8.1	Deposits +8.1		

Net change:

Bank A		Bank B		Bank C		Public	
		Assets 0	Deposits 0	Cash +8.1	Deposits +8.1	Deposits +8.1	Loans +8.1

Bank reserve positions
(cumulative change to the end of Stage III)

Cash reserves

	Deposits	Actual	Required	Excess
Bank A	+10	+1	+1	0
Bank B	+9	+0.9	+0.9	0
Bank C	+8.1	+8.1	+0.81	7.29
System	+27.1	+10	+2.71	+7.29

The money supply
(cumulative change to the end of Stage III)

	Deposits
Stage I	+10
Stage II	+9
Stage III	+8.1
Total	+27.1

STAGE n: This process continues until excess reserves are exhausted.

Bank reserve positions
(cumulative change to the end of Stage n)

Cash reserves

	Deposits	Actual	Required	Excess
Bank A	+10	+1	+1	0
Bank B	+9	+0.9	+0.9	0
Bank C	+8.1	+0.81	+0.81	0
Bank D	+7.29	+0.73	+0.73	0
Bank E	+6.56	+0.66	+0.66	0
...	...	...	...	...
Bank n	0	0	0	0
System	+100	+10	+10	0

The money supply
(cumulative change to the end of Stage n)

	Deposits
Stage I	+10
Stage II	+9
Stage III	+8.1
Stage IV	+7.29
Stage V	+6.56
...	...
Stage n	+0
Total	+100

Multipliers

Deposit expansion multiplier $= \dfrac{\Delta D}{\Delta R} = \dfrac{100}{10} = 10$

Savings and Time Deposits

To this point in our analysis, we have assumed that banks issue only chequable demand deposits. In fact, they also issue nonchequable savings and time deposits. In a narrow definition of the money supply, these deposits would not be considered money because they are not in a form which can be used as a medium of exchange. In a broader definition of money, however, they would be considered part of the money supply. They are very liquid, and indeed a large portion of them are payable on demand. If they are not money, they are least a very close substitute for it. How do they affect the process of deposit creation?

This question is actually twofold: (1) how does the presence of time deposits affect the creation of *demand deposits*, and (2) how does the presence of time deposits affect the creation of *total deposits*? Throughout, we take the level of cash reserves in the banking system as given, and to minimize complexities we ignore cash drain. However, we must allow for the possibility of different cash reserve requirements for time and demand deposits.

Time Deposits and Money Creation.   Any bank depositor is free to choose whether he will hold his funds in a demand deposit on which no interest is paid[3] but which is designed to be used as a medium of payment, or in a time deposit bearing a positive rate of interest but not designed to be a medium of payment. What is the effect on the supply of money and credit of a transfer of funds from demand deposits to time deposits?

The immediate impact is obvious. If holders of demand deposits convert them into time deposits there is an immediate reduction in the stock of demand deposits outstanding. The narrow money supply is reduced. but how permanent is this reduction? Can the banks then make additional loans, creating new demand deposits to replace those which have been converted into time deposits?

The answer to this follows directly from our earlier analysis of the process of deposit creation. *Additional deposits can only be created if the transfer to time deposits produces excess reserves in the banking system.* If time deposits are subject to the same reserve requirements as demand deposits, no excess reserves will be created by the transfer. The restriction of the narrow money supply will be "permanent" (i.e., will last as long as the funds are kept in time deposits, or until more cash reserves are available), but the total deposits in and total credit extended by the banking system will be unchanged. However, if the time deposits are subject to a lower reserve requirement, the transfer will produce excess reserves. Additional deposits can be created. If the reserve requirement for time deposits is greater than zero, however, the demand deposits lost in the transfer cannot be fully replaced (some "permanent" reduction in the narrow money supply ($M1$) will result). Nonetheless, total bank deposits will have increased, and with it total bank earning assets. If the reserve ratio behind time deposits is zero, no monetary restriction will occur, and total bank deposits will be greater by an amount equal to the amount of deposits transferred to time deposits.

An Example.   These points are illustrated in Example 17-5, which considers three possible cases: where the reserve ratios for demand and time deposits are the same;

where the reserve ratio for time deposits is less than that for demand deposits; and where the reserve ratio for time deposits is zero. The effects of a transfer of $10 000 from demand to time deposits is traced through for each case. When the reserve ratios are assumed to be the same (Case 1), total deposits are unchanged but demand deposits fall by the amount of the transfer. When the reserve ratios are assumed to be 10% and 3% (Case 2), the bank is able to create deposits to replace 70% of the demand deposits

---

EXAMPLE 17-5   **Time deposits and deposit expansion ($ Thousands)**

Case 1

Reserve Ratios: Demand deposits   0.10
                      Time deposits   0.10

$10 thousand is transferred from demand deposits to time deposits.

Bank			Public		
Deposits			Deposits		
Demand	−10		Demand	−10	
Time	+10		Time	+10	

Bank deposits				*Bank reserve position* (net change)			
	Demand	Time	Total		Demand	Time	Total
Net change	−10	+10	0	Deposits	−10	+10	0
				Reserves			
				Actual			0
				Required	− 1	+ 1	0
				Excess			0

Case 2

Reserve Ratios: Demand deposits   0.10
                      Time deposits   0.03

STAGE I: $10 thousand is transferred from demand deposits to time deposits.

Bank			Public		
Deposits			Deposits		
Demand	−10		Demand	−10	
Time	+10		Time	+10	

Bank deposits (net change)				*Bank reserve position* (cumulative change to end of Stage I)			
	Demand	Time	Total		Demand	Time	Total
Stage I	−10.0	+10.0	0	Deposits	−10	+10	0
				Reserves			
				Actual	—	—	0
				Required	− 1	+ .3	−0.7
				Excess	—	—	+0.7

STAGE II: The bank makes loans in the amount of its excess reserves from Stage I. $0.7 thousand are credited to *demand deposits* of the general public.

Bank					Public			
Loans	+0.7	Deposits			Deposits			
		Demand	+0.7		Demand	+0.7	Loans	+0.7

Bank deposits (net change)				*Bank reserve position* (cumulative change to the end of Stage II)			
	Demand	Time	Total		Demand	Time	Total
Stage I	−10.0	+10.0	0	Deposits	−9.3	+10.0	+0.7
Stage II	+ 0.7	+ 0	+0.7	Reserves			
Cumulative	− 9.3	+10.0	+0.7	Actual	—	—	0
(to end of				Required	−0.93	+ 0.3	−0.63
Stage II)				Excess	—	—	+0.63

STAGE III: The bank makes loans in the amount of its excess reserves from Stage II. $0.63 thousand are credited to *demand deposits* of the general public.

Bank					Public			
Loans	+0.63	Deposits			Deposits		Loans	+0.63
		Demand	+0.63		Demand	+0.63		

Bank deposits (net change)				*Bank reserve position* (cumulative change to the end of Stage III)			
	Demand (Money)	Time	Total		Demand	Time	Total
Stage I	−10.0	+10.0	0	Deposits	−8.67	+10.0	+1.33
Stage II	+ 0.70	0	+0.70	Reserves			
Stage III	+0.63	0	+0.63	Actual	—	—	0
Cumulative	− 8.67	10.0	+1.33	Required	−0.67	+ 0.30	−0.57
(To end of				Excess			+0.57
Stage III)							

STAGE *n:*   The process continues until excess reserves are exhausted.

Bank deposits (net change)				*Bank reserve position* (cumulative change to end of *n* Stages)			
	Demand (Money)	Time	Total		Demand	Time	Total
Stage I	−10.0	+10.0	0	Deposits	−3	+10.0	+7
Stage II	+ 0.70	0	+0.70	Reserves			
Stage III	+ 0.63	0	+0.63	Actual	—	—	0
Stage IV	+ 0.57	0	+0.57	Required	−0.30	+ 0.30	0
...	...	...	...				
Stage *n*	0	0	0	Excess	—	—	0
Cumulative	− 3.0	+10.0	+7.0				

Case 3

Reserve Ratios: Demand deposits   0.10

Time deposits   0

STAGE I: $10 thousand is transferred from demand deposits to time deposits.

Bank			Public		
	Deposits			Deposits	
	Demand	−10		Demand	−10
	Time	+10		Time	+10

Bank deposits				*Bank reserve position*		
(net change)				*(cumulative change to the end of Stage I)*		
	Demand	Time	Total		Demand	Time	Total
Stage I	−10	+10	0	Deposits	−10	+10	0
				Reserves			
				Actual			0
				Required	− 1	0	−1
				Excess			+1

STAGE II: The bank loans in the amount of its excess reserves from Stage I. $1 thousand is credited to *demand deposits* of the general public.

Bank				Public			
Loans	+1	Deposits		Deposits		Loans	+1
		Demand	+1	Demand	+1		

Bank deposits				*Bank reserve position*		
(net change)				*(cumulative change to the end of Stage II)*		
	Demand	Time	Total		Demand	Time	Total
Stage I	−10	+10	0	Deposits	−9	+10	+1
Stage II	+ 1	0	+1	Reserves			
Cumulative	− 9	+10.0	+1	Actual			0
(To end of				Required	−0.9	0	−0.9
Stage II)				Excess			+0.9

STAGE n: The process continues until excess reserves are exhausted.

Bank deposits				*Bank reserve position*		
(net change)				*(cumulative change to the end of n Stages)*		
	Demand	Time	Total		Demand	Time	Total
Stage I	−10.0	+10.0	0	Deposits	0.0	+10.0	+10.0
Stage II	+ 1.0	0	+1	Reserves			
Stage III	+ 0.9	0	+0.9	Actual	—	—	0
Stage IV	+ 0.81	0	+0.81	Required	0	0	0
...	...	...	...				
Stage n	0	0	0	Excess	—	—	0
Cumulative	0	+10.0	+10.0				

which were transferred to time deposits.[4] Total deposits increase by $7000, and the *net* reduction in demand deposits is only $3000. When it is assumed that no reserves are held against time deposits (Case 3), the bank is able to create deposits to replace all of the demand deposits transferred to time deposits. As a result, total deposits increase by the full $10 000.

In brief, if time deposits are subject to lower reserve requirements than demand deposits, any transfer of funds from demand deposits to time deposits will:

—reduce the narrowly defined money supply (*M1*), but by less than the net transfer of funds;

—increase total deposits (and hence the broadly defined money supply, *M3*); and

—increase total bank credit.

The Limits to Deposit Creation.   If the transfer of funds from demand deposits to time deposits will increase total deposits and hence the earning assets of a bank, other things being equal, such transfers would appear to be profitable for the banks. If so, what limits such transfers? What restricts the expansion of credit through this mechanism?

We must remember that the banks cannot reclassify accounts at will. To increase their time deposits they must induce people to give up demand deposits in favor of time deposits. The prime incentive to do so is the rate of interest paid on time deposits.

This suggests the nature of the limiting mechanism. Additional time deposits can only be gained by offering higher interest rates on time deposits. This increases the opportunity cost (the interest foregone) of holding demand deposits, and induces depositors to economize on their demand deposits balances, transferring a portion to time deposits. However, this cannot be done without limit or without inconvenience and cost to the depositor. Demand deposits are mainly held by business firms to facilitate the transactions of the firms. They cannot be dispensed with readily. As a result, the banks will find that to attract more time deposits they will have to pay higher interest rates and hence incur higher costs.[5]

Banks are business firms, striving to maximize profits. As you will recall from your principles of economics course, if marginal revenue (the revenue derived from producing and selling an additional unit of output) exceeds marginal cost (the cost of producing an additional unit of output) the firm can increase its profits by increasing output. If marginal revenue is less than marginal cost, the firm can increase its profits by reducing output. Only when marginal revenue equals marginal cost will profits be maximized.

This rule can be applied to banks. Our assertions about the cost to the bank of attracting more time deposits can be interpreted to mean time deposits are subject to rising marginal cost. The additional earning assets which can be acquired as a result of the increase in time deposits produce an increase in interest income (marginal revenue). It is only profitable, then, for the bank to strive for higher levels of time deposits if the expected marginal revenue exceeds anticipated marginal cost. With rising marginal cost, and a given yield on new earning assets, this establishes a definite limit to the share of time deposits in the total deposits of the banking systems.

In short, *the limit to credit creation through the time deposit mechanism lies in the increasing cost of attracting additional time deposits.* Attempts to expand time deposits beyond some point will simply not be profitable.

Time Deposits and the Money Multiplier.   This analysis of the impact of time deposits on deposit creation assumed a single lump-sum transfer of funds from demand deposits to time deposits (perhaps in response to a change in interest rates; perhaps for a variety of other reasons). What if there is a systematic relationship between demand deposits and time deposits? For example, what if, other things being equal, some fraction of any increase of demand deposits is normally transferred to time deposits?

It should be obvious from what has gone before that such a relationship between time deposits and demand deposits will alter the size of the deposit multiplier. As long as time deposits are subject to reserve requirements, any transfer of funds from demand deposits to time deposits will reduce the amount of demand deposits which can be created on the basis of a given increase in bank reserves. The narrow money supply multiplier ($M1$) will be reduced. At the same time, if the reserve ratio applied to time deposits is less than that applied to demand deposits, any such transfer will increase the total deposits of the banking system. What we might call the total deposit multiplier will be increased. The smaller the reserve ratio applied to time deposits, the larger the money supply multiplier and the total deposit multiplier. At the extreme, if the reserve ratio for time deposits is zero, the money supply multiplier will be the same as if time deposits did not exist.

Algebraic Representation.   In this analysis we ignore currency drain. Suppose there is a simple proportional relationship between time deposits (T) and demand deposits (D).
That is:

$$T = tD \qquad\qquad (17.12)$$

Let the reserve ratio applicable to time deposits be r_t and that applicable to demand deposits be r_d, where:

$$0 < r_t < r_d < 1 \qquad\qquad (17.13)$$

In equilibrium, total reserves (R) will be divided between demand deposits and time deposits such that no excess reserves remain. That is,

$$R = r_d D + r_t T \qquad\qquad (17.14)$$

Substituting

$$R = r_d D + r_t(tD)$$
$$= D[r_d + r_t t] \qquad\qquad (17.15)$$

or:

$$D = R\left[\frac{1}{r_d + r_t t}\right] \qquad\qquad (17.16)$$

The expression in square brackets is the *demand deposit multiplier*, allowing for time deposits. As long as $t > 0$, or $r_t > 0$, then:

$$\frac{1}{r_d} > \frac{1}{r_d + r_t t} \qquad\qquad (17.17)$$

That is, if positive cash reserves are maintained behind time deposits, the drain of funds into time deposits will reduce the demand deposit multiplier.

The total deposit multiplier will be greater than this. Total deposits are the sum of demand deposits and time deposits.

From 17.16 and 17.12:

$$D + T = R\left[\frac{1}{r_d + r_t t}\right] + tR\left[\frac{1}{r_d + r_t t}\right]$$

$$= R\left[\frac{1+t}{r_d + r_t t}\right] \tag{17.18}$$

The expression in square brackets is the *total deposit expansion multiplier*, allowing for time deposit drain. It can be shown quite easily that this will be greater than the basic multiplier, if $r_d > r_t$.

Combining the analysis of the effects of currency drain and of time deposits, we can derive an even more complicated set of multipliers.

From 17.5 and 17.14:

$$H = cD + r_d D + r_t t \tag{17.19}$$

Substituting 17.4 and 17.12 in 17.19:

$$H = cD + r_d D + r_t tD$$
$$= D(c + r_d + r_t t)$$

or:

$$D = H\left[\frac{1}{c + r_d + r_t t}\right] \tag{17.20}$$

The expression in square brackets is the *demand deposit multiplier*, allowing for both cash drain and the time deposit drain.

Substituting 17.4 and 17.20 in 17.9:

$$M = C + D$$
$$= cD + D$$
$$= H\left[\frac{1+c}{c + r_d + r_t t}\right] \tag{17.21}$$

The expression in square brackets is the *narrow money supply multiplier (M1)*, allowing for cash drain and time deposit drain.

We can also derive a total deposit multiplier by a similar process. The result is:

$$D + T = H\left[\frac{1+t}{c + r_d + r_t t}\right] \tag{17.22}$$

Secondary Reserve Requirements

Throughout this analysis of the deposit-expansion mechanism we have implicitly assumed that all of the reserves held by the banks, either as a hedge against banker's risk or to conform to legal requirements, are in the form of high-powered money (either cash in the vault or deposits with the central bank). However, we know that in Canada the banks also have a secondary reserve requirement, which can be satisfied by holding treasury bills, day-to-day loans, or cash. Moreover, the chartered banks in fact hold very large reserves of call loans and short-term, marketable securities as their primary hedge against banker's risk. In contrast to cash reserves, the banks normally have substantial excess reserves of liquid assets, which, unlike cash, are earning assets. Thus, the secondary reserve requirement is less onerous for banks than a corresponding cash reserve requirement would be. Does it have the same effect in restricting the expansion of deposits?

In general, the answer to this question is no. *Unless the supply of eligible liquid assets is less than the amount which the banks require, the liquid asset ratio will not impose a constraint on the amount of deposits which the banks can create on the basis of a given amount of high-powered money.*

This is not to say that the secondary reserve requirement has no significance. It clearly affects the composition of any increase in the banks' asset portfolios, and in this sense affects the form of the credit which may be extended. It could prevent the banks from increasing their loans as rapidly as they might otherwise do, thus restricting the availability of credit to certain sectors of the economy. By preventing the banks from taking on a larger proportion of high yielding assets it may also affect bank earnings.

NEAR BANKS AND DEPOSIT CREATION

One of the more contentious issues in the theory of the supply of money is whether near banks can create deposits.

Many economists argue that only true commercial banks have deposit-creating powers. In this regard, commercial banks are said to be unique among financial intermediaries. Near banks can increase their deposit liabilities by attracting deposits from commercial banks. They cannot "create" deposits.

Other economists disagree, denying the validity of the sharp dichotomy between banks and near banks, asserting that any differences are just a matter of degree, and that near banks participate actively along with banks in a complex process of deposit creation.

Near Bank Liabilities and Bank Money.   One factor in the debate is the definition of money. While most near banks have deposits which are transferable by cheque, their rate of turnover is not high as compared to demand deposits with chartered banks. Some economists do not include them in their definition of the money supply. A possible answer to the question, "Can near banks create money?" is yes, if you define deposits with near banks as money, and no, if you do not.

This answer is not helpful, however. It does not clarify the central issues. To focus on these issues, we will consider an example involving near banks which do not have chequable deposits.

An Example.   In Example 17-6 we trace the effects of a transfer of $10 000 from a demand deposit with a chartered bank to a nonchequable time deposit with a trust company. Two assumptions are particularly important. First, we assume that the trust company keeps any addition to its cash reserves in a demand deposit with a chartered bank. This is quite realistic. Currency in their vaults — the only other form of cash reserves — is typically a very small portion of total cash reserves of trust companies. For this example we have chosen a *desired* cash reserve ratio of 2% for the trust company. Second, we assume that when the trust company makes a mortgage loan, or otherwise invests its excess reserves, the recipients of these funds use them to purchase goods and services (e.g., building materials). The funds are deposited in demand deposits with chartered banks, and enter the general circulation.

EXAMPLE 17-6   Deposit creation by near banks: Case 1 ($ Thousands)

STAGE I: $10 thousand is transferred from *demand deposits* with chartered banks to time deposits with a trust company. The trust company deposits the funds in its demand deposit with its banker.

Trust Co.		Bank		Public	
Reserve Deposits +10	Deposits +10	Deposits Public −10	Deposits Bank −10		
		Trust +10	Trust +10		

The trust company desires to maintain cash reserves in the form of correspondent balances with its banker in the amount of 2% of its deposit liabilities.

	Public deposits (net change)				Reserve position (cumulative change to the end of Stage I)		
	Trust co.	Bank	Total		Trust co.	Bank	Total
Stage I	+10	−10	0	Total deposits	+10	0	+10
				Reserves			
				Actual	+10	0	+10
				Desired	+ 0.2	0	+ 0.2
				Excess	+ 9.8	0	+ 9.8

STAGE II: The trust company makes mortgage loans in the amount of its excess reserves. The $9.8 thousand is deposited in *demand deposits* of the general public, entering general circulation.

Trust Co.		Bank		Public	
Reserve Deposits −9.8		Deposits Trust −9.8	Deposits Bank +9.8	Loans +9.8	
Loans +9.8		Public +9.8			

	Public deposits (net change)				Reserve position (cumulative change to the end of Stage II)		
	Trust co.	Bank	Total		Trust co.	Bank	Total
Stage I	+10	−10	0	Total deposits	+10	0	+10
Stage II	0	+ 9.8	+9.8	Reserves			
				Actual	+ 0.2	0	+ 0.2
Cumulative	+10	− 0.2	+9.8	Desired	+ 0	0	+ 0
				Excess	+ 0	0	+ 0

In Example 17-6, the *immediate impact* of the transfer of funds from banks to near banks is to increase the deposit liabilities of the near banks *without reducing the deposit liabilities of the banks*. It is true that the ownership of deposits in the banking system has changed significantly. A trust company now owns deposits which were previously owned by members of the general public, and in consequence *the publicly-owned money supply has fallen*. However, the banks have the same total deposits, their cash reserve position is not changed (they have neither excess reserves nor deficient reserves), and they have no incentive to contract credit and deposits.

At the same time, *the trust company* has *excess reserves*. Its portfolios is in disequilibrium. The profit motive will dictate that it acquire more earning assets, and in making new loans or acquiring securities, it will be adding to the total stock of credit available to the economy. In this sense, by attracting deposits from the banking system, the trust company expands the total supply of credit.

What happens to the money supply as the trust company lends its excess reserves, and the borrowers — probably housebuyers — spend the borrowed funds which then enter the general monetary circulation as demand deposits? The ownership of deposits at the chartered bank again changes from the trust company to members of the public, except for the small part of these deposits held by the trust company as part of its cash reserves. The trust company loses the excess reserves in their entirety, but the bank does not gain any excess reserves. There is no secondary expansion of money and credit. Indeed, there is a small net contraction of the publicly-held money supply, narrowly defined, equal to the increased cash reserves which the trust company holds against its time deposits.

In sum, Example 17-6 illustrates that a transfer of funds from a demand deposit with a chartered bank to a time deposit with a near bank will:

—increase the total supply of credit to borrowers,
—increase the total supply of liquid deposits in the financial system (banks + near banks)
—reduce the narrowly defined money supply held by the general public.

As Example 17-7 makes clear, the expansion in total deposits and credit will occur even if the funds which are attracted from chartered banks come out of time deposits rather than demand deposits, and if the near banks choose to hold the same cash reserve ratio against time deposits as the chartered banks are required to hold. In the example, we have assumed that both the bank and the trust company hold cash reserves of 3% behind time deposits. The expansion occurs because the trust company holds its cash reserves in a deposit with the chartered bank.

Let us define the *effective total reserve ratio* as the ratio of high-powered money to total deposits in banks and near banks. Then, we can say that the transfer of funds from banks to near banks creates both credit and deposits because it reduces the equilibrium effective total reserve ratio of the financial system. If, as in Example 17-7, the transfer of deposits to the trust company results in a net shift of funds from time deposits in chartered banks, there may be a net contraction of the narrowly defined money supply. In other words, the effective total reserve ratio is affected both by the distribution of deposits between banks and near banks, and by the distribution of deposits between time deposits and demand deposits at banks.

In order to consolidate your understanding of these points, it might be useful for you to do the following two exercises. First, trace through what would happen if near banks held their cash reserves in the form of currency in their vaults. Second, trace through what would happen if the chartered banks held most of their cash reserves in the form of correspondent balances with each other. In assessing the relevance of the latter, remember that while correspondent balances are mainly connected with international banking operations in Canada, in the United States they are an important part of domestic banking. Indeed, in some states, state banks can count correspondent balances as part of their required cash reserves.

Limits on Near-Bank Credit Creation.   This analysis demonstrates that any transfer of funds from banks to near banks will lead to an expansion of the supply of credit and the stock of liquid assets in the economy. We have seen that the amount of credit which can be created from any given transfer is strictly limited by the reserve ratios of the banks and near banks. However, we have not established that there is any limit to the amount of funds which will be transferred. Will such transfers go on indefinitely? What limits the ability of the near banks to attract deposits and expand credit?

The answer is exactly the same as that which we developed in the case of time deposits at chartered banks. It is a matter of profitability.

If a near bank is to gain more deposits, it must persuade depositors to shift their accounts. To do this, it must offer terms which are sufficiently attractive to depositors to induce them to alter their banking habits. This may involve many factors in addition to interest rates paid on deposits, including such conditions as the location of branches, the hours of business at branch offices, service charges on accounts, advertising, gifts for opening new accounts, etc. To all of this, the banks can be expected to respond in some degree. As a result, the near banks can only obtain more deposits by being successful in a process of competitive bidding, and in doing so they will encounter rising costs. In brief, *near bank deposits are subject to rising marginal costs.*

Given the yield which can be expected on new assets acquired by the near bank — marginal revenue — there is some point beyond which the competition for deposits is no longer profitable. Thus, competition for more deposits will only appear profitable if expected marginal revenue exceeds marginal cost. When marginal revenue equals marginal cost, equilibrium will have been established, including an equilibrium distribution of deposits between banks and near banks.

This, then, establishes the limit to credit creation by near banks. It is inherent in the profit motive.

THE MONEY MULTIPLIER AND MONETARY POLICY

In this chapter we have examined the process by which the supplies of money and credit are expanded and contracted by private financial institutions. What does this analysis tell us about the implementation of monetary policy?

EXAMPLE 17-7 Deposit creation by near banks: Case 2 ($ Thousands)

STAGE I: $10 thousand is transferred from *time deposits* with chartered banks to *time deposits* with a trust company. The trust company deposits the funds in a demand deposit with its correspondent bank.

Trust co.

Reserve Deposits +10	Deposits +10

Bank

	Deposits
	Time −10
	Demand +10

Public

	Time Deposits
	Bank −10
	Trust Co. +10

The trust company desires to maintain cash reserves in the form of correspondent balances with its banker, in the amount of 3% of its deposit liabilities. The bank maintains a 3% reserve behind time deposits and 10% behind demand deposits.

Public deposits
(net change)

	Time deposits		Demand deposits	Total
	Trust Co.	Bank		
Stage I	+10	−10	0	0

Reserve position
(cumulative change to the end of Stage I)

Bank

	Trust Co.	Time	Demand	Total
Total Deposits	+10	−10	+10	+10
Reserves				
Actual	+10	0	0	+10
Desired	− 0.3	− 0.3	+ 1	+ 1
Excess	+ 9.7		−0.7	+ 9

STAGE II: The trust company makes mortgage loans in the amount of its excess reserves. $9.7 thousand is transferred from demand deposits owned by the trust company to demand deposits owned by the general public.

Trust co.

Loans +9.7	
Reserve deposit −9.7	

Bank

	Demand deposits
	Trust Co. −9.7
	Public +9.7

Public

Demand deposit +9.7	Loans +9.7

Public deposits
(net change)

	Time deposits		Demand deposits	Total
	Trust Co.	Bank		
Stage I	+10	−10	0	0
Stage II	0	0	+9.7	+9.7

Reserve position
(cumulative change to the end of Stage II)

Bank

	Trust Co.	Time	Demand	Total
Total deposit	+10	−10	+10	+10
Reserves				
Actual	+ 0.3	0	0	+ 0.3
Desired	+ 0.3	− 0.3	+ 1	+ 1.0

STAGE III: "Simultaneously the banks reduce their portfolios of earning assets, refusing to renew loans in the amount of their reserve deficiency.

Trust co.	Banks	Public
Loans −0.7	Loans −0.7	Demand Deposits −0.7
	Demand Deposits Public −0.7	Loans −0.7

Public deposits (net change)

	Time deposits		Demand deposits	Total
	Trust Co.	Bank		
Stage I	+10	−10	0	0
Stage II	0	+ 9.7	+9.7	+9.7
Stage III	0	0	−0.7	−0.7
Cumulative	+10	−10	+9.0	+9.0

Reserve position
(cumulative change to the end of Stage III)

	Bank			
	Trust Co.	Time	Demand	Total
Total Deposits	+10	−10	+9	+9
Reserves				
Actual	+ 0.3	0	0	+0.3
Desired	+ 0.3	− 0.3	+0.9	+0.9
Excess	0		−0.6	−0.6

STAGE n: This process of bank deposit contraction continues until the reserve deficiency is eliminated.

Public deposits (net change)

	Time deposits		Demand deposits	Total
	Trust Co.	Bank		
Stage I	+10	−10	0	0
Stage II	0	0	+9.7	+9.7
Stage III	0	0	−0.7	−0.7
Stage IV	0	0	−0.6	−0.6
⋯	⋯	⋯	⋯	⋯
Stage n	0	0	0	0
Cumulative	+10	−10	+3.0	+3.0

Reserve position
(cumulative change to the end of stage n)

	Bank			
	Trust Co.	Time	Demand	Total
Total Deposits	+10	−10	+3.0	+3.0
Reserves				
Actual	+ 0.3	0	0	+0.3
Desired	+ 0.3	− 0.3	+0.3	+0.3
Excess	0	0	0	0

The Money Multiplier: A Generalized Concept

Using the concept of the money supply multiplier, which we developed in several different formulations, we can think of the money supply as being determined by two factors, the stock of high-powered money (H) and the money supply multiplier (k). That is:

$$M = kH, \tag{17.23}$$

where $k > 1$. This is a very general statement of a complex relationship, but it provides a useful framework for thinking about the implementation of monetary policy.

This model of the money supply process makes a very important point. If the multiplier, k, is a *constant*, changes in the money supply will be simply reflections of changes in high-powered money. In particular, *the rate of growth of the money supply will be equal to the rate of growth of high-powered money.*

In Canada, high-powered money (currency in circulation plus bank cash reserves) consists mainly of liabilities of the central bank, the Bank of Canada. The central bank has relatively prompt information about the amount of high-powered money outstanding, and by the techniques to be discussed in the next two chapters the bank can control that magnitude. *If the multiplier is a constant, control over high-powered money is sufficient to give the central bank control over the money supply.* One of the most popular prescriptions for monetary policy in recent years is that the central bank should maintain an appropriate steady rate of growth in the money supply. If the money supply multiplier is a constant, the central bank can achieve the appropriate rate of growth in the money simply by using its powers to maintain that rate of growth in high-powered money.[6]

But there is another implication of the multiplier model. Any random disturbance to the stock of high-powered money — including mistakes by the central bank — will also have a magnified effect on the supply of money and credit, which could be very disturbing to the economy. On the one hand, the central bank must avoid major errors, and on the other hand it must carefully monitor developments to detect and offset extraneous disturbances if it is to effectively control the money supply.

Is the Money Multiplier a Constant?

The Two Basic Multipliers.   We have seen that it is possible, on certain simple assumptions, to develop a great variety of multipliers.[7] However, in the context of contemporary discussions of monetary control policies, two are basic, depending on the concept of money which is the focus of concern. Thus, if we want to focus on the narrow concept of money, M1, where

$$M1 = C + D \tag{17.9}$$

then, as we saw above, the multiplier (k_1) is:

$$k_1 = \left[\frac{1+c}{c+r_d+r_t t} \right] \tag{17.21}$$

However, if we focus on a broader concept of money, perhaps including time deposits with chartered banks (M3), so that,

$$M = C + D + T,$$ (17.24)

then the multiplier (k_3) becomes:

$$k_3 = \left[\frac{1+c+t}{c+r_d+r_t t} \right]$$ (17.25)

Let us briefly explore the behavior of these two multipliers in recent years.

Some Evidence.   Figure 17-2 shows the ratio of the money supply to high-powered money in Canada, monthly, from 1970 to 1979, on two definitions of money, M1 and M3.[8] If we assume that the average ratio over a month (which is a relatively long period of time in financial markets) reflects the money supply process in equilibrium, we can use these ratios as approximations to the multipliers, k_1 and k_3.

FIGURE 17-2   Money multipliers in Canada, 1970-1980: *K3* and *K1*

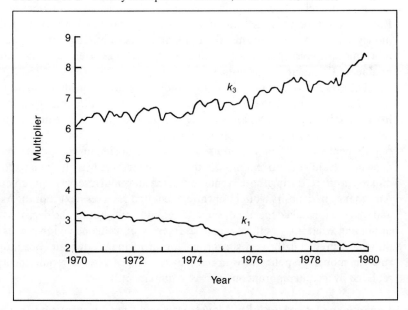

As we would expect, k_3 is much larger than k_1 — both have the same base, *H*, but k_3 relates to a much broader concept of the money supply. At the end of 1979, $k_3 = 8.5$ whereas $k_1 = 2.2$. But neither multiplier was constant. Both were subject to very pronounced, but opposite, trends. Thus, k_3 rose from 6 to 8.5 over the period, and k_1 fell from 3.3 to 2.2. A given steady rate of growth in high-powered money would have produced very different trends in M1 and M3. Moreover, both multipliers, but particularly k_3, showed significant short-term variability about the trend.

In short, on the evidence from 1970 to 1979, on a month-by-month basis, it is difficult to argue that the money supply multiplier, in either a broad or a narrow definition of money, is a constant.

Predictability versus Constancy.   But *stability* of the multiplier is not necessary for effective management of the money supply through control over high-powered money. Trends and fluctuations in k are all right, providing they are *predictable*.

Part of the observed fluctuations in the multipliers represents regular seasonal movements which are more or less predictable. However, the seasonal component is only part of the picture. Research by the staffs of the Bank of Canada and of Federal Reserve Banks suggests that both in Canada and in the United States, even allowing for seasonal variations, the instability of the multiplier is sufficient that during the short periods of time (up to several months) over which the central bank must be concerned about the behavior of the money supply, the rate of growth in high-powered money is a very poor predictor of the rate of growth in the money supply.[9] Over longer periods of time, a year of more, there is greater predictability. The Bank of Canada regards the multiplier model as a very unreliable guide for the implementation of monetary policy. Rather than setting a target rate of growth of high-powered money, and allowing the money supply to adjust to this, the Bank attempts to influence the money supply by other means. This approach to monetary control has been severely criticized by a number of Canadian economists.[10]

The reasons for the instability of the multiplier have been analyzed to some degree. All of the critical ratios make some contribution, but of major importance is instability in the effective marginal reserve ratios, r_d and r_t. You should remember from Chapter 9 that in Canada during this period, reserve requirements were calculated with a lag. The requirement was 12% of *last month's* demand deposits plus 4% of *last month's* time deposits. During the current month, the required reserve was always a fixed number of dollars; in effect, during the current month, the marginal reserve requirement was zero. Any change in deposits would only affect required reserves next month. As a result, r_d and r_t in the formula depend not on legal requirements but on the decisions of bankers in holding what are in effect excess reserves — and this behavior proves to be very difficult to predict in the very short run. Not surprisingly, advocates of a monetary base rule for monetary policy also argue that the lagged reserve requirement should be replaced by a contemporaneous reserve requirement.[11]

Limitations of the Multiplier Model.   It should not be surprising that we observe considerable instability in the money multipliers. These multipliers are constructed from several ratios, each of which is an assumption about the behavior of participants in the financial system. Thus, the reserve ratios are presumed to represent decisions made by banks with respect to the level of their cash reserves, and the cash drain coefficient and the time deposit coefficient represent decisions made by members of the public as to the form in which they are going to hold liquid assets (currency, time deposits, or demand deposits). It would be very surprising indeed if we could capture such complex behavior in such a simple formulation.

The money multiplier model makes a very important point about the relationship between the money supply and high-powered money, and the role of portfolio decisions by banks and the public in this relationship. But we must not take the multiplier model too literally. The danger of the multiplier approach to the analysis of the supply of money and credit is that it seems to suggest that the expansion (or contraction) of the supplies of money and credit is a simple *mechanical* process. A complex multiplier, constructed from several ratios, regulates the relationship between changes in the quantity of high-powered money and changes in the supply of money and credit in the economy, just as the gears in an automobile regulate the relationship between the speed of the engine and the speed of the wheels. This mechanical analogy is unfortunate. It assumes constant things which are demonstrably not constant. *We can only consider the multiplier model to be a first approximation to a much more complicated model of portfolio selection, incorporating a great variety of other factors explaining the critical ratios.*

ENDNOTES

1. It is logical to ask: What about the interest on the loan? Because the businessman must repay more than he has borrowed, will not the net effect of the extension and repayment of the loan be to reduce the money supply?

   To the extent that the bank makes a profit on the loan and does not distribute that profit as dividends to its shareholders, any payment received by the bank tends to reduce the money supply. The bank debits the relevant demand deposit. However, any payment by the bank tends to expand the money supply. The bank credits the relevant demand deposit. Thus, the receipt of interest will tend to reduce the money supply. However, the payment of wages, salaries, and other expenses, and the payment of dividends out of profits, will offset this. Thus, the net reduction in the money supply amounts to the value of retained earnings. The bank's total assets remain the same; its liabilities contract and its capital account expands by the amount of the retained profit.

2. In Canada, the penalty is the equivalent of a 10% per annum interest rate on the deficiency for the whole averaging period during which it occurs.

3. We are ignoring chequable deposits on which interest is paid (at a lower rate than on nonchequable deposits).

4. We have chosen the 3% reserve ratio to reflect the 1980 *Bank Act*. That bill calls for cash reserves equal to 2% of time deposits plus 1% of time deposits in excess of $500 000. For large banks, then, the marginal ratio will be 3%.

5. The banker may think he is attracting funds which would otherwise be invested in other financial instruments, such as stocks or bonds (we will consider the special case of deposits in other financial intermediaries in the next section). However, if someone is to sell stocks or bonds to place the funds in a time deposit, he must find someone with money (demand deposits or currency or another time deposit) to sell it to. If there is to be a net addition to

time deposits, the funds must come out of demand deposits (or currency in circulation) directly or indirectly.
6. Perhaps the most influential presentation of this argument in Canada is that of T. Courchene of the University of Western Ontario. See, T. Courchene, *The Strategy of Gradualism: An Analysis of Bank of Canada Policy from Mid-1975 to Mid-1977* (Montreal: C. D. Howe Research Institute, 1977), pp. 109-112.
7. We see no point in going through the tedious exercise of developing other versions of the multiplier. The interested student can do this himself. For some additional multipliers see J. Galbraith, "A Table of Banking System Multipliers," *Canadian Journal of Economics*, Vol. 1 (November, 1968), pp. 763-71.
8. You should recall the concepts of *M1* and *M3* from Chapter 2. The relevant data are published monthly in the *Bank of Canada Review*. The data used for the calculations of the multipliers in Figure 17-2 do not correspond exactly to the Bank of Canada's definitions of *M1* and *M3*. k_1 is calculated from a definition of *M1* which includes all *chequable* deposits with chartered banks, i.e., what the Bank of Canada calls *M1B*. k_3 is calculated using a definition of *M3* which excludes all foreign currency deposits at chartered banks, what the Bank of Canada calls *M3C*.
9. Clinton and K. Lynch, *Monetary Base and Money Stock in Canada*, Bank of Canada, Technical Report 16 (Ottawa, 1979); A. E. Burger, "The Relationship between Monetary Base and Money: How Close?" Federal Reserve Bank of St. Louis, *Review*, 57 (October 1975).
10. T. Courchene, "On Defining and Controlling Money," *The Canadian Journal of Economics*, XII (November 1979), pp. 604-15.
11. The lagged reserve requirement was specified in the 1967 *Bank Act*. It could not be altered except with a revision of the Act. The 1980 *Bank Act* permits the federal cabinet to make regulations relating to such matters. The lagged reserve requirement can be changed by Order-in-Council.

APPENDIX

DEPOSIT EXPANSION AS A GEOMETRICAL PROGRESSION

In the text we developed the formula for the basic deposit expansion multiplier, assuming only one type of deposit (demand deposits) and ignoring cash drain.

$$D = R\left(\frac{1}{r}\right) \tag{17.2}$$

We developed this multiplier from the basic equilibrium condition that there should be no excess reserves in the banking system. It is sometimes developed in a different way, as the sum of a geometrical progression.

STAGE 1 Currency is deposited in the banking system. Cash reserves (R) and deposits (D) increase by the same amount.

$$\triangle D_1 = \triangle R \tag{17A.1}$$

Excess Reserves:
Required reserves (R_r) increase by a fraction (r) of the increase in deposits.

$$\triangle R_r = r \triangle D_1$$
$$= r \triangle R \tag{17A.2}$$

Leaving excess reserves (R_e):

$$R_e(1) = \triangle R - r \triangle R$$
$$= \triangle R (1-r) \tag{17A.3}$$

STAGE 2 Loans are made, and deposits created, in the amount of excess reserves from Stage 1.

$$\triangle D_2 = \triangle R (1-r) \tag{17A.3}$$

Cumulative Expansion:
At the end of Stage 2, total deposits have increased:

$$\triangle D_1 + \triangle D_2 = \triangle R + \triangle R (1-r) \tag{17A.4}$$

Excess Reserves:
At the end of Stage 2, excess reserves remain in the amount of:

$$R_e(2) = R_e(1) - r[R_e(1)]$$
$$= \triangle R (1-r) - r[\triangle R (1-r)]$$
$$= \triangle R (1-r)^2 \tag{17A.5}$$

STAGE 3 Loans are made, and deposits created, in the amount of the excess reserves from Stage 2.

$$\triangle D_3 = \triangle R (1-r)^2 \tag{17A.6}$$

Cumulative Expansion:

$$\triangle D_1 + \triangle D_2 + \triangle D_3 = \triangle R + \triangle R (1-r) + \triangle R (1-r)^2 \tag{17A.7}$$

Excess Reserves:

$$R_e(3) = R_e(2) - r[R_e(2)]$$
$$= \triangle R (1-r)^2 - r[\triangle R (1-r)^2]$$
$$= \triangle R (1-r)^2 (1-r)$$
$$= \triangle R (1-r)^3 \tag{17A.8}$$

STAGE n
Cumulative Expansion:
If we allow this process to continue for n periods, the cumulative expansion of deposits appears as the sum of a geometric progression, with first term $\triangle R$ and common ratio $(1-r)$. It is shown in elementary algebra that the sum of such a geometric series is:

$$\triangle D = \frac{\triangle R [1 - (1-r)^n]}{1 - (1-r)} \tag{17A.9}$$

Excess reserves will remain until n approaches infinity, and hence $(1 - r)^n$ approaches zero. The expression for the cumulative expansion of deposits then becomes:

$$\triangle D = \triangle R \left[\frac{1}{1-(1-r)} \right]$$
$$= \triangle R \left(\frac{1}{r} \right) \tag{17A.10}$$

The deposit expansion multiplier is $\left(\frac{1}{r} \right)$.

This method of formulating the multiplier model makes a very important point. The multiplier is an equilibrium concept. It shows the relationship between two states of equilibrium, before and after a change in high-powered money. However, the adjustment to the new equilibrium is not instantaneous. It involves many transactions and takes time. How much time? We don't know. However, observing the monetary system on any given day may well catch it in a state of disequilibrium.

Development of other multipliers using the geometric progression approach is very complex, particularly if different speeds of adjustment apply to the various elements in the multiplier. We do not develop such models here.

The Money Supply Process
PART 2: DETERMINANTS
OF THE MONETARY BASE **18**

In the previous chapter we analyzed the process by which the money supply is expanded or contracted in the private sector of the financial system. That process involves a complex interaction among banks, near banks and the general public; but we discovered that the fundamental factor is the supply of high-powered money. High-powered money consists of currency in circulation and the cash reserves of banks, a sum which is also called *the monetary base*. The purpose of this and the following chapters, is to analyze the determinants of the monetary base and, in particular, to demonstrate how the monetary base can be controlled by the central bank and hence used as an instrument of monetary policy.

THE MONETARY BASE EQUATION

The Bank of Canada

The first important point to note is that, with the exception of subsidiary coinage (which because of its small magnitude we can ignore), *the monetary base consists of liabilities of the Bank of Canada*, i.e., Bank of Canada notes (currency) and the reserve deposits of the chartered banks with the Bank of Canada.

We have encountered the Bank of Canada at several points in our analysis of the financial system. It is Canada's central bank, the organization and functions of which were outlined in Chapter 14. In brief, it is the bank for the financial system. It holds the bulk of the chartered banks' cash reserves; handles the settlement of interbank clearing balances; makes advances to the chartered banks and approved security dealers; manages the nation's central reserve of foreign exchange; and issues notes to be used as currency. In addition, the Bank of Canada acts as the fiscal agent of the Government of Canada (manages the government's cash balances, handles government security transactions, etc.) and acts as the Canadian correspondent of foreign central banks. However, the aspect of the Bank of Canada which is of immediate concern to us is its function as manager of the money supply. When we ask what controls bank reserves one possible answer is the Bank of Canada. To see how, we must first analyse the Bank of Canada's balance sheet.

TABLE 18-1   **The Bank of Canada: balance sheet June 30, 1982**

	$ Millions	Percent
Assets		
Government of Canada bonds	16 443	90
Advances to banks and security dealers	42	—
Foreign currency deposits	781	4
Items in process of collection	511	3
All other assets	559	3
Total assets	18 336	100
Liabilities		
Bank of Canada notes outstanding		
In circulation	9 985	54
Held by chartered banks	1 554	8
Deposits		
Chartered banks	4 551	25
Government of Canada	216	1
Other	119	1
Items in process of collection	673	4
All other liabilities (including capital accounts)	1 238	7
Total liabilities	18 336	100

SOURCE: *Bank of Canada Review,* November, 1982.

The Balance Sheet of the Bank of Canada

Assets.   The asset portfolio of the Bank of Canada is exceptionally simple. Indeed, from this vantage point the Bank appears to be little more than a warehouse for government bonds. At the end of 1981, 88% of the Bank's assets were government bonds, almost a fifth of the public debt of Canada.[1] Interest paid by the government is the major source of income for the Bank of Canada.

The account *Advances to banks and security dealers* reflects the Bank's activities as lender of last resort for the financial system. The Bank is empowered to make short-term advances to the chartered banks and other members of the Canadian Payments Association, and to enter into purchase and resale agreements with approved government security dealers. While these agreements are not in the form of advances, they have the same effect and purpose, so we have included them in the advances account. It should also be noted that the Bank has the power to make advances directly to the government, a power which it has not used in recent years.

Foreign currency deposits are working balances which the Bank of Canada keeps with foreign correspondents, mainly other central banks. Although they are part of Canada's foreign exchange reserves, the Bank's foreign currency assets must not be confused with the Exchange Fund Account of the Department of Finance which holds the bulk of Canada's official foreign exchange reserves. We will examine the role of the Exchange Fund in the money supply process later.

The remainder of the Bank of Canada's assets have been grouped together into two accounts. *Items in process of collection* includes cheques which have been received by the Bank of Canada, either for its own account (e.g. in payment for securities sold by the Bank) or for the government's account (e.g., for taxes paid to the government), which have not yet been collected from the banks on which they are drawn. In later analysis we will set this account off against the corresponding liability account, and call the difference the Bank of Canada *float*. The *Other assets* are primarily accrued interest on the Bank's portfolio and the Bank's premises.

Liabilities.   The liability side of the Bank of Canada's balance sheet is only slightly more complicated. The primary liability is *Bank of Canada notes*, which we have seen are legal tender and comprise the bulk of the supply of currency in the country. Most of these notes are in active circulation, although a significant portion is held by the banks as part of their cash reserves.

The other liability of major consequence is the *deposits of the chartered banks*. Along with Bank of Canada notes held in their vaults, these are the cash reserves of the banking system, held to satisfy legal requirements. Together, chartered bank deposits and Bank of Canada notes outstanding account for 87% of the total liabilities of the Bank of Canada.

The Bank of Canada also has *other depositors*. Principal among these is the Government of Canada itself. Indeed, the management of the government's cash balances raises some particular problems for the Bank of Canada which we will have occasion to examine in the next chapter. The other depositors are primarily Government of Canada Crown corporations and foreign central banks which have business in Canada, either on their own account or for the account of their governments.

The account *Items in Process of Settlement* includes outstanding cheques upon which the Bank of Canada will have to make payment when they are cleared through the banking system. The *Other liabilities* include the capital accounts, the government's net equity in the assets of the Bank.

We are not interested in the structure of the Bank of Canada's balance sheet for its own sake. Rather, we want to use the balance sheet to examine the mechanism by which the Bank of Canada can control the money supply. Because the two sides of the balance sheet are equal, by definition, we can interpret the balance sheet as an equation (an identity) which, like other equations, can be manipulated algebraically to derive more, useful equations.

The Monetary Base Equation

In Table 18-2 we transform the balance sheet identity into an equation explaining the monetary base in terms of other accounts in the balance sheet of the Bank of Canada. The resulting equation, which we call the monetary base equation, expresses the *monetary liabilities* of the Bank of Canada (bank reserves + currency in circulation = monetary base) in terms of the remaining *non-monetary assets and liabilities*. It is as follows (the figures in brackets are millions of dollars and refer to June 30, 1982:

$$\begin{array}{c} \textit{Monetary Base} \\ (16\,090) \end{array} = \begin{array}{c} \textit{Non-Monetary Assets and Liabilities} \\ (16\,090) \end{array}$$

$$\begin{array}{c} \text{DEPOSITS} \\ \text{of banks} \\ (4\,551) \end{array} + \begin{array}{c} \text{NOTES} \\ \text{outstanding} \\ (11\,539) \end{array} = \begin{array}{c} \text{SECURITIES} \\ (16\,443) \end{array} + \begin{array}{c} \text{ADVANCES} \\ (42) \end{array} + \begin{array}{c} \text{FOREIGN} \\ \text{ASSETS} \\ (781) \end{array}$$

$$- \begin{array}{c} \text{DEPOSITS of} \\ \text{government} \\ (216) \end{array} + \begin{array}{c} \text{FLOAT} \\ (-162) \end{array} + \begin{array}{c} \text{OTHER ASSETS} \\ \text{(Net)} \\ (-798) \end{array}$$

(18-1)

Most of these variables have already been defined. *Float* is the difference between the asset "items in process of collection" and the liability "items in process of settlement." The rest of the assets and liabilities ("other assets," "other liabilities," and "other deposits") are included on a net basis as *Other Assets (Net)*. Both Float and Other Assets (Net) are technical items which affect the monetary base but are not part of the monetary control process.

The major point to note is that size of the monetary base cannot change without a simultaneous and equal change in at least one of the non-monetary asset or liability accounts.[2] If the Bank of Canada can control its non-monetary assets and liabilities it will thereby control the monetary base.

TABLE 18-2   **Derivation of the monetary base equation**

Symbols

Government securities	$= S$	Notes in circulation	$= N_c$
Advances	$= A$	Notes in banks	$= N_b$
Collection items (asset)	$= C_a$	Bank deposits (at Bank of Canada)	$= D_b$
Foreign assets	$= E$	Government deposits	$= D_g$
Other assets	$= OA$	Other deposits	$= D_o$
Float	$= F$	Settlement items (liab.)	$= C_l$
Other assets (net)	$= OA_n$	Other liabilities	$= OL$
Monetary base	$= B$		

Derivation

The Bank of Canada balance sheet (Table 18-1) can be rewritten as an equation:

$S + A + E + C_a + OA = N_c + N_b + D_b + D_g + D_o + C_l + OL$

By definition:

$B = N_e + D_b + N_b$

Substituting equation (2) in equation (1), and rearranging the terms:

$B = S + A + E + C_a - C_l + OA - OL - D_o - D_g$

By definition:

$F = C_a - C_l;$ and $OA_n = OA - OL$

Substituting (4) and (5) in (3), and rearranging the terms:

$B = S + (E - D_g) + A + (F + OA_n)$

This is the monetary base equation.

Stated another way, a change in the magnitude of any of the Bank of Canada's non-monetary asset or liability accounts, unless offset by an equal and opposite change in some other non-monetary account on the right-hand side of the equation, must produce an equal change in the monetary base. Thus, an increase in any of the bank's assets — whether through the purchase of securities, the granting of an advance, or, indeed, the purchase of a new building — taken by itself, will involve an equal increase in the monetary base. Likewise, an increase in any of the bank's non-monetary liabilities — perhaps an increase in government deposits or in deposits of other central banks — taken alone, will involve an equal reduction in the monetary base.

These principles should be familiar. They are exactly the same as those which we encountered in Chapter 17 in the analysis of the expansion and contraction of the money supply by private financial institutions. The motives of the firms and the details and ultimate limits of the process may be very different. However, it is important to remember that the principles by which the central bank can create high-powered money are exactly the same as the principles by which commercial banks can create payments money. Thus, the effective decision taken by the central bank in order to increase the money supply is a decision to increase its asset holdings or to reduce its non-monetary liabilities.

The Bank Reserve Equation

The monetary base is comprised of currency in circulation and bank reserves. However, as we have seen, a reduction in bank reserves will have a much more powerful impact on the supply of money and credit than will an equal increase in the amount of currency in circulation. Thus, the transfer of currency from bank reserves to active circulation will actually lead to a contraction of the total money supply, other things being equal. For this reason, it is frequently more important to examine changes in bank reserves than in the monetary base *per se*.

By subtracting currency in circulation from each side, we can transform the monetary base equation into a bank reserve equation:

$$
\underset{(6\,105)}{\textit{Bank Cash Reserves}} = \underset{(16\,090)}{\textit{Monetary Base}} - \underset{(9\,985)}{\textit{Currency in Circulation}}
$$

$$
\begin{array}{l}
\underset{(1\,554)}{\substack{\text{BANK OF}\\ \text{CANADA}\\ \text{NOTES}\\ \text{held by}\\ \text{Banks}}} \quad
\underset{(4\,551)}{\substack{\text{DEPOSITS}\\ \text{OF BANKS}\\ \text{at the Bank}\\ \text{of Canada}}} = \underset{(16\,443)}{\text{SECURITIES}} + \underset{(42)}{\text{ADVANCES}} + \underset{(781)}{\substack{\text{FOREIGN}\\ \text{ASSETS}}} \\[2em]
\qquad\qquad - \underset{(216)}{\substack{\text{DEPOSITS of}\\ \text{government}}} + \underset{(-162)}{\text{FLOAT}} + \underset{(-798)}{\substack{\text{OTHER ASSETS}\\ \text{(Net)}}} \\[2em]
\qquad\qquad - \underset{(9\,985)}{\substack{\text{CURRENCY IN}\\ \text{CIRCULATION}}}
\end{array}
$$

(18-2)

The Instruments of Monetary Control

These equations can be used to make a point of considerable importance for our analysis. Control of the monetary base or of bank reserves is an essential function of the central bank. However, equations 18.1 and 18.2 demonstrate that *not all of the determinants of the monetary base or of bank reserves are under the direct control of the central bank*.

Consider first the monetary base equation (18.1). As we will demonstrate more clearly in subsequent sections, normally the Bank of Canada can directly control only three of the terms in the equation: their holdings of government securities, foreign assets, and government deposits. They are the *positive instruments* of monetary control. Bank of Canada advances fall into a different category. The initiative for making and repaying such advances rests with the banks and security dealers, not with the Bank of Canada. While the Bank of Canada can influence the level of advances outstanding, it has only *partial control*. Advances cannot be considered a positive instrument of monetary control.

Bank of Canada float is a phenomenon of the postal service and of the clearing system. While the speed with which major cheques are cleared and collected can sometimes be influenced by the Bank of Canada, in general we must regard the behavior of float as beyond central bank control. It is normally a very small element in the monetary base equation, yet in the very short run, it can have a significant impact on changes in the monetary base. Let us classify it as a *technical factor* in the equations. We have grouped all other asset and liability accounts together to consider them on a net basis. Again, with this residual we have a factor in the determination of the monetary base over which the central bank has little, if any, direct control. Some of the components in this sum involve longer-term arrangements (e.g., interest accrued on investments, or the value of bank premises) and others involve decisions made by outside agencies (e.g., the deposits of foreign central banks and others). Like float, Other Assets (Net) must be considered a *technical or external factor*. It cannot be considered an instrument of monetary control.

In order to summarize these propositions, we can rewrite the monetary base equation as follows:

$$
\underset{\text{Influenced by Bank of Canada}}{\underbrace{\overset{\text{Positive instruments of monetary control}}{\text{MONETARY BASE} = \text{SECURITIES} + \text{FOREIGN ASSETS} - \text{DEPOSITS of GOVERNMENT}}}}
$$

$$
\overset{\text{Technical and external factors}}{+ \text{ADVANCES} + \text{FLOAT} + \text{OTHER ASSETS (Net)}}
$$

(18-3)

As the bank reserve equation makes clear, the determination of bank reserves involves an additional factor beyond the control of the central bank, the amount of currency in circulation outside banks. This is determined by the general public when they decide whether to hold their money balances in the form of currency or in the form of bank deposits. The Bank of Canada and the chartered banks are passive agents in this process.

With this in mind, we can rewrite the bank reserve equation, identifying the loci of control as follows:

Positive instruments of monetary control

$$\underset{\text{RESERVES}}{\text{BANK}} = \text{SECURITIES} \quad + \quad \underset{\text{ASSETS}}{\text{FOREIGN}} \quad - \quad \underset{\text{GOVERNMENT}}{\text{DEPOSITS of}}$$

Influenced by   Technical and external factors
Bank of Canada

$$+ \quad \text{ADVANCES} \quad + \quad \text{FLOAT} \quad + \quad \underset{\text{(Net)}}{\underset{\text{ASSETS}}{\text{OTHER}}} \quad - \quad \underset{\text{CIRCULATION}}{\underset{\text{in}}{\text{CURRENCY}}}$$

$$(18\text{-}4)$$

Defensive versus Dynamic Operations

Given that some important variables in these equations — particularly float and currency in circulation — are beyond the control of the central bank, can we really say that the Bank of Canada determines the monetary base or bank reserves and hence the money supply?

The answer must be a qualified yes. It should be obvious that although some factors are beyond central bank control, *it can still control the monetary base if it can anticipate changes in the external factors and if it can use the account over which it has control to offset the external effects on the monetary base. Operations* designed to defend a given monetary base from extraneous influences have been called *defensive operations* as distinguished from the more familiar *dynamic operations* designed to change the monetary base and the money supply.[3] For example, the monetary effects of a reduction in float could be offset by an equal increase in holdings of government securities. Or, the effects on bank reserves of a decline in currency in circulation could be offset by a corresponding increase in government deposits at the Bank of Canada. This suggests that in spite of its inability to control each and every item in the basic equations, the Bank of Canada can exert quite detailed control over the aggregate levels of the monetary base and bank reserves.

This answer must be qualified under some circumstances. If the actions of the central bank indirectly induce a partially offsetting reaction in some other account, then the central bank's control is obviously weakened. Thus, for example, if the attempt to reduce the monetary base by sales of government securities produced an increase in central bank advances, the intentions of the central bank would be partially frustrated. This is a matter which requires more detailed investigation.

THE GOVERNMENT AND
THE MONETARY BASE

The involvement of the Government of Canada in the economy is both very important and very complex. Depending on the purpose of the analysis, various aspects of it can be emphasized. In macroeconomics, the role of the government which is stressed is the formulation and implementation of *fiscal policy*. What is of interest is the direct impact of the government on the flow of income and expenditure. For this purpose, government economic activity can be summarized in terms of its "national accounts budget," i.e., the balance between revenues, primarily from taxes, and expenditures on goods, services, and transfer payments as reported in the national income accounts. Government transactions in assets and liabilities are not directly relevant.

Our concern is different. It is frequently asserted that a deficit in the government's budget is inflationary not only because of its direct fiscal impact on income and expenditure but also because it involves an increase in the money supply. This suggests that the government's budget is a part of the money supply process. However, the government's budget has not appeared in our analysis of the money supply process, either in the private sector (Chapter 17) or at the level of the Bank of Canada. Indeed, we have just seen that an increase in the monetary base can only occur at the initiative of, or at least with the acquiescence of, the Bank of Canada. How, then, might the government's budget have a role in the money supply process?

The Government's Cash Requirements

For an analysis of the potential impact of the government's economic activities on the money supply, the national accounts concept of the government budget is not adequate. What we require is a measure of the total amount of money which the government must raise during a given period of time to meet all of its payments commitments, whether or not these payments are included in the national accounts budget. The difference arises because the government's transactions are not limited to those directly affecting the flow of income and expenditure in the economy, but also involve transactions in financial assets. Two categories of financial transactions are important: changes in official foreign exchange reserves and loans made under various government lending programs. Funds must be provided to finance any net acquisition of foreign currency assets and to finance any excess of new loans over repayments in the lending programs. We call the broader concept the net *cash requirements of the government*. The impact of the government on the monetary base depends on how these cash requirements are financed.

Perhaps the concept is best explained by an example. The cash requirements of the Government of Canada for 1979 and, by way of contrast, for 1969 are summarized in Table 18-3. This table has three panels: the top panel shows the sources of the cash requirements of the government; the second panel shows how these requirements were financed; and the third panel reminds us that there were other factors affecting the monetary base.

The analysis starts with the government's budget as reported in the national income and expenditure accounts. This shows a deficit of $9169 million in 1979. However, the

TABLE 18-3   **The monetary consequences of the federal government's budget, 1969 and 1979 ($ Millions)**

	1969	1979
Cash requirements Arising from income and expenditure transactions		
Balance of revenue less expenditure, national accounts basis	$1 021	−$9 169
Adjustment to a cash basis	− 109	− 937
Cash surplus or cash requirements (−) arising from income and expenditure transactions	912	−10 106
Cash requirements Arising from financial transactions		
Increase (−) or decrease in loans	− 827	− 1 261
Increase (−) or decrease in official foreign exchange position	314	− 525
Cash surplus or cash requirements (−) arising from financial transactions	− 513	− 1 786
Net cash requirements Arising from income and expenditure transactions and financial transactions	399	−11 892
Financing Not affecting the monetary base:		
Decrease or increase (−) in government deposits with chartered banks	− 642	4 048
Increase or decrease (−) in government bonds held by the banks and the public		
Canada Savings Bonds	324	− 1 329
Marketable bonds	− 217	7 461
Total: non-monetary financing	− 535	10 180
Financing Affecting the monetary base:		
Decrease or increase (−) in government deposits with the Bank of Canada	− 34	4
Increase or decrease (−) in government bonds held by the Bank of Canada	170	1 708
Net Impact on the monetary base	136	1 712
Addendum:		
Other factors affecting the monetary base (from monetary base equation)	76	− 490
Net change in the monetary base	212	1 222

national accounts are recorded on an accrual basis. That is, certain transactions, particularly tax collections, are recorded as of the date on which the liability for payment is incurred rather than as of the date on which the payment is actually made. Since we are concerned with the actual cash position of the government, appropriate adjustments must be made. In 1979, adjustment to a cash basis added $937 million to the budget deficit and hence to the cash requirements of the government.

The deficit arising from income and expenditure transactions does not include all of the cash requirements of the government. Two types of financial transactions also have to be allowed for. In 1979, the government provided loans in excess of repayments amounting to almost $1. 3 billion under various lending programs. Some of the loans were to the private sector (e. g., through the Central Mortgage and Housing Corpora-tion, the Farm Credit Corporation, and similar programs), some to crown corporations, and some to provincial and municipal governments. In addition, there was a net increase in the government's foreign exchange reserve position of $525 million. The purchase of foreign exchange, like the purchase of any asset, involves a corresponding payment of Canadian dollars, which, of course, has to be financed. If, as in 1969, the government sells foreign exchange on balance, the proceeds help finance the cash requirements arising from other sources. In 1979, the two types of financial transactions added $1.8 billion to the cash requirements of the government.

The last line in the top panel displays the figure with which we are concerned, the net cash requirements of the government. It is the sum of the cash deficit on account of income and expenditure transactions and the cash required to complete the financial transactions.

The year 1979 provides a striking example of large cash requirements — $11.9 billion — arising from a large budget deficit and the activities of the government's lending agencies. However, large deficits and large cash requirements are not inevitable. Table 18-3 provides an example of a year, 1969, in which the national accounts budget showed a surplus sufficient to finance the government's lending activities. Indeed, the sale of foreign exchange produced a net cash surplus for the government.

But, what is the impact of the cash requirements, or the cash surplus, on the monetary base?

The Government's Cash Requirements and the Monetary Base

The monetary consequences of the government's net cash requirements depend on how these requirements are financed, or, if there is a cash surplus, on how the surplus is disposed of.

The middle panel of Table 18-3 divides the financing of the cash requirements into that part which has no direct impact on the monetary base, and that part which tends, directly, to increase the monetary base. It should come as no surprise that the distinction depends on whether the Bank of Canada is involved in the financing, i.e., whether the transaction shows up in the monetary base equation. In 1979, of the total cash requirements of $11.9 billion, only $1.7 billion could be said to have expanded the monetary base. Almost all of this was a result of the acquisition of government bonds by the Bank of Canada. A reduction in government deposits at the Bank of Canada worked in the same direction, but the effect was small.

The rest of the cash requirements ($10.2 billion) were financed in two ways: drawing down government deposits with chartered banks ($4 billion) and selling bonds to the public and the banks ($6.1 billion). It is interesting to note that on balance the public cashed in Canada Savings Bonds in 1979, in effect adding $1.3 billion to the cash requirements of the government, and forcing the government to sell $7.5 billion of marketable bonds to raise the required $6.1 billion. It should also be remembered that the ability of the government to draw on funds on deposit with banks is strictly limited by the amount on deposit and the government's normal requirements for cash. Unless the government has abnormally large sums on deposit to begin with, drawing down bank deposits is but a temporary expedient.[4] *The fundamental source of financing, if expansion of the monetary base is to be avoided, has to be the sale of bonds to the public*, including banks and non-residents.[5]

In this regard, it is again relevant to compare 1969 and 1979. In 1979 a very large deficit was translated into a relatively much smaller increase in the monetary base. The suggestion that there is a direct link between a budget deficit and the monetary base might appear correct in direction, but very wrong in magnitude. In 1969, even the direction is wrong. The combination of a budget surplus and lending activities produced a small cash surplus ($399 million). However, the monetary base did not fall. Transactions in government bonds (in particular, the Bank of Canada's purchase of marketable bonds from the public) produced a small increase in the monetary base ($136 million) and permitted the government to add to its cash balances with the banks.

It is obvious from these examples that there need be no simple, mechanical link between the government's budget and the monetary base. Indeed, we have discovered a simple and obvious principle. *The cash requirements of the government will only increase the monetary base if those cash requirements are financed, in whole, or in part, by the Bank of Canada* (and vice versa for a cash surplus).

These, however, are only accounting relationships. Is the Bank of Canada free to decide whether it will acquire government bonds? Will that decision be made independently of the state of the government's budget? Are there circumstances under which the Bank of Canada would be forced to provide part of the funding for large cash requirements?

The Bank of Canada and the Government's Cash Requirements

We are not yet in a position to fully analyze these questions. However, the basic point is quite obvious.

If the Bank of Canada does not purchase government bonds in the face of large net cash requirements of the government, the government will have to compete in the open market with all private borrowers for the limited funds which private lenders have available. The government may have to offer significantly higher interest rates on its bonds to induce private lenders to purchase them. Interest rates will be bid up. In the short run, the purchase of government bonds by the Bank of Canada, with a corresponding increase in the monetary base, might seem to be an attractive alternative to higher interest rates (and remember: the Bank of Canada is owned by the government, and is responsible to Parliament through the Minister of Finance).

This provides us with a very important conclusion. *There will be a direct link between large cash requirements of the government and expansion of the monetary base, if the maintenance of a low level of interest rates rather than control of the growth of the money supply is the objective of monetary policy.* If the Bank of Canada is free to decide on an appropriate rate of growth of the money supply and chooses to do so, the interest rate on the public debt will be determined in the open market. The Bank of Canada will decide on the appropriate growth of the monetary base, take careful note of other factors affecting the monetary base, and purchase only the quantity of government bonds necessary to achieve the target. The same propositions apply in reverse to a situation in which the government has large cash surpluses.

There are many historical examples in Canada and elsewhere of central banks attempting to peg interest rates at low levels. In a later section (Chapter 21) we will demonstrate that a policy of keeping interest rates low through monetary expansion can be self-defeating.

There is one other point which must be explored briefly before we leave this topic. We have noted, but essentially glossed over, the implications of changes in foreign exchange reserves. In some years, changes in these reserves are very large (in 1978, the foreign exchange reserve position fell by $5.5 billion, financing more than half of the national accounts deficit!), and there is an important and growing body of economic literature which stresses the monetary consequences of changes in foreign exchange reserves. While much of the analysis must wait till later, the present discussion would be seriously incomplete without some consideration of foreign exchange reserves.

FOREIGN EXCHANGE RESERVES AND THE MONETARY BASE

In the modern world, all governments hold foreign exchange reserves and large pools of foreign currencies (and foreign liquid assets) which can be sold in the foreign exchange market for the purpose of influencing the foreign exchange rate. The management of foreign exchange reserves is a major issue in international monetary policy, and we will consider some aspects of it in Chapter 22. At this point we want to consider the implications of changes in official foreign exchange reserves for the money supply process.

The Exchange Fund Account

We have already noted that the Bank of Canada holds some foreign currency assets primarily for use in its day-to-day operations (although, as we shall see in the next chapter, the Bank's foreign currency assets can have an important role in the implementation of monetary policy). Normally, the Bank's holdings are not large, but they are considered to be part of the official foreign exchange reserves of Canada. Purchases and sales of foreign assets by the Bank of Canada are fully accounted for in the monetary base equation. They need not detain us further. Our concern now is the much larger foreign exchange reserves held by the Department of Finance which are not directly accounted for in the monetary base equation.

The bulk of Canada's foreign exchange reserves are held by the Department of Finance in the *Exchange Fund Account*. The Exchange Fund was established in 1935 from the accounting profits which occurred when the Bank of Canada's gold reserves were revalued from the historical statutory price ($20.67 per ounce) to the new market price U.S. $35 per ounce). In effect, part of the Bank's gold was assigned to the Fund. In 1940, the Bank of Canada's gold reserve requirement was suspended by Order-in-Council and all of the Bank's gold was transferred to the Fund. Subsequently, the Minister of Finance was empowered to make advances to the Fund as necessary for its operations. Thus, if the Fund was to increase its holdings of foreign exchange, the Minister had to supply the Canadian dollars required to make the purchase. As we saw in the previous section, increases in the Fund thus add to the cash requirements of the government. Correspondingly, sales of foreign exchange out of the Fund provide Canadian dollars to meet some of the cash requirements of the government.[6]

The link between the Exchange Fund and the monetary base, then, is the cash requirements of the government. The analysis of the previous section applies in full, but it only tells us the circumstances under which a change in foreign exchange reserves will affect the monetary base. What produces the change in foreign exchange reserves?

The Foreign Exchange Rate and Foreign Exchange Reserves

Again, this is a subject which we cannot explore in any depth at this point. More analysis will come later (Chapter 22). However, one general observation is of some importance to us now.

The function of foreign exchange reserves is to permit the government to intervene in the foreign exchange market to influence the level of the foreign exchange rate. If, because of developments in the balance of international payments, there is upward pressure on the price of the U.S. dollar (and hence downward pressure on the Canadian dollar), and the government does not want the price to rise, it can sell U.S. dollars out of its foreign exchange reserves to attempt to stabilize the exchange rate. Similarly, if there is downward pressure on the price of the U.S. dollar (and hence upward pressure on the price of the Canadian dollar), the government can purchase U.S. dollars in the market in an attempt to stabilize the exchange rate.

This suggests a general conclusion. *Foreign exchange reserves can influence the cash requirements of the government, and hence possibly the monetary base, if the level of the foreign exchange rate is a target of government policy.* If the government is prepared to accept whatever exchange rate is determined in the market, changes in foreign exchange reserves will not be induced by shifts in the balance of international payments, and will not be an independent factor determining the monetary base.

DETERMINANTS OF THE MONETARY BASE

The analysis in this chapter is fundamental to the understanding of the money supply process in Canada. We have developed the monetary base equation — and derived from it the bank reserve equation — to provide a framework for the analysis of the determinants of the monetary base. Five general conclusions should be remembered.

1. The monetary base equation contains a number of factors which are beyond Bank of Canada control. But, if the Bank can anticipate these factors, it can offset their impact and hence maintain complete control over the monetary base.
2. However, the Bank of Canada's ability to control the monetary base depends on there being no conflicting objectives of monetary policy.
3. In particular, Bank of Canada control over the monetary base may be impaired, and, indeed, destroyed, if the level of interest rates on government bonds is a primary objective of policy. Such a policy objective creates a direct link between the cash requirements of the government and the monetary base.
4. Further, if the foreign exchange rate is a target of policy, the balance of international

payments will induce changes in foreign exchange reserves. There will then be a direct link between the balance of international payments and the cash requirements of the government.

5. It follows from (3) and (4) that if both the level of interest rates and the exchange rate are pegged, there will be a direct link between the balance of international payments and the monetary base.

It is thus policies that attempt to peg certain key prices — interest rates on government bonds or the foreign exchange rate — which may impair the Bank of Canada's ability to manage the monetary base. There is much more to the story, of course. Our analysis in this chapter is incomplete. It ignores many of the subtle interactions in a market economy. In particular, it ignores the complications which may arise in attempting to peg interest rates, including the possibility that such a policy may be self-defeating. It also suggests that the government may peg the exchange rate and allow foreign exchange reserves to fluctuate without monetary consequences, if it is prepared to let the interest rate fluctuate as well. A more complete analysis will reveal that there are limits to such a policy. At best, what is commonly called a sterilization policy, can only be effective in the short run. However, all of that comes later.

ENDNOTES

1. Remember: The Bank of Canada is owned by the Government of Canada. The $17 billion of government securities held by the Bank of Canada is *intra-governmental debt*, owed by one branch of the government to another. If we want to calculate the *net* public debt (claims on the government held outside the government) we should deduct the value of the securities held by the Bank of Canada (along with those held by other agencies).

   By the same reasoning, the liabilities of the Bank of Canada to the general public (currency in circulation), the chartered banks and other depositors should be included in the public debt, and this is a somewhat larger figure. However, there is one significant difference between the liabilities of the Bank of Canada and the rest of the public debt. The former do not bear interest. If we are concerned with the interest-bearing public debt, the Bank of Canada's holdings should be deducted. In this connection you may recall the historical controversy discussed in the section on "The Banks and Government Finance" in Chapter 14.

   Finally, in this connection, it should be remembered also that all profits from the Bank of Canada's operations revert to the central treasury of the Government (prior to 1956 part of the profits were retained to build up a financial reserve). In effect, the payment of interest on the Bank of Canada's holdings of government bonds is simply a complicated method of meeting the expenses of the Bank of Canada out of the public treasury, although it gives the Bank the appearance of financial independence and profitability.

2. This statement requires qualification. Remember that we are ignoring *coin* in circulation and in bank vaults, which is part of the monetary base but not a liability of the Bank of Canada. However, since this is a relatively small component of the monetary base, and, more importantly, since the volume of coin in circulation can be expected to adjust fairly systematically to the amount of other money in circulation, its existence as part of the monetary base does not impair Bank of Canada control over the monetary base.

3. The terminology is that of Robert Roosa, who was for many years an important officer of the Federal Reserve Bank of New York. His pamphlet *Federal Reserve Operations in the Money and Government Securities Markets* (New York: Federal Reserve Bank of New York, 1956) is one of the best available discussions of the inner workings of a central bank. As Roosa makes clear, most of the day-to-day operations of such a bank are defensive in nature.

4. It should also be remembered that a reduction in government deposits with chartered banks tends to add directly to the privately held money supply, as the ownership of deposits changes from the government to private individuals and firms.

5. Remember the analysis of Chapter 17. The expansion of the monetary base adds to the capacity of private financial institutions, and particularly the banks, to acquire earning assets. As they do so, the money supply expands, by a multiple of the expansion of the monetary base. Some of the additional earning assets acquired by the banks will be government bonds. To this extent, the monetary expansion in the private sector, induced by the expansion of the monetary base, will also finance the cash requirements of the government.

6. The government can also obtain additional foreign exchange reserves by borrowing them, either from the International Monetary Fund (see Chapter 23, pp. 974-84), from other central banks, or in the open market. Indeed, in recent years, government borrowing of foreign exchange has been very important. Such transactions complicate the analysis in the text, but do not alter its basic conclusions. If foreign exchange is borrowed, the government incurs a foreign currency liability in order to acquire the foreign currency asset — the net foreign exchange reserve position has not changed. Subsequent sale of foreign currency assets in exchange for Canadian dollars produces the same effects as discussed in the text. However, because the foreign currency liability remains intact, sale of the foreign currency assets may actually make the official foreign exchange reserve position negative (a net liability rather than a net asset).

The Money Supply Process PART 3: THE MECHANICS OF MONETARY CONTROL

19

The monetary base equation is an accounting framework for the quantitative analysis of basic determinants of the money supply. It also helps identify those determinants which are beyond the control of the central bank and those which are potential instruments of central bank policy. The purpose of this chapter is to explore further the potential use of each of the policy instruments.

OPEN MARKET OPERATIONS

From the point of view of monetary policy, the most important factor in the monetary base equation is the Bank of Canada's holdings of government bonds. Not only is it the *largest* element in the equation but it also plays the central role in changes in the monetary base.

Transactions in the Open Market

The Bank of Canada can obtain government securities either by purchasing them directly from the government (new issues or outstanding issues held in various trust funds administered by the government) or by purchasing outstanding issues in the government securities market. Likewise, the Bank can reduce its holdings either by not replacing maturing issues when they are redeemed by the government, or by selling bonds out of its portfolio to other participants in the government securities market. Transactions in the government securities market —commonly called *open market operations* — are particularly important in this respect because they permit the Bank of Canada to make frequent adjustments to the monetary base *on its own initiative*. As long as there is a broad, active market with a large volume of transactions occurring every day, the Bank need only enter the market as a buyer or seller on the same basis as any other participant in order to effect the appropriate adjustments in the monetary base.

Given the importance of the government securities market in the analysis, it may be useful for you to review the discussion of the organization of Canadian financial markets presented in Chapter 3. You will recall that there is outstanding a very large stock of marketable government bonds (over $50 billion in private hands at the end of 1981), covering almost the entire range of possible maturities, and held by a wide variety of assetholders, both in Canada and abroad. These bonds are actively traded in the market — indeed, the secondary bond market is dominated by government bonds — through the intermediary of investment houses which act both as dealers and brokers. The largest volume of continuous trading is in the short-term maturities, including treasury bills. As with other participants in the market, when the Bank of Canada engages in open market operations, it submits bids and offers through the intermediary of the government security dealers.

An Example: The mechanics of the process by which the Bank of Canada can expand the monetary base by purchasing government bonds in the open market is illustrated in Example 19-1.

The monetary repercussions of the transaction follow from the method by which the Bank of Canada makes payment for the securities purchased. The Bank of Canada does not hold chequable deposits with commercial banks. Unlike a private purchaser, it does not make payment by writing cheques, ordering a chartered bank to make payment to the seller of the bonds. Rather, it draws a cheque on itself, and when that cheque is presented for payment by the seller's bank, an equal sum is credited to the bank's cash reserve deposit with the Bank of Canada. High-powered money has been created in the transaction, and, other things equal, bank reserves have increased. As we saw in Chapter 17, this lays the basis for a further multiple expansion of the supply of money and credit.

The effects of a sale of securities by the Bank of Canada are exactly the opposite. The purchaser of the securities makes payment to the Bank of Canada by a cheque drawn on a chartered bank, and, when the cheque is collected, the appropriate sum is deducted from the bank's reverse deposit with the Bank of Canada. Bank reserves are reduced, and, other things being equal, there follows a further contraction of the supply of money and credit by private financial institutions.

Open Market Operations and Interest Rates.   It is true, in principle, that in open market operations changes in bank reserves occur at the initiative of the Bank of Canada. But there is an important qualification.

Open market operations cannot be undertaken in any significant volume without affecting the market price and hence the yield on government bonds. The sale of bonds by the Bank of Canada will depress prices and hence raise yields; the purchase of bonds will raise prices and reduce yields. Subsequent portfolio adjustments by private asset-holders, coupled with the effects of changes in the supply of money from private financial institutions, will generalize the change in government bond yields to a change in the general level of interest rates. *The Bank of Canada is free to take the initiative in open market operations only if it can ignore the repercussions on interest rates.*

EXAMPLE 19-1   Open market operations: the purchase of government bonds in the open market by the Bank of Canada

STAGE I: The Bank of Canada purchases from government security dealers government bonds worth $100 thousand. These bonds were previously held in the private sector of the economy, and offered for sale to any buyer in the market. The Bank of Canada pays for the bonds with cheques drawn on itself.

Bank of Canada		Security dealers	
Government bonds +100	Cheques outst. +100	Bank of Canada cheques +100	
		Government bonds −100	

STAGE II: The government security dealers deposit the cheques in their accounts with chartered banks.

Security dealers		Chartered banks	
Bank of Canada cheques −100		Bank of Canada cheques +100	Deposits+100
Bank deposits +100			

STAGE III: The outstanding Bank of Canada cheques are cleared and collected, and the $100 thousand is credited to chartered bank reserve deposits with the Bank of Canada.

Bank of Canada		Chartered banks	
	Cheques outst. −100	Bank of Canada cheques −100	
	Deposits of banks +100	Cash reserves +100	

Net change:

Bank of Canada		Security dealers		Chartered banks	
Government bonds +100	Deposits of banks +100	Government bonds −100		Cash reserves +100	Deposits+100
		Bank deposits +100			

NOTES:
1. There has been no change in the society's wealth. The private sector of the economy has taken non-interest-bearing claims on the government in exchange for interest-bearing claims.
2. The security dealers will use their new bank deposits to purchase other securities (or to pay off other debts). The new deposits will go into general circulation.
3. The deposit liabilities and the cash reserves of the chartered banks have increased by the same amount. The chartered banks will therefore have excess cash reserves, and will further expand the supply of money and credit.
4. The overall effects would have been the same if the Bank of Canada had purchased the bonds from members of the general public (other than the security dealers) or from the chartered banks.

This caveat has three important implications. First, if open market operations are to be an instrument of monetary control, *the Bank of Canada's operations must not be guided by a profit motive*. The Bank cannot be deterred from selling bonds by the knowledge that in doing so it will incur substantial financial losses. Profits have no place in the policy objectives of the central bank.

Second, the Bank of Canada can only have freedom of initiative in open market operations *if the level of interest rates on government bonds is not an overriding objective of government policy*. Indeed, in the extreme case in which the level of interest rates is pegged as a matter of policy, the Bank of Canada may have to assume a completely passive position in the open market. It will have to respond to every initiative emanating from the market, buying bonds whenever private selling pressures would otherwise depress prices and raise yields. The central bank's open market operations become an instrument for implementing a particular interest rate policy, and the size of bank reserves adjusts to whatever level is consistent with the chosen level of interest rates. The level of interest rates and the size of bank reserves cannot be chosen independently of each other.

Third, there is a risk that the *immediate impact* of sizeable open market operations that have not been anticipated by market participants may be *a sharp change in bond prices and yields*, from which the market will soon rebound. Thus, open market sales will tend to increase interest rates, but the immediate impact of the sale may be to drive up rates by an unusual amount for a short time. Such impact effects serve no useful purpose, and they can be disturbing to financial markets. For this reason, it may be useful for the central bank to have an alternative policy instrument which will have the same effect on bank reserves but which does not have the same immediate impact on financial markets. It is partly for this reason that the Bank of Canada has come to rely on the transfer of government deposits between the Bank and the chartered banks as the normal instrument for day-to-day adjustments in bank reserves.

GOVERNMENT DEPOSITS

Among its many functions, the Bank of Canada serves as the banker for the Government of Canada. However, while the Bank of Canada holds the government's chequing account, it normally holds only a small fraction of the total cash balances of the

FIGURE 19-1   Government of Canada deposits.* 1975-1980

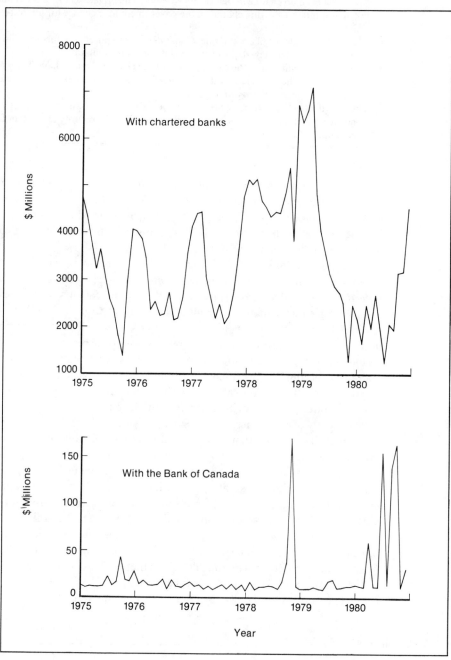

* Average of Wednesdays

Source: *Bank of Canada Review,* various issues.

government. The bulk of the government's funds are in deposits with the major chartered banks, divided among them on the basis of an agreed formula. At the end of 1981, the government had over $7.5 billion in its bank accounts, of which only 0.4 billion (just over 5%) was with the Bank of Canada.

The Bank of Canada is the government's own bank and all profits from its operations revert to the government. Why, then, does the government rely so heavily on the chartered banks as depositories for its cash balances? Why does it not have the Bank of Canada do all of its banking business?

The Management of Government Cash

The division of the government's cash balances between the Bank of Canada and the chartered banks is a matter of deliberate policy. Indeed, the obvious policy of holding all of the government's cash with the Bank of Canada would create severe and unnecessary complications for the Bank of Canada in managing bank reserves. It would require frequent, massive "defensive" open market operations.

To understand this, you should keep in mind two basic points: government deposits are highly volatile; and changes in government deposits at the Bank of Canada have a direct impact on bank reserves.

Volatility of Government Deposits.   The volatility of total government cash balances is obvious from Figure 19-1. In the period 1975-1980 government deposits with the chartered banks, and hence total government deposits, underwent very wide swings. A change of several hundred million dollars in the space of a month was not unusual. There is evidence of a strong seasonal movement in the balances, reflecting systematic differences in the timing of tax collections and government expenditures, but there are also other irregular influences, including the issuance and retirement of government bonds.

Government Deposits and Bank Reserves.   If the government held all of its cash balances at the Bank of Canada, the volatility of its deposits would be very troublesome, because any change in government deposits at the Bank of Canada has an equal and opposite effect on bank reserves. An increase in government deposits at the Bank of Canada tends to reduce bank reserves by an equal amount; a reduction in these deposits tends to increase bank reserves. These relationships are apparent in the monetary base equation, and are demonstrated in more detail in Example 19-2.

If the government kept all of its cash balances at the Bank of Canada, the Bank would have to engage in massive open market operations to offset the monetary repercussions of government transactions. Since monthly changes in government cash balances are frequently many times greater than the total of transactions in government securities which the Bank of Canada would enter into a similar period for all other reasons, we are not talking about a minor complication.

The Two-Deposit Policy.   These complications can be minimized (but not avoided entirely) by the simply expedient of a two-deposit policy. All government expenditures are made out of the account with the Bank of Canada. However, the bulk of the

EXAMPLE 19-2   Government deposits

Case A
Tax collections — deposited at the Bank of Canada

STAGE I: Taxes are paid by members of the general public, with cheques drawn on accounts at chartered banks. The government deposits these cheques in its account with the Bank of Canada.

Bank of Canada		Public	
Cheques on banks +100	Deposits of govern-ment +100		Tax liability −100
			Cheques outst. +100

STAGE II: When the outstanding cheques are cleared and collected, bank reserve deposits at the Bank of Canada are reduced by an equal amount.

Bank of Canada		Public		Chartered banks	
Cheques on banks −100	Deposits of banks −100	Bank deposits −100	Cheques outst. −100	Reserve deposits −100	Deposits of public −100

Net change:

		Public		Chartered banks	
	Deposits of banks −100	Bank deposits −100	Tax liability −100	Reserve deposits −100	Deposits of public −100
	of govern-ment +100				

NOTE: The deposit liabilities and cash reserves of the chartered banks have been reduced by the same amount. The banks will now be deficient in their reserve positions, and multiple credit contraction will follow.

Case B
Tax collections — deposited at chartered banks

Taxes are paid by members of the general public, with cheques drawn on accounts at chartered banks. The government deposits these cheques in its accounts with chartered banks.

Bank of Canada		Public		Chartered banks	
		Bank deposits −100	Tax liability −100		Deposits of public −100
					of govern-ment +100

NOTE: The total deposit liabilities and cash reserves of the chartered banks are unaffected by this transaction. No general credit contraction will occur. The publicly owned money supply has been reduced by the amount of the tax collection.

Government expenditures would have opposite effects. If they are made out of deposits with chartered banks only the ownership of the money supply is changed (as in Case B): if they are made out of deposits with the Bank of Canada, total chartered bank reserves and deposit liabilities will be increased by the same amount, leaving excess reserves and inducing further credit expansion.

Case C
Transfer of government deposits

Government deposits with chartered banks are withdrawn and redeposited with the Bank of Canada.

Bank of Canada		Chartered banks	
Deposits of banks −100		Reserve deposits −100	Deposits of govern- ment −100
of govern- ment +100			

NOTE: The deposit liabilities and cash reserves of the chartered banks are reduced by the same amount, leaving the banks with deficient reserves. Multiple credit contraction will follow.

A transfer of deposits from the Bank of Canada to the chartered banks would have the opposite effect, creating excess reserves and inducing general credit creation.

---

government's cash is kept in accounts with the chartered banks, and transferred to the Bank of Canada only as needed. As a result, government cash outlays tend to reduce government deposits at the chartered banks, transferring the ownership of bank deposits from the government to the general public, but without any repercussions on the monetary base. Government cash inflows are deposited with chartered banks, again transferring ownership of bank deposits without affecting the monetary base.

As a result, the major fluctuations in government cash balances are confined to accounts with chartered banks. Balances at the Bank of Canada are kept small and *relatively* stable (see Figure 19-1). The monetary complications of government transactions are thereby minimized.

Government Deposits as a Policy Instrument

There is thus good reason for the government to maintain bank accounts at both the Bank of Canada and the chartered banks. But the existence of the two sets of accounts also creates a potential instrument of monetary control. Bank reserves can be adjusted just as effectively by a transfer of funds between the government's accounts with the chartered banks and the Bank of Canada as by open market operations. As the fiscal agent for the government, the Bank has the authority to make such transfers for policy reasons. In recent years, indeed, the transfer of government deposits has become the primary mechanism for day-to-day adjustments of bank reserves.[1] There are two reasons for this. First, as we noted above, unexpected open market operations may cause a temporary disturbance in securities markets, which may be avoided by the deposit transfer. Second, while securities transactions take a few days to affect bank reserves (because of the standard settlement arrangements in securities markets), the transfer of deposits can affect reserves the next day (after the cheque transferring the deposit has cleared). Deposit transfers are simpler and quicker.

There are, however, some obvious technical problems in using government deposits as an instrument of monetary control. Consider first the transfer of deposits from the chartered banks to the Bank of Canada to reduce bank reserves. For the transfer to have a continuing effect on bank reserves, the deposits would have to be held idle in the Bank of Canada, and not spent by the government. In spending these funds, the government would draw cheques against them, which would be deposited in bank accounts by their recipients, thus returning the funds to bank reserves. But, generally speaking, the government's cash balances are not excess funds which can be held idle at the Bank of Canada indefinitely. The government has to be free to draw on them in the normal course of its business. Accordingly, the Bank of Canada can only regard the transfer of funds from the chartered banks as a temporary measure. Over a longer period of time, it would engage in open market sales of securities, permitting the government deposits to be spent or transferred back to the chartered banks while maintaining the desired level of bank reserves. The purpose of the initial transfer of government deposits to the Bank of Canada, then, is to make it possible for the Bank of Canada to choose the timing of its open market operations. The transfer of government deposits is an initial, temporary adjustment; the open market operations a more permanent adjustment.

In the case of the opposite deposit transfer from the Bank of Canada to the chartered banks, for the purpose of increasing bank reserves, the technical problem is rather different. We have just seen that, normally, government deposits at the Bank of Canada are very small. What if there are not sufficient funds in the government's account to be transferred to the chartered banks? Does this very real possibility impair the potential use of this instrument?

One solution to the problem is obvious. The Bank of Canada could make an advance to the government, and, with a simple bookkeeping entry, deposit the funds in the government's account at the Bank. The necessary funds would then be available for transfer to the government's accounts with the chartered banks. We noted earlier (p. 641) that the Bank has the power to make such direct advances to the government, and indeed that an account is provided in the Bank's balance sheet and hence in the monetary base equation. However, this power is never used, and the account is always empty. The Bank achieves the same effect by another, indirect method, known as a "swap" with the Exchange Fund Account.

"Swaps" with the Exchange Fund[2]

You will recall from the discussion in Chapter 8 that in the jargon of the foreign exchange market a swap involves the pairing of a spot transaction in foreign exchange with an opposite forward contract. The spot purchase of foreign exchange would be matched with a forward sale contract; or, the spot sale of foreign exchange would be paired with a forward purchase contract.

In order to increase bank reserves, the Bank of Canada would purchase foreign exchange from the Exchange Fund, and simultaneously contract to resell the foreign exchange to the Fund at a convenient date in the future, at a price stipulated in the contract. As Example 19-3 illustrates, the spot transaction adds to the foreign currency assets of the Bank of Canada as it subtracts from the foreign currency assets of the Exchange Fund. (Canada's total foreign exchange reserves are not changed; ownership is simply transferred from the Exchange Fund to the Bank of Canada.) The Bank pays for the foreign currency assets by crediting the government's deposit with the Bank. Bank reserves are not affected yet. In terms of the monetary base equation, there have been offsetting increases in the Bank's foreign currency assets and the government's deposit at the Bank. However, the Bank is now in a position to transfer government deposits from the Bank of Canada to the chartered banks, thereby increasing bank reserves.

The forward contract between the Bank of Canada and the Exchange Fund does not affect bank reserves. It is a contract for a transaction to occur in the future. Its only significance for us is as a reminder that when it is convenient, the transaction will be reversed.

Since late 1964, the Bank of Canada has used swap transactions on a fairly large scale for temporary adjustments to bank reserves. While these swaps are a highly technical and rather arcane subject, there should be no mystery about them. *Swaps with the Exchange Fund are simply a complicated method for the Bank of Canada to make temporary advances to the government* — to do indirectly what they seem unwilling to do directly. In the examples described above, the swaps are presented as an aspect of the day-to-day management of bank reserves; they could easily be used as a method of temporarily financing the cash requirements of the government. Moreover, there is no reason why such swaps have to be confined to the Exchange Fund. Purchase and resale agreements could be made with any of the special funds administered by the Minister of Finance. Also, on occasion the Bank of Canada has adjusted the timing of the transfer of its profits to the government as a technique of monetary control. When the Bank's profits are paid over to the government and deposited in the government's account with the chartered banks, bank reserves increase by a like amount. By choosing the time at which such transfers will be made, the Bank can harmonize this impact on bank reserves with other aspects of its monetary control policies.

Foreign Currency Assets

When swaps between the Exchange Fund and the Bank of Canada are part of the process of adjusting bank reserves, the monetary base equation will suggest that the factor which is inducing the change in bank reserves is the Bank of Canada's purchase of foreign currency assets. In fact, as we have just seen, there will have been no market transaction in foreign currency assets. The role of the foreign currency asset account is purely nominal, reflecting a complex bookkeeping arrangement. However, in principle, the Bank of Canada could engage in open market transactions in foreign exchange for the purpose of adjusting bank reserves. It should be remembered that whenever the Bank of Canada purchases foreign exchange for its own account, it makes payment with a cheque drawn on itself. When this cheque is deposited in the vendor's account with a chartered bank and is cleared and collected, bank reserves are augmented by an

EXAMPLE 19-3   **Bank of Canada, Exchange Fund swaps**

STAGE I: The Bank of Canada purchases foreign currency assets from the Exchange Fund ("spot" transaction) and credits the government's deposit with the Bank. Simultaneously, the parties enter into a forward contract to reverse the transaction at a convenient date in the future.

Minister of Finance

Advance to Exchange Fund −100	
Deposit: Bank of Canada +100	

Exchange Fund account

Foreign currency assets −100	Advance from Minister −100

Bank of Canada

Foreign currency assets +100	deposits: government +100

NOTES:
1. The Bank of Canada has a forward commitment to sell, and the Exchange Fund account a forward commitment to purchase, foreign currency assets of 100. The forward commitments do not show on the spot balance sheet.
2. The "advances" entry in the books of the Exchange Fund and the Minister simply serves to balance the books.

STAGE II: The Bank of Canada transfers government deposits to the chartered banks. When the cheques are cleared, the banks' reserve deposits at the Bank of Canada are increased.

Minister of Finance

Deposits: Bank of Canada −100 chartered banks +100	

Bank of Canada

	Deposits: government −100 banks +100

Chartered banks

Reserve deposit +100	Deposits: government +100

Net change:

Minister of Finance

Advances to Exchange Fund −100	
Deposits: Bank of Canada 0 chartered banks +100	

Exchange Fund account

Foreign currency assets −100	Advance from Minister −100

Bank of Canada

Foreign currency assets +100	Deposits: government 0 chartered banks +100

Chartered banks

Reserve deposits +100	Deposits: government +100

NOTES:
1. The reserves of banks have increased by 100, which will have the usual effects on bank credit expansion.
2. In terms of the reserve equation, it will appear that the increase in bank reserves is a result of an increase in the Bank of Canada's foreign currency assets. In fact, it is a result of an implicit advance to the government, with these funds transferred to the chartered banks. The government's total cash balances (at the Bank of Canada + the chartered banks) have increased by 100.

STAGE III: The Bank of Canada purchases government bonds in the open market, permitting the transfer of government deposits back to the Bank of Canada and the resale of the foreign currency assets to the Exchange Fund, while leaving the banks' cash reserves at the new level.

Minister of Finance

Advances to Exchange Fund +100	Deposits: Bank of Canada −100
	chart. banks +100 / −100

Exchange Fund account

Foreign currency assets +100	Advance from Minister +100

Bank of Canada

Foreign currency assets −100	Deposits: government +100 / −100
Securities +100	

Chartered banks

Reserve deposits 0	Deposits: government −100
	public +100

Public

Securities −100
Bank deposits +100

Net change (through Stage III)

Minister of Finance

Advances to Exchange Fund 0	Deposits: Bank of Canada 0
	chartered banks 0

Exchange Fund account

Foreign currency assets 0	Advances from Minister 0

Bank of Canada

Foreign currency assets 0	Deposits: government 0
Securities +100	banks +100

Chartered banks

Reserve deposit +100	Deposits: government 0
	public +100

Public

Securities −100
Bank deposits +100

NOTES:
1. The forward commitment between the Bank of Canada and the Exchange Fund has been honored, and the transactions of Stage I reversed.
2. The Bank of Canada's open market operations have made "permanent" the increase in bank reserves which resulted from the temporary swap and the temporary deposit transfer.

equal amount. Bank of Canada sales of foreign exchange in the open market have the opposite effect. Payment is received in the form of a cheque drawn on a chartered bank, and that amount will be deducted from the bank's reserve deposit at the Bank of Canada. In principle, then, the Bank of Canada could conduct its open market operations in the foreign exchange market rather than in the securities market.

The Bank of Canada's power to trade in the foreign exchange market on its own account in order to alter bank reserves is, in fact, severely circumscribed under normal circumstances. In the first place, the Bank's holdings of foreign exchange are relatively small, no more than required for operational purposes. This means that the Bank cannot easily sell foreign exchange to contract bank reserves which, of course, does not prohibit foreign exchange purchases to increase bank reserves. However, more important than this technical detail, for which there are obvious solutions, is the fact that the Bank cannot buy and sell foreign exchange without influencing the foreign exchange rate. This raises two problems. If the government has an independent policy with respect to the exchange rate, the Bank's operations might bring it into direct conflict with the government's policy. Also, the level of the exchange rate is a matter of interest to another government, that of the United States. Bank of Canada operations which have a direct and obvious influence on the exchange rate for purely domestic monetary reasons might create diplomatic problems.

CENTRAL BANK ADVANCES

In contemporary monetary systems, central bank advances account for only a small fraction of total bank reserves. Yet, these advances, and the conditions on which they are made, have been the subject of a vigorous controversy among monetary economists. Defenders of the *status quo* argue that these advances perform a vital auxiliary function in the process of monetary control, permitting a more vigorous pursuit of monetary restraint when necessary. Critics argue that the provision of central bank credit on demand at a posted interest rate weakens the central bank's control over bank reserves. There are also a few economists who suggest that the advances mechanism ought to be much more important in the financial system, and that the interest rate on advances ought to be rehabilitated to its classical role as the basic instrument of monetary policy.

Our task in this section involves not only the exploration of how the mechanism works in Canada today, but also an exploration of the issues underlying the controversy. For this purpose we must consider the operations of the "discount window" of the Federal Reserve Banks of the United States. But first we must review the relationship between central bank advances and the monetary base.

Advances and Bank Reserves

Forms of Advances.   There are three basic types of central bank advances: rediscounts, loans secured by appropriate collateral, and purchase and resale agreements. In Canada, today, only the last two are relevant.

The *rediscounting* of commercial paper is the classic form of central bank advance.

It involves the purchase from a bank of the promissory notes of the bank's commercial customers which have been endorsed by the bank so that they are simultaneously the liability of the bank and the commercial customer. The notes are purchased by the central bank at a discount from their face value and are called "rediscounts" because the central bank is discounting notes which the commercial bank itself had previously "discounted." In popular parlance, however, and particularly in the United States, all central bank advances (except, perhaps, purchase and resale agreements) have come to be called "discounts," the interest rate for all advances the "discount rate," and the mechanism for such advances the "discount window."

In contrast to rediscounts, *direct loans* by the central bank involve only the promissory note of the bank which is borrowing. However, the bank must normally pledge acceptable assets as security for the loan. The most common type of collateral is government bonds, although some central banks will accept other assets.

The *purchase and resale agreement* is the normal method by which a central bank makes advances to security dealers. The central bank purchases securities from the dealer, but at the time of the purchase the dealer signs an agreement to repurchase the securities from the central bank on a particular date and at a specified price. The difference between the buying and selling prices determines the rate of interest on such advances. Short-term government bonds are the most common type of security used in these arrangements, although some purchase and resale agreements are also made with banker's acceptances.

Monetary Effects.   As the monetary base equation makes clear, the extension of central bank advances expands the monetary base, and the repayment of these advances contracts it. The process is illustrated in more detail in Example 19-4. Central bank advances appear to be no different from open market operations. The extension of advances has the same effects as the purchase of government bonds (or the acquisition of any asset), and the repayment of advances has the same effect as the sale of bonds.

Locus of Initiative.   However, there are important qualitative differences. Unlike open market operations, central bank advances involve direct, face-to-face negotiations between borrower and lender. They are not impersonal transactions in the securities of a third party which are traded actively in the open market.

The locus of initiative for the two types of central bank operations is correspondingly different. Open market operations are normally entirely at the initiative of the central bank. Advances are at the initiative of the banks and security dealers. The central bank establishes the line of credit available to each borrower, sets the conditions for advances, and posts the interest rates at which advances will be made. While it can make the terms for advances more or less favorable, for example by lowering or raising the relevant interest rates, the central bank must then sit back and await the decisions of possible borrowers. It can *offer incentives* but *cannot initiate* the advances which will change the quantity of high-powered money outstanding. For this reason, most contemporary economists do not regard central bank advances as an important instrument of monetary policy.

This was not always the case.

EXAMPLE 19-4   Central bank advances

A purchase and resale agreement between the Bank of Canada
and government security dealers

STAGE I: A government security dealer enters into a purchase and resale agreement with the Bank of Canada. The Bank of Canada purchases $100 thousand worth of government bonds from the dealer, and the dealer simultaneously signs an agreement to repurchase the securities from the Bank of Canada in five days. The Bank of Canada pays for the securities with a cheque drawn on itself.

    In the following accounts, in order to minimize complications, we treat this transaction as though it were a direct advance from the Bank of Canada to the dealer — which in effect it is.

Bank of Canada			Security dealer	
Advances +100	Cheques outstanding +100		Bank of Canada cheques +100	Advances from Bank of Canada +100

STAGE II: The dealer deposits the cheque with his bank

Security dealer			Chartered bank	
Bank of Canada cheques −100 Bank deposits +100			Bank of Canada cheques +100	Deposits +100

STAGE III: The outstanding Bank of Canada cheque is cleared and collected, and the $100 thousand is credited to the chartered bank's cash reserves.

Bank of Canada			Chartered bank	
Cheques outstanding −100 Deposit of bank +100			Bank of Canada cheques −100 Cash reserves +100	

Net change:

Bank of Canada		Security dealer		Chartered bank	
Advances +100	Deposits of banks +100	Bank deposits +100	Advances from Bank of Canada +100	Cash reserves +100	Deposits +100

NOTES:
1. There has been a direct increase in the money supply of $100 thousand. It is presently in the hands of the security dealer, but he will use it to pay off other (private) debts or to purchase securities. The money will go into general circulation.
2. The deposit liabilities and the cash reserves of the chartered banks have increased by the same amount. The banks now have excess cash reserves which provide the base for a further expansion of the supply of money and credit.
3. While the initial impact would have been different, the overall effect would have been the same if the Bank of Canada had made the advances directly to the chartered banks.

REPAYMENT:
When the advance is repaid (i.e., the securities repurchased) exactly the opposite set of transactions will occur. The dealer will pay by cheque, when the cheque is cleared and collected, chartered bank reserves will be reduced, and credit contraction should ensue. You should note that, because of the interest charges involved, a larger sum will be repaid than was lent.

United States' Experience

The American central bank, the Federal Reserve System, was established in 1913 in a classical mould. It was envisaged that the Federal Reserve Banks would extend credit only to commercial banks, rediscounting the promissory notes of the banks' commercial customers, at a discount rate set by the Federal Reserve Banks from time to time "with a view to accommodating business and commerce." In this way the supply of Federal Reserve credit was supposed to adjust automatically to meet the legitimate demands of business — an extension of the commercial loan theory of commercial banking to the central bank. In the early 1920s over 70% of the member banks had occasion to borrow from the Federal Reserve System during each year, and discounts accounted for roughly the same proportion of total bank reserves.

The original charter implied a passive role for the Federal Reserve System in the financial system. The supply of Federal Reserve credit was to be regulated primarily by the supply of "eligible paper" rather than by the judgment of a centralized monetary authority. Indeed, although their actions were subject to review by the Federal Reserve Board, each of the 12 Federal Reserve Banks was free to establish its own discount rate, applicable for loans to member banks in its district. The institutions were hardly designed for the implementation of a vigorous national monetary policy.

In the 1920s, some experiments were conducted with the use of the discount rate as a regulating device. Gradually, however, reliance came to be placed on open market operations, supervised by an *ad hoc* "open market committee" of the Federal Reserve Banks. With this change in emphasis, a new policy emerged with respect to the discount window. Continuous borrowing by member banks was discouraged, with the discount window to be used for "seasonal and temporary requirements of members," and particularly to meet "unusual circumstances," such as those caused by "adverse economic circumstances in their localities and among their customers."

The importance of the discount window as a source of bank reserves declined somewhat in the mid-1920s, but nonetheless extensive use of the facility continued until the early 1930s. Following the banking crisis, and major revisions in the legislation governing the operations of the Federal Reserve System, reliance on the discount window by member banks declined sharply.[3] The volume of discounts remained insignificant, until the early 1950s, by which time the new concept of the role of the discount window in policy formation was firmly established. The principles underlying access to the discount window have not changed significantly from those evolved in the 1920s and 1930s.

Cyclical Behavior of Advances. In recent years, bank borrowing from the Federal Reserve has been much less important as a source of bank reserves than in the 1920s. However, bank borrowing undergoes systematic and relatively wide fluctuations, and these fluctuations are closely related to the monetary policies of the Federal Reserve System. Periods of substantial increase in advances tend to be periods when the Federal Reserve is pursuing a restrictive monetary policy, using the instruments of monetary control to restrict the growth of bank reserves relative to rising demands for money and credit. Periods of major decline in advances tend to be periods when the Federal Reserve is pursuing an easier monetary policy, using the instruments of monetary control to actively expand bank reserves.

As we have seen, an increase in central bank advances adds to bank reserves whereas a reduction in such advances decreases bank reserves. For this reason, then, *monetary policy and the discount window seem to work in opposition to each other.*

During a period of monetary restraint, several forces bear upon banks simultaneously. In general, the demand for loans will be strong and expanding rapidly. The central bank will resist the credit and monetary expansion implicit in the rising loan demand by restricting the growth of bank reserves. The banks will compete vigorously with each other for the available deposits, particularly in the market for negotiable certificates of deposits. They may rearrange their asset portfolios, disposing of short-term liquid assets in the money market (and probably also some longer-term marketable bonds) in order to make room for additional loans. The liquidity of the banks' asset portfolios will be reduced; cash reserves will be scarce; bond prices will be depressed; and, correspondingly, interest rates will be bid up.

To a banker, borrowing from the Federal Reserve is but one method of adjusting his cash reserve position. It is an alternative to calling outstanding call-loans; selling short-term liquid assets; borrowing from other banks through the federal funds market or the Eurodollar market; or competing for large blocks of corporate cash balances through the issuance of negotiable certificates of deposit. Various considerations will affect the choice, including the size of the bank (a small country bank is unlikely to enter either the certificate of deposit or the Federal funds markets), the size and expected duration of the reserve deficiency, and the size of the bank's liquid asset holdings. However, one of the basic considerations is the *relative cost* of the alternative adjustment techniques. In the case of borrowing, the obvious cost is the interest which must be paid. In the case of selling short-term liquid assets, it is the opportunity cost of interest foregone. Borrowing from the Federal Reserve System should then be affected by the relationship between the discount rate and other monetary market interest rates.

The discount rate is changed only at discreet intervals, and then usually by relatively large amounts (¼ or ½ percentage point). When it takes such a jump, the discount rate cannot help but affect the level of other short-term interest rates. However, between jumps a significant gap frequently opens between the discount rate and the continually changing market rates. Overall, the discount rate gives the appearance of a runner who makes occasional spurts to the fore, but who generally lags behind the pack. In a period of generally rising interest rates, this creates an obvious inducement for banks to borrow from their Federal Reserve Banks, and for this reason alone, central bank advances can be expected to increase in periods of monetary restraint. In addition, the incidence of credit restraint among banks may be very uneven. Some banks may experience severe cash drains and, given their reduced holdings of liquid assets, may find they cannot cope with their cash deficiencies other than by borrowing from their Federal Reserve Bank or by making a fundamental retrenchment in their lending policies or in their investment portfolios. Given the relatively high cost implied in calling loans or disposing of longer-term bonds in a depressed bond market, they will be driven to borrowing from their Federal Reserve Banks. Such borrowing would occur even if the discount rate were continuously kept equal to short-term money market rates such as the treasury bill rate.

In a period of monetary restraint, then, more banks will be borrowing larger sums for longer periods of time. Federal Reserve advances will increase, providing additional high-powered money, and thus offsetting some of the restriction of bank reserves.

This relationship is apparent in Figure 19-2. The top panel shows Federal Reserve

FIGURE 19-2   Federal Reserve advances to member banks,
United States, 1970-80

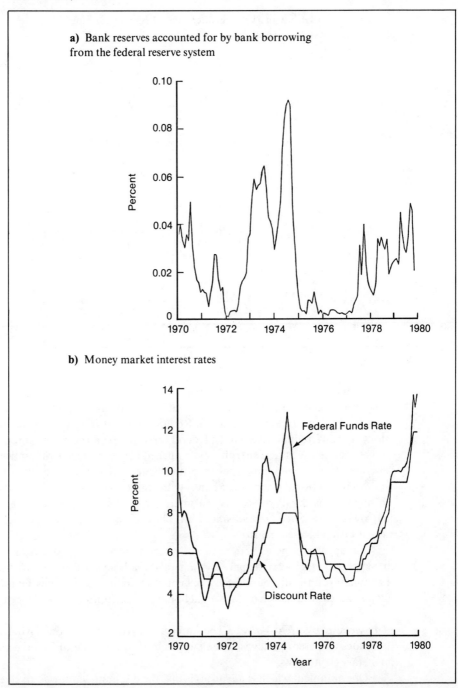

a) Bank reserves accounted for by bank borrowing
from the federal reserve system

b) Money market interest rates

FIGURE 19-2   *continued*

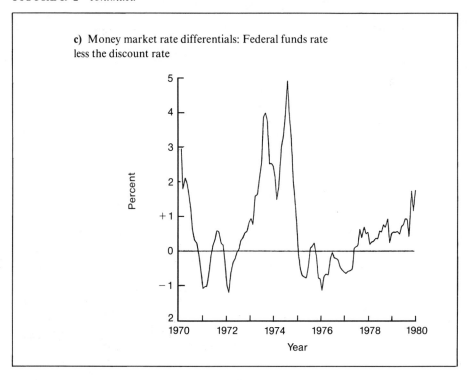

c) Money market rate differentials: Federal funds rate less the discount rate

advances to member banks over the period 1970-79. The middle panel shows the federal funds rate, a key money market interest rate at which banks lend reserves to each other, and the discount rate of the Federal Reserve Bank of New York. The bottom panel shows the differential between the federal funds rate and the discount rate. Whenever money market rates rose sharply, a gap opened between the federal funds rate and the discount rate, making advances from the Federal Reserve relatively attractive as a source of additional reserves for banks with temporary reserve deficiencies. Advances to member banks increased. When interest rates fell sharply, the interest rate gap narrowed or reversed, and advances fell. The cycle of 1972-75 is only one of several in recent Federal Reserve history.

The apparently perverse cyclical movement of Federal Reserve advances to member banks, then, is at least in part a result of the administration of the discount rate. Presumably, if the discount rate were kept more in line with money market rates, the major swings in bank borrowing would be dampened, although perhaps not eliminated.

Advances as a Safety Valve.   The implications that the discount window partially frustrates monetary policy is vehemently denied by the Federal Reserve and by many monetary economists.

One argument which is advances is that the discount window is an essential *safety valve*. By providing them with a reliable emergency source of funds, it cushions the impact of monetary restraint on individual banks which might otherwise be very adversely affected. It is argued that this permits the Federal Reserve System to ignore some of the harsher individual consequences of its monetary actions, and thus permits it to pursue a more vigorous policy than it would otherwise be able to do.

Moreover, it is asserted that the reserves which the banks borrow from the Federal Reserve System are not the same thing as reserves which the banks own outright, because bankers are reluctant to be in debt to any other bank, including the central bank.[4] Tradition has it that such indebtedness is a sign of poor bank management.

Like many similar "traditions," the precise meaning of this one is difficult to define. Bankers certainly do borrow from the central bank and from other banks, when there is some advantage in doing so. However, whatever the precise meaning of the bankers' "reluctance to borrow," the Federal Reserve Systems regulations governing the use of the discount window are calculated to reinforce it. The regulations emphasize that borrowing is a "privilege" of membership in the Federal Reserve System, not a "right." Members may borrow only on short-term and for "appropriate" purposes. Borrowing from the Federal Reserve is not to be a continuing source of funds to finance bank operations, and continuous or frequent borrowing is a matter for official concern and scrutiny. Under these circumstance, it is argued, banks which are in debt to the Federal Reserve System will feel themselves under continuous pressure to restrict credit in order to repay their debt and to make a more fundamental adjustment to their deposit situation. The object of policy will be achieved, albeit gradually rather than abruptly. *Bank borrowing from the federal Reserve System does not offset the restrictive effects of open market operations. It simply alters the way in which such effects are transmitted to the economy.*[5]

Purchase and Resale Agreements.   The Federal Reserve System also makes advances to security dealers by means of purchase and resale agreements (normally called repurchase agreements or buy-backs in the United States), and since the mid-1970s they have increased in importance to rival advances to member banks as a source of bank reserves. However, the administration of purchase and resale agreements is fundamentally different from the administration of advances to member banks. While the initiative in taking an advance rests with the security dealer, the Federal Reserve does not take a passive role, making advances continuously available at a posted interest rate and under specified rules. Decisions on the availability of purchase and resale agreements are made periodically by the Open Market Committee, a joint committee of the Board of Governors and the Federal Reserve Banks which is responsible for policy decisions on open market operations. Instructions on timing, amounts, and interest rates are issued to the responsible officials at the Federal Reserve Bank of New York, where the agreements are made. Traditionally, when available, purchase and resale agreements were made at the discount rate, but in recent years they have been offered for competitive bidding. When this occurs, the quantity of credit is effectively determined by the Federal Reserve; the market sets the price — the reverse of the situation with advances to member banks.

Although they involve some initiative from the market, in the United States purchase and resale agreements are in effect a type of open market operation. Temporary, and hence automatically reversible, they are particularly suitable for short-term adjustments to the monetary base. As we shall see, they have a somewhat different character in Canada.

Canadian Experience

In some respects, Canadian experience with central bank advances has been very similar to that of the United States. This partly reflects a common underlying philosophy of the administration of the advance mechanism. In other respects, however, Canadian experience has been different, reflecting market differences in the structures of the two financial systems (and particularly the small number of banks in Canada) and different approaches to the setting of the interest rate on advances. The Bank of Canada has made notable innovations in bank rate policy.

Early History: The Finance Act.   In the United States, the discount mechanism was created to provide "elasticity" to the money supply, i.e., to make the supply of money sensitive to changing commercial demands for funds, particularly seasonal demands. In Canada, in spite of more pronounced seasonal factors, elasticity in this sense was never a problem. The Federal Reserve was supposed to provide elasticity by discounting on the commercial loan principle; in Canada, the elasticity was provided by the flexible arrangements under which the chartered banks operated, including adherence to the commercial loan principle of banking.

Although there was no central bank in Canada until 1935, a discount facility was created almost as early as in the United States. Passed as a wartime emergency measure in 1914 (but continued by a 1923 Act), the *Finance Act* permitted the chartered banks to obtain advances of Dominion notes, the legal tender of the day, from the Department of Finance at a rate of interest set from time to time by the government. Superficially this provided Canada with the essential institution of a classical central bank. Advances were made against various collateral. In the early years, substantial seasonal loans were secured by grain, very much in the commercial loan spirit; but after the early 1920s, loans were almost exclusively secured by government bonds. The interest rate on advances was changed from time to time. However, in spite of recent evidence of two or three *ad hoc* attempts to implement monetary policy by means of the *Finance Act*, it is clear that the Act created an institution without a mission and without a guiding philosophy. To the banks it provided a method to adjust cash reserves, and frequently it was a low-cost method. To the government it was a financial convenience; changes in the interest rate on advances were generally designed to induce the banks to purchase new issues of government securities. No serious consideration was given to using the Department of Finance as a central bank, manipulating the interest rate to control the financial system.

An Inactive Discount Window 1935-1955.   When the Bank of Canada was established, it took over the *Finance Act's* function as lender of last resort for the banking system. However, until the mid-1950s, its role in this capacity was almost hypothetical. Aside from a few wartime advances to support bank financing of Victory Loan campaigns, the discount mechanism was rarely used by the banks, which had, in any case, substantial excess cash reserves throughout the period.

Likewise, the discount rate was not used as an instrument of policy prior to the mid-1950s. When the Bank of Canada opened for business, it continued the 2½% discount rate then in effect under the *Finance Act*. This rate continued until February

1944, when it was reduced to 1½% because 2½% was "out of line with the current market."[6] The Governor took pains to emphasize that this did not signal a change in credit policy. A second change of the rate occurred in October 1950, when it was increased to 2%. Although it was announced that this was part of a new policy of higher interest rates, the change did not in fact foreshadow active use of the rate as an instrument of policy. No further change occurred until the rate was reduced to 1½% in February 1955, following which the official conception of the role of the discount rate entered a new phase.

Thus, during the first 20 years of the Bank of Canada the discount rate was changed only three times — in 1944, 1950, and 1955. This record could hardly be called aggressive use of the rate as an instrument of credit policy! (In order to maintain perspective on the discount rate, however, it should be noted that interest rates were effectively pegged at a low level through most of this period, with the result that there was virtually no active use of any of the formal instruments of quantitative monetary policy). In this context, the discount window had no clearly defined function in the financial system. It was an inactive and apparently redundant appendage to the central bank.

Reforms of 1953-54.   On several previous occasions we have referred to the major changes which were introduced into the Canadian financial system in 1953 and 1954. Among other things chartered bank cash reserve requirements were altered and made more effective in the sense that the banks stopped holding large excess reserves, and the Bank of Canada took measures to develop an active, open short-term money market. The banks were encouraged to work close to their required holdings of cash reserves, and were provided with a short-term money market in which they could invest any temporary excess liquidity and in which they could obtain additional cash on short notice (by calling day loans or selling short-term securities) as necessary.

A revision of the provisions for central bank advances was an integral part of these reforms. By making advances available to approved government security dealers (in the form of purchase and resale agreements), the Bank of Canada made it clear that it was underwriting the stability of the market. Such a guarantee was important to the banks if they were going to depend on the market for day-to-day reserve adjustments. It should be noted also that in encouraging the banks to work closer to their minimum cash reserve requirements, and thus removing the cushion of excess cash reserves, the Bank of Canada almost guaranteed that the discount window would receive more use than it had in the previous 20 years.

The Role of the Discount Window.   In breathing life into its redundant appendage, the Bank of Canada adopted the American concept of the function of central bank advances. Thus, in his 1956 Annual Report, the Governor of the Bank of Canada warned:

> The purpose of Bank of Canada advances to the chartered banks is not to provide loanable funds to the banking system but simply to enable an individual bank to replenish its cash reserves or its total liquid assets at a time when these have been depleted by unexpected withdrawals.[7]

The rules governing advances to banks

> …are designed to limit the Bank's role as lender of last resort to exceptional circumstances and to encourage the chartered banks to use, whenever practicable, alternative methods of adjusting their cash reserves in the market such as calling day-to-day loans or selling securities.[8]

The bank rate applies to the first advance to a bank during any month; renewals, or additional advances, are at high rates of interest. Advances must be taken for a minimum of two or three days.

Likewise, advances to dealers are not be regarded as an important, continuous source of dealer finance. Rather, they are designed to

> provide an underlying assurance of liquidity to the money market and to encourage the use of the money market mechanism in the adjustment of cash reserves.[9]

To this end, the arrangements for purchase and resale agreements are more flexible than the arrangements for advances to banks. Agreements may be made for any period up to 30 days, and there are no penalty interest rates for repeated advances. At times when the bank rate has been pegged, the rate for purchase and resale agreements has been more flexible. Although neither is of major importance, in recent years purchase and resale agreements have dwarfed advances to banks as a source of bank reserves.

Although the underlying philosophy of central bank advances is similar in the United States and Canada, there has been notable diversity in the behavior and importance of advances as a source of bank reserves in the two banking systems. To some extent these differences reflect differences in the structures of the banking systems, and to some extent differences in policy with respect to interest rates on advances.

Continuity of Advances. The advances accounts in the balance sheets of the Federal Reserve Banks are seldom empty. There are always some banks with outstanding indebtedness. This cannot be said of Canada. For example, in 1975, a year of moderate borrowing, advances were outstanding to chartered banks on only 28 business days and to security dealers on 76 days (there were 252 business days in the year). On all other days there were no advances outstanding.

The discontinuity of advances in Canada does not mean that individual Canadian banks borrow less frequently than do U.S. banks. In Canada, in the late 1970s, there were less than a dozen chartered banks (and only a few more security dealers) eligible to borrow; in the United States there were over 5 600 member banks. Like Canadian banks, individual member banks borrowed relatively small sums, infrequently.[10] However, there were always some banks in debt to the Federal Reserve, and for this reason alone we should expect central bank advances to banks to be more important as a source of bank reserves in the United States than in Canada. In periods of monetary restraint, more banks borrow larger sums for longer periods of time, producing the characteristic cyclical pattern to advances.

Cyclical Behavior of Advances. Bank of Canada advances to the chartered banks are sufficiently small, and sufficiently irregular, so that, although a slight cyclical pattern might be detected in Figure 19-3, it cannot be argued that advances to the banks in any

TABLE 19-1 Bank of Canada advances to chartered banks and government security dealers, 1956-1981

	Number of days advances outstanding		Average amount outstanding per business day	
	to banks	to security dealers*	banks	security dealers*
1945	74	—	0.6	—
1946	12	—	—	—
1947	6	—	0.1	—
1948	12	—	0.1	—
1949	14	—	0.1	—
1950	6	—	—	—
1951	—	—	—	—
1952	—	—	—	—
1953	30	293	0.2	15.2
1954	62	124	2.4	14.5
1955	98	48	4.2	1.9
1956	105	62	7.6	2.0
1957	59	103	3.5	6.5
1958	40	50	1.4	2.6
1959	53	64	2.1	3.0
1960	25	75	1.5	4.7
1961	5	55	0.2	3.0
1962	37	50	3.0	3.4
1963	20	48	0.4	2.4
1964	15	49	0.2	2.4
1965	48	42	1.8	2.8
1966	5	48	0.1	3.7
1967	24	72	1.1	7.6
1968	14	35	0.2	4.3
1969	35	93	1.2	9.4
1970	35	125	1.8	16.7
1971	27	78	0.6	16.0
1972	19	115	0.7	17.1
1973	53	126	5.2	27.7
1974	49	110	7.4	25.9
1975	28	76	1.6	11.6
1976	23	128	1.5	43.4
1977	74	172	10.2	90.7
1978	29	143	3.0	65.6
1979	32	169	6.4	112.3
1980	39	161	13.8	109.9
1981	35	192	14.8	150.8

* Purchase and resale agreements

SOURCE: Bank of Canada, *Annual Reports,* 1945-1981.

FIGURE 19-3 Bank of Canada advances to chartered banks, Canada, 1965-1980

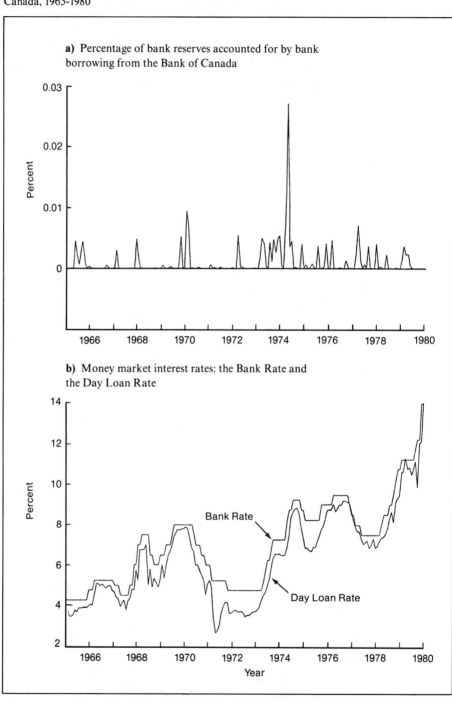

FIGURE 19-3   *continued*

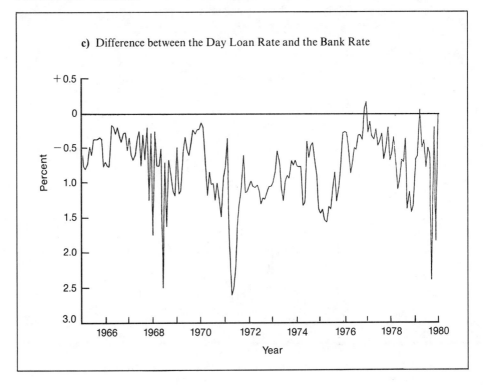

c) Difference between the Day Loan Rate and the Bank Rate

way impair the Bank of Canada's control over aggregate reserves. In Figure 19-3, advances to banks are shown in the top panel as a percentage of bank reserves. (It is useful to compare the percentages in Canada, which seldom exceeded ½%, with those in the United States in Figure 19-2, which seldom dipped as low as ½% and on one occasion reached as high as 9%). The level of money market interest rates, represented by the day loan rate, and the bank rate are shown in the middle panel. Comparison with Figure 19-2 will reveal parallel movements in money market interest rates in the two countries. (Why? It may be useful to review the material on international interest arbitrage in Chapter 8.) But the panel (c) of Figure 19-3 reveals a striking difference between Canada and the United States. Whereas in the U.S. money market interest rates generally exceeded the discount rate, markedly so in periods of monetary restraint, in Canada the bank rate almost always exceeded the comparable money market rates. This suggests a significantly different policy in Canada with respect to the bank rate than in the United States with respect to the discount rate.

Thus, in addition to the fewness of Canadian banks and the restrictive rules governing access to advances, we have discovered another reason why Bank of Canada advances to the chartered banks have not displayed the strong cyclical pattern which is so obvious in the United States. Bank rate policy has been fundamentally different from the Federal Reserve's discount rate policy. Whereas, in periods of monetary restraint,

FIGURE 19-4   Bank of Canada advances to security dealers,
Canada, 1965-1980: purchase and resale agreements

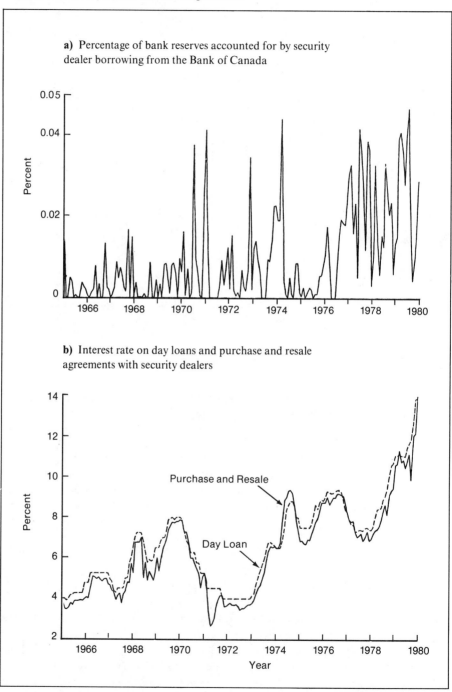

FIGURE 19-4   *continued*

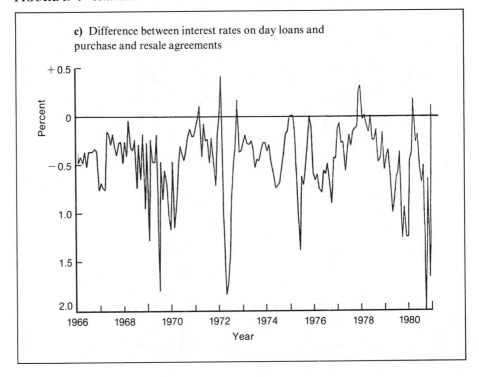

c) Difference between interest rates on day loans and purchase and resale agreements

the U.S. discount rate tends to lag behind sharply rising money market rates, creating an interest rate inducement for banks to borrow from the Federal Reserve (Figure 19-2), the Bank of Canada's bank rate normally remains above key money market rates, avoiding a systematic cyclical inducement for banks to borrow.

The behavior of purchase and resale agreements has been different. Not only have they increased in importance relative to advances to banks in recent years, they show much more cyclical sensitivity than do advances to banks (Figure 19-4). In this regard, it should be remembered that dealer access to purchase and resale agreements is less restrictive than bank access to advances, and the penalty interest rates for repeated advances do not apply to purchase and resale agreements. It is clear that, as the money market comes under severe pressure from restrictive money policy, the Bank of Canada systematically increases in importance as an underwriter of the liquidity of the market. To the extent that there is a cyclical offset to Bank of Canada restrictions on bank reserves, it is through purchase and resale agreements with security dealers, not through advances to banks.

Bank Rate Policy.   We saw that during the first 20 years of the Bank of Canada's existence, the discount window was virtually a redundant appendage to the central bank. When the mechanism was rehabilitated in 1955, the Governor of the Bank of Canada warned that the public would have to become accustomed to more flexible use of the bank rate in the future. Certainly the early record was not difficult to beat. From early August 1955, through mid-October 1956, the bank rate was increased on six separate occasions. In a little over a year there were twice as many changes as had occurred in the first 20 years of the Bank's history. On November 1, 1956, the Bank of Canada took the final step in the direction of flexibility and formally tied the bank rate to market interest rates. The bank rate was fixed at $\frac{1}{4}\%$ above the yield on 90-day treasury bills as established at the last weekly auction of treasury bills.

The Canadian experiment with floating discount rate was regarded with interest by economists. However, in late June 1962, at the height of a foreign exchange crisis, the experiment was abruptly terminated and shortly thereafter the Governor of the Bank of Canada stated publicly, "I regard the argument about the relative merits of a fixed bank rate and floating bank rate as over."[11] How wrong predictions can be! In March 1980, under circumstances which were strikingly similar to those in the fall of 1956, in that interest rates were rising sharply and the bank rate had been increased 10 times in the space of two years, a new Governor again announced the adoption of a floating bank rate.[12] The bank rate was set at $\frac{1}{4}\%$ above the average rate on 90-day treasury bills as established at the weekly auction.

Actually, the term "fixed" is a misnomer for the bank rate system of the period 1962-1980. The bank rate was not rigidly fixed, but was "discretionary." It was posted, and in that sense fixed, but it was subject to change from time to time at the discretion of the Bank of Canada. Moreover, the bank rate only applied to advances to the banks (and a higher, unspecified, rate applied to repeated borrowings within a month). Security dealers borrowed at what we can call the pra rate. This rate remained a floating rate, set weekly at $\frac{1}{4}\%$ above the 90-day treasury bill rate, but subject to a ceiling (bank rate plus $\frac{1}{2}\%$) and a floor (bank rate minus $\frac{3}{4}\%$).[13] Under the system adopted in March 1980 the pra rate is the bank rate.

What are the relative merits of discretionary and floating bank rate systems? Why did Canada adopt a floating rate, abandon it in favor of a mixed system, then adopt it again?

The Floating Bank Rate.   There are two major advantages of a floating bank rate. First, it automatically guarantees that the bank rate will continuously be a "penalty rate." This does not mean that it will be higher than the rates earned by banks or security dealers on all of their short-term assets. Rather, it means that it will consistently be somewhat higher than the rates on certain key money market instruments commonly used for reserve adjustments (e.g., treasury bills and day loans). While movements in the bank rate may not be predictable from week to week, its relationship to certain other rates is consistent and predictable.

This could presumably be achieved through frequent changes in a discretionary bank rate. However, there is a potentially disturbing "mystique" about announced changes of the bank rate.

A change in a discretionary bank rate is a deliberate, calculated act of intervention on the part of the central bank, dramatized through a public announcement. Invariably, this stimulates a spate of speculation in the financial papers. What does the rise in the bank rate "mean"? Does the central bank see storm clouds on the economic horizon? Or is it really an indication of continued economic expansion? Is the central bank simply adjusting to rising interest rates in the market? Or is it attempting to push the market to higher levels of interest rates? Is the country in for a period of tighter money and credit? The central bank normally finds it necessary to dispel uncertainty through a public statement of the purpose of the move (which sometimes provokes further speculation as the financial editors attempt to read between the lines to discover what the Bank "really" intends). By itself, the bank rate is an inefficient device for communicating complex information.

The two major advantages of allowing the bank rate to float are that it guarantees a suitable "penalty rate" at all times, and that changes in the rate will not provoke disturbing speculation about the economic prognosis and about the central bank's intentions.

The Bank Rate as a Signal.   Paradoxically, the latter "advantage" of the floating rate is also cited by its critics as a major disadvantage. That is, it is argued that if the bank rate is allowed to float, the central bank loses a valuable weapon from its limited armory. It can no longer use changes in the bank rate as a dramatic signal of its intentions.

There is considerable confusion regarding what information can be communicated by changes in the bank rate. As we have already seen, as a technique of communicating the central bank's views on the state of the economy and on appropriate economic policy, the bank rate is at best inefficient and at worst confusing and perhaps perverse. As the Governor of the Bank of Canada has acknowledged:

> The easiest method of communicating ideas is that of using the English language. If the central bank has something...to say...the most natural thing for the central bank to do is to make a speech or to issue a statement.[14]

Some economists call this "open mouth operations."

What, then, can be efficiently signalled by way of a discretionary change in the bank rate?

The bank rate can be used to provide guidance to participants in the money market as to the level of short-term interest rates which the central bank thinks is appropriate under the circumstances. By eliminating uncertainty about the central bank's intentions in this regard, the bank rate provides a clear focus for participants in the market, without tying the market rigidly to any particular level or structure of rates.

Normally, the central bank adjusts the bank rate in response to changes emerging in the money market (perhaps under central bank pressure). However, the bank rate can also be used to lead the money market to new levels of rates — something which could be accomplished through open market operations, but which might be effected more simply and more directly through the device of an abrupt, dramatic change in the bank rate. Perhaps the clearest instance of this use of the rate was provided by the circumstances in which the floating rate was abandoned in June 1962. At the height of the foreign exchange crisis, the Bank of Canada led the money market to much higher levels of interest rates by dramatically raising the bank rate from $3\frac{1}{2}\%$ to 6%.

Central Bank Advances: Summary

Central Bank advances should not be thought of as a positive instrument for monetary control. They provide a safety valve for individual banks and security dealers faced with severe but temporary cash deficiencies. Under some circumstances, however, these advances can have a perverse effect on the total supply of bank reserves in terms of the objectives of monetary policy, and to this extent they may weaken the central bank's control over the monetary base. In Canada, the perverse behavior of central bank advances has never been a problem for monetary control. In part, this is a result of the rules governing advances, and in part a result of bank rate policy. The bank rate, and the associated pra rate, have consistently been "penalty" rates, fixed slightly higher than key money market interest rates. A major controversy surrounds the use of a discretionary bank rate as a signal of central bank policy. In March 1980, the Bank of Canada abandoned the possibility of using the rate as a signal by adopting a floating bank rate, tied to the 91-day treasury bill rate. This does not mean that the Bank of Canada has abrogated responsibility for the bank rate. Through open market operations and direct participation in the treasury bill auction the Bank of Canada can effectively determine the level of treasury bill yields. The bank rate is thus set indirectly; but the direct consequences of irregular movements in the bank rate are avoided.

DISCRETIONARY CASH
RESERVE REQUIREMENTS

With the possible exception of bank rate policy, all of the techniques of monetary policy which we have discussed so far involve direct control of bank reserves and the monetary base. To a very large extent, this is what central banking is about. However, control of bank reserves is but a method of regulating the supplies of money and credit in the economy. Two other types of measures have also been used by central banks, in certain situations, to affect supplies of money and credit without affecting bank reserves. In this section we consider the possibility of varying the minimum legal cash reserve ratios of banks as an instrument of policy. This is a power which is not presently available to the Bank of Canada, but it is available to some central banks and it is an approach to monetary policy which is advocated by some economists. In the following section we will consider selective credit controls.

Reserve Ratios as a Policy Instrument.   We demonstrated in Chapter 17 that the money supply can be related to bank reserves by a "multiplier," the value of which depends, among other things, on the cash reserve ratio maintained by banks. The higher the cash reserve ratio, the smaller the multiplier, and vice versa. Under normal circumstances, banks will have little incentive to hold substantial excess cash reserves. This means that the size of the multiplier depends on the minimum cash reserve ratio required by law.

Provided that they have the authority to vary the required reserve ratio, this relationship gives the monetary authorities an additional instrument for monetary control. By lowering the required cash reserve ratio, the central bank can create excess cash reserves in every bank simultaneously, inducing monetary expansion throughout the banking system. Similarly, by raising the required cash reserve ratio, the central bank can create deficient reserves in every bank in the system, forcing monetary contraction. A variable cash reserve ratio, then, can be a powerful and pervasive instrument of policy, which is independent of central bank operations in the open market.

American Experience.   The United States is one of the few countries to make aggressive use of variable cash reserve requirements as a policy instrument. A brief review of American experience, therefore, is useful in highlighting both the potential use of the instrument and the attendant problems.

The Federal Reserve System was given the authority to vary the required cash reserve ratios of member banks within certain limits in 1935.[15] This power was used almost immediately, as the ratios were doubled in three stages in 1936 and 1937, raising them to their new legal maximums. Over the next 33 years there were about 50 changes in reserve requirements applicable to some category of member bank or some class of deposits or similar liability. Although the Board of Governors has noted that it does not consider the variable cash reserve ratio to be a normal instrument of monetary control but one to be used in exceptional circumstances, this is hardly a record of inactivity.[16]

A summary of the record of changes in cash reserve requirements is presented in Table 19-2. Three periods can be identified. The first period, from 1937 through the early

TABLE 19-2   **The variable cash reserve requirement in the United States, 1935-1971**

Ratios in effect as of:*		Demand deposits			Time and savings deposits
		Central reserve city banks	*Reserve city banks*	*Country banks*	
1917		13	10	7	3
		First period			
1935	Dec	13	10	7	3
1937	May	26	10	14	6
1938	Apr	22¾	17½	12	5
1942	Oct	20	20	14	6
1948	Sept	26	22	16	7½
1949	Sept	22	18	12	5
1951	Feb	24	20	14	6
		Second period			
1951	Dec	24	20	14	6
1960	Dec	16½	16½	12	5

Third period

Ratios in effect as of:*		Demand deposits				Time deposits			Euro-dollar liability
		Reserve city		*Country*		*Savings*	*Other Time*		
		0-5	*over 5*	*0-5*	*over 5*		*0-5*	*over 5*	
1965	Dec	16½		12		4	4		
1966	Jul	16½		12		4	4	5	
	Sept	16½		12		4	4	6	
1967	Mar	16½		12		3	3	6	
1968	Jan	16½	17	12	12½	3	3	6	
1969	Apr	17	17½	12½	13	3	3	6	
	Sept	17	17½	12½	13	3	3	6	10
1970	Oct	17	17½	12½	13	3	3	5	10
1971	Jan	17	17½	12½	13	3	3	5	20

1950s, contained several episodes of large, across-the-board changes in reserve requirements, including three occasions on which the requirements were increased by several percentage points to their legal ceilings. These occurred during bouts of intense inflationary pressure associated with war (1941 and 1951) or postwar adjustment (1948) when restrictive open market operations were impossible because of government policy to peg interest rates (see Chapter 18). The second period extended from the early 1950s through the mid-1960s, and involved a series of 10 relatively small reductions in reserve requirements, generally timed to correspond with periods of monetary ease. There were no increases in reserve requirements, even in periods of restraint.[17] In effect, the Board of Governors had forsworn the active use of variable reserve requirements as a policy instrument, and were gradually moving the system to a lower level of requirements. The Board was concerned about the loss of member banks, many of which were withdrawing from the System to take advantage of less onerous state reserve requirements.

The third period began in 1966, and is characterized by both more active and more *selective* use of variable cash reserve requirements as a policy instrument. Some of the changes have been simply an adjunct of general policies of monetary restraint. Thus, requirements against demand deposits were increased by ½% January 1968, April 1969, and July 1973, and subsequently relaxed. However, some of the changes and other specific purposes, and as a result the structure of reserve requirements has become very complex. The period was ushered in by increases in reserve requirements for large concentrations of time deposits (more than $5 million in a single bank). Subsequently special requirements were imposed on increases in borrowings in the Euro-dollar market and on large denomination certificates of deposit, and a variety of nondeposit liabilities were classified as time deposits for reserve purposes. The purpose was to discourage intense competition for funds among banks using these instruments in periods of tight money and high interest rates. When interest rates fell, the requirements were relaxed. In 1972, the whole system of reserve requirements was revised, and the requirements for banks with small deposit holdings sharply reduced in order to minimize the penalties for smaller banks remaining in the system. The result is a maze of very complicated reserve requirements (the complications of which are only partially captured in Tables 19-3 and 19-4).

Canadian Experience. The attitude of the American authorities toward variable reserve requirements has thus changed over the years. Originally, it was a tool to be used when other operations were paralyzed; when open market operations became possible in the mid-1950s, the variable reserve requirement receded to the background; but in the late 1960s, it became an active instrument for selective as well as general monetary control. The Canadian experience is dramatically different.

The Bank of Canada first gained the power to vary the required cash reserve ratios of the chartered banks, within the limits of 8% to 12%, in 1954. The maximum increase in any one month was limited to 1%, and a month's notice had to be given before any increase could be brought into effect. This power was withdrawn in the 1967 revision of the *Bank Act without ever being used.* In its place a variable secondary reserve requirement was introduced, which we will examine shortly.

Should the power to vary cash reserve requirements be restored? (It is not included in the 1980 revision to the *Bank Act.*) Should the Bank of Canada be encouraged to make vigorous use of such an instrument, in the American style?

TABLE 19-3 The variable cash reserve requirement in the United States, 1971-1980 (Fourth period)

		Demand deposits					*Time deposits*								
		0-2	*2-10*	*10-100*	*100-400*	*Over 400*	*Savings*	*30-179 days*	*180-days-4 yrs*	*4 yrs or more*	*30-179 days*	*180 days-4 yrs*	*4 yrs or more*	*Large certif. deposit*	*Euro-dollar liability*
1972	Nov	8	10	12	13	17½	3		3			5			20**
1973	Jun	8	10	12	13	17½	3		3			5		8**	8
	Jul	8	10½	12½	13½	18	3		3			5		8**	8
1974	Dec	8	10½	12½	13½	17½	3		3		6		3		8
1975	Feb	7½	10	12	13	16½	3		3		6		3		8
	May	7½	10	12	13	16½	3		3		6		3		4
	Oct	7½	10	12	13	16½	3	3		1	6	3	1		4
1976	Jan	7½	10	12	13	16½	3	3	2½	1	6	2½	1		4
	Dec	7	9½	11¼	12¼	16¼	3	3	2½	1	6	2½	1		4
1977	Dec	7	9½	11¼	12¼	16¼	3	3	2½	1	6	2½	1		1
1978	Aug	7	9½	11¼	12¼	16¼	3	3	2½	1	6	2½	1		
1979	Oct	7	9½	11¼	12¼	16¼	3	3	2½	1	6	2½	1	8**	8**

* 1917-1960: high or low point of reserve ratios. 1966-1979: dates of major changes in reserve ratios.

** Marginal reserve ratio, applicable to increases in specified liabilities above a reserve-exempt base.

A Policy Instrument?   The multiplier model of monetary expansion suggests that open market operations and reserve ratio variations are equivalent methods of achieving a given objective, i.e., a particular change in the size of the money supply. That is, a desired increase in the money supply could be obtained either by holding the reserve ratio constant and increasing bank reserves or by holding bank reserves constant and reducing the reserve ratio. The opposite would be true for a desired reduction in the money supply. For this reason, it is sometimes suggested that open market operations and cash reserve ratio variations are perfect substitutes as policy instruments, and that the central bank should be indifferent as to which it uses in any particular circumstance.

There are, however, important differences between open market operations and variable cash reserve requirements considered as policy instruments. First, open market operations are conducted continuously in the market, without public announcement. Changes in reserve requirements, by contrast, are discrete events, which involve a formal public announcement. Like changes in the discount rate, then, they involve *announcement effects*. Indeed, on occasion, increases in reserve requirements in the United States appear to have been made with the primary purpose of making it clear to all concerned that the Federal Reserve was prepared to take dramatic and drastic measures to implement anti-inflationary policies.[18] As we noted in the case of discretionary changes in the discount rate, however, many economists argue that because their impact on economic activity is unreliable, such announcement effects should not be relied upon as a major element in policy.

Second, open market operations have much greater *flexibility*. They can be conducted in large or small amounts, and both the magnitude and the direction of the operations can be changed from day to day or week to week as necessary. This makes possible relatively delicate adjustments to bank reserves and permits a gradual approach to monetary restriction or monetary ease. Mistakes can be quickly and easily corrected.

By contrast, changes in cash reserve ratios are only feasible at distinct intervals. That is, changes must be made to coincide with the start of a new averaging period, which in Canada is now 15 days. Frequent changes in the continuous use of a variable reserve ratio as an instrument of policy would only be feasible with very short reserve averaging periods. Moreover, the monetary repercussions of seemingly small across-the-board changes in the required cash reserve ratios can in fact be rather large. Thus, an increase of ½% in the required reserve ratios in 1979 would have added $535 million to the required reserves of the chartered banks, a 9.1% increase. If the Bank of Canada did not make the additional reserves available through open market operations, this would have forced a contraction of total deposits of chartered banks of almost $9 billion, or 8.4% — all in one jolt.[19] So powerful is the initial impact of such an across-the-board change in the reserve ratio that the Federal Reserve, in using the instrument in recent years, has normally given advance notice, made relatively small changes (½% and, on one occasion, ½%), and either made the change at a time of year where there would be large seasonal adjustments in bank reserves in any case, or engaged in open market operations to partially offset the effects of the change in the reserve requirements.

Of course, the central bank need not be constrained to reserve ratio changes in the traditional magnitudes of multiples of ½%. It could change the ratios by smaller fractional amounts, such as 0.1%. Indeed, with a lagged reserve ratio, under which the banks are always working to a fixed dollar amount of required reserves during the current averaging period, the central bank could specify increased reserve requirements as a small percentage of the required reserve deposit rather than as a percentage of the banks' deposit liabilities. Alternatively, as the U.S. Federal Reserve has demonstrated in recent years, a central bank does not have to limit itself to across-the-board increases in reserve requirements. It can increase the requirements on some categories of deposits and not on others; and, indeed, specify other bases for the calculation of additional required reserves (such as Euro-dollar borrowings by banks), thereby reducing the total impact of an increase in required reserves.

In other words, it is possible to make variable cash reserve requirements a more flexible instrument of monetary policy. however, two other important points should be noted: the implications of *uncertainty* about required reserve ratios and the *selective impact* of differentiated ratios.

The possibility of frequent, though small, variations in the required reserve ratios introduces an important new source of uncertainty for bankers, which cannot help affecting their management policies, and particularly induce them to hold a larger share of their assets, on the average, in liquid form. If it induces the banks to hold larger amounts of excess cash reserves, it may also make the deposit expansion multiplier less certain, depending on how predictable the banks' demands for excess reserves is.

This reaction to *uncertainty* about the required cash reserve ratio is related to but conceptually different from the direct impact of higher reserve ratios on bank portfolio management policies. This points to what is perhaps the most significant difference between open market operations and cash reserve ratio variations. While both can be used to change the size of the bank's asset portfolios, changes in the reserve ratio also impose a *constraint on the composition of the bank's asset portfolios.* An increase in the reserve ratio reduces the share of earning assets in the bank's operations. (Consider, for example, the implications of raising the cash reserve ratio to 100%.) It is not difficult to understand why commercial bankers are strongly opposed to increases in cash reserve ratios as a technique of monetary restraint (although they are generally quite happy to see cash reserve ratios reduced in periods of monetary ease). In general, variable cash reserve ratios have an unsettling effect on bank operations.

The *selective* nature of differentiated reserve requirements must also be emphasized. As long as interest is not paid on reserve deposits with central banks (or if interest is paid, but at a rate below that which the banks could earn on the assets which they would otherwise hold), cash reserve requirements act like a tax on the banks. They force the banks to hold sterile, nonearning assets. If the reserve requirements are differentiated among types of deposits (e.g., demand deposits versus time deposits; or Euro-dollar borrowings versus domestic deposits) or among sizes of deposits, they will significantly affect the *relative profitability* of different types of banking activity, or of different sizes of banks. Variation of selected reserve requirements, as opposed to across-the-board variations, will therefore have an impact not only on the money creation process (by affecting the total cash reserves which the banks must hold) but also on the structure of banking activity (by affecting the relative profitability of different activities or different types of banks). Thus, the reserve requirement policies of the Federal Reserve System since 1966 have to be considered as *selective credit controls*, not just as general controls over the money supply. We will turn to the topic of selective credit controls in the next section.

Defense of Discretionary Reserve Ratios.   The arguments presented above are critical of reliance on discretionary cash reserve ratios as an instrument of monetary policy. We conclude that the power to vary reserve requirements is not necessary; and, if available, should not be commonly used. Not all economists agree that variable cash reserve ratios are of limited use in central banking.[20] Some argue that the pervasive, dramatic, and rapid impact of reserve ratio changes is a positive attribute. All banks are affected simultaneously and immediately, in contrast to open market operations, which have their immediate impact at the financial centers and then gradually filter out to the rest of the banking system. (Given the difference in the structure of the banking systems, this argument is much less persuasive in Canada than in the United States. Why?) It is argued that bankers will soon become accustomed to reserve ratio changes, that errors of magnitude can be adjusted through appropriate open market operations, and that unfortunate effects on individual banks can be taken care of through the discount window.

Without attempting to evaluate the relative merits of the pro and con arguments, it is instructive to briefly review the circumstances under which the Federal Reserve System in fact used its power to vary cash reserve ratios.

The initial use of the variable cash reserve ratio prior to World War II was an attempt to impound the very sizable "excess reserves" which had suddenly been created in the banking system as a result of a flood of gold into the country from war-threatened Europe. The Federal Reserve System was concerned about the inflationary potential in the credit expansion which these excess reserves seemed to portend. The Federal Reserve action has been roundly criticized as overly drastic, and as responsible for the subsequent recession.

The actions taken in 1948 and 1951 were again attempts to impound what the Federal Reserve System regarded as excessive liquidity in the banking system under inflationary conditions. In this case, the liquidity took the form of large holdings of government bonds, the prices of which were virtually pegged by government policy. The pegging of bond prices immobilized the Federal Reserve System's primary instrument of policy, open market operations.

The across-the-board increases in 1968, 1969, and 1973 were somewhat different. They were relatively moderate in size, and aimed primarily at the larger banks. They had a psychological purpose. Concerned that widespread expectations of inflation were weakening the impact of higher interest rates, the increases in reserve ratios were intended as dramatic evidence of "the system's determination to resist inflationary pressures."[21] In other words, the Federal Reserve System was deliberately capitalizing on the so-called announcement effects.

In summary, the Federal Reserve System has used what it regards as a drastic, blunt tool, across-the-board increases in cash reserve requirements, primarily to impound large blocks of liquid assets in the banking system, and secondarily to have strong announcement effects. The Federal Reserve's use of more complex variations in cash reserve requirements as a selective credit control raises another range of issues.

SELECTIVE CREDIT CONTROLS

Another option for the implementation of monetary policy which is sometimes open to central banks is the direct or indirect regulation of the lending and borrowing activities of banks and other financial institutions. The regulations may have their roots in legislation which compels compliance and imposes formal legal penalties in proven cases of noncompliance, and they may be administered by an agency other than the central bank. Alternatively, the "controls" may be based on the moral authority of the central bank to command voluntary compliance. The latter type of "control" is looser, more flexible and, in some cases, of uncertain effectiveness. It is commonly called "moral suasion."

Selective controls restrain or encourage particular types of financial activities. The objectives of the controls may vary. At times, controls have been used in the attempt to restrain aggregate expenditures on goods and services, as a substitute for, or a supplement to, control of the money supply an anti-inflationary program. It is assumed that by restricting the availability of certain key types of credit, perhaps consumer credit or general bank loans, aggregate expenditures will also be restricted. In recent years, however, selective controls have been used more commonly to influence the allocation of credit, and hence the allocation of real resources in the economy, to uses which the authorities deem to be socially beneficial. Attempts may be made to influence the allocation of credit directly, or indirectly by affecting the profitability of different types of lending or the interest rate which may be charged.

Direct Controls

Some examples may help clarify the nature and scope of direct controls. *Consumer credit* has been a favorite target for such controls. For example, during the Korean War, the government imposed high downpayments and short repayment periods on installment credit extended to consumers by financial institutions, and on residential mortgage credit. The use of *foreign exchange* has also been a common target of controls, and in many countries over the past 50 years there have been long periods when there was no legal free foreign exchange market. In Canada, foreign exchange control was imposed as a wartime measure in 1939, and not completely abandoned until 1951. When the Canadian controls were in full effect, all foreign exchange had to be sold to the Foreign Exchange Control Board, and could only be purchased with a permit from the Board, which would only be issued if the use of the foreign exchange conformed to national priorities.

These are examples of formal direct controls over the allocation of funds. Much different in nature, but nonetheless selective in impact, are the variable *differential cash reserve requirements* imposed by the Federal Reserve System, as discussed in the previous section. From time to time, the Federal Reserve has used differential reserve requirements to discourage interbank competition for large corporate cash balances, to discourage borrowing in the Euro-dollar market, to encourage borrowing in the Euro-dollar market, to improve the competitive position of U.S. banks abroad, to improve the competitive position of small banks, and to improve the competitive position of member banks relative to non-member banks. Although Canada has not had discretionary cash reserve requirements since 1967, the 1967 revision of the *Bank Act* introduced differential requirements between time and demand deposits, with the effect of improving the competitive position of chartered banks relative to near banks. The 1980 revisions carry the process a step further, differentiating cash reserve requirements according to the size of deposit holdings. The apparent purpose is to foster competition by giving a slight competitive advantage to smaller institutions.

Secondary Reserve Requirements.   These should also be considered a form of direct selective credit control. In Canada, a secondary reserve requirement was introduced informally in 1955, and legislated in 1967. Under the 1967 law, the Bank of Canada could specify a ratio between 6% and 12% of Canadian dollar deposits which the banks would have to hold in cash, treasury bills, or day loans *in addition* to their required cash reserves. One of the effects of this requirement is to impound liquid assets in the banking system: to prevent the banks from selling off liquid assets to make loans. In this sense, like cash reserve requirements, secondary reserve requirements are a constraint on portfolio choice. However, in one important sense they are much less drastic than cash reserve requirements. While the secondary reserve ratio may force banks to hold a larger share of the eligible securities (directly or indirectly these are government bonds) than they would voluntarily choose to do, at least, unlike cash, these are interest-bearing assets. The income penalty is not as great as in the case of an increase in the required cash ratio.

It should be noted that an increase in the secondary reserve ratio would normally have no implications for the money supply unless the eligible securities are in very limited supply. For this reason, those who argue that the only proper concern of the central bank is the size of the money supply also argue that secondary reserve requirements have no value as a tool of monetary policy. They are merely a device for creating a market for government bonds. Those who argue that the supply of bank credit is an important variable in its own right feel that a variable secondary reserve ratio may be a valuable instrument of policy if it can be used flexibly. It can be used to regulate the volume of bank loans extended with any given level of the money supply.

It was on this theory of central banking, commonly called the "credit conditions" approach, that the Bank of Canada, from time to time, changed the secondary reserve requirement. Thus, in early 1969, the Bank increased the required ratio from 7% to 8%, and, effective July 1, 1970, raised it again to 9%, as a measure of credit restraint. Subsequently, the requirement was lowered in small jumps until, in February 1977, it was set at 5%. When monetary policy shifted from the management of credit conditions to the management of the money supply in 1976, variations in the secondary reserve requirement became essentially irrelevant as an instrument of monetary policy. however, provision for a variable requirement remains in the 1980 revisions to the *Bank Act*; and as long as it remains in effect, the requirement has its essential selective credit control property. It provides a captive market for government securities, which directly (held by the banks) or indirectly (held by security dealers and financed by the banks through day loans) satisfy the requirement.

These examples of formal direct controls, backed by legislation. More common, certainly in Canada, is the informal type of control which we call "moral suasion." It involves the use by the central bank of its "moral authority" to command "voluntary" compliance — although there may be subtle threats in the background.

Moral Suasion

Examples of moral suasion are abundant in Canadian central banking history. Indeed, in times such as the late 1950s, moral suasion appeared to be the primary operating technique of the Bank of Canada. Three periods can be identified in the history of moral suasion in Canada.

Period 1: Monetary Controls Paralyzed. The early history of moral suasion in Canada coincided with the official policy of pegging interest rates on government bonds, which effectively immobilized normal controls over the quantity of money during a period of powerful inflationary pressures. This was the same coincidence of events which led the Federal Reserve to raise cash reserve requirements in order to immobilize bank liquidity. The Bank of Canada did not have this power, but resorted instead to moral suasion. In 1947 and 1948, years of heavy capital expenditures and rapid inflation, the Bank of Canada "suggested" that banks refrain from extending bank credit to finance capital expenditures.[22] The "suggestion" was withdrawn in 1949. Again in February 1951, during the Korean War inflation, the Bank of Canada supplemented the government's direct controls over consumer and mortgage credit with a "suggestion" to the banks that total bank credit for all purposes would not increase, and that particularly severe restrictions should be placed on term loans to finance capital expenditures, loans to finance stock market speculation, and installment credit.[23] These "suggestions," including the ceiling on total bank loans, were effective. In spite of boom conditions in the economy with associated strong demands for bank credit, and the absence of vigorous policies to control bank reserves no increase in bank loans occurred for a full year, the duration of the "suggestion."

Period 2: Credit Conditions and Moral Suasion. The second period, which began in the mid-1950s, involved intensive use of moral suasion at a time when the immediate postwar shackles on quantitative monetary controls had been removed, and restrictive monetary policies could be pursued vigorously. Moral suasion was used to supplement quantitative measures, not to substitute for them. The dominant theory of monetary policy, which was gradually articulated during this period, held that monetary policy influenced the economy by affecting "credit conditions," and cost, and availability of credit in fragmented and imperfect financial markets. The money supply was not considered a relevant variable in its own right, only in its effect on credit conditions. The impact of general monetary restraint on the economy would only be felt with a long, and possibly variable, time lag, and the effects would not be distributed equally across all sectors of the economy or all regions of the country, with possibly unfortunate social consequences. In this context, moral suasion was considered to be a basic instrument of policy, particularly in periods of monetary restraint. The role of moral suasion was to reinforce and perhaps speed up the impact of general monetary restraints; to direct credit restraint to particular "key" areas, such as capital expenditures, consumer credit, or the balance of payments; to restrict adjustments in the financial system which might mitigate the effects of general monetary restraint; and, when credit restraints were most severe, to modify the sectoral or regional impact of the restraints.

Without attempting a complete history of moral suasion in this period, perhaps we can give some examples that will illustrate the scope and importance of such measures.

The first major episode began in the autumn of 1955. At first the Governor of the

Bank of Canada urged banks to anticipate the forthcoming monetary restrictions by restricting lines of credit to businesses, presumably to shorten the time lag in the restraints taking effect.[24] This was followed by agreed ceilings on term loans to businesses, particularly loans to finance capital expenditures, and attempts to control consumer credit.[25] The Governor held discussions with finance companies and major department stores with a view to restricting installment credit, but "It turned out that agreement of all concerned could not be reached."[26] However, a suggestion to the banks apparently was effective, so that the Governor could report in early 1957 that "the banks have not increased in 1956 their lines of credit to finance companies and retail stores providing installment finance facilities."[27] What could not be achieved directly was attempted indirectly, with some success.[28]

The most enduring "suggestion" during this episode was the 1955 proposal that the chartered banks maintain a 7% secondary reserve ratio in addition to their 8% cash reserve ratio. As we have seen, this became a permanent feature of chartered banking operations and was finally written into the law in 1967. It provided a guaranteed market for government bonds and helped stimulate the development of the money market, but the official rationalization of the policy was as a measure to restrict banks from selling government bonds to obtain resources to extend more loans to business.[29]

In the next episode of intense monetary restraint, 1968-1970, the Bank again resorted to moral suasion. In this case, primary attention was devoted to interbank competition for large blocks of corporate funds. In order to restrict the rise in short-term interest rates, and presumably to limit the rise in the velocity of circulation of money, the banks agreed to a ceiling on interest rates paid on short-term certificates of deposit and a ceiling on the quantity of "swapped" deposits (foreign currency deposits with a forward contract for conversion back to Canadian dollars). The Governor also attempted to modify the distributional consequences of tight money, urging the banks to "soften the impact...on less prosperous areas of the country," "to maintain reasonable continuity of lending on housing mortgages," "to pay particular attention to loan applications from small businesses," and "to give priority...to the credit-worthy demands of their Canadian customers.[30]

The third episode of tight money in this period was in 1972-74, and again the Bank invoked moral suasion to restrain interbank competition for funds and to modify the distributional impact of tight money. Under the "Winnipeg Agreement" of June 1972, the banks agreed to a ceiling on the interest rate paid on large, short-term deposits; and the banks were repeatedly urged to "minimize the impact on small business...less buoyant regions...and mortgage lending."[31]

Period 3: Monetarism and Market Allocation.   In 1975-76 there was a dramatic transformation of the Bank of Canada's theory and practice of monetary policy, from "credit conditions" to "monetarism." Instead of the regulation of credit flows in imperfect financial markets, the Bank focused on the growth of the money supply, which was to be contained within predetermined limits. Subsequently, there have been no reported instances of the use of moral suasion. Of course, because they are not reported does not necessarily mean that they do not occur. Indeed, in a financial system as concentrated as Canada's, with regular meetings between officials of the Bank of Canada, bankers, and security dealers, some moral suasion may be inevitable.

Why Moral Suasion?   In this review of the history of moral suasion in Canada, we have interpreted the use of moral suasion in terms of the dominant theory of monetary policy. The credit conditions theory, with its emphasis on flows of credit, through markets which are fragmented and imperfect, was consistent with an emphasis on moral suasion to directly regulate the flow of credit to key sectors of the economy. Monetarism, coupled with the view that financial markets are less segmented than casual inspection might suggest, sees no role for moral suasion or other types of direct controls. Money is fungible. It cannot be contained in rigid compartments. Constraints on borrowing in one form will simply produce adaptations in the system to provide the funds in another way. The only feasible control is over the aggregate supply of money. This suggests that the changing role of moral suasion reflects changes in the theory guiding monetary policy.

There is another important interpretation of the reasons for the Bank of Canada's heavy reliance on moral suasion.[32] It has been argued that the choice of policy instruments by the Bank must be analyzed in the context of the theory of bureaucracy. Unconstrained by market disciplines, and not guided by profit motives, a "bureau" will strive for self-preservation and prestige. In this search, it will try to operate by covert means, which are not easily identified and hence not easily criticized, rather than overt means, which are easily identified and which may leave explicit records of mistakes. Moral suasion is a covert technique of intervention; open market operations an overt technique. When the institutional setting, and particularly a high degree of concentration in the banking system, make moral suasion efficient, this theory predicts that the central bank will rely heavily on this technique. Presumably, the theory of bureaus implies that monetarism will only temporarily suppress the Bank of Canada's natural preference for moral suasion.

Effectiveness of Moral Suasion.   In general, moral suasion is designed to override the profit motive. It is used to restrain financial institutions from activities which they would normally undertake, or to induce them to undertake activities which they would not do voluntarily. If the discrepancy between the dictates of the profit motive and the dictates of central bank "suggestions" is great, there is a strong incentive to evasion — an incentive which is accentuated if some firms suspect that others are evading or will evade the regulations. The central bank has the best chance of success if the financial institutions are vulnerable to central bank sanctions, if evasions can be detected easily, and if the financial institutions constitute a relatively small, closely knit and hence self-policing group. It should not be surprising that the Bank of Canada obtained agreement from the chartered banks for all but the most drastic suggestions for reorganizing their business (e.g. the separation of commercial and savings business) but could not obtain full cooperation from department stores and finance companies. The latter firms were not directly dependent on the central bank (although they proved to be indirectly vulnerable), and therefore were not obliged to provide a continuous flow of detailed statistical information on their operations. Furthermore, they were not as highly concentrated and centrally organized as the chartered banks.

It should also be noted that even though direct controls are successful in achieving their proximate objective, such as the control of term loans by chartered banks, they will not necessarily be effective in achieving their ultimate objective, the elimination of inflationary pressures on the economy. Selective controls attack the symptoms of the economic ailment, not the causes. If the problem is an excessive supply of money and credit, the suppression of its expression in certain forms (e.g., particular types of credit, or credit extended by particular types of firms) will result in its expression in other forms. Borrowers will seek out alternative sources of credit: lenders will find loopholes and disguised forms for extending the prescribed type of credit; pressures for the evasion of the regulations will build up, and "black markets" (and perhaps corruption) will be encouraged. There is evidence that selective controls can have the desired macroeconomic effects in the short run. In the face of sustained use, the market system is highly inventive, and the success of the controls is far less certain.

The Morality of Moral Suasion.   Finally, we should question the morality of moral suasion in a democracy. Carried to the length it has been in Canada, moral suasion involves the appropriation by the central bank of powers which many citizens would argue properly belong with Parliament. The imposition of a secondary reserve ratio in 1955 is a case in point — a case which actually provoked a bitter exchange between the Governor of the Bank and the Minister of Finance. A 1957 suggestion to the banks, which was rejected, that they formally separate their commercial banking business from their savings banking business, something not required by the *Bank Act*, is another extreme example. But do not all of the other examples only differ from these by a matter of degree?

Selective Controls and the Allocation of Credit

Perhaps the most serious aspect of moral suasion and other forms of selective controls is that, if they are subject to comprehensive, sustained, and effective use, they introduce a new dimension to central banking. The central bank is no longer simply an arbiter of macroeconomic balance in the economy; it becomes an important arbiter of the allocation of credit and hence of resources. The collective judgement of "the market" as reflected in the interaction of supply and demand and the behavior of prices and profits is overruled by a centralized judgement as to the "national interest." If the competitive market is the most reliable mechanism for achieving an efficient allocation of resources in the economy, effective and sustained moral suasion is likely to produce serious distortions in resource allocation (unless it somehow compensates for distortions resulting from a lack of effective competition). It is not surprising that vigorous advocates of the freely competitive market system denounce selective controls as harmful to the economy — and, indeed, argue that they do the least damage when they are evaded!

THE PROCESS OF
MONETARY CONTROL _____

This has been a long chapter, but, taken together with Chapters 17 and 18, it suggests a few important conclusions which should be highlighted.

What Can the Central Bank Control?   We have seen that the Bank of Canada has a variety of methods for controlling the monetary base, or, alternatively, bank reserves.

Unless there is an overriding policy of pegging interest rates or the foreign exchange rate, there is no reason to suspect the Bank's ability to control these magnitudes. The only potential weak link in the chain of control, the discount window, is effectively controlled by restrictive regulations and bank rate policy.

However, does control over bank reserves necessarily imply control over the money supply? There remains an issue of definition, which we have not addressed yet. Which money supply? M1, M2, M3, or some other concept? If we leave that big question aside, the Bank's ability to control the money supply by controlling bank reserves depends on the stability of the multiplier. Research suggests that, with the lagged reserve requirement, multipliers are not stable in the short run, but have a high variance. In the long run, they are reasonably stable. Is there, then, some slippage in the Bank's ability to control the money supply in the short run?

We should remember that the Bank of Canada knows the size of the money supply weekly, with a one-week delay. If the movement of the money supply is off target, the analysis of Chapter 17 suggests that the Bank can induce expansion, or contraction simply by providing a small amount of excess cash reserves (+ or −). When the desired adjustment occurs, it can withdraw the excess and stop the process. In other words, the Bank is in a position to directly control the money supply, and then provide bank reserves consistent with that money supply. More serious than controlling the money supply is deciding upon what is an appropriate money supply, given all of the seasonal and special factors bearing on the situation.

There can be little question of the Bank of Canada's ability to exert careful control over the money supply. In the process, it will also have a powerful effect on the flow of credit in the economy, and, at least in the short run, on the level of interest rates. We still have to ask: What should the Bank of Canada control, and, with what objectives in mind? These are much more serious questions, which we cannot begin to answer until we have explored the theory of monetary policy.

ENDNOTES

1. "Cash Reserve Management," *Bank of Canada Review* (June, 1975), pp. 3-12.
2. F. Faure, "Technical Note on Temporary Bank of Canada-Exchange Fund Swaps," *Bank of Canada Review* (July, 1977), pp. 15-20.
3. Important among the changes were a broadening of the lending authority of the Federal Reserve Banks (by eliminating the restrictive link to "eligible" commercial paper); the formalization of the institution of the open market committee; and the introduction of variable cash reserve requirements. A brief history of discount window policy in the United States is contained in Bernard Shull, *Reappraisal of the Federal Reserve Discount Mechanism: Report on Research Undertaken in Connection with a System Study* (Washington D.C.: Board of Governors of the Federal Reserve System, 1968).
4. Perhaps the best known study is A. J. Meigs, *Free Reserves and the Money Supply* (Chicago: University of Chicago Press, 1962). Other studies are briefly reviewed in D. M. Jones. *A Review of Recent Academic Literature on the Discount Mechanism* (Washington: Board of Governors of the Federal Reserve System, 1968), pp. 13-17.
5. Proponents of this view argue that the purpose of monetary policy is to affect the cost and availability of credit, and particularly the availability of loans from commercial banks. The

willingness of banks to extend new credit can be gauged by the level of "free reserves" in the banking system. This is a new concept for us, which strictly has relevance only in the American banking system but which has sometimes been used in discussion Canadian banking developments as well. A formal definition is:

$$\frac{\text{FREE}}{\text{RESERVES}} = \frac{\text{EXCESS}}{\text{RESERVES}} - \frac{\text{BORROWED}}{\text{RESERVES}}$$

Excess reserves are cash over and above those required by law, and borrowed reserves are outstanding advances from the Federal Reserve System.

Thus excess reserves of American commercial banks tend to be relatively stable. Thus, major changes in free reserves result from changes in the level of indebtedness to the Federal Reserve System. When banks have large free reserves, they have excess cash and they are not heavily in debt to the Federal Reserve System. Because they are not worried about a shortage of cash, nor under pressure to repay outstanding advances, they are willing to extend more credit. By contrast, it is argued, when free reserves are small, and particularly when they are negative (i.e., borrowings exceed cash reserves) the banks are under substantial pressure. They have pared down their cash somewhat, and are heavily in debt. They must give top priority to repaying Federal Reserve advances and rebuilding their cash positions, and hence are reluctant to extend more credit.

6. Bank of Canada, *Annual Report, 1943*, p. 4.
7. Bank of Canada, *Annual Report, 1956*, p. 13. On one recent occasion, when the Bank of Canada was called upon to provide extended credit to a bank with serious liquidity problems, the Governor took pains to record the fact in his annual report. The bank subsequently merged into another bank. See, Bank of Canada, *Annual Report, 1977*, p. 23.
8. Bank of Canada, *Submissions to the Royal Commission on Banking and Finance* (Ottawa: 1964), p. 40.
9. Bank of Canada, *Annual Report, 1956*, p. 13.
10. For a study of member bank borrowing in one Federal Reserve District, see R.A. Gilbert, "Access to the Discount Window for All Commercial Banks: Is it Important for Monetary Policy?" Federal Reserve Bank of St. Louis, *Review*, 62 (February, 1980), pp. 15-24; "Benefits of Borrowing from the Federal Reserve When the Discount Rate is Below Market Interest Rates," Federal Reserve Bank of St. Louis, *Review*, 61 (March, 1979), pp. 25-32.
11. Bank of Canada, *Evidence of the Governor Before the Royal Commission on Banking and Finance* (Ottawa, 1964), p. 55.
12. Bank of Canada, "Press Release: 10 March 1980," *Bank of Canada Review*, (March, 1980), pp. 29-30.
13. Initially there was only a ceiling. On June 24, 1962 the purchase and resale agreement rate was set at 1/4% above the 91-day treasury bill rate, subject to a maximum of the bank rate. On November 12, 1970 a floor of bank rate less 3/4% was established, and on May 12, 1974 the ceiling was raised to bank rate plus 1/2%.
14. Bank of Canada, *Annual Report*, 1956, p. 46.
15. A provision for increases in reserve ratios in a "national emergency" was introduced in 1933, but the Federal Reserve was not granted the authority to vary the ratios at its own discretion until 1935. At present the limits within which the ratios can be varied are:

Demand Deposits	
at country banks	7%-14%
at reserve city banks	10%-22%
Time and Savings Deposits	
at all member banks	3%-10%

Originally, the classification of banks into "reserve city" and "country" categories reflected the nature of the banking business in the city in question. Since November, 1972, however, it simply reflects the size of the bank. A reserve city bank is one with net demand deposits of more than $400 million; all others are country banks.

16. The Board has provided a clear statement of their concept of the use of variable reserve requirements in Board of Governors of the Federal Reserve System, *The Federal Reserve System: Purposes and Functions* (Washington: 1963), pp. 52-55.

17. An apparent increase in requirements for country banks in 1960 was, in fact, designed to absorb cash reserves released by a change in the method of computing the required reserves.

18. In the United States, notes on the deliberations of the Open Market Committee are released 30 days after each meeting, and are published periodically in the *Federal Reserve Bulletin*. However, at the time of operations there is no public statement. Statements of the reasons for changes in reserve requirements are issued immediately, and published in the Federal Reserve Bulletin. The psychological reasons for increasing reserve ratios in 1968, 1969, and 1973 are apparent in the Annual Report of the Board of Governors of the Federal Reserve System, 1967, pp. 81-82; 1968, pp. 95-97; 1969, pp. 74-76; 1973, pp. 47-49.

19. The deposit contraction of $9 billion was estimated using the average reserve ratio (demand and time deposits) for 1979. From the multiplier analysis of Chapter 17, it should be obvious that we cannot know the precise implications of a given increase in the reserve ratios without knowing the impact of the ensuing monetary contraction on the division of deposits between time deposits and demand deposits, and on the amount of currency in circulation.

20. D. S. Ahearn, *Federal Reserve Policy Reappraised, 1951-1959.* (New York: Columbia University Press, 1963), pp. 145-63.

21. "Record of Policy Actions of the Federal Open Market Committee: Meeting held on April 1st, 1968," *Federal Reserve Bulletin*, Vol. 55 (July, 1969), p. 601.

22. Bank of Canada, *Annual Report*, 1948, p. 7.

23. Bank of Canada, *Annual Report*, 1951, p. 9. It is noted in the *Report* that the Governor "found the banks in agreement with the suggestion that further expansion of total bank credit was undesirable under existing conditions."

24. Bank of Canada, *Annual Report*, 1955, pp. 10-11.

25. Bank of Canada, *Annual Report*, 1956, pp. 32-36.

26. Bank of Canada, *Annual Report*, 1956, p. 34. A similar suggestion to the stock markets that credit for stock market trading should be restricted appears to have met with easier agreement, perhaps reflecting the quasi-regulatory authority of the stock markets in this industry.

27. *Ibid.*, p. 35.

28. Many finance companies have external sources of finance but bank credit remains an essential part of their operations, particularly for the smaller companies. The impact of the credit squeeze was severe, as is testified to by the fact that the iniquity of the 1956 "suggestion" to the banks was a major theme in the finance companies' brief to the Royal Commission on Banking and Finance.

29. Bank of Canada, *Annual Report*, 1955, p. 16.

30. Bank of Canada, *Annual Report*, 1969, pp. 12-13.

31. Bank of Canada, *Annual Report*, 1972, pp. 15-17; 1973, pp. 5-6; 1974, p. 25.

32. Chant, J.F. and K. Acheson, "The Choice of Monetary Instruments and the Theory of Bureaucracy," *Public Choice* (Fall, 1971), pp. 13-33.

THE DEMAND FOR MONEY **20**

In the previous three chapters we explored the mechanism by which the supply of money is controlled in Canada, and particularly the possibilities open to the Bank of Canada to implement monetary policy. We now begin to consider the consequences of managing the money supply.

With money, as with other goods, the analysis of the effects of varying supply must begin with an analysis of demand. To some extent such analysis must be theoretical — what factors do we expect to influence the quantity of money demanded, and why? — but for a full understanding of monetary policy, we must also be concerned with empirical evidence. How important are the various determinants of demand suggested by theory? How stable is the demand function in fact? In the final section of the chapter we review some empirical evidence for Canada.

We explored some aspects of the demand for money in our analysis of the microeconomics of the financial system. Thus, in Chapter 2, we considered the basic characteristics of money and its role in facilitating the flow of transactions in a complex exchange economy, and in Chapter 5 we considered the attributes of money as an asset which an individual might want to include in his portfolio of assets. In this chapter we want to expand some aspects of the earlier analysis, and building on these microeconomic foundations identify the determinants of the *aggregate demand for money* in the economy as a whole. As in previous discussions, it turns out that the definition of money is a substantive issue; both the theory of the demand for money and the empirical results depend on the definition of money adopted. Accordingly, we begin by considering theories applicable to a narrow definition of money as a medium of exchange, and then consider modifications appropriate to a broader definition.

THE TRANSACTIONS DEMAND: CLASSICAL THEORY

Money, narrowly defined, is an asset which is designed to be used as a medium of payment. Under normal conditions, it is the only generally accepted means by which purchasing power is transferred from one spending unit to another in exchange for goods, services, or securities, and the basic demand for money derives from this fact. The *transactions demand for money is a demand for money to be held to bridge a gap in time between successive receipts of income, permitting a flow of expenditures which is independent of the time pattern of the flow of income.*

Stocks and Flows Again

Throughout this discussion of the demand for money, keep in mind the distinction between *stocks* and *flows*. Money is a *stock* variable; a quantity which appears on a balance as an asset (to the holder) or a liability (to the issuer). The stock of money is measured at a point in time, but can be held over a period of time. Expenditure, like income, is a *flow* variable, something which happens over a period of time. Thus, the two variables are in different time dimensions.

The two variables, the stock of money and the flow of expenditure, can be related to each other in two different ways. The flow of expenditure can be regarded as the rate of flow over an infinitesimally short period at the point in time at which the stock of money is measured. Alternatively, the stock of money can be regarded as the average stock held at successive instants during the time period over which the flow of expenditures is measured. Most formal economic theory involves the first interpretation. However, because all data on flows of income and expenditure refer to finite periods of time — usually a month, a quarter, or a year — most empirical research involves the latter interpretation.

The concept of the stock of money as a bridge in time between successive receipts of income can best be illustrated with reference to the income-expenditure cycle of a typical household.

The Household's Demand for Transactions Balances

Consider a household which receives a regular monthly salary income of $1200, all of which is spent on goods and services during the month. For simplicity, assume that all of the salary is paid into a chequing account at a bank on the first day of each month and is spent in 30 equal daily installments of $40 during the month. The behavior of the household's bank balance is described by the step-wise line in Figure 20-1. On the first day of the month it will jump to $1200 (the heavy vertical line); by the last day it will be zero. It is easy to demonstrate that the *average daily cash balance* during the month will be $600. Early in the month it will be greater; late in the month it will be less. However, if we define the household's transactions demand for money as the average daily cash balance held in anticipation of expenditures to be made before the next regular receipt of income, then it is $600 — half the household's monthly income, or one-twenty-fourth of its annual income.

FIGURE 20-1   The income-payments cycle of a household:
Daily cash balances assuming a monthly income of $1200 and daily
expenditures of $40

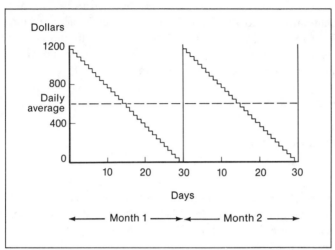

Days

← Month 1 → ← Month 2 →

If we can further assume that with a change in its income the household will not
alter the *pattern* of its expenditure within the month but will change the amount of its
daily expenditure proportionately then we can represent its transactions demand for
money function by the equation:[1]

$$m_t = .0417 \, y, \tag{20.1}$$

where m_t is the household's average daily cash balance demanded for transactions
purposes and y the household's *annual* income, which, by assumption, is also the
household's total annual expenditure on goods and services.

Generalizing the Example.   The example is artificial, but it sets in clear relief the basic
idea that money is held as a time-bridge between regular receipts of income, on the
assumption that income and expected payments have different time patterns. We could
make the example much more complicated. As a mental exercise, consider the impact
on the household's transactions demand for money if:

— in addition to the regular daily expenditures, there is one large payment on the
first day of the month equal, say, to half the monthly income (rent or the
mortgage payment).
— all expenditures are made on Saturday.
— all purchases are made using a charge account, which is paid off regularly on the
first day of each month.

We could also develop examples, applying the same concept to business firms
rather than households, although, in this case, the time patterns of receipts and
payments are likely to be reversed (a steady flow of receipts, with less regular large
payments). This is particularly true of retail firms whose receipts are the expenditures of

the households. To further approach reality, we should also allow for the effects of uncertainty on the demand for transactions balances, particularly the uncertainty of the flow of expenditures for households and the flow of receipts for business firms. However, the development of more complicated models of the income-expenditure cycle of households and firms serves no particular purpose in our analysis. Our concern is the aggregate demand for money in the economy.

Aggregate Demand for Transactions Balances.   The aggregate demand for transactions balances is the sum of individual demands by households and firms. What does our microeconomic example tell us about the aggregate demand function?

First, it tells us that the demand for transactions balances should depend directly on the aggregate flow of transactions in the economy. As the total flow of transactions increases (with economic growth, or a rise in the price level), the quantity of money demanded for transactions purposes should also increase.

Second the demand for transactions balances should depend on the patterns of payments in the economy, including such institutional arrangements as the frequency with which payrolls are met, the degree to which payments are made by cheque and the efficiency of the postal service as it affects the speed with which cheques are cleared and collected, the degree to which credit cards are used as a substitute for money in making purchases, etc. In the short run, it can be assumed that these institutional patterns are given, establishing a direct relationship between the flow of transactions and the demand for transactions balances. However, the institutional arrangements are not arbitrary. In the long run, they change, reflecting in part technological changes (e.g., electronic funds transfer systems), and in part economic choices made by households and firms in the face of changing relative costs of alternative methods of effecting transactions.

Beyond these two points, little can be said about the aggregate demand for transactions balances on the basis of the simple income-expenditure cycle model. In particular, we cannot deduce the form or shape of the demand function. Is the aggregate demand for transactions balances a linear function of the flow of transactions, or a nonlinear function? That depends not only on the shapes of the individual demand functions (which we do not know), but also on the distribution of transactions among spending units with differing income-expenditure cycles and patterns (which we also do not know).[2] In the face of total ignorance a simple assumption is probably the best assumption; it is commonly assumed that the relationship is linear, at least in the short run. That is,

$$M_t = t'PT \qquad \text{(20.2)}$$

where M_t is the aggregate demand for transactions balances, on a daily average over some time period, PT is the aggregate value of transactions in the economy during the same time period, and t' is a constant. Much pre-Keynesian monetary theory, perhaps best represented by the works of the great American economist Irving Fisher, was built around this assumption. We can call this the *classical theory of the demand for transactions balances.*

Income and the Transactions Demand.   The classical theory relates the transactions demand for money to the aggregate flow of *transactions* during a given period of time.

However, in most modern formulations, the transactions demand for money is related to the level of *income* rather than the flow of transactions. Although the latter will normally be several times the former (remember all of the double counting which has to be eliminated in deriving an estimate of national income from the flow of total expenditures), it is generally thought that this substitution is acceptable (to be perfect substitutes the relation between the two would have to be constant over time and we cannot be certain of that). Most transactions occur in connection with the generation of income, i.e., in the process of producing and distributing goods and services. Hence, the level of income should be highly correlated with the aggregate value of transactions. Either variable can be used as an index of the impact of the level of economic activity on the demand for money.

Moreover, the use of an income variable in the demand for money has a major advantage. A demand-for-money equation is seldom desired for its own sake. Whether in theoretical or empirical analysis, it is normally wanted as one equation in a macro-economic model (a mathematical description of the economy in terms of the interaction among highly aggregative variables). Such a model may be relatively simple, involving only a few equations, or may be very detailed, involving a hundred or more equations. In either case, it is helpful to express the demand for money in terms of variables which are explained in the model. Income is normally such a variable; the aggregate value of transactions is not.

With this substitution in mind, we can then rewrite our aggregate transactions demand for money function as follows:

$$M_t = tY, \tag{20.3}$$

where Y is a measure of aggregate income (perhaps gross national product).

Three Implications of the Classical Model

The classical model should be regarded as a long-run model of the demand for money, i.e., a statement which applies when equilibrium has been achieved. The major classical exponent of the model, Irving Fisher, made this perfectly clear, describing at length departures from the equilibrium demand for money in the face of disturbances. Considered in this light, there are three important implications of the classical model.

(1) The equation will not hold continuously. In the face of a disturbance to equilibrium, the demand for money will adjust to the new equilibrium with a *time lag*.

(2) *Y can be disaggregated into the price level (P) and real income (Y_r).* In equilibrium, the real income elasticity of the demand for money = 1. That is, an increase in real income will increase the quantity of money demanded proportionately

(3) In equilibrium, the price level elasticity of the demand for money is also 1.

With implications (2) and (3) in mind, the classical demand for money equation (19.3) is often written in the form:

$$\frac{M}{P} = t\ Y_r, \tag{20.4}$$

where M/P is what we will call later *real* money balances demanded, and Y_r is *real* income ($= Y/P$). We will discuss the significance of the price level for the demand for money later.

THE TRANSACTIONS DEMAND: INVENTORY CONTROL

The classical theory of the demand for transactions balances is plausible at first glance, but considered carefully, it is far from convincing as a theory of the transactions demand for *money*.

The Demand for Transactions Balances or the Demand for Money?

The classical theory demonstrates that a household or a firm with patterns of income and expenditure which are not coincident in time will have a demand for transactions balances in some form. This is not the same thing as a demand for money because *money is not the only form in which transactions balances can be held*. Indeed, if money yields no interest, or a relatively low rate of interest, it may not be the most desirable form in which to hold transactions balances. Why should the household of our example hold money which it knows will not be spent until the end of the month, when it can invest the idle money in short-term, highly liquid assets, which yield interest income, and which can be sold at the very moment that expenditures are to be made to obtain the money required for the expenditures. Indeed, why hold any cash at all? At the beginning of the month the household can invest $1160 (the monthly salary less the first day's expenditures) in a *series* of short-term $40 loans or securities, one to mature on each day of the month. These securities will provide cash as needed to meet anticipated expenditures, while putting the transactions balances of the household to work earning interest income. In this extreme case, the household's demand for *money* balances on a daily average basis during the month would approximate zero!

This possibility is not allowed for in the simple classical formulation.

Transfer Costs and the Transactions Demand for Money

If we lived in a "frictionless" world in which there were no costs involved in buying and selling financial instruments, the rational policy would indeed be to hold no money among transactions balances. As long as there were a positive rate of interest, people would hold money for only an instant before they made an expenditure, and the average cash balance of every spending unit would approach zero.

Thus, the *crucial assumption implicit in the classical theory of the transactions demand for money is that transfer costs are so high that such transfers between money and non-money liquid assets are impracticable. It implies a world of extreme frictions.* Although it is true that the real world is not frictionless, the implicit classical assumption of complete immobility between money and other assets is clearly not valid either.

Transfer Costs   The costs involved in transfers among asset forms were discussed in

Chapter 9. These costs proved to be important in explaining financial intermediation. They are also essential in explaining the transactions demand for money.

Some transfer costs are quite *explicit*, such as the fees and commissions of brokers, dealers, and investment advisers. Some, however, are *implicit*, such as the inconvenience of changing habitual arrangements, the time and bother involved in making the detailed calculations necessary for sophisticated decisions, or even the time involved in going to the bank to cash in a savings bond. Transfer costs are incurred both when assets are acquired, and when they are sold. There is also a problem of indivisibilities. Thus the wealth-owner may find that minimum investment requirements force him to hold money until he has accumulated sufficient wealth to purchase a desired asset, e.g., treasury bills with a minimum denomination of $10 000.

The important point is that unlike interest income, these transfer costs normally do not depend directly on the value of the assets or the length of time which they are held. Given the schedule of fees, they depend mainly on the *number of transactions*.

The Inventory Model   Given the existence of different time patterns of cash expenditures, a positive interest rate on non-money assets and transfer costs which depend on the number of transfers between money and other assets, how much money should an individual hold?

This problem in economic theory was explored independently in two pioneering articles by William Baumol[3] and James Tobin.[4] Because of its affinity to the problem faced by the retailer or manufacturer in deciding on the appropriate level of inventories to be held, their approach to the problem has been labelled the "inventory-theoretic" model of the transactions demand for money. We will not explore the formal mathematics of the inventory-theoretic model of the transactions demand for money. However, the basic argument should be intuitively obvious.

It is assumed that a household with an income-payments cycle like that examined in the earlier example seeks to maximize the net yield on its transactions balances. This depends on finding the optimum combination of money and earning assets in which to hold the transactions balances. If too much money is held, the loss of interest income will reduce the yield. If too little money is held, the transfer costs between earning assets and money will more than offset the additional interest income, thus reducing the net yield. It turns out that given the level of transfer costs, the interest rate on earning assets, and the total value of transactions, that there is a definite optimum level of cash balances. What is important, however, is that for an individual household or firm:

(1) *The optimum level of money balances increases with the total value of expenditures* to be made during the period. However, the relationship is quite complex. The optimum level of cash balances for a household increases as the *square root* of total expenditures.

(2) *The optimum level of money balances increases with the level of transfer costs* between money and non-money assets.

(3) *The optimum level of money balances varies inversely with the level of interest rates* on non-money assets.

The first of these three conclusions has a familiar ring. However, it should be noted that in the Baumol-Tobin analysis, the optimum level of cash balances does not increase in proportion to the total value of expenditures as classical theory implies. Rather, it increases much less than proportionately, implying *economies of scale* in individual transactions demands for cash (i.e., a doubling of the level of income and expenditure for a household will not double the optimum level of cash balances).[5]

The second and third conclusions, taken together, show that: "when the yield disadvantage of cash is slight, (i.e., when interest rates are low) the costs of frequent transactions will deter the holding of other assets, and average cash holdings will be large. However, when the yield disadvantage of cash is great, it is worthwhile to incur large transactions costs and keep average cash holdings low."[6] That is, the transactions demand for money on the part of individual households and firms — and hence the aggregate transactions demand for money — will display some interest elasticity. The higher the level of interest rates, the lower the average cash holdings. However, the existence of transfer costs will induce people to hold some transactions balances even at relatively high interest rates.

Baumol and Tobin both conclude that the advantages of such sophisticated management of cash holdings may be negligible for the average spending unit. We should not expect to find a high degree of interest elasticity with their cash holdings. However, for spending units with a large cash flow, such as corporations or municipal and provincial governments, the advantages from efficient cash management would be substantial. It is with their cash balances that we would expect to find substantial elasticity with respect to changes in interest rates.

Interest Elasticity.   The Baumol-Tobin model, strictly speaking, applies to individual households and firms. What does it tell us about the nature of the aggregate demand for cash balances?

Again, consider the aggregation problem which we noted earlier in connection with the classical theory of the transactions demand for money. The information necessary to draw any firm conclusions about the aggregate demand for cash balances from such general microeconomic information is totally unobtainable.

However, one conclusion at least seems warranted. It is highly probable that the aggregate transactions demand for money has some negative interest elasticity.[7]

This suggests that we must revise our earlier formulation of the aggregate transactions demand for money. Using the common mathematical notation for a *general* functional relationship (i.e., a mathematical statement that one variable depends on another, without specifying the exact nature of this dependence) we can express the relationship between the quantity of money demanded for transactions purposes (M_t), the level of aggregate income (Y) and the level of interest rates (r) (taking the level of transactions costs as given), as follows:

$$M_t = T\,(Y, r) \tag{20.5}$$

While we do not know the exact shape of the relationships (e.g., if they are linear or not), we are confident that the demand for cash balances varies directly with the value of expenditures, and inversely with the level of interest rates.

These assumptions about the aggregate transactions demand for money are incorporated in Figure 20-2. The demand for money is shown to increase with the level of aggregate income, and at each level of income to vary inversely with the level of interest rates. At any level of income there should be a maximum quantity of money demanded for transactions purposes (i.e., when the interest rate is so low that all transactions

FIGURE 20-2   The transactions demand for money: interest rate and income effects

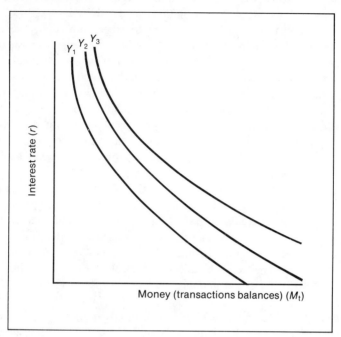

balances are held in money form), but the existence of transfer costs should guarantee that the demand for money will never be zero at "reasonable" levels of the interest rate.

ASSET DEMANDS FOR MONEY

We introduced this chapter with the observation that money, narrowly defined, is an asset which has been specially designed to serve as a medium of exchange. But this means that to its holders money must be the most liquid of assets. Our analysis of the portfolio balance decision in Chapter 5 demonstrated that assetholders have reasons for holding liquid assets in their portfolios in addition to the accommodation of specific expenditures plans in the near future (i.e., in addition to a generalized "transactions motive"). In particular, the provision of a *hedge against uncertainty and speculation on changes in interest rates* were suggested as important motives for holding liquid assets. But if money is the most liquid of assets, does this mean that there will be corresponding "precautionary" and "speculative" demands for money in addition to what we have called the transactions demand?

We will not repeat the analysis of uncertainty and speculation from Chapter 5. We take as proven the proposition that they can give rise to demands for liquid assets. Because of the uncertainty about the future course of income and expenditures, each assetholder will want to hold part of his portfolio in liquid form. Likewise, in periods when interest rates are expected to rise, assetholders can be expected to shift out of long-term securities and into short-term instruments, giving rise to additional demands for liquid assets. Conversely, when interest rates are expected to fall, holdings of liquid assets will be abnormally reduced, as assetholders shift into longer-term securities in anticipation of capital gains.

The Demand for Liquid Assets

In his famous book, *The General Theory of Employment, Interest and Money*, J.M. Keynes came to the conclusion that the very facts of uncertainty and speculation on interest rate changes were by themselves sufficient to explain the existence of asset demands for money. However, Keynes derived this conclusion from a model in which the assetholder's range of choice is limited to two financial instruments, money and long term bonds. Money is the only possible hedge against uncertainty, and money is the only possible vehicle for speculation on a rise in interest rates.

But again, we must remind ourselves that while money may be the most liquid of assets, it is not the only highly liquid asset. Normally, the range of alternatives is wide, including short-term claims on governments, businesses and financial intermediaries which may be payable with as little notice as one day, and *unused* lines of credit, whether directly from a bank or on a charge card such as Visa (which has a minimal fee) or Mastercharge. Given a wide range of non-money liquid assets which either yield interest income or, in the case of lines of credit, involve no opportunity cost, we might well ask Keynes himself his famous question: if money is narrowly defined, "Why would anyone outside a lunatic asylum wish to hold money as a store of wealth?"[8] Surely it is more attractive to hold precautionary balances in the form of earning assets or a costless line of credit than in the form of non-interest bearing money; and surely it is attractive to supplement possible speculative capital gains with the interest earned on short-term investment of the speculative balances.

The Definition of Money Again. The above discussion implies that money is an asset which normally yields no interest income, i.e., a narrow definition of money, encompassing only currency and demand deposits. As we saw earlier, many economists choose to define money more broadly, including in the concept of money deposits with banks (and perhaps with other financial institutions) which are not designed to be used as a medium of exchange but which normally pay interest and are available on demand or with short notice. These deposits are designed to be held as liquid assets to satisfy precautionary and speculative motives. It should not be surprising, therefore, that those economists who emphasize the asset approach to the demand for money also use a broad definition of money (see box).

Wealth and the Asset Demand for Money

The asset demand for money, then, is properly seen as a problem in portfolio selection, in which one of the assets which may be included in the portfolio is money. The decision to hold money as a store of wealth is presumably sensitive to the opportunity cost of holding money i.e., the difference between the yield on other assets, financial and real,

The Demand for Money: Three Classics

One of the most insightful and influential early analyses of the demand for money was that of Irving Fisher, in his classic work on monetary theory, *The Purchasing Power of Money*, published in 1911. Fisher chose a very narrow payments definition of money — "what is *generally* acceptable in exchange for goods." Writing before the cheque was as common an instrument for making payment as it has become, he was inclined to exclude deposits from his definition of money because cheques are "specially acceptable" (i.e., "only by the consent of the payee") not "generally acceptable." However, they are "an excellent substitute" for money, and hence Fisher developed his analysis in a way which readily encompassed deposits.

In analyzing the demand for money, Fisher focused on the determinants of the reciprocal of the coefficient *t* in our equation 19.2; what he called the *velocity of circulation of money*, the ratio of the value of total payments to the average stock of money. He identified three classes of determinants of velocity:

I. Habits of Individuals
   — thrift and hoarding
   — use of book credit
   — use of checks
II. System of Payments in the Community
   — frequency of receipts and payments
   — regularity of receipts and payments
   — synchronization of receipts and payments
III. General Causes
   — density of population
   — efficiency of the transportation system

Fisher was concerned primarily with the demand for money as a medium of exchange — the *transactions demand for money*. In the long run, he argued, this demand (the velocity of circulation) is institutionally determined, and relatively stable. However, he did foreshadow later analysis of the demand for money as a liquid asset. Thus, the concept of "hoarding" implies an asset demand. He notes in passing the role of interest rates as an opportunity cost of holding money, and in discussing the irregularity of receipts and expenditures he notes that in the face of uncertainty "prudence requires the worker to keep a larger sum on hand to insure against mishaps." He also discusses at length the demand for money in the transition period between two long-run equilibria following a major monetary disturbance. In this context, he emphasizes the role of expected changes in the general level of prices as a factor affecting velocity.

Fisher's long-run equilibrium demand for money function, then, is:

$$M = \frac{PT}{V}, \qquad \text{(20-B1)}$$

where PT is the aggregate value of transactions (the quantity of transactions, T, time the general level of prices, P), and V is the institutionally determined velocity of circulation.

* * *

J.M. Keynes, in his 1936 masterpiece, *The General Theory of Employment, Interest and Money*, developed the asset demand themes of Fisher and other early writers on the subject, to produce a radically different emphasis in the theory of the demand for money. In comparing Keynes' analysis to that of Fisher, it is important to emphasize that Keynes had in mind a much broader definition of money. Rejecting Fisher's notion that there is some theoretically correct definition of money, e.g., as a medium of exchange, Keynes suggested that the appropriate definition is whatever "is most convenient for handling a particular problem." Thus, he notes that it is often convenient to include time deposits and "even such instruments as (e.g.) treasury bills," instruments which are not designed as a medium of exchange. Keynes is concerned with the demand for financial assets which have the property of a high degree of *liquidity*, and hence the name which he applied to his demand function, the *liquidity preference function*.

Keynes argued that, in addition to the transactions demand for money, which he saw as depending on the level of income, there is an asset demand for money which is partly *precautionary* ("the desire for security as to the future case equivalent of a certain proportion of total resources") and partly *speculative* ("the object of securing profit from knowing better than the market what the future will bring forth") with respect to the level of interest rates. Both asset demands for money, Keynes argued, depend on the level of interest rates, increasing as interest rates fall. A particularly controversial aspect of the Keynesian analysis is the conclusion that at some very low level of interest rates, the demand for money becomes perfectly elastic — what has been called the "liquidity trap."

Keynes' demand for money function, in general form, is:

$$M = L\ (Y, r), \qquad \textbf{(20-B2)}$$

where Y is aggregate income and r the long term interest rate. Remember also, Keynes' concept of money is broader than Fisher's.

* * *

The modern classic on the demand for money is Milton Friedman's paper, "The Quantity Theory of Money — A Restatement." Accepting Keynes' view that there is no conceptually pure definition of money, he suggest that we think of money as "a temporary abode of purchasing power" rather than as a medium of exchange. He also puts some flesh on Keynes' criterion of "whatever is most convenient for the problem at hand," suggesting that for macroeconomic analysis what is "convenient" is a concept of money for which there is a relatively simple and relatively stable aggregate demand function. That is, to Friedman, the appropriate definition of money is an *empirical* issue. In general, Friedman's research leads him to favor a broader definition of money than did Fisher, including currency

and all deposits with commercial banks.

Friedman elaborated Keynes' concept of the asset demand for money into a more comprehensive and more consistent framework. First, he argued, the demand for money should be considered an aspect of the demand for capital; the decision to be made is the *form* in which *wealth* is to be held. This implies that wealth should replace income as the scale variable in the demand for money function. (In this context, note Keynes' use of the term "resources" in describing the asset demand, although he used only income and interest rates in his demand function). Second, Friedman argued that the demand for money should be thought of as a demand for *real balances*, M/P, and that, correspondingly, wealth should be expressed in real terms. Mathematically, this is an assertion that the demand for money is homogeneous to degree one in prices. Third, a decision to hold money involves an opportunity cost which is multidimensional, not just the long-term interest rate. At a minimum, allowance must be made for the yields on bonds and on equities, expected changes in these yields, which will produce capital gains or losses, and the expected rate of change in the general level of prices (which, of course, affects the expected real rate of return on assets, including money). If the assets included in the concept of money bear interest, this "own rate of interest" must be included also.

The measurement of wealth is a particularly difficult problem in empirical research. Demand for money analyses in the Friedman tradition tend to use an estimate of *permanent income* (see Chapter 4) as an index of wealth. In this framework, then, the demand for money becomes:

$$\frac{M}{P} = M\ (\ \frac{Y_p}{P}, r_b, r_e, g_b, g_e, r_m, P), \quad \textbf{(20-B3)}$$

where r_b and r_e are the yields on bonds and equities; g_b and g_e are the corresponding expected capital gains or losses; r_m is the yield on money; and P is the expected rate of change of the general level of prices.

and the yield on money. However, it is not obvious that the asset demand for money should depend *directly* on the level of income. Rather, the variable which determines the scale of the asset demand for money is not income but *wealth*.

The foremost exponent of this approach to the analysis of the demand for money is Milton Friedman (see insert). Friedman argues that to a business firm money is a capital good, a source of productive services, facilitating transactions, hedging against uncertainty, and bridging irregularities in the operations of the firm. The firm's demand for money, like its demand for any capital good, involves a balancing process, equating the marginal productivities of all factors of production, including money, at the margin.

To the household, money yields utility directly, like a durable consumer good. The household's wealth, to Friedman, is the present value of all expected future income, regardless of the source or the form of the income (i.e., whether it is received in money or in the form of intangible services). Thus, his analysis includes human as well as non-human sources of income. Each source of wealth is an asset, with a measureable yield, and to maximize the utility derived from its portfolio each household must so arrange the composition of its portfolio as to equate the expected yields at the margin. In the process, each household elects to hold some portion of its wealth in the form of money.

A crucial problem in the empirical application of this approach is the measurement of wealth. Friedman surmounts this problem by substituting a summary measure of the stream of expected future income from which the concept of wealth is derived, i.e., the concept of *permanent income* which we encountered in Chapter 4 in our discussion of the saving decision. Assuming peoples' expectations are heavily influenced by developments in the recent past, Friedman estimates permanent income on the basis of a weighted average of past incomes, with most recent income weighted most heavily. This measure is used in the demand for money function as a proxy for wealth.

On the basis of a large body of empirical research, Friedman concludes that permanent income is the single most important determinant of the aggregate demand for money. Current income is only significant as one of the components of permanent income.

THE AGGREGATE DEMAND FOR MONEY

The aggregate demand for money is a combination of the transactions demand and the asset demand. What can we conclude about the nature of the aggregate demand for money?

First we must underscore an important point. The nature of the demand for money depends on the definition of money. If we define money narrowly as the active medium of exchange, currency plus demand deposits, the demand for money should be predominantly a transactions demand. The aggregate demand for M1 then, will be:

$$M1 = M(Y, r) \tag{20.6}$$

If, however, we accept one or another of the broader definitions of money, including deposits which are not designed to be used as a medium of exchange, then we must allow for asset demands as well as the transactions demand. Then the aggregate demand for money, M2, will be:

$$M2 = M2\,(W,\ Y,\ r,\ r_m) \qquad (20.7)$$

where r_m is the ("own") interest rates on money and r the interest rate on non-money assets. We include both income (Y) and wealth (W) in this equation because, given the transactions demand for money as well as the asset demand, income is likely to have a direct impact on the demand for money which is independent of any indirect effect through its impact on wealth (or permanent income). That is, current income will have a greater weight in determining the demand for money that it has in determining wealth.

In the short run we can take wealth as given. Then the short-run aggregate demand for money becomes simply,

$$M2 = M2\,(Y,\ r,\ r_m) \qquad (20.8)$$

The important theoretical point for our subsequent analysis is that the aggregate demand for money should have a positive association with the level of aggregate income and a negative association with the level of interest rates in financial markets (or better, the differential between interest rates on non-monetary and monetary assets). Taking the level of interest rates on money as given, this demand function is illustrated in Figure 20-3.

FIGURE 20-3   The aggregate demand for money: income and interest rate effects

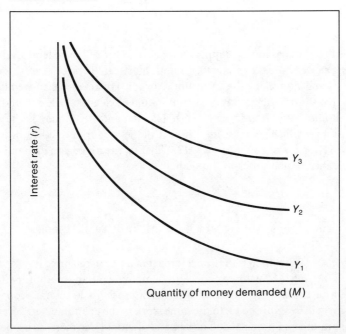

PRICES AND THE
DEMAND FOR MONEY

Up to this point we have discussed the demand for money on the implicit assumption that the general level of prices was stable. In the real world, such an assumption is hardly reasonable. Inflation seems to be an ever-present phenomenon, and at times in some countries the rate of change of the price level has been so great as to merit the sobriquet "hyper-inflation." As we noted in Chapter 5, changes in the price level can be an important consideration in portfolio selection decisions. It follows that they should also affect the demand for money.

We must distinguish two different effects of the price level on the demand for money: the *direct impact* of a change in the price level, and the impact of *expectations* of continuing price level changes.

Direct Impact

"Nominal" versus "Real" Money Supply.   An increase in the general level of prices involves a decline in the real value — the purchasing power — of anything whose nominal value is fixed in terms of the unit of account. Money is such an item. For this reason, economists find it necessary to distinguish between the "nominal money supply" and the "real money supply." The former is simply the money supply as we would conventionally measure it — the number of dollars (currency plus chequable bank deposits) in circulation. The real money supply is the nominal money supply adjusted for changes in its real purchasing power. That is, we define the real money supply (M_r) as:

$$M_r = \frac{M}{P} \tag{20.9}$$

where M is the nominal money supply and P is an index of the general level of prices.

As long as we made the implicit assumption of a stable price level, this distinction between real and nominal values was not relevant. However, when we allow for the possibility that the price level may change, it should be clear that the demand for money function, should be written in real terms. The demand for money is the amount of purchasing power which people want to hold in monetary form, whether for transactions purposes (M1) or for asset purposes (M2). That is, the aggregate demand for money narrowly defined (equation 20-6) should be:

$$\frac{M1}{P} = M\left(\frac{Y}{P}, r\right), \tag{20.10}$$

and the demand for money more broadly defined (M2) similarly adapted.

Direct Impact.   What then is the direct impact of a rise in the price level? At any given level of real income (i.e., with given levels of employment and output, perhaps at full employment) a rise in the price level will increase nominal income proportionately. More dollars will be required to do the same work in the economy. However, the price level and the number of nominal dollars demanded should also increase proportionately.

That is, *the demand for real balances at each level of interest rates should not change* as a result of a rise in the price level. This is the conclusion of the classical theory of the demand for money noted earlier.

The impact of *expectations* of continuing increases in the price level is very different.

Expectations of Price Level Changes

As we saw in Chapter 5, a rise in the price level is like a negative interest rate — it reduces the purchasing power of financial instruments over a period of time. Expected increases in the price level, then, must be taken into account in assessing the probable real yield on financial instruments and real assets, and hence in portfolio balance decisions. With respect to the demand for money, *the expected rate of inflation is equivalent to a negative interest rate on money balances.* It is a cost of holding money, and as such it should have the same effect on the demand for money as an increase in interest rates on other assets which can be held as substitutes for money. That is, the expectation of inflation should reduce the real quantity of money demanded at each (nominal) market rate of interest.

This effect is illustrated in Figure 20-4. The dotted line is the demand for money in the absence of expectations of inflation. The solid line is the demand for money when inflation is expected at the rate of $100e\%$ per annum.

How important should be the expected rate of inflation as a separate determinant of the demand for money? In thinking about this question, remember that our discussion of substitutes for money, whether in transactions balances or more generally as liquid assets, emphasized the substitutability between *money* and short-term *bonds*. But a money-holder cannot avoid the ravages of inflation by shifting to bonds; holders of bonds will lose purchasing power in the face of inflation just as will holders of money. Given the interest rate on bonds, the expectation of inflation should not induce a shift from money to bonds in asset portfolios.

However, we cannot take the interest rate as given. As we saw in Chapter 5, the workings of financial markets will probably incorporate the expected rate of inflation into the nominal interest rate on bonds. That is, given the real interest rate, the nominal interest rate will increase by the expected rate of inflation. With high nominal interest rates, people will hold less money and more bonds. Thus, one effect of inflation on the quantity of money demanded will be a result of higher nominal interest rates.

However, we have already allowed for this by using the nominal interest rate in the demand for money function. Thus, it is the nominal interest rate which is on the vertical axis of Figure 20-4. Is there any other effect of expected inflation on the demand for money?

If there is an *independent* effect of expected inflation on the demand for money, which is in addition to its effect through the nominal rate of interest, it must be because the expectations of inflation induces money holders to substitute *real assets* (or their equivalent in variable price financial assets) for money in their transactions balances or their asset portfolios. If, as seems likely, there is a low degree of substitutability between money and real assets, the expected rate of inflation will have a small independent effect on the demand for money unless the expected rate of inflation is very high.

FIGURE 20-4   The demand for money with expectations of
inflation

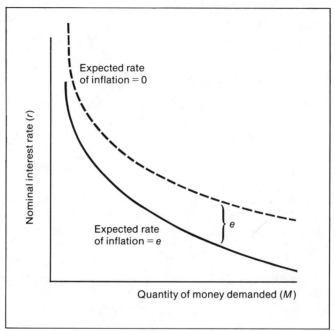

The measurement of the *expected* rate of inflation is obviously difficult, conceptually as well as empirically. Expectations, generally speaking, cannot be observed.
However, empirical economists have developed a variety of approaches to attempt to
represent expectations, on a variety of assumptions. We will not explore these matters
here. Suffice it to note that for rates of inflation in the range experienced in Canada
since World War II, investigators have had little success in identifying an effect of
expected inflation on the demand for money which is independent of the nominal
interest rate. For hyper-inflations, where the rate of inflation is measured in the
hundreds or thousands of percents per annum, however, very significant effects can be
detected.[9]

EVIDENCE ON THE DEMAND
FOR MONEY IN CANADA

Our survey of the theory of the demand for money has revealed a number of ambiguities
and some controversies. However, it has also suggested some conclusions of importance
for macreconomics. In particular, whatever else may affect the demand for money, such
as attitudes toward risk and the technology and institutions of exchange, two factors
emerge as the focus of attention for monetary policy — interest rates and income. But,
granted their theoretical role in the demand for money, what is their quantitative
importance? What is the elasticity of the demand for money with respect to interest

rates? With respect to income? How stable are these relationships? Can they be used to predict the demand for money?

These issues, which are of vital importance for the implementation of monetary policy, are empirical questions. They cannot be deduced from theory. Empirical answers to these questions require the application of sophisticated econometric techniques to estimate the demand for money function. Many studies have been undertaken, and to report in detail on each would require a capsule course on econometric techniques, which is not the function of a text on money and banking. We can do little more than summarize the findings of a few major studies. In doing so we concentrate on Canadian evidence, although it is important to emphasize that there is a rich empirical literature on the demand for money in the United States and other countries.

Although the results of empirical work on the demand for money have shown remarkable consistency over the years, all empirical research tends to become "dated" rapidly, as new studies produce new estimates. The serious student of monetary economics should be aware of this, and be prepared to search the professional journals for more recent evidence.

Interest Rate and Income Elasticities of Demand

Perhaps the most important recent study of the demand for money in Canada is that of W.R. White, a member of the staff of the Bank of Canada.[10] This study is important not only because of its thoroughness and comprehensiveness but also because of its apparent impact on the formulation of monetary policy by the Bank of Canada.

White estimated demand for money functions for Canada for the period 1959-1974, using monthly data and a variety of definitions of money. His statistical method permitted him to allow for time lags in the adjustments of the quantity of money demanded to changes in the independent variables, and hence to distinguish between the immediate impact and the equilibrium effect of any such changes. Table 20-1 presents some estimates of the equilibrium elasticities of demand with respect to income and interest rates which are representative of White's results. The estimates are presented for two time periods, before and after 1967 revision of the *Bank Act*, and for two definitions of money.

"Nominal" versus "Real" Balances.   Several points should be noted about the White results. First, White estimated the demand functions in a way which permitted him to test empirically the proposition that an increase in the general level of prices will result in a proportionate increase in the nominal quantity of money demanded in the economy. White's results support this proposition in equilibrium. That is, although the immediate impact of a change in the general level of prices is — a less than proportionate increase in the quantity of money demanded, after adjustment to equilibrium the effect is proportionate. In other words, the equilibrium elasticity of the demand for money with respect to the price level is one, whether money is defined narrowly or broadly. Moreover, the adjustment period was found to be short, perhaps no more than four months. These results provide strong empirical support for a basic proposition from economic theory, that, in equilibrium, the demand for money should be a demand for *real balances*.

The income and interest rate elasticities reported in Table 20-1 are after allowance for price level changes. In effect, they are elasticities of demand for real balances.

TABLE 20-1   **Equilibrium elasticities of demand for money, Canada, 1959-1974**

Concept of money	Time period	Income elasticity[c]	Interest market[d]	Elasticity own[e]
Narrow[a]	1959-68	0.59	− 0.08	
	1969-74	0.98	− 0.06	
Broad[b]	1959-68	0.57	− 0.01	0.04
	1969-74	0.95	− 0.003	0.01

[a] Narrow money = $M1A$ = currency + demand deposits
[b] Broad money = $M2$ = $M1A$ + personal savings deposits + chequable term and notice deposits
[c] Income = real domestic product
[d] Market interest rate = interest rate on 90-day finance company paper
[e] Own interest rate = interest rate on non-chequable personal savings deposits.

SOURCE: W.R. White, *The Demand for Money in Canada and the Control of Monetary Aggregates: Evidence from the Monthly Data.* (Ottawa: Bank of Canada, 1976).

Income Elasticity of Demand.   Second, the income elasticity of demand for real balances has increased over time, and for the post-1967 *Bank Act* period, for both definitions of money, it is approximately 1. Indeed, in statistical terms, it is not significantly different from 1. White used real domestic product as his measure of aggregate income. Some other studies, using a different measure of income (real gross national product) and covering different time periods, found somewhat different estimates of the income elasticity, closer to 0.7 for narrow money and 1.0 or slightly higher for broader money.[11]

Interest Elasticity of Demand.   Third, White's estimates of the interest elasticities of demand for real balances are consistent with the predictions of economic theory. That is, a rise in the market rate of interest (the opportunity cost of holding money) by itself reduces the quantity of money demanded, and an increase in the rate of interest on money balances (the "own" interest rate) by itself increases the quantity of money demanded. The study assumes that the own rate on currency and demand deposits is zero, so this term only applies to the broader definition of money.

White's results suggest that the interest elasticities are very small. The precise estimates depend not only on the definition of money adopted but also on the interest rates used in the equation. The results reported in Table 20-1 involve the interest rate on 90-day finance company paper as the market rate and the interest rate on non-chequable personal savings deposits as the own rate. For money narrowly defined, White suggests an interest elasticity smaller than −0.1. Other studies, covering more recent time periods, suggest that the elasticity may be somewhat larger, perhaps as large as −0.2, particularly if full allowance is made for the impact of strikes in the postal service on the demand for money.[12] Estimates in this range are broadly consistent with results of similar studies for the United States.

Estimating interest elasticities for money more broadly defined poses difficult statistical problems. It is difficult to identify the independent effects of the market interest rate and the own interest rate given that the two interest rates tend to move together. White's estimates for the market rate elasticity are surprisingly low, smaller that the elasticity for narrow money. It is commonly assumed that the relationship would be reversed, a result obtained in several studies which did not make allowance for the effects of the own interest rate. It is also interesting to note that the estimated own interest elasticity is considerably larger than the market interest elasticity. If the interest rate on bank deposits increases in step with increases in market interest rates, the demand for broad money will increase!

Stability of the Demand for Money

Empirical research thus supports the major predictions of the theory of the demand for money — unit elasticity of the demand for nominal money balances with respect to the price level; positive elasticity of the demand for real balances with respect to real income (or some similar index of transactions); and negative elasticity of the demand for real balances with respect to market interest rates. Studies in Canada and elsewhere in recent years, have produced estimates of the various elasticities which are broadly consistent with each other.

For the monetary authorities, however, this general agreement between theory and fact, and among studies, is not sufficient. As central banks rely more explicitly on estimates of the demand for money in the implementation of monetary policy (see box) they must also know how *dependable* the estimates are. Are the estimates reasonably precise, or are they subject to large error? Is the demand function stable, or is it likely to shift over short periods of time? Can the demand function be used to predict the demand for money, under various circumstances, and over periods of time which are of interest to the monetary authorities? Which concept of money is best from this perspective?

Two Types of Instability. The concept of instability in the demand for money is used in at least two different ways.

On the one hand is the important question of the ability of the investigator to obtain statistically precise estimates of elasticities of demand, which will permit him to make reliable forecasts of the demand for money in periods when the basic institutional environment is relatively stable. In their attempts to obtain the "best fit" and to minimize forecasting errors, investigators test various types of demand functions (e.g., linear versus logarithmic), including alternative explanatory variables (e.g., different interest rates, indexes of expectations of inflation, or income variables), with real and nominal specifications of variables, and for narrow and broad definitions of money. The result is an immense literature, not easily summarized. However, one point is of interest. Generally speaking, studies have found that narrow concepts of money (especially M1) yield demand functions with superior statistical properties. Thus, in an early study for Canada, K. Clinton of the Bank of Canada concluded that for the period

The Demand for Money and Monetary Policy

What many economists regard as a highly significant "revolution" in central banking practice occurred in several countries, including Canada, in the mid-1970s. As a result, the demand for money has been brought more explicitly to center stage in the formulation and implementation of monetary policy. In Canada, the formal implementation of the new strategy was announced in November 1975.

The "strategy of gradualism" called for a steady reduction in the rate of growth of the money supply from the highly inflationary range of 10-15% per annum, which had been achieved in 1973-75, to a rate consistent with price level stability, thought to be about 5% per annum. (This was the estimated long-term average rate of growth of production of goods and services in Canada.) What does this imply about the assumed income elasticity of demand for money?

The main features of the policy of gradualism are:

— The relevant concept of money is a narrow concept, M1.
— The policy has a long-run focus, seeking a non-inflationary equilibrium over a number of years. This recognizes both significant random errors in the estimated demand for money relationships, and time lags in adjustment to equilibrium.
— Annual targets for the rate of growth of M1, are expressed as a range within which the growth rate is to be kept. Again, the range is designed to allow for random errors both in the demand functions and in the implementation of policy.

Period	Target Growth Rate for M1	Actual Growth Rate for M1
	percent per annum	
Mar 1975- Mar 1976	10-15%	11.1%
Mar 1976- June 1977	8-12%	7.9%
June 1977- June 1978	7-11%	9.0%
June 1978- June 1979	6-10%	8.4%
May 1979- Sept 1980	5-9%	6.5%
Sept 1980- Sept 1981	4-8%	

Source: *Financial Post*, February 28, 1981

The target ranges have been summarized above.

The new policy proved to be highly controversial, for reasons which we will explore later. For our present purposes, the important point is the central role played not only by the concept of the demand for money but also by empirical estimates of the demand function in the formulation for monetary policy. Esoteric subjects like the relative "goodness of fit" of demand for money functions for different definitions of money suddenly became the subjects for columns in the financial press.

1955-1970, "money, narrowly defined, has a stable demand function," but "inclusion of a wider range of chartered bank liabilities expunges this stability."[13] White's later study supports the general conclusion, but finds a smaller margin of superiority for narrow money than Clinton implies.

On the other hand is instability which results from occasional "structural" changes. A prime example, which has been studied intensively, is the 1967 revision of the *Bank Act*. As you will recall from earlier discussions, this revision involved several major changes, including the differentiation of reserve requirements behind chequable and non-chequable deposits and increased emphasis on interbank competition for deposits. The banks responded by changing their interest rate policies, sharply differentiating between chequable and non-chequable personal savings deposits, and by offering a wider range of deposit arrangements and services to their customers. Clinton found that the 1967 *Bank Act* produced a major structural shift in demand for money functions in Canada. His results provoked several other studies, but this conclusion has stood up well to critical analysis, including analysis using more recent data.[14]

Other research has directed attention to other institutional considerations, such as the impact of strikes in the postal service and changes in the exchange rate regime. It has been clearly established that postal strikes, by disrupting the basic payments mechanism, significantly increase the demand for money for the duration of the strike.[15] It has also been suggested that the choice of fixed or flexible exchange rates, by altering the relative liquidity of Canadian and American dollars, might alter the traditional relationships.[16]

The "Missing Money."   Studies of the demand for money in the United States suggest that in the 1970s historically reliable estimates of demand for money functions deteriorated seriously. Prediction errors increased dramatically, and, for various periods of time, the historical equations significantly overestimated the quantity of money demanded in the economy. That is, the demand equations predicted much larger holdings of money than actually occurred — which led one American economist to write a long analysis of "The Case of the Missing Money."[17] Various suggestions have been offered, including the unusual behavior of interest rates in a period of rapid inflation, the development of electronics payments technology, new cash management techniques on the part of businesses, and the emergence of new institutions in the money market (so called "financial institutions").

Published literature has not explored these issues thoroughly in the Canadian case.[18] However in his 1979 annual report, the Governor of the Bank of Canada noted with concern the problem of predicting the demand for money in the face of major changes in banking practices which were having the effect of permitting depositors to hold smaller balances on deposit than the traditional demand for money relationships predicted.[19]

CONCLUSIONS

In classical economic theory, the role of money was essentially that of a medium of exchange. The demand for money was a transactions demand which varied directly with the total value of transactions in the economy (or, alternatively, with the level of aggregate income). The inventory-theoretic analysis suggests that the demand for money for transactions purposes should also have negative elasticity with respect to the level of interest rates. If money is defined more broadly to include bank deposits which are not designed to be used as a medium of exchange, then the argument that the demand for money should be sensitive to the opportunity cost of holding money, i.e., market interest rates on other liquid assets, is strengthened. However, allowance should also be made for the direct effects on the quantity of money demanded of the "own" interest rate on bank deposits.

In analyzing the demand for money, careful attention has to be devoted to the effects of the price level. In principal, the demand for money should vary proportionately with the general level of prices, so that the demand is a demand for "real balances." In addition, *expectations* of inflation should reduce the demand for real balances, because inflation acts like a negative interest rate on holdings of money balances. In general, the effects of expected inflation on the demand for money appear to be small, except in periods of hyper-inflation.

Empirical estimates of the demand for money provide strong support for the theoretical conclusions that the demand for nominal balances should have unit elasticity with respect to the price level, and that the demand for real balances should have positive elasticity with respect to income and negative elasticity with respect to market interest rates.

ENDNOTES

1. We have used small letters in this equation to signify that it relates to an individual household rather than to the aggregate.

   The coefficient is $(\frac{1}{2} - \frac{1}{12}) = .0417$. You should note that the size of the coefficient depends on the *period* for which the flow of income and expenditure is measured, increasing as the period gets shorter (and hence, as the income variable becomes proportionately smaller). Thus, if y is the household's *quarterly income* the coefficient would be $(\frac{1}{2} - \frac{1}{4}) = .125$; and if y is the household's *monthly income* it is $\frac{1}{2}$ or .5. We assume that the salary is paid in monthly installments, and that expenditures are made in the same pattern each month.

   It can be readily seen that if several large payments are made early in the month, the average cash balance will be less than $\frac{1}{2}y_m$. In the extreme, if the entire monthly income is paid out in a single lump sum payment during the first day, the average cash balance will approximate 0. Likewise, if few payments are made early in the month, with the bulk spent in several large payments late in the month, the average cash balance will be greater than $\frac{1}{2}y_m$. In the extreme, if only one large lump sum payment were made at the end of the month, the average cash balance would approximate y_m, the household's monthly income.

2. The issues which arise in attempting to derive an aggregate transactions demand for money from this simple model of the income-expenditure cycle of the household are considered in W.T. Newlyn, *Theory of Money* (Oxford: Clarendon Press, 1962), pp 38-50.

3. W.J. Baumol. "The Transactions Demand for Cash: An Inventory Theoretic Approach," *The Quarterly Journal of Economics,* Vol. 56 (November, 1952), pp. 545-56.

4. James Tobin, "The Interest Elasticity of Transactions Demand for Cash," *The Review of Economics and Statistics,* Vol. 37, (August, 1956), pp. 241-47.
5. The theoretical importance of the Baumol-Tobin derivation of the square root rule has been challenged by K. Brunner and A.H. Meltzer, who demonstrate that economics of scale should diminish sharply as the level of transactions increases, and for large values of transactions the demand for cash balances (at any given interest rate) becomes proportional to the value of transactions. K. Brunner and A.H. Meltzer, "Economics of Scale in Cash Balances Reconsidered," *Quarterly Journal of Economics,* 81(August, 1967), pp.422-36. The empirical evidence on economics of scale in cash balances is ambiguous. See, W.J. Frazer, Jr., *The Demand for Money* (Cleveland: World Publishing Co., 1967), pp. 218-56.
6. Tobin, *op. cit.,* 242.
7. The macroeconomic implications of the square root rule are particularly hard to interpret. The usual problem of relating to the distribution of income and expenditures among households arises, of course. However, even ignoring that, we cannot tell whether the fact that the optimum level of cash balances for *each household* varies with the square root of the household's expenditures also implies that the *aggregate demand* for cash balances varies with the square root of total expenditures. Clearly, if the increase in total expenditures is spread over a larger number of firms and households (with no individual household's expenditures increasing) the square root rule would not apply. Without solid empirical evidence to the contrary, perhaps the classical linear assumption is most useful at the aggregate level.
8. J.M. Keynes, "The General Theory of Employment," *Quarterly Journal of Economics* (February, 1937), 215-16.
9. A widely quoted study of hyper-inflation is Philip Cagan, "The Monetary Dynamics of Hyperinflation," in M. Friedman, ed., *Studies in the Quantity Theory of Money* (Chicago: University of Chicago Press, 1956), pp. 25-120. The literature on attempts to identify the independent effects of expectations of inflation is surveyed in D. Laidler, *The Demand for Money: Theories and Evidence,* Second Edition. (New York: Harper & Row, 1977), 135-37.
10. W.R. White, *The Demand for Money in Canada and the Control of Monetary Aggregates: Evidence from the Monthly Data* (Ottawa: Bank of Canada, 1976).
11. N. Cameron, "The Stability of Canadian Demand for Money Functions," *Canadian Journal of Economics,* 12(May, 1977), pp. 258-81; A.R. Gregory and J.G. MacKinnon, "Where's My Cheque? A Note on Postal Strikes and the Demand for Money in Canada," *Canadian Journal of Economics,* 13(November, 1980), pp. 683-87; S. Poloz, "Simultaneity and the Demand for Money in Canada," *Canadian Journal of Economics,* 13(August, 1980), pp. 407-20.
12. Cameron, *op. cit.;* Gregory and MacKinnon, *op. cit.;* Poloz, *op. cit.;* B.K. Short and D.P. Villanueva, "Further Evidence on the Role of Savings Deposits as Money in Canada," *Journal of Money Credit and Banking,* 9(August, 1977), pp. 437-46; D,K, Foot, "The Demand for Money in Canada: Some Additional Evidence," *Canadian Journal of Economics,* 10(August, 1977), pp. 475-85.
13. K. Clinton, "The Demand for Money in Canada, 1955-70: Some Single Equation Estimates and Stability Tests," *Canadian Journal of Economics,* 6(February, 1973), pp. 53-61.
14. Foot, *op. cit.;* Cameron, *op. cit.;* Poloz, *op. cit.*
15. *Gregory and MacKinnon, op. cit.*
16. Clinton, *op. cit.* Poloz, *op. cit.,* also argues that changes in the exchange rate regime and in the principles governing the Bank of Canada's operations make it more difficult to obtain statistically reliable estimates of the elasticities in the demand for money function.

17. S.M. Goldfeld, "The Case of the Missing Money," *Brookings Papers on Economic Activity,* 3(1976), pp. 683-739; J. Wenninger, L. Radecki, and E. Hammond, "Recent Instability in the Demand for Money," Federal Reserve Bank of New York, *Quarterly Review,* 6(Summer, 1981), pp. 1-9; R.D. Porter, T.D. Simpson and E. Mauskopf, "Financial Innovation and Monetary Aggregates," *Brookings Papers on Economic Activity,* 1(1979), pp. 213-229.

18. L. Landy, "Financial Innovation in Canada," *Federal Reserve Bank of New York Quarterly Review,* 5(Autumn, 1980), pp. 1-8.

19. Bank of Canada, *Annual Report,* 1979, pp. 23-25.

The Theory of Monetary Policy
21
PART 1: THE DOMESTIC MACROECONOMY

Monetary policy is the management of the money supply by the central bank. We saw in Chapters 18 and 19 how the central bank can *implement* monetary policy, and some of the constraints on the bank's actions. In this and the following two chapters we explore some of the *effects* of monetary policy, both domestically and internationally. The starting point for our analysis is the demand for money, which we saw in Chapter 20 appears to be a relatively predictable function of, among other things, the levels of aggregate income and interest rates. The question before us, then, is: Given the demand for money, what happens when the central bank changes the supply?

We can divide the repercussions into three interrelated categories: financial adjustments, aggregate demand adjustments, and real adjustments. By *financial adjustments* we mean the changes which occur in the portfolios of assets and liabilities held by all types of assetholders. By *aggregate demand adjustments* we mean the changes which occur in the level of aggregate demand for goods and services. By *real adjustments* we mean the ultimate effects on production, employment and the general level of prices. The linkage between monetary policy and real economic activity is a subject of major controversy among monetary economists. We will explore the analysis of two major schools of thought, those in the Keynesian tradition, inspired by the works of J.M. Keynes, and those in the monetarist tradition, inspired by the works of Irving Fisher and more recently Milton Friedman.

FINANCIAL ADJUSTMENTS

The direct impact of central bank monetary actions is to produce disequilibrium in asset portfolios throughout the economy. The repercussions which follow result from asset-holders' adjustments in the face of portfolio disequilibrium.

Portfolio Disequilibrium Within the Banking System

Consider first the financial repercussions of central bank measures to expand the money supply. As you will recall, such actions can take various forms, initially probably a transfer of government deposits from the Bank of Canada to the chartered banks, but possibly the purchase of government securities in the open market.

Bond Prices and Yields.   The central bank cannot purchase government securities in the open market without raising their prices and hence somewhat depressing their yields. However, we will leave that aspect of the matter aside for the moment. As we shall see, the direct impact of the central bank on government bond yields becomes swallowed up in the larger effects resulting from private portfolio adjustments.

Excess Bank Reserves.   *The major initial impact of the central bank's actions is to produce disequilibrium in the asset of portfolios of commercial banks.* The banks have a larger proportion of cash reserves among their assets than they would like, given the existing levels of interest rates. As we saw in Chapter 17, in this situation the profit motive will induce the banks to acquire additional earning assets. This has three important financial repercussions.

First, to some extent the banks will satisfy their demand for earning assets by purchasing securities, probably short-term government bonds, in the open market. Like the initial purchase by the central bank, this will tend to *raise the price and hence lower the yield on government securities.* Second, the banks will probably demonstrate increased willingness to extend loans. That is, at any given level of interest rates, they will be willing to extend more credit. The supply curve for bank loans shifts outward. Depending on the competitive environment, This should lead to some reduction of interest rates and an easing of other terms for bank loans. In the jargon of central banking, there will follow *a reduction in the cost and an increase in the "availability" of bank credit.* Third, on the other side of the balance sheet, the increase in the banks' earning assets will be matched by *an increase of the money supply.*

These are all familiar propositions, developed in detail in Chapter 17. What then happens outside the banking system?

Portfolio Disequilibrium Among Other Assetholders

We now have three developments which combine to produce disequilibrium conditions within the portfolios of private assetholders other than banks: they are holding a larger than normal amount of money; the yields on government bonds have declined somewhat; and bank credit is available on more favorable terms. Together, these factors will induce private assetholders to rearrange their portfolios.

Excess Supply of Money.   Perhaps the most important effect, and certainly the one most stressed in traditional monetary theory, is the increase in private holdings of money. This money was put into the hands of individuals when they responded to offers from the central bank or the commercial banks for securities in their possession at marginally favorable prices, or through the extension of loans by the commercial banks. In general, for the private assetholders, the new money is a temporary repository of purchasing power between the sale of one asset and the purchase of another. Given the levels of income and interest rates they have no reason to hold the additional money itself. The new assets which they seek to acquire may be securities, or — and this is important as a link to the "real" side of the adjustment process — they may be real assets, capital goods or consumer durables.

The Level of Interest Rates.   We can leave aside the effects on demands for real assets for the moment. In the market for securities, the attempts of private assetholders to purchase securities in exchange for the money which they do not want to hold will add to the upward pressure on security prices and hence to the decline in yields initiated by the central bank and aggravated by the portfolio adjustments of the commercial banks. Note also that through private portfolio adjustments, the decline of government bond yields will be generalized to securities of all types and all maturities. Assetholders will attempt to dispose of any securities whose yield has been abnormally depressed and attempt to purchase securities which still have relatively favorable yields. Given that the supply of each security is temporarily fixed, all that can happen as a result of such trading is a change in relative prices. Through the market adjustment, yields will tend to be equalized (allowing for risk and liquidity, of course) at new lower levels. In other words, *the end result is a decline in the general level of interest rates.* Indeed, *if* there were no real adjustments, *the level of interest rates would have to fall until private assetholders were content to hold the enlarged money supply.* (Remember: as we demonstrated in Chapter 17 there is no way that private assetholders can reduce the size of the money supply. They can only pass the unwanted money among themselves, until interest rates are bid down sufficiently that some assetholders are willing to hold the money in their portfolios.)

This is an important "if." There may be repercussions on real economic activity, and, as we shall see, these real repercussions also serve to adjust the demand for money to the expanded supply of money.

AGGREGATE DEMAND AND REAL ADJUSTMENTS

Given that an increase in the money supply will cause disequilibrium in the financial sector, what happens next? Will the disequilibrium be totally absorbed by adjustments in asset portfolios, with no real consequences? Will production and employment be affected? Will the general level of prices change?

There are two radically different hypotheses to be considered, each of which contains an important message — the quantity theory and the Keynesian theory. In this section we consider the quantity theory in its original or classical form. In the next section we consider the Keynesian analysis, before returning to the more modern version of the quantity theory.

The Classical Quantity Theory

The simplest and most direct statement of the classical quantity theory is that of Irving Fisher:

> One of the normal effects of an increase in the quantity of money is an exactly proportional increase in the general level of prices.[1]

This is a very strong prediction. What type of model of the economy would lead to such conclusions?

There are two fundamental assumptions underlying the classical model: a tendency of the economy to full employment and stability of the demand for money in real terms.

Long-Run Full Employment. Fisher's statement is a proposition about the *long run.* A fundamental assumption underlying the analysis is that if the forces inherent in a reasonably competitive market economy are allowed to work themselves out, the economy will tend to full employment of its productive resources, and particularly full employment of the labor force. This means that in the long run, the *level of output and employment does not depend on the size of the money supply.* In Fisher's words: "An inflation of the currency cannot increase the product of farms and factories, nor the speed of freight trains or ships. The stream of business depends on natural resources and technical conditions, not on the quantity of money. The whole machinery of production, transportation, and sale is a matter of physical capacities and technique, none of which depend on the quantity of money."[2]

This proposition should not be interpreted as an assumption of *continuous* full employment. Indeed, Fisher recognized that changes in the quantity of money might have temporary, "transitional" effects on levels of output and employment,[3] but these transitional effects are not of primary concern. Rather, attention is directed to the long run, when all of the economic forces inherent in the situation have worked themselves out. The mechanism which guarantees full employment as the "normal" equilibrium state of the economy is the general flexibility of prices. Unemployment implies an excess supply of labor at existing wage rates. Given time, and price flexibility, the relative price of labor (the *real* wage rate) will fall sufficiently that the excess supply will be absorbed into productive employments. Inevitably, full employment will be reestablished.

The Demand for Money. We discussed the second fundamental assumption of the classical analysis in Chapter 20. It is that the demand for money is a simple and stable function of the aggregate flow of transactions, which can be represented by the level of aggregate income. A useful concept in this regard is the *income velocity of money (V),* the ratio of income to the stock of money.

$$V = \frac{Y}{M} \tag{21-1}$$

For Fisher's statement of the quantity theory with which we introduced this section to be literally true, the velocity of money would have to be *constant.* Indeed, the classical quantity theory has frequently been interpreted in this way. However, this was not quite the proposition intended by the classical quantity theorists. They were asserting that aside from temporary "transitional" effects, *the velocity of circulation is determined by factors which are independent of the supply of money.* Velocity has a long-run equilibrium value determined by relatively slow-changing technical and institutional factors, by the requirements for money to facilitate the flow of transactions in the economy. Thus, as long as the basic institutional and technical determinants of the demand for money are given, the quantity of money demanded in the economy in the *long run* depends directly on the level of income. that is,

$$M_d = \frac{Y}{V} \tag{21-2}$$

To express the equation in real terms, we can divide through by the general level of prices (P), so that:

$$\frac{M_d}{P} = (\frac{Y}{P})(\frac{1}{V}) \tag{21-3}$$

The Mechanics of the Quantity Theory.   In order to explore the economic process assumed in the classical quantity theory, let us consider the effects of a sizeable increase in the supply of money.

The initial impact of an increase in the supply of money, given the existing levels of prices and incomes, would be the creation of an *excess supply of money.* There would be more money in the economy than was demanded under existing circumstances. Remember, the supply of money is determined primarily by the banking system and the monetary authorities. While each individual can dispose of money which he does not want to hold by purchasing goods, services, or securities, he does so by passing the money on to someone else. Collectively, the public cannot reduce the nominal money supply. If the supply cannot be reduced, then the demand must increase to absorb the excess supply. How does this happen?

In one sense, the classical quantity theory does not answer this question. Although Fisher and others offered many insights into the transition period, the quantity theory *per se* only focused on the end result. It started with an economy in equilibrium, introduced a disturbance in the form of a change in the money supply, and then examined the new equilibrium. The process by which the economy got there was not part of the theory.

Remember, in the long run the classical demand for money is defined only in terms of an equilibrium velocity of circulation and the level of income. Under the assumption of full employment, the aggregate quantity of goods and services available cannot expand to satisfy the increased demands for goods and services on the part of those holding excess money. In terms of the demand for money function (21.3), real income cannot increase. Given the equilibrium velocity of circulation, all that *can* happen is that the general level of prices of goods and services is bid up. Indeed, the price level must increase until the excess supply of money is entirely absorbed by the demand function. That is, the price level must rise until:

$$\frac{M_s}{P} = \frac{M_d}{P} = (\frac{1}{V}) (\frac{Y}{P}) \tag{21.4}$$

This conclusion can be expressed in a slightly different way. At the initial price level, the increase in the *nominal money supply* has the temporary effect of increasing the *real money supply*. However, given the basic technical and institutional determinants of velocity, equation 21.3 tells us that the demand for real money will not have changed. Thus it follows: *Given an increase in the nominal money supply, equilibrium between demand and supply will only be re-established when the price level rises sufficiently that the real money supply is reduced to its original level. This means that the price level must eventually rise in proportion to the initial increase in the nominal money supply.* You should take careful note of the fact that in this model, *the price level is the one and only variable which adjusts to maintain long-run equilibrium between the demand for and the supply of real money.* Thus, Irving Fisher concludes that in the long run "The price level is normally the one *absolutely passive* element" in the economy.[4]

Implications for Monetary Policy.   The implications of this analysis for monetary policy are quite straightforward. Whatever happens in the short run, in the long run, in an economy which automatically tends to full employment, monetary policy can only affect the general level of prices. Stability of the price level can be achieved if the authorities provide that supply of money which is demanded at the full employment level of income with the existing price level. It is pointless for the monetary authorities to attempt to regulate levels of output and employment. In the long run, these are matters which cannot be controlled by monetary policy.

As we have stated it, Fisher's analysis applies to a static economy, with a given full employment level of income. Perhaps we should set it in the context of a growing economy. In this context, stability of the price level, in the long run, depends simply on the choice of an appropriate *rate of growth* for the money supply. The growth rate of the nominal money supply should be the rate at which the availability of productive resources and technical advances will permit aggregate output to grow, adjusted, of course, for any changes in the institutional and technical conditions underlying the demand for money function.

Keynesian Theory

To many economists of the 1930s and 1940s the classical quantity theory, with its assumptions of a stable velocity of money and long-run tendencies to full employment, seemed either wrong or utterly irrelevant. Regardless of the measure of the money supply, income velocity was not a constant, or even a relatively stable magnitude (Figure 21.1 shows the income velocity for M3), and in the face of the massive and prolonged unemployment of the 1930s there was considerable speculation that the chronic unemployment of a high proportion of the labor force rather than full employment was the normal equilibrium state of the economy. In this context, the Keynesian model which focused on the level of employment, swept the field in macroeconomic analysis.

The classical quantity theory of money was a theory of long-run equilibrium, in which the price level is the central variable. The economics of "transitional" periods between one long-run equilibrium and another, including the possibility of prolonged, large-scale, involuntary unemployment, received little attention. To Keynes, by contrast, the analysis of this period contained the essence of the macroeconomic policy problem

FIGURE 21-1   The income velocity of money ($M3$) in Canada, 1920-1980

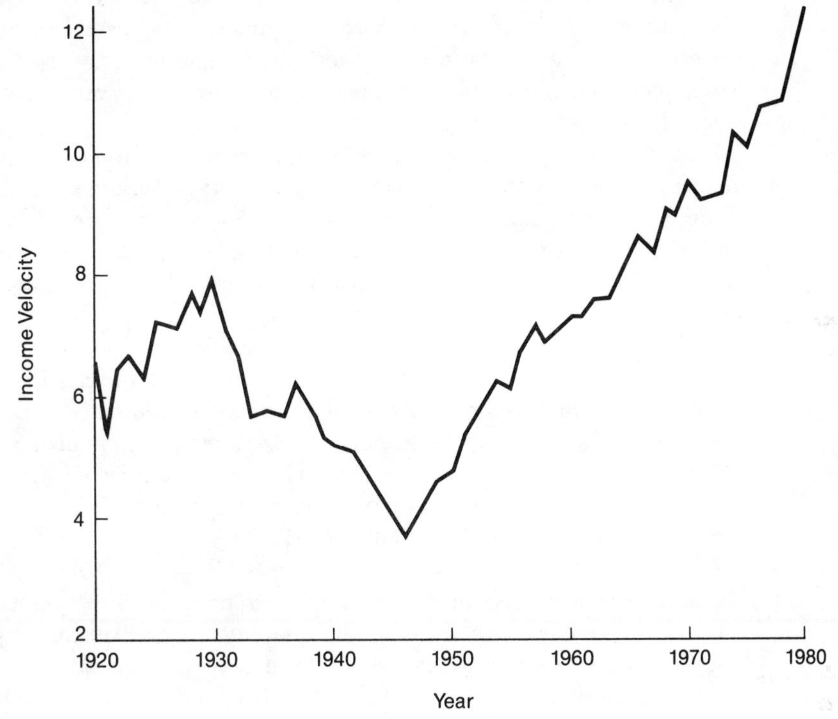

Source: *Bank of Canada Review*, various issues. M.C. Urquhart and K.A. Buckley, *Historical Statistics of Canada* (Toronto: Macmillan, 1965).

— a point which is underlined by the famous Keynesian aphorism, "In the long run we all are dead." The Keynesian theory is a theory about the short run in which output and employment are the central variables. Indeed, in the extreme version of the Keynesian theory, the price level is presumed to be fixed by institutional rigidities. This is the model of the macroeconomy which we want to explore in some detail.

Some Points of Contrast

We have already stressed the fundamental difference in the "time period" considered by the two models, and the associated assumptions about the behavior of the price level. We will have much more to say about this later. However, there are also other important points of contrast between the classical and the Keynesian analysis which should be kept in mind.

The Transmission Mechanism.   As we have just seen, because it focuses on the long-run equilibrium — on the state of affairs after all of the economic forces inherent in the situation have worked themselves out — the classical quantity theory has very little to say about what we can call the *transmission mechanism*. How, exactly, does a change in the money supply lead to a change in the price level? What is the chain of economic events? It is clear that there is a change in aggregate demand for goods and services, represented in the classical model by a single aggregate, MV. However, what components of aggregate demand are likely to be affected by monetary policy? In what degree? And why?

In models in the Keynesian tradition, there is a much more detailed analysis of aggregate demand, considering demand separately from various sectors of the economy. Moreover, the impact of a change in the money supply on aggregate demand is largely *indirect,* and may occur only in some sectors. Indeed, under some circumstances, it is argued, a change in the money supply may have negligible real consequences.

Role of Interest Rates.   An essential link in the Keynesian transmission mechanism is the bond market and the level of interest rates. Whereas the classical quantity theory implies that an increase in the supply of money will be translated directly into demand for goods and services, the Keynesian model assumes that initially it will be translated into a demand for bonds. The resulting change in the price of bonds, and hence of interest rates, will *indirectly* induce changes in aggregate demand, depending on the sensitivity of spenders to the level of interest rates.

General Equilibrium Analysis.   As a result, models in the Keynesian tradition are much more complex than in the classical quantity theory. Even the simplest models, of the type which we will consider, must allow for several sectors which interact with each other. Equilibrium in the economy must involve simultaneously equilibrium in each of the sectors. More complex Keynesian models may involve hundreds of equations and require modern computers with very large capacity for their solutions.

Of course, all of the interactions which are made explicit in the Keynesian models are implicit in the classical model. They are suppressed because the model focuses only on the end result, the final long-run equilibrium. As we will see, it is possible to use the Keynesian model to obtain the classical result; although, the Keynesian model also suggests that over periods of time of interest to policy makers, very different results may be obtained. In this, the fundamental differences between the approaches rest in the analysis of the determinants of the price level.

Some Basic Identities

The central concept in the Keynesian model is aggregate demand. This is a concept which we have used on several occasions. We must now consider it more carefully.

Aggregate Demand.   By aggregate demand we mean the aggregate expenditures from all sources during a given period of time for the purchase of goods and services newly produced by factors of production owned by residents of Canada. Note that aggregate demand has a time dimension. It is a flow concept.

Depending on the purpose of the analysis, aggregate demand can be broken down into many categories of expenditure. For most purposes, at least four sources of demand must be recognized: household expenditures for all types of consumer goods and services (commonly called *consumption* and represented by the symbol *C*); business expenditures for new capital goods, machinery, equipment, buildings,and inventories (*investment* — *I*); government expenditures for all types of goods and services, but excluding purely transfer payments like unemployment insurance compensation which are not payments for goods or services rendered (*government expenditure* — *G*); and the expenditures of non-residents of Canada to purchase Canadian-produced goods or the services of Canadian productive factors (*exports* — *X*). Mention of the foreign sector should remind us that not all expenditures by Canadian households, business firms, and governments constitute demand for the services of Canadian productive factors. Part of this demand is for the importation of foreign-produced goods or the services of foreign-owned productive services (*imports* — *Im*). In measuring aggregate demand we must deduct this part of the aggregate expenditures of Canadian spending units.

By this definition,

$$\text{AGGREGATE DEMAND} = D = C + I + G + X - Im \tag{21.5}$$

Aggregate Income. Another concept which we have used on several occasions is aggregate income. By this we mean the total income of all types (wages, rent, interest, profits) earned by factors of production owned by residents of Canada during a given period of time. Like aggregate demand, it also is a flow concept.

The owners of factors of production earn income because of the participation of their factors in the production process. Indeed, because we have included profits in the category of income, it should be obvious that if it were not for problems relating to certain taxes, subsidy payments and depreciation accounting,[5] the sum of all incomes earned should equal the value of output produced. All income payments besides profit show on the books of business firms as costs. But the difference between the value of output and costs measured in this sense is profit. Hence, if we add profit to factor costs, we should have a measure of both the value of output *gross national product* (= GNP) and the value of *aggregate income* (*Y*).[6]

Thus,

$$\text{AGGREGATE INCOME} = Y = \text{GNP} = \text{AGGREGATE OUTPUT} \tag{21.6}$$

We also know, however, that the value of aggregate output in the same thing as the value of aggregate expenditures. These two concepts are merely two sides of the same set of market transactions. GNP is the value of what has been produced and sold; *D* is the value of what has been purchased.

It follows then, that:

$$\text{AGGREGATE INCOME} = Y = C + I + G + X - Im = \text{AGGREGATE OUTPUT} \tag{21.7}$$

What we have in the middle of this expression is aggregate demand.

Output and Employment.   Remember, we are assuming that *the price level is fixed.* Since we can think of gross national product as the price level multiplied by the quantity of output produced, the assumption of a fixed price level means that any change in aggregate demand must involve a proportional change in output.

But, in the short run, given the established techniques of production and existing productive equipment, any change in output will be reflected in a change in the level of employment. For various reasons, the change in employment may not be proportional to the change in aggregate demand, but it will be in the same direction. Thus, a decline in aggregate demand means a drop in the level of output, and it means unemployed labor and idle machinery and factories.

A Simplified Framework.   Striving for closer and closer approximations of reality, modern Keynesian models recognize many more sub-categories of aggregate demand. However, our interest in the Keynesian model is very general. We only want to identify the basic principles of how monetary policy is supposed to influence the level of income and employment. We can simplify rather than complicate the model, by delaying consideration of the government sector and the international sector.

The simplified framework which we will consider is as follows:

$$\text{AGGREGATE DEMAND} = C + I = Y = \text{GNP} \tag{21.8}$$

This equation is an identity. It provides a framework for analysis, but tells us nothing about the economic processes which determine the levels of income and employment. For this we need assumptions about the behavior of the relevant macro-economic variables. So far we have made two important assumptions: that the price level is fixed and that the level of employment depends directly on the level of output and hence on the level of aggregate demand. What is assumed about the determinants of consumption and investment in the aggregate demand equation 21.8?

The basic distinction between the two categories of aggregate demand in equation 21.8 between those expenditures which are presumed to be directly and primarily affected by the current level of income (consumption) and those which are less directly dependent on the current level of income, being influenced primarily by expectations of future developments (investment). We will consider the latter category first.

Behavioral Assumptions: The Investment Decision

In the Keynesian model, investment is *expenditures to acquire real capital* — houses, factories, transportation facilities, machinery, equipment, and inventories of goods in the process of production of distribution. What determines the level of investment expenditures? Is there a link to monetary policy? In this section we present a theory of investment which builds on the firm's demands for capital goods.[7] An important, if indirect link with monetary policy is established through the interest rate.

Desired Stock of Capital.   A firm's demand for real capital derives from the role of capital as a factor of production. Although the limit is far from rigid in most cases, the production capacity of the firm is limited by its stock of real capital. We can think of a typical firm as having a planned or *designed production capacity,* at which it operates most efficiently, based on its stock of real capital and the capital's technological characteristics. In the short run, output can fluctuate widely, using more or less of the designed capacity. Indeed, production may well exceed designed capacity for extended periods of time, although production in excess of designed capacity normally involves relatively high costs of production. A substantial and sustained increase in output beyond designed capacity will require new real capital for efficient production. Projections of opportunities for sustained profitable increases in output will be an incentive for firms to increase their production capacity. Conversely, projections of stagnant or shrinking markets will provide incentives to just maintain, or perhaps reduce production capacity, perhaps failing to replace capital equipment as it wears out.

At any time there is presumably a stock of capital which the firm regards as optimal, given the market prospects and its planned level of output now and in the relevant future. We can call this the *desired stock of capital.* It may be greater or less than the *actual stock of capital* held by the firm. If the desired stock exceeds the actual stock, the firm will invest in new real capital. Investment in the Keynesian sense will occur.

The same concepts can be applied at the aggregate level. The sum of the desired stocks of capital of individual firms is the aggregate desired stock of capital. It is a difference between the desired stock and the actual stock of capital which induces aggregate investment expenditures.

Investment as an Adjustment Process.   Seen in this light, investment is an adjustment process — a process of adjusting the actual stock of capital to the desired stock of capital. The rate of investment, then, must depend directly on the size of the gap between the aggregate desired stock of capital and the actual stock of capital. But investment also involves a process of production, which takes time. The capital goods have to be designed, produced, and installed, processes which may take weeks, months, or years, depending on the capital goods in question. Thus, a gap between the desired and the actual stock of capital can seldom be filled instantaneously. Indeed, in any given period of time, a month, a quarter, or a year, only some fraction of the gap may be filled. That is, in any given time period, the adjustment process may only be partial. Symbolically,

$$I = \lambda \, (K^* - K) \qquad\qquad (21.9)$$

where K^* is the desired and K the actual stock of capital, and λ is an adjustment coefficient, indicating that in the given time period the adjustment is only partial (i.e., $0 < \lambda < 1$).

The flow of investment expenditures, then, will depend primarily on the size of the gap between the desired and the actual stock of capital but will also depend on factors affecting the speed of adjustment. Some types of capital (e.g., standard pieces of minor equipment) can be produced quickly; others (e.g., hydroelectric dams) may require years of construction.

Volatility of Investment.   One of the most important macroeconomic characteristics of the flow of investment is, its *volatility.* Investment shows much wider fluctuations from year to year than other major components of aggregate demand. We cannot develop a complete analysis of this phenomenon here, but our characterization of investment as an adjustment process should make it obvious why investment is so volatile. When a gap occurs between the desired and the actual stock of capital, investment will spurt forward. But the investment itself eliminates the gap, reducing the need for further investment. Investment is thus the seed of its own destruction.

To understand the point, think of an economy in which the actual stock of capital is approximately equal to the desired stock of capital. Investment expenditures will be very small, primarily for the replacement of worn-out equipment. Now allow any development which increases the desired stock of capital. This might be a significant new product, a major technological innovation, population growth, the opening of a new foreign market, a rise in the world price of an underdeveloped natural resource, a marked improvement in domestic markets — in short, any of the myriad developments which frequently buffet our economy.

The increase in the desired stock of capital will induce a spurt of investment expenditures. The investment component of aggregate demand will jump from a low level to a high level. However, even though all of the firm's expectations with respect to the underlying development are fulfilled, this high level of investment will not be maintained. As investment occurs, the actual stock of capital will increase, approaching the desired stock, and the need for further investment disappear. At some point, investment will begin to fall off, and it may fall off rapidly, approaching again the low level required for the maintenance of the existing stock of capital. Of course, should market conditions turn very sour, so that most firms would have substantial excess production capacity and hence redundant capital equipment, investment expenditures may not even be held at this level. Firms will not replace worn out capital goods, deliberately reducing their productive capacity. Thus, for extended periods during the severe depression of the 1930s private investment expenditures were almost non-existent.

But what does all of this have to do with monetary policy? Nothing we have said so far establishes a link between monetary policy and investment — and that is what we are seeking.

Interest Rates and the Capital.   In order to establish the link between monetary policy and investment it is useful to think of the firm's decision on the desired stock of capital in a slightly different way. From the foregoing discussion it should be apparent that the complex of factors which will bear on the firm's choice of a desired stock of capital can be capsulized as the firm's expectation of making profits from the production of goods and services, using the capital. These profits are in the future, and for that reason are only conjectural. Their magnitude, timing, and duration cannot be known with certainty. To the firm, then, real capital —real production capacity — is simply *an asset with an uncertain yield.* In this sense, real capital is like any of the variable income assets discussed in Chapters 3 and 5, which have a distribution of possible alternative yields, and hence an expected yield.

Keynes called the expected yield on additions to the stock of real capital the *marginal efficiency of capital.* The Keynesian theory of investment is rooted in this concept. It represents the demand side of the investment decision — the demand for new production capacity.

FIGURE 21-2   The investment demand function

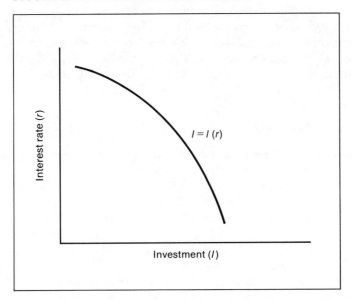

But there is another aspect to the determinants of aggregate investment, the supply side. We must remember that the creation of real capital involves a commitment of resources which have alternative uses in the economy. Most immediately, funds have to be borrowed, at the current rate of interest, or, if the firm has sufficient funds of its own, they could be lent to banks or other firms at the current rate of interest. Thus, in making a rational decision about its stock of real capital the firm must pay careful attention to the *opportunity cost* of investment in real capital; that is, it must pay careful attention to the level of interest rates in financial markets. Given the marginal efficiency of capital, the higher the level of interest rates, the smaller the desired stock of real capital.

Considered in this way, it is apparent that the firm's decision on the desired stock of real capital is but another example of the portfolio balance decision of Chapter 5 — choice among risky assets, based on expected yields, allowing for both credit risk and market risk (liquidity).

Investment and Interest Rates.   If the interest rate affects the desired stock of capital then it also affects the size of the gap between the desired and the actual stock of capital and hence the flow of investment expenditures. But note, the link between investment expenditures and interest rates is at best indirect. Moreover, given the volatility of the marginal efficiency of capital, the effects of changes in interest rates may well be swamped by other considerations. It should not be surprising, therefore, that most empirical studies suggest low sensitivity of many types of investment expenditures to interest rates.

In general, however, these studies confirm that *the higher the level of market interest rates, the lower the level of investment expenditures.* This assumption is represented graphically in Figure 21.2, with the flow of investment expenditures planned by firms measured along the base axis, and the level of interest rates along the vertical axis. *This is the investment demand function for any given "state of expectations" relating to the yields of potential new capital projects.* Among other things a change in the economic outlook will shift the function — a buoyant outlook shifting it to the right, and pessimistic expectations shifting it to the left. Similarly, a significant technological revolution might suddenly increase the amount of investment that would be worthwhile at various interest rates.

The Consumption Function

We discussed the Keynesian postulate with respect to consumption in Chapter 4. In brief, Keynes asserted that the dominant factor determining the level of consumption expenditures is the level of income, but that consumption increases less than proportionately with the level of income. That is, what he called the marginal propensity to consume has a magnitude less than 1. In linear form, the Keynesian consumption function is:

$$C = C_0 + cY \tag{21.10}$$

where C_0 is a constant (that part of consumption which is independent of the level of income — "autonomous" consumption) and c is the marginal propensity to consume, the slope of the consumption function in the top panel of Figure 21.3.

As we also noted in Chapter 4, given that the decision between saving and consumption involves an inter-temporal choice — consumption now versus consumption in the future — the level of interest rates should also affect consumption expenditures. However, the effect is generally thought to be small. In the usual exposition of the Keynesian model this effect is neglected.

A Saving Function.   Applying an identity which we developed in Chapter 4, we also know that:

$$Y = C + S \tag{21.11}$$

where S is aggregate saving. It follows, then, that:

$$\begin{aligned} S &= Y - C \\ &= Y - (C_0 + cY) \\ &= Y(1-c) - C_0 \end{aligned} \tag{21.12}$$

In our simplified model, which ignores the government sector and external trade, this is the saving function. If we let s represent the marginal propensity to save, such that:

$$s = (1-c), \tag{21.13}$$

we can rewrite equation 21.12,

$$S = -C_0 + sY \tag{21.14}$$

The saving function is thus derived directly from the consumption function, as is shown in Figure 21-3.[8]

FIGURE 21-3 "Keynesian" consumption and saving functions

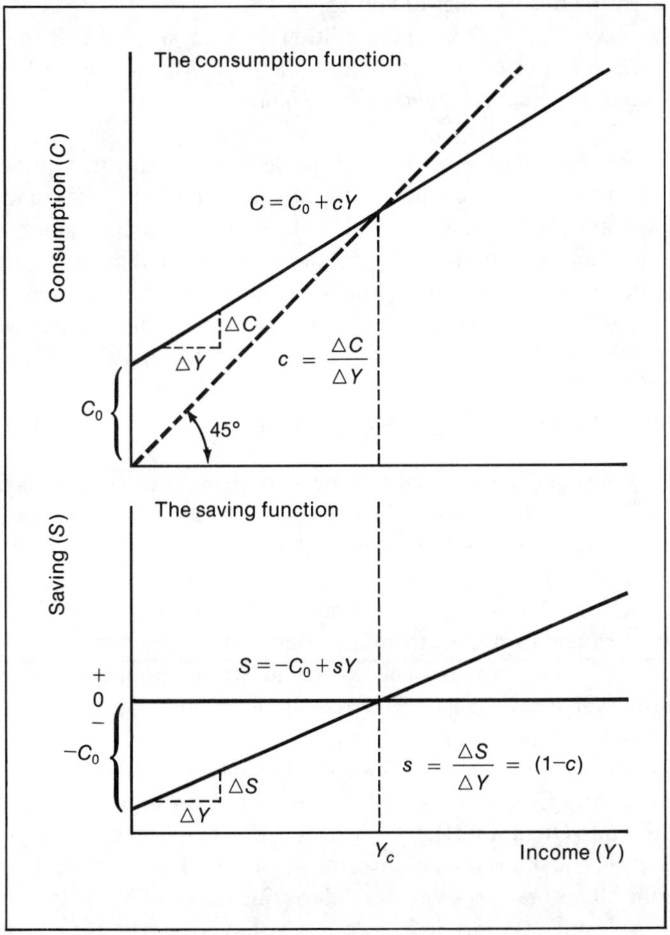

The consumption function

$$C = C_0 + cY$$

$$c = \frac{\Delta C}{\Delta Y}$$

45°

The saving function

$$S = -C_0 + sY$$

$$s = \frac{\Delta S}{\Delta Y} = (1-c)$$

Income (Y)

Equilibrium in the "Commodity Market"

An equilibrium level of income is one which does not have an inherent tendency to change. We know from equation 21.8 that aggregate income is the sum of consumption and investment expenditures, and we know from the above discussion that these two components are determined independently. Consumption depends on the level of income, and investment on the state of expectations and the level of interest rates. However, for *any given level* of income to be an equilibrium level, it must be true that the level of investment expenditures which businesses want to undertake is exactly equal to the level of savings which households want to make.

A moment's thought should convince you of the validity of this proposition. If businesses want to invest more than households want to save, at the given level of income, the sum of planned consumption and planned investment will have to exceed that level of income. Income will, of necessity, rise. The opposite is true if investment falls short of the planned savings of households.

Thus we have the equilibrium condition in what we will call the commodity market. *An equilibrium level of income is one at which the planned investment of businesses equals the planned saving of households.*

Indeterminacy of Equilibrium Income.   If the level of investment depends on the rate of interest, then there must be many different equilibrium levels of income which are consistent with any given investment and saving functions. Indeed, since there will be a different equilibrium level of income for each possible level of interest rates, we cannot identify a unique equilibrium level of income unless we have determined the level of interest rates. At best, we can draw a curve which shows all of the possible equilibrium levels of income, one for each level of interest rates. Such a curve is commonly called an *I-S* curve because it shows all of the combinations of interest rates and income levels at which planned Investment equals planned Saving.

Derivation of the I-S Curve.   One method of deriving the *I-S* curve is illustrated in Figure 21.4. This involves what is at first glance a rather complicated geometrical construction, a four-quandrant diagram, with the origin at the center (0) and with the scales on each axis increasing as you move away from the origin. (Note that this is in contrast to the usual four-quadrant diagram of elementary geometry in which movements downward and to the left from the origin have a negative sign.) However, it is basically a simple construct, designed to demonstrate graphically the necessity for equilibrium interest rates and income levels to simultaneously satisfy both the investment demand function and the savings function.

Equilibrium requires that $I = S$. For any selected interest rate, say r_1, the investment demand function in Quandrant II tells us the associated level of investment, i.e., I_1. Projecting this into Quadrant III, the saving function tells us the only level of income at which saving will equal this level of investment, i.e., Y_1. This is the equilibrium level of income for the interest rate, r_1. We can similarly find the equilibrium level of income for all other possible interest rates. In Figure 21.4 we have done this for two other levels of interest rates, r_2 and r_3.

The line in Quadrant IV is simply a geometrical device to project the equilibrium incomes to the base axis of Quadrant I. This line makes a 45° angle with each of the two axes, so that the distance $0 Y_1$ in Quadrant I is the same as the distance $0 Y_1$ in Quadrant III. The resulting curve in Quadrant I, then, identifies the equilibrium level of income associated with each possible level of interest rates. It is the *I-S* curve. At any point above the *I-S* curve, saving will exceed investment, and income will have to fall. Likewise at any point below the *I-S* curve investment will exceed saving, and income will have to rise (to demonstrate your understanding of the analysis, you should be able to explain why these statements are true). *The* I-S *curve is the locus of equilibrium points in the commodity market.*

Position and Shape of the I-S curve.   The *position* of the *I-S* curve depends on the positions of the investment demand and saving functions (and on the size of the marginal propensity to save). An increase in investment demand will shift the *I-S*

FIGURE 21-4   Derivation of the *I-S* curve

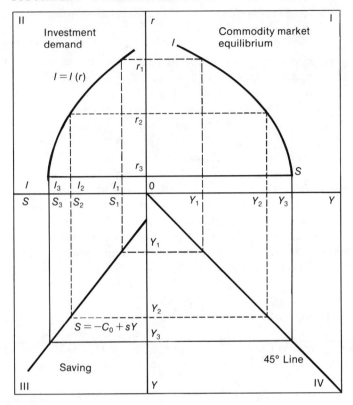

function to the right. By contrast, an increase in the demand for saving, in the sense of an increase in saving at every level of income, will shift the *I-S* function to the *left*.[9] You should be able to demonstrate these propositions.

Likewise, the shape of the *I-S* function depends on the *shapes* of the investment demand and the saving functions. If investment were very *inelastic* with respect to the rate of interest (if the *I* function were very steep), the *I-S* function would likewise be very inelastic. The increase in income for any given drop of the interest rate would be relatively small. Correspondingly, the smaller the marginal propensity to save (the closer the *S* function is to the axis), the more elastic will be the *I-S* function. The increase in income for any given drop of the interest rate will be relatively large.

Equilibrium in the "Money Market"

This analysis of equilibrium in the "commodity market" makes clear the central variable in the Keynesian model: the level of interest rates. Without specification of the level of interest rates, the equilibrium levels of income and employment are indeterminate. But what determines the level of interest rates?

We cannot answer this question until we have explored the financial side of the

Keynesian model. In particular, we have to establish the conditions for equilibrium between the demand for and supply of money. We call this equilibrium in the "money market."

The Demand for Money.   As we stated in Chapter 20, Keynes accepted the classical argument that the demand for money depended on the level of income, but argued that the level of interest rates was also a major factor in the demand function. Moreover, Keynes argued that at low interest rates the demand for money would become highly elastic with respect to the interest rate. Indeed, some of Keynes' followers hypothesized, there may be some low interest rate at which the demand for money becomes perfectly elastic — what has been called the "liquidity trap."

Indeterminacy of Equilibrium.   In what follows, we take the supply of money as given by the central bank. If the demand for money depends on both the level of income and the level of interest rates, equilibrium in the money market depends on finding *combinations* of income and interest rates at which the demand for money equals the supply of money. As in the commodity market, we cannot identify a unique equilibrium in the money market considered alone. The best we can do is to draw a curve similar in concept to the *I-S* curve, which describes all possible combinations of income and interest rates which will produce equilibrium in the money market. Such a curve is normally called an *L-M* curve.[10]

Derivation of the **L-M** *Curve.*   One method of deriving the *L-M* curve is presented in Figure 21.5. The graphic technique is similar to that employed in Figure 21.4.

For the purposes of this exercise, it is assumed that the Keynesian demand for money function takes a particular form: i.e., that the interest rate and income effects on the quantity of money demanded are independent of each other, and hence separable. That is, it is assumed that the impact of a given interest rate on the quantity of money demanded is the same regardless of the level of income, and vice versa. This makes it possible to draw a curve showing the interest rate effect (as in Quadrant II) without regard to the level of income,[11] and to add the interest rate effect directly to the income effect (Quadrant IV) to obtain the total quantity of money demanded. We also make the "classical" assumption that the relationship between income and the quantity of money demanded is linear. It must be emphasized that these are very special assumptions, adopted to make the graphic analysis manageable.

Consider Quadrant II first. If the interest rate is r_1, the quantity of money demanded because of the interest rate effect alone is M_1^*. The total supply of money made available by the central bank is M. Therefore, if equilibrium is to exist in the money market, in the sense that the demand for money equals the supply of money, the quantity of money demanded because of the level of income must be $M-M_1^*$. The problem is to identify the level of income which will produce this demand for money.

Quadrant III, labelled "The Supply of Money," is the only part of Figure 21.5 which should require special explanation. Again, this contains a special construct, making use of elementary geometry. The Line MM makes a 45° angle with each of the axes of Quadrant III. It joins up points indicating the total money supply as measured

FIGURE 21-5   Derivation of the *L-M* curve

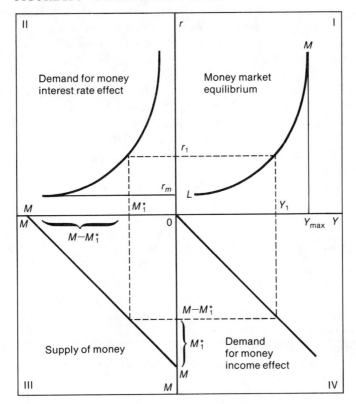

from the origin along each of these axes. It also serves to reflect the two components of the demand for money from the horizontal axis to the vertical axis of Quadrant III. Thus, because the line MM makes a 45° angle with the vertical axis, the distance from the point M to the point $(M\text{-}M_1^*)$, represents the quantity of money demanded because the level of interest rates is r_1. The remainder of the distance to the origin $O - (M\text{-}M_1^*)$, represents the quantity of money which has to be demanded because of the income effect if equilibrium is to prevail. From the curve in Quadrant IV, which shows the relationship between income alone and the quantity of money demanded, we can identify the level of income which will induce this demand for money. This level of income Y_1, is indicated on the horizontal axis of Quadrants I and IV. Y_1 is the equilibrium level of income, given the interest rate r_1.

This provides us with one point on the *L-M* curve. By the same process we could find other combinations of interest rates and income levels which would permit equilibrium in the money market. The end result would be a curve like that labelled *L-M* in Quadrant I.

In order to demonstrate your understanding of the construction of the *L-M* curve you should be able to show that any point above the *L-M* curve (i.e., to the left of the curve) implies a combination of income and interest rates at which the quantity of money demanded is less than the available money supply. It cannot be an equilibrium situation. Similarly, you should be able to demonstrate that any point below the *L-M* curve implies a combination of income and interest rates at which the quantity of money demanded exceeds the quantity supplied by the central bank. *The* L-M *curve describes the locus of equilibrium points in the money market.*

The* L-M *Curve and the Money Supply.   Note particularly, the shape of the *L-M* curve. It slopes upward to the right, with a virtually horizontal portion at very low interest rates, and a virtually vertical portion at high interest rates. The flat portion of the curve reflects the Keynesian assumption of a liquidity trap. It implies that there is a minimum level of interest rates. The vertical portion implies that there is a maximum level of income for any given money supply.

You should also remember that the *L-M* curve is drawn for a given money supply. If the money supply is increased (the M-M curve of Quadrant III shifts to the left), the *L-M* curves will shift to the right. The minimum interest rate may not change (why not?), but the maximum income level will increase. Similarly, a reduction in the money supply will shift the *L-M* curve to the left.

The* L-M *Curve and the Price Level.   Remember, the Keynesian model assumes a fixed price level. What happens, however, if the price level changes?

In Chapter 20 we noted two different effects of a change in the price level. We can use Figure 21.5 to illustrate the differences between them.

Consider first the impact of a *once-and-forever rise in the price level,* what we called in Chapter 20 the direct impact of a rise in prices. For this purpose we should interpret all of the curves in Figure 21.5 as showing the relationships between *real* magnitudes. That is, the money supply is the real money supply, and the income level is real income. Then, with the *nominal supply of money fixed* by the central bank, a rise in the general level of prices would imply a reduction in the real money supply. The curve *MM* in Quadrant III would shift to the right, implying higher interest rates and lower real incomes. Neither of the demands for money functions, *expressed in real terms,* would shift.

By contrast, consider the effects of a general *expectation of a continuing rise of the price level* in the future. The opportunity cost of holding money at any given level of market interest rates has increased by the expected rate of inflation. As a result, the demand curve in Quadrant II will shift to the right. That is, at any given market interest rate, a smaller quantity of money would be demanded. The end result would be a higher level of income and a higher level of interest rates. The mere expectation of inflation can have powerful economic effects. (What would be the impact of the expectation of deflation?)

Macroeconomic Equilibrium in the Keynesian System

Macroeconomic equilibrium requires equilibrium simultaneously in both the money market and the commodity market. If one of the markets is in disequilibrium, at least one of the variables in the system, income or the level of interest rates, will change, and when it changes the equilibrium will be disturbed in the other market. Therefore, full equilibrium requires a combination of income and interest rates which simultaneously satisfies both the *I-S* function and the *L-M* function, i.e., that combination identified by the intersection of the two curves. Thus, in the upper panel of Figure 21.6, the equilibrium income and interest levels are Y and r_1 respectively.

FIGURE 21-6   Monetary policy in the Keynesian model

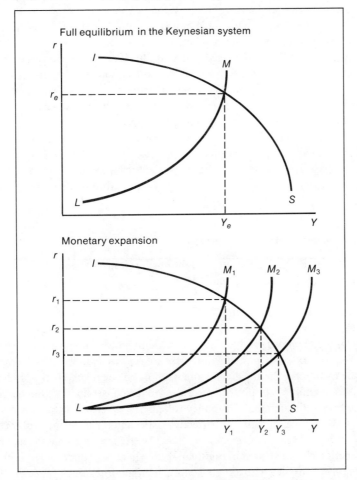

Monetary Policy in the Keynesian System

We are now in a position to use the analytical apparatus of the *I-S* and *L-M* curves to examine the effects of monetary policy in the Keynesian model. In particular, let us consider the effects of an expansion of the money supply by the central bank.

We start with the economic system in equilibrium at income level Y_1 in the bottom panel of Figure 21.6. An increase in the money supply shifts the *L-M* curve outward, from L-M_1 to L-M_2. The money market is now in disequilibrium. There is more money in the economy than is demanded at existing levels of income and interest rates.

Attempts of money holders to purchase bonds, the supply of which is given in the short run, will bid up the price of bonds and hence reduce interest rates. This is a key element in the Keynesian analysis. *It is the level of interest rates which provides the link between the financial sector and the real sector.*

As interest rates fall, the quantity of money demanded increases (Quadrant II, Figure 21.5) and the level of investment expenditures rises (Quadrant II, Figure 21.4). As Figure 21.4 shows, an increase in investment expenditure produces an increase in income. Again, remember that in this model the price level is fixed. The increase of income means an increase in employment.

The system will gravitate toward a new equilibrium, with the levels of income and interest rates at Y_2 and r_2 respectively on the bottom panel of Figure 21.6. A further increase of the money supply would produce a further adjustment in the same direction, perhaps to Y_3, r_3. Of course, a reduction of the money supply would shift the L-M function and hence the equilibrium point in the opposite direction.

The economics of the Keynesian model, with its assumption of a fixed price level, is the economics of an under-employment economy. The problem is to increase the level of income from a level which involves substantial unemployment, to one which implies full employment of the labor force. Is monetary policy always capable of achieving this objective?

The Effectiveness of Monetary Policy

The Keynesian analysis suggests two conditions for monetary policy to be effective as a regulator of aggregate demand and hence of economic activity: (1) the demand for money cannot be highly elastic, and (2) expenditures cannot be highly inelastic with respect to the level of interest rates.

Elasticity of the Demand for Money.   If the demand for money is highly elastic with respect to interest rates — implying that there are very close substitutes for money as an asset — the L-M curve for any given money supply will be relatively flat, and, in spite of variations in the money supply, interest rates will be constrained within narrow limits. In the extreme, if the demand for money were perfectly elastic with respect to interest rates, the L-M curve would also be perfectly elastic, and the monetary authorities could have no control over the level of interest rates. The effects of a highly elastic demand for money function are illustrated in Figure 21-7, in which L-M curves are derived for two different money supplies with a highly elastic demand for money function. The upper and lower limits to interest rates are indicated. (As an exercise, derive the L-M curve for a perfectly elastic demand for money, and demonstrate the effects of changing the money supply.)

A relatively flat L-M curve implies that a wide range of levels of income is consistent with any given money supply. The supply of money is not a significant constraint on aggregate demand and hence on economic activity. Indeed, the only significant determinant of aggregate demand is the *position* of the I-S curve, that is to say the marginal efficiency of capital (which, you will remember, depends heavily on business *expectations* regarding the economic outlook). This stands in stark contrast to the classical model, in which aggregate demand (MV) depends directly on the money supply.

FIGURE 21-7   The *L-M* curve with a highly interest-elastic demand for money

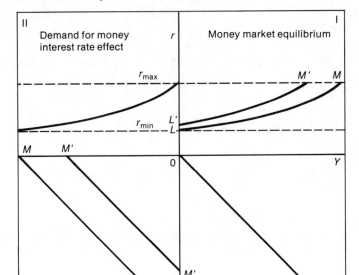

Velocity and Monetary Policy.   In the classical model, the velocity of circulation of money is assumed to be given as its long-run equilibrium value. As we saw in Figure 21-1, historically, velocity has been far from constant. The analysis of Figure 21-7 illustrates, indirectly, a Keynesian explanation for the observed fluctuations in velocity. To the extent that the demand for money is interest elastic, variations in aggregate demand will not be proportional to variations in the money supply. Not only will velocity change, but, contrary to the classical quantity theory argument, these *variations in velocity are induced by changes in the money supply*. Indeed, they serve to offset at least part of the impact of monetary policy, since velocity falls as the money supply expands, and rises as the money supply contracts. In the extreme case of a perfectly elastic demand for money, the money supply can change with no effect on income. In these circumstances, according to the Keynesian model, *there is no limit to the velocity of money*. Indeed, the very concept of velocity is meaningless as an analytical tool.[12]

The Classical Model in a Keynesian Framework.   It is also possible to obtain the classical result within the Keynesian framework. If the demand for money function is perfectly inelastic with respect to the level of interest rates, so that the *L-M* curve is vertical, aggregate demand cannot change without a change in the money supply. Indeed, with some interest elasticity of the *I-S* function, any change in aggregate demand would be proportional to the change in the money supply. (We have not illustrated this case; however, the student can readily verify the statement. How do interest rates behave given an increase in the money supply according to this interpretation of the classical model?)

The Interest Elasticity of Investment.   The second factor which qualifies the effectiveness of monetary policy as a regulator of aggregate demand, within the Keynesian framework, is the interest elasticity of expenditures. If expenditures are very insensitive to changes in the level of interest rates, the I-S curve will be very steep. This is illustrated in Figure 21-8. Because of the steepness of the I-S curve, an increase in the money supply, shifting the L-M curve from L-M_1 to L-M_2, lowers the level of interest rates, but does not significantly increase the level of investment or income.

Again, there will be a change in velocity. If the increase in the money supply is not accompanied by an increase in income, by definition velocity falls. The converse would be true for a reduction in the money supply in the same range of the I-S curve, for example, a shift of the L-M curve from L-M_2 to L-M_1.

Clearly, the interest elasticity of expenditures is crucial consideration in assessing the efficacy of monetary policy.

FIGURE 21-8   Monetary policy with an interest-inelastic I-S curve

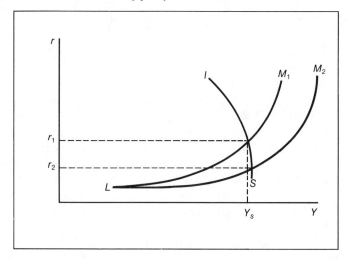

The Fiscal Policy Alternative

An important conclusion of our analysis to this point is that there is a significant risk that monetary policy will not be effective as a regulator of economic activity. Is there an alternative? Historically, one of the important results of the Keynesian monetary analysis was to thrust *fiscal policy* to the fore as the primary regulator of economic activity. The economics of fiscal policy is subject enough for a book in itself. However, because some of the recent controversies in monetary economics relate to the relative effectiveness of monetary and fiscal actions, it is important that we review the rudiments of the Keynesian analysis of fiscal policy.

The Nature of Fiscal Policy.   By fiscal policy we mean decisions with respect to the levels of revenues and expenditures of the government sector of the economy. It is argued that by varying government expenditures or the level of taxation (or both) the government can have a direct and powerful impact on aggregate demand, and hence, in the short-run (i.e., with a given price level), on production and employment.

Government Expenditures and Aggregate Demand.   The impact on aggregate demand of changes in the level of government expenditures on goods and services should be obvious from the aggregate demand equation (21.5). If the government increases its expenditures without doing anything which would induce private spenders to reduce their expenditures (whether consumption, investment or exports), then aggregate demand *must* increase. Indeed, as the early Keynesians emphasized, the resulting increase of income and output might well induce further increases of private expenditures, particularly consumption expenditures which are assumed to depend directly on income, thus reinforcing the initial increase of aggregate demand. This is the familiar "multiplier" process, noted earlier in discussing the shape of the *I-S* function. A reduction of government expenditures on goods and services would have the opposite effect, i.e., it would reduce the levels of aggregate demand, production, and employment.

Taxes, Transfer Payments, and Aggregate Demand.   The impact on aggregate demand of changes in the level of taxation is only slightly more complicated. Taxes do not appear directly in the aggregate demand equation, but changes in tax rates should have an indirect effect on aggregate demand because of their impact on expenditures by private spenders (households and firms). Taxes limit the share of earned income which private spenders have available to support their expenditures. A reduction of tax rates thus increases the funds available for other purposes and hence should stimulate private spending. By contrast, an increase in tax rates restricts the funds available in the private sector, and hence should restrict private spending.

In this context it is also important to distinguish between government expenditures on goods and services and government transfer payments. Transfer payments are typified by family allowances or unemployment compensation. They are payments by the government which are not payments for goods or services rendered to the government. In this sense they are negative taxes. They do not add directly to the aggregate demand for productive services, but they do add to the disposable incomes of private spenders and hence should stimulate private demands for goods and services. In the rest of our analysis we will not consider transfer payments explicitly. Rather we will assume that they are deducted from taxes to obtain "net taxes."

Government Expenditure and Tax Functions.   There is an important asymmetry in the treatment of government expenditures and tax revenues as instruments of stabilization policy in the Keynesian model.

It is usually assumed that the *level* of government expenditures on goods and services is a policy variable with respect to which decisions can be made independently of government tax revenues and independently of such other economic variables as the level of income or the level of interest rates. This is not to deny that many categories of government expenditures are substantially affected by economic developments. The government is not a monolithic sector, in which a single set of consistent decisions is made, controlling all expenditures at all levels of government in all parts of the country. Canada is, after all, a federal state. However, it is not necessary for all government expenditures to be a policy instrument. All that is necessary is that the central government have the *potential* to control the *total* of government expenditures — perhaps partly by varying its own expenditures on goods and services, and perhaps partly by influencing expenditures at other levels of government through intergovernmental transfers (grants-in-aid, etc.).

FIGURE 21-9 The government sector: exenpenditure, tax, and budget functions

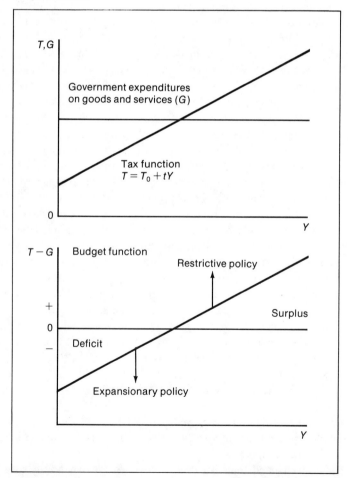

Therefore, in drawing the government expenditure function as a horizontal line in Figure 21-9 we are assuming that the central government has the potential to control the level of aggregate government expenditures on goods and services as an instrument of fiscal policy.[13]

By contrast, it is generally assumed that the instrument of government policy is not the level of tax revenues but the *rate* of taxation of national income, i.e., that the government establishes a schedule of tax rates as a matter of policy, with the level of tax revenues then depending on variations in the level of income.

The relationship between tax collections and income can be quite complex. It depends partly on the mix of taxes established by the government (e.g., the relative importance of sales and excise taxes, property taxes, corporation income taxes, personal income taxes, etc.,) on changes in the composition of economic activity and income (e.g., relative changes in retail sales, or in corporation profits) and partly on the progression of tax rates with income in the personal income tax. For simplicity, we have assumed a familiar linear tax function in Figure 21-9, of the form:

$$T = T_0 + tY \tag{21.15}$$

where T = tax collections and Y = gross national product. The coefficient t is a constant marginal tax rate, the slope of the tax function in Figure 21-9.

A particular fiscal policy, then, implies a decision on both the level of government expenditures and the position and shape of the tax function.

Budgetary Surpluses and Deficits.   Figure 21-9 summarizes our assumptions about the government sector, including the balance on the government's budget (lower panel). It is important to note that active use of fiscal measures for economic stabilization implies that the government cannot be concerned with maintaining an exact balance of expenditures and tax revenues. As the lower panel of Figure 21-9 demonstrates, the balance on the government's budget for any given fiscal policy (level of expenditures and tax function) depends on the level of income. At high levels of income, high tax revenues will produce a budget surplus. At low levels of income, low tax revenues will produce a budget deficit. An expansionary policy can be implemented either by increasing government expenditures or by shifting the tax function downwards. The effect is to increase the budget deficit or decrease the budget surplus at each level of national income, or, alternatively, to increase the level of income at which the government's budget is balanced. A restrictive policy can be implemented either by reducing government expenditures or by shifting the tax function upward. The effect is to reduce the budget deficit or increase the surplus at each level of national income, or, alternatively, to reduce the level of national income at which the government's budget is balanced.

In this sense, *the size of the surplus or deficit in the government budget is the central consideration in fiscal policy.* The strong functional relationship between the balance on the government's budget and the level of national income should be noted. This means that the government sector tends to be an automatic stabilizer of economic aggregate demand. A decline in aggregate demand from private sources tends to be cushioned by the combination of stable government expenditures and declining tax collections, and hence by the emergence of a deficit in the government's budget.

Similarly, an upsurge of aggregate demand tends to be restrained the full employment deficit or surplus.

The sensitivity of the balance on the government's budget to changes in the level of national income also means that the actual magnitude of the budget deficit or surplus is not an adequate measure of the degree of ease or restrictiveness in fiscal policy. Since a deficit, for example, may emerge from a drop in national income with a given set to fiscal policy (i.e., given government expenditures, given tax schedules), it cannot be evidence of an expansionary policy. An expansionary policy would require a larger deficit than that which would emerge automatically as a result of the level of aggregate demand and income. It is frequently argued that a suitable summary measure of the degree of ease or restrictiveness of fiscal policy is the estimated balance on the budget with present expenditures and tax schedules if the economy were at full employment. This concept is called the full employment deficit or surplus.[14]

The Government Sector and the* I-S *Function. To carry through with the analytical technique which we developed earlier, we must introduce a government sector into the *I-S/L-M* model. The important result of doing this is to change the shape of the *I-S* curve. This is illustrated in Figure 21.10.

In constructing Figure 21.10 we have simply taken government expenditure and tax functions, such as those discussed above, and superimposed them on the basic *I-S*

FIGURE 21-10   Derivation of the *I-S* curve with a government sector

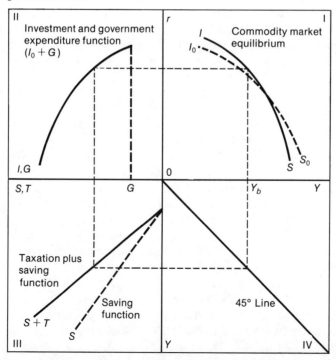

model of the commodity market developed in Figure 21-4. In Quadrant II of Figure 21-10 we have added a fixed amount of government expenditures (G) to the original investment demand function. The result is a new investment and government expenditure function ($I + G$) which lies to the left of the original investment demand function. In Quadrant III, the tax function has been added to the savings function to obtain a new tax-plus-savings function.[15] *The new equilibrium condition is that the level of investment plus government expenditures must equal the level of tax collections plus savings* (you should be able to demonstrate why this is the new equilibrium condition). In Quadrant IV we have the familiar 45° line, which reflects the equilibrium income levels to the base axis in Quadrant I. The *I-S* curve, as before, shows those combinations of interest rates and income levels at which equilibrium can be achieved in the commodity market, taking account of both government expenditures and taxes.

As a reference base, we have also plotted the original *I-S* curve from Figure 21-4 in Quadrant I of Figure 21-10 (the line $I_0 - S_0$). The change in shape as a result of the introduction of the government sector should be obvious. At relatively low levels of income, the new *I-S* curve lies outside the old curve. Because of the assumed shape of the tax function, the income-generating effects of the given level of government expenditures outweigh the restrictive effects of taxation. As a result, the effect of government fiscal operations is to raise the equilibrium level of income associated with each possible level of interest rates in this range.

As we move down the *I-S* curve, the restrictive effects of increasing tax revenues eventually offset and overwhelm the expansionary effects of the given level of government expenditures (this phenomenon has come to be known as "fiscal drag"). At relatively high levels of income, the new *I-S* curve lies inside the old curve. In this range, the effect of government fiscal operations is to lower the equilibrium level of income associated with each possible level of interest rates.

The basic conclusion, then, is that the introduction of the government sector makes the *I-S* curve steeper. The equilibrium level of income is less sensitive to changes in interest rates, or, in other words, to shifts in the *L-M* curve.

The level of income at which the government sector's budget is balanced (tax collections = government expenditures) is indicated at Y_b by the broken line. It is interesting to note that at this level of income, the new *I-S* curve lies outside the old. A balanced budget in the government sector is not neutral with respect to the level of income. It has a slight net expansionary effect.[16]

Fiscal Policy. In this framework, fiscal policy — whether implemented through government expenditures or through tax rates — involves a deliberate shift of the *I-S* function. Figure 21-11 illustrates the impact of a restrictive fiscal policy implemented through an increase of tax rates. In Quadrant III, the original tax-plus-savings function (broken line, $T_0 + S$) has been shifted to the left, with an increased slope. The effect is to shift the *I-S* function inward (from $I_0 - S_0$), and to make it steeper. At each possible level of interest rates, the equilibrium level of income has decreased.

Figure 21-12 illustrates an expansionary fiscal policy implemented through an increase of government expenditures. The investment-plus-government-expenditures function in Quadrant I has been shifted to the left by the amount of the increased expenditures, with the result that the *I-S* curve is shifted outward. At each possible level of interest rates, the equilibrium level of income has increased.

FIGURE 21-11   Restrictive fiscal policy and the *I-S* curve: increase in tax rate

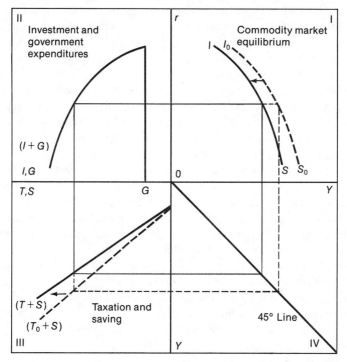

The possibilities for an expansionary fiscal policy in a situation in which monetary policy would be ineffective, a highly elastic *L-M* curve, as illustrated in Figure 21-13. By shifting the *I-S* function, fiscal policy can increase the level of aggregate demand even though interest rates are held stable. Of course, the same conclusion applies to the case in which investment expenditures are sufficiently insensitive to interest rates to make monetary expansion ineffective. Fiscal policy can, nonetheless, shift the *I-S* function, as in Figure 21-13.

Coordination of Monetary and Fiscal Policies.   Normally, both monetary and fiscal policies, used independently, will have some impact on aggregate demand. *Coordinated* monetary and fiscal actions will have an even more powerful impact on aggregate demand than either instrument used (in the same degree) independently. This point is illustrated in Figure 21-14. Starting with the initial curves. I_0-S_0 and L_0-M_0 and with the initial equilibrium level of national income, Y_0 we can trace through the independent effects of monetary expansion (shifting the *L-M* curve to L_1-M_1) and fiscal expansion (shifting the *I-S* curve to I_1-S_1). Monetary expansion alone will raise income from Y_0 to Y_m. Fiscal expansion alone will raise income from Y_0 to Y_f. The combination of the same monetary expansion and the same fiscal expansion, however, will raise income to Y_{m+f}. This is the traditional argument for the coordination of monetary and fiscal

FIGURE 21-12   Expansionary fiscal policy and the *I-S* curve:
increase in government expenditures on goods and services

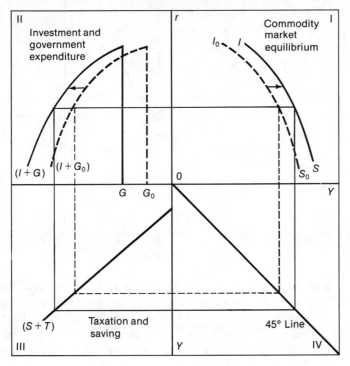

FIGURE 21-13   Fiscal policy when monetary policy is ineffective

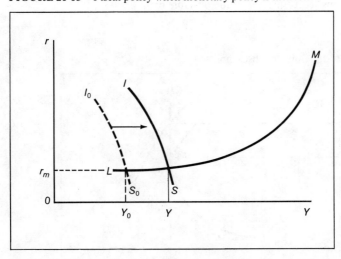

policies. By parallel analysis, you should be able to show how conflicting monetary and
fiscal policies can neutralize each other.

FIGURE 21-14   Coordinated monetary and fiscal policies

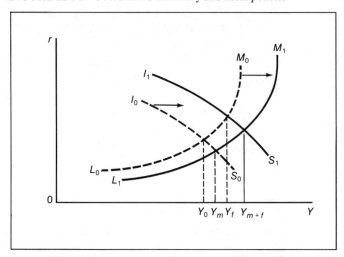

Impotent Fiscal Policy.   There is one other situation which merits brief attention. The Keynesian model suggests one case in which fiscal policy would be ineffective, illustrated in Figure 21-15. In this case, fiscal expansion is incapable of raising the level of national income, output and employment, because at the existing level of income, the L-M curve is perfectly inelastic with respect to the level of interest rates. An expansionary fiscal policy could only drive up the interest rate until private investment expenditures are reduced sufficiently to make room for the additional government expenditures (or for the additional consumption made possible by tax cuts).

FIGURE 21-15   Impotent fiscal policy

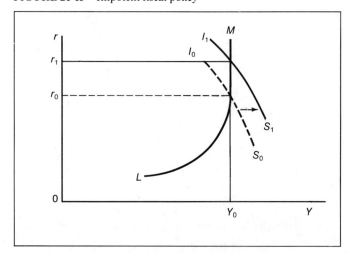

We should recognize Figure 21-15 from our earlier discussion. It is simply the classical case. The demand for money has no interest elasticity and, as a result, money is perfectly complementary to aggregate economic activity. Any increase in income and output *requires* an increase in the money supply.

In general, neither of the extreme cases seems likely to be a common occurrence. However, the classical case does contain an important lesson. Fiscal expansion may be largely reflected in interest rates rather than income growth, unless it is supported by appropriate monetary policies.

Financing the Deficit.   In our discussion of fiscal policy, we have studiously avoided discussing the methods to be used to finance any government budgetary deficit (or alternatively, to discuss what would be done with a budgetary surplus). But as we have seen, an expansionary fiscal policy implies a budgetary deficit, an excess of government expenditures over revenues, and that deficit must somehow be financed. Our elementary accounting identities tell us that the net government debt, in one form or another, must expand. Correspondingly, a restrictive fiscal policy implies a surplus in the government's budget, an excess of revenues over expenditures. The net government debt must contract. We have considered only the impact of government revenues and expenditures on aggregate demand. Must we not also take into account the separate effects of changes in the government debt outstanding? If so, will this not seriously alter our basic conclusions on the impact of fiscal policy?

Such an argument has been advanced vigorously by many critics of the Keynesian analysis, and it has been given the label of "the crowding out effect."[17] In particular, it has been argued that used independently (i.e., without coordinated monetary policy), fiscal policy is almost always ineffective. The financing of a government deficit will absorb funds which would otherwise be available to finance the investment expenditures of firms. Private expenditures will be depressed sufficiently to offset the impact of increased government expenditures or of reduced taxation. Correspondingly, a government surplus, involving the retirement of government debt, will indirectly provide funds to finance private expenditures, and these expenditures will expand sufficiently to offset the restrictive effects of reduced government expenditures or increased taxation.

Consider the case of an expansionary fiscal policy, involving a budgetary deficit. The government must sell bonds to finance the deficit, and private assetholders must be persuaded to purchase these bonds. Will it not require higher interest rates on government bonds to induce private assetholders to purchase them, and will not interest rates on other bonds rise correspondingly as the private assetholders sell them to make room for more government bonds? And will not the higher interest rates in turn restrict private spending?

The Keynesian answer is that this argument assumes that private asset portfolios are fixed in size. To the contrary, it is argued, an expansionary fiscal policy will generate additional income, which will in turn induce more saving, thus providing the required additional demand for government bonds to be held as financial assets. Remember the earlier discussion of the consumption function and the saving function. A rise in income implies higher levels of *both* consumption and saving. Remember, also, one of the lessons of Chapter 4: saving is a demand for wealth and, in this context, a demand for financial instruments. As income and savings expand, private asset portfolios expand, thus creating the demand for the bonds which the government must issue in order to finance its deficit.[18] Indeed, one way to state the condition for a new equilibrium to be established in the commodity market is that income must rise to the point at which sufficient savings are forthcoming to absorb the increases in the government debt.

In other words, in the pure Keynesian case, the problem of financing the deficit is not a limitation on the effectiveness of fiscal policy. If a constraint arises, it is because assetholders demand to hold part of their expanding asset portfolios in the form of the one asset which is in absolutely limited supply, i.e., money, and the restriction will be greater the less willing are the assetholders to substitute other financial assets for money. That is, it will be the interest elasticity of the demand for money function and hence the L-M function which limits the effectiveness of fiscal policy in raising aggregate demand and income. We are right back where we started. Taking into account the problem of financing the government's deficit does not suggest any new conclusions; it simply provides a different perspective on the same analysis.[19]

Exactly the same analysis applies in reverse to the problem of disposing of the surplus created by a restrictive fiscal policy. We will leave it to you to trace through the analysis yourself.

Conclusions.   Keynesian theory suggests that fiscal policy is a powerful instrument for economic stabilization even when monetary policy is rendered impotent by a liquidity trap or the insensitivity of private expenditures to monetary variables. In general, the analysis suggests that monetary and fiscal measures should be used in conjunction with each other. Coordinated monetary and fiscal policies are much more powerful than either policy used alone.[20]

UNEMPLOYMENT AND THE PRICE LEVEL

As we have developed the analysis, both the classical quantity theory and the Keynesian theory can be considered, in the first instance, to be theories of the impact of monetary policy on aggregate demand for goods and services. According to the quantity theory, the impact is direct and certain — in the long run. According to the Keynesian theory, the impact is indirect and uncertain — in the short run. The quantity theory of aggregate demand becomes a theory of the determination of the price level because of an assumption about the behavior of output and employment. The presumed tendency of the economy to full employment suggests that the only feasible objective of monetary policy is the price level, and that stability of the price level can be achieved simply by permitting the money supply to grow at the long-run equilibrium growth rate of aggregate output. There is no role for short-term stabilization policies, and no need for instruments of policy other than monetary policy. The Keynesian theory of aggregate demand becomes a theory of the determination of aggregate output and employment because of an assumption about the behavior of the price level. Because the economy does not tend to full employment over the relevant short run, there is an important role for active management of aggregate demand. In this activity, however, monetary policy may not be sufficient. Short-term stabilization policies may require coordinated use of both fiscal and monetary policies.

Clearly, the relative behavior of output and employment on the one hand and the price level on the other is at the essence of the difference between the two major analytical traditions. Does the economy tend to full employment? How long is the long run? Is the price level a monetary phenomenon? Or is the price level determined independently of the money supply? How can we explain the coexistence of rapid inflation and historically high levels of unemployment, a phenomenon which emerged in the mid-1970s in apparent defiance of both extreme models? Is there a role for the active use of monetary policy for the short-term management of aggregate demand? Or should we refrain from all attempts at short-term stabilization policy, gearing monetary growth to a long-term objective?

These are questions which perplex the economics profession. They are at the roots of controversies over the impact and formulation of monetary policy which divide the profession into intellectually warring camps. The issues are unsettled. However, following our development of the two polar cases of the classical quantity theory and the classical Keynesian theory, these are issues to which we must turn.

Trade-off Theory

The Phillips Curve.   In the 1950s and 1960s, the analysis of the relationship between the level of employment and the rate of change of the price level was a major preoccupation of macroeconomists. Primarily on the basis of the pioneering research of a New Zealand economist, A.W. Phillips, it was argued that there is a strong and historically rather stable *negative relationship* between the *level* of unemployment (measured as a percentage of the labor force) and the *rate of change* of wage rates.[21] At low levels of unemployment, wage rates will increase rapidly. At higher levels of unemployment the rate of increase of wage rates will be smaller. At some level of unemployment wage rates will increase at approximately the long-run rate of increase in labor productivity. At some high level of unemployment, wage rates might be stable, and at a very high level of unemployment they might actually fall.

Because of the importance of wage rates in determining the costs of production of goods and services, the Phillips curve predicts a similar negative relationship between the level of unemployment and the rate of change of the general price level. Low levels of unemployment will be associated with rapid inflation; higher levels of unemployment with lower rates of inflation; and at some level of unemployment the general level of prices will be stable. Some economists defined this level of unemployment as "full employment." At higher levels of unemployment the price level will fall.

The derived relationship between the level of unemployment and the rate of change in the price level thus has the same general shape as the Phillips curve. However, there is one significant difference. The level of unemployment at which the price level will be stable is generally much lower than the level of unemployment at which wage rates will be stable. The major reason for this difference is the growth of labor productivity (output per work-hour), largely as a result of long-term developments in the economy (capital formation and technical change). To the extent that labor productivity is increasing, wage rates can also grow without increasing costs of production and hence without putting upward pressures on the price level.

Statistical studies of the Phillips curve were undertaken for many countries over various time periods, with broadly similar results. Although there were some skeptics, the Phillips curve became a basic building block of stabilization policy. Indeed, in 1970 one leading economist described the concept as "...the only significant contribution...to the theory of economic policy...to emerge from post-Keynesian theorizing."[22]

Widely cited 1967 estimates of the relationship between unemployment and the rate of change in wage rates (the Phillips curve) and between unemployment and the rate of change in the consumer price index (a measure of the general price level) for Canada for the years 1953-67, based on a study done at the University of Western Ontario for the Economic Council of Canada, are presented in Figure 21-16.[23] Take particular note of the shapes of the two curves. Both fall to the right, but the price level curve is significantly steeper. The study suggests that stability of the price level could be achieved with unemployment in the neighborhood of 5% of the labor force. At this level of unemployment, wage rates would be increasing at approximately the long-run rate of growth of productivity (about 3.2% at that time). At higher levels of unemployment, prices would fall somewhat although wage rates would still increase (but at less than the rate of growth of productivity).

The Phillips Curve and Stabilization Policy.   The significance of the Phillips curve for stabilization policy should be obvious. On a theoretical level, it seemed to complete the Keynesian model. It provided a plausible and empirically based assumption about the behavior of wages and prices which suggested the conditions under which an increase in aggregate demand would increase employment and the conditions under which it would produce inflation.

On a practical level, the Phillips curve implied a *constraint* on stabilization policy. The management of aggregate demand through monetary and fiscal policies would have effects on *both* the price level and employment. Without additional policy instruments capable of shifting the Phillips curve, the government could not decide on price level and employment objectives separately. They had to think in terms of *combinations* of objectives. Thus, the Phillips curve seemed to offer the policy makers a well defined *menu of policy options.* Low levels of unemployment could be attained, but only at the cost of predictable higher rates of inflation. The Phillips curve implied that there was a well defined *trade-off* between inflation and unemployment, and the government seemed free to choose any position on the trade-off function which it preferred. Indeed, some research was undertaken in the attempt to quantify the relative social costs of inflation and unemployment, information which would help governments make better informed choices. Some attention was also given to measures which might shift the Phillips curve, or change its shape, improving the trade-offs facing the government. Some economists attempted to justify wage and price controls on these grounds, and some argued that "supply policies," designed to improve the competitiveness of markets in the economy, would be a valuable supplement to monetary and fiscal policies.[24]

FIGURE 21-16   1967 estimates of the unemployment-price level tradeoffs in the Canadian economy

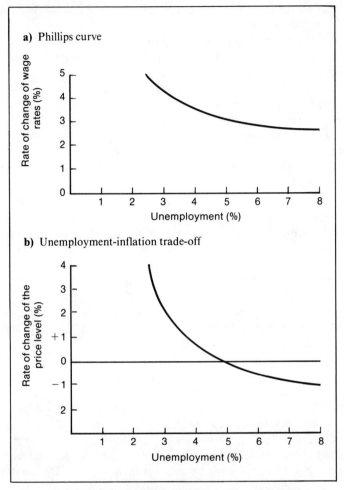

Source: R.G. Bodkin, E.P. Bond, G.L. Reuber, T.R. Robinson, *Price Stability and High Employment: The Options for Canadian Economic Policy.* (Ottawa: Economic Council of Canada, Special Study No. 5, 1967).

The Theory of the Phillips Curve.   It is one thing to discover the Phillips curve as an empirical regularity in the historical statistics of the economy; it is another thing to regard it as a basis for the formulation of economic policy. If we are going to base policy on the Phillips curve, we want to be sure that it is not just a historical accident, a result of peculiar historical circumstances which may disappear when we try to exploit the curve for policy purposes. We must understand why it exists, and why it has the shape suggested by the data. That is, we require a *theory* of the Phillips curve. The Phillips curve concept proved to be seriously vulnerable on this level. While the concept had some empirical plausibility, attempts to develop a theoretical explanation for the phenomenon which were consistent with other aspects of the theory of markets and prices were generally unsatisfactory. Eventually, even the empirical plausibility of the concept was called into question.

The theory of markets and prices developed in most elementary books on economics is *equilibrium theory*. It asks the question: At what price will the quantity demanded equal the quantity supplied? Or, What is the new equilibrium price, given, a change in demand or a change in supply? Little attention is paid to the process by which the price adjusts or to the time taken in the adjustment. The Phillips curve, by contrast, is concerned with markets which are not in equilibrium, when demand does not equal supply. In this sense the theory of the Phillips curve is *disequilibrium theory*. It is a theory of the adjustment of prices — in this case wage rates — in the face of *excess* demand or *excess* supply, in markets which are not perfectly competitive.[25]

Observers of labor markets note that wage rates are not highly flexible. They are established through a process of collective bargaining, and are subject to contracts of varying length. Thus, underlying the market is a pricing process which occurs at discrete intervals, not continuously. This does not mean that effective wage rates cannot change between contract dates. Contracts are sometimes opened for re-negotiation, special bonuses are sometimes permitted, workers may be reclassified into different wage categories (even though the tasks performed do not change), and variable amounts of overtime work at premium wage rates will introduce variability into hourly earnings even with a fixed scale of wage rates. The essential point is, however, that the institutions of the market make the wage rate "sticky." It does not adjust quickly or smoothly in the face of excess demand or excess supply in the labor market. As Keynesian theory suggests, a change of demand is likely to be reflected initially in a change in the level of employment rather than in a change of the wage rate.

However, this does not mean that wage rates are established arbitrarily, or that they do not respond to market forces. Rather, it is argued that the adjustment of wage rates to new market conditions takes time, and that the *speed of the adjustment* is a variable which also depends on market conditions. Very strong excess demand for labor will induce rapid wage rate increases. Modest excess demand will induce slow wage adjustments. Thus, it is argued, the rate of change in the wage rate depends on the degree of excess demand (+ or −) in labor markets.

In this argument, the level of unemployment is taken as a measure of the degree of excess demand in labor markets in the aggregate. However, the relationship between the level of unemployment and the level of excess demand is not simple and direct. There is always some "frictional" unemployment in the economy — workers who are between jobs, having terminated one job (for one reason or another) and searching for another suitable position. Government policies, such as unemployment insurance, may increase the level of such unemployment, facilitating workers to take longer in searching for new jobs. There is also always some "structural" unemployment — a mismatch between the skills required for vacant positions or the locations of these positions and the skills and locations of unemployed workers. Again, government policies may aggravate such unemployment, reducing incentives to move or to retrain. Minimum wage laws may also create a group of unemployed workers who are, in a sense, "unemployable" because the value of their marginal product is less than the minimum wage.

An increase in aggregate demand, in the face of substantial unemployment, may reduce unemployment, as in the Keynesian model. However, as unemployment falls, total unemployment is increasingly frictional or structural in nature. Further attempts to reduce unemployment are, in effect, attempts to use aggregate demand as an instrument to speed up adjustments in the labor markets. The result is strong upward pressure on wage rates, as employers attempt to bribe workers to change jobs, to move, or to move more quickly. The level of unemployment at which the increase in wage rates is approximately equal to the rate of productivity advances (and hence the level at which there will be no upward pressure on costs and prices) will not be zero. Indeed, in the University of Western Ontario study referred to above, price stability was found to require 5% unemployment.

The Modern Quantity Theory

In broad outline, this is the theoretical explanation for the Phillips curve and the associated trade-off theory of stabilization policy. It is based on a simple *ad hoc* characterization of the rate of adjustment of wage rates in relation to the strength of excess aggregate demand. The late 1960s saw two very powerful theoretical attacks on this analysis, by E.S. Phelps and M. Friedman.[26] Although somewhat different in presentation, both critiques pointed to the same essential flaws in the theory of the Phillips curve, and came to the same conclusion that the Phillips curve is a temporary illusion. If used as the basis for a high employment policy — a policy of keeping the rate of unemployment below what Friedman calls the *natural rate of unemployment* — the curve will shift upward to the right so that the desired rate of unemployment can only be maintained with high and probably accelerating inflation.

Nominal and Real Wages.   To explore the Phelps-Friedman analysis, we again require what should now be a familiar distinction between *nominal* and *real* magnitudes, in this case between a *nominal wage* and a *real wage*. The former, of course, is simply the wage paid to labor per unit of time, expressed in dollars and cents of *current purchasing power*. The latter is the nominal wage adjusted for changes in the level of prices, the nominal wage expressed in dollars and cents of *constant purchasing power*. The Phillips curve is a proposition about the adjustment of *nominal* wages. However, as Phelps and Friedman emphasize, all of the participants in the labor market (employers and workers) are concerned with *real* wages. It is not sufficient to focus directly on nominal wages, as in the Phillips curve. It is also necessary to consider the impact of a change in the nominal wage rate and the associated change in prices on the real wage rate if we are to understand the adjustment of the labor market to a change in aggregate demand.[27]

For workers, the real wage directly affects their economic well-being, their command over goods and services. Higher real wage rates will normally elicit a larger supply of labor, and vice versa. While the real wage rate will be directly affected by the behavior of prices, workers cannot control prices. Bargaining for increases in nominal wages in excess of increases in the price level is their only method of increasing the real wage rate.

For firms, the real wage rate directly affects the optimum levels of employment and production. Given the production function, and hence the marginal productivity of the labor function, the higher the real wage the lower the level of employment offered, and vice versa. The real wage, therefore, is important to the maximization of profits. However, to many firms, prices are also an instrument for profit maximization. The real wage can be lowered if prices can be increased by more than the negotiated increase in the nominal wage.

The Shifting Phillips Curve: Inflation.   The heavy solid line *PP* in Figure 21-17 is a typical Phillips curve. In order to sketch the analysis of the inflationary case we can start with the economy resting at the point *N*, at which the rate of change in the nominal wage rate, W^*, is approximately equal to the rate of productivity advance, leaving the price level constant. The level of unemployment associated with price level stability, then, is U^*.

FIGURE 21-17   The shifting Phillips curve: inflation

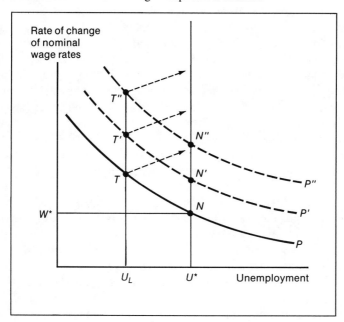

Suppose, however, that the government considers this level of unemployment to be excessive, and sets as a target U_L in full recognition that this level of unemployment implies some inflation. Monetary expansion is used to shift the *LM* curve, increase aggregate demand, and move the economy to the left along the Phillips curve, *PP*, toward point *T*.

For firms to offer more employment, prices must rise more rapidly than nominal wages. The real wage rate must fall. (In this connection note again the relative shapes of the curves in Figure 21-16.) Initially, workers may respond to the higher nominal wage rate as though it involved a higher real wage rate. That is, they may respond as though they expected the existing level of prices to remain stable — as though they held what have been called *static expectations* about the price level. The economy will move along the static Phillips curve, *PP*, toward point *T*. Eventually, however, workers will recognize that the real wage is falling, and they will respond with demands for higher nominal wages in order to maintain the real wage. As a result, the given level of unemployment, U_L, will be associated with a higher rate of increase of nominal wages than that predicted by the original Phillips curve. The Phillips curve will have shifted to the right, perhaps to *P'P'*. There will be an associated increase in the rate of inflation of the general price level.

With a given rate of growth of the nominal money supply, a higher rate of inflation means a slower rate of growth of the *real* money supply. Money will be tighter, and eventually aggregate demand and employment will fall. The unemployment rate will have a tendency to increase from U_L in the direction of U^* (a tendency represented by the dotted arrow). If the government persists in its policy of keeping the unemployment rate at U_L, it must repeat the process. That is, it must engage in further monetary expansion, eventually producing more inflation, and again shifting the Phillips curve, perhaps to *P"P"*. And so on. Eventually, workers experiencing continuing inflation will begin to expect it, and will demand wage rate increases in *anticipation of future inflation*. These expectations of inflation will accelerate the shifting of the Phillips curve. In the extreme, it may be difficult to keep the unemployment rate below the natural rate, in which case the Phillips curve has become vertical.

Thus, attempts by the government to maintain a low rate of unemployment will simply result in high, perhaps accelerating, inflation, as they engage in accelerating monetary expansion in the attempt to overcome the powerful tendency of unemployment to return to its natural rate. This is a modern quantity-theory explanation for the phenomenon of stagflation — the coexistence of high unemployment and high, perhaps accelerating, inflation.

The Shifting Phillips Curve: Deflation   The argument in the case of deflation is parallel. We will only sketch the outline, as an exercise the student should fill in the details.

Suppose the economy is at a point like *I* on Figure 21-18. At this point, the rate of increase in nominal wages, W_I, greatly exceeds the rate of productivity advance, so that the prices of goods and services are rising — a situation of inflation. If, in the interests of restraining inflation, the government reduces the rate of monetary expansion, the economy will be pushed to the right, along the static Phillips curve *PP*, perhaps to point U_H. As the level of unemployment rises, the rate of inflation falls. As the real money supply, price level expectations, and nominal wage demands adjust, the Phillips curve will (eventually) shift to the left. With a given money supply, the unemployment rate will tend to fall toward the natural rate, U^*, but with a lower rate of inflation.

The Natural Rate of Unemployment.   A key concept in this analysis is the "natural" rate of unemployment. It is deeply embedded in the structure and institutions of the economy, although it can change over time. The natural rate will increase, for example, as a result of more liberal unemployment insurance arrangements; and it will decrease with more competitive and more flexible labor markets.

If the government attempts to keep the unemployment rate below U^*, it will have

FIGURE 21-18   The shifting Phillips curve: deflation

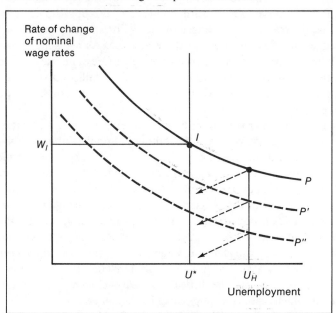

to engage in repeated bouts of monetary expansion, and inflation will accelerate as the Phillips curve shifts. It is important to note, however, that the natural rate of unemployment itself is not associated with any particular rate of inflation. It is consistent with a wide range of possible rates of change in the price level, both inflation and deflation. Indeed, the vertical Phillips curve implies that, apart from a purely temporary relationship, the rate of inflation and the level of unemployment are independent of each other. The rate of inflation depends on the rate of monetary induced expansion in aggregate demand; the level of unemployment depends on structural and institutional characteristics of the economy. The analysis is somewhat different, but the conclusion is essentially the same as that of the classical quantity theory. In the long run, the economy tends to full employment, defined now as the natural rate of unemployment, and the rate of change in prices depends simply on monetary policy.

Theories of Expectations.   How rapidly does the Phillips curve shift? The answer is to be found in the critical role of expectations in the process. How are expectations formed? How are they altered?

In his original exposition of this analysis, Friedman argued, in the tradition of Irving Fisher, that expectations are based on experience — an extrapolation of past events. This notion has come to be known as the *extrapolative expectations* theory. Friedman suggested that people adjust slowly, that it might take as long as two decades for expectations to fully adapt to a new inflationary situation. This suggests considerable scope for governments to increase employment through monetary expansion without a strong initial inflationary impact. However, this illusion is also a trap. Once embedded in the collective psychology, inflationary expectations are equally slow to be removed. Hence, an anti-inflationary policy, moving the economy to the right around the vertical Phillips curve, will require a prolonged period of high unemployment if it is to be successful. The notion that expectations are slow to form and slow to change thus has profound implications for the effectiveness of stabilization policies.

In recent years, a new variant on classical monetarism has emerged, stressing a different mechanism for the formation of expectations. It is argued that people do not simply extrapolate experience. Rather, they base their expectations on the best available information, including their understanding of how the economy works and their anticipations of the actions of the monetary authorities. That is, they form *rational expectations*.

If expectations are formed rationally, and the information available to workers and businesses is good, the Phillips curve will shift very quickly. Because expectations of inflation are based in part on the government's conduct of policy rather than on the slow evolution of experience, an expansionary monetary policy will immediately trigger expectations of inflation which will raise the Phillips curve. The government will have very little scope to influence the level of employment, even temporarily — and then only to the extent that their actions are not anticipated. It follows that an anti-inflationary monetary policy, if it is believed, can be successful without widespread unemployment. The adjustment of expectations in response to the policy will, relatively painlessly, shift the Phillips curve and purge the economy of inflationary pressures.

Monetarism: The New Quantity Theory.   In brief compass, this is the essence of the new monetarism. It is based on the proposition that there is a natural rate of unemployment to which the economy tends to move inexorably. As a result, monetary expansion can only affect the rate of increase in the price level. Perhaps, aside from a temporary effect, monetary expansion cannot alter the level of production and employment. The prescription for price level stability is to increase the money supply at the rate of increase in the demand for money at stable prices, approximately the rate of growth of aggregate output. The prescription for full employment is that you cannot do better than the natural rate of unemployment unless you engage in "supply" policies, reducing the institutional impediments to employment and to wage flexibility, and the tax and transfer payment incentives to be unemployed.

Expectations play a crucial role in this analysis. If expectations are based on experience and are slow to change, monetary expansion will affect employment for a considerable period of time, and monetary contraction will induce widespread unemployment. If expectations are formed "rationally," the impact of monetary actions on the price level may be more direct and, in the case of deflation, less painful. However, this implies that the policies of the government are both understood and believed.

Inflationary Expectations and Inflation

It is not necessary to accept the Phelps-Friedman analysis of the vertical Phillips curve, or the strong monetarist conclusions which derive from it, to assign to inflationary expectations a powerful role in the inflationary process. The literature of economics abounds with theories of inflation, which defy cataloguing or brief summary. However,

Stagflation: A Conundrum for Theory and Policy

The history of inflation and unemployment in Canada for the past 35 years is shown in Figure 21-B1. The solid line shows for each year the percentage increase in the consumer price index and the dashed line shows the average level of unemployment, expressed as a percentage of the labor force. The main point to note is the pronounced change in Canadian experience in the early 1970s. The measured unemployment rate rose to levels previously associated with serious recession in the economy; but the inflation rate, instead of falling off, rose to levels previously associated with strong excess demand in a fully employed economy. The phenomenon of high unemployment associated with rapid inflation has been labelled "stagflation." Is it a

new economic problem, which requires a major revision in our macroeconomic theories and in our approach to stabilization policy?

In the years between World War II and the early 1970s, the rate of inflation tended to vary inversely with the level of unemployment (the Phillips curve), although the relationship was far from exact. In periods of recession (1949-50, 1953-55, 1957-61, 1970-71) the level of unemployment increased and the rate of inflation fell. Levels of unemployment in excess of 6% of the labor force occurred only in the period of serious economic stagnation, 1957-1962, when the rate of inflation fell to a level that we would now regard as trivial. To find other instances with comparable unemployment rates, we have to reach back to the great

FIGURE 21-B1   Unemployment and inflation in Canada, 1946-1981

depression of the 1930s. In periods of relative prosperity, (1946-48, 1950-53, 1956-57, 1962-69) the rate of inflation increased and unemployment fell. The only experiences with inflation rates above 10% per annum were associated with wars — the postwar adjustment period (1946-48) when prices and wages were released from wartime controls, and at the height of the Korean War (1951). In both cases unemployment was in the range of 2%-3.5% of the labor force.

One might argue that Canada's inflationary experience in the 1970s is but a continuation of a longer-term trend which began in the mid-1950s. However, during the early 1960s, accelerating inflation was accompanied by falling unemployment (this was the heyday of the Phillips curve); as unemployment rose in the late 1960s, the acceleration of inflation stopped; and in the recession of 1970-71, when unemployment rose above 6%, the rate of inflation dropped. Nonetheless, the inflation rate in the low year of 1971 averaged about the same as during the intense resource development boom of 1956 when inflation was thought to be a very serious problem. Clearly, the inflationary characteristics of the Canadian economy had changed over the intervening 15 years.

The recession of 1970-71 proved to be a watershed in our inflation-unemployment experience. The recovery from the recession saw inflation accelerate at an alarming rate — indeed, at a rate more commonly reflecting the excess demands for goods and restricted supplies of labor associated with wars. Unemployment, instead of falling to levels which had previously been indicative of tight labor markets, remained high, and as the rapid inflation continued, rose to new high levels. The very serious recession of 1974-75 saw some respite in the inflation rate, but subsequently acceleration of inflation re-emerged, with unemployment persisting at unusually high levels. What had happened?

In 1969, concerned about the accelerating inflation, the government appointed a Prices and Incomes Commission "to inquire into and report upon the causes, processes and consequences of inflation." In its 1972 *Report* the Commission concluded that it was excessive aggregate demand pressure, beginning about 1964 in Canada but seriously aggravated by a 1966-67 inflationary boom in the United States associated with the Vietnam war, that explained the acceleration of inflation. The persistence of inflation in the face of restrictive monetary policies and the slack demand of the recession of 1970-71, was attributed to time lags in the response of prices and wages to short-term changes in demand, together with "strongly held 'inflationary expectations' formed on the basis of experience during the inflationary expansion of the 1960s."

The concept of "inflationary expectations" became a major theme in most explanations of "what happened." However, explanations for the development of these expectations vary and a number of other factors have been assigned major significance. Many economists have concluded that for a variety of reasons — notably changes in the age and sex structure of the labor force (a larger proportion of young and of female workers) and the liberalization of unemployment insurance — the "natural rate of unemployment" has increased from around 3% in the early postwar period to over 6%. As a result, the unemployment statistics are said to be misleading as a guide to policy. A 6% level of unemployment, which earlier reflected serious recession in the economy, now reflects the economy in overall balance. Monetarists argue that the government's response to the recessions of 1970-71 and 1974-75 reflected an exaggerated view of the amount of unemployment in excess of the "natural rate," and involved grossly excessive monetary expansion. The absorption of rates of growth in the money supply in the range of 13-15% per annum, well above historical norms even for years of recession, not only produced accelerating inflation but also persistent inflationary expectations.

Other economists have emphasized a

number of international "supply side shocks" emanating from raw materials markets in this period, and particularly a reduction in supply and increase in price of basic foodstuffs in 1972-74 and a sudden quadrupling of the price of petroleum in 1973-74. It is argued that given the process of price formation in other markets in the economy, dominated by oligopolistic structures and long-term labor contracts, the inevitable response to these price changes was an upward adjustment in the price level, quite independent of aggregate demand and monetary expansion. Indeed, the monetary expansion may have been necessary to prevent further large-scale unemployment.

The debate over the causes of the new macroeconomic situation will continue, and eventually a consensus will probably emerge. In the meantime, the policy makers face a conundrum: which of the opposing schools' advice on the cures for persistent inflation and reported high unemployment should be accepted?

there is an alternative to the monetarist interpretation of the contemporary inflationary process, which also assigns a central role to expectations but which is much more eclectic and less theoretically coherent than the analysis derived from Phelps-Friedman. Although much of the analysis has a long history, perhaps we can call this the new Keynesian view.[28]

The roots of the analysis are several, and perhaps it would be more accurate to refer to it as a collection of views rather than to suggest that it is a single model. Much is owed, in fact, to the work of Phelps and Friedman. The analysis is so powerful that it cannot be ignored, even by those who deny its more extreme conclusions. When the papers appeared, much research was already underway designed to identify and quantify the influence of expectations in what has come to be called the "expectations augmented Phillips curve," but Phelps and Friedman gave immense impetus to such work. The importance of expectations in affecting the shape and position of the Phillips curve is now well established, even though the magnitude of the effects, time lags, the nature of the process of expectations formation, and the implications for theory and policy remain highly controversial.[29]

But expectations are not the only forces seen as shifting the Phillips curve over time. Other roots of this view are institutional in nature — involving interpretations of how the economy and its institutions actually function, with particular emphasis on market imperfections. It is argued that through a broad range of markets, including most labor markets, oligopolistic or monopolistic structures produce administered prices, prices which are not flexible downward in the face of excess supply, but which are flexible upward in the face of excess demand. The range of markets in which there is a high degree of price flexibility is limited, and shrinking over time as more and more raw materials markets are brought under various types of government regulation or cartelization. A general increase in demand will increase the general price level; a reduction in demand will only affect prices in the diminishing "flexprice" sector. As a result, it is argued, the economy has a built-in inflationary bias — an inflationary drift. The level of unemployment at which inflation will not tend to accelerate — the natural rate — seems to be steadily increasing.

The new Keynesian view thus finds an important source of inflation on the supply side. It does not deny the possibility of demand-induced inflation, through excessive monetary expansion, but it denies that this is the *exclusive* source of inflation. In the recent past, special significance has been accorded to major shocks from the supply side, such as the major jump in petroleum prices in the early 1970s. Because other prices could not adjust downward, the price level was ratcheted upward. If the monetary system had not accommodated the jump in prices, significant unemployment would have resulted as the economy was pushed along the now higher Phillips curve by deficient aggregate demand. It is important in this connection to remember the earlier analysis of the interaction between the money supply adn aggregate demand. There are two possibilities for monetary accommodation. Either the central bank permits an expansion of the monetary base, or a combination of elasticity in the demand for money and elasticity in its supply (perhaps the creation of monetary substitutes) produces the accommodation. If the monetary expansion does not occur, however, the result is not a restraint on inflation — which occurs almost exogenously — but unemployment.

What we are calling the new Keynesian view accepts much of the analysis about the role of expectations in the inflationary process, but denies the strong monetarist conclusions bout the exclusive role of monetary expansion in determining the pace of inflation. It is particularly vehement in denying the rational expectations formulation of monetarism, with its implication that there can be a relatively smooth adjustment to a lower rate of inflation through the direct impact of consistent monetary restraint on expectations. Inflation can be a supply side phenomenon, not only through the workings of expectations but also through the structure of institutions. It follows that once inflation is deeply imbedded in the economy and in expectations, the attempt to remove it by monetary restraint alone can be very painful indeed. Many adherents to this view also advocate some type of direct intervention in price and wage formation as necessary to restrain inflation.

Expectations and Interest Rates

Before leaving this survey of the theory of monetary policy, we must note the implications of the analysis of inflationary expectations for interest rates. The Keynesian analysis of aggregate demand, developed earlier in this chapter, suggests that given the *IS* curve and the demand for money, the level of interest rates depends on the supply of money. That is, the level of interest rates is a monetary phenomenon, something that the central bank can regulate. However, in developing the *IS-LM* curve analysis we implicitly assumed static expectations of the price level. Suppose we replace static expectations with expectations of inflation? How must we modify our analysis of the determination of interest rates?

Nominal and Real Interest Rates.   Again we must invoke the distinction between nominal and real variables, in this case between nominal and real interest rates. This distinction was established in Chapter 7. It would be useful to review that discussion at this time.

Briefly, the *nominal interest rate* is simply the now familiar concept of the yield implied in the relationship between the market price of a financial instrument (a bond) and the expected payments associated with that instrument, until its maturity. The *real interest rate* allows for the decline in the purchasing power of the payments over the life of the contract as a result of the increase in the general level of prices. However, the payments are to be received in the future. Thus, in calculating the real interest rate we must be concerned with the *expected* change in the price level over the contract period.

As we noted in Chapter 7, the relationship between the nominal and the real interest rates can be approximated in a simple equation:

$$i_n = i_r + p^e \qquad\qquad (21.16)$$

where i_n is the nominal interest rate, i_r the real interest rate, and p^e the rate of change in the price level expected over the relevant time period. This equation defines the variables, but does not tell us anything about causation. Will expectations of inflation increase the nominal interest rate or reduce the real interest rate?

Interest Rates and Inflation. In principle, it should be the real interest rate which is relevant to saving and investment decisions and to the decisions of assetholders about the forms in which to hold their wealth. Suppose we start with an economy, in equilibrium without inflation and without expectations of inflation. Introduce into this economy inflationary expectations. Assetholders will attempt to shift out of assets with fixed nominal prices — bonds and money (Chapter 20) — and into assets whose market value will appreciate with inflation, including real assets such as land and houses. The attempts to sell bonds will reduce their prices; given the contractual future payments, this will increase the yield on bonds, which is to say, the nominal interest rate. At the same time, prices of real assets, such as land and houses, will increase, reflecting the expected impact of inflation on the future rental payments on these assets. In principle, the prices of the assets should adjust until the real interest rates on each are equal. In the case of bonds this means lower market prices and higher nominal interest rates; in the case of real assets it means higher prices.

Economic theory suggests, moreover, that in the *long run* the real interest rate will be the anchor for these adjustments. The real interest rate will have a long-run equilibrium value, i^*, which depends on very fundamental forces in the economy — the marginal productivity of capital and the savings propensities of the population, or (as we shall discover in the next chapter) in an open economy, on the level of real interest rates internationally.[30] For the purposes of equation 21.16, in the long run, we can take the real interest rate as given, and conclude that the nominal interest rate will be determined by the expected rate of inflation.

Two implications of this analysis are very important. First, high rates of inflation, with accompanying *expectations* of high rates of inflation, will result in high nominal rates of interest. As we noted in Chapter 7, this generalization corresponds to experience in Canada and other countries in recent years. As inflation accelerated, interest rates increased; countries with relatively high inflation rates also experience relatively high nominal interest rates.

Second, in the long run, interest rates, nominal or real, are beyond the direct control of the monetary authorities, except to the extent that monetary policy affects the inflation rate (and the expected inflation rates) and hence indirectly the level of nominal interest rates. What then of the proposition from *IS-LM* curve analysis that the monetary authorities, through control of the money supply, can directly control interest rates?

Interest Rates and Monetary Policy.   *IS-LM* curve analysis is short-run analysis. It takes as given the expected rate of inflation (p^e) and the long-run equilibrium real interest rate (i_r^*). If these are given, the central bank, through monetary actions, can *temporarily* raise or lower the nominal interest rate, and in doing so, raise or lower the actual real interest rate (i_r) relative to the long-run equilibrium real interest rate (i_r^*). For example, the central bank could expand the monetary base, purchasing securities in the open market, and lower the nominal interest rate. Indeed, experience suggests that the nominal interest rate can be reduced below the rate of inflation. If the expected rate of inflation is in the neighborhood of the actual rate, this would result in a *negative* real interest rate in financial markets. The purpose, of course, is to stimulate investment expenditures and hence to move the economy down the *IS* curve, stimulating aggregate demand and, it is to be hoped, production and employment. Conversely, to restrain aggregate demand, the central bank can sell securities and reduce the monetary base, driving up the nominal interest rate so that — given expectations of inflation — the real interest rate is temporarily above its long-run equilibrium value.

Monetarism and the Theory of Interest Rates.   Earlier, we considered at some length the 1968 paper of Friedman in which he argued that the Phillips curve is a dangerous illusion. It seems to give to the government a power which it does not have, except in the very short run — the power to regulate the level of employment. In that paper Friedman used the same analysis to argue that the *IS-LM* curve analysis of interest rates is also a dangerous illusion. It seems to give to the central bank the power to set interest rates. However, Friedman argues, if the government engages in monetary expansion to lower interest rates, it will eventually induce both inflation and expectations of inflation. Rather than reducing nominal interest rates, the monetary expansion will actually increase them by adding the inflationary premium to the given real interest rate. Attempts to use monetary policy according to the Keynesian prescription to regulate interest rates will be self-defeating.

This analysis raises the familiar issues. Are inflation and the inflationary expectations monetary phenomena? According to the new Keynesian view, the answer is largely no. The central bank has power to influence interest rates without fear of perverse consequences, provided there is some slack in the economy. According to the rational expectations school, the answer is decidedly yes. The economy always tends to full employment (the natural rate of unemployment); and the very fact of monetary expansion will itself induce inflationary expectations which will very rapidly increase nominal interest rates. If this argument is correct, the central bank's power to influence nominal interest rates according to the Keynesian prescription would be fleeting indeed, depending only on public misperceptions of the nature and consequences of monetary policy. The way to lower nominal interest rates would be to restrict the money supply, not to expand it.

Monetary Policy in Canada:
From Credit Conditions to
Monetarism and Beyond

The early history of monetary policy was a search for effective institutions and control techniques. In the 1920s and early 1930s the *Finance Act* provided a lender of last resort facility for the banking system but no agency was charged with the responsibility for managing monetary conditions. When the gold standard was effectively suspended in early 1929, Canada was left with no formal monetary control institutions. The Bank of Canada was established in 1935, and was initially preoccupied with discovering the role of a central bank in an open economy with a flexible exchange rate in the late stages of a catastrophic international depression. As one historian of the Bank noted, "economic conditions did not demand consummate brilliance in technique from the Bank, a happy state of affairs for this fledgling."* With the outbreak of World War II in 1939, the primary objective of the Bank became the provision of financial means to mobilize resources for the war effort, and the Bank became an arm of a system of direct governmental controls over economic and financial activity in Canada. The aftermath of the war, from 1945 through 1949, was a period of decontrol and reconstruction, with emphasis on the avoidance of a recurrence of the depression of the 1930s. The Bank's primary role was to facilitate the government's full employment policies by maintaining stable, low interest rates. In spite of rapid inflation (Figure 21-B2), the money supply was not controlled by the Bank of Canada but was determined by the demand for money at the

*E.P. Neufeld, *Bank of Canada Operations and Policy* (Toronto: University of Toronto Press, 1958), p. 81.

pegged interest rates, although the Bank made extensive use of direct controls and moral suasion to regulate bank credit. The process of postwar adjustment was no sooner over than Canada experienced a massive inflow of foreign capital for resource development and, almost simultaneously, became involved in the Korean War. With little direct experience with active monetary policy, the Bank found itself attempting to cope simultaneously with inflationary pressures arising from the war and a strong balance of payments surplus, while experimenting with a regime of flexible exchange rates but without effective institutions for the management of monetary conditions.

To the extent that the Bank made significant efforts to control monetary conditions prior to 1954, it placed heavy reliance on moral suasion. In the early 1950s, however, deliberate efforts were made to develop institutions for the effective *quantitative* control of domestic monetary conditions. In the revision of the *Bank Act* in 1954, the cash reserve requirement was raised from 5% of deposits to 8%, and lagged reserve accounting was introduced. At the same time, the Bank cultivated a domestic short-term money market in which it could carry out open market operations and in which the banks could, quite reliably, make cash reserve adjustments. Among a number of technical measures, the Bank agreed to underwrite the liquidity of the market by providing lender of last resort arrangements for selected security dealers, and encouraged the development of the "day loan" from chartered banks as the normal method of financing dealer inventories of short-term securities and of adjusting bank reserve positions. The banks

FIGURE 21-B2   Long-term interest rates and the rate of growth
of the money supply (*M1*), Canada, 1946-1981

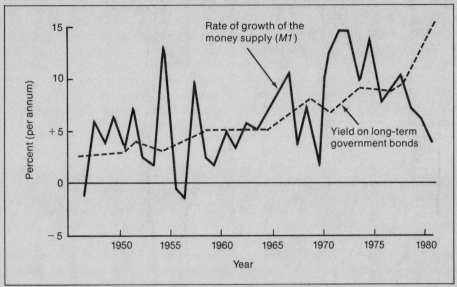

had previously held cash reserves in excess of 10% of deposits, more than double what they were legally required to hold. Following the reforms of 1954, they gradually reduced their holdings of excess cash reserves, making them more responsive to Bank of Canada-induced changes in the supply of cash reserves.

The recession of 1953-54 provided the first opportunity to test the new institutional arrangements, and the Bank of Canada undertook what was effectively its first experiment in counter-cyclical monetary policy. The Bank encouraged monetary expansion and a reduction of interest rates, but it is generally agreed that the policy of monetary expansion was excessive given the mildness of the recession and too late, the major expansion occurring after the business recovery was well underway.

Inflationary pressures emerged in the strong investment boom of 1955-56 which the Governor of the Bank of Canada, J. Coyne, partly attributed to excessive monetary expansion in 1954-55. An abrupt reversal of Bank of Canada policy, involving both moral suasion and quantitative measures, saw a sharp reduction in the rate of growth of the money supply and a rise in interest rates. Although there was a very sharp jump in the rate of growth of the money supply in 1958, this reflected a temporary policy of stabilizing interest rates to assist in the refinancing of a major portion of the public debt of Canada (the conversion loan of 1958) and was not a conscious counter-cyclical monetary policy. This episode aside, the policy of restricted monetary growth continued for about six years and provoked an intense controversy involving many Canadian economists (who were severely critical of the Bank's concern for inflation in the face of high unemployment, and who petitioned for the removal of the Governor) and the government (which was concerned about high unemployment and dismayed by the Governor's public criticisms of its fiscal and international policies). In 1961, in the aftermath of a government attempt to have Parliament dismiss him, the Governor resigned. Following a foreign exchange crisis in May 1962, the Bank attempted to pursue a more flexible policy of monetary management, with the objective of stabilizing the growth of the economy at a high level of employment and without serious inflation.

The doctrine of monetary management which emerged has been labelled the *credit conditions approach.* In brief, it asserts that monetary policy should be used for counter-cyclical stabilization policy and that it is the *cost and availability of credit* which is the appropriate indicator of monetary tightness or ease. Bank of Canada operations should be directed at modifying credit conditions in a counter-cyclical way. When excessive unemployment is threatened, credit conditions should be eased — the cost of credit lowered and credit availability increased to stimulate expenditures. When excessive inflation is threatened, credit conditions should be tightened — the cost of credit increased and credit availability reduced to restrain expenditures. Note the assumptions that there is a trade-off between unemployment and inflation, that credit conditions will have a substantial effect on aggregate demand in a reasonable period of time, and that the management of aggregate demand in a counter-cyclical way is the essence of stabilization policy.

In the early 1960s the policy seemed to be notably successful. However, as we saw earlier (Figure 21-B1), as the decade wore on inflation accelerated to levels that the government then regarded as unsatisfactory (3½-4½%!). In appointing the Prices and Incomes Commission in 1969, the government asked it not only to study the problem but also to "inform those making current price and income decisions, the general public and the Government on how price stability may best be achieved." The Commission stressed the futility of having too low a target level for

unemployment, and counselled a longer-term perspective on demand management, with the objective of reducing the *instability* in the growth of aggregate demand. However, for an economy already in the grips of a severe inflation "originally generated by an overshoot of demand but persisting stubbornly because of widely held inflationary expectations and response lags," the Commission saw an important role for a temporary program of direct price and wage controls. The purpose of the controls was to be to facilitate the adjustment to a lower rate of inflation without the necessity of prolonged and possibly severe unemployment.

The Bank of Canada's response to the recession of 1969-1970 was like that of 1955 — a major expansion of the money supply (Figure 21-B2). As we saw earlier (Figure 21-B1), unemployment remained high after the recession; monetary expansion continued at an unusually high rate. It has been argued that the high and rising *nominal interest rates* evident in Figure 21-B2 were misinterpreted by the Bank of Canada as evidence of tight credit conditions, whereas widespread inflationary expectations meant that *real interest rates* were low and possibly falling so that credit conditions were relatively easy. This is one of the major criticisms of the credit conditions approach — that in the absence of information about expectations it is impossible to measure real interest rates and hence the degree of credit tightness. In any case, in retrospect, the monetary expansion of this period was clearly excessive.

Alarmed by the acceleration of inflation from 1970 to 1974, the government introduced price and wage controls in October 1975. Almost simultaneously the Bank of Canada announced that it was abandoning the credit conditions approach in favor of a policy which focused on the longer-run rate of growth of the money supply (defined as M1). The two policies were in the spirit of the recommendations of the Prices and Incomes Commission, although fiscal policy was not made to conform. Target growth rates for M1 were announced in November 1975 and gradually reduced in subsequent years (see Chapter 20). In general, the targets were met. The new policy is in the spirit of monetarism, but, stressing the gradual implementation of the monetarist rule, the Bank has referred to it as a policy of "gradualism."

Studies of the price and wage controls suggest that they were modestly effective in reducing the rate of increase in wages and prices. They were terminated in 1978. The effects of the new monetary policy have been hotly debated. Following a dip in 1975-76, inflation again began to accelerate. Neo-Keynesians argued vociferously that the policy was an utter failure; that it increased unemployment without reducing inflation. Some monetarists also argued that the policy was a failure — because it was not monetarist enough. That is, it was not sufficiently severe and consistent, and the wrong monetary aggregate was chosen. Although M1 was being controlled, broader measures of the money supply (M2 or M3) were growing at uncontrolled rates; and the Bank of Canada was too slow in reaching the appropriate long-term growth rate and too often departed from its commitment to monetarism to worry about the level of interest rates or the foreign exchange rate. In the place of a money supply target some monetarists have strongly advocated a target rate of growth in the monetary base.

In his 1981 *Annual Report* and in subsequent speeches, the Governor of the Bank of Canada reported that the Bank had suspended its reliance on M1 as a target for monetary policy, because "For more than a year now we have been aware that the M1 target system that existed was not giving good direction signals...,"[*] that "...the relationship between our target monetary aggregate — M1 — and the levels of spending and interest rates has not turned out to be as stable as it appeared in the mid-1970's."[**] For the time being, the Bank has withdrawn its monetary targets and has not announced new ones. Is this a fundamental shift in the conduct of monetary policy? Or, is it but a temporary, technical adjustment in the policy of gradualism? What lies beyond monetarism?

[*] G. Bouey, Statement to the Standing Senate Committee on National Finance (mimeographed); Ottawa: Bank of Canada, December 8, 1982), p. 4.

[**] G. Bouey, "Monetary Policy — Finding a Place to Stand," *Bank of Canada Review,* (September, 1982), p. 11.

SUMMARY

This has been a long chapter, dealing with a complicated range of material, reflecting the analysis of two divergent schools of thought on the nature and potential of monetary policy. We have only scratched the surface of a rich field of intellectual enquiry and controversy. Moreover, as complex as the issues may seem, we have only considered half of the problem. In our discussion of monetary theory and policy we have not considered at all the international aspects. In a country such as Canada, these are of overwhelming importance. We turn to them in the next two chapters.

Before going on, however, it may be useful to sketch briefly some of the highlights of the discussion in this chapter.

The notion that the money supply is a major determinant of aggregate demand has a long history in economics. In Classical monetary theory the velocity of money was assumed to be given in the long run by institutional factors, so that aggregate demand, MV, varies directly with changes in the money supply. Keynesian economics shifted emphasis from the long run to the short run. In this tradition, control of aggregate demand had to be seen in a general equilibrium context, in which the level of interest rates is the crucial variable. Because of the interest elasticity of the demand for money, and the less-than-perfect interest elasticity of investment expenditures, control of aggregate demand through control of the money supply appears to be less than perfect.

An assumption that the economy tends to full employment in the long run converts the classical analysis of aggregate demand into a monetary theory of the price level, the quantity theory of money. An assumption about the inflexibility of prices in the short run converts the Keynesian analysis of aggregate demand into a theory of aggregate production and employment, in which the control of the money supply is of doubtful power. Neither theory is fully satisfactory for the analysis of macroeconomic problems in recent years, and particularly for the analysis of the coincidence of inflation and substantial unemployment.

The Phillips curve analysis which developed in the 1950s and 1960s, seemed to provide a reconciliation of theories of unemployment and theories of inflation. However, theoretical analysis by Phelps and Friedman offered a powerful challenge to the Phillips curve, suggesting that as a basis for the conduct of monetary policy it was a dangerous and temporary illusion. As a government attempted to exploit the Phillips curve to increase employment at the cost of a low rate of inflation, inflation would accelerate and the Phillips curve would shift, translating short-term employment gains into a high rate of inflation. The Phelps-Friedman analysis has, among other things, shifted the emphasis in the theory of monetary policy to the nature and role of expectations. Even in the new Keynesian theories, expectations play a central role along with other institutional factors in explaining the inflationary drift of the economy.

Contemporary monetary economics is rife with controversies over major points of theory and policy. Intellectually, this is healthy. It is through controversy that the discipline develops. For policy, however, it can be distressing. The prescriptions from the opposing camps are markedly different. the modern quantity theory, particularly with rational expectations, suggests that inflation can be contained relatively easily by a consistent and determined policy of monetary restraint. The modern Keynesian theories suggest that serious monetary restraint will produce large-scale unemployment with doubtful effects on inflation in the short run.

ENDNOTES

1. Irving Fisher, *The Purchasing Power of Money* (New York: Macmillan, 1911), p. 183.
2. *Ibid.,* p. 155.
3. *Ibid.,* pp. 55-73; pp. 159-161.
4. *Ibid.,* p. 172.
5. The student who is not familiar with elementary national income accounting should review the relevant section of any standard principles of economics textbook.

The problem arises because in the conventional methods of accounting there are certain "costs" involved in the production of output which do not directly accrue as income to any factor of production. Primary among these is the capital consumption or depreciation allowance. It is because it is included in the measure of output that this measure is called the "gross" national product. Indirect taxes have the same effect. To the business firm they are costs; but they do not accrue as income to any factor of production. (Note that income taxes are different. As long as we measure income received before income tax is paid, the same problem does not arise.) Government subsidies to businesses are in effect negative indirect taxes.

It must also be remembered in this context that interfirm sales of semi-processed goods net out in measuring aggregate income. That is, only the value added at each stage is included in the measure of aggregate output; and it is this figure which is equal to aggregate income (measured gross of depreciation and indirect taxes).

6. Again, remember, both income and output must be measured in the same way: either net or gross of depreciation, indirect taxes, and subsidies.

7. In this brief statement of the theory of investment we can only consider the bare essentials. The student who wants to explore the theory at greater depth is advised to consult a good recent text on macroeconomics, such as R. Dornbusch, S. Fischer and G. Sparks, *Macroeconomics,* First Canadian Edition, (Toronto: McGraw Hill, 1982); M. Parkin, *Modern Macroeconomics* (Scarborough, Ont.: Prentice-Hall, 1982); D.A. Wilton and D.M. Prescott, *Macroeconomics: Theory and Policy in Canada* (Don Mills, Ont.: Addison-Wesley, 1982.

8. The dotted line in the top panel is drawn at a 45° angle to the base axis. Where this line crosses the consumption function, income and consumption are equal, and savings are zero. This point has been projected onto the lower panel. At all levels of income lower than Y_0, consumption exceeds income and saving is negative. Householders are drawing on their accumulated savings or are borrowing to finance consumption in excess of their income. At all income levels higher than Y_0 consumption is less than income and savings is positive. The saving function measures the vertical distance between the consumption function and the 45° line.

9. A larger marginal propensity to save will also shift the *I-S* curve to the left, and a smaller *marginal* propensity to save will shift it to the right. Why? (Hint: review the discussion of the investment-income multiplier, usually just called "the multiplier," from your principles of economics course.)

10. Keynes called his demand for money function the "liquidity preference function." Thus, the *L-M* function connects points at which (*L*) iquidity preference = the (*M*) oney supply.

11. This point is tricky. Remember that the direct effect of income on the demand for money is otherwise allowed for. What is depicted in Quadrant II is the effect of the interest rate pure and simple. It is to be added to the effect of income.

If our assumption did not hold, we would have to draw a different curve in Quadrant II for each level of income. Curves for successively higher levels of income might lie inside or outside the given curve, and might have a different shape. This would complicate the analysis unnecessarily.

12. A particularly powerful statement of this proposition was contained in a 1957 Report of the British Committee on the Working of the Monetary System (the Radcliffe Commission): "...we cannot fund any reason for supposing, or any experience in monetary history indicating, that there is any limit to the velocity of circulation; it is a statistical concept that tells us nothing directly of the motivation that influences the level of total demand" (p. 133).

More recently economists have pointed to such developments as widespread use of credit cards and electronic funds transfer arrangements as factors which are drastically changing conventional notions about restraints on the velocity of money.

13. In some macroeconomic models of the economy, total government expenditures are consi-
dered an exogenous policy instrument. Cf., J.F. Helliwell, L.H. Officer, H.T. Shapiro and
I.A. Stewart, *The Structure of EDXI,* Bank of Canada, Staff Research Studies, No. 3
(Ottawa, 1969); J.F. Helliwell, R.G. Evans, F.W. Gorbert, R.F.S. Jarrett, and D.R. Ste-
phenson, *Government Sector Equations for Macroeconomic Models,* Bank of Canada,
Staff Research Studies, No. 4 (Ottawa, 1969).

    In some other macroeconomic models, the expenditures of junior governments are
endogenous. Separate equations are included to "explain" their behavior. Only the expenditures of the central government are considered an exogenous policy instrument. Cf., F. de
Leeuw and E. Gramlich, "The Federal Reserve — M.I.T. Econometric Model," *Federal
Reserve Bulletin,* Vol 54 (Jan. 1968), pp. 11-40.

14. The concept of the full employment budget as the guide to fiscal policy has been developed
and applied by the Council of Economic Advisers in the United States. A relevant excerpt
from their 1962 *Annual Report* is reprinted in W.L. Smith and R.L. Teigen, *Readings in
Money, National Income and Stabilization Policy* (Homewood, Illinois: Richard D. Irwin,
1965), pp. 281-84. A similar approach to the analysis of fiscal policy has been urged in
Canada by the Economic Council of Canada. See their *First Annual Review, Economic
Goals for Canada to 1970* (Ottawa: Queen's Printer, 1964), pp. 197-98; *Second Annual
Review, Towards Sustained and Balanced Economic Growth* (Ottawa: Queen's Printer,
1965), pp. 160-67. The concept is also explored at some length by the Royal Commission on
Taxation, *Report, Volume 2, The Use of the Tax System to Achieve Economic and Social
Objectives* (Ottawa: Queen's Printer, 1966), pp. 67-85.

15. The savings function in Figure 21-10 is different from that in Figure 21-4. In constructing
Figure 21-4 it was not necessary to distinguish between earned income and disposable (or
after-tax) income. There was no government sector to collect taxes. In constructing Figure
21-10, however, this distinction is essential. We assume that the income concept which is
relevant for private saving and consumption decisions is disposable income. Thus, if there is
a linear consumption function such as that developed in Figure 21-3, it is a relationship
between consumption and disposable income. The income concept in Figure 21-10 is gross
national income. Disposable income is less than national income. The savings function in
Quadrant III, then, shows the effects of both the relationship between disposable income and
national income, and the saving decision out of disposable income. We assume that the
existence of government reduces the level of private saving at each level of gross national The
saving function in Figure 24-10 is closer to the vertical axis than that in Figure 21-4.

16. This is the proposition commonly called the "balanced budget multiplier." The mathematics
of it are developed in most textbooks on macroeconomic theory. The common sense of the
argument is as follows:

    There is a systematic quantitative difference in the *immediate impact* of government
expenditures and tax collections on aggregate demand. Government expenditures have a
direct, dollar for dollar impact, increasing aggregate demand. Taxation has the opposite
direct dollar for dollar impact on *disposable income.* However, people react to the reduction
of their disposable income partly by reducing consumption expenditures, and partly by
reducing saving. The impact on aggregate demand (via reduced consumption expenditures)
is less than the total amount of the tax collections. Therefore, a balanced budget, in which
government expenditures equal tax collections, has a net expansionary effect on aggregate
demand. The reduction of consumption is less than the increase of government expenditures.

17. Perhaps the clearest and most explicit statement is that of M. Friedman in M. Friedman and
W. Heller, *Monetary and Fiscal Policy: A Dialogue* (New York: W.W. Norton & Co., 1969),
pp. 43-62, 71-80.

18. Changes in the relative supply of government bonds (increased) and private bonds (unchanged) may well have some effect on relative interest rates on the securities. Thus, the government may find that interest rates on the public debt have risen *relative* to rates on private debt.

19. We have ignored the problem of time lags in this discussion of fiscal policy. If there are very long time lags in the effects of fiscal measures on aggregate income, then the initial effects of a deficit in the government budget may fall heavily on interest rates. The total effect, then, is very complex, depending as it will on the time lags in the impact of interest rates on private spending as well as the time lags in the impact of fiscal measures on aggregate demand.

20. It is sometimes argued that monetary and fiscal measures should not be co-ordinated in this sense, i.e., they should not be used to achieve the same objective. From time to time, economists have argued that monetary policy should be geared to keeping interest rates low in order to stimulate investment and economic growth, with fiscal policy used to stabilize aggregate demand in the short-run. Similarly, it is sometimes argued that monetary policy should be used to maintain equilibrium in the balance of international payments, while fiscal measures are used for domestic stabilization. We will return to the latter argument in the next chapter.

21. A.W. Phillips, "The Relation Between Unemployment and the Rate of Change of Money Wage Rates in the United Kingdom, 1861-1957," *Economica*, N.S., Vol. 25 (November, 1958), pp. 283-99.

22. H.G. Johnson, "Recent Developments in Monetary Theory — A Commentary," in D.R. Croome and H.G. Johnson, eds., *Money in Britain, 1959-1969* (Oxford: University Press, 1970), p. 110.

23. R.G. Bodkin, E.P. Bond, G.L. Reuber and T.R. Robinson. *Price Stability and High Employment: The Options for Canadian Policy,* Economic Council of Canada, Special Study No. 5 (Ottawa, 1966).

    The trade-off function in Figure 21-16 is drawn on the assumption that corporate profits are "average;" that import prices are stable; and that wage rates in the United States are increasing at 3.2% per annum (a widely quoted guideline for "non-inflationary" wage rate increases in the United States).

24. Economic Council of Canada. *Third Annual Review, Prices, Productivity and Employment* (Ottawa: Queen's Printer, 1966), pp. 168-69.

25. B. Corry and D. Laidler, "The Phillips Relation: A Theoretical Explanation," *Economica* (New Series), 34(1967), pp. 189-97.

26. E.S. Phelps, "Phillips Curves, Expectations of Inflation and Optimal Unemployment Over Time," *Economics* (New Series) 34(1967), pp. 254-281; M. Friedman, "The Role of Monetary Policy," *American Economic Review* 58(March, 1968), pp. 1-17.

27. The following two paragraphs draw on very basic microeconomic theory. For a review of the relevant analysis see P.A. Samuelson and A. Scott, *Economics,* Fourth Canadian Edition (Toronto: McGraw-Hill Ryerson 1975), pp. 503-8, 524-40.

28. A readable statement of this view is J. Tobin, "Stabilization Policy Ten Years After," *Brookings Papers on Economic Activity,* 1(1980), pp. 20-71. Also important is F. Modigliani, "The Monetarist Controversy or, Should We Forsake Stabilization Policies?" *American Economic Review,* 67(March, 1977), pp. 1-19.

29. See the discussion in the excellent survey by D. Laidler and M. Parkin, "Inflation: A Survey," *Economic Journal,* 85(December, 1975), pp. 741-809.

30. Friedman, following the terminology of the great Swedish economist of the early part of this century, Knut Wicksell, calls this the "natural rate of interest." ("The Role of Monetary Policy," *American Economic Review,* 58(March, 1968), pp. 1-17.)

The Theory of Monetary Policy 22
PART 2: THE INTERNATIONAL MACROECONOMY

In the previous chapter we explored the theory of monetary policy for the domestic economy, ignoring its international ramifications. In this chapter we extend the analysis to allow for international trade in goods and services and international capital flows. Since this discussion presumes an understanding of the institutions of the foreign exchange market and of the balance of international payments (Chapter 8), it might be useful to review that material.

EXCHANGE RATE REGIMES

In our earlier discussion we defined the foreign exchange rate as the Canadian dollar price of one unit of foreign money, which, for convenience, we can take as one U.S. dollar. The nature of the interaction between monetary policy and international trade and capital flows depends to a significant degree on the institutional arrangements governing the determination of the foreign exchange rate, on what we will call the "exchange rate regime." In particular, it depends on whether the foreign exchange rate is constrained within narrow limits or is free to find its own level on the basis of demand and supply pressures in the foreign exchange market. While, in reality, exchange rate arrangements are seldom "pure," for purposes of analysis it is useful to think in terms of two polar extremes, a regime of *fixed exchange rates* and a regime of *flexible exchange rates*.

Fixed Exchange Rates

The concept of the exchange rate regime is shorthand for the obligations with respect to the exchange rate which have been assumed by the government. Under a fixed exchange rate regime, the government, directly or indirectly, undertakes to keep the foreign exchange rate, as determined in the foreign exchange market, very close to a predetermined price called the *par rate of exchange.* Historically, Canada has had experience with two types of fixed exchange rate regimes. In the 19th century and the first part of the 20th century, we adhered to the international gold standard and, after World War II, we were members of the Bretton Woods system. We will examine both systems in Chapter 23. Suffice it to say that for extended periods of time, Canada's foreign exchange rate was fixed within very narrow limits on either side of an official par rate — and, while the exchange rate is not presently fixed, a similar system could be introduced in the future. It is important that we understand the macroeconomics of fixed exchange rate regimes.

Flexible Exchange Rates

Under a flexible exchange rate regime, the government has no obligation to control movements in the foreign exchange rate. The concept of a "par" rate becomes meaningless. Indeed, if the regime is "pure" the government has an obligation not to intervene in the foreign exchange market, but to allow the foreign exchange rate to find its own level under the pressures of demand and supply. Flexible exchange rate regimes are seldom "pure," however. In the years 1950-1962 and again from 1970 on, Canada described its exchange rate regime as "floating," implying a modest degree of official intervention to smooth out erratic fluctuations in the rate. From time to time, however, intervention has been much more substantial. When the Bretton Woods system collapsed internationally in the years 1971-73, and floating became the general state of affairs in world foreign exchange markets, a major problem in international diplomacy became that of designing a set of rules governing official intervention in foreign exchange markets. The task of monitoring the situation was assigned to the International Monetary Fund, but an agreed upon and operational set of rules has not yet been devised. In exploring the economics of flexible exchange rates, then, we must pay careful attention to whether the regime is pure or is subject to substantial governmental intervention.

In what follows, we first consider the case of fixed exchange rates, and then turn to flexible exchange rates.

FIXED EXCHANGE RATES
THE PRICE LEVEL

The Small Open Economy Assumption

For our purposes, Canada can be assumed to be a small open economy. The concept of *openness* implies that a significant portion of the country's economic activity involves international transactions. This is obviously true for Canada. Exports and imports of goods and services each account for over 25% of gross national product, and a similarly high proportion of transactions in security markets involves international transactions. The concept of *smallness* implies that Canada is a price taker in world markets for goods, services, and securities. That is, the assumption that Canada is a small open economy is an assumption that Canada does not have sufficient market power to significantly affect prices in world markets for goods and services that are exported or imported, or for securities.

The Foreign Exchange Rate

The concept of the foreign exchange rate is a source of endless confusion, partly because there are two equally acceptable ways of quoting the exchange rate. In this book, we treat foreign exchange as a particular financial instrument which is bought and sold in a market at a price which we call the foreign exchange rate. That is, we mean by the foreign exchange rate the Canadian dollar price of a unit of foreign currency. Unfortunately, the concept of the foreign exchange rate is also widely used to refer to the reciprocal of our definition, that is, the foreign currency price of a Canadian dollar. Our definition involves a Canadian perspective, looking outward; the alternative definition involves an external per-

FIGURE 22-B1   Two Measures of the Foreign Exchange Rate: the Price of a U.S. Dollar and the IMF Index of the effective exchange rate

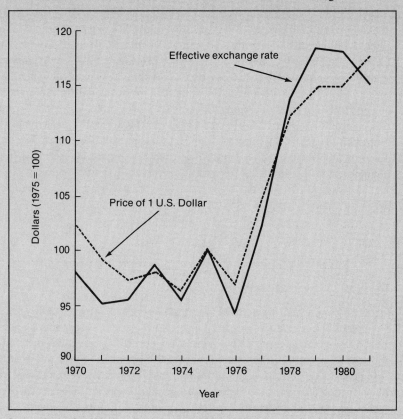

Source: International Monetary Fund, *International Financial Statistics,* (various issues).

spective, looking inward. When the foreign exchange rate on our definition goes up, on the alternative definition it goes down. Obviously, to keep your thinking straight, it is vitally important to be absolutely clear on which definition you are using, and to use that definition consistently.

But there is another problem with the concept of the exchange rate. Although we refer to "the" foreign exchange rate, there are as many foreign exchange rates as there are foreign currencies. Obviously, not all currencies are equally important for Canada's international transactions, and as a result of the very large importance of transactions with the United States, we tend to refer to the Canadian dollar price of a U.S. dollar as "the" foreign exchange rate. However, while the rate on the U.S. dollar is of primary importance to Canada, it is not the only exchange rate of importance — and the rate on the U.S. dollar and the rates on other important currencies like the Japanese yen and the British pound can move in opposite directions, occasionally by sizeable amounts.

This problem in the meaning and measurement of "the" foreign exchange rate has become particularly serious since the 1971-73 collapse of the Bretton Woods system and the general adoption of floating exchange rates. In response, attempts have been made to develop measures of the *"effective" exchange rate*, a weighted average of the rates on currencies of importance in international trade and investment. One measure of the effective exchange rate for Canada, a weighted average of the rates on 17 currencies, has been developed by the International Monetary Fund. It is presented in Figure 22-B1, along with the rate on the U.S. dollar, for the years 1970-1980. Both measures of the exchange rate are expressed as index numbers, 1975 = 100.

Inspection of Figure 22-B1 should suggest that the rate on the U.S. dollar and the effective exchange rate do behave somewhat differently — but not that differently. Perhaps the use of the price of a U.S. dollar as "the" foreign exchange rate is not a bad first approximation for Canada.

Determination of the Price Level

The assumption that Canada is a small open economy has very important implications for the determination of the Canadian price level with a fixed exchange rate.

Export Prices. First consider the determination of the Canadian price of export goods. Export goods are sold in world markets, and foreign money is received in payment. The proceeds, after all transactions costs have been paid (including foreign tariffs), are converted into Canadian funds at the fixed exchange rate. In Canada, then, the price of the export good will be:

$$P_{x,c} = R(P_{x,w} - T_x), \tag{22-1}$$

where $P_{x,c}$ is the price received by Canadian exporters (expressed in Canadian dollars); $P_{x,w}$ is the world market price for the export good (quoted in foreign currency); R is the Canadian price of foreign exchange; and T_x is the cost of exporting the good (expressed in foreign money). If the small country assumption is valid, moderate changes in Canadian demand or supply will not affect the world market price, $P_{x,w}$. With the exchange rate (R) and transactions costs (T_x) given, the Canadian price is determined in world markets.

Import Prices.   Similarly, imported goods are purchased in world markets, where payment must be made in foreign money. For imported goods, then, it must be true that:

$$P_{m,c} = (P_{m,w} + T_m) R, \qquad\qquad (22\text{-}2)$$

where $P_{m,c}$ is the price of the imported good delivered in Canada (expressed in Canadian dollars); $P_{m,w}$ is the price of the good in world markets (quoted in foreign currency); R is the Canadian price of foreign currency (the foreign exchange rate); and T_m is the cost of importing the good (expressed in foreign currency). With R and T_m given, the Canadian price of imported goods delivered in Canada will be determined by their prices in the rest of the world. It should be obvious that the price of a Canadian-produced good which is a perfect or very close substitute for an imported good will also be determined by equation 22-2.

The Price Level.   Together, prices of export goods ($P_{x,c}$), the prices of imported goods ($P_{m,c}$), and the prices of import competing goods account for a very substantial portion of prices which enter into the Canadian price level. Although it is true that there are many purely domestic goods and services, whose prices are determined in Canada, we can assert as a first approximation that *under a regime of fixed exchange rates the Canadian price level is determined abroad.*

This is a very important conclusion. Among other things, it tells us that variations in Canadian aggregate demand, perhaps induced by Canadian monetary policy, cannot directly affect the price level. The price level is an exogenous variable, determined outside the Canadian economic system. As you will recall, this is the condition necessary for the Keynesian model of aggregate demand to apply. What adaptations do we have to make to the Keynesian model to allow for the international sector?

FIXED EXCHANGE RATES: THE CURRENT ACCOUNT

A major concern of the pure theory of international trade is to explain the level and composition of imports and exports in the long run in a fully employed economy. The analysis usually assumes national economies which have different endowments with factors of production, and explains mutually advantageous trade flows between these economies in terms of the principle of comparative advantage. However, this is a long-run theory which deals with a range of analytical problems which are not of concern to us in the present context. We will take the structure of comparative advantage as given, and will focus exclusively on short run fluctuations in the aggregate levels of imports and exports, in an economy which is not necessarily at full employment. The term "exports" refers to all current account receipts from the sale of goods and services abroad, and the term "imports" refers to all current account payments for the purchase of goods and services from abroad. Remember, we are assuming that the foreign exchange rate is fixed within very narrow limits, and the prices of goods and services, abroad and in Canada, are given.

Imports, Exports, and Aggregate Demand

We saw in Chapter 21 that exports add to aggregate demand, whereas imports are a leakage from aggregate demand. Ignoring the government sector again, we can write the basic aggregate demand identity:

$$\begin{matrix} \text{AGGREGATE} \\ \text{INCOME} \end{matrix} = D = C + (X - Im) = Y = \begin{matrix} \text{AGGREGATE} \\ \text{DEMAND} \end{matrix} \qquad \text{(22-3)}$$

This identity provides a framework for our analysis. We carry over the assumption which we made earlier regarding the behavior of investment, consumption, and saving. What we need now are assumptions about the short-run behavior of aggregate imports and aggregate exports.

The Import Demand Function. Our basic assumption is that in the short run, with other things being equal (i.e., the level of prices, the foreign exchange rate, and the long-run determinants of the structure of comparative advantage), *the level of imports and hence the demand for foreign exchange on current account, depends directly on the level of aggregate demand.* As aggregate demand rises, the demand for imports rises. As aggregate demand falls, the demand for imports falls.

In contemporary Canada, the magnitudes involved in this relationship between imports and aggregate expenditures are not small. Thus, in recent years imports have ranged between 24% and 31% of gross national expenditure. It is also important to note that some components of aggregate demand have a stronger impact on imports than others. Thus, it has been estimated that almost one-third of all investment expenditures in Canada directly or indirectly involve the purchase of imported goods and services. The corresponding figures for other categories of expenditure are significantly less: 20% for consumption, 15% for exports, and 11% for government expenditures.[1] It follows that the demand for imports depends not only on the level but also on the *composition* of aggregate demand. A rise in investment expenditures will have a particularly strong impact on the demand for imports. A corresponding increase in government expenditures will have a significantly smaller effect.

We can incorporate both of these assumptions into an import demand function distinguishing between imports which depend on investment expenditures (Im_1) and imports which depend on consumption expenditures (Im_2). That is,

$$Im = Im_1 + Im_2 \qquad \text{(22-4)}$$

For simplicity we will assume that in each case imports are proportional to the relevant expenditures.

$$Im = m_1 I + m_2 C \qquad \text{(22-5)}$$

The coefficients m_1 and m_2 are not necessarily equal (in the example considered below we assume that m_1 is greater than m_2, in accordance with the information noted above).

Equation 22-5, then, is our import demand function. It tells us that *imports depend on the level of consumption expenditures and the level of investment expenditures.*

Exports. In the same way that Canada's imports depend on the level of aggregate demand in Canada, so Canada's exports depend on the level of aggregate demand in the rest of the world, and particularly in the United States. Exports help determine the level of income and employment in Canada, but they are not in turn determined by the levels of income and employment in Canada.[2] In this sense, given the assumptions of the Keynesian model, exports are an exogenous variable — a variable whose magnitude is determined by external factors. In our analysis we simply take the value of exports as given.

The Current Account and the I-S Curve

The addition of an exogenous export variable and an import demand function such as equation 22-5 makes no difference in principle to the "real" side of the basic Keynesian model. In terms of the concepts which we developed in the previous chapter, they simply alter the *position* and *elasticity* of the *I-S* function. Figure 22-1 is a demonstration of this, using the now familiar four-quadrant diagram.

FIGURE 22-1   Commodity market equilibrium with international trade

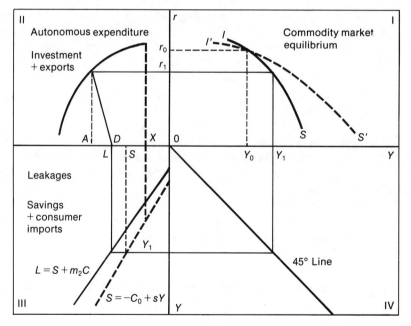

In discussing the significance of external trade for macroeconomic equilibrium, it is useful to distinguish between the effects of autonomous exports and the effects of the import demand function.

Exports as "Autonomous" Expenditures.   When we first constructed the *I-S* curve, in Figure 21-4, we had only one category of expenditures which we assumed to be independent of the level of income, i.e., investment expenditures. In the present case we have two types of "autonomous" expenditures, investment, and exports. Moreover, exports, unlike investment, are independent of the level of interest rates.

In quadrant II of Figure 22-1, the given value of exports is indicated by the distance OX. In deriving what we might call the "autonomous expenditure function" of that quadrant, we have simply added the given magnitude of exports to investment (derived from the original investment demand function of Figure 21-4) at each level of interest rates. That is,

$$A = I + X \qquad (22\text{-}6)$$

The effect on conditions for commodity market equilibrium is the same as if investment expenditures had increased at every level of interest rates. That is, the I-S curve will be shifted to the right. *The effect of including exogenous exports in the Keynesian model is simply to increase the equilibrium level of income at each possible level of interest rates.*

The Demand for Imports as "External Leakage".   The effects of adding an import demand function of the type which we have specified to the Keynesian model is somewhat more complex. In general, the effects of imports is the opposite of the effects of exports. They reduce the equilibrium level of income for each level of interest rates, shifting the I-S curve to the left. However, the fact that imports vary directly with investment and consumption expenditures also has an important effect on the *shape* of the I-S curve. *By limiting the increase in domestic consumption expenditures consequent on any given increase of investment expenditures, imports reduce the interest-elasticity of the* I-S *function.*

An important part of the impact of imports on the I-S curve arises because that portion of investment expenditures which is devoted to the purchase of imports is irrelevant to the process of income generation in Canada. The import content of investment is an "external leakage" which must be deducted from income-generating "autonomous" expenditures. In Quadrant II of Figure 22-1 we show the effect of this adjustment for the arbitrarily selected level of interest rates, r_1. At this level of interest rates, autonomous expenditures $(X + I)$ would be OA. However, from this must be deducted the import content of investment expenditures, leaving OD as the domestic component of autonomous expenditures. It is this magnitude — the sum of exports and the *domestic component* of investment expenditures — which is projected into Quadrant III at each level of interest rates.[3]

The second part of the import demand function, the import content of consumption expenditures (m_2C), has the effect on the I-S curve as would an increase in the marginal propensity to save. It increases the share of any increment to income which is diverted away from income-generating consumption expenditures, and thus limits the total increase of income which can result from a given increase of autonomous expenditures. Accordingly, in Quadrant III we have added the import content of consumption (m_2C) to the original saving function from Figure 21-4, (the broken line in Quadrant III), to obtain the total leakage function,

$$L = S + M_2C \qquad (22\text{-}7)$$

This function is represented by the solid line in Quadrant III.

Equilibrium in the Commodity Market with International Trade.   You will recall from Chapter 21 that equilibrium in the commodity market at any level of interest rates requires a level of income such that the (income-depressing) planned savings of households exactly offset the (income-generating) planned investment expenditures of business firms. With the introduction of international trade we have to redefine the conditions for equilibrium. Investment can exceed saving without pushing up income providing the excess of investment over saving is just offset by net inflow of goods from abroad. The income-generating effects of excess investment are just offset by the net leakage of aggregate demand through the current account. The opposite is also true. That is, an excess of saving over investment is also consistent with equilibrium in the commodity market providing it is offset by an excess of exports over imports. The income-depressing effects of excess saving are just offset by the income-generating effects of excess exports.

We can state our new equilibrium conditions as:

$$X + I = Im + S$$
$$= m_2C + m_1I + S \qquad\qquad (22\text{-}8)$$

Rearranging the terms:

$$X + I - m_1I = m_2C + S \qquad\qquad (22\text{-}9)$$

or:

$$A - m_1I = m_2C + S \qquad\qquad (22\text{-}10)$$

In Quadrant III we see that the equilibrium level of income, given interest rate r_1, is Y_1. At this level of income, leakages $(S + m_2C = OL)$ equal the domestic component of autonomous expenditures $(A - m_1I = OD)$. By a similar process we could find equilibrium levels of income for all other possible levels of interest rates.

The* I-S *Curve.   The line in Quadrant IV is the now familiar 45° line, used to reflect equilibrium levels of income from the vertical axis of Quadrant III to the horizontal axis of Quadrant I. Since investment depends on the levels of interest rates, there will be a different equilibrium level of income for each possible level of interest rates. As usual, the *I-S* curve, the solid line in Quadrant I, is the locus of all combinations of interest rates and income levels which are consistent with equilibrium in the commodity market.

The broken line, *I'-S'*, in Quadrant I is the original *I-S* curve from Figure 21-4, drawn on the assumption of the same investment and saving functions, but no international trade. It provides a convenient reference base for identifying the effects of introducing the international trade into the Keynesian model.

The two *I-S* curves have one point in common: that combination of interest rate (I_0) and income (Y_0) at which imports equal exports. This tells us that *international trade makes no difference to the macroeconomic equilibrium in the economy if the current account is in balance.* In our model, the level of income at which the current account is in balance depends on the level of exports. The larger the value of exports, the higher will be the level of income at which exports will equal imports, and the farther to the right will be the intersection of the two *I-S* curves.

In general, however, imports and exports are not equal, and whenever the current account is not in balance the presence of international trade affects the combinations of interest rates and income levels at which the commodity market will be in equilibrium. Thus, to the left of the intersection of the two *I-S* curves in Quadrant I, exports exceed imports. Because of this fillip to income, the new *I-S* curve lies above the old. *International trade will limit the decline of income and employment which would be the normal consequence of a rise in the level of interest rates.* To the right of the point of intersection, the new *I-S* curve lies below the old. Imports exceed exports. Because of the import content of both investment and consumption expenditures, *international trade limits the increase of income and employment which would be the normal consequence of reduction of interest rates.*

Implications for Monetary Policy.   These conclusions on the significance of international trade for macroeconomic equilibrium (with fixed prices and a fixed exchange rate) do not introduce any new principles into our analysis of monetary policy. However, they do provide additional reasons for thinking that the *I-S* curve may be relatively interest *inelastic*, and this is an important matter. As we saw in Chapter 21, the lower the elasticity of the *I-S* function, the less is the likelihood of a strong macroeconomic response to monetary policy.

There is also another dimension to the macroeconomic implications of international trade which we have glossed over. One conclusion which can be drawn from our analysis is that, given the level of exports, the behavior of imports tends to stabilize the level of income and employment in Canada. It tends to dampen any increase of income, and to limit any decline of income, consequent on any given change of autonomous expenditures. However, international trade also exposes the Canadian economy to another source of instability, through fluctuations in the level of exports. Any change in exports will shift the *I-S* function in the same direction, and hence will alter the equilibrium levels of income and employment. To the extent that exports depend on aggregate demand in the rest of the world, and particularly in the United States, this provides a strong link between income and employment in Canada and economic activity abroad. If the *I-S* function were relatively inelastic, it would be difficult to counteract external effects on Canadian income and employment through monetary action alone.

FIXED EXCHANGE RATES:
THE CAPITAL ACCOUNT

In our analysis of the role of international trade in the Keynesian macroeconomic model, we imposed no constraints on the current account balance. We implicitly assumed that there was no limit to the magnitude of the current deficit or surplus which could be induced by a rise or fall in the level of aggregate demand. However, our discussion of the balance of payments identity in Chapter 8 revealed that the current account deficit *must* be matched by an equal surplus in the capital account, or else official foreign exchange reserves *must* be drawn down. Similarly, any current account surplus *must* be matched by an equal capital account deficit, or else official foreign exchange reserves *must* increase. Do these facts not affect the extent to which current deficits or surpluses can be incurred?

The answer is "yes." As a result, in analyzing the conditions for macroeconomic equilibrium in the Canadian economy, we cannot consider the current account in isolation. We must consider it in relation to international capital flows and possible changes in official foreign reserves.

The role of official foreign exchange reserves in this context poses special problems which are better deferred for separate treatment. What regulates private international capital flows?

The Determinants of International Capital Flows

We have already considered the international investment decision in some detail in Chapter 8. There is no need to repeat that discussion here. If we regard international capital flows of all types — direct investment as well as portfolio investment — simply as international transactions in financial instruments (in the broad way in which we have defined the concept of a financial instrument), then what is involved in international capital flows are the portfolio balance decisions of Canadian and foreign assetholders and debtors. Thus, capital outflows result when Canadian assetholders choose to take foreign securities into their portfolios, when foreign assetholders choose to reduce their holdings of Canadian securities, or when Canadian debtors decide to retire foreign-held debt. Similarly, capital inflows result when foreign assetholders choose to take Canadian securities into their portfolios, when Canadian assetholders choose to reduce their holdings of foreign securities, or when foreign debtors decide to retire Canadian-held debt.

Many types of financial instruments, many different assetholders and debtors, and hence many individual decisions are involved in the aggregate of international capital flows in any given year. Each decision calls for the weighing of a variety of considerations, some economic, some political, some long-term, and some short-term. However, the central consideration in most of these decisions — whether they relate to direct investment or portfolio investment — must be the *expected yield* on the investment (considered relative to risk and liquidity, of course). Foreign capital will be attracted to Canada by relatively high expected yields on Canadian investments. Canadian capital will be attracted abroad by relatively high expected yields on foreign investments.

Interest Rates and Capital Flows.   This line of argument suggests that there should be a direct link between Canadian monetary policy and international capital flows. A tight money policy, as we have seen, implies higher interest rates in Canada. Given interest rates prevailing abroad, this should induce foreign assetholders to purchase relatively higher-yielding Canadian securities, and should induce Canadian borrowers to raise more funds from foreign banks and financial intermediaries. The net result should be an enlarged inflow of capital to Canada. Similarly, an easy money policy implies lower interest rates in Canada. Given the interest rates prevailing abroad, this should reduce the incentive for foreign assetholders to hold Canadian securities and the incentive for Canadian borrowers to raise funds abroad. Indeed, a sufficient reduction of Canadian interest rates could induce substantial foreign borrowing in Canada. The end result of an easy money policy should be a reduction of the capital inflow, and perhaps a net capital outflow.

Not all international capital flows are highly sensitive to international interest rate differentials. For example, empirical researchers have found little statistical evidence of a strong response of direct investment to interest rates. However, there is substantial evidence of high interest-elasticity of portfolio investment, in both long-term and short-term forms. This effect is sufficiently strong to have a decisive impact on the balance of payments and the foreign exchange market should Canadian interest rates depart significantly from those prevailing in the United States.

The Net Capital Flow Function. These basic assumptions about the dependence of international capital flows on the level of Canadian interest rates are incorporated in the net capital flow function presented in Figure 22-2.

FIGURE 22-2   The net capital flow function

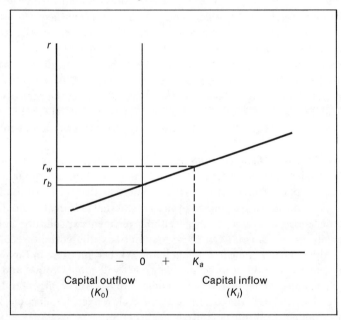

We assume that international capital flows are highly sensitive to international interest rate differentials, and hence we have drawn the line with a relatively low slope. However, we have not adopted the extreme assumption of perfect international capital mobility which is sometimes employed in the analysis of this problem. Such an assumption would produce a perfectly horizontal line at the world interest rate (or perhaps at the world rate plus a small "risk premium"). Furthermore, we have drawn the net capital flow function as a straight line purely for convenience.

The level of interest rates in Canada (r) is measured along the vertical axis, and the net international flow of capital along the horizontal axis. At interest rate r_w, the level of interest rates in Canada is the same as that in the rest of the world (i.e., for all practical purposes, in the United States). That is, the international differential between yields on comparable securities is zero. We have assumed that at this level of interest rates there is still a net inflow of capital into Canada (K_a). We might call this the "autonomous" capital inflow. It may take the form largely of direct investment.

At higher levels of interest rates in Canada, a greater net inflow of capital (K_1) will occur. At lower levels of interest rates there will be a smaller net inflow, until, at interest rates lower than r_b, a net capital outflow (K_0) from Canada results.

Balance of Payments Equilibrium

The important new concept, balance of payments equilibrium under a fixed exchange rate regime, can be defined as *a condition in which normal market forces tend to keep the foreign exchange rate within the permitted range about the official par rate, without direct controls and without direct intervention by the government*. Balance of payments equilibrium requires that the international capital flows resulting from the free choices of Canadian and foreign assetholders and debtors are just sufficient to offset the net balance on current account at the pegged rate of exchange. No change in official reserves is required to achieve a balance of international payments.

The conditions for balance of payments equilibrium thus depend partly on the behavior of the capital account, and partly on the behavior of the current account. We have a function, the net capital flow function, which describes the behavior of international capital flows in response to Canadian interest rates. What we require to complete our analysis is a companion function describing the behavior of the current account.

The Current Account Balance Function. The required current account balance function can be derived directly from our earlier analysis of the determinants of imports and exports, and partly from Figure 22-1. You will recall that we assumed that the value of exports was exogenous, determined by factors external to Canada, and that the value of imports depended separately on the levels of investment expenditures and consumption expenditures in Canada. On these assumptions, the current account balance depends on the level of income in Canada in the manner indicated in Figure 22-3.[4]

At one particular level of income, Y_0, imports will equal exports and the current account will balance. At higher levels of income, imports will be larger, and hence there will be a negative balance in the current account. At lower levels of income, imports will be smaller, producing a surplus in the current account.

The B-K Function. Balance of payments equilibrium, then, must depend on the level of interest rates and the level of income in Canada. At any given level of income, there will be a unique level of interest rates which will induce a capital inflow equal to the current account deficit associated with that level of income (or a capital outflow equal to the current account surplus). Thus, balance of payments equilibrium requires a different level of interest rates for each possible level of income, and we can derive a function, similar in concept to the *I-S* and *L-M* functions, which identifies all possible combinations of interest rates and income levels consistent with balance of payments (or foreign exchange market) equilibrium. We call such a curve a *B-K* function.[5]

FIGURE 22-3   The current account balance function

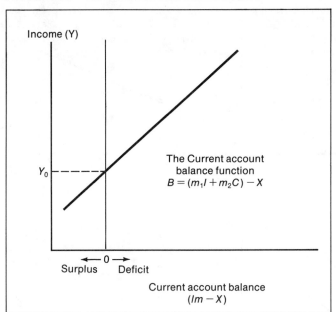

The derivation of the B-K curve from the net capital flow function of Figure 22-2 and the current account balance function of Firure 21-3 is demonstrated in Figure 22-4. The technique is the same as that employed earlier, and should require no explanation. The net capital flow function is in Quadrant II, with the net international flow of capital measured along the base axis and interest rates along the vertical axis. The current account balance function is in Quadrant III, with the current account balance measured along the base axis, and the level of income measured in a downward direction along the vertical axis. We can use these two curves to find combinations of interest rates and income at which the net capital flow and the current account balance are equal. Equilibrium income levels for each level of interest rates are projected from the vertical axis of Quadrant III to the base axis of Quadrant I, using the 45° line of Quadrant IV. The result is the balance of payments equilibrium line, B-K described by the solid line in Quadrant I.

At points above the B-K function the level of interest rates is too high relative to the level of income. The net inflow of capital from abroad will exceed the current account deficit (in order to demonstrate your understanding of the B-K function you should be able to show that this is the case). Excess supply in the foreign exchange market will put downward pressure on the foreign exchange rate. If such a condition is to exist, in the absence of direct controls and without a change in the foreign exchange rate, the excess supply must be absorbed by an increase of official foreign exchange reserves.

At points below the B-K function, the level of interest rates is too low relative to the level of income. The net inflow of capital will fall short of the current account deficit, and excess demand in the foreign exchange market will put upward pressure on the

FIGURE 22-4   Derivation of the balance of payments
equilibrium function $(B-K)$

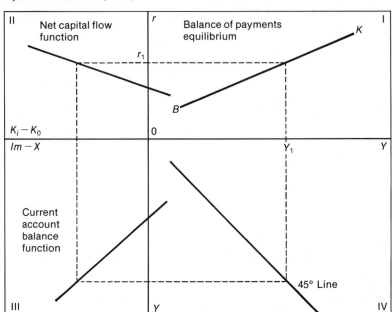

foreign exchange rate. If such a condition is to exist, official foreign exchange reserves
must be drawn down to satisfy the excess demand at the maximum permitted foreign
exchange rate.

You should note that according to our assumptions, at higher levels of income,
balance of payments equilibrium requires higher levels of interest rates.The more
sensitive are international capital flows to interest rate differentials, the flatter this line
will be. In the extreme case of perfect international capital mobility, the B-K line will be
horizontal at the world level of interest rates, r_w.

FIXED EXCHANGE RATES: OPEN ECONOMY EQUILIBRIUM

We are now in a position to incorporate international trade in goods and services and
international capital flows into our analysis of macroeconomic equilibrium.

Macroeconomic Equilibrium

We discovered in Chapter 21 that full macroeconomic equilibrium in a *closed economy*
requires that equilibrium be achieved simultaneously in the money market and the
commodity market. In an *open economy* we add a third condition: equilibrium must be
achieved simultaneously not only in the commodity and money markets, but also in the
balance of international payments. That is, *full macroeconomic equilibrium in an open*

economy requires a combination of interest rates and income levels which will simultaneously satisfy the I-S *function, the* L-M *function, and the* B-K *function.*

A state of full macroeconomic equilibrium is illustrated in Figure 22-5. At any combination of income and interest rates other than Y_e and r_e at least two of the three markets must be in disequilibrium (and with many conceivable combinations, all three markets will be in disequilibrium). For example, at the levels of interest rates and income indicated by r_1 and Y_1 equilibrium would be achieved in the commodity market. However, given the money supply, the money market would not be in equilibrium (the supply of money would exceed the demand, creating downward pressure on interest rates) and given the foreign exchange rate and foreign interest rates, the balance of payments would not be in equilibrium (the inflow of capital would exceed the current account deficit, creating downward pressure on the foreign exchange rate). At levels of interest rates and income represented by r_2 and Y_2 the commodity market would again be in equilibrium, but there would be excess demand in both the money market and the foreign exchange market. Full macroeconomic equilibrium would not exist. (To demonstrate your understanding of this discussion you should be able to explain the nature of the disequilibrium conditions represented by other combinations of interest rates and income.)

In the conditions depicted in Figure 22-5, full macroeconomic equilibrium is possible. Indeed, any departure from equilibrium income and interest rates would eventually be corrected. Thus, at points like r_1 Y_1, downward pressure on interest rates resulting from the excess supply of money and the excess capital inflows would increase investment, income, and imports, and would tend to move the system toward equilibrium at r_e Y_e. Similarly, at points like r_2 Y_2, upward pressure on interest rates would move the system toward equilibrium at r_e Y_e.

FIGURE 22-5 Full macroeconomic equilibrium in an open economy

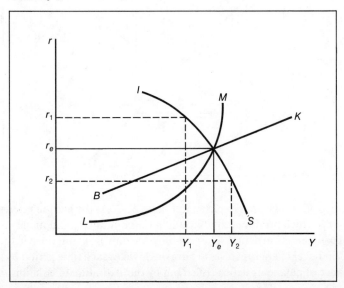

The Impossibility of Equilibrium

However, the tendency of the economy toward general macroeconomic equilibrium as depicted in Figure 22-5 is an *accident* — a product of the way in which we have drawn the three curves. Given the underlying behavioral functions (i.e., the demand for money function, the investment function, the import demand function, etc.), and given any arbitrarily selected money supply and foreign exchange rate, *general macroeconomic equilibrium may be impossible.* That is, *given the money supply and the foreign exchange rate, there may be no combination of interest rates and income which will simultaneously satisfy the I-S function, the L-M function, and the B-K function.*[6]

An example of a situation in which general macroeconomic equilibrium is impossible is depicted in Figure 22-6. The three functions do not have a common point of intersection. In this situation, with interest rates and income at r_1 Y_1 respectively, the money and commodity markets will be in equilibrium but the balance of international payments will be in surplus. The economy can only be maintained in this condition if official foreign exchange reserves increase in each time period by the amount of the balance of payments surplus (which we have ruled out by our definition of equilibrium).

FIGURE 22-6   Macroeconomic equilibrium impossible.
Domestic equilibrium: balance of payments surplus

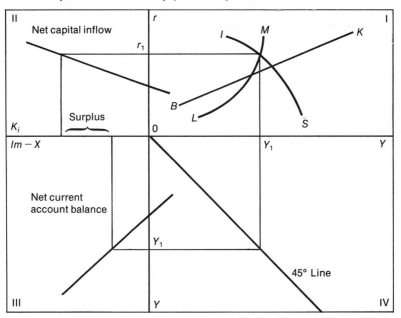

The opposite situation is depicted in Figure 22-7. At the level of interest rates and income $(r_2$ $Y_2)$ which produces equilibrium in the commodity and money markets, the balance of payments is in deficit. The economy can only be maintained in this condition if official foreign exchange reserves are drawn down in each time period by the amount of the balance of payments deficit (ruled out by our definition of equilibrium).

FIGURE 22-7   Macroeconomic equilibrium impossible.
Domestic equilibrium: balance of payments deficit

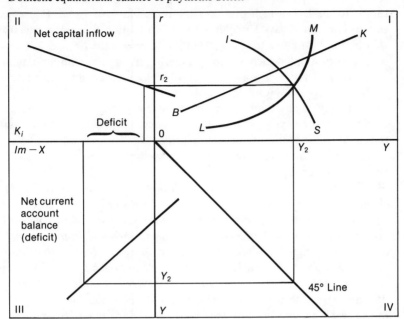

It should also be noted that if macroeconomic equilibrium is achieved, as in Figure 22-5, it will be a fragile condition. Underlying each of the functions in Figure 22-5 is a great variety of variables and behavior patterns, some domestic and some external, each of which is subject to substantial change over short periods of time. A significant change in any major macroeconomic variable will disturb the equilibrium. Thus, for example, a rise in investment demand will shift the I-S function; a decline in exports will shift the B-K function; and an increase in the demand for money will shift the L-M function. Moreover, a shift in any one of these functions will convert a condition of full equilibrium into a condition (such as Figures 22-6 or 22-7) in which equilibrium may be impossible without further intervention on the part of the government.

Implications for Monetary Policy

Let us continue our earlier assumption that the level of official foreign exchange reserves must not change significantly (as we shall see in the next section, this is not an unreasonable assumption). What, then, are the implications of this analysis for monetary policy?

Governmental Policy and Macroeconomic Equilibrium.   The important point to be derived from this analysis is not that under certain plausible conditions macroeconomic equilibrium may be impossible in an open economy, but rather that *the achievement of equilibrium may require a particular set of governmental policies.* In this regard, we must remember that the position of the L-M curve is a matter of governmental policy. It depends on the size of the money supply. Thus, in a situation typified by Figure 22-6, full equilibrium is only impossible if the government insists on restricting the money supply to the level which produces the indicated *L-M* curve. Full macroeconomic equilibrium can always be achieved in this situation through monetary expansion, shifting the *L-M* curve to the right until it intersects the *I-S* and *B-K* curves. There is some money supply which is compatible with full macroeconomic equilibrium — but that money supply implies a lower level of interest rates and a higher level of aggregate demand in the economy.

Similarly, in situations like that depicted in Figure 22-7, full equilibrium can always be obtained by the appropriate monetary policy. In this case, the money supply must be restricted, shifting the *L-M* curve to the left until it intersects with the *I-S* curve and *B-K* curves. Full equilibrium implies a higher level of interest rates and a lower level of aggregate demand.

This discussion suggests a very important conclusion. *In a relatively small, open economy, with a pegged exchange rate and with official foreign exchange reserves which cannot undergo major fluctuations, the central bank does not have the power to determine independently the course of monetary policy. Rather, monetary policy is dictated by the necessity of finding a money supply which is compatible with equilibrium in both the commodity market (the* I-S *curve) and the balance of payments (the* B-K *curve).* Indeed, the very purpose of monetary policy ceases to be the regulation of domestic aggregate demand in the interests of employment and price level stabilization in the fashion discussed in Chapter 21. Monetary policy becomes a tool for the harmonization of the balance of payments and domestic aggregate demand in the interests of macroeconomic equilibrium.

In principle, macroeconomic equilibrium can also be achieved through fiscal policies designed to shift the *I-S* curve. However, for short-run adjustments, this is seldom a practical alternative. The very flexibility of monetary policy normally throws the bulk of the shorter-term adjustments on it. Nonetheless, the potential use of fiscal policy for this purpose — and particularly for the solution of longer-term problems — should not be overlooked.

Conflicts Between Domestic and External Policy.   This new perspective on monetary policy has another important implication. In Chapter 21 we discovered several reasons, within the Keynesian framework, why monetary policy might be relatively impotent as a tool for achieving domestic macroeconomic objectives like full employment and price level stability. The balance of international payments obviously imposes another constraint on the effectiveness of monetary policy for domestic economic stabilization. Indeed, *under certain circumstances, the balance of payments constraint may actually dictate monetary policies which are perverse from a domestic point of view.*

Two important cases must be considered. The first is represented in Figure 22-8. In this situation, the equilibrium level of income (Y_e) falls short of the level required to maintain full employment in the economy (Y_r). (Remember that we are dealing with a Keynesian economy, in which the price level is fixed.) Domestic considerations call for monetary expansion, shifting the *L-M* curve to L'-M', inducing lower interest rates and increased credit availability, and higher levels of investment income, and employment. Balance of payments considerations prevent this. Equilibrium can only be maintained in the foreign exchange market at the pegged exchange rate with high interest rates. There is a clear conflict between the use of monetary policy for domestic objectives and for external objectives. Overriding balance of payments considerations render monetary policy *perverse* from a domestic point of view.

That is not to say that full employment and balance of payments equilibrium cannot be achieved simultaneously in this situation. As noted above, fiscal policy can be used to move the *I-S* curve. What would be required in this situation would be expansionary fiscal policy (lower taxes, higher government expenditures) to move the economy toward full employment, coupled with a restrictive monetary policy to maintain balance of payments equilibrium.

FIGURE 22-8   Conflicts between policy objectives: balance of payments deficit and unemployment

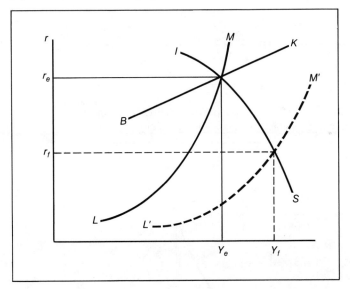

Another case of conflict in the use of monetary policy is illustrated in Figure 22-9. The equilibrium level of income (Y_e) is greater then the full employment level of income (Y_f). Full equilibrium calls for a larger money supply (L-M) than that which is required for full employment (L'-M'), and the lower interest rates and larger level of aggregate demand are inconsistent with price level stability. The monetary policy required to maintain stability of the foreign exchange rate in the absence of substantial increases in official foreign exchange reserves is an inflationary monetary policy.

Again, harmonization of the domestic and external objectives is possible in principle through the combined use of monetary and fiscal policies. As in the previous case, monetary and fiscal policies must be used in the opposite directions.

Conflicts between external and internal objectives are not inevitable, of course. In the case illustrated by Figure 22-10, at the existing level of income, (Y), there is neither

FIGURE 22-9   Conflicts between policy objectives: balance of payments surplus and inflation

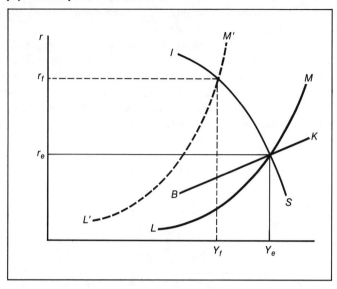

FIGURE 22-10   Conflicts between policy objectives · Agreement on direction of policy: conflict on intensity of expansion

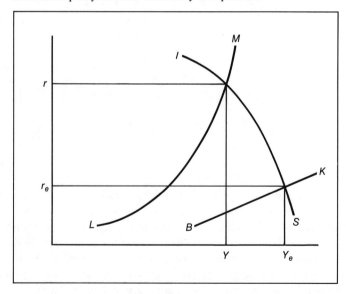

full employment nor full macroeconomic equilibrium (the combination (r, Y) lies above the B-K function, and hence the balance of payments is in surplus). The achievement of full employment and macroeconomic equilibrium both call for monetary expansion. There is no conflict on the *direction* of policy.

It should be noted, however, that in such a situation, the degree of monetary expansion appropriate to each objective may be different. This is also illustrated in Figure 22-10. Thus, once full employment is achieved (Y_f) further monetary expansion is still called for to eliminate the balance of payments surplus. The conflict between internal and external objectives reemerges at full employment.

Obviously, examples of this sort can be multiplied *ad nauseam*. However, the manipulation of graphs is only useful if it produces important conclusions about the functioning of the economy. Have we discovered anything of significance?

An Important Conclusion.   The results of our analysis to this point are very important. They demonstrate that *in an economy like Canada's there is little scope for a vigorous, independent monetary policy designed to regulate domestic aggregate demand if the foreign exchange rate is pegged, and if official foreign exchange reserves cannot undergo short-term fluctuations.*

This is a powerful conclusion, particularly if there is a constraint on the use of official foreign exchange reserves to fill the balance of payments gap.

FIXED EXCHANGE RATES:
OFFICIAL RESERVES

Official foreign exchange reserves are a pool of foreign exchange and other foreign currency assets which can be readily converted into foreign exchange, in the hands of the government and its agencies, and are available to finance direct government intervention in the foreign exchange market. We want to explore their role in ameliorating the potential conflict between domestic and external objectives of monetary policy.

Foreign Exchange Reserves and Balance of Payments Deficits

Let us first consider the case illustrated by Figure 22-8. This is a situation in which full employment calls for monetary expansion, but monetary expansion implies excess demand for foreign exchange at the maximum permissible foreign exchange rate. There is a clear conflict between the domestic and the external objectives of policy. Full employment implies a balance of payments deficit.

Foreign Exchange Reserves as a Buffer Stock.   The conflict is more apparent than real if the implied balance of payments deficit can be financed readily by drawing down official foreign exchange reserves. In this sense, official foreign exchange reserves can serve as a buffer stock, absorbing the balance of payments consequences of domestic economic policies (or, alternatively, shielding domestic policy from adverse developments in the balance of payments). Indeed, this *is* the economic function of official foreign exchange reserves. They are supposed to make the government's commitment to maintain the pegged exchange rate credible, without imposing continuous tyranny of the balance of payments over domestic monetary and fiscal policies.

If foreign exchange reserves are to perform this function they must be large relative to potential balance of payments deficits. Remember that at any point in time official foreign exchange reserves are a *stock* of finite magnitude. A balance of payments deficit (a *flow*) during any period will reduce the level of reserves available to finance a deficit in the following period. A continuing deficit will deplete the stock of reserves more or less rapidly, depending on the size of the deficit relative to the stock of reserves. Thus, Canada's foreign exchange reserves of just over $3 billion at the end of 1980 would only last 12 months in the face of a steady monthly deficit of $250 million, or three months in the face of a steady monthly deficit of $1 billion.

This implies that the independence of domestic monetary policy from the balance of payments constraint under a fixed exchange rate regime is simply a matter of having adequate foreign exchange reserves. The larger the stock of reserves, the greater the scope for independent action in pursuit of domestic full employment, unhampered by concern over potential balance of payments deficits.

There is an important element of truth in this proposition. Large reserves will finance larger or more prolonged deficits than will small reserves. However, the degree of independence provided by even quite large reserves can be illusory. A simple comparison of the size of the reserves with the size of probable deficits which will result from vigorous pursuit of a domestic full employment policy neglects the effect of the vital force of speculation in the foreign exchange market.

Speculation in the Foreign Exchange Market.   We referred briefly to the possibility of speculative demands for foreign exchange in anticipation of a rise in the foreign exchange rate in Chapter 8. From time to time, particularly in the closing stages of the Bretton Woods system, speculation proved to be a powerful, and occasionally decisive, force in foreign exchange markets. We cannot discuss the role of official foreign exchange reserves as a buffer stock between the balance of payments and domestic policy without considering the possibility that a drop in foreign exchange reserves will incite speculation on a major change in the exchange rate.

The Bretton Woods system was peculiarly vulnerable to speculative activity. While exchange rates were pegged, unlike the situation under the classical gold standard, they were not sacrosanct. Periodic adjustments were permissible, and did occur with reasonable frequency, even for major currencies. Such changes tended to occur in sudden, discrete jumps of relatively large magnitude (e.g. 10% to 15%).

In this environment, with the exchange rate pressed against the ceiling and foreign exchange reserves falling, speculators may see a possibility for large gains *with virtually no risk of a major loss*. If a rise in the par rate of exchange occurs, they stand to make a substantial gain. Under the circumstances, there is virtually no possibility that the par rate of exchange will be reduced. As a result, the worst they can expect is a small decline in the market rate away from the ceiling. Given the very one-sided risk, this is a speculation which might even appeal to "risk averters." Indeed, much speculative activity (in the sense of a transfer of funds in anticipation of a change in the exchange rate) was undertaken by conservative corporate treasurers who argued that they were not seeking speculative gains, but were simply protecting the financial position of the corporation.[7] It should not be surprising, therefore, that a country which was losing foreign exchange reserves with its exchange rate pressed against the ceiling would find its currency under intense speculative attack.

The important point is that the government must make available all of the foreign exchange which the speculators demand if it is to prevent the exchange rate from rising above the ceiling. In other words, speculation induced by a drop in the level of official foreign exchange reserves will accelerate the decline of those reserves — and further declines will intensify the speculative activity. From the point of view of the monetary authorities, it is a vicious circle. Experience in several countries has demonstrated that the pressures of speculation can be overwhelming.

It is not necessary that the speculative attack culminate in a change in the par rate of exchange for it to be relevant and important. Whether or not it alters the exchange rate, in the face of intense speculation the government will be forced to adjust domestic monetary and fiscal policies to take the pressure of the balance of payments, if it is to avoid resort to direct foreign exchange controls. Indeed, the balance of payments crisis may dictate temporarily more severe domestic restraint than would have been necessary otherwise.

The degree of insulation from balance of payments constraints which may seem to be provided by a given level of foreign exchange reserves can be a dangerous illusion.

Intervention in the Forward Exchange Market.   It is unlikely that speculation will be confined to the spot exchange market. Anticipations of a rise in the foreign exchange rate are also likely to lead to speculative demands for *forward exchange* (Chapter 8). Indeed, from the point of view of the speculator, forward exchange has an advantage over spot exchange as a vehicle for speculation in that it does not call for immediate payment. Payment will not occur until the contract expires and the actual delivery of foreign exchange occurs (at which time the speculator will presumably immediately sell the foreign exchange, taking his gains or losses). Because it involves no immediate payment, speculation in forward exchange might seem irrelevant to the problem of maintaining adequate foreign exchange reserves. If there is no immediate delivery of spot exchange, speculation in forward exchange cannot directly constitute a drain on the official foreign exchange reserves.

However, speculation in forward exchange will put upward pressure on the forward exchange rate, and this has two important consequences. First, by providing a clear signal that "the market" expects the spot rate to rise in the near future, a significant rise in the forward rate might intensify speculation in the spot market. Second, as we saw in Chapter 8, given the levels of short-term interest rates in Canada and abroad, a rise in the forward exchange rate will create an incentive to move funds out of Canada on a covered interest-arbitrage basis. Thus, speculation in forward exchange will *indirectly* induce a capital outflow, add to the balance of payments deficit, and accelerate the drain of foreign exchange reserves.

For these reasons the government will probably find it expedient to intervene in the forward exchange market as well as in the spot market. The Exchange Fund will offer to "sell" forward exchange in order to stabilize the forward exchange rate. That is, the Fund will enter into contracts to deliver foreign exchange at some specified date in the future at a price agreed upon now. At times, the Canadian Exchange Fund has been called upon to take a very large position in forward exchange.

Do Forward Sales Reduce Foreign Exchange Reserves? When it "sells" forward exchange, the Exchange Fund has entered into a contract to deliver part of the nation's foreign exchange reserves to speculators at some future date. It can be argued, therefore, that the Fund's forward exchange position ought to be taken into account in computing the nation's foreign exchange reserves. That is, the Fund's forward sales contracts ought to be deducted from the published holdings of spot foreign exchange in order to obtain the nation's *net foreign exchange reserves* (and likewise the Fund's forward purchases ought to be added to reserves).

This is not done. Indeed, the Fund's forward position is normally not published until long after the event. Moreover, some economists would argue that the two should be kept quite separate: that regardless of its holdings of spot exchange, in the face of speculative buying of forward exchange, the Fund can enter into almost unlimited forward exchange contracts without prejudicing the nation's underlying foreign exchange position. If the forward contracts are truly speculative, the purchaser has no intention of actually taking the funds out of the country. He will be happy to sell back the foreign exchange to which he is entitled after the anticipated change in the exchange rate has occurred, or at any time that he is convinced that no change will occur. Thus, it is argued, there is no real risk that the Exchange Fund will ever be called upon to deliver the foreign exchange which it has sold forward; and there is nothing to stop it from taking a very large position in forward exchange, perhaps selling forward substantially more foreign exchange than it actually has in its spot reserves.

The proposition can be pushed a step further. It is sometimes argued that in the face of a strong speculative attack, the government ought to intervene vigorously in the forward market, taking as large a position as necessary to drive the forward exchange rate *down*, producing an inflow of funds on an interest-arbitrage basis, and perhaps breaching the solid front of expectations underlying the wave of speculation. Adapting the concepts introduced in Chapter 18 to describe central bank operations, it is argued that intervention in the forward exchange market can be used as a dynamic instrument of policy rather than simply as a defensive measure.

While aggressive action in the forward exchange market sometimes plays an important role in central banking operations, central bankers generally argue that extreme policies such as those sketched above are not practical. The risks to the Exchange Fund involved in a very large forward position are too great to be regarded with the equanimity displayed by economic theoreticians.

Inter-Central Bank Credits: Another Buffer.   Finally, before we leave the general topic of governmental measures to stabilize the foreign exchange rate in the face of a balance of payments deficit, we must relax the assumption that at any point in time official foreign exchange reserves are absolutely fixed in amount. In addition to its *explicit* reserves in the form of gold, foreign exchange and drawing rights at the International Monetary Fund available for immediate use at any time, Canada has a second line of defence which is *implicit* in the Bank of Canada's close cooperation with the central banks of other industrialized nations, and in Canada's membership in the International Monetary Fund. In effect, Canada belongs to an international mutual assistance society of central bankers, and Canada, like other members, can normally rely upon substantial credits being extended by the International Monetary Fund, the Bank for International Settlements and other central banks in time of emergency, providing additional foreign currency assets to support the government's intervention in the foreign exchange market.

Credits which are potentially available in this way are commonly called *conditional reserves* because the extension of credit is conditional on the lenders being convinced that the borrowing government will implement effective monetary and fiscal policies which assign top priority to the correction of the balance of payments problem. While conditional reserves have proven to be a valuable and flexible device for combatting waves of speculation, and for the stabilization of exchange rates, they are not designed to liberate domestic monetary and fiscal policy from the discipline of the balance of payments.

Conclusions: The Significance of Speculation. Speculation, whether in the spot market or the forward market, is a powerful force which cannot be ignored in assessing the adequacy of foreign exchange reserves as a buffer between domestic monetary and fiscal policy and the balance of international payments. The "adjustable peg" arrangement of the Bretton Woods system was particularly vulnerable to speculation, and periodic speculative attacks on one currency or another became almost commonplace in international finance in that era. From our point of view, the important point is not that speculative attacks occasionally force a change in par rates of exchange. Rather, it is that speculation, or the threat of speculation, forces monetary and fiscal authorities to assign a higher priority to the balance of payments in deciding on policy than might seem desirable on other grounds or than might seem necessary given the magnitude of the buffer stock apparently provided by official holdings of foreign exchange. The presence of conditional reserves eases the problem of coping with a speculative attack, but it does little to modify the primacy which must be assigned to balance-of-payments equilibrium in policy deliberations.

Foreign Exchange Reserves and Balance of Payments Surpluses

So far, our discussion of the role of foreign exchange reserves as a buffer between domestic policy and the balance of international payments has been cast in terms of coping with balance of payments deficits in a period of less than full employment. Before we leave the subject, however, we must refer briefly to the opposite case, in which the balance of payments is in surplus when the economy is at full employment. This is the situation depicted in Figure 22-9. Monetary expansion would eliminate the balance of payments surplus, but monetary expansion would be inflationary.

Foreign Exchange Reserves as a Buffer Stock. Again, foreign exchange reserves appear in the role of a buffer stock. The balance of payments surplus can, in principle, be added to the official foreign exchange reserves and stored up to be used subsequently in times of balance of payments deficit.

However, the accumulation of foreign exchange reserves is not without its problems. In this case, the problem is to finance the acquisition of reserves in a manner which is not inconsistent with domestic policy objectives.

Monetary Effects.   We discussed the monetary implications of changes in foreign exchange reserves in some detail in Chapter 18. The central point to emerge from that analysis was that operations of the Exchange Fund have no necessary direct effect on the monetary base. Monetary repercussions, if any, depend on the financial adjustments which are made to accommodate the change in the Exchange Fund. Thus, purchases of foreign exchange by the Exchange Fund will expand the monetary base if they are financed, directly or indirectly, by the Bank of Canada. However, if the government simply draws on its cash balances with the chartered banks to pay for the foreign exchange acquired by the Exchange Fund the monetary base will be unaffected. (What will happen to the publicly-owned money supply?) In general, the government does not have large excess cash balances. Thus, if there is a sustained surplus in the balance of payments the government can only avoid monetary expansion if it can generate a budgetary surplus (by raising taxes or reducing other government expenditures), or if it can borrow the required funds in the Canadian capital market. What has to happen is a diversion of part of the income of the nation from the acquisition of consumer and capital goods to the acquisition of foreign exchange. The nation must be induced to accumulate wealth in the form of official foreign exchange reserves (although it is far from evident that the yield on official foreign exchange reserves is sufficiently great to justify the diversion of resources from alternative uses, whether in consumption or in real capital formation). If it borrows heavily, the government may force up interest rates on government bonds, and indeed may aggravate the balance of payments problem by attracting more foreign capital. If it raises taxes to finance the accumulation of foreign exchange reserves, the government may meet strong political resistance. In principle, it should be possible to finance the accumulation of foreign exchange reserves in a noninflationary manner: in fact, the technical and political problems of doing so may be very great. The problem of coping with a balance of payments surplus in a fully employed economy will obviously be aggravated if there is a wave of speculation that the exchange rate will have to be reduced.

The problem of avoiding inflation in the face of a substantial balance of payments surplus in a fully employed economy are clearly illustrated in Canada in 1950 and in 1970. While we will not examine them here, these examples are well worth investigation on the part of the student of monetary economics.

Conclusions

With a fixed foreign exchange rate, the independence of monetary policy depends on the existence of foreign exchange reserves as a buffer stock between domestic policy and the balance of payments. Large foreign exchange reserves are important, but it should be obvious from our discussion of speculation that the independence of domestic monetary and fiscal policies does not depend on the size of reserves alone. The essential question is whether the government can tolerate wide swings in the level of reserves in a short time period. As the Governor of the Bank of Canada observed in his testimony before the Royal Commission on Banking and Finance,

> with a structure of international transactions as large as ours, and containing as many potentially volatile elements, it must be expected that from time to time the changes in the level of our reserves will be very large, and we must be prepared therefore to accommodate them.

If the system is to work,

> Canadian public opinion must prepare itself to accept large fluctuations in our reserves....It will militate against the smooth operation of the fixed [exchange] rate system if, instead of focusing on the underlying position of the country's balance of payments, public attention should be pre-occupied to an exaggerated degree with short-term changes in reserves....[8]

If sharp changes in exchange reserves engender strong speculation, foreign exchange reserves are more likely to be useful in financing relatively small balance of payments deficits of relatively short duration, rather than relatively large, persistent deficits. This is a slim reed on which to tie the independence of domestic monetary policy.

As we will note later, throughout the 20th century Canada has shown an aversion to a regime of fixed exchange rates. Perhaps you now know enough to develop a plausible explanation why.

FIXED EXCHANGE RATES: MONETARIST ANALYSIS

We saw in Chapter 21 that economists of the monetarist school came to very different conclusions from those of the Keynesian school about the impact and role of monetary policy in a closed economy. Are there corresponding differences in the analysis of the interaction between monetary policy and the balance of international payments under a fixed exchange rate regime?

The answer is emphatically yes! Although some of the differences in conclusions may seem less extreme than those in the analysis of the closed economy, an alternative to the Keynesian analysis of the open economy has developed in recent years, called "the monetary approach to the balance of payments."[9] Two closely related propositions constitute the core of the monetary approach.

The Balance of Payments as a Monetary Phenomenon

The first, and most fundamental, proposition is that, with a fixed exchange rate, the balance of international payments is strictly a monetary phenomenon. A balance of payments deficit is a direct consequence of excessive monetary expansion, and a balance of payments surplus is a direct consequence of inadequate monetary expansion. The main elements of the analysis leading to this conclusion should be familiar already, and a brief sketch of the major points should be sufficient.

Tendency to Full Employment.   Like the monetarist analysis of a closed economy, the monetarist analysis of the open economy assumes that the economy tends automatically to the "natural" rate of unemployment. This is the equivalent of an assumption of full employment. In this sense, the monetary approach to the balance of payments is "long run" analysis.

Exogenous Prices and Interest Rates.   As in our previous analysis of the small economy, the monetarist analysis assumes that the prices of goods and services are given, determined in large world markets. Beyond this, however, it also assumes that interest rates are given, determined in world capital markets. This is equivalent to an assumption of a perfectly elastic *B-K* curve, resulting from perfectly interest-elastic international capital flows.

The Demand for Money and the Balance of Payments.   The analysis also assumes a stable demand for money function. With the level of income determined by the full employment assumption, and prices and interest rates fixed in world markets, the quantity of money demand in the economy is also determined.

Suppose the central bank supplies a larger quantity of money than is demanded. In the monetarist model of the closed economy the price level will adjust; in the Keynesian model, it is the interest rate that will respond first. In the open economy monetarist model, no adjustment can occur in domestic production, employment, prices, or interest rates. The excess supply of money must become an excess demand for foreign goods, services, or securities. There is no other outlet for the excess supply of money. It must generate either a current account deficit or a net capital outflow, or both. In the monetary approach the distinction between an impact on the current account and an impact on the capital account is not important. The important point is that an *excess supply of money must result directly in a balance of payments deficit and hence in a loss of foreign exchange reserves.*

The opposite is also true. (We leave it to you to sketch out the analysis). *An excess demand for money must result directly in a balance of payments surplus and hence in a gain of foreign exchange reserves.*

An Endogenous Money Supply

The second fundamental proposition of the monetary approach to the balance of international payments is that within a period of time "relevant for policy analysis" *the monetary authorities cannot sterilize the monetary consequences of changes in foreign exchange reserves.*[10] A loss of foreign exchange reserves will reduce the money supply; a gain of foreign exchange reserves will increase the money supply. Thus, over the "relevant" time period, *a balance of payments disequilibrium will be self-correcting—* the very monetary factors which produced the disequilibrium will be reversed so that, over the "relevant" time period, there cannot be a fundamental conflict between internal and external objectives of monetary policy. Indeed, *the central bank cannot pursue an independent monetary policy.* The quantity of money will be determined by the demand for money, given the levels of income, prices, and interest rates.

The Scope for Sterilization.   We explored the relationship between changes in official foreign exchange reserves and the monetary base in Chapter 19. When foreign exchange reserves increase, the government is purchasing foreign money in the foreign exchange market, making payment in Canadian dollars. If the Canadian dollars are provided by the Bank of Canada, the Canadian monetary base (and hence the money supply) increases. However, if the Canadian dollars are provided out of the government's own cash balances (deposits with the chartered banks), borrowing in the open market (not from the Bank of Canada), or an excess of tax collections over government expenditures, there will be no increase in the monetary base, and the increase in foreign exchange reserves will have been *sterilized*. At any time, of course, the government's cash balances are limited, and earmarked for other purposes. In a fully employed economy, government borrowing or an excess of tax collections over expenditures involves the diversion of part of national income from consumption or capital formation into the accumulation of foreign exchange reserves. It is unlikely that the accumulation of foreign exchange reserves is the use of national savings which has the highest yield. The monetary approach assumes that there are strict limits to the ability of the government to invest in foreign exchange and hence to sterilize the monetary effects of the accumulation of foreign exchange, perhaps because of taxpayer (or lender) resistance.

Reductions in foreign exchange reserves pose the opposite problem. The government is selling foreign exchange out of its reserves and receiving payment in Canadian dollars. If the Canadian dollars are deposited in the Bank of Canada, or used to retire government debt held by the Bank of Canada, the monetary base will contract, and the monetary adjustment of the monetary approach will occur. However, if the Canadian dollars are deposited in the chartered banks, used to retire government debt held by the general public, or used to finance expenditures in excess of tax collections, the monetary base will not be affected, and the change in foreign exchange reserves will be sterilized. At any time, the government's foreign exchange reserves are limited. However, as we saw in the previous section, foreign exchange reserves can generally be augmented by government borrowing in foreign capital markets. In asserting that sterilization is not possible, the monetary approach is asserting that such borrowing cannot occur or is strictly limited.

There is ample evidence that governments, including the government of Canada, have been successful in sterilizing large changes in foreign exchange reserves. Except under conditions of a classical gold standard, when gold was simultaneously foreign exchange and domestic money, the second fundamental proposition of the monetary approach is not convincing in the face of this historical evidence (if it is interpreted literally that the monetary authorities *cannot sterilize*). However, there is another interpretation that merits closer attention: monetary authorities *should not sterilize* the monetary effects of changes in foreign exchange reserves. On this interpretation, the second fundamental proposition is not a technical statement about what is possible, but, rather, a prescription for what ought to be done.

Sterilization and the Perpetuation of Disequilibrium.

Both the Keynesian model of the open economy and the monetary approach to the balance of payments agree that a persistent change in foreign exchange reserves is a sign of macroeconomic disequilibrium in an open economy. Keynesian concern for short-term unemployment problems would induce a search for alternative solutions — fiscal policy or devaluation. The monetarists argue that the authorities should not be concerned with the short run — that is not the period of time "relevant for policy analysis." If the monetary authorities focus on the short-term, they will respond to transitory developments rather than fundamental problems, and as a result exacerbate the situation. In particular, a balance of payments disequilibrium which is not corrected will cumulate into a severe crisis. Because, it is argued, the disequilibrium is monetary in origin, only a monetary adjustment will correct it.[11] If the disequilibrium involves a balance of payments surplus, the money supply should be increased to correct it; if the disequilibrium involves a balance of payments deficit, the money supply should be contracted to correct it. Remember, it is argued that the functioning of the labor market is such that the economy will return to full employment regardless.

The Monetarist Analysis: Conclusions

The monetarist analysis of the closed economy leads to the conclusion that while the monetary authorities can control the normal money supply, in the long run they cannot control the real money supply. The price level adjusts, making the real money supply endogenous (determined within the economy). On one interpretation, the monetarist analysis of the small open economy with a fixed exchange rate suggests an even stronger conclusion. In the long run, the monetary authorities cannot even control the nominal money supply. On another interpretation, short-term sterilization of changes in foreign exchange reserves is technically possible, but undesirable. Balance of payments disequilibrium is a monetary phenomenon. Correction of the disequilibrium requires appropriate monetary policy; monetary expansion for a surplus, contraction for a deficit. In either case, the economy will tend to full employment regardless.

It is perhaps worth noting that with fixed exchange rates the closed economy monetarist analysis applies only at the *world* level. An individual country cannot create inflation through monetary expansion (unless the rest of the world uses its currency as money); it can only create a balance of payments deficit. However, simultaneous monetary expansion by all countries will create worldwide inflation.

FIXED EXCHANGE RATES: PRICES AND WAGES

We introduced our analysis of the macroeconomics of a fixed exchange rate regime with the strong assumption that the prices of Canadian imports and exports are determined in world markets and as a result, given the importance of internationally traded goods in the Canadian economy, movements of the Canadian price level (the rate of inflation or deflation) are determined abroad. We then developed our analysis using the Keynesian assumption that the price level is given. However, even for an economy like Canada's, which is heavily engaged in international trade, this can only be a first approximation.

Non-Tradeable Goods

Not all goods and services, the prices of which are significant in the Canadian price level, enter into international trade. Many services must be performed locally, and for some goods transportation costs are so heavy relative to the value of the goods as to make them "non-tradeable." For some other goods, tariffs and governmental barriers to international trade, stand between Canadian producers and world markets, although this does not necessarily isolate Canadian prices for these products from competitive prices set in world markets. The prices of many tariff-protected products are set at levels just below those which would elicit competitive imports, and these prices can be

FIGURE 22-11   Relative rates of inflation with fixed and flexible exchange rates: rate of change in the Consumer Price Index, Canada and the United States, 1955-1980

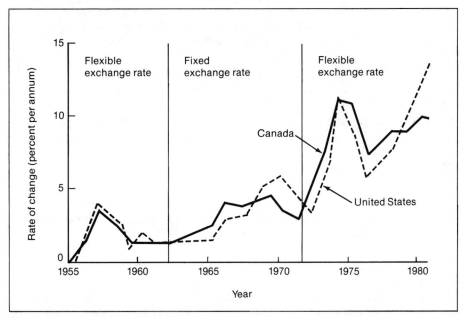

Source: Federal Reserve Bank of St. Louis, *International Economic Conditions*

expected to be adjusted if world prices change. However, there are some items which are truly "non-tradeable" — some goods and many services — the prices of which are set in Canada. To the extent that these prices are important in the Canadian price level, movements in the level will not be rigidly tied to world prices, even with a fixed exchange rate.

It is difficult to identify the set of "non-tradeable" goods, and it undoubtedly changes over time. Hence it is difficult to assess the quantitative importance of "non-tradeable" goods in the Canadian price level. However, while there are technical problems in comparing price indexes for different countries, Figure 22-11 can be used to illustrate the point. During the most recent period in which Canada had a fixed exchange rate, 1962-1970, the consumer price indexes for Canada and the United States displayed the same underlying movements, but were clearly not rigidly tied together. We can conclude that while the assumption that the Canadian price level is determined abroad is not literally valid under a fixed exchange rate, the degree of freedom for the Canadian price level to move independently of world prices is small.

International Substitution Effects.   To the extent that Canadian prices can move independently of world prices under a fixed exchange rate, domestic inflation will involve a change in *relative* prices. Prices of domestic "non-tradeable" goods will rise relative to prices of imports and exports. One of the basic propositions of elementary economic theory is that a change in relative prices will induce substitution among the goods in question. Exactly the same thing will happen if the prices of Canadian-produced goods and services change relative to the prices of goods and services produced in the rest of the world. *A rise in the Canadian price level will induce international substitution effects.* These effects may show up in various ways but, basically, domestic consumers will be induced to purchase more imported goods as substitutes for relatively more expensive Canadian-produced goods. The impact on international trade, and on aggregate demand for Canadian productive resources, will depend on the magnitude of the change in prices and the relevant elasticities of demand and supply. However, the general effect of a rise in Canadian costs and prices relative to world prices will be some decline in exports and some rise in imports, reducing a surplus or increasing a deficit in the current account of the balance of payments. A decline in Canadian prices relative to world prices would have the opposite effects. That is, it would tend to increase exports and reduce imports, increasing a surplus or reducing a deficit in the current account of the balance of payments.

However, far more powerful than the change in relative prices of non-tradeable and imported goods is the impact which domestic inflation may have on costs of production.

Wage Rates

Although most commodity prices are set in world markets, there is one set of prices, changes in which are of profound importance, which are set independently in Canadian markets — *wage rates.* By and large, labor is not *directly* an item in international trade (there are some important exceptions) and Canadian wage rates are not set *directly* in large international markets for labor. Of course, a major part of the demand for labor in Canada is derived from the demand for exports or for import-competing goods; and the cost of labor is a major component of the total costs of production of exports and import-competing goods. But that is the point! Independent changes in Canadian wage rates can have a profound influence on the international competitive position of Canadian producers of export and import-competing goods, and hence can affect both the current account of the balance of international payments and the *I-S* curve.

Determination of Wage Rates. In Chapter 21 we noted that the process by which wage rates are set and the pressures under which they change are central issues in the fundamental controversies in macroeconomics between Keynesian and monetarist analysis. This is an unsettled area, and the subject of intensive theoretical and empirical research. The role of labor unions and their potential to induce movements of wage rates independently of market conditions is particularly controversial.

Three points seem clear from the evidence, however. (1) Wage rates are not highly flexible in the short run. They do not respond sensitively and quickly to excess demand or excess supply pressures in labor markets. (2) Over longer periods of time, and in the face of persistent demand or supply pressures, wage rates do respond in the expected manner. (3) As a result, earlier developments in labor markets — perhaps excess demand pressures accompanied by general inflation some time ago — can give momentum to wage rates, making them continue to rise long after economic slack has emerged.

In particular, it is recognized the inflationary expectations, stubbornly held, can be built into labor contracts, leading to wage rate increases in the face of unemployment. In this sense, short-run movements in wage rates have at least the appearance of being independent of the state of the economy.[12]

Wage Rates and the Balance of Payments.   Suppose such an apparently independent increase in wage rates occurs. To business firms, an increase in wage rates — or at least an increase in wage rates in excess of the increase in output per manhour (labor productivity) — implies an increase in costs of production. Cost curves in export industries and in import-competing industries shift upward. With a fixed exchange rate, and prices of exports and imports set in large world markets, there will be no commensurate change in prices received by exporters and import-competing firms. The profitability of production for export and competition with imports will fall. The export function of Figure 22-1 will shift inward, and the import demand functions will

FIGURE 22-12   The effects of higher wage rates

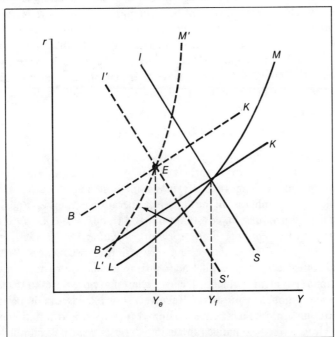

The shifts in the *I-S* and *B-K* curves are a result of higher wage rates in Canada (with a fixed exchange rate and given world prices of exports and imports). *I-S* shifts to *I'-S'*; *B-K* shifts to *B'-K'*.

The shift in the *L-M* curve is an act of policy. For macroeconomic equilibrium, *L-M* must shift to *L'-M'*, resulting in equilibrium at point *E*, and lower levels of real income (*Y_e* rather than *Y_f*), production and employment.

shift upward; the *I-S* curve will shift to the left, reducing potential equilibrium levels of production and employment in Canada for any given level of interest rates (or, in the complete model, for any given money supply). But the shift of export and import functions also means that the current account of the balance of international payments will deteriorate at any given level of income; the current account function of Figure 22-4 will shift to the left, producing a larger current account deficit at each level of income. Given the net capital flow function, the *B-K* curve is also shifted to the left. At any level of income, balance of payments equilibrium will require a larger net inflow of capital to offset the larger current account deficit, and to induce this net capital inflow a higher level of interest rates will be required.

The combined effects of the shift in the *I-S* curve and the *B-K* curve create the classic conflict of policy in an open economy (Figure 22-12). Macroeconomic equilibrium requires a contraction of the money supply (shifting *L-M* to the left); full employment requires an expansion of the money supply (shifting *L-M* to the right). Given short-term inflexibility in fiscal policies designed to shift the *I-S* curve, the government authorities are faced with a fundamental policy dilemma.

It is important to emphasize that the shifting of the *I-S* and *B-K* curves does not depend exclusively on the movement of Canadian wage rates. *It is the relationship between Canadian wage rates and world prices for exports and imports which is crucial.* A fall in world prices, given a fixed exchange rate and inflexible Canadian wage rates, will produce exactly the same effect. Of course, a rise in world prices, given a fixed exchange rate and inflexible Canadian wage rates, will produce the opposite effect. (As an exercise, it is well worth setting out the analysis which leads to this conclusion.)

Relative Inflation Rates and the Fixed Exchange Rate

This discussion leads to an important conclusion. In a small open economy, with export and import prices set in world markets, inflation of domestic origin must show up primarily as increases of wage rates in excess of increases in productivity. While there is always some slippage inherent in the imperfect operation of markets and in time lags in the adjustment of production, consumption, and trade, *with a fixed exchange rate a small open economy cannot choose a rate of inflation independent of the rate of inflation in the rest of the world* without very serious consequences. Relatively rapid increases in domestic wage rates will lead to unemployment and a deteriorating balance of international payments, which will elicit deflationary pressures in the labor market and deflationary monetary pressures. Relatively slow increases in domestic wage rates will lead to high employment, excess demand for labor, and inflationary monetary pressures. Thus, a fixed exchange rate regime imposes a stern discipline on Canadian macroeconomic policy. But the point is much more general than that. Every country with a fixed exchange rate will be in the same situation. Even without accepting the extreme assumptions of the monetarist model, it should be apparent that by forcing all countries to have essentially the same rate of inflation, the fixed exchange rate regime imposes a severe discipline on macroeconomic policies internationally. Is it surprising that stresses and policy conflicts develop frequently under a multilateral fixed exchange rate regime? Can we now explain more fully why Canada has shown such an aversion for fixed exchange rates in the 20th century?

But all of that assumes that the exchange rate is fixed. What happens if the exchange rate is flexible, adjusting quickly and sensitively to excess demand or excess supply in the foreign exchange market?

FLEXIBLE EXCHANGE RATES: KEYNESIAN ANALYSIS

If the exchange rate is fixed, the Canadian price level cannot change significantly relative to the world price level. However, a change in the foreign exchange rate is equivalent to a change in the world price level; and a flexible exchange rate can permit the Canadian price level to move independently of the world price level. This fundamentally alters the environment in which monetary policy is conducted, and significantly alters the potential impact of monetary policy.

Changes in the Exchange Rate Versus Changes in Price Levels

A rise in the price of foreign exchange (= a *fall* in the external value of the Canadian dollar) raises the delivered price of foreign goods to Canadian buyers just as effectively as a rise in foreign price level itself. Thus, it will tend to restrict Canadian imports. Similarly, a rise in the foreign exchange rate lowers the delivered price of Canadian goods to foreign markets just as effectively as a decline in the Canadian price level. It will tend to increase Canadian exports. Taking the two effects together, a rise in the foreign rate will improve the current account balance, and hence will tend to increase a balance of payments surplus or reduce a balance of payments deficit. In terms of its impact on the balance of payments, *a rise in the foreign exchange rate is a substitute for a fall in Canadian wage rates and prices or for a rise in the world price level.*

The opposite arguments hold for a fall in the foreign exchange rate (= a *rise* in the external value of the Canadian dollar). By making Canadian goods more expensive for foreign buyers, it will tend to restrict exports. By making foreign goods less expensive for Canadian buyers, it will tend to increase imports. Thus, a fall in the foreign exchange rate will tend to worsen the balance on current account, and hence will tend to reduce a balance of payments surplus or increase a balance of payments deficit. In terms of its impact on the balance of payments, *a fall in the foreign exchange rate is a substitute for a rise in Canadian wage rates and prices, or a fall in the world price level.*

The Exchange Rate and Policy Conflicts.   It follows that changes in the exchange rate can be used to resolve balance of payments problems which would otherwise force a drastic change in domestic monetary and fiscal policies. Thus, a balance of payments deficit (whatever its cause) can be removed by an appropriate rise in the foreign exchange rate; and a balance of payments surplus can be removed by an appropriate drop in the foreign exchange rate.

However, these are once-over changes. If domestic policy involves a rate of price level change which is different from that in the rest of the world, balance of payments equilibrium will require *continuous adjustment* of the exchange rate. A more rapid rate of inflation in Canada than in the rest of the world is only consistent with balance of payments equilibrium if the exchange rate continuously rises. A slower rate of inflation in Canada than in the rest of the world would call for a continuous fall in the exchange rate.

In other words, the independence of domestic policy from external constraints is only possible if the exchange rate can be adjusted continuously to changing pressures in the foreign exchange market.

Flexible Exchange Rates and Monetary Policy

Flexibility of the exchange rate creates a fundamentally different environment for monetary and fiscal policy from that provided by a regime of fixed exchange rates. Let us now explore some of the implications of flexible exchange rates for monetary policy.

The Exchange Rate and Balance of Payments Equilibrium.   The crucial difference between the fixed and flexible exchange rate regimes is the mechanism for maintaining equilibrium in the balance of international payments. Although some proponents of the monetary approach to the balance of payments would disagree, our earlier analysis of the fixed exchange rate regime suggests that the maintenance of equilibrium in the balance of payments must be the responsibility of *government policy*, and particularly of monetary policy. Unless there is considerable flexibility in the levels of wages and prices, there is no automatic mechanism to ensure the equilibration of demand and supply forces in the foreign exchange market in the short run. With a flexible exchange rate, by contrast, *the foreign exchange rate* can be expected to adjust automatically to maintain equilibrium in the balance of payments even though domestic wages and prices are inflexible in the short run.

Consider the case in which the balance of payments is in deficit, perhaps because the deficit on current account is greater than the surplus on capital account. There will be excess demand for foreign exchange at the existing exchange rate. It is this pressure of excess demand which will tend to increase the foreign exchange rate, and in the absence of an official constraint on the rate, the rate will rise.

Will the increase of the exchange rate tend to eliminate the balance of payments deficit?

The Current Account.   As we noted above, a rise of the foreign exchange rate is equivalent to a rise in the world price level relative to prices and wage rates in Canada. As a result, there should be substitution effects in the current account of the balance of payments. Exports, which are now relatively cheaper to the rest of the world, should increase, and imports, which are now relatively more expensive to Canadians, should fall. The current account should adjust so as to eliminate the excess demand for foreign exchange.

The Capital Account.   The behavior of the capital account is more problematic. In general, the *level* of the foreign exchange rate *per se* should not be relevant to international portfolio investment decisions. As long as the investor *expects* to bring his funds back at the same exchange rate at which he takes them out of the country, the level of the foreign exchange rate will not be a factor in his calculations. This should be obvious from the examples explored in Chapter 8 (e.g., Example 8-1). If the investor expects the exchange rate to be the same when he brings his funds home as when he sends them out, the exchange rates applicable to the two foreign exchange transactions (out — in) simply cancel each other out. All that is relevant to the calculation of the expected net return is the difference in interest rates (although the *risk* of change in the exchange rate will be relevant to the investment decision, of course).

It is different if the investor has reason to expect a change in the foreign exchange rate. Any increase of the foreign exchange rate will give an added premium to Canadian investments in foreign securities, and will impose a penalty on nonresidents' investments in Canadian securities. Similarly, a reduction of the exchange rate will impose a penalty on nonresidents' investment in Canadian securities, and will add a premium to Canadian investments in foreign securities.

To know what will happen in the capital account as the exchange rate rises, then, we must know what happens to investors' *expectations* about the future course of the exchange rate. If they expect a continuing rise in exchange rate there will be an incentive for more Canadian investment abroad and less nonresident investment in Canada. Capital outflows should be increased or capital inflows reduced. However, if investors feel that the rise is temporary, and that the rate will eventually subside, there will be an incentive for less Canadian investment abroad and more nonresident investment in Canada. Capital inflows should be increased or capital outflows restricted. If, by contrast, they expect the exchange rate to be unchanged at any particular level established at any particular time, then capital inflows and outflows will be unaffected by the change in the exchange rate. In other words, if the net capital inflow does not increase or decrease it will stay the same!

The crucial consideration is that of investors' expectations of future changes in the exchange rate, not the present level of the exchange rate. Unfortunately, we know very little about the determinants of these expectations. With this in mind, perhaps it is best to first consider the case in which we can ignore expectations. That is, we will assume that investors take the existing exchange rate to be the best estimate of what future exchange rates will be, regardless of the present level or the past history of the exchange rate. In this case, the entire adjustment in the balance of payments occurs in the current account. The net capital inflow will be unaffected by the rise in the exchange rate: imports must fall and exports rise until the current account deficit is tailored to the net capital inflow. Exactly the opposite arguments would apply if we had chosen a case of balance of payments surplus. What are the implications of these balance of payments adjustments for monetary policy?

To explore this matter, we return again to the *IS-LM* model of the open economy, on the assumption of short-term inflexibility in domestic wages and prices, and particularly wage rates. What modifications have to be introduced to allow for the flexibility of exchange rates?

The Balance of Payments Constraint on Monetary Policy.   The first important point is that the *B-K* curve (the locus of combinations of interest rates and income levels which are consistent with equilibrium in the balance of payments) is no longer a useful concept. Balance of payments equilibrium will be maintained continuously by adjustments in the foreign exchange rate.

To see this, consider again how we constructed the *B-K* curve. We started with the *net capital flow function* (Figure 22-2), reflecting the sensitivity of international capital flows to international differences in interest rates. If we can ignore expectations of future changes in the exchange rate, this function will be unchanged under a regime of flexible exchange rates.

The second component of the *B-K* curve was the *current account balances function*, which we built up on the assumption that exports were given and imports depended on the levels of investment and consumption expenditures. However, with a flexible exchange rate, and inflexible domestic wage rates, both imports and exports depend directly on the level of the foreign exchange rate. Moreover, because the foreign exchange rate will always rise when there is an excess demand for foreign exchange (e.g., the current account deficit exceeds the capital account surplus) and fall when there is an excess supply of foreign exchange (e.g., the current account deficit is less than the capital account surplus), the exchange rate will always adjust until the current account balance is equal in size and opposite in direction to the capital account balance.

It should be emphasized that this could require wide fluctuations in the exchange rate from time to time, depending on the sensitivity of import and export demands to change in the exchange rate.

With a flexible exchange rate, then, the current account balance is a residual, determined by the capital account balance. The current account balance function is the mirror image of the net capital flow function. The sole determinant of the aggregate current account balance will be the level of Canadian interest rates relative to world interest rates.

This is illustrated in Figure 22-13. In this figure, the net capital flow function, K, is the same as that developed earlier (Figure 22-2). However, the current account balance function, B, is based on the assumption that the flexible exchange rate will adjust until the current account balance is just equal in size and opposite in direction to the capital account balance. At high levels of interest rates in Canada, r_1, there will be a net capital inflow. However, as a result of the automatic adjustment of the exchange rate, the surplus in the capital account will be exactly offset by an equal deficit in the current account. At low levels of interest rates in Canada (r_2), there will be a net capital outflow. However, as a result of the automatic adjustment of the exchange rate, the deficit in the capital account will be exactly offset by an equal surplus in the current account. The net balance of payments surplus or deficit (lower panel) will always be zero, regardless of the level of interest rates in Canada (and hence, by implication, regardless of the level of income and output in Canada). *A flexible exchange rate will ensure that the balance of payments is always in equilibrium.*

This points to our first important conclusion. *If the government is willing and able to ignore wide fluctuations of the foreign exchange rate, a flexible exchange rate frees domestic monetary policy from the balance of payments constraint.*

This is not the only implication of flexibility in the foreign exchange rate, however. A flexible exchange rate, coupled with highly interest-elastic international capital flows, will reinforce the impact of monetary policy on domestic income and output.

Effectiveness of Monetary Policy.   The implications of flexible exchange rates for the domestic impact of monetary policy should be obvious if you keep in mind that both exports and imports are factors determining the level of aggregate demand.

FIGURE 22-13   The current account, the capital account and the
balance of payments, with flexible exchange rates

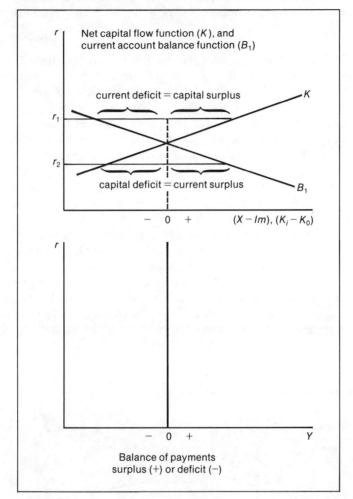

We have seen that restrictive monetary policy which raises Canadian interest rates
relative to interest rates in the rest of the world will induce capital inflows and thus, by
creating an excess supply of foreign exchange, will depress the foreign exchange rate.
The exchange rate will have to fall until the combination of increased imports and
reduced exports produces a current account deficit large enough to offset the capital
inflow. But remember: both the increase in imports and the reduction of exports
depress aggregate demand. These exchange-rate-induced effects on aggregate demand
are in addition to any effects which might result from the direct impact of tight money
on investment expenditures. In other words, the flexibility of the exchange rate,
coupled with the sensitivity of international capital flows to Canadian interest rates has
strengthened the restrictive impact of a tight money policy.

You should be able to trace through a similar analysis for the case of an expansionary monetary policy under a regime of flexible exchange rates. The conclusion is the same: flexibility of exchange rates reinforces the impact of an expansionary monetary policy.

The **IS-LM** *Model Again.*   These arguments are illustrated in Figure 22-14, which is another adaptation of the much-used four-quadrant diagram. First consider Quadrant II. The investment demand function, the broken line, I_0-I_0, is the same as that used in chapter examples. In the present analysis, however, instead of showing the individual components of the current account balance, as in Figure 22-1, we have adopted the conclusion of the previous section that, in a regime of flexible exchange rates, the current account balance will be determined simply by the net capital inflow. Accordingly, we have deducted the current account balance function of Figure 22-13 from the investment demand function in Quadrant II, to obtain what might be called the *investment — trade balance function (I-T)*. It plays the same role in the analysis as the *autonomous expenditure function* of Figure 22-1.

The construction of the *I-T* curve should be obvious. At high levels of interest rates there will be heavy capital inflows. As a result, exports must fall and imports must rise, producing a negative trade balance. This negative trade balance is a deduction from aggregate demand, and accordingly we have deducted it from the investment function to obtain the relevant point on the *I-T* curve. By contrast, at very low levels of interest rates there will be strong capital outflows. Exports will have to rise and imports fall until there is an equally large trade surplus. This trade surplus is an addition to aggregate

FIGURE 22-14   Commodity market equilibrium with flexible exchange rates

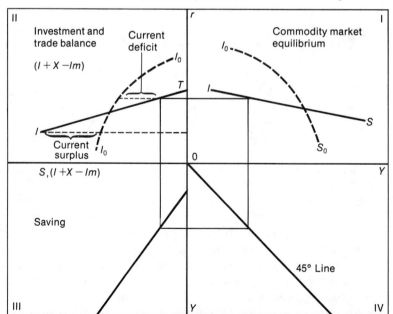

demand, and accordingly it has to be added to the investment demand function to obtain the relevant point on the *I-T* curve.

In Quadrant III we now have only the saving function of our earlier analysis. We do not have to include induced imports in this Quadrant, as we did in Figure 22-2, since total imports are allowed for in the construction of the *I-T* curve.

The new equilibrium condition is that the level of investment expenditures plus the net trade balance (= the net capital flow) must equal gross saving. (You should be able to explain why this is the equilibrium condition.) In Quadrant IV we have the 45° line which is used to reflect the equilibrium levels of income to the base axis of Quadrant I. Taking these together with the associated interest rates, we can trace out the *I-S* curve for the flexible exchange rate case.

We have also plotted the original I-S curve for the fixed exchange rate case (broken line, I_0-S_0) in Quadrant I as a reference base. The important point to note is that in the flexible exchange rate case the *I-S* curve is much more elastic with respect to the interest rate. A given increase in the money supply, shifting the *L-M* curve, will have a much more powerful impact on income and employment than in the fixed exchange rate case.

A flexible exchange rate not only frees monetary policy from the international constraint, it also increases the effectiveness of monetary policy as an instrument for manipulating aggregate demand.

A Classical Case. The elasticity of the *I-S* function in the flexible exchange rate case depends directly on the elasticity of the net capital flow function. In the extreme, we might conceive of a net capital flow function which is perfectly elastic with respect to Canadian interest rates. That is, any deviation of Canadian interest rates from some given level (world interest rates, or world interest rates plus a risk premium) would induce a massive movement of capital either in or out of the country. In such a situation, the level of interest rates in Canada would be rigidly tied to the world level of interest rates, and the *I-S* curve would also be perfectly interest-elastic at this level of interest rates.

In this case, the level of income depends simply on the demand for and supply of money (i.e., on the position of the *L-M* function). Monetary policy would be all powerful, while fiscal policy would have absolutely no impact. An increase in government expenditures, for example, would tend to increase income. But with a given money supply, this would imply higher interest rates. The resulting flood of capital flowing into the country would prevent interest rates from rising, but it would induce a drop in the foreign exchange rate. The result would be an offsetting deficit in the current account of the balance of payments. There could be no net change in the level of income and output unless there was a sympathetic increase in the money supply. With a perfectly elastic net capital flow function, and flexible exchange rates, we are back in the world envisioned by the classical quantity theorists.

Exchange Rate Expectations. In this analysis of the economics of flexible exchange rates, we have ignored what we said earlier was a crucial consideration in international capital flows — investors' expectations of future changes in the exchange rate. What modifications of the analysis are necessary if we drop the assumption that investors always expect the existing exchange rate to continue into the relevant future?

Let us consider the case in which an expansionary monetary policy initiates a rise in the flexible exchange rate. Aside from the assumption about exchange rate expectations which we have already explored, there are two possibilities. Either the rate is expected to continue to rise, or it is expected to fall back toward a more "normal" level.

Expectations of future rises in the exchange rate will induce speculative capital movements. Capital outflows will increase and capital inflows will be retarded. The net capital flow function of Figure 22-13 will shift outward to the right (larger capital outflows or smaller capital inflows at each possible level of interest rates) and the current account will have to respond. The I-T curve of Quadrant II, Figure 22-14 will shift to the right, inducing a similar shift in the I-S curve of Quadrant I. The impact of the expansionary monetary policy which initiated the whole process will be accentuated.

This is not the end of the story, however. If rises in the exchange rate induce expectations of further rises, the whole process could become cumulative. The exploration of the possible interactions between expectations and adjustments in the exchange rate requires a class of dynamic models which are well beyond the scope of an elementary money and banking textbook. It should be clear, however, that if a rise in the exchange rate induces strong expectations of a continuing rise in the future, there is a serious danger of severe instability in the foreign exchange market.

Expectations of a continuing rise in the exchange rate will reinforce the impact of monetary policy in a regime of flexible exchange rates. The opposite is true if the rate is expected to fall back to "normal" in the near future.

If a rise in the exchange rate induces expectations of a return to a lower, more "normal" level, the effects will be the opposite of those discussed above. The net capital flow function will be shifted to the left (smaller capital outflows or larger capital inflows at each possible level of interest rates) as speculators seek to avoid losses on holdings of foreign currency assets. As a result the I-T curve and the I-S curve will also be shifted to the left. The rise of the exchange rate will be dampened, and the overall effectiveness of the expansionary monetary policy will be reduced.

As we noted earlier, little is known about the determinants of expectations of changes in the foreign exchange rate. However, students of Canada's experience with flexible exchange rates between 1950 and 1962 have generally concluded that the second type of behavior was most characteristic; that is, expectations of a return to "normal" tended to dampen fluctuations in the exchange rate. The full benefits of a flexible exchange rate regime could not be attained.

FLEXIBLE EXCHANGE RATES: MONETARIST ANALYSIS

In our earlier discussion of the monetarist model of an open economy with fixed exchange rates, we noted that the analysis produced two fundamental propositions: (1) the balance of payments is a monetary phenomenon, in the sense that balance of payments deficits reflect an excess supply of money and balance of payments surpluses reflect an excess demand for money; and (2) in the "relevant" time period, because sterilization of changes in foreign exchange reserves is not possible, the central bank cannot control the nominal money supply. The monetarist model of the flexible exchange rates system can also be summarized in two fundamental propositions, but these propositions have a very different thrust: (1) the foreign exchange *rate* is a monetary phenomenon, and (2) as a result, the closed economy monetarist model is fully applicable. Again, by drawing on our earlier analysis, our discussion of this model can be very brief. This does not mean that it is unimportant.

The Exchange Rate and the Money Supply

The basic assumptions of the monetarist model remain unchanged. In the domestic economy, there is a stable demand for money function and prices and wages are flexible so that the economy tends to the natural rate of unemployment. Internationally, the "law of one price" holds, which implies that Canadian prices of imports and exports must equal the product of world prices for these goods (quoted in foreign currencies) and the price of foreign exchange (the foreign exchange rate), with appropriate allowance for international transactions costs (equations 21-1 and 22-2) and Canadian interest rates must equal comparable world interest rates.

To explore the first proposition of the monetarist flexible exchange rate model, we can go through the same mental experiment that we performed earlier for the fixed exchange rate case. Suppose the central bank supplies a larger quantity of money than is demanded at the existing levels of production, prices, and interest rates. The excess supply of money involves an excess demand for goods and securities (again, the analysis does not need to distinguish between the impacts on goods and securities markets). What will adjust to move the economy to a new equilibrium? Production cannot increase (full employment); interest rates cannot fall (law of one price); and prices of imports, exports, and import-competing goods cannot rise (law of one price). The excess supply of money may show up as excess demand in the market for non-tradeable goods, producing increases in prices in these markets; but it must also show up as an increase in the demand for *foreign* goods and securities. But this also implies an increase in the demand for foreign exchange to purchase the foreign goods and securities — and the foreign exchange rate is flexible. An excess demand for foreign exchange will lead to an increase in the price of foreign exchange.

As a result of the provision of too much money by the central bank, the foreign exchange rate rises (the Canadian dollar depreciates). In this sense, the foreign exchange rate is a monetary phenomenon. (To be sure that you understand the analysis, you should carefully set out the analysis for the case for a reduction in the money supply by the central bank).

The Flexible Exchange Rate and the Closed Economy Model

That is not all there is to the story, however. How far will the exchange rate rise?

The basic concept is again the "law of one price." According to equations 22-1 and 22-2, an increase in the foreign exchange rate (given world prices and transactions costs) implies a proportionate increase in Canadian prices of exports, imports, and import-competing goods. Taken together with the direct increase in prices of non-tradeable goods and services resulting from the pressure of excess demand in these markets, the overall result is an increase in the Canadian price level. But this is precisely the prediction of the closed economy monetarist model!

We can push the analysis one step further. The closed economy analysis led to the conclusion that the price level had to rise until the excess supply of money was eliminated — until the *real money supply* returned to its original value. In the open economy, with a flexible exchange rate, the rise in the exchange rate is primarily responsible for adjusting the price level. Other things being equal (e.g., the distribution of expenditures between tradeable and non-tradeable goods), the rise in the exchange rate will be proportionate to the original increase in the nominal money supply.

This is a very important conclusion. In the long-run economy of the monetarist model, the exchange rate is a monetary phenomenon, just as the price level is a monetary phenomenon. *The flexible exchange rate* makes the results of the closed economy monetarist model fully applicable to the open economy.

Continuing Monetary Expansion and the Exchange Rate

Our analysis to this point has been *static* — we have considered the adjustment to new equilibrium values of the exchange rate and the price level in the face of a once-over increase in the supply of money. However, what if the central bank continues to increase the money supply?

In the closed economy analysis, a continuous increase in the supply of money at a rate more rapid than the increase in the demand for real money balances (approximately the potential rate of growth of aggregate output) resulted in a continuous increase in the general level of prices. In the open economy, with flexible exchange rates, the same result occurs. However, the continuous inflation is associated with a continuous rise in the exchange rate. A country which chooses a rate of inflation that is more rapid than that obtaining in the rest of the world will experience continuous depreciation of its currency in foreign exchange markets.

It should also be remembered from earlier discussions that as inflation comes to be anticipated, the expected rate of inflation will be built into nominal interest rates. A country which chooses a relatively rapid rate of inflation will not only experience continuous depreciation of its currency in foreign exchange markets, it will experience relatively high levels of nominal interest rates. As an exercise, it is useful to compare the experience of countries with relatively high and relatively low rates of inflation during, say, the post-1971 period. (*International Financial Statistics*, published by the International Monetary Fund, is a handy source of such information.) Are these predictions of the monetarist model supported by the experiences of say Switzerland, Germany, Canada, the United States, Brazil, and Israel?

It should also be obvious that the interest rates which are relevant for the analysis of international capital flows are real interest rates. A country with relatively high inflation requires relatively high nominal interest rates to compensate for the expected loss of purchasing power in the future. To the foreign investor, this loss of purchasing power shows up in the form of a continuous, inflation-induced decline in the external value of the currency.

CONCLUSION: AN INTERNATIONAL MONETARY CONSTITUTION?

This has been another long and complicated chapter. Is it possible to distill a few significant conclusions from our discussion?

The broad conclusion of overriding importance is that for a country like Canada, heavily involved in international trade and international capital flows, the choice of the foreign exchange rate regime is a matter of major importance. That choice will affect both the possibilities for independent monetary policy and the effects of such policy. Both the short-run model, with inflexible prices, and the long-run model, with flexible prices, suggest that an independent national monetary policy is only possible with a regime of flexible exchange rates — although the two models differ sharply on what can be accomplished with monetary policy. The short-run, Keynesian model implies that, working through the flexible exchange rate, domestic monetary policy can be very powerful in regulating levels of production and employment. The long-run, monetarist model, suggests that levels of production and employment cannot be regulated through monetary policy, but that the price level can be. By contrast, the models indicate that a regime of fixed exchange rates immobilizes monetary policy in terms of domestic policy objectives. The behavior of the price level is determined by the behavior of world prices. The short-run model suggests that a serious conflict can arise between domestic objectives of monetary policy (the maintenance of full employment) and equilibrium in the balance of international payments — a conflict which can be ignored temporarily if foreign exchange reserves are large enough, but which must be corrected eventually, perhaps through the use of other policy measures, such as fiscal policy. The long-run model suggests that the conflict of objectives should not be a focus of attention for monetary policy. In the long run, the conflict cannot exist, because monetary policy must conform to the dictates of the balance of payments.

We cannot understand Canadian monetary policy, either in the past or in the future, without seeing it in its international context. The rules governing international monetary affairs — and particularly the exchange rate regime — do matter. What is the nature of the contemporary international monetary constitution? Where did it come from? These are the topics of the next chapter.

ENDNOTES

1. T.R. Robinson, "The Foreign Trade Sector and Domestic Stability: The Canadian Case," *Yale Economic Essays*, Vol. 9 (Spring 1969), pp. 46-87.
2. This is not strictly correct. A rise in Canadian income will increase Canada's imports from abroad. But this rise in the rest of the world's exports to Canada will increase income in the rest of the world, and hence imports from Canada (= Canadian exports). We are assuming that any "reflex" effect of this sort is so small that it can be ignored.

    There is also a possibility that there is an offsetting "supply effect." A rise in Canadian income increasing the demand for all types of goods and services, may also increase the share of exportable goods which is absorbed within Canada. The supply available for export will accordingly be reduced.

These are complexities which we can safely ignore in our analysis.

3. Remember, we are ignoring the fact that exports may also have some import content. OX in Figure 22-1 should be interpreted as exports net of the value of any imported materials or component parts used in the production of those exports.

4. Our assumptions also imply that the current account balance will depend on the *composition* of aggregate demand, since the import content of investment and consumption expenditures, in general, will be different. However, with given investment demand and consumption function, the composition of aggregate demand is also given for any particular level of income. For this reason, we can ignore this complication to the analysis.

5. It shows combinations of interest rates and income at which the Current Account (B)alance equals the Net (K)apital Inflow.

6. The student with some algebra will note that the basic problem is that we have only two variables but three equations which must be solved simultaneously. It is only by accident that a solution will be found.

7. Speculation occurs whenever someone takes an "open" position in foreign exchange or when one covers what would otherwise have been an open position, because he anticipates a rise in the exchange rate. Thus, a corporate treasurer who purchases foreign exchange now, whether spot or forward, knowing that the corporation will need it in the future and anticipating a rise in the exchange rate, is speculating. Similarly, a corporate treasurer who buys forward exchange to cover short-term foreign currency liabilities, when he would not normally do so, is speculating. In each case the treasurer would argue that he is merely protecting the financial position of the corporation against a reasonably foreseeable risk, and in this argument he is correct. Nonetheless, he has the same impact on the foreign exchange market as a professional speculator. To say that the corporation is speculating in foreign exchange is not to say that it is doing anything illegal or immoral.

   On the importance of corporations as speculators in foreign exchange, see Royal Commission on Banking and Finance, *Report* (Ottawa, 1964), pp. 297-299; J. H. Young and J. F. Helliwell, "The Effects of Monetary Policy on Corporations," in Royal Commission on Banking and Finance, *Appendix Volume* (Ottawa: Queen's Printer, 1964), pp. 419-426.

8. Bank of Canada, *Evidence of the Governor before the Royal Commission on Banking and Finance* (Ottawa, 1964), p. 11.

9. The classic statement of the monetary approach to the balance of payments is H.G. Johnson, "The Monetary Approach to Balance of Payments Theory," *Journal of Financial and Quantitative Analysis* (March, 1972), pp. 1555-64. A concise and readable statement of the theory is D.S. Kemp, "A Monetary View of the Balance of Payments," Federal Reserve Bank of St. Louis, *Review* (April, 1975), pp. 14-22. Both have been reprinted in T.M. Havrilesky and J.T. Boorman, *Current Issues in Monetary Theory and Policy*. (Arlington Heights, Illinois: A.H.M. Publishing Corp., 1980).

10. Johnson, *op. cit.*

11. As we will show in the next section, devaluation (a rise in the foreign exchange rate) will increase the price level. An increase in the price level, with the nominal money supply held constant, is a reduction in the real money supply. In this sense, a devaluation is a monetary adjustment, and there is some devaluation which will eliminate an excess supply of money and hence eliminate the balance of payments disequilibrium. However, if the monetary authority continues to create an excess supply of money, continuous devaluation will be necessary to maintain balance of payments equilibrium. This is the result if there is a flexible exchange rate.

12. A very readable analysis of wage rate determination in Canada is presented in *Inflation, Unemployment and Incomes Policy*, Final Report of the Prices and Incomes Commission (Ottawa: Information Canada, 1972).

THE QUEST FOR AN INTERNATIONAL MONETARY CONSTITUTION 23

At the risk of oversimplification, we can draw three very broad but basic conclusions from the analysis of the previous six chapters.

The first conclusion, drawn from Chapters 20 and 21, is that the behavior of the money supply has important macroeconomic implications. If the supply of money increases less rapidly than the demand for money, the economy will suffer from deflationary pressures. While in the long run, this may involve only a fall in the general level of prices, in the short run, with wage rates stable, it may mean widespread unemployment. If the money supply increases more rapidly than the demand for money, unless there is widespread unemployment, the price level will rise. Rapid, and particularly erratic, inflation is also widely regarded as a serious social problem.

The second conclusion, from Chapters 17-19, is that in a modern economy the government can control the money supply, either directly or, more commonly, through the agency of a central bank. The government can exert its control for good or ill. The money supply is a potential instrument of macroeconomic policy for the stabilization of the economy. But, as history the world over testifies, governments can use monetary expansion blindly, as an apparently costless method of financing budgetary deficits, with inflationary consequences and, in the extreme, the destruction of the monetary system. For this reason, many economists argue that control over the money supply is far too important to be left to the discretion of governments, or of central banks controlled by governments. Indeed, some economists argue that even an independent central bank ought to have little or no discretion. Rather, the conduct of monetary policy ought to be governed by a simple and widely understood set of rules — a monetary constitution.

The third conclusion, from Chapter 22, is that domestic monetary policy cannot be conducted in a vacuum. A two-way interaction between the money supply and the balance of international payments is at the very heart of Canadian macroeconomics, and the nature of that interaction depends on such international monetary arrangements as the flexibility or rigidity of exchange rates. Rules for the conduct of monetary policy cannot be established without regard to the exchange rate regime. But exchange rates are two-sided. Domestic monetary policy which affects the exchange rate (or the balance of payments if the exchange rate is fixed) will also affect other countries to a greater or lesser degree. Perhaps, if a monetary constitution is to be established, it must be by international agreement.

From this point of view, we can interpret the evolution of the international monetary system in the 20th century as a flight from the discipline of a strong international monetary constitution, the classical gold standard, followed by international discord, uncertainty, and experimentation as the world searched for a workable international monetary constitution to put in its place. That search is far from over. The purpose of this chapter is to review some of the highlights and issues in this process, particularly as they have impinged on Canadian monetary affairs.

THE CONCEPT OF A MONETARY CONSTITUTION

By a monetary constitution we mean a set of *rules* governing the conduct of monetary policy. These rules may give to the central bank (and hence the government) great discretion in regulating the money supply, or they may give it very little discretion. Indeed, the context in which the concept of a monetary constitution has had the most intensive discussion in recent years has been a proposal to eliminate all discretion over the money supply — to have all changes in the money supply governed by a simple, fixed rule, such as a fixed rate of increase, year in, year out, regardless of economic conditions. The long-standing debate over this proposal has come to be known as the "rules versus authority" controversy.

The Philosophy of the Free Market Economy

The foundation of the "rules" position is a philosophy of the appropriate role of government in the economy. It is argued that, in general, an economy in which production and distribution are organized and directed by competitive markets will simultaneously maximize individual freedom and economic efficiency.[1] This is not to say that the government does not have a vital role to play in the economy. However, with some exceptions, the appropriate role of the government is simply "to provide a stable framework of rules within which enterprise and competition may effectively control and direct production and distribution of goods."[2] Part of that stable framework must be in the monetary sphere, because, in the words of H.C. Simons, an early proponent of the rules philosophy:

> An enterprise system cannot function effectively in the face of extreme uncertainty as to the action of monetary authorities...where every business venture becomes largely a speculation on the future of monetary policy...[D]efinite, stable, legislative rules of the game as to money are of paramount importance to the survival of a system based on freedom of enterprise.[3]

Simons considered various possible rules, including the fixing of the quantity of money at some arbitrary level. Although he was not completely happy with it (because it left the central bank with a considerable amount of discretion), he finally settled on one which focused on the *results* of governmental intervention — stability of the price level. That is, he argued that as a simple and comprehensible rule, the central bank ought to be compelled to manage the money supply in such a way as to achieve stability of a general index of prices of goods and services. The Simons rule involves an important empirical judgment — that the central bank can in fact manage the money supply so as to achieve stability of the price level, a conclusion which, as we have seen, many economists doubt, at least in the short run. (Most monetarists, who argue that the relationship between money and prices is strong in the long run, emphasize that the time lags are long and variable.)

Recent advocates of the Simons approach to monetary policy have been firmly in the modern quantity theory tradition, which suggests that the money supply does control the price level, in the long run. The problem is to force monetary policy to focus on the long run. Central banks with discretionary powers have many short-term temptations, such as concern over high levels of interest rates or high levels of unemployment, to deflect them from the Simons long-term course. However, it is argued, monetary policies based on these short-term objectives are misguided. It is not that the short-term objectives are undesirable, but that central banks are inherently incapable of achieving the desired results. It is the combination of unattainable objectives and the power of money which makes discretionary monetary policy such a threat to freedom, stability, and efficiency.

The argument is not that central bankers are devious or anti-social in their intentions, or that they are not competent in their jobs. Rather, it is argued, in spite of the best of intentions and the highest technical skill, monetary policy directed at short-term objectives like interest rates or unemployment, cannot work. Two fundamental problems have been suggested.

Expectations and Discretionary Monetary Policy. In one of his most influential papers, Milton Friedman asserted, as a theoretical proposition, that there are two fundamental limitations to monetary policy:

> "(1) It cannot peg interest rates for more than very limited periods; (2) It cannot peg the rate of unemployment for more than very limited periods."[4]

We discussed the analysis underlying these conclusions in Chapter 22, and will not repeat that discussion here. Suffice it to say that Friedman bases his argument on the assumption that there are "natural" levels of real interest rates and of unemployment in the economy, to which real interest rates and unemployment will tend in the long run. If the central bank attempts to use monetary expansion to maintain low levels of interest rates or low levels of unemployment, when the natural levels of these variables are higher than the central bank's objectives, the policies will be frustrated by adjustments in the market. Price levels will rise, and eventually expectations of a rise in the price level will be built into nominal interest rates and wage rates, and both the real interest rate and unemployment will return to their natural levels. If the central bank persists in the pursuit of its unattainable objectives, it will accelerate the expansion of the money supply, producing accelerating inflation and rising nominal interest rates.

In the long run, then, monetary policy can do little but affect the price level. Concern for monetary stability dictates that monetary policy be directed at the long-run behavior of the price level, not at unattainable short-term interest rates or unemployment objectives.

Time Lags and Discretionary Monetary Policy.   There is also an important argument about the short-run impact of policy. Even accepting the Keynesian dictum that, in the short run, monetary policy can affect real economic variables like interest rates and employment levels, it is argued that discretionary monetary policy will produce perverse results. Central bankers, attempting to use discretion, are trapped by the fact that the *timing* of the impact of their actions is *uncertain*. It is not simply that time lags exist and may be distributed over an extended period of time. If that were the only problem, improved techniques of prediction would presumably contain a solution. It is argued, however, that the lags are both long and *irregular,* and it is the latter attribute which causes the trouble. If the timing of the impact cannot be predicted with any degree of accuracy, a discretionary monetary policy is likely to be perverse: imparting contractionary forces when expansion is the order of the day, and imparting expansionary forces when contraction is appropriate. The central bank is as likely to be a source of economic instability as it is to counteract such instability, and the central banker cannot do better because he cannot know when his actions will affect economic activity.[5]

Obviously, central bankers do not have to yield to the temptation to pursue short-term objectives if they are convinced by Friedman's analysis. However, the political pressures, including pressures coming through elected governments, may be intense from time to time, and a central banker with the legal power to pursue discretionary policies may find these pressures overwhelming. A central banker who attempts to pursue an independent course may find himself replaced. The example of the conflict between the Governor of the Bank of Canada and the Government of Canada in the late 1950s and early 1960s is instructive in this regard.[6] Moreover, as long as the *possibility* of discretionary policy is there (the central banker may change his mind!), the certainty said to be necessary for efficiency in the economy will be lacking. It would be better for all concerned, it is argued, if the central banker (and the government) had no option — if there was a monetary constitution which forced the central bank to follow an appropriate money supply rule.

A MONEY SUPPLY RULE AS A MONETARY CONSTITUTION

What is the appropriate rule which ought to be imposed on monetary policy?

Given the present state of knowledge, perfection cannot be expected. However, it is argued that the simple rule of *increasing the money supply at a constant rate* would vastly improve the performance of monetary policy. Thus;

> A fixed rate of increase in the stock of money would almost certainly rule out...rapid and sizeable fluctuations, though it would not rule out mild cyclical or secular fluctuations [in economic activity], and it would give a firm basis for long range planning on the part of the public.[7]

This raises several technical questions. How should the money supply be defined? What is the appropriate growth rate? What should be done about seasonal, weekly, and daily fluctuations in the demand for money?

The central issue is, of course, the growth rate. It is argued that the money supply should be allowed to increase at approximately the same rate as the demand for money would increase, if the general level of prices were constant. In practice this means a rate of growth roughly equal to the long-run rate of growth of potential gross national product. This assumes an income elasticity of demand for money of one, which may not be correct. However, precision is not necessary. The economy is capable of adjusting to *moderate* upward or downward trends in the general level of prices without any serious loss of efficiency.[8] Friedman proposed a rate in the range of 3% to 5% per annum.[9] However, what is essential is that the rate, once chosen, be *stable* and hence *predictable*.

The other questions are technical details. The exact definition of the money supply is not important, as long as it contains the major monetary media, currency and demand deposits (although advocates of the rule usually include time deposits at commercial banks). Seasonal and similar adjustments are appropriate, providing they are to accommodate regular shifts in the demand for money and hence are fully predictable.

It is not argued that this money supply rule will provide the best of all worlds. However, it will protect us from major blunders, and will neutralize the central bank as a source of monetary instability. Thus, the Economic Council of Canada stated in their *First Annual Review*, that such a policy of expanding the money supply in line with the growth of potential output would, "help both to minimize the dangers of shorter term instability and to assist in the successful attainment of orderly progress towards consistent high standards of performance in the Canadian economy."[10]

The Case Against a Money Supply Rule

Attacks on the concept of a fixed money supply rule have not been lacking. Thus, the distinguished British scholar of central banking, R.S. Sayers, has asserted:

> We are doomed to disappointment if we look for rules that are applicable to all times and places. We have central banks for the very reason that there are no such rules.[11]

Elsewhere he states that "the essence of central banking is discretionary control of the monetary system."[12]

In a slightly different vein, Professor P. Samuelson has derided the black and white contrast which is drawn between "discretion" and "rules":

> for when men set up a definitive mechanism which is to run forever afterward by itself, that involves a single act of discretion which transcends, both in its arrogance and its capacity for potential harm, any repeated acts of foolish discretion that can be imagined.[13]

In other words, the quest for immutable rules — attractive as they may be — is at best idle dreaming, and at worst highly dangerous.

In part, these criticisms are a rejection of the underlying "optimistic" assumption that in the absence of monetary instability, a market economy would be inherently stable, in the sense that it would tend to return to the natural rate of unemployment after a reasonable period of time whenever this equilibrium was disturbed. These criticisms reflect a Keynesian model of the economy, rather than the monetarist model inherent in the money supply rule. However, the criticisms also rest on empirical judgments about what a central bank can and cannot accomplish.

Tests of the Money Supply Rule

Empirical evidence of the effectiveness of a rules approach to monetary policy is of two types. On the one hand, a number of economists have attempted retrospective studies, assessing whether monetary policy would have been better in selected historical periods if a rule had been followed. On the other hand, a small literature has developed offering preliminary assessments of the experience with the widespread adoption of an approximation to a rules approach by central banks in the late 1970s.

The retrospective studies analyzed the behavior of the money supply in relation to economic activity during various time periods, comparing the actual behavior of the money supply to what would have happened under several possible money supply rules. The results are inconclusive. E.S. Shaw, in an early study, stated that a simple money supply rule (a stable growth rate) would have been in the "right" direction more often than was the Federal Reserve System over its entire history. [14] A similar conclusion was reached for Canada in the 1950s and early 1960s by Johnson and Winder. [15] Some subsequent work came to more tentative or opposite conclusions. [16] Perhaps the most influential critical assessment of the monetary rule approach is that of Modigliani. Reporting on experiments using an econometric model of the U.S. economy for the period 1959-1971, Modigliani observes that "...with a constant money growth the economy...(would have been)...far from stable — in fact, it...(would have been)... distinctly less stable than actual experience, by a factor of 50 percent." [17]

This range of empirical findings (a problem to which we should be well conditioned, by now) is disquieting, particularly given the importance of the issues at stake. However, in a sense, all of the evidence may be irrelevant. The tests presume that central bankers cannot improve on their past performance. It can be argued, however, that much of the historical record was, in fact, a learning process. It contains errors in judgment, misconceptions of the nature, purpose, and effects of monetary policy, and conflicts (or confusions) over the objectives to be pursued, rather than (or, as well as) inherent defects in discretionary policy emanating from long and variable time lags. Objectives can be clarified and conflicts in priorities resolved, and techniques of central bank decision-making and intervention can be refined.

But, as we noted in Chapters 20 and 21, the Bank of Canada, like many other central banks, adopted a money supply policy in the late 1970s, the so-called policy of gradualism. Can we not assess the merits of the money supply rule proposal by examining the results of the policy of gradualism?

Unfortunately, from this point of view, the policy of gradualism is seriously flawed. It is not a constitutional constraint on the discretion of the central bank. Rather, it is a manifestation of that discretion. The Bank of Canada established the policy; the Bank of Canada decides whether it will adhere to the policy in any given situation; and the Bank of Canada is free to alter the policy. Indeed, there are strong suggestions in the

1981 *Annual Report* of the Bank of Canada that the policy of gradualism was significantly altered, if not abandoned, in late 1981.[18] In any case, even within the policy of gradualism, the central bank has very considerable latitude in managing the money supply. Rather than a fixed rate, the policy provides relatively wide bands (e.g., between 4% and 8% per annum in 1981-82) within which the rate of growth of the money supply can fluctuate without violating the policy. Moreover, the target growth rates are set by the central bank for a short period of time and are subject to revision at the discretion of the central bank.

It is perhaps too early to adequately assess the effects of the policy of gradualism, particularly if the time lags are long and variable. Opinions of economists vary. Some are willing to ascribe a measure of success to the policy. Others argue that it has been a complete failure in containing inflation and very damaging for maintaining full employment. With the rate of increase in the consumer price index in 1981 *higher* than it was at the start of the new policy in 1975, the balance of professional opinion on the success of the policy seems to be skeptical.[19] In the words of the Governor of the Bank of Canada, "The problem of containing inflation in Canada has certainly not been resolved."[20]

The reasons offered for the failure to achieve more tangible results vary. Economists of a Keynesian persuasion argue that the policy is faulty in conception. Because the inflation is not monetary in nature, we should not expect monetary policy to control it. Restricted monetary growth can only create unemployment.[21] Economists of a monetarist persuasion contend that the policy is fundamentally sound, but that it has not been properly implemented. It is sometimes argued that the Bank has used the wrong concept of the money supply; that it has strayed from single-minded concern with the money supply into such policies as the stabilization of the exchange rate; or that it has allowed too much variability in the rate of growth of the money supply to have the necessary consistent impact on expectations.[22]

Whatever the reasons, Canada's experiment with monetary gradualism does not provide strong evidence in support of a money supply rule.

The Money Supply Rule in an Open Economy

In an economy such as Canada's, the adoption of a money supply rule raises another class of issues. As we saw in Chapter 22, monetary policy in an open economy with a *fixed exchange rate* will be largely dictated by the balance of international payments. Except by chance, the monetary policy required for balance of payments equilibrium will be inconsistent with any arbitrarily chosen money supply rule. It follows that in an open economy the adoption of a money supply rule implies a flexible exchange rate — and it is not by accident that the major exponent of the rules approach to monetary policy is also a major exponent of flexible exchange rates.[23] This was acknowledged by the Governor of the Bank of Canada in 1975 in announcing the policy of gradualism:

> I should also note that the pursuit of a policy of stable monetary expansion requires that interest rates and the exchange rate be allowed scope for such movement as may be needed in either direction, not only over the course of business cycles but also over shorter periods.[24]

Fixed Exchange Rates as a Monetary Constitution.   There is, then, a paradoxical aspect to flexible exchange rates. They are necessary if the monetary authorities are to have discretion over the money supply; but they are also necessary if there is to be a money supply rule which prohibits discretionary monetary policy.

Both the money supply rule and fixed exchange rates substantially eliminate discretion over monetary policy. In this sense, both are monetary constitutions. However, a regime of fixed exchange rates is a very different type of monetary constitution from that advocated by supporters of a money supply rule. The growth of the money supply is constrained by the balance of international payments, not by long-term determinants of the demand for money. Moreover, given that more than one country is necessarily involved, a regime of fixed exchange rates is an *international* monetary constitution.

International monetary history is replete with experiments with alternative exchange rate regimes. We cannot explore them all in brief compass. However, in the present context, it is useful to review the broad outlines of the evolution of the international monetary system in the 20th century, beginning with the classical gold standard, perhaps the most rigid international monetary constitution imaginable.

THE CLASSICAL GOLD STANDARD

During the second half of the 19th century and until World War I, the classical gold standard provided an international monetary constitution. Although the use of gold as money, and the concept and theory of the gold standard, go back far in history, what we now call the "classical" gold standard had its origins in the restoration of gold convertibility by the Bank of England in 1821, following the Napoleonic Wars (a period of inconvertible paper money and severe inflation). Canada became a gold standard country in 1853 and thereafter the gold link between Canada and the United States was a dominant factor in Canadian monetary affairs. However, it was not until the 1870s, as international telegraphic communication improved (the transatlantic cable was successfully laid in 1866) and more countries linked their money to gold, that the gold standard began to function as a truly international monetary system, and it was not until the mid-1890s that its development could be said to be complete. In spite of its relatively short history, by 1914 "the gold standard was...the prevailing idea of normal."[25] World War I effectively ended the classical gold standard period, although there were attempts to restore it after the war.

What do we mean by the classical gold standard?

Gold as Standard Money

Basic to the concept of the gold standard was the principle that gold was the "standard" money of the nation. Gold coin was legal tender, and the national monetary unit (e.g., the dollar, the pound, etc.) was defined as the equivalent of a fixed amount of gold. Thus, the legal definition of the Canadian dollar made it equivalent to 23.22 grains of pure gold.[26] But the definition of the monetary unit in terms of a fixed amount of gold also implied that gold had a price fixed by law — we can call it the "statutory" or "mint" price of gold. Because there are 480 grains in a troy ounce, with the dollar defined as 23.22 grains of pure gold, the statutory price of gold was $(480/23.22) = \$20.67$ per ounce. This was the statutory price of gold in Canada from 1853 until 1952 (although, through part of that time, and particularly after 1935, the statutory price was irrelevant).

In most gold standard countries, gold coins with legal tender status were minted and circulated as a medium of exchange. It is interesting to note that Canada did not establish a mint until 1908, and the first gold coins were not struck until 1912. Little gold coin appears to have actually circulated in Canada, and the gold coins which had legal tender status were, with minor exception, all of foreign vintage (mainly British and American).

A Monetary Control Mechanism

The classical gold standard involved much more than a definition of the national monetary unit in terms of gold. It also involved a commitment to two basic principles: (1) all other monies used in the economy were, directly or indirectly, convertible into gold, on demand, at the fixed statutory price of gold (and vice versa); and (2) gold could be freely imported and exported. Taken together, these principles provided a second meaning for the concept of the gold standard. It was a mechanism for the control of the money supply, based on the ability of the economy to attract and retain gold rather than on the fiat of a government or a central bank.

Gold standard countries had different rules for the conduct of their internal monetary affairs. In one respect, Canada had a particularly rigid link between gold and money; in another respect, the system was very flexible. The rigidity arose because the law required a 100% gold reserve behind Dominion notes issued in excess of a basic fiduciary issue. For any increase in Dominion notes, the government had to hold gold, dollar for dollar; any reduction in the stock of gold held by the government required a reduction of the Dominion note issue, dollar for dollar. The flexibility arose because similar rules did not apply to money issued by the chartered banks, whether notes or deposits. While there were other restrictions on the banks' ability to issue bank notes (related to their paid-up capital), there were no legal minimum reserve requirements for notes or deposits.

The banks, of course, were faced with the necessity of converting both notes and deposits into gold or Dominion notes, on demand. As a matter of prudence — as a hedge against their banker's risk — the banks held substantial reserves of gold and Dominion notes. However, their reserve ratios were not fixed, but varied with the bankers' own assessments of need. Nonetheless, the money supply process worked much as described in Chapters 17-19. The monetary base was gold, held either by the banks or by the government as backing for Dominion notes. The money supply was bank notes, bank deposits, and Dominion notes in circulation outside banks. Linking the money supply and the base was a money supply multiplier which depended on the banks' demands for cash reserves and the public's demands for currency. Given the multiplier, the money supply depended on the stock of gold in the system. This was true in Canada, and in every country on the classical gold standard.

But what determined the stock of gold in any country's monetary system?

An International Adjustment Mechanism

The concept of the gold standard has a third meaning. It was also a mechanism for international adjustment — for the maintenance of equilibrium in the balances of payment of member countries. The adjustment mechanism, commonly called the "specie flow mechanism," involved a two-way interaction between the money supply and the balance of international payments, with international gold flows the connecting link.

Some of the earliest macroeconomic theory was the theory of the specie flow mechanism — the intellectual precursor of the modern monetary approach to the balance of international payments, which we discussed in Chapter 22.[27] Indeed, the theory of the specie flow mechanism can be regarded as simply a very rigid version of the monetary approach to the balance of payments. According to the theory, any macroeconomic disturbance — domestic or international — which created a disequilibrium in the balance of international payments would induce international gold flows which would, through the money supply process, set in motion adjustments which would correct the disequilibrium.

Exchange Rates.   To understand the theory of the specie flow mechanism it is important to keep in mind that the international gold standard was a regime of fixed exchange rates. With the Canadian and U.S. dollars both defined as 23.22 grains of pure gold, there was a fixed "mint par" rate of exchange between them of Can $1 = US $1. At the mint, an ounce of gold could be converted into the same number of dollars on each side of the border. Similarly, with the British pound defined as 113 grains of pure gold, the mint par rate of exchange between the pound and the dollar was (113/23.22), or $4.8666 = £1.

Gold, however, was seldom used in making international payments. It was heavy and hence costly to ship, and there was always danger of loss from theft or natural disaster, giving rise to insurance costs. Normally foreign transactions were completed through the purchase and sale of foreign exchange — relatively inexpensive paper transfers, often via the telegraph. There was a market for foreign exchange, with the balance of supply and demand in the market moving the exchange rate up and down around the mint par rate of exchange. However, if the market rate of exchange departed from the mint par rate of exchange by more than the cost of shipping gold, it would be less expensive to make foreign payments by obtaining gold from the government and shipping it than by purchasing foreign exchange from the banks. Gold would flow internationally. As a result, there were effective upper and lower limits to fluctuations in the market rate of exchange, commonly called the "gold points." Strong demand for foreign exchange would drive up the market rate of exchange to the *gold export point.* Beyond that, the premium on foreign exchange would exceed the cost of shipping gold, and gold would be exported. A strong supply of foreign exchange would drive down the market rate of exchange to the *gold import point.* Below that, the discount on foreign exchange would exceed the cost of shipping gold, and gold would be imported. In Canada, given the close proximity of Montreal and New York, the gold points were very narrow, ± 5/64ths of a cent per dollar. That is, if the price of a U.S. dollar rose to $1.00078, gold would flow out of Canada, and if it fell to $.99922, gold would flow into Canada. The scope for movements in the exchange rate was very narrow indeed!

The Specie Flow Mechanism.   The theory of the specie flow mechanism should be familiar from our discussion of the monetary approach to the balance of payments in Chapter 22. They are the same theory. Two examples of how the mechanism was supposed to work — one assuming a domestic monetary disturbance and the other an external disturbance to the balance of payments — should be sufficient to illustrate the principle.

For the first example, suppose that, in a fully employed economy, the government or the banks increase the supply of paper money, with consequent inflationary pressures, and upward pressures on commodity prices and wage rates. With a fixed exchange rate (given the law of one price), prices cannot increase significantly. If the excess supply of money cannot induce more domestic production (full employment) and cannot raise domestic prices (law of one price) it must directly or indirectly result in increased demand for foreign produced goods. The demand for foreign exchange to pay for the foreign goods and services will eventually push the market exchange rate up through the gold export point. Gold will flow out of the country to pay for the imports. However, if gold flows out of the country, the government and the banks are losing gold reserves. The money supply must contract because the monetary base is contracting, and the contraction of the money supply will correct the original inflationary pressures.

You should recognize this example as an example of the monetary approach to the balance of payments — an example in which the monetary approach appears to hold fully. Excess domestic monetary creation is self-defeating because of the specie flow mechanism. Money creation in a fully employed economy causes a balance of payments deficit; and the balance of payments deficit will result in a drain of gold which will correct the initial monetary disturbance. The same process will occur in reverse if the domestic money supply is too small. In theory, the adjustment is automatic.

As a second example, consider a very different kind of disturbance, one which occurs initially in the balance of payments rather than in the monetary system. Suppose there is a very strong inflow of financial capital from abroad for investment in railway construction and other national development projects, as in late 19th century Canada. If there is to be a real transfer of capital to Canada, there must be an excess of imports of goods and services over exports in the *current account* of the balance of international payments. It is this excess of imports over exports which represents the transfer of real resources to Canada for investment in railways, etc. But what the foreign investors provide is foreign money. How does this get transformed into a current account deficit?

There are various possible adjustment processes. Most obvious is the possibility that the corporations receiving the foreign funds will use them directly to purchase, and import, foreign-produced capital goods (e.g., the railway companies purchase rails and locomotives in Europe). To the extent that this happens there is no transfer problem. The capital inflows have a direct and offsetting impact on the current account of the balance of payments. However, suppose part of the funds are for expenditure in Canada, to pay workers and to acquire local building materials. Then how does the real transfer occur?

To make expenditures in Canada, the foreign money must be converted into Canadian money. The attempts to purchase Canadian dollars will reduce the foreign exchange rate (increase the price of Canadian dollars will reduce the foreign exchange rate (increase the price of Canadian dollars in the foreign exchange market). When the foreign exchange rate falls through the gold import point, gold will flow into Canada. This will add to Canadian bank reserves, and, through the familiar process, will lead to an expansion in the Canadian money supply. In an otherwise fully employed economy, the result will be an increased demand for foreign goods and services, and an increase in imports, as required for the real transfer to occur.

Examples of the working of the gold standard mechanism could be multiplied (perhaps, as an exercise, you should work out some other examples for yourself — the effects of a sharp increase in foreign interest rates; the effects of a crop failure, reducing grain exports and increasing imports; the effects of an export boom). The important point is that, in theory, the classical gold standard was an automatic mechanism for the mutual adjustment of the money supply and the balance of international payments. Disequilibrium in the demand for and supply of money would automatically induce corrective forces through the balance of international payments and international gold flows; and disequilibrium in the balance of international payments would automatically set up corrective forces through gold flows and their impact on the domestic monetary system. If the system was to function automatically, there was no scope for discretionary monetary policy — no *policy role* for a central bank.

Theory and Reality: The "Rules of the Game"

The gold standard never operated as automatically as the theory of the specie flow mechanism suggested. Perhaps the closest approximation to the theory in reality was the Canadian case. Canada had no central bank, and the law established a strong link between gold reserves and government issued paper money (Dominion notes). But even in this case, recent research suggests that there was more flexibility in the system, through the banks' adjustment of their cash reserve ratios, than the theory allows.[28]

Other gold standard countries had central banks which held a significant portion of the nation's gold reserves and which issued both notes and deposits commonly held by other banks as cash reserves. Often these central banks — like the Bank of England — were privately owned, profit-seeking institutions, not the modern government-owned institutions which we are accustomed to think of as the managers of the monetary system. The gold standard central banks were in a position to manage the money supply independently of international gold flows, at least in the short run, by allowing their gold reserve ratios to vary. If the gold standard was to work as in the specie flow theory, each central bank should have followed three rules. It should have permitted free international gold flows; when it received gold, it should have expanded the money supply; and when it lost gold, it should have contracted the money supply. Research has shown, however, that as often as not, central banks did not follow these rules. They used various devices to interfere with international gold movements, and they attempted to neutralize the monetary effects of gold movements with offsetting discount or open market operations.[29]

Nonetheless, the gold standard was a stern and relentless monetary disciplinarian. While a central bank might violate the "rules of the game" for a time, if it continued to ignore a gold drain, it would eventually lose all of its reserves. If it ignored the "rules" it ran the risk of a crisis, forcing a sudden brake on the monetary system. There were repeated financial crises during the gold standard period, as the logic of the system caught up with errant central banks. The central banks could not for long manage the money supply independently — and, perhaps equally important, the government could not seize control of the money supply mechanism to finance government expenditures. Inflation had to be an international phenomenon, not rooted in the creation of paper money but in the discovery of abundant new sources of gold.

Thus, although the classical gold standard was far from the mechanical system suggested by the theory of the specie flow mechanism, it was effectively *an international monetary constitution*. Implicit in adherence to the gold standard was adherence to certain rules for the conduct of domestic monetary affairs. Some slippage was possible in the short run; but in the long run, national governments could not manage the money supply for their own purposes. They had to manage the money supply with a view to maintaining very rigidly fixed exchange rates (and hence the statutory price of gold).

THE COLLAPSE OF THE GOLD STANDARD

World War I marked the end of the classical gold standard. Attempts were made to restore the gold standard, in modified form in the interwar period, but both the economic and the policy environments had changed. The war and the accompanying inflation had a wrenching effect on preexisting international economic relationships, and most governments were no longer willing to subordinate all economic policy objectives to the maintenance of gold convertibility. The definitive collapse of the new gold standard was part of the financial turmoil which accompanied the international depression of the 1930s.

The Financial Implications of War

Canada, like most belligerents, suspended the convertibility of government-and-bank-issued money into gold in early August 1914 (see Chapter 14). The immediate rationale for suspending the gold money control mechanism was to prevent a major international drain of gold reserves as a panic reaction to the war. The important effect, however, was to make exchange rates flexible and to give to the government direct or indirect control over the supply of money. The prewar monetary constitution was suspended, and the creation of money was an important aspect of the financing of the war effort. The predictable result was inflation; and the currencies of all belligerent countries depreciated relative to that of the only major nation to remain on gold, the United States (which did not enter the war until 1917).

Widely different relative rates of inflation coupled with both the physical destruction of production facilities in some countries and the disruption of prewar international trade and investment relationships meant that it was a very different world economy which emerged from the war. Nonetheless, the classical gold standard, with the same prewar mint par rates of exchange, was still widely regarded as "normal," and attempts were made in many countries to recreate the prewar system. A general return to gold convertibility occurred in the mid-1920s, sometimes accompanied by monetary reform (a new monetary unit), sometimes by devaluation relative to the prewar par, and in the important case of Britain (1925), by a prolonged period of deflationary monetary policies. Canada resumed gold convertibility in 1926, quite effortlessly. By 1928, a form of the gold standard was again the international monetary system — but times had changed. Central banks were little inclined to follow the dictates of the gold standard "rules of the game," and there was general concern about the long-run adequacy of the supply of gold. The interwar gold standard was not the classical gold standard.

The Supply of Gold

Under the classical gold standard the growth of the money supply — in the world as a whole — was constrained by the growth of the stock of monetary gold (gold in circulation and in the reserves of governments and banks). Although not rigid, the link between gold reserves and the world money supply was strong. The money supply could not grow much faster than the stock of monetary gold. Although not all newly produced gold was added to the monetary stock (according to one estimate, between 1839 and 1929 about 44% of new gold production went to non-monetary uses, such as jewellery), the production of gold was the key to the expansion of the international monetary system.

Gold Production.   The production of gold increased dramatically during the classical gold standard period (top panel of Figure 23-1). Thus, in the 50 year period 1851-1900, the world's output of gold was almost nine times as great as in the previous 50 years, and that total was almost matched again in the next 15 years, 1901-1915. However, the production of gold could not be regulated in accordance with the requirements of the international monetary system, and rather than providing for steady long-run growth in the base of the world's monetary system, it displayed very wide fluctuations.

Historically, the supply of gold was influenced by two contrary forces. On the one hand, occasional major discoveries, whether of rich new deposits of gold or of new techniques for the extraction of gold, induced spasmodic bursts of production and periods of rapid growth in the stock of monetary gold. On the other hand, between such bursts, in spite of irregular discoveries of smaller importance, the steady depletion of the ore bodies in established mines led to falling production, which retarded the growth of the world's stock of monetary gold and of the world's money supply. In the period of the classical gold standard, two concentrations of discoveries are particularly important, one in the late 1840s and early 1850s, particularly in California and Eastern Australia, and one in the late 1880s and 1890s, particularly the opening of the rich South African fields and major mines in the western United States. One of the important contributors to the second burst was the practical implementation of the cyanide process for the recovery of gold from quartz ores. As is evident in the chart, each major burst was followed by a prolonged period of stagnation of production of gold.

FIGURE 23-1 The supply of gold during the classical gold standard

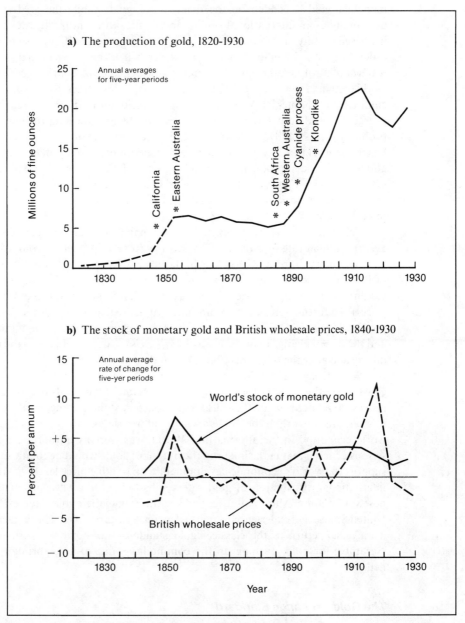

a) The production of gold, 1820-1930

b) The stock of monetary gold and British wholesale prices, 1840-1930

Source: Jastram, R.W., *The Golden Constant: The English and American Experience, 1560-1976* (New York: Wiley, 1977); Kitchen, J, "The Supply of Gold Compared with the Prices of Commodities," in League of Nations, *Interim Report of the Gold Delegation of the Financial Committee* (Geneva, 1930), 79-85; Ridgway, Robert H., *Summarized Data of Gold Production*, U.S. Department of Commerce, Bureau of Mines, Economic Paper 6 (Washington: 1929).

Gold, Money, and Prices.   The economic significance of the behavior of the supply of monetary gold depended on the demand for gold. While the gold standard was developing as an international system, in the mid-19th century, the demand for gold increased rapidly, as country after country attempted to build up its gold reserves in order to go on the gold standard. However, when the international gold standard reached maturity, in the late 19th century, the demand for gold was derived from the world demand for money, which was determined by the forces discussed, for individual countries, in Chapter 20. Most important, over a long-time horizon, was the growth in aggregate world output. In contrast to the supply of gold, the long-run demand for gold probably grew steadily. Following a major discovery, the stock of monetary gold, and hence the world money supply, increased much more rapidly than world output of goods and services, producing a period of price inflation. In the intervening period, the stock of monetary gold, and hence the world money supply, increased much less rapidly than aggregate world output of goods and services, producing a prolonged period of price deflation.

This pattern is clearly evident in the lower panel of Figure 23-1. The solid line is the average annual rate of growth of the world's stock of monetary gold, for successive five-year intervals from 1840-1930. The dashed line is the average annual rate of change of British wholesale prices, for which there is a long historical record (assuming the validity of the law of one price, we can use British prices as an approximation to world prices). Unfortunately, we have no index of aggregate world output. However, the pre-World War I association between the rate of growth in the stock of monetary gold and the rate of change in prices is obvious — as is the decisive break in the relationship during and after the war, when the gold standard was suspended.

While the classical gold standard provided a monetary constitution which severely constrained the ability of governments to generate inflation through the creation of money, it did not provide the world with monetary stability. There was no mechanism to guarantee growth in the monetary base appropriate to the potential growth of the world economy. In the aftermath of World War I, many authorities expressed the serious concern that in the long run the output of gold "would be totally insufficient to support the world's economic development with a stable price level."[30] Moreover, the international distribution of gold reserves had changed as a result of the war and postwar inflation. Many countries had lost the bulk of their gold reserves, and one, the United States, had experienced a marked increase in its reserves. The danger involved in a universal return to the classical gold standard was obvious — an international "scramble for gold, pushing up the commodity value of gold through competitive deflation."[31]

The Gold Exchange Standard

An international monetary conference in 1922 strongly urged on the world a new international monetary system, based on gold, but designed to economize on the world's stock of monetary gold. It was called the "gold exchange standard."[32] The basic principles were similar to those of the classical gold standard, but there were important differences.

Some major countries were to maintain the monetary arrangements of the classical gold standard, including the convertibility of their currencies into gold and free international gold movements. Every other participating country would declare a par rate of exchange and would maintain the market rate of exchange "within a prescribed fraction of parity" (not necessarily the gold points) by purchasing and selling foreign exchange in the market (not necessarily through international gold flows). For this purpose, each of these countries would hold official reserves "of approved assets, not necessarily gold." These reserves would be foreign exchange, in the form of "bank balances, bills, short term securities or other suitable liquid resources," i.e., claims on the gold standard countries which could be drawn upon to finance official intervention in the foreign exchange market in support of the home currency. There was to be a fixed exchange rate, but no commitment to direct convertibility into gold.

The gold exchange standard was a gold standard once removed. The currency of a gold exchange standard country was convertible, at a fixed exchange rate, into currencies which were convertible into gold. The gold reserves of the full gold standard currencies did double purpose, backing their own currencies and those of the gold exchange standard countries. As long as monetary conditions were stable, the system should have economized on gold. Smaller reserves, in relation to the money supply, should have been necessary than were required under the classical gold standard when each country held its own gold reserves.

The Realities of the International Monetary System.   While the monetary arrangements of the 1920s are often described as the gold exchange standard, it is not clear that this label is apt. In the years 1920-24, flexible exchange rates were common. As stabilization occurred in the years 1924-1926, many countries opted for the gold exchange standard. For some, like France, it was apparently a transitional measure, on the way to a full gold standard. Countries, like the United Kingdom, which returned to the full gold standard, did so with restrictions on gold convertibility.[33] Canada was one of the very few nations which restored the original gold standard arrangements, although, as we saw in Chapter 14, with the fateful addition of the *Finance Act.*

Internationally, the effective ratio of gold to the money supply fell significantly from prewar norms, and in some countries it fell dramatically.[34] Thus, to some extent, the objective of economizing on the stock of gold was achieved — but it was a once over adjustment. As the 1920s came to an end, some countries, and most notably France, made deliberate efforts to replace foreign exchange with gold in their official reserves. By the end of the decade, the fear of a general shortage of gold reemerged.

The "Rules of the Game" Again.   More than just the form of the gold standard had changed. There was also a fundamental change in the "spirit" of the system. Although the "rules of the game" had not been followed slavishly in the classical period, the severe monetary discipline of the gold standard was accepted as natural and normal. In the interwar period, central banks began to concern themselves more with monetary policies for domestic stabilization, and violations of the "rules of the game" occurred on a large scale.[35] International gold flows were restricted, and were not permitted to be decisive in regulating domestic money supplies. Instead of reinforcing the direct effects of gold flows on the domestic money supply, central banks sterilized the monetary effects of gold flows, and frequently took contrary monetary actions — expanding in the face of a loss of gold, and contracting in the face of a gain of gold. The international specie flow mechanism was not allowed to work as in its classical conception. Thus,

Canada's covert suspension of the gold standard in early 1929 (Chapter 14), was but an extreme example of a policy which had become commonplace.

The Depression of the 1930s

The depression of the 1930s was the most traumatic economic event of the 20th century. From our present perspective, the development of the international monetary constitution, its impact was profound. Three aspects should be emphasized.

First, it destroyed any semblance of the gold standard as an international monetary constitution. Faced with drains of gold in a situation already dominated by powerful deflationary forces, country after country suspended gold convertibility, particularly following Britain's suspension in September 1931. Rather than accepting the discipline of the gold standard, some countries allowed their exchange rates to fluctuate in the market, others attempted to manage their exchange rates through official intervention in the exchange market, and some adopted foreign exchange controls. The patchwork international monetary system that was the gold exchange standard became even more variegated.

Second, there was the beginning of an intellectual revolution with respect to economic policy. The theoretical analysis of Keynes' *General Theory of Employment, Interest and Money* seemed to offer the world a new approach to the management of monetary affairs, stressing the use of fiscal and monetary policies to maintain full employment. The focus of policy shifted from international commitments to domestic concerns; from the exchange rate to the level of employment.

Third, contemporary interpretations of experience during the 1930s with exchange rates which were not firmly anchored to par values strongly suggested that a regime of flexible exchange rates was inherently destructive of international economic integration — a view which dominated plans for the reconstruction of the international monetary system after World War II.

The influential analysis was that of the Norwegian economist Ragnar Nurkse, undertaken for the League of Nations and published in 1944 as *International Currency Experience: Lessons of the Inter-War Period*. Nurkse concluded that few exchange rates were allowed to fluctuate freely, except for short periods. Those that did were subject to "violent" fluctuations. Foreign exchange markets were "swayed by speculative anticipations." A movement of the exchange rate in any direction was "liable to create expectations of a further movement in that direction," inducing speculative capital flows to take advantage of the anticipated movement in the exchange rate. The capital flows, in turn, would induce the expected movement in the exchange rate. Thus, speculative capital movements were "disequilibrating"; and movements in the exchange rate were "cumulative and self-aggravating."[36]

This picture of disequilibrating international capital movements was disturbing in itself. But Nurkse argued further that their effects on the exchange rate might be reinforced by the current account. It is generally assumed that a rise in the exchange rate (a fall in the external value of the home currency) will stimulate exports and reduce imports, improving the balance of trade. However, in the short run at least, the demand for imports (and possibly for exports) may be sufficiently inelastic so that the rise in the exchange rate increases the foreign exchange required to pay for imports (and reduces the foreign exchange earned from exports), making the balance of payments worse. This would aggravate the fluctuation in the exchange rate. Thus, the combination of "extrapolative expectations" with respect to the exchange rate dominating capital accounts and short-run "elasticity pessimism" with respect to current accounts led to the conclusion that a regime of unregulated flexible exchange rates would be violently unstable, and this instability would serve no useful economic purpose. In particular, fluctuations in a flexible exchange rate could not be relied upon to sensitively adjust the current account of the balance of payments to equilibrium.

The case against flexible exchange rates was even stronger, however. Nurkse's analysis led to the conclusion that exchange rates had to be managed by governments, through direct intervention in the foreign exchange market, supported by appropriate monetary policies (shades of the gold standard?). However, governmental intervention could be used to deliberately depreciate a currency in an attempt to increase exports and reduce imports and hence stimulate domestic employment. Like protective tariffs, which were also widely adopted at this time, deliberate devaluation was a "beggar thy neighbor" policy. It was an attempt to shift the burden of unemployment to other countries, and for this reason it invited retaliation, and hence competitive devaluations. Nurkse concluded that the only hope for exchange stability rested in international coordination, including "simultaneous and coordinated international action" to establish appropriate exchange rates, — and "coordination between national policies affecting income, employment and prices."[37]

The Bretton Woods System

Like World War I — but in even greater degree — World War II brought about dramatic changes in international economic and financial relationships. During the War, because all major countries adopted direct controls over foreign exchange trans-actions (and over most aspects of economic activity), an international monetary system in the traditional sense could hardly be said to exist. Market forces were not permitted to affect domestic monetary affairs, nor to determine exchange rates. As a result, exchange rates became increasingly arbitrary as time passed, and by the end of the War a major realignment of currencies was necessary if financial stability without controls was to occur. The problem of reconstructing the international monetary system was urgent, and it was viewed against the background of the 1930s. There was a general fear that the depression would recur without appropriate policies designed to promote full employment and industrial reconstruction, and there was determination that neither the chaotic international monetary situation of the 1930s nor the deflationary strictures of the gold standard would be permitted to interfere with such policies. The mistakes made after World War I were to be avoided — what Nurkse described as a solution to the reconstruction problem,

> ...arrived at by the sovereign choice of independent powers rather than by international agreement.... The piecemeal and haphazard manner of international monetary reconstruction...(which)...sowed the seeds of subsequent disintegration.[38]

An international conference was convened at Bretton Woods, New Hampshire, in 1944 to design a new international monetary system.

The Principles of Bretton Woods

As part of our analysis in Chapter 22 of the macroeconomic implications of a regime of fixed exchange rates, we sketched some of the features of the Bretton Woods system. We must now consider the system in greater detail to identify its flaws and the reasons for its failure as an international monetary constitution.

The Bretton Woods system was based on four fundamental principles.

The Adjustable Peg.   In principle, the Bretton Woods system was a *fixed exchange rate* regime. The basic obligation assumed by member governments was to declare a par rate of exchange and to ensure that the actual rate at which transactions were consummated in the foreign exchange market did not depart from the par rate by more than 1% in either direction. The upper and lower limits had the same effect as did the gold points under the gold standard, but, particularly in the Canadian case, they were much wider. This provided some flexibility to a central bank in managing the nation's monetary affairs, although the scope which it provided for independent monetary policy was very limited.

Thus, in some important respects the Bretton Woods system mimicked the gold standard. However, in other respects it was very different. Under the classical gold standard, a balance of payments deficit *forced* deflationary monetary measures (and a balance of payments surplus forced inflationary measures). With the exchange rate fixed and without direct controls, domestic monetary adjustments were the only mechanism for adjusting the balance of payments to equilibrium (and the adjustment was supposed to occur automatically as a result of the specie flow mechanism). In effect, the domestic economy was the residual in the system — its variables (prices, income, employment, etc.) were to be adjusted through monetary pressures so that the economy could maintain its international relationships at the fixed exchange rate. In the aftermath of the Great Depression, such an approach to international adjustment was not acceptable.

The Bretton Woods system provided a short-term cushion against balance of payments pressures, through the pooling of foreign exchange reserves (to be discussed below), and it provided an alternative to the gold standard adjustment mechanism for more severe problems. Under the classical gold standard the exchange rate was *immutable* — under Bretton Woods it was not. Changes in the par rate of exchange were possible, but such changes were to be *infrequent*, subject to *international consultation and approval*, and made only in response to *exceptional and intractable* balance of payments pressures. Under Bretton Woods the exchange rate, rather than fixed, is better described as *pegged* — and the peg was *adjustable*.

National Policy Sovereignty.   The world had experienced a regime of adjustable exchange rates before, during the 1920s and 1930s, and, as we have seen, the experiment was widely condemned. The major complaints, as echoed by Nurkse, were that at best the setting of exchange rates was haphazard and uncoordinated leading to instability, and at worst exchange rates were adjusted to secure some national advantage at the expense of production and employment in other countries, inviting retaliation and hence further instability. The Bretton Woods system prescribed *international consulta-*

tion and agreement on change. in par rates, and it provided an institution — the International Monetary Fund — as a vehicle for such consultations and as a watchdog, maintaining surveillance over the exchange rate policies of member countries. Par exchange rates were not supposed to be changed without the prior approval of the International Monetary Fund.

In the spirit of Nurkse's conclusions about the necessary conditions for a stable international financial system, the IMF attempted to assume an even more comprehensive coordinating role, encompassing domestic monetary and fiscal policies of member countries. Its staff continuously monitored developments in all member countries, and held regular consultations with member governments. However, the power of the IMF to impose its will was very limited, except when a member country, faced with a balance of payments problem, was seeking IMF assistance. On such occasions the concept of *conditionality* came to bear.[39] IMF assistance was provided on the condition that appropriate policies, and particularly monetary policies, were adopted and implemented to correct the balance of payments problem. In this sense, the IMF was able to develop a broad role in coordinating domestic policies — but it must be emphasized that this role related directly only to the policies of member countries who were in balance of payments trouble, and did not encompass the policies of countries with balance of payments surpluses. The degree to which the Bretton Woods system effectively restricted national sovereignty over fiscal and monetary policies proved to be relatively small.

Avoidance of Direct Controls.   There is frequently an "easy" way out of the dilemma posed by a conflict between the domestic and the external objectives of monetary policy through the use of direct foreign exchange controls. Thus, for example, when the problem is excess demand for foreign exchange at the maximum permitted foreign exchange rate, it is possible to maintain stability of the foreign exchange rate by substituting official rationing of the restricted supply of foreign exchange for rationing by the price mechanism. By giving itself the power to approve or disapprove applications for foreign exchange, the government adds another weapon to its policy armory, making it possible to keep the foreign exchange market in a continuous state of disequilibrium (i.e., with demand in excess of supply at the pegged exchange rate). Since it is then unnecessary to use monetary policy to maintain equilibrium in the foreign exchange market, monetary policy is freed from the international constraint, at least in the short run.

Direct controls involve arbitrary interference with the allocation of resources in the economy. In general, they impair economic efficiency. In an international context, such controls permit arbitrary interference with the free flow of international trade and impair economic efficiency in other countries. They can be used as devices for "beggar thy neighbor" policies or for politically based discrimination in international commerce. Widely used by major countries they would distort the international division of labor and prevent the development of international trade as the engine of world economic growth.

However, the Bretton Woods system did not involve an absolute prohibition against direct controls. A distinction was made between controls over current account and controls over capital account transactions. The former were prohibited, except temporarily, to deal with an exceptional balance of payments problem. Perhaps reflecting Nurkse's analysis of the disruptive effects of speculative international capital flows in the interwar period, and the desperate shortage of capital in postwar Europe, the agreement was more flexible with respect to controls over capital account transactions.

The Link to Gold.   Although attempts were made at the Bretton Woods conference to dislodge gold from its paramount position as international money, proposals for a new flat international money were rejected. Gold had a central role in the Bretton Woods system. Indeed, we can characterize the system as an elaboration of the gold exchange standard advocated by the Genoa Conference in 1922 and partially adopted in the interwar period. The Bretton Woods system suffered from some of the same flaws as the interwar gold exchange standard, including a growing imbalance between the demand for and supply of gold.

On a symbolic level, the U.S. dollar of gold content prescribed by U.S. laws in effect in 1944 was the official unit of account for the International Monetary Fund, and all members were obliged to declare a par rate of exchange in terms of this gold dollar. In practical terms, however, the important aspects of the link to gold were threefold.

First, gold was international money, which could be used in international settlements among central banks. Part of each country's subscription to the IMF had to be in gold or in currencies convertible into gold, and both the IMF and most central banks accumulated a substantial portion of their official foreign exchange reserves in gold.

Second, although the U.S. government had terminated its formal obligation to convert private holdings of U.S. dollars into gold in the early 1930s (and residents of the United States were prohibited from owning or trading in gold, other than for artistic, industrial, and numismatic purposes), the government continued to guarantee the convertibility of dollars in the hands of foreign governments "for legitimate monetary purposes" and to purchase all gold offered to it at the official price of $35 per ounce. The U.S. gold stock, which, at the end of World War II, amounted to almost three quarters of the gold in monetary reserves in the western world, became in effect the central gold reserve for the world monetary system.

Third, an active private market in gold existed, centered primarily in London. The interaction between the private gold market and official holdings of gold was an important factor in the breakdown of the Bretton Woods System.

The International Liquidity Problem

Adoption of these principles meant that the Bretton Woods system was to be an elaboration on the gold exchange standard of the 1920s, with most of the same flaws. Like the gold standard, it was to be a fixed exchange regime, but with two important differences. In the short run, there was to be more independence for domestic stabilization policies than was possible under the gold standard. In the long run, there was to be an alternative to deflation as an adjustment mechanism, i.e., coordinated changes in the par values of exchange rates. As we saw in Chapter 22, in the absence of direct controls over foreign exchange transactions, a precondition for the independence of domestic monetary policy with a fixed exchange rate is that the government have access to very sizeable external reserves, gold and foreign exchange which can be drawn upon freely to permit direct intervention in the foreign exchange market in support of the domestic currency. Moreover, the potential need for external reserves increased as the international economy recovered and international trade increased in volume and in value, and as international capital markets were freed from controls and improved their effectiveness in moving funds from country to country, in large volumes, on short notice, and at low cost. A growing supply of reserves was obviously critical to the successful operation of the Bretton Woods system, and it would have been pointless to design an international monetary system on Bretton Woods principles without providing a solution to this problem of international liquidity. What happened to official external reserves during the Bretton Woods period? And, what mechanisms did the Bretton Woods system have for creating additional reserves as they were needed?

The Growth of External Reserves.   The increase in the aggregate external reserves of all governments from 1950 through 1980 is shown in Figure 23-2. During the Bretton Woods period, the accumulation of official external reserves was steady but slow — until the last two years. From 1950 through 1969, the external reserves of all countries taken together increased from the equivalent of U.S. $48 billion to U.S. $79 billion, about 63% (or an annual average rate of increase of 2.6% per annum). As an index of the growth of the international economy, over the same period the total value of exports from all countries increased more than fourfold (an average annual growth rate of almost 8% per annum). As an alternative index, the world's money supply increased more than threefold (an average annual growth rate of over 6% per annum).

Thus, through most of the Bretton Woods period, official holdings of external reserves increased much less rapidly than might be expected, given the expansion of the world economy. However, there was a dramatic change in the last two years. In 1970 and 1971 total reserves increased by 70% — more than over the previous 19 years! This late spurt in the accumulation of external reserves is an interesting paradox. Given the theoretical importance of external reserves to the functioning of the Bretton Woods system, why would the system begin to disintegrate just when the growth of reserves was accelerating? We will explore this question, along with the behavior of external reserves in the post-Bretton Woods period, later.

Sources of Reserves.   Figure 23-2, together with Table 23-1, also makes an important point about the sources of increased external reserves during the Bretton Woods period. Although gold was the basic international money of the Bretton Woods agreement, the increase in the stock of gold in central banks was not the primary factor in the growth of official reserves. The issue of the scarcity of gold, which was of such serious concern during the 1920s, reemerged during the Bretton Woods period — and, as we shall see, the consequences were similar. An international scramble for a very slowly increasing stock of gold — involving private as well as official purchasers — led to an international redistribution of gold reserves, which contributed to the instability of the system.

Member nations also had unconditional rights to draw reserves out of the International Monetary Fund. Because they provided almost immediate access to foreign exchange, these drawing rights are normally counted as part of a nation's external reserves. Drawing rights at the IMF (to be discussed later) increased steadily during the Bretton Woods period, but they constituted a small fraction of aggregate reserves and their growth made but a small contribution to the overall increase in reserves.

FIGURE 23-2   Official external reserves, all countries: Bretton
Woods and after, 1950-1980

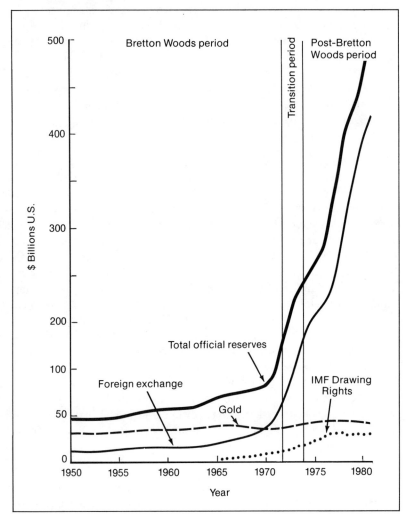

By far the most important factor in the growth of official external reserves was the
accumulation of foreign exchange. Several national currencies were held, but by far the
most important currency was the U.S. dollar. This gave the United States a special role
in the system. As the primary "reserve currency country" it was, in effect, the banker for
the system. Not only was its money used as external reserves by other countries, but also
the major source of increases in external reserves in the system had to be a deficit in the
balance of international payments of the United States. This is an important point to
note. As we shall see, it helps explain the spurt in the accumulation of external reserves
in 1970, and it contributed to the instability of the Bretton Woods system.

TABLE 23-1   **Source of official external reserves during the Bretton Woods period, 1950-1971 (billions of U.S. dollars)**

	Stock of Reserves			*Increase in Reserves*	
	1950	*1969*	*1971*	*1950-69*	*1969-71*
Total official reserves (all countries)	48.3	78.7	133.6	30.4	54.9
Gold	33.3	38.9	39.0	5.6	0.1
Drawing rights at the International Monetary Fund*	1.7	6.7	13.3	5.0	6.6
Foreign exchange	13.3	33.0	81.4	19.7	48.4
(U.S. dollars)	(4.9)	(16.0)	(50.6)	(11.1)	(34.6)
(Other currencies)	(8.4)	(17.0)	(30.8)	(8.6)	(13.8)

* Includes Special Drawing Rights.

SOURCE: International Monetary Fund, *International Financial Statistics* (various issues).

Conditional Reserves.   The concept of external reserves used in the above discussion includes only "unconditional" reserves, gold and foreign exchange held by governments and central banks, and drawing rights at the IMF which were unconditionally available to them. In addition, the authorities of all nations held what we can call "conditional reserves," funds available to them if certain conditions were satisfied. To some extent, these conditional reserves represented credit which would be extended by the International Monetary Fund above and beyond the basic unconditional drawing rights. However, they, largely represented the ability to borrow foreign exchange from other central banks or possibly in the open market. From time to time, formal lines of credit were negotiated among central banks. In general, however, the available sums were unspecified — the lines of credit were implicit rather than explicit. As a result, while we can measure some components of conditional reserves from time to time, there is no way to develop a consistent measure of the aggregate of conditional reserves over time. However, they were very important throughout the Bretton Woods period, and they undoubtedly increased in importance as the period advanced. As a result, Figure 22-2 probably understates the rate of growth of aggregate external reserves during the Bretton Woods period by a considerable margin.

In comparison to the gold exchange standard of the 1920s, the development of sophisticated and coordinated arrangements for the mobilization of conditional reserves was the most distinctive feature of the Bretton Woods system. A major institution for this purpose was the International Monetary Fund.

The International Monetary Fund

Although it was by no means the only mechanism for the provision of conditional external reserves, the International Monetary Fund was the cornerstone of Bretton Woods. Since 1947, when it opened for business, the IMF has changed in size, structure, and methods of operations, with particularly marked changes occurring after the Bretton Woods system disintegrated in the early 1970s. In this discussion of the IMF we have reference primarily to its operations while the Bretton Woods system was functioning more or less as originally conceived, i.e., prior to mid-1971. We will return to the "new" IMF later.

In a sense, the IMF was to be the central bank for the international monetary system. It was given lender of last resort responsibilities and limited powers of supervision and coordination with respect to the monetary and foreign exchange policies of member governments. However, until 1969, it was denied the basic power of a central bank to issue liabilities of its own which were usable as international money. In that year it was given the power to make a limited issue of "Special Drawing Rights," an instrument which had some of the characteristics of international money. But it was not until after the breakdown of the Bretton Woods system that the SDR took on a major role in the international monetary system.

Quotas.   From a financial point of view, the IMF is essentially a pool of gold and national currencies, available to be borrowed by member countries. When the IMF was established (or when a country joined), each member was assigned a quota, based on its national income, its importance in international trade, and its holdings of gold and U.S. dollar reserves. Twenty-five percent of each member's quota (the so-called gold tranche) had to be subscribed in gold, or currencies convertible into gold, and the balance in its own currency. For each member country, the size of the quota not only established its "drawing rights" (i.e., rights to borrow gold or foreign exchange from the Fund) it also determined its voting rights in the affairs of the IMF. Although, as time passed, other sources of funds were developed, the aggregate of the national quotas provided the basic financial resources with which the IMF could carry on its operations. In 1947, the aggregate value of all quotas was U.S. $8.8 billion. As a result of new members joining and several general increases in the quotas of members, by 1971 (the beginning of the end of Bretton Woods) this had increased to U.S. $28.8 billion. (By the end of 1980 it was SDR 59.6 billion, the equivalent of about U.S. $75 billion.)

Drawing Rights.   IMF resources are available to members to supplement their own external reserves. Under the Bretton Woods agreement, and as IMF policies developed, the basic rights of any member to draw on the Fund were defined on the one hand by the member's quota and on the other hand by the Fund's holding of the member's national currency. A member draws on the Fund by paying in its own currency in exchange for appropriate foreign currencies (or, during the Bretton Woods period, gold). A member can draw on the Fund virtually without question, providing the drawing does not increase the Fund's holding of the member's currency beyond its quota. In effect, the gold tranche is available to a member *unconditionally*. (Remember: what the member is drawing from the Fund is simply the gold and convertible foreign exchange which it had earlier subscribed to the Fund. It is simply reclaiming what had originally been part of its foreign exchange reserves.) Drawings which would increase the Fund's holding of the member's currency beyond its quota are *conditional*. Normally, the right to make such drawings is negotiated in advance, under a *standby agreement*, which specifies both the amounts which can be drawn and a program of domestic policies which the member is expected to implement in order to correct its balance of payments problem, including a timetable of performance which the staff of the IMF can monitor.

It should be noted that the unconditional drawing right is not a fixed amount. It depends on the Fund's holdings of the member's currency as well as its quota. If other nations draw a member's currency out of the Fund, the reduction in the Fund's holding increases the member's unconditional borrowing right. Conversely, if other nations repay their drawings by putting the member's currency into the Fund, the increase in the Fund's holding reduces the member's unconditional borrowing right.

Limits to Borrowing.   The Bretton Woods Agreement contained two limits on the drawing rights of any member, but both could be waived at the discretion of the IMF. First, the rate of increase in the Fund's holding of a member's currency was to be limited to 25% per year. Waivers to this provision were common, and after 1953 most drawings exceeded it. Second, no drawings were to make the Fund's holding of a member's currency exceed more than 200% of its quota. Again, waivers to this limit were not uncommon, particularly after 1963.

Obligations to Repurchase.   Each drawing from the Fund simultaneously reduces the Fund's holdings of other currencies (thus increasing other member's drawing rights from the Fund) and increases the Fund's holdings of the drawing member's currency. Drawings which increase the Fund's holdings of the member's currency above 75% of its quota, create an obligation to repurchase. The amount and timing of the repurchase is governed by another complicated set of rules, but all repurchases must be made with convertible foreign exchange. Interest is charged on the Fund's excess holdings of a member's currency as an inducement to early repayment, the interest rate increasing with both the magnitude of the excess and the time that it is outstanding. Thus, drawings on the Fund are appropriately regarded as short-term loans.

International Credit Creation.   When a member draws on its gold tranche, it is drawing gold and foreign exchange which it had previously accumulated through its own national efforts and subscribed to the Fund. The gold tranche is simply a part of the nation's reserves held in a different form. However, when a member draws foreign exchange in excess of this — in what are called the "credit tranches" — *new reserves are created*. The drawing member obtains foreign exchange which was previously not part of any nation's foreign exchange reserves, and it is free to use this foreign exchange for intervention in the foreign exchange market. Other members have, in effect, extended credit in their own currencies through the intermediary of the IMF, and thus they temporarily help finance the drawing member's balance of payments deficit. It is in this way that the pooling of national currencies in the IMF makes a net contribution to the supply of international liquidity.

This is an important point. It was the credit tranches of the Fund which were its distinctive contribution to the solution of the liquidity problems of the Bretton Woods system. Over time, these credit tranches increased as new members joined and as general increases in quotas were agreed upon. From less than U.S.$7 billion in 1947, they increased to U.S. $34 billion in 1971 and U.S. $77 billion in 1980. In the latter years

Canada and the IMF in 1968

The arrangements governing transactions with the IMF are complicated. Perhaps an example will help clarify them. Canada's transactions with the IMF in 1968, while relatively remote in time, were one of the few examples of Canada's defending a pegged exchange rate while the Bretton Woods system was in full flower.

At that time, Canada's quota in the IMF was U.S. $740 million. At the end of December, 1967, the Fund held U.S. $341.6 million worth of Canadian dollars. Thus, Canada's basic drawing right was U.S. $399.6 million. However, Canada also had outstanding loans of Canadian dollars to the I.M.F. under the General Arrangements to Borrow equivalent to U.S. $35 million. This was a special arrangement to augment the resources of the IMF through borrowing. However, under the G.A.B. the IMF was obliged to repay its borrowings in Canada if Canada was itself forced to borrow from the Fund. Since repayment of

EXAMPLE 23-B1   Canada's transactions with the International Monetary Fund, 1968 (Millions of U.S. dollars)

December 31, 1967	
Canada's quota	740.0
Outstanding loans under the G.A.B.	35.0
Augmented quota	775.0
I.M.F. holdings of Canadian dollars	341.6
Unconditional Drawing Right	433.4
January 1, – February 29, 1968	
Transactions affecting I.M.F. holdings of Canadian dollars	
Third country repayments in Canadian dollars	+ 7.3
Canadian drawing of foreign exchange	+426.0
I.M.F. repayment of G.A.B. loan	− 35.0
Net change in Fund holdings of Canadian dollars	+398.3
February 29, 1968	
Canada's quota	740.0
I.M.F. holdings of Canadian dollars (341.6 + 398.3)	739.9
Unconditional Drawing Right	0.1
Canada's obligation to repurchase [739.9 − (0.75 - 740)]	184.9
March 1 –December 31, 1968	
Transactions affecting I.M.F. holdings of Canadian dollars	
Third country drawings of Canadian dollars	−138.5
Canadian repurchase of Canadian dollars	− 67.6
Net change in Fund holdings of Canadian dollars	−206.1
December 31, 1968	
Canada's quota	740.0
I.M.F. holdings of Canadian dollars (739.9 − 206.1)	533.8
Unconditional Drawing Right	206.2

the G.A.B. loan would reduce the Fund's holdings of Canadian dollars, the loan in effect augmented Canada's IMF quota. As a result, Canada's unconditional drawing right at that time amounted to U.S. $433.4 million.

In the early part of 1968 other members of the IMF repaid outstanding debts to the Fund in Canadian dollars. This increased the Fund's holdings of Canadian dollars by U.S. $7.3 million, and reduced Canada's unconditional drawing right by the same amount. During the foreign exchange crisis of early 1968, Canada drew U.S. $426 from the Fund, and the Fund repaid the outstanding G.A.B. loan. As a result of these transactions, the Fund's holdings of Canadian dollars increased by U.S. $398.3, to U.S. $739.9 or 100% of Canada's quota. Canada had exhausted her unconditional drawing right, and since the Fund's holdings of Canadian dollars exceeded 75% of Canada's quota,

had created an obligation to repurchase from the Fund. Further Canadian borrowing would normally be conditional on the presentation of an acceptable program for correction of the balance of payments problem.

During the balance of the year other countries borrowed Canadian dollars from the Fund, and Canada repaid part of her earlier borrowings. Both sets of transactions reduced the Fund's holdings of Canadian dollars, and by year-end, unconditional drawing rights had been reestablished to the extent of U.S. $206.2 million.

This example should make clear the relationship between Canada's quota, the I.M.F.'s holdings of Canadian dollars, and Canada's drawing rights. It also illustrates how Canada's position at the I.M.F. can be affected by the transactions of third countries with the Fund.

they amounted to more than a quarter of the explicit external reserves of members — a not inconsiderable addition to international liquid assets held by governments and central banks.

It should be noted in passing that not all of the aggregate of credit tranches at the IMF can be considered "liquid." In the early years, almost the only generally useful currency in the Fund was the U.S. dollar (from 1947 through 1960, 87% of all drawings from the Fund were of U.S. dollars). The IMF was a vehicle by which the United States extended short term credit to the rest of the world. With the economic recovery of Western Europe and Japan, more currencies became freely convertible in active foreign exchange markets, and hence potentially useful to the Fund. While the U.S. dollar remained of primary importance, other currencies were also drawn. From 1960 through 1971, the currencies of nine industrialized countries were heavily used (97% of all drawings), and subsequently others added to the list, including the currencies of some nonindustrialized oil-producing countries. However, it remains an important fact that a significant fraction of the Fund's resources are not readily usable. This complicates the interpretation of the Fund's role in the international monetary system, and it helps explain some of the political controversies which have surrounded the IMF from time to time. However, given our purpose, these issues need not detain us.

Special Drawing Rights

Until 1969, drawing on the credit tranches was the primary method by which the IMF made a general contribution to the international liquidity problem. Following prolonged negotiations, however, a 1969 amendment to the Articles of Agreement introduced a new principle into the operations of the International Monetary Fund. It permitted the Fund to create a limited amount of a new reserve asset, to be allocated to members in proportion to their quotas, as an addition to their external reserves. Special Drawing Rights were created without members' subscribing either gold, foreign exchange, or their own currencies to the Fund. In this sense, they involved the IMF in the *direct* creation of international reserve money.

There have been two allocations of SDRs. The first, in three annual installments beginning in January 1970, totalled SDR 9.3 billion (12% of total external reserves at the end of 1968). The second allocation, again in three annual installments beginning in January 1979, totalled SDR 16.1 billion (6% of total external reserves at the end of 1978), bringing the total allocation to SDR 21.4 billion. The creation of the SDR thus made a small but significant contribution to the growth of international reserves — but this contribution came as the Bretton Woods system was failing, and its effect was swamped by other developments.

These statistics highlight the dual character of the Special Drawing Right. On the one hand, it is an abstract *unit of account* in which values are measured, and on the other hand it is a *financial asset* which governments can hold as part of their external reserves.

A Unit of Account.   As a unit of account, the SDR has a value in terms of the currencies of all of the members of the IMF. When it was first created in 1970, the SDR was defined as the equivalent of 0.88671 grams of fine gold, which made it identical to the U.S. dollar. When the official U.S. price of gold was increased in mid-1971 and again in early 1973, the U.S. dollar value of the SDR increased from $1.00 to $1.086 and then to $1.206. The value of an SDR in terms of any other currency was simply the product of that currency's exchange rate on the U.S. dollar and the U.S. dollar price of the SDR. In 1974, the fixed link between the SDR and gold (or between the SDR and the U.S. dollar) was broken. The SDR was defined as a basket of specified quantities of 16 major currencies. The relative amounts of each currency in the basket depended on the relative importance of that country in international trade (with somewhat heavier weight given to the U.S. dollar). In 1981, the basket was simplified to include only the five major currencies (see insert on page 647). All of the accounts of, and many of the statistics published by, the IMF are recorded in SDRs, and the SDR has come into use in some private international transactions. Just as the dollar is the unit of account for Canadian domestic transactions, the SDR has become the unit of account for many international transactions.

A Reserve Asset.   Considered as a financial asset, SDRs are simply entries in a set of books maintained by the International Monetary Fund. They cannot be spent directly to finance intervention in the foreign exchange market, because, with minor exceptions, ownership of SDRs cannot be transferred to private individuals and firms. Rather, governments holding SDRs may transfer them to other member governments designated by the IMF in exchange for currencies which can be used in the foreign exchange market. The designated members are obliged to accept the SDRs in return for their

The Value of an SDR

The determination of the value of an SDR is best illustrated by an example.

Effective January 1, 1981, the SDR was defined as the equivalent of a basket of the five major currencies involved in international trade. The number of units of each currency in the basket is as follows:

U.S. dollar	0.54
Deutsche mark	0.46
Japanese yen	34
French franc	0.74
Pound sterling	0.071

These quantities of each monetary unit are used as weights to calculate the value of an SDR in terms of any national monetary unit, given the market rates of exchange for these currencies. To illustrate the calculation, consider the exchange rates for these currencies which prevailed in the New York foreign exchange market at the end of February, 1981. The U.S. dollar price of one unit of each currency in the basket was:

U.S. dollar	1.00
Deutsche mark	0.47
Japanese yen	0.0048
French franc	0.20
Pound sterling	2.20

The value of a Special Drawing Right in terms of the U.S. dollar on that day was then:

$$(0.54 \times 1.00) + (0.46 \times 0.47) + (34 \times 0.0048) +$$
$$\text{dollar} \qquad \text{mark} \qquad \text{yen}$$
$$(0.74 \times 0.20) + (0.071 \times 2.20) = \$1.223$$
$$\text{franc} \qquad \text{pound} \qquad \text{SDR}$$

On the same day, a U.S. dollar was worth $1.20 in Canada. As a result, the Canadian dollar value of an SDR was (1.20 × 1.233) = $1.47. In a world of flexible exchange rates, the value of an SDR changes every day, and the IMF announces an official rate for each day based on the exchange rates for each of the five countries which prevailed in the London market at noon that day.

currency, and thus extend reserve credit to the deficit country. However, the amount of credit which a member may be called upon to extend in this way is subject to a number of safeguards. No member may be required to accept additional SDRs in excess of twice its allocation and each member is required to maintain its holdings of SDRs at 30% of its allocation on the average over a five-year period. The latter provision means that a member drawing down his allocation of SDRs is obliged to reconstitute his position through purchases of SDRs with convertible currency from other members or from the IMF itself. This ensures that SDRs will not become a large-scale chronic source of credit from one set of members to another.

Interest is paid on holdings and charged on allocations of SDRs. Initially, the interest rate was set at a nominal 1½% per annum. As a result of the reforms of 1974 and 1978 it is now set quarterly at 80% of the average of short-term interest rates in the five major countries whose currencies are included in the SDR basket. Members who draw down their holdings will pay interest to the Fund, and members who are required to accept additional SDRs will receive interest from the Fund. All charges and interest are payable in SDRs.

International Liquidity

As we noted earlier, the growth of explicit external reserves during the Bretton Woods period was very slow, until the very end. Even if we allow for Special Drawing Rights (which are included in our measure of external reserves) and the credit tranches at the IMF, the story does not change significantly. It is easy to get the impression that the slow growth of international reserves slowly strangled the Bretton Woods system. However, this ignores a very important part of the story. The growth of international liquidity was not limited to the growth of explicit reserves, or indeed to the willingness of members to increase their quotas with the IMF. There was another mechanism for the provision of international liquidity — inter-central bank credits. It was these credits which effectively solved most liquidity problems of the Bretton Woods system, and hence made the system work.

Multilateralism and the Liquidity Problem.   The resources of the International Monetary Fund are available to all members in proportion to their quotas. An increase in quotas increases the resources of the Fund and thus increases international liquidity on a multilateral basis. However, under the Bretton Woods system, the liquidity problems of the industrialized nations and of the less developed nations were rather different, in ways not adequately reflected in their relative quotas. The industrialized nations accounted for the bulk of international trade, but more importantly their national financial markets were connected in a network of international capital flows which, as the period advanced, became relatively free of direct controls. Most less developed countries maintained direct controls of varying degrees of severity over international transactions, and particularly over capital transactions, as they attempted to mobilize resources in accordance with national development plans. It was the freely convertible currencies of industrialized nations which were actively used in international finance, and which were subject to large-scale speculative attacks (or used as large-scale speculative refuges). Free convertibility of currencies exposed the currencies and the financial markets of the industrialized nations to the full blast of international speculation.

The response was to develop credit facilities which were specific to the industrialized nations.

Inter-Central Bank Credits.   The provision of special international credit facilities began as an *ad hoc* response to a British balance of payments crisis in early 1961. Meeting at the Bank for International Settlements in Basle, Switzerland, the central bankers of the major industrialized nations resolved that no member of the group (the "Basle Club") would be forced to change its par value because of speculative capital flows, and entered into reciprocal agreements to support each other's currencies and to extend credits to each other as necessary. From this informal beginning, the inter-central bank credit network developed in various ways, essentially (but not completely) outside the IMF.[40]

Some of the arrangements were *ad hoc*, to deal with a problem as it arose. Each major foreign exchange crisis involving the currency of a member of the "Club" was met by close consultation among central banks and frequently by a large "package" of assistance. For example, during the 1968 Canadian crisis, U.S. $900 million in credits were extended by other central banks, although the Bank of Canada did not find it necessary to draw upon them. It is not possible to quantify the potential magnitude of such *ad hoc* credits (if only because they were *ad hoc* and not a matter of continuing commitment), but in the later years of the Bretton Woods period special credits of upwards of U.S. $9 billion were mobilized in support of various currencies (mainly the British pound and the French franc), the equivalent of about 60% of the aggregate of quotas in the IMF.

In 1962, 10 members of the IMF (called the "Group of Ten" even though they were later joined by Switzerland, a non-member, making them 11) entered into an agreement with the IMF, called the General Arrangements to Borrow.[41] This permitted the IMF to borrow up to specified sums from each signatory to supplement the resources of the Fund. The total credit provided under this arrangement was about U.S. $6.2 billion, approximately 40% of the aggregate of national quotas in the IMF. The important point to note, however, is that although the arrangement was made through the IMF, this large sum could only be mobilized in support of the currencies of the signatory nations — the Group of Ten.

As a third arm of the inter-central bank credit network, the Federal Reserve System developed extensive reciprocal lines of credit with the central banks of industrialized countries under which assistance would be provided on a bilateral basis between the United States and the member countries. These arrangements were like the *ad hoc* credits, but were explicit lines of credit, arranged in advance, and on a bilateral basis. By 1970, the aggregate value of such reciprocal arrangements exceeded U.S. $11 billion.

Taken together, then, inter-central bank credits — including the *ad hoc* credits, the potential magnitude of which we can never know — involved the creation of international liquidity greatly in excess of that which was possible through the International Monetary Fund. Moreover, all of this liquidity was concentrated at the core of the international financial system, among the industrialized countries with freely convertible currencies. From this perspective, the Bretton Woods system was very flexible, generating vast sums of external reserves. Its problem was not one of strangulation through inadequate growth in reserves. The reasons for its failure must be sought elsewhere, particularly in the incredible stresses which speculative capital flows put on the system from time to time, stresses that no conceivable system of providing international liquidity could cope with.

THE DISINTEGRATION OF THE BRETTON WOODS SYSTEM

The Bretton Woods Agreement was an international monetary constitution which seemed to offer the benefits of a fixed exchange rate regime but with much more flexibility and scope for domestic stabilization policies than was possible under the classical gold standard. However, the Bretton Woods system had serious flaws which made it difficult for the system to cope effectively with stresses which developed in the international economy from time to time, and which independently generated serious stresses within the system itself. The disintegration of the system began in the late 1960s, but the decisive break occurred in mid-1971. Although there were dedicated attempts to reconstruct the system with even more flexibility about fixed "central" values for currencies, the international economic environment had changed significantly. By early 1976 the failure of reconstruction attempts was acknowledged, and the *de facto* flexible exchange rate system was accepted.

What were the flaws in the Bretton Woods system? We identify four: the vulnerability of the system to *speculation*; the asymmetrical nature of the *adjustment mechanism*; the lack of a rationally controlled mechanism for the *creation of international money*; and the link to *gold*.

Speculation

Nurkse suggested that a critical difference between the classical gold standard and the experience of the interwar period was that under the gold standard speculative international capital movements were stabilizing (helping to keep the exchange rate at par), whereas in the interwar period they were often destabilizing (accentuating the movement of the exchange rate in whatever direction it was moving). There is an obvious explanation. Under the gold standard everyone accepted the par value of the exchange rate as *immutable*. If the market rate deviated from par, it was widely expected to return to par sooner or laer. During the interwar period this was no longer true. There was much experience to show that exchange rate changes of very large magnitude could occur in either direction. The concept of immutable par values no longer provided an anchor for expectations. Like the gold standard, the Bretton Woods system was based on the concept of par values for exchange rates; however, the par values were not regarded as immutable, and because of the consequences for speculation, this proved to be a serious flaw.

We discussed the nature and consequences of speculation under the Bretton Woods system in connection with our analysis of the role of foreign exchange reserves in Chapter 22. We will not repeat that discussion here. Suffice it to remember that whenever a par value seemed out of line with fundamental developments in a country's international economic relationships — whether the currency appeared to be overvalued or undervalued — a basis for speculation existed. To the speculator, the risk of loss was minimal, and the possible gains were great. The exchange rate would either remain the same or it would change in the expected direction in a discrete and substantial jump. The possibility that the speculator would be caught by the exchange rate moving in the opposite direction was extremely remote. If the expected change did not occur, the maximum loss to the speculator was the interest foregone and other transactions costs, a small gamble for a potentially very large return. If the exchange rate were flexible, the speculative pressure itself would have altered the exchange rate, eventually removing the basis for the speculation and exposing the speculators to the risk of opposite movements. Under the Bretton Woods system, par values acted like dams, behind which the speculative pressure would accumulate. The government, of course, had to accomodate the speculators, supplying all the foreign exchange (or the domestic money, as the case might be) that the speculators demanded. From time to time, the speculator's demand for foreign exchange could be very large. Occasionally, the dam broke, the par value was changed, and the speculators won.

As the period advanced, the bouts of intense speculation became more frequent and the sums of money involved became immense. Billions of dollars could appear in speculative pools almost instantaneously. It is reported, for example, that on May 4, 1971 the German central bank was forced to absorb $1 billion dollars to prevent the mark from rising through the ceiling. The next day, it took in $1 billion in its *first hour* of operations, then gave up attempting to restrain the rate.[42] This degree of speculative activity put intense strain on the system — strain which even the imagination, cooperation, and immense resources of the central banks of the industrialized countries could not cope with.

The Adjustment Mechanism

Under the classical gold standard, in principle, if not always in fact, the adjustment process was symmetrical between surplus and deficit countries. The loss of gold, monetary contraction and deflation corrected the balance of payments of countries in deficit; the receipt of gold, monetary expansion, and inflation corrected the balance of payments of countries in surplus. The Bretton Woods system was designed to avoid this strong adjustment discipline. Many countries, particularly the less developed countries, suppressed chronic balance of payments problems behind direct controls. Among the industrialized countries with fully convertible currencies, direct and indirect access to external reserves or international credit meant that adjustment was not an automatic process but a matter of policy decision. If the assistance of the International Monetary Fund was sought, the negotiated discipline of "conditionality" came into play. However, that included the possibility of an adjustment of the exchange rate if the consequences of domestic policies were prices and wages which were inconsistent with balance of payments equilibrium at the old par rate of exchange. This encouraged delay in adjustment, and perhaps avoidance of severe domestic measures. In any case, the Bretton Woods system placed no formal pressures on surplus countries to pursue corrective adjustment policies.

As a result, the adjustment process under Bretton Woods was generally *delayed* and *asymmetrical*. The full burden of adjustment tended to fall on the deficit countries. The significance of the sluggish nature of the adjustment process is that it created or perpetuated stresses in the system, producing the situation in which adjustments in par values were almost inevitable, and hence laying the groundwork for the bouts of intense speculation discussed above. Divergent domestic policies, resulting, for example, in divergent rates of inflation, were tolerated if not encouraged, and contributed to the downfall of the system.

There was, however, one country which the system almost required to be in deficit, and for which the adjustment process, when it was necessary, created special problems — the major reserve currency country, the United States.

The Creation of External Reserves

As we noted earlier, the primary currency held as an external reserve asset by governments around the world during the Bretton Woods period was the U.S. dollar, and the major source of growth in explicit external reserves was an increase in holdings of U.S. dollars. This put the U.S. economy in a unique situation in the world. In order to supply the world's central banks with the additional external reserves which they demanded, the United States had to have a balance of payments deficit. That is, the balance of transactions on current account (goods and services) and on capital account (securities) had to be negative — the United States had to purchase more than it sold, year after year, on balance leaving liquid claims on the U.S. economy or gold from the U.S. reserve in the hands of other governments, to be held as their external reserves.

Figure 23-3 provides a summary of the U.S. balance of payments during this period. The upper panel shows the balances on current account and on capital account (with net errors and omissions included as a net capital flow). The bottom panel shows the net balance on current and capital accounts combined, which is to say the net balance of official monetary transactions (if you don't remember the accounts, perhaps you should quickly review Chapter 8). In the early years there was a small balance of payments deficit, comprised of small deficits on both current and capital accounts. The growth of external reserves in the rest of the world was slow (Figure 23-2), and there was much discussion of the implications of the "dollar shortage" for the viability of the Bretton Woods system. That is, there was concern that because of the dominant position of the U.S. economy in the world, the U.S. balance of payments would not produce large enough deficits to provide the necessary growth of external reserves in the rest of the world.

In the 1960s, the U.S. balance of payments situation changed significantly. Although the current account moved into a strong surplus, the capital account moved into an even stronger deficit, producing a larger balance of payments deficit and some acceleration of the growth of external reserves in the rest of the world (Figure 23-2). Indeed, there was concern in the United States that the net export of capital was excessive, and the accumulation of official claims on the United States too rapid. Measures were taken to restrain the export of capital, including special taxation provisions and moral suasion. Had these measures not been introduced the deficit would probably have been larger. Following a strengthening of the U.S. balance of payments in the late 1960s, the dramatic developments which precipitated the collapse of the Bretton Woods system occurred in 1970 and 1971. The current account surplus disappeared, and the capital account deficit reemerged, in accentuated degree (much of it short-term capital transactions, suggesting the presence of strong speculation against the U.S. dollar). The result was a deep deficit in the balance of international payments, reaching a remarkable $30 billion in 1971, and the equally remarkable jump in the external reserves of the rest of the world (Figure 23-2) which we commented upon earlier.

The supply of external reserves to the rest of the world was thus erratic, depending as it did on the multitude of factors which affected the U.S. balance of international payments (including the domestic monetary and fiscal policies of the United States). It can be argued that, during the 1950s, the growth of external reserves in the rest of the world was too slow; in the mid-1960s, somewhat too rapid; and in the early 1970s, far too rapid for the smooth functioning of the Bretton Woods system. However, there was no mechanism to deliberately regulate the supply of external reserves. Commenting on the failures of the gold exchange standard in the interwar period, Nurkse pointed to two significant problems: excessive private liquidity, which provided the means for large-scale international speculation, and instability in the reserve currency countries, which induced and magnified instability in the whole system.[43] Writing in 1944, he could have been forecasting the failures of the Bretton Woods system.

FIGURE 23-3 The U.S. balance of payments in the Bretton Woods period, 1950-1972

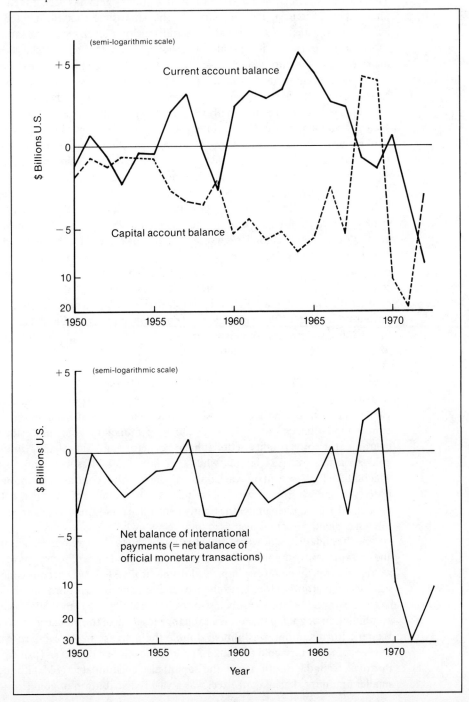

The Link to Gold

The role of the United States in the Bretton Woods system has been linked to that of an international financial intermediary. At the same time that the United States was lending to the rest of the world by acquiring long-term securities (and less liquid short-term securities), it was also borrowing from the rest of the world, issuing international monetary liabilities. As we saw in earlier chapters, borrowing on short-term liquid instruments and lending on long-term and less liquid instruments is the classic pattern of a bank-type financial intermediary. If the supply of U.S. dollars to the rest of the world could be rationally regulated, in general there is no reason to think that such an arrangement would be impractical in the long run, providing the world's central bankers were willing to accept the U.S. dollar as the exclusive international money. Indeed, the adoption of an international "dollar standard" with the U.S. dollar as the exclusive, inconvertible international money had many proponents.[44]

However, the Bretton Woods system had *two* types of international money — U.S. dollars and gold. This proved to be a fatal flaw. Some central bankers displayed a strong preference for gold among their foreign exchange reserves. Given the rate of growth of foreign exchange reserves in the rest of the world, the required gold could only be provided by drawing down the U.S. gold stock. Eventually, the United States was placed in the position of a banker faced with a precipitous decline in his cash reserves. The smaller the reserve ratio, the less credible is the banker's promise to convert all of his monetary liabilities into cash (i.e., gold) on demand. The problem was serious in the mid-1960s; it became severe at the beginning of the 1970s. The act which finally killed the Bretton Woods system was the U.S. renunciation of the convertibility of the U.S. dollar into gold at a fixed price.

International Redistribution of Gold Reserves.   In the immediate postwar period the role of the United States as banker to the new international gold standard seemed quite viable. As we noted earlier, the United States had emerged from World War II with almost three-quarters of the world's stock of monetary gold, more than ample to guarantee the convertibility of dollar balances in foreign official hands (in 1950 the U.S. gold stock was over $21 billion, while U.S. liquid liabilities were only $8.4 billion of which $4.9 billion were in official hands). Moreover, the economic disruptions produced by the war had left Europe with a seemingly chronic balance of payments deficit *vis à vis* the United States. Even under the tightly controlled conditions which prevailed, official foreign exchange reserves increased only very slowly.

By the mid-1950's, however, the situation began to change. With economic recovery and, in some cases, important monetary reforms, the balance of payments of continental western European countries improved dramatically. This was accompanied by large-scale accumulations of foreign exchange reserves, almost two-thirds of which were held in gold, with the balance largely in United States dollars. From 1950 through 1966 the accumulation of gold in the foreign exchange reserves of the industrialized countries of Western Europe alone was almost double the increase in the western world's total reserves of monetary gold (Table 23-2). Other developed countries (principally Spain, Portugal, Canada, South Africa and Japan) also accumulated gold, although in much smaller amounts. The overall effect was a vast redistribution of gold from the United

TABLE 23-2   **Gold and foreign exchange reserves, 1950-1966 ($ Millions U.S.)**

	I. Total monetary gold stock*	II. Reserve centers United States		United Kingdom	
		Total reserves	Gold	Total reserves	Gold
1950	35 300	24 265	22 820	3 443	2 862
1966	43 185	14 881	13 235	3 100	1 940
Net change 1950-1966	7 885	−9 384	−9 585	−343	−922

	III. Other countries				
	Industrial Europe		Other developed countries		Less developed countries
	Total reserves	Gold	Total reserves	Gold	Total reserves	Gold
1950	5 160	3 510	5 520	1 522	9 715	3 045
1966	31 287	19 076	11 057	4 095	11 655	2 555
Net change 1950-1966	26 127	15 566	5 537	2 573	1 940	−490

* Excludes U.S.S.R., China, Eastern Europe. Includes holdings of international institutions not listed separately in the table.

States, to other developed nations. As the reserves of the rest of the world increased, those of the United States declined setting the scene for the gold crisis of 1967-68.

Only a much more rapid rate of increase in the supply of monetary gold could have staved off the crisis by permitting the European central banks to increase their gold reserves without impairing the reserve position of the United States. What governed the rate of increase of the aggregate stock of monetary gold?

The Supply of Monetary Gold.   The problem of the scarcity of gold, which had been of such serious concern in the 1920s, reemerged during the Bretton Woods period. The price of gold had been fixed at U.S. $35 per ounce in 1935, and was unchanged. Costs of production had increased inexorably, partly as a result of the general rise of prices and wage rates, and partly as a result of the exhaustion of the richest and most accessible deposits of ore. The implications for the profitability of gold mining are obvious. In spite of subsidies to gold mining in several countries (including Canada), the production of new gold outside South Africa has been declining steadily for two decades.

In South Africa, the situation was different, but only by accident. Major new gold fields were brought into production beginning in 1953, and as a result total South African output increased substantially for several years. Whereas in 1953, South African mines accounted for half of the world's output of new gold, by the mid-1960s they were producing three-quarters of the total. However, the entire increase in this period occurred in the new mine fields. Output from the old fields fell off as rapidly as in the rest of the world. By 1966 the output from the new fields began to level off also.

FIGURE 23-4   The gold market: supply and demand

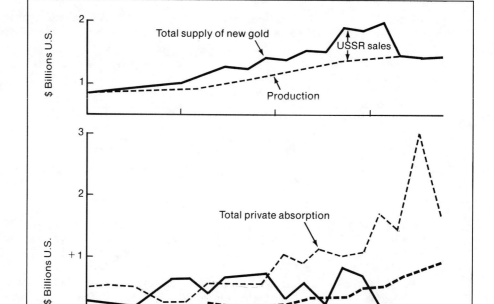

Apparently, this fillip to the base of the world's monetary system had run its course, and the underlying long-run retardation of gold production had re-asserted itself.

Although the production of new gold increased steadily, net additions to the world's stock of monetary gold were much more erratic, for two reasons. On the one hand, new production was augmented periodically by U.S.S.R. sales of gold, and on the other hand gold was absorbed by private demands. Although generally modest in amount, U.S.S.R. sales of gold were occasionally a significant factor in the market (Figure 23-4), and the abrupt termination of these sales in 1965 produced an important change in the supply situation. Much more important, however, and much more erratic, was the private absorption of gold. It consisted of two parts, a steadily growing industrial demand, and a highly volatile "hoarding" or "speculative" demand. Two important institutions which helped translate these private demands into drains on the world's stock of monetary gold were the London gold market and the Gold Pool.

The London Gold Market and the Gold Pool.   The London gold market is a private market for gold, which is the hub of a network of such markets around the world. Its importance to the Bretton Woods system was as a conduit through which gold was drained from official reserves to private hoards.

Most countries imposed severe restrictions on the private ownership and trading of gold before and during World War II. In an environment of monetary instability and rampant inflation, black markets for gold, a traditional and relatively durable international store of value, flourished nonetheless. Although there were some important exceptions (notably the United States and the United Kingdom), many countries relaxed or abolished restrictions on gold ownership and trading in the early 1950s and even those countries which maintained rigid controls found it almost impossible to eliminate large-scale illegal transactions. In 1954, after a period of stability in free gold markets, the London gold market was opened for trading among nonresidents through the intermediary of British brokers (British citizens were still prohibited from owning or trading gold). It quickly became the dominant wholesale market.

The basic stock-in-trade of the London gold market and its satellite markets throughout the world was the annual output of the Western world's gold mines, augmented by periodic U.S.S.R. gold sales. From time to time, various central banks also sold gold in the free market to gain foreign exchange. As long as the free market price was above the U.S. treasury's buying price ($34.9125 per ounce) suppliers of gold would offer it for sale in the market. If the price dropped below this, gold would flow into the United States' stock. As a result, the U.S. treasury's buying price set an effective floor under the free market price. On the demand side, the market was dominated by the various private demands for gold, although some European central banks also satisfied a large part of their demands for gold in this market. Because they had the option of dealing directly with the U.S. Treasury, these central banks provided a bridge between the gold market and the U.S. gold reserve. If they could satisfy their demands for gold in the open market at a price less than the U.S. treasury's selling price ($35.0875) they would do so. If the open market price rose above this, they would switch their demands to the U.S. treasury. This put an effective ceiling on the market price —unless private demands exceeded the flow of gold on the market.

In October 1961 this happened for the first time after the London gold market opened in 1951. Private speculation drove the market price to over $40 per ounce. Fearing that price instability would aggravate speculative pressures, the U.S. government intervened, supplying gold to the market through the Bank of England to stabilize the price close to the official price. In 1961 and 1962, in a series of agreements with major European central banks, the Federal Reserve System organized joint intervention as necessary to keep the market price close to the official price. The United States agreed to provide half of the gold required by the so-called Gold Pool, but of course the U.S. commitment to supply gold to central banks meant that in the long run a drain on the Gold Pool was a drain out of the U.S. reserve.

In this way, given the flow of gold onto the market, private demands for gold determined the rate of growth of aggregate stock of official gold reserves: and the sum of private demands and the demands of other central banks determined the rate of change of the U.S. gold stock.

Bifurcation of the Gold Stock.   Although the Gold Pool succeeded in stabilizing the price of gold, it did not prevent further waves of speculation. As Figure 23-4 indicates, the absorption of gold into private hoards continued, and indeed increased. A devaluation of the pound sterling in 1967 precipitated a particularly intense bout of speculation on the price of gold, which resulted in a substantial drain of gold out of monetary reserves and provoked a new gold policy.

The basic decision was to cease the *de facto* pegging of the price of gold in the free market. The members of the Pool announced that they would no longer sell gold to the free market nor buy gold from the free market, and that they would not supply gold to other central banks to replace gold sold in private markets. At the same time, gold then in the hands of central banks would continue to be treated as a reserve asset. The United States would still buy and sell gold "for legitimate monetary purposes" at $35 per ounce, and all would feel free to use gold for official international settlements. Other central banks were invited to subscribe to the new principles, and most, but not all, did.

Under the new "two-tier" policy for gold, the existing monetary stock of gold became, in effect, expensive yellow tokens, with a fixed nominal value of $35 per ounce, usable only for inter-central bank clearings. Private gold could be traded freely in the open market at a price determined by the interaction of supply and demand. The London price of gold increased to over $40 per ounce through mid-1969. There was then a period of calm, when the price dropped back to the neighborhood of $35 per ounce. In mid-1970, however, the price began to rise steadily again, breaking through $40 in mid-1971, and continuing on upwards.

The Breaking Point.   The bifurcation of the gold stock into an almost frozen monetary stock and a residual private stock arrested the decline in the gold reserves of the United States (Figure 23-5). However, it did not resolve the underlying problems of the Bretton Woods system. When the large U.S. balance of payments deficit emerged in 1970 and 1971, the U.S. gold stock did not fall, but the ratio of gold to external monetary liabilities of the United States continued to fall. The contradictions of the system were again laid bare. The need for reform was urgent.

We noted earlier that a U.S. balance of payments deficit was the primary source of reserves to the international monetary system. The counterpart of this was that when the United States ran a balance of payments deficit, the rest of the world ended up holding U.S. dollars, almost whether they wanted to or not. They could take gold from the United States instead; but the 1968 agreement discouraged that, and the very low level of U.S. reserves made it impractical. They could attempt to dispose of the U.S. dollars in the private gold market in exchange for gold, but only by driving up the price of gold and exciting speculation. They could attempt to dispose of the U.S. dollars in the foreign exchange market, but only by driving up the prices of the currencies that they were attempting to purchase, and exciting speculation. The system was locked-in, and the only solutions seemed to be a large-scale readjustment of exchange rates (which also excited intense speculation), sharp deflationary policies in the United States (on gold standard principles); or the suspension of the Bretton Woods system. On the initiative of the United States, the latter course was chosen.

FIGURE 23-5   The external monetary liabilities and gold reserves of the United States during the Bretton Woods period, 1950-1972

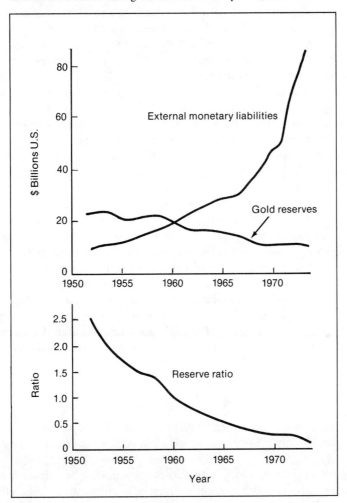

The End of Bretton Woods

As part of a complex package of economic policies directed at the correction of the U.S. balance of payments deficit and controlling domestic inflation, on August 15, 1971 the President of the United States announced the suspension of convertibility of the U.S. dollar into gold.[45] Major foreign exchange markets were closed for a week as other governments digested the implications of the U.S. policy. When they reopened on August 23, all major currencies were permitted to float against the dollar. This launched almost four years of turmoil in foreign exchange markets, as the international monetary system vaccilated between floating exchange rates and attempts to reconstruct the par value system. The death blow was delivered to Bretton Woods by the 1973 rise in the price of petroleum, launching the world on an era of flexible exchange rates.

We will not review developments in detail, but some highlights are useful.[46] A basic factor conditioning all developments in this period was an increase in the rate of inflation throughout the world, but with widely divergent rates in different countries. In December 1971, the Group of Ten met in Washington, and, in the so-called Smithsonian Agreement, proposed a revival of the par value system, but with much wider bands of flexibility about what were now called "central values" — 2¼% for major currencies and 4½% for all others. The United States agreed to fix the price of gold at $38 per ounce, a devaluation of the dollar relative to its old gold par of 7.9%. By June 1972, the new system was put under severe stress when the pound was allowed to float independently. A study of further reform was initiated by the International Monetary Fund (the so-called Committee of Twenty). In early 1973, the United States announced a further 10% devaluation, raising the price of gold to $42 per ounce, and further turmoil in foreign exchange markets ensued. In March, the members of the European Economic Community (the Common Market) began a new system under which they would peg their currencies relative to each other (within the 2¼% Smithsonian bands) but jointly float against the U.S. dollar (an arrangement which was called the "snake in the tunnel"). This promised an interesting compromise between par values and flexibility; in effect, two major currency areas, with flexibility between them. However, the final devastating blow was delivered in late 1973 when the oil-producing nations announced cutbacks in production and a series of increases in the price of petroleum which raised the price more than fivefold. Given the importance of petroleum among the imports of most nations, this foreshadowed international payments imbalances and a redistribution of international liquid assets of orders of a magnitude not seen previously. Shortly after, attempts to restore the principles of Bretton Woods were abandoned. At a conference in Jamaica in January 1976, new principles governing an international system of flexible exchange rates were agreed to.

The Lesson of Bretton Woods

So much for the history of the Bretton Woods system. What can we learn from it? While there are undoubtedly many points which merit consideration, we will focus on only one.

A regime of fixed exchange rates has many attractive features, not the least of which is the constraint which it places on inflationary domestic policies. However, the experience of Bretton Woods suggests that a regime of fixed exchange rates will only provide this constraint if the member governments regard the fixed exchange rates as immutable — as the cornerstone of their monetary constitution. The combination of uncoordinated domestic monetary policies and adjustable exchange rates has the potential for serious contradictions and hence international monetary instability.

THE NEW INTERNATIONAL MONETARY ORDER

What emerged from the Jamaica Agreement and the subsequent second amendment to the Articles of Agreement of the International Monetary Fund is general acceptance of flexible exchange rates and a new role for the International Monetary Fund. We have touched on the economics of flexible exchange rates at several points in our discussion of international monetary economics, and in so doing we have noted several concerns which economists have about the implications of flexible exchange rates. Before noting the institutional changes of the last few years, perhaps we should briefly remind ourselves of these concerns.

Concerns About Flexible Exchange Rates

Economists have at least four major concerns about flexible exchange rates.

Speculation and Instability.   First is the concern that flexible exchange rates may be inherently unstable. In part, this concern reflects an assumption that flexible exchange rates invite speculation and the worry that, as Nurkse concluded about the interwar period, such speculation will frequently be disequilibrating, driving the exchange rate away from equilibrium rather than toward it. This amounts to the assumption that, at least within some range, expectations will be extrapolative rather than rational — that a change in the exchange rate will generate expectations of a further change in the same direction, causing an overshooting of the new equilibrium. In part, it also reflects pessimism about the sensitivity of the balance of payments to changes in the exchange rate, particularly in the short run. Short-run inelasticity in demands for imports may produce perverse changes in the demand for foreign exchange, again causing the exchange rate to overshoot its longer-term equilibrium. (Remember the property of an inelastic demand function: an increase in price may result in a smaller quantity being purchased but it will also result in an *increase* in total expenditures on imports, which is to say an increase in the quantity of foreign exchange demanded.) In part, however, it reflects the concern that the flexibility of exchange rates will induce governments to adopt policies which will produce instability in foreign markets. We will return to this point below.

Uncertainty and Economic Efficiency.   Second is the concern that flexibility of the exchange rate will create a very uncertain environment for business and investment planning, particularly for any business directly involved in international trade or competitive with foreign firms for a domestic market. The added business risks, it is argued, may lead to economic inefficiency and slower economic growth.

Promotion of Nationalistic Economic Policies.   Third is the concern, again based on the experience of the inter-war period, that in times of economic stress, flexible exchange rates can be used as an instrument of nationalistic economic policies to the detriment of the international economy. Direct or indirect manipulation of a flexible exchange rate can be used like a tariff to protect domestic industries and domestic employment, permitting a country to export unemployment to other countries. The legacy of such beggar-thy-neighbor policies and of the retaliation which they invite is economic inefficiency on an international scale.

Inflationary Bias.   Fourth is the related concern that an international regime of flexible exchange rates may be inherently inflationary. As we have seen, fixed exchange rates impose severe fiscal and monetary discipline on governments. Flexible exchange rates relax that discipline, encouraging governments to use monetary expansion (with the consequent depreciation of their currency) as an attempted solution to all kinds of economic problems. On an international scale, the illusion of independence from constraints can result in accelerating inflation.

With such serious concerns about the consequences of an international regime of flexible exchange rates, what safeguards are built in to the new international monetary system?

The "New" International Monetary Fund

Three important changes have occurred in the operations and role of the International Monetary Fund.

Access to Fund Credit.   Among the first changes to be made (before the second amendment was ratified) were measures to increase the IMF's ability to help members to cope with the unusually severe balance of payments imbalances which sometimes resulted from the disruptions to petroleum and raw materials markets in the 1970s and 1980s. The Fund's resources were augmented through increases in quotas, and special borrowing and lending arrangements were developed to deal with special problems. Thus, for example, the "Oil Facility" permitted the Fund to provide special assistance to members with severe petroleum-induced balance of payments problems. In general, the limits on total fund lending to any single member were increased, and the "conditionality" provisions which were the basis of the Fund's role in the balance of payments adjustment process were relaxed, in effect lengthening the time allowed for adjustment. In this way, it was hoped that the IMF would become a more flexible instrument for economic stability in very troubled economic times, and the short-term pressures on exchange rates would be reduced without eliminating the central role of the exchange rate in longer-term adjustment of the balance of payments.

Demonetization of Gold.   Along with the acceptance of flexible exchange rates, the most dramatic break with the past was the official demonetization of gold. The concept of an official price of gold was abolished, its role as a reserve asset was discouraged (and within the IMF itself abolished), it was denied any role as a unit of account, and the Fund (as well as several countries, including Canada) began to dispose of its holdings of gold. In the place of gold, the amendment sought to push the Special Drawing Right to the fore as the primary reserve asset and the standard unit of account for official international transactions. A new issue of Special Drawing Rights was made, more than doubling the number outstanding, and the rules were altered to make the SDR more usable for reserve asset purposes.

Surveillance over Exchange Rate Policies.   If the new system is to work, however, it is on the third change that the burden must fall. While members are explicitly left free to adopt whatever exchange arrangements they want (fixed or flexible), they are supposed to commit themselves to maintain "...orderly economic and financial conditions that will promote a stable system of exchange rates."[47] The IMF is assigned the responsibility of maintaining surveillance over member governments to see that their policies, both domestic and external, comply with this obligation.

The important question is: will it work? The power of the IMF to force compliance is limited — perhaps nonexistent. What is clearly necessary is the cooperative determination of all governments to make the system work. Experience of the interwar period suggests that such cooperation is difficult to obtain, particularly in periods of economic stress.

The Quest for an International Monetary Constitution

What are we to conclude from the discussion in this chapter? We have surveyed theoretical arguments in favor of a monetary constitution designed to eliminate the discretionary authority of governments and central banks over the money supply. We have also surveyed experience at the international level — the classical gold standard, the interwar gold exchange standard, and the Bretton Woods system — with monetary constitutions designed to limit domestic control over money. All of these systems broke down. Apparently, control over money is an element of national sovereignty that few governments of the 20th century are willing to surrender to an abstract rule like the fixity of an exchange rate (or a rate of increase in the money supply?). The collapse of the Bretton Woods system in the early 1970s seems to open the door to serious monetary instability around the world. Perhaps the conversion of central bankers in several countries to a type of money supply rule (but not a "constitutional" rule) in the mid-1970s is really an attempt to find some method of resisting the temptation or the political pressure to directly or indirectly "manage" the exchange rate as an aggressive instrument of stabilization policy.

ENDNOTES

1. For a highly readable but sophisticated exposition of the general thesis see M. Friedman, *Capitalism and Freedom* (Chicago: University of Chicago Press, 1962). This work is a modern economics classic.
2. H. C. Simons, "Rules versus Authorities in Monetary Policy." in *Journal of Political Economy*, Vol. 44 (1936). Reprinted in American Economic Association, *Readings in Monetary Theory* (Philadelphia, 1952), pp. 337-68. Subsequent page references are to the latter publication.
3. *Ibid.*, p. 338.
4. M. Friedman, "The Role of Monetary Policy," *American Economic Review*, 58 (March, 1968), p. 5.
5. M. Friedman, "The Supply of Money and Changes in Prices and Output," *The Optimum Quantity of Money* (Chicago: Aldine, 1969). pp. 171-87. For an argument along this line with reference to Canada see: D. J. Daly, "The Scope for Monetary Policy — A Synthesis," Economic Council of Canada. *Conference on Stabilization Policies* (Ottawa: Queen's Printer, 1966).
6. P. C. Newman, *Renegade in Power: The Diefenbaker Years* (Toronto: McClelland and Stewart, 1963), pp. 295-321; P. Wonnacott, *The Canadian Dollar, 1948-1962* (Toronto: University of Toronto Press, 1965), pp. 203-53.
7. M. Friedman, *A Program for Monetary Stability* (New York: Fordham University Press, 1960), p. 92.

8. M. Friedman, "The Supply of Money and Changes in Prices and Output," p. 186.

9. M. Friedman, *A Program for Monetary Stability*, p. 91.

10. Economic Council of Canada, *Economic Goals for Canada to 1970, First Annual Review of the Economic Council of Canada*. (Ottawa: Queen's Printer, 1964), p. 198.

11. R. S. Sayers, *Central Banking After Bagehol* (Oxford: Oxford University Press, 1957), p. 7.

12. *Ibid.*, p. 1.

13. P. Samuelson, "Reflections on Central Banking." *National Banking Review*. Vol. 1, (September, 1963), p. 16.

14. E. S. Shaw, "Money Supply and Stable Economic Growth." in N. H. Jacoby, ed., *United States Monetary Policy*, rev. ed. (New York: American Assembly, 1964), pp. 73-93.

15. H. G. Johnson and J. L. Winder, *Lags in the Effects of Monetary Policy*. Royal Commission on Banking and Finance Working Paper (Ottawa: Queen's Printer, 1694). See also H. G. Johnson, "Alternative Guiding Principles of the Use of Monetary Policy," in *Essays in International Finance*, No. 44 (Princeton: Princeton University Press, 1963).

16. M. Bronfenbrenner, "Statistical Tests of Rival Monetary Rules," *Journal of Political Economy*, Vol. 69 (February, 1961). pp. 1-14; "Statistical Tests of Rival Monetary Rules: Quarterly Data Supplement" *Journal of Political Economy*, Vol. 68 (December, 1961), pp. 621-25; F. Modigliani, "Some Empirical Tests of Monetary Management and Rules Versus Discretion," *Journal of Political Economy*, Vol. 72 (June, 1964), pp. 211-45.

17. F. Modigliani, "The Monetarist Controversy, or Should We Forsake Stabilization Policies," *American Economic Review*, 67 (March, 1977), pp. 1-19.

18. "Experience to date confirms the Bank in its view that sole reliance on monetary aggregates in judging the appropriate degree of monetary expansion is not warranted. But the Bank also continues to believe that *M1* is particularly useful as a check against cumulative error in monetary policy over the longer term. The ultimate interest of the Bank is the performance of the economy, and it continues to take account of a wide range of economic and financial consideration in its conduct of monetary policy." Bank of Canada, *Annual Report, 1981* (Ottawa: 1982) p. 32.

19. The range of professional opinion is included in a symposium on "Has Monetarism Failed?" *Canadian Public Policy*, 7 (April, 1981), pp. 215-64.

20. Bank of Canada, *Annual Report, 1980* (Ottawa: 1981), p. 10.

21. C. Barber and J. McCallum, *Unemployment and Inflation: The Canadian Experience*, (Toronto: Canadian Institute for Economy Policy, 1980); Donner, A.W. and D. Peters, *The Monetarist Counter-Revolution: A Critique of Canadian Monetary Policy, 1975-1979* (Toronto: Canadian Institute of Economic Policy, 1979).

22. T. J. Courchene *Money, Inflation and the Bank of Canada, Volume II: An Analysis of Monetary Gradualism, 1975-1980*. (Montreal: C.D. Howe Institute, 1981).

23. M. Friedman, "The Case for Flexible Exchange Rates," in *Essays in Positive Economics* (Chicago: University of Chicago Press, 1953), pp. 157-201.

24. Bank of Canada, *Annual Report, 1975* (Ottawa: 1976), p. 11.

25. Yeager, L. B., *International Monetary Relations: Theory, History and Policy*, Second Edition (New York: Harper and Row, 1976), p. 296. Yeager's discussion of the gold standard is both concise and readable. We recommend it highly.

26. The *Currency Acts* actually defined the Canadian dollar in terms of the pound sterling, establishing a par rate of exchange of $4.867 per pound sterling. Given the gold content of the pound, this was the equivalent of a dollar of 23.22 grains of pure gold. The *Currency Acts* also gave legal tender status to the American gold eagle (a $10 piece) as the equivalent of Can. $10, and permitted the government to establish similar equivalents for other foreign gold coins. For purposes of coinage, "standard" gold was to be 9/10ths fine (90% pure gold).

27. The first careful exposition of the specie flow mechanism is usually attributed to David

Hume in 1752, although he did not originate the theory. For a discussion of the early history of the analysis see J. Viner, *Studies in the Theory of International Trade* (New York: Harper & Bros. 1937), pp. 74-87.

28. This research, so far unpublished, is that of Dr. Georg Rich, of the National Bank of Switzerland.

29. Bloomfield, A.J., *Monetary Policy Under the International Gold Standard, 1880-1914.* (New York: Federal Reserve Bank of New York, 1959).

30. Kitchen, J., "Production and Consumption of Gold — Past and Prospective," in League of Nations, *Interim Report of the Gold Delegation of the Financial Committee* (Geneva, 1930).

31. Nurkse, R., *International Currency Experience: Lessons of the Inter-War Period* (Geneva: League of Nations, 1944), p. 27.

32. The quotations from the resolutions of the Genoa conference of 1922 are from Nurkse, *op. cit.*, p. 28.

33. Britain adopted a "gold bullion standard." Bank of England notes, instead of being converted into internationally acceptable gold coin, were to be converted into gold bars (bullion) containing about 400 ounces of fine gold, worth about $3300. France adopted similar arrangements (League of Nations, *Legislation on Gold* (Geneva, 1930).

34. Loveday, A., "Gold: Supply and Demand," in League of Nations, *Interim Report of the Gold Delegation of the Financial Committee* (Geneva, 1930), pp. 88-120.

35. Nurkse, *op. cit.*, 66-112.

36. *Ibid*, 117-122.

37. *Ibid*, 117, 229.

38. *Ibid.*, 117.

39. Guitan, M., *Fund Conditionality: Evolution of Principles and Practices.* IMF Pamphlet Series, No. 38 (Washington, 1981).

40. Fred Hirsch quotes the French Minister of Finance on the informality of the agreement: "There never was any gentlemen's agreement of Basle, but at Basle there are only gentlemen." (F. Hirsch, *Money International* (London: Penguin Press, 1967), p. 341.

41. The Group of Ten consisted of the United States, Germany, France, Italy, Canada, Great Britain, the Netherlands, Belgium, Sweden and Japan, with Switzerland (which was not a member of the IMF) joining in 1964.

42. Meier, G.M. *Problems of a World Monetary Order*, Second Edition (New York: Oxford University Press, 1982), p. 341.

43. Nurkse, *op. cit.*

44. For example, R. I. McKinnon. *Private and Official International Money: The Case for the Dollar*. Princeton University International Finance Section, Essays in International Finance, No. 74. (Princeton, 1969).

45. The measures included the introduction of wage and price controls, reductions in taxation and in government expenditures, a 10 percent surcharge on import tariffs, and the suspension of convertibility of the dollar into gold.

46. For a more complete discussion, see W.M. Scammel, *International Monetary Policy: Bretton Woods and After* (London: Macmillan, 1975).

47. J. Gold, "The Second Amendment of the Fund's Articles of Agreement: A General View," *Finance and Development* (London: Macmillan, 1979), p. 13.

INDEX

collapse, 627-35
definition, 622-26
gold exchange standard, 630-35
Government lending institutions,
268-69
Government savings depositories, 247
Group banking, 331, 337

High-powered money, 418-21, 425

Inflation
and bond yields, 132-44
and Bretton Woods System, 657-58
and choice among financial instruments, 86-87, 500-502
and foreign exchange rate, 569-72,
598-603, 611-12, 659-60
and gold standard, 627, 630
and interest rates, 132-44,
anticipated and unanticipated, 133
definition, 86
impact on financial markets, 86
redistributive effects, 133
trade-off theory, 545-59
Insurance, 260-62
Insurance companies
as financial intermediaries, 262-65
assets, 198, 262-65
competition, 265
Interest arbitrage, 162-70, 175-78
Interest rates
and demand for money, 7, 492-99,
503-505, 532
and inflation, 132-44
and international capital flows, 146-
48, 158-74, 578-80, 604-606
and investment expenditures, 522-24,
534
and macroeconomic equilibrium,
530-32, 582-89, 608-609
and money supply, 512, 518, 559
and risk premium, 130-31
and saving decision, 7
and yield on financial instruments,
70, 75
bank rate (Canada), 467-69
B-K function, 580-82
definition, 7, 74-75
discount rate (United States), 455-59

expectations and, 557-59
inflation and, 557-59
international differentials, 146-48,
158-74
I-S function, 526-27
L-M function, 528-30
nominal and real, 135, 501-502
term structure, 125-30
yield curve, 125
International capital flows
accounts, 154-56
and interest rates, 146-48, 173-74,
578-80
and macroeconomic equilibrium,
577-89, 604-605
International Monetary Fund, 639-47,
660-61
International monetary system
Bretton Woods system, 635-58
classical gold standard, 622-30
gold exchange standard, 630-35
post-Bretton Woods, 658-61
Investment funds,
closed-end, 254-55
mutual funds, 250-54

Keynes, J.M., 386
demand for money, 495-97

Liquidity
and risk, 84-86
definition, 11, 50
L-M function, 527-30

Marketable security, 47
Monetary base, determinants:
bank rate policy, 467-69
central bank advances, 452-70
equation, 425-29
foreign exchange, 436-37, 449-52
government accounts, 432-33, 443-52
open market operations and, 440-43
Monetary policy
definition, 511
Monetary policy, instruments:
bank rate, 223-24, 467-69
central bank advances, 56, 211, 224,
452-70